Lecture Notes in Computer Science 9188

Commenced Publication in 1973
Founding and Former Series Editors:
Gerhard Goos, Juris Hartmanis, and Jan van Leeuwen

More information about this series at http://www.springer.com/series/7409

Aaron Marcus (Ed.)

Design, User Experience, and Usability

Interactive Experience Design

4th International Conference, DUXU 2015
Held as Part of HCI International 2015
Los Angeles, CA, USA, August 2–7, 2015
Proceedings, Part III

 Springer

Editor
Aaron Marcus
Aaron Marcus and Associates
Berkeley, CA
USA

ISSN 0302-9743   ISSN 1611-3349 (electronic)
Lecture Notes in Computer Science
ISBN 978-3-319-20888-6   ISBN 978-3-319-20889-3 (eBook)
DOI 10.1007/978-3-319-20889-3

Library of Congress Control Number: 2015942472

LNCS Sublibrary: SL3 – Information Systems and Applications, incl. Internet/Web, and HCI

Springer Cham Heidelberg New York Dordrecht London

Printed on acid-free paper

Springer International Publishing AG Switzerland is part of Springer Science+Business Media
(www.springer.com)

Foreword

The 17th International Conference on Human-Computer Interaction, HCI International 2015, was held in Los Angeles, CA, USA, during 2–7 August 2015. The event incorporated the 15 conferences/thematic areas listed on the following page.

A total of 4843 individuals from academia, research institutes, industry, and governmental agencies from 73 countries submitted contributions, and 1462 papers and 246 posters have been included in the proceedings. These papers address the latest research and development efforts and highlight the human aspects of design and use of computing systems. The papers thoroughly cover the entire field of Human-Computer Interaction, addressing major advances in knowledge and effective use of computers in a variety of application areas. The volumes constituting the full 28-volume set of the conference proceedings are listed on pages VII and VIII.

I would like to thank the Program Board Chairs and the members of the Program Boards of all thematic areas and affiliated conferences for their contribution to the highest scientific quality and the overall success of the HCI International 2015 conference.

This conference could not have been possible without the continuous and unwavering support and advice of the founder, Conference General Chair Emeritus and Conference Scientific Advisor, Prof. Gavriel Salvendy. For their outstanding efforts, I would like to express my appreciation to the Communications Chair and Editor of HCI International News, Dr. Abbas Moallem, and the Student Volunteer Chair, Prof. Kim-Phuong L. Vu. Finally, for their dedicated contribution towards the smooth organization of HCI International 2015, I would like to express my gratitude to Maria Pitsoulaki and George Paparoulis, General Chair Assistants.

May 2015

Constantine Stephanidis
General Chair, HCI International 2015

HCI International 2015 Thematic Areas and Affiliated Conferences

Thematic areas:

- Human-Computer Interaction (HCI 2015)
- Human Interface and the Management of Information (HIMI 2015)

Affiliated conferences:

- 12th International Conference on Engineering Psychology and Cognitive Ergonomics (EPCE 2015)
- 9th International Conference on Universal Access in Human-Computer Interaction (UAHCI 2015)
- 7th International Conference on Virtual, Augmented and Mixed Reality (VAMR 2015)
- 7th International Conference on Cross-Cultural Design (CCD 2015)
- 7th International Conference on Social Computing and Social Media (SCSM 2015)
- 9th International Conference on Augmented Cognition (AC 2015)
- 6th International Conference on Digital Human Modeling and Applications in Health, Safety, Ergonomics and Risk Management (DHM 2015)
- 4th International Conference on Design, User Experience and Usability (DUXU 2015)
- 3rd International Conference on Distributed, Ambient and Pervasive Interactions (DAPI 2015)
- 3rd International Conference on Human Aspects of Information Security, Privacy and Trust (HAS 2015)
- 2nd International Conference on HCI in Business (HCIB 2015)
- 2nd International Conference on Learning and Collaboration Technologies (LCT 2015)
- 1st International Conference on Human Aspects of IT for the Aged Population (ITAP 2015)

Conference Proceedings Volumes Full List

1. LNCS 9169, Human-Computer Interaction: Design and Evaluation (Part I), edited by Masaaki Kurosu
2. LNCS 9170, Human-Computer Interaction: Interaction Technologies (Part II), edited by Masaaki Kurosu
3. LNCS 9171, Human-Computer Interaction: Users and Contexts (Part III), edited by Masaaki Kurosu
4. LNCS 9172, Human Interface and the Management of Information: Information and Knowledge Design (Part I), edited by Sakae Yamamoto
5. LNCS 9173, Human Interface and the Management of Information: Information and Knowledge in Context (Part II), edited by Sakae Yamamoto
6. LNAI 9174, Engineering Psychology and Cognitive Ergonomics, edited by Don Harris
7. LNCS 9175, Universal Access in Human-Computer Interaction: Access to Today's Technologies (Part I), edited by Margherita Antona and Constantine Stephanidis
8. LNCS 9176, Universal Access in Human-Computer Interaction: Access to Interaction (Part II), edited by Margherita Antona and Constantine Stephanidis
9. LNCS 9177, Universal Access in Human-Computer Interaction: Access to Learning, Health and Well-Being (Part III), edited by Margherita Antona and Constantine Stephanidis
10. LNCS 9178, Universal Access in Human-Computer Interaction: Access to the Human Environment and Culture (Part IV), edited by Margherita Antona and Constantine Stephanidis
11. LNCS 9179, Virtual, Augmented and Mixed Reality, edited by Randall Shumaker and Stephanie Lackey
12. LNCS 9180, Cross-Cultural Design: Methods, Practice and Impact (Part I), edited by P.L. Patrick Rau
13. LNCS 9181, Cross-Cultural Design: Applications in Mobile Interaction, Education, Health, Transport and Cultural Heritage (Part II), edited by P.L. Patrick Rau
14. LNCS 9182, Social Computing and Social Media, edited by Gabriele Meiselwitz
15. LNAI 9183, Foundations of Augmented Cognition, edited by Dylan D. Schmorrow and Cali M. Fidopiastis
16. LNCS 9184, Digital Human Modeling and Applications in Health, Safety, Ergonomics and Risk Management: Human Modeling (Part I), edited by Vincent G. Duffy
17. LNCS 9185, Digital Human Modeling and Applications in Health, Safety, Ergonomics and Risk Management: Ergonomics and Health (Part II), edited by Vincent G. Duffy
18. LNCS 9186, Design, User Experience, and Usability: Design Discourse (Part I), edited by Aaron Marcus
19. LNCS 9187, Design, User Experience, and Usability: Users and Interactions (Part II), edited by Aaron Marcus
20. LNCS 9188, Design, User Experience, and Usability: Interactive Experience Design (Part III), edited by Aaron Marcus

Design, User Experience and Usability

Program Board Chair: Aaron Marcus, USA

- Sisira Adikari, Australia
- Claire Ancient, UK
- Randolph G. Bias, USA
- Jamie Blustein, Canada
- Jan Brejcha, Czech Republic
- Marc Fabri, UK
- Patricia Flanagan, Hong Kong
- Emilie Gould, USA
- Luciane Maria Fadel, Brazil
- Brigitte Herrmann, Germany
- Steffen Hess, Germany
- Nouf Khashman, Canada
- Francisco Rebelo, Portugal
- Kerem Rızvanoğlu, Turkey
- Javed Anjum Sheikh, Pakistan
- Marcelo Soares, Brazil
- Carla G. Spinillo, Brazil
- Katia Canepa Vega, Brazil

The full list with the Program Board Chairs and the members of the Program Boards of all thematic areas and affiliated conferences is available online at:

http://www.hci.international/2015/

HCI International 2016

The 18th International Conference on Human-Computer Interaction, HCI International 2016, will be held jointly with the affiliated conferences in Toronto, Canada, at the Westin Harbour Castle Hotel, 17–22 July 2016. It will cover a broad spectrum of themes related to Human-Computer Interaction, including theoretical issues, methods, tools, processes, and case studies in HCI design, as well as novel interaction techniques, interfaces, and applications. The proceedings will be published by Springer. More information will be available on the conference website: http://2016.hci.international/.

General Chair
Prof. Constantine Stephanidis
University of Crete and ICS-FORTH
Heraklion, Crete, Greece
Email: general_chair@hcii2016.org

http://2016.hci.international/

Contents – Part III

Designing the Learning Experience

Designing the Playing Experience

Designing the Urban Experience

Designing the Driving Experience

Designing the Healthcare Patient's Experience

Designing for the Healthcare Professional's Experience

Designing the Social Media Experience

Social Media Interactions and the Use of Third-Party Management Applications on Effectiveness and Perception of Information

Çakır Aker and Özgürol Öztürk[✉]

Faculty of Communication, Galatasaray University, Ciragan Cad. No: 36,
34357 Ortakoy, Istanbul, Turkey
cakiraker@gmail.com, ozozturk@gsu.edu.tr

Abstract. Social media has a significant impact in our daily social lives, which challenges the traditional face-to-face interaction and/or other conventional media. Most of the social media platforms provide unique and effective web sites that enable the users to connect and interact with one another yet they also update their sites with Web 2.0 improvements and innovative ways of interaction. Twitter and Facebook have launched their own applications that became really popular among users. However, there are also third-party applications, which enable the use of diverse social networking sites through one platform. These platforms are within the reach of everyone and can be accessed directly from desktop without any browser needed. This research focuses on the usability of these third-party management applications. In this context, it will explore whether the desktop versions (third-party software) of those platforms enhance the interaction capabilities and improve user experience. In this regard the focus will be on an application that enables the use of multiple social media sites simultaneously through a single graphical user interface, 'Yoono'. The user interaction with multiple accounts and social media services at the same time presents the ability to show the information in one screen rather than having separate tabs like has been done in typical browser view. Also it might be possible to have an estimate about if the user prefers to have separate tabs or just one tab to show all of the information regarding the social media that he/she is using. In order to understand this, a qualitative usability test, based on multi-method approach, was carried out with a sample of 8 participants who were experienced mobile social network site (SNS) users. Tests were conducted on a desktop computer with Yoono. After a background questionnaire, the participants were observed during the task executions and additional data was collected through eye-tracking. After the session, participants were asked to fill out a post-test form while having a small debriefing interview to gain a detailed insight into their experience. Findings support the notion that the usability problems might shroud the new and innovative capabilities of Yoono and prevents it to become an application that users would chose to use instead of browser interaction and needs further development in order to be an alternative to browsing.

Keywords: User experience · Dashboard applications · Social networking

© Springer International Publishing Switzerland 2015
A. Marcus (Ed.): DUXU 2015, Part III, LNCS 9188, pp. 3–12, 2015.
DOI: 10.1007/978-3-319-20889-3_1

1 Introduction

Especially in the past decade, we feel the effects of social media more day by day. Developing communication technologies allowed us to innovatively interact with our surroundings as well as social media. Philip, E. Agre at his book 'Cybersociety', explained how these genre improvements should be made. He mentioned that the slogan is to do more in which he referred to creating something that does more than its predecessor in order to open up a new way for the genre. It can be said that, one should look at a community, explore existing genres, which actually fit in, and lastly try to find how to exceed this function and offer more to the people. This remarks call for further engagement. Philip E. Agre in 1995 was mentioning that people should consider the media design in terms of a new communication method not just by focusing on its social impacts and design principals but as a whole term and its place in live. *"Perhaps these media will undergo a shake-out, leading back to the relatively homogeneous days of yore. But more likely, I think, media will continue to multiply. Everybody's daily life will include a whole ecology of media; some of these will be voluntarily chosen and others will be inescapable parts of life in public spaces and the workplace"*. He pointed out the fact that these technologies will continue to change non-stop (1). The new uses of communication technology should be able to offer its user a better usability in a better way and to a wider market. This is how social network sites (SNS) entered to our lives. Social media, according to A. Kaplan and M. Haenlein, can be defined as follows; *"a group of Internet -based applications that build on the ideological and technological foundations of Web 2.0, and that allow the creation and exchange of user- generated content"*(2). This article focuses on the social side of new technological advancements in terms of SNS and third-party applications –specifically dashboard and mash-ups, promising better usability and interaction to its user. Dashboard and/or mash-up applications (API) do not simply offer an alternative way of interaction of SNS but also transmute and combine the best aspects of each site in one application making the clutter much more manageable. In order to understand these API's and to be able to comprehend their effects, one should focus on social networking as information service, on heuristics of interaction dashboards for managing these SNS and the expectations towards these platforms.

The number of 727 million daily active users on average in September 2013 using Facebook shows how popular this site became and how it turned out to be a necessity of being connected with each other in daily live. Twitter now averages approximately 50 million tweets per day (4) proving the involvement of SNS. Twitter offers its users a simple text entry system which is limited to 140 characters, enabling them to share whatever they feel like sharing with their followers while being able to follow the feeds including all the shared entries retweeted (shared) or written by their friends. This creates an information flow, mainly customizable via selection of whom to follow. Dave Jones and Lisa Potts in their article define one key to Twitter's success as its support of third-party developers who build applications for organizing and interacting with Twitter content (5) pointing out the demand for improvement on SNS interaction methods. Also it is possible to synchronize Twitter with other mainstream SNS's such as Facebook. Facebook offers much more variety since it has no character limitation such as Twitter and enables to share media in a much more effective way. Sharing videos, getting comments about them, creating photo albums, chatting, creating event pages etc. offer a deep social interaction experience to users which results in a much more sophisticated information flow. Just like Twitter, this information depends on whom the user has as a 'friend' in his/her list including companies and people. To assist users of multiple social media sites effectively, dashboards and mash-up applications were created, especially for Twitter such as 'Hootsuite' and 'Yoono'. With such a dashboard application, the input from various social media sources can be monitored simultaneously and content can be post or replied through this dashboard, instead of having to go to every individual site one by one. Most of these applications are often free and offer an integrated interaction with browser capabilities or have independent software that offer unique possibilities. The main goal of a dashboard application is to give the users a new way of managing complex social networking interactions as well as promoting accessibility in terms of receiving the information on one screen and speeding up the comprehension process.

2 Third-Party Applications for SNS and Yoono

Third party applications endeavor to improve manageability of SNS from different approaches such as adding tools and more customizability. By offering a specific graphical user interface (GUI), those applications re-organize task flow and thus improve user experience. Yoono, specifically offers the user to connect to social media without any need for external software, it works stand-alone and is a freeware software. Yoono offers its users a single inter-changeable GUI through which it allows both web-based view and its special column view. In web-based view, it works just like a simple browser software: It displays http addresses, the user may go to any webpage (s)he desires without the need for another software, it also saves system resources and clicks (Fig. 1).

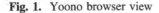

Fig. 1. Yoono browser view   **Fig. 2.** Yoono column view

As seen in the figures, Yoono has static and constantly updating column structure, which presents a mix of all the social media 'feeds' with SNS logos. The left column enables to reach all SNS at the same screen as well as the input field, which is already launched, offering information entry and direct share opportunities. It also allows users to automatically share their entries via several networks at the same time without the necessity of logging into each webpage and copy-paste and/or synchronize several feeds. Yoono also has its specific 'column view' (Fig. 2) which bolsters its most underlined capability of being able to connect to various SNS's on one screen. Through this screen users are able to manage information feeds regarding the SNS and the SNS specific feed titles such as 'updates' or 'direct messages'. Users have to sign-in with their site-specific credentials via Yoono and, have to arrange and open up new view options in order to manage these feeds in the column view. Also in those columns new updates would appear with light yellow background, so that the recent updates can be reached easily. Main feed column stays at the right side of the interface at all times, while the user can modify the rest of columns. At the top right corner, there are 'minimize', 'full screen' and 'close' buttons but there is also the 'single column view' option which makes the screen to shrink to the width of the main feed column at the left. This makes the software look like a side scrolling news gadget. There is also an updates pop-up function, making the updates appear as alert pop-ups just like system based messages, allowing the user to follow up updates effortlessly while the program runs at the background.

3 Analysis Framework

Social media users can read, view, interact and create various contents in various media platforms anytime. SNS may lead its users to various content through hyperlinks, banners, blogs, wiki's and other information resources play a crucial role as part of the overall function for SNS. In this context it is a necessity to use those related media with SNS to effectively engage with the community. To evaluate this, the analysis framework was derived directly from the Nielsen's heuristics (7), which include the following parameters; Visibility of System Status, Match Between System and The Real World, User Control and Freedom, Consistency and Standards, Error Prevention, Recognition Rather Than Recall, Flexibility and Efficiency of Use, Aesthetic and Minimalist Design, Help Users Recognize/Diagnose And Recover from Errors, Help and Documentation on Yoono Dashboard application.

4 Methodology

In order to understand the usability issues of dashboard applications, two research questions were asked. The first question was; how do design aspects and information architecture affect user experience in terms of its emancipating capabilities? Second question was; does having a third party application, with the capabilities like manageability of several SNS accounts and feed information on one screen, make SNS interaction more practical and easy to use rather than browser-based interaction?

This qualitative study on the usability issues of Yoono version 1.8.43 was based on a multi-method approach, which consisted of the following data collection instruments: A pre-test survey, task observation and a structured debriefing interview. The sample included 8 participants, who are between 25 and 40 years old and have at least university degree. All of them were active users of social networks especially Twitter and

Facebook. A pre-test survey was executed with the participants in order to understand their involvement to social media and if they used a dashboard application before. Eight specific tasks were given to the participants: Logging in, opening the column view, arranging the columns according to their personal preference, posting a tweet (Twitter), posting a status update (Facebook), Synchronizing and posting a photo over twitter and Facebook at the same time, commenting on the photo (Facebook), navigating photos/videos and lastly logging out. In this task execution phase, the navigation was directly observed and recorded on a structured observation sheet by the researchers. Besides the observation, additional data was collected through a desktop eye-tracker and video recording. In the post-test debriefing interview, the users were asked for their opinions regarding their experience, perceived difficulty of the tasks and attitudes towards the platform.

5 Results and Discussion

Yoono was a good case for understanding the heuristics of dashboards related to SNS services and how heuristics can and should be applied to those applications. Mainly the application was problematic rather than emancipating its user. The success rate of the tasks is % 50 in general, since 8 participants were able to complete 4 out of 8 tasks in the given order successfully. For each task 3 min was given. Some participants were considered (n = 4) failed when they exceeded the given time for each task. Average time for completing the tasks was 20 min.

5.1 Visibilities and System Status

Yoono was partially able to inform its users about where they are at any time and what is going on. New feeds/messages or any other update is highlighted so that it is easy to follow what is recent. Since Twitter and Facebook services depend mainly on the 'what's happening now' context, this should be considered as an advantage. Also every column has its specific topic indicated at the top. There is also the 'search' field at the top of each column making it possible to search for specific quarries. Main problem is that the recent updates were received randomly and the connection speed affected the performance of the feed update. Users were unable to refresh the posts as they please and unable to check the sent messages to see if they are indeed posted correctly. This confused the users and made them to switch to browser mode to re-connect and look for the update by themselves most of the time.

5.2 Match Between System and the Real World

Yoono did not support languages other than English. Small indicator buttons were clear enough to guide participants such as adding a photo and the iconography was understandable. The problem was that some of those did not function as the participants expected such as again the photo upload option. There are two different upload buttons but none of them functioned properly during the tests. The 'share something' button has an unexpected iconography, which the users related as 'refresh' button. The button at the top left corner of the screen, which was depicted as a wrench icon was not clear enough to indicate its function, causing problems during the logging out task and reaching other options about the application.

5.3 User Control and Freedom

During the tests, most users (n = 6) face with the problem of accessing the column view and without any assistance; they were not able to find it. It was possible to move the columns between each other yet most of the participants indicated that they preferred to be able to resize the columns one by one instead of having a fixed width. This fixed layout revealed a non-functional white space on the screen. In addition to that some of the participants not only wanted to re-arrange the space for columns in a horizontal layout but in vertical as well. The placement of each column with a different title may be changed by dragging, but the flickering issues that occurred during the process caused the participants to hesitate from doing it. This action was mostly perceived as an error. The most important observation of the task execution phase within this context is about the logging out task. The log out option has been placed in the options menu, under the "add another social media/IM" option (Fig. 3). None of the participants were able to find it without assistance and instead they tried to log out from their account via browser screen. This would be less crucial if the application allowed it but instead Yoono stayed connected even after they logged out from the browser view.

Fig. 3. The path to follow in order to log-out from accounts

5.4 Consistency Standards

After the text and/or media entry, half of the participants looked for the 'send' button instead of 'update' which was the applications alternative for that. Also for adding columns about updates, some participants indicated that they were looking for the term 'feed'. As mentioned in the "Match Between System and the Real World" sub-selection above, participants mostly chose to use the icon of a camera instead of the text button saying 'upload photo' while trying to upload a photo from Facebook and

Twitter accounts. The application does not allow its users to upload any photos while the accounts were synced even it mentions the photo has been uploaded. When the user chose to send a photo via only Facebook for instance the icon remains but another option appears, the 'photo upload' button that and it functions successfully. Another issue about the consistency is that while accepting the terms regarding the SNS, nothing really happens rather than a mere text message telling the users that they are logged in, at the browser view. The user has to click on the 'finish' button before reaching the entry box. The sentence 'finish' most commonly caused an alarm, which leads the participants to an impression that clicking this would terminate their session. Therefore they chose not to click it until they could seek the way for text entry goal and/or asking for assistance. The term simply led the users to think that the session will be terminated. The hesitation of the users can be clearly seen in Fig. 4. This points out that the participants gaze is on the button and yet still not making him/her press it, in order to 'finish the logging in process. 6 out of 8 participants have encountered the hesitation and told that this problem really made them feel confused.

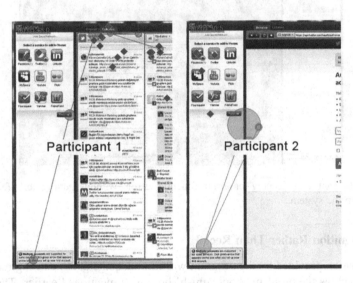

Fig. 4. Two participants trying to find the text entry field. Looking at the 'finish' button yet not clicking it.

5.5 Error Prevention

Although there were errors regarding the third-party applications connection to SNS, these were expected by the participants. The problem in this context is that whenever the user wanted to send a text input in one of the SNS there was no confirmation option feedback. This was also a problem about uploading a media. Although sharing icon was miss-interpreted, this option had the confirmation feedback and progress indicator. Adding a confirmation pop-up box might prevent accidental text entry and upload failures. One of the participants pointed out that: "*Uploading a photo and not seeing it at the feeds is better than uploading a photo with text and just seeing the text on my timeline*". This calls for the urge to prepare a reviewing screen before publishing the information. Also another functionality problem occurred during one test, resulting the program to not open any columns even after a successful login sequence. The software did not provide any feedback about the issue. This made the participant to focus on only on one column which is the fixed left column that the application provides, and he kept up with using this one to finish his tasks during the tests (Fig. 5). The diamonds seen represent the mouse clicks done by the participant during the related tests. From these it can be easily observed that the common sense on typing an entry problem, is searching for information at the small indicator text at the bottom left of the screen. Participants mostly thought that this information would lead them to the solution almost all the time.

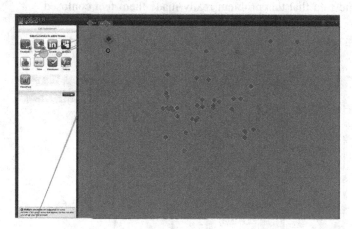

Fig. 5. Participant experiencing program function error, without getting any feedback or message from the system.

5.6   Recognition Rather Than Recall

The information provided by the program was not adequate at all, causing recognition problems such as the problem about 'finish' button as mentioned earlier. The column view has the means for recognition; users were feeling comfortable about the guides yet there were no indicators for additional information on the features. The profile thumbnails can be changed in terms of size from the options button, allowing the user to customize their profile picture. This sub-tab was quite clear to the participants since enlarging the profile picture size was depicted using varied sizes of thumbnails as selection buttons and size of the font depicted from X large to Small. The options button placed under the wrench icon confused the participants since under the tab there is also the button for options but this caused no frustration at all.

5.7   Flexibility and Efficiency of Use

At the top right corner, there was the option to turn the application into a single-column view. This button and the icon were recognizable after several uses and speeded up some of the participants' navigation. However participants had the tendency to open photos and videos in the same screen just like Facebook does, or in a light-box pop-up screen without any switches between views. Yoono was programmed to open the related media in the browser view, just like the user tried to avoid while clicking the link. In general the application dictates the user to adapt to the pre-given interface and placement rather than enabling full customization.

5.8   Aesthetics and Minimal Design

In terms of graphical user interface, the program had no customization options. The color scheme was preset to grayscale. Since the columns were dominant in the interface design, the rather static view of them, as mentioned before, created compositional problems such as the use of non-functional white space. Also the hierarchy of elements of the design was not pre-defined, causing some problems on what to look first. For example the 'finish' button after logging in was not getting enough attention (Fig. 4). The use of the logo thumbnails of the SNS networks received positive feedback during the tests but some of the participants said that they would be happy if columns related to the SNS were somehow colored with the logo color instead of plain white background, leading them to the observation that the title space for each SNS was not designed in the right hierarchical order.

5.9   Help Users Recognize, Diagnose, and Recover from Errors

The participants were engaged with only one error/confirmation message during the tests, which was the terms and conditions for the third-party application connecting to their accounts. This error message was clear and enabled perceived affordance. There were no apparent complaints and problematic issues regarding this context.

5.10   Help and Documentation

As mentioned above, there were no apparent error messages besides logging in messages. Also there were no tips for the users to explain what a specific button did. After logging in, the participants seemed to lost control of the application, and didn't know what to do next. In the de-briefing interview, they emphasized the need for a tutorial. It should also be noted that there was no help button in the application.

6   Conclusion

Although Yoono is a resourceful application, it is still immature and needs to be improved. It allows users to reach all the information from their SNS's in a single view and is really practical in nature. Problems, that were mentioned above, during the tests led participants tend to quit and made them think about opening the browser view in order to complete the tasks. Most of the participants (n = 5) mentioned that the engagement was fun and Yoono could be the application for interacting with social networks but only few considered adopting as it stands. In several occasions, the interaction methods of the application were not related to the original SNS capabilities, preventing the participants to use the application efficiently. This problem might be resolved by adopting the SNS related Web 2.0 capabilities and allowing users a more natural interaction, such as light-box pop-up screens for browsing media content instead of opening a new browser tab in the application. Yoono can be a good solution for navigating through the most complex social networks, only after fixing the major software and interaction problems as well as adopting those common capabilities from SNS's. For Yoono, and other SNS dashboard applications, consistency standards should be improved primarily in order to fulfill the expectation about manageability of SNS accounts through one screen. Also the need for flexibility and help documentation prevent new users to engage easily. The aesthetics problems is seemingly less important than the issues above but a much more minimalistic design would lower the cognitive load for the users and prevent them from confusion and frustration. The GUI elements seemed to make the application look like it was designed for experienced SNS users and drives newcomers away.

At first glance, the new and innovative approach for SNS and manageability offered by Yoono seems well suited for the task for avoiding the information clutter. It enables the user to interact with the SNS's via one common screen and keeps them updated with the help of pop-up indicators appearing whenever a new feed is received. But consequently, the usability problems seem to enshroud these capabilities and make the application a more complex system to interact regardless of its practical nature.

Acknowledgements. This study has been realized under the coordination of Dr. Barış Kara with the support of Galatasaray University Scientific Research Fund.

References

1. Agre, P.E.: Designing genres for new media. In: Jones, S. (ed.) CyberSociety 2.0: Revisiting CMC and Community. Sage (1998)
2. Kaplan, A.M., Haenlein, M.: Users of the world, unite! The challenges and opportunities of social media. Bus. Horiz. **53**(1), 59–68 (2010)
3. Dierdorp, S.E.: A framework for a social media dashboard for entrepreneurs (2013)
4. Wauters, R.: Twitter spawned 50,000 apps to date, will open up firehose for more. TechCrunch. Accessed (2009). http://techcrunch.com/2009/12/09/twitter-le-web-2009
5. Jones, D., Potts, L.: Best practices for designing third party applications for contextually-aware tools (2010)
6. Morville, P.: Ambient Findability. O'Reilly, Sebastopol, CA (2005)
7. Nielsen, J.: Usability Engineering, pp. 115–148. Academic Press, San Diego (1994)

Design Process of a Social Network System for Storage and Share Files in the Workplace

Heloisa Candello(✉), Silvia Bianchi, and Leandro Cassa

IBM Research, Rua Tutóia 1157, São Paulo, Brazil
{hcandello,ssardela,lcassa}@br.ibm.com

Abstract. This paper explores the design process of a social network based storage and share application in the workplace. One of the big challenges of our era is to handle the amount of data available. This may result in a high cost with additional servers to store the data and guarantee availability and reliability. We interviewed ten employees to understand better their share and storage practices in everyday life, and also identify opportunities to inspire the design of storage applications. As a result, we provided 20 recommendations to develop social network storage systems. Additionally, we created personas and scenarios inspired by interviewed participants. We envisioned how the system should work and we illustrated it by interaction cycles with a low-tech prototype. Finally, we provide lessons learned towards the design of storage and share files in the workplace leveraging the social relationship amongst co-workers.

Keywords: Design process · Social networks · Distributed storage systems

1 Introduction

Social networking has been adopted in different contexts inside the enterprises not only to improve the relationships among co-workers across different departments but also to allow them to share ideas, documents and information. With such systems, workers can connect with each other, create and participate in several communities related to projects, teams and subjects they are interested in. One possible solution to store these documents is to have a dedicated storage. However, with the rapidly increasing number of files produced by the user, the dedicated storage may become a bottleneck: single point of failure and high bandwidth consumption.

In addition, the expectation of employees in the organizations, as attested by our study, is that storage needs to expand continually. Thus, this storage should be elastic and increase with the amount of data since users hardly erase old versions and documents that are no longer relevant. This may result in a high cost with additional servers to store the data and guarantee availability and reliability. According to a SpiceWorks[1] report, the organizations have in average 55 percent of the storage in laptops and desktops that are unused. So, leverage unused storage may lead to solution with no additional cost. In this paper we wanted to understand the user experience of current ways of storage and share files in the workplace to gather insights and look for

---

[1] http://www.spiceworks.com.

© Springer International Publishing Switzerland 2015
A. Marcus (Ed.): DUXU 2015, Part III, LNCS 9188, pp. 13–24, 2015.
DOI: 10.1007/978-3-319-20889-3_2

opportunities to build a new mobile storage tool that might overcome some storage problems in the workplace. Our main research questions are:

- What are the everyday practices of storage and share files in the workplace?
- What are the practices to deal with storage and sharing files in the workplace?
- In which ways a future mobile storage tools may improve practices of storage and share files in workplace?

We followed a Design Research methodology. The preliminary research was a semi-structured interview with 10 employees working in the same company. Afterwards, we provided 20 recommendations to develop social network storage systems. Additionally, we created personas and scenarios inspired by interviewed participants. As a result, we proposed a decentralized storage and share system based on social network and illustrated it by interaction cycles with a low-tech prototype.

2 Methodology

In this work, we follow a Design Research Methodology with the intent to have a distributed system to store and share files in the workplace, and doing so minimizing the cost of a centralized structure and to take advantage of unused space in worker's devices and their social relationships. Design research aims to improve the design process of manmade artifacts and extend the knowledge acquired to projects with a similar approach. Several authors contribute with definitions of Design Research [6, 8, 14]. Some of them explore design research applied to the Human Computer Interaction field [22]. There is a lack to apply this approach to the design of mobile systems. Most writers emphasize the lessons learned in the design process as a contribution to knowledge. Methods, theories and better development of certain artificial products are carefully studied to improve the design process, solve problems and extend the knowledge generated to other similar artifacts. Additionally, in their opinion, previous research is necessary to boost new achievements in developing objects. In [8], Design Research (also referred to as the design experiments approach) was developed as a way to carry out formative research to test and refine educational designs based on theoretical principles derived from prior research. In general, authors agree that design research process consists of three main stages: Preliminary Research, Prototyping phase and Assessment phase [6, 12, 14] add one more stage: reflection and documentation.

The prior research phase [8], also known as preliminary research [12] and predictive research [16], may be an investigation of literature and main principles existent in the field; similar products that are already in the market and/or field studies to understand better the target users. In [6], the authors suggest that the designer has to start by analyzing human behavior, from which he could derive "quantities, qualities, and relationships". Empirical research is essential to this first stage.

The stage of refinement is also called the prototyping phase. Elements identified in the preliminary research are implemented in the prototype in order to test their validity and improve the artifact. The designers implement some elements as intended, some are adapted to circumstances and others will not be implemented due to their lack of relevance in the context. This approach is described as progressive refinement in [8]. This implies bringing the first version of a design into the world to see how it works. Therefore, the design is constantly revised based on experience to solve possible problems. Expert evaluations or user evaluation with early prototypes might be applied. From these studies, design principles are indicated. Prototype designs represent a specific framing of the problem, and are compared to other research artifacts that emphasize the same problem. They provoke a discussion in the community of methods and approaches employed to solve common problems [9]. Those artifacts become design exemplars, providing an appropriate conduit for research findings to easily transfer to the HCI research and practice communities [22].

Reference [19] suggests that while design researchers do focus on specific objects and process in specific contexts, they try to study these as integral and meaningful phenomena.

The last stage, the assessment phase, is more usually named the evaluation phase. The outcomes of this stage are: identification of main problems occurring; confirming design issues and principles emerging in the experimental phase with the prototype; and recommendations for artifact and design process improvements [14]. The result of the whole process, after a systematic reflection and documentation of each phase, will be the production of theories or/and validated design principles [12].

In this paper we show the preliminary research step (user research and conceptual design) and the prototyping phase.

3 Preliminary Research

In our study, we decide to interview workers to understand better the practices of storage and share in the workplace. We also reviewed the main literature in the field.

3.1 Related Work

In this section we situate our study of investigating work practices of sharing and storage files among the field of research surrounding to social network activities in the workplace. We begin by reviewing related research. Then, we describe some market applications that aim sharing and store files.

Research on management of information in work environments has been explored for the last three decades [1, 3, 4]. Technology has been changing over since, and new challenges emerged in the workplaces. Workers normally adopt several tools in their everyday practice and those tools not always work as expected. As a consequence workers found themselves diverted from their tasks because of missing information, broken tools, or needed expertise [2]. Current practices in file sharing are studied in [20] and the authors examined tools used to share files. They noted that people shared a wide variety of file types, that they determine their sharing practices with respect to a combination of individual users and groups, and that they typically select from a small number of mechanisms for sharing, most commonly sending files by email due to its simplicity and universality. The breakdowns in sharing that were reported were often related to the poor visibility of sharing settings in the user interface. Users identified a set of characteristics of file sharing mechanisms and push and pull activities. Users chose which sharing modality to use based on the affordances of this sharing modality. Based on it, they developed a tool – sharing palette – that supports interaction for a variety of file sharing styles that allow users to select a sharing modality based on the affordances of that modality.

One common tool example is the e-mail application. Reference [3] investigated "e-mail overload" in-depth fieldwork and uncovered six key challenges of task management in e-mail: threaded task-centric collections, equality for all content, task-centric meta-information for all items and aggregations of information for an overview.

Other studies have been proposed with attempt to understand how users organize their files. In [1] the authors interviewed managers and employees to understand how the information is used. This results in how they will be organized and stored in the file systems. Reference [4] interviewed 27 employees from 5 different organizations in order to understand the information scraps life cycle. Jones [10] investigated how users organize information in support of projects. The study suggests that users continuously reorganize the folder's structure to reflect with the projects completion. Reference [5] investigated personal information management across several tools and over time. Results showed that users devote little time to maintain their information.

Another study points to the way people think about and use shared folders. Questions of ownership and privacy are highly discussed in this work. Even though people can modify, delete and modify other people's files in shared folders, there are implicit rules and assumptions guiding their behaviors. Access permissions affect how people incorporate share folders to their personal management. Reference [21] identified it in cases involving sharing between just two people. More studies are needed with large group of people sharing folders. Reference [15] did an online experiment related to understand if information management tasks are governed by the same communication processes as conversation. The study suggested that people think of labeling and organizing not just as storage and categorization, but as a communicative activity.

In [13], the authors asked 30 people to describe instances of when they shared something that they later regretted sharing. As a result, people do not want a transgression made public or their e-mail to be widely shared, but are comfortable with people having their work e-mail address and desk phone number. Additionally, authors discovered that people willingness to share depends on who they are sharing the information with. Reference [7] proposes a Facebook-based social storage cloud. The integration with Facebook application allowed users to discover and trade storage contributed by their friends, taking advantage of preexisting trust relationships. A credit-based trading approach has been adopted to discourage free loading.

In [17] the authors studied how workers store and manage their files in the workplace. They have examined what files the users have in common and they found an aggregate redundancy of 54 % in number of files and 32 % of total storage space. Moreover, the study showed a tendency to share files is more common on people sharing same or similar role. So, these characteristics can be considered to create a distributed storage system where files are stored in people working in similar role or project in order to minimize the network and storage overhead. Another aspect that should be taken into account while designing such systems is to avoid free riding or lurking behavior, i.e., avoid users that uses the system's resources (store files only) without contributing to the system (provide resources for other users). For example, studies done on Cattail, a social file sharing system of an enterprise showed that 72 % of users presented a lurking behavior [11].

Reference [15] studied users' multi-device utilization in workplaces. Users use multiple storage and share solutions and the choice depends on the type of the file.

Systems such as CrashPlan, Symform and SpaceMonkey are relatively recent distributed storage services that allow data to be stored and retrieved among peers. Even that most of these systems can be deployed inside the organizations, they do not take into account the co-workers relationship such as participating in the same projects or communities. Other distributed storage systems tries to leverage the social network relationships between friends. Friendbox [18] is a hybrid friend-to-friend personal storage system that combines friend's storage with cloud storage.

3.2 Semi-structured Interviews

Occasionally, the time available to carry out experiments is not enough for users to write long answers. At other times, users do not feel encouraged to write their own opinions. An alternative is to use semi-structured interviews that are employed to support users in answering questionnaires and to give users opportunities to share their experience in a more natural way.

In our study, participants answered a semi-structured interview. The interview was audio recorded. Participants signed a consent form. The interviews took place in a cafe inside the company, to add an informal atmosphere to the study, and to let participants get confortable. The study lasted about one hour and participants answered in average twenty questions. The questions covered issues of everyday life at work; experience with share and storage tools at work; organization of files in their computers and management of digital files. The results of interviews gave us directions to user modelling and insights of a storage and share prototype features.

3.3 Participants

A convenience and snowball sample was used to collect the data. Ten participants were interviewed. Four participants have been working at the company from 9 months to 4 years. Three participants have been working at the company from 6 to 8 years and three from 13 to 27 years. Participants had different job roles: Sales out report analysts (2 participants); Supply Chain analyst (1); Project manager (1); Research scientist (1); Problem analyst (1); Contractor Manager Specialist (1); Business control (1); Credit and Invoice executer (2). All the participants had a smartphone and work at the same company.

3.4   Data Analysis

The data sets available were audio transcriptions of semi-structured interviews. The method selected to examine the interviews was content analysis, in which the data was analyzed using a categorization scheme. The categorization scheme arose from the data itself and the research questions also guided the study to find new relations and categories. The researchers wanted to identify opportunities, advantages and drawbacks of having a distributed way of sharing and storage files in the workplace. Therefore, a set of research questions were formulated to guide the study:

- How do people organize, share and storage files in the workplace? Why?
- What are the drawbacks and opportunities to improve sharing and storage practices in the workplace?

3.5   Findings

With the purpose of presenting the findings, categories were classified but also dissolved in the text, as the boundaries among them are not so clear. Findings were described according to the research questions in sections.

How Do People Organize, Share and Storage Files in the Workplace? Participants use a number of tools in everyday work to communicate and share files with co-workers. Most participants usually start their day checking their calendars and e-mails. They use the company chat service to communicate with co-workers and share files. The size of the file determines which tool will be choosing to transfer files. If the file is important and relevant to the topic of the chat conversation, the files are send in the same time to the chat partner. If the file is not relevant in the moment, or/and people are not online, or even if they want to register/track the receive file they transfer it by e-mail. When the file is big, they use USB flash drivers or a storage app to transfer it. Some official tools were created to share files, but were not fully adopted for this purpose, were used as a file repository instead. Problems with storage space were common problem using these tools. Participants were not aware of limit storage and limit of size files for sharing using company official tools. The drawback of using the chat tool and e-mail to share files is the tracking of the file. When they shared their files through a cloud system or the social network official tool it was possible to recover it. On the other hand, storing files in a server/cloud and send the hyperlink, sometimes takes more time (uploading and downloading) and affect computer performance than sending files via chat and e-mail.

Generally they store their files in their computer and an external hard drive. Three participants store files on cloud systems and two on social networks apps. Only one person store her files in an external hard drive and does not have a copy of them in her computer. More than half of the participants do not backup their files often, normally only when they need space or remember of it. The same happens related to the frequency to erase old versions of files in their computers. To save file versions is a common practice in the workplace. We identified several practices related to file versions and replicas. Some save relevant files versions on the desktop. Hence, they are aware that those files are temporary and means that actions have to be done. They group the files in a folder, when the desktop has many files saved, and then later they decide to erase them or not. Others save file versions in the same folder, and keep them in the backups. Despite of doing versions, sometimes they override files by mistake and cannot recover the previous version. To avoid this, others have original version of the files in a server/cloud, shared or not with their team co-workers. Half of the participants do not use any tool to synchronize their files.

Participants reported that they do not use the entire storage space of their device. As aforementioned, usually people use about 40 % of the storage space. In our study, most of participants have the impression they use between 50 % and 75 %. This shows the opportunity to use unused storage space. Only one participant thinks he uses more than 75 % of storage availability. Some of them have difficulties to manage their own files; they try to find a pattern for labeling them - including the date in the name; the name of the person who sent the file. Additionally, they save versions files by numbering (1, 2, 3...) or lettering (A, B...). Folder was a metaphor people are used to in other applications. In their view, it is important to keep the same folder name in the backups, otherwise you cannot find the files you need in the backup easily.

Not all the participants use mobile phones for work purpose, but they mentioned interest of using it if the company gave them the device. The ones who use mobile phones for work, they usually review, edit and share files from their devices.

What are the Drawbacks and Opportunities to Improve Sharing and Storage Practices in the Workplace? It is clear that participants use numerous software alternatives to share and store files in the workplace. And also the residual space in their devices might be availed. The study suggested an integration of tools to share and storage files in the workplace. Additionally, it is clear that social network structure is used for safety and recovers files. In order to recover files, they ask co-workers to send them last versions, in case they do not have anymore. Even though, most of them have personalized way to organized files in their computer, most of the interviews already share a server space with their team to save files. The main problems are many similar versions of files available, each team member store in their machines. Moreover, not always they are aware of who has the updated version. Furthermore, some participants have not only the computer machine but also mobile phones for work purposes, which gives room for use the unused space of those devices and avoiding servers.

Our study expands findings described in the literature review. We confirm common sharing and storage practices unveiled before, such as usage of many tools at work and their drawbacks [2]. They do not clean files when they do not need them anymore [5]. People label their files in an intuitive way for better search [15]. People duplicate files in their devices to assure they will not be corrupted; lost according to files importance or they saved it in a shared folder or cloud. The preferred mode of sharing files in our study was a Chat service not e-mail as previous studies pointed out [20]. File size was the main factor to choose tools to use to share and storage files.

Thinking of those practices, tools constraints and cost of storage we suggest design requirements for developing storage systems for the use in the workplace.

4 Recommendations

The interviews gave us a better view of people's behaviors of sharing and storing files in the workplace. We examined the findings and listed the main drawbacks employees mentioned. From that, a list of recommendations was formulated.

We describe 20 design recommendations for storage and share files systems based on the literature review and the findings of our data analysis interviews.

1. The system should be integrated to other tools such as e-mail and chat.
2. The system should work in diverse platforms, mobile or not.
3. The system should provide more flexible storage space avoiding limiting the space size
4. The system should assure safety, when stores files in other people computer.
5. The system should allow chat between users if they wish to ask for permission to store a file and also send files anywhere, anytime.
6. The system should have transparence/people awareness of who has permission of editing files.
7. The system should be customizable to let user to import contacts from other social networks.
8. The system should be available 24/7 or during work period.
9. The system should not affect the performance and storage (available space).
10. The system should provide mechanism to share files and folder. The owner may give access to other people.
11. Provide some access control: e.g., password.
12. The system should protect the files (guarantee redundancy, automatic backup) in case there is a problem with the local storage or laptop.
13. The files should be encrypted.
14. Guarantee that there is always a safe copy in case someone deletes or the file is corrupted.
15. Automatic backup and restore.
16. The system should trace the transfers (who sent to whom) and the versions (who has the last version).
17. Access to people outside the enterprise: clients or business partners.
18. The system should guarantee that at least one copy of the file is available remotely or locally as a backup. The system should have copies of the files, in case the file is corrupted.
19. The system should allow to create the structure of storage similar to the structure of the project.
20. Provide incentives for people to give more space. e.g. Users may have space from the system proportional to the amount of space he/she provides (available x times the space provided).

We applied those recommendations to develop a new storage and share system based on social network. For better envision of the new system, we created personas and scenarios based on real situations described during the interviews.

5 Personas

Personas' characteristics were envisioned based on our interviewees, as well the scenarios exemplifying the personas using the future system. Vanessa, Laura and Ricardo our personas, are co-workers in the same company. Vanessa is a financial analyst, works in the company for two years and is very keen on social network tools. One of the tools she uses, is an internal social network that helps her to share files with her peers and create private communities. When she is storing files on her own computer, she usually keep several versions of the same file with different names, so she does not lose milestones of the work she is doing. Her philosophy is: Personal is personal, company is company. Therefore, she does not mix personal documents such as pictures to work documents. Laura is a manager and works for 8 years in the same company. Uses the corporative chat system to talk with people from her team. She is very competent and cautious in his work. She does backups every week and does not save many version of the same file in his hard disk. She only erases files if she needs space in her machine. Ricardo is a team leader and has been working in the same company for 15 years. He is a member of public social networks, but did not use the corporative social network. He tried to use, but does not see value to be apart of a social network environment as he can share, store his files in other corporative applications. He can talk with his team and share files by the corporative chat system. The only community he is a compulsory member, he adopts a lurking behavior. Additionally, he asks members of his team to save files in their computers to assure they will not be corrupted. He prefers store files in his machine and in the hard drive than use a dedicated system, a cloud to save his files. He uses 75–100 % of space in her laptop hard drive.

6 Scenarios

We describe here, one scenario that highlights a task in the system using the social network. Laura is interacting with 'Ruy' a co-worker.

Laura arrives at work and checks her priorities for the day. She opens her e-mail and the Storage system pops up appears. It is her colleague Ruy asking permission to save a file in her device. She sees in the pop up screen her storage capacity and remembers she has to backup her hard-drive. So, she types: Good Morning Ruy. How was the weekend? - He answers -Great and yours? She says - Good. About store your file, I'm sorry Richard, Im afraid I wont be able to do, as you know, even I have space to store it, I don't really like to store personal files in my work machine. I can indicate some people the company that is part of my Storage system network to you. Ruy - No problem, I was suspecting you wouldn't store for me. Laura select back up settings, change Weekly by Now, and the backup files process start.

7 Low-Tech Prototype

After identifying the system requirements based on the use-case scenarios and basic functionalities that the system should fulfill, we have developed a low tech-prototype. Our system is multiplatform, for personal computers and mobile devices as the working

Fig. 1. Low-tech prototype (a,b,c and d).

environment is changing to a more collaborative, social and mobile workplace. It uses unused space in hard-drive machines to store files of people working together. The edges or workers will have a direct communication in order to share resources that can be content such as file. Each worker acts both as a server providing resources and as a client requesting services. Thus, in contrast to the traditional client-server architecture, this system has no centralized control. The files will be encrypted and the host will know who is storing information in their machine. Primary files and also backup copies will be stored; the number of copies stored will be proportional to the importance owners will rate to the file. Files that are more important might have more copies. In Fig. 1 we illustrate some of these functionalities according to the developed scenarios.

Figure 1(a) illustrates some of the system's settings where the user can access his storage, chat with other users, manage his storage space and configure the system. In the low tech-prototype we have assumed that the system has a limited storage, but with the possibility to increase if the user provides more available space in his/her disk. The Fig. 1(b) shows a selected file and the user can easily upload a new version, download, delete or access old versions. In addition, the user can share the file with other users in the social network as illustrated by a person and the number 5. The idea is that the system stores the replicas of the files in these people storage in order to minimize the overhead of storing and downloading the file. The old versions of the file can be accessed in a separate screen, as shown in Fig. 1(c). In this screen the user visualizes a timeline of the versions and the size of the files and the user can click on a version in order to download or delete and old version it. When the user wants to upload a new file or version, the system will provide a list of users based on the social network where the user can interact with via chat (see Fig. 1 (d)). So, when the other user receives a request to store a file, he can decide to chat with this requesting user.

8 Discussion and Future Work

Interesting facts are not only the ones that appeared more during the interviews. Due to our sample (ten people), any issue raised by interviewees is interesting to examine. In addition to practical factors (integration of tools, possibilities of convergence of tasks to the same system) and subjective factors (sense of privacy, safety, confidence) concerns of basic tasks also appeared in the study. In participants view, if the company requests them to use a system they will use it, they will learn and will accept it as it occurred with many other tools they use with similar functionality. The problem is that using many tools to do similar tasks (e.g. depending on the file size they choose the tool to share it) affects their work performance. Sending or sharing a file might turn out a time-consuming activity and a cognition overload. As any tool has to use machine performance to work and people have to learn and remember diverse ways to do the same task. It might be a solution to use a social network approach to help in the action of sharing and storage files. It provides a low cost solution to the high cost of additional servers to store the data and guarantee availability and reliability in the workplace. As they aggregate storage from edge devices such as laptops, desktops and smart-phones.

Our solution, distributed social network storage, still has to be investigated very carefully. It intents to use the spaces unused in employees devices, therefore cautious with safety and privacy are matter issues. Also issues such as backup management, redundancy and duplication of files and performance will be addressed in this project follow up activities. According to the literature and our interviews, people do not use the whole space available in their machines and generally save duplicate files. For example, in a team of 15 people we could have 2 files duplicate instead of 15, it would save storage. Otherwise, those 2 copies should be available for the team whenever they need, at least in the work hours.

We are planning to run user evaluation sessions, assessment phase, with a group of employees in order to refine the prototype. We expect this process will also generate recommendations to develop similar systems, documentation and reflection phase.

9 Conclusion

Our studies aimed to find opportunities for supporting work through appropriate design and technology. For this purpose, we applied a Design Research methodology. The use of a Design Research methodology leads us to think about the design process and insights that might emerge from it. We interviewed 10 employees about their everyday sharing and storage activities. Our main findings are (1) collaboration was a primary activity among employees; (2) employees worked with many tools to do similar tasks; (3) employees save many versions of the same file in their computers (4) the residual space in employees devices might be availed; (5) integration of work tools would save time. Furthermore, (6) the tools available to employees do not fulfill their work practices in these areas. They have to use several tools to storage and share files according to the size of the file or their real time priority for someone to see it.

We propose twenty recommendations for developing social network storage systems based on the interviews and literature review. Those recommendations were applied to develop a social network storage tool. Conceptual design was also inspired by the interviews. We created personas and scenarios to envision a new share and storage system based on social network. A social network storage tool might overcome some employee's issues while storing and sharing files in the workplace and decrease cost of storage servers in the workplace. The follow up activity will be to evaluate the prototype and identify lessons learned for similar approaches (reflection and documentation).

References

1. Barreau, D., et al.: Finding and reminding: file organization from the desktop. In: SIGCHI (1995)
2. Barrett, R.B., et al.: Field studies of computer system administrators: analysis of system management tools and practices. In: CSCW (2004)
3. Bellotti, V.B., et al.: Quality versus quantity: e-mail-centric task management and its relation with overload. Hum.-Comput. Interact. **20**(1), 89–138 (2005)
4. Bernstein, M.B., et al.: Information scraps: how and why information eludes our personal information management tools. ACM Trans. Inf. Syst. **26**(4), 1–46 (2008). Article 24
5. Boardman, R.B, Sasse, A.M.S.: Stuff goes into the computer and doesn't come out: a cross-tool study of personal information management. In: SIGCHI (2004)
6. Broadbent, G.B.: The morality of design. In: Design: Science: Method, pp. 309–328 (1981)
7. Chard, K.C., et al.: Social cloud computing: a vision for socially motivated resource sharing. IEEE Trans. Serv. Comput. **5**(4), 551–563 (2012)
8. Collins, A.C., et al.: Design research: theoretical and methodological issues. J. Learn. Sci. **13**, 15–42 (2004)
9. Cross, N.C., et al.: From a design science to a design discipline: understanding designerly ways of knowing and thinking. In: Design Research Now. Birkhäuser Basel (2007)
10. Jones, W.J., et al.: Don't take my folders away!: organizing personal information to get things done. In: SIGCHI (2005)
11. Muller, M., et al.: We are all lurkers: consuming behaviors among authors and readers in an enterprise file-sharing service. In: GROUP (2010)
12. Nieveen, N.: Educational design research: the value of variety. In: Van Den Akker, J., et al. (eds.) Introducing Educational Design Research, pp. 151–157. Roultedge, New York (2006)
13. Olson, J.S.O., et al.: A study of preferences for sharing and privacy. In: CHI (2005)
14. Plomp, T.P. Educational design research: an introduction. In: Seminar Conducted at the East China Normal University, Shanghai (2007)
15. Rader, E.R.: The effect of audience design on labeling, organizing, and finding shared files. In: SIGCHI (2010)
16. Reeves, T.R.: Design research from a technology perspective. In: Van Den Akker, J., et al. (eds.) Educational Design Research, pp. 52–66. Roultedge, New York (2006)
17. Tang, J.C.: Exploring patterns of social commonality among file directories at work. In: CHI (2007)
18. Tinedo, T., et al.: Friendbox: A hybrid F2F personal storage application. In: CLOUD (2012)
19. Van deer Akker, J.A., et al.: An introduction to educational design research. In: Proceedings of the Seminar Conducted at the East China Normal University (2009)
20. Voida, S.V., et al.: Share and share alike: exploring the user interface affordances of file sharing. In: SIGCHI (2006)
21. Zhang, H., Twidale, M.: Mine, yours and ours: using shared folders in personal information management. In: Personal Information Management (PIM) (2012)
22. Zimmerman, Z.: Research through design as a method for interaction design research in HCI (2007)

Evolution of e-Research: From Infrastructure Development to Service Orientation

Hashim Iqbal Chunpir[1,2(✉)], Thomas Ludwig[1,2],
and Dean N. Williams[3]

[1] German Climate Computing Center (DKRZ), Bundesstr. 45a,
20146 Hamburg, Germany
{chunpir, ludwig}@dkrz.de
[2] Department of Informatics, University of Hamburg, Hamburg, Germany
[3] Lawrence Livermore National Laboratory (LLNL), Livermore, CA, USA
williams13@llnl.gov

Abstract. E-Research has reframed the process of research. Researchers can now access distributed data around the globe with the help of e-Research infrastructure. This paper presents an overview of the developmental process and evolution of an e-Research platform: Earth System Grid Federation (ESGF) that evolved from a research infrastructure test-bed to a services oriented platform, in subsequent phases. ESGF is a leading distributed peer to peer data grid system in Earth System Modelling having around 27000 users distributed all over the world. Currently, it is a challenge faced by most of the e-Research facilities to provide user oriented services. Moreover, there is a strong need to conduct user experience and usability studies of e-Research facilities like ESGF, which is in demand. However, very few steps have been taken in practice to create a better user experience (UX), so that users' interest can be generated to interact with e-infrastructures, on an intuitive basis. Hence, thriving the practice of e-Research and making it more interesting overtime. Finally, this paper indicates at the service oriented and usability aspects of e-Science infrastructures.

Keywords: Service orientation of e-Science systems · E-Research · User support · Help desk · User experience · User-centered design · Federated e-Research facilities

1 Introduction

Usability and user service orientation of big data has always been an interesting topic in Human Computer Interaction (HCI), Computer Supported Cooperative Work (CSCW), e-Research, big data and other fields as it refers to use of technology via which a user can achieve big discoveries. The recent discovery of Higgs Boson Particle was also accomplished via an e-Research facility at CERN (reported by BBC on 1st August 2012). Users of e-Research technology are chiefly researchers and they realize multifarious tasks of their research that they need to complete within a specific time-frame, via e-Research infrastructures. In the past, in e-Research facilities, a massive development effort and money has been invested in making infrastructure

© Springer International Publishing Switzerland 2015
A. Marcus (Ed.): DUXU 2015, Part III, LNCS 9188, pp. 25–35, 2015.
DOI: 10.1007/978-3-319-20889-3_3

stable and reliable [1, 2]. Currently, in most of e-Research facilities, a relatively stable and reliable state has been achieved such that they can serve researchers by fulfilling their research needs [3]. Moreover, research and development in improving the user oriented services in e-Research facilities has been done to some extent [2, 3]. However, the usability aspects of e-Research infrastructure have hardly been addressed [4].

The organization of this paper is as follows: Sect. 2 provides a brief background on this study related to the field of e-Research. The research methods used in this study are explained in Sect. 3. An overview on the historical development of ESGF is given in Sect. 4. Discussion and future work on ESGF is given in Sect. 5. Finally, concluding remarks are provided in Sect. 6.

2 Background

This paper analyzes the historical development of a well-known e-Research facility Earth System Grid Federation (ESGF) that is serving data projects in climate science domain. ESGF facilitates to study climate change and impact of climate change on human society and Earth's eco system [5]. Moreover, this paper provides an overview of the structural, organizational, functional development achieved in ESGF, including the expansion in volume as well as number of data projects that is served with respect to user oriented services. With the passage of time the users of ESGF have also increased in number and currently there are 27,000 users using this e-Research facility for research purposes.

The structural, organizational and functional development of ESGF includes, for instance; programming, architectural design, connectivity of distributed components, strategic planning including governance with organization, node administration and others. The process of operating, maintaining and further expanding the e-Research facility including its data is iterative in nature [1, 6]. Apart from the structural, organizational and functional development in ESGF, progress in servicing end-user requests has also been done. The progress includes offering user support in the form of self-help via support websites, online tutorials, wikis or contacting an expert in the form of traditional help-desk [7, 8] and service-desk [9–11]. In this paper, the environmental complexity and the contemporary practices of user support services is presented. The paper then emphasizes on the need to enhance the usability and user experience in e-Research.

3 Research Methodology

In this research, case study research method is used and an important practical use-case in e-Research, in the field of climate science is ESGF project. This study is based on a single, in-depth, synchronic case in the e-Research infrastructure user services sector. A case study is "a research strategy which focuses on understanding the dynamics present with single settings" [12]. It can also be defined as "an empirical inquiry that investigates a contemporary phenomenon within its real-life context" [13].

The methods of data collection used in this study are: Participatory observations, informal meetings and archival analysis of documents relevant to ESGF.

A reason for the choice of the case study approach as a research method is that it suits well for studying service processes that are linked to a complex organizational context, as these cases offer in-depth view of development in organisations [14]. Moreover, the use of the case study is appropriate since e-Research infrastructure support involves a large number of actors in the form of distributed users and support teams and practices where the boundaries between these constituents are not easily distinguishable.

4 Evolution of ESGF

In this section the history of development of the ESGF along with the significant changes in the infrastructure and organization structure through time are described. It is important to see the developmental steps that the ESGF has been undergone. At first ESGF (then known as ESG) project was initiated as a grid computing research case, just to test the ability of grid computing and its associated technologies. Overtime, the technology matured enough to enable hosting data for research purposes, initially chosen to host climate data. Another important aspect to notice is the dynamic and ever changing structure of ESGF with time, if we observe the history of ESGF.

The history of ESGF is divided into four phases. The summary of salient features of the historical development of ESGF in these phases is discussed in the forthcoming sections. Phase 1 from 1999 to 2001 when it was called ESG-I is presented in Sect. 4.1, phase 2 from 2001 to 2006 when it was called ESG-II is given in Sect. 4.2, phase 3 from 2006 to 2011 when it was called ESG-CET is described in Sect. 4.3 and finally the current phase of ESGF which is from 2011 onwards is given in Sect. 4.4.

4.1 ESG-I Phase 1 (1999–2001)

There are varieties of problems faced by climate scientists, one of them is the need to efficiently access and manipulate climate data for research purposes. Climate scientists must collect number of datasets and analyze them, but these datasets are scattered and are accessible via different platforms using different tools which indeed are time consuming and inefficient in many cases. Therefore, in order to combat this problem a need was felt to create a common environment which could provide a common platform to not only access climate data sets but also analyze those using analysis tools. Consequently, an initiative began in 1999 with the name of "Prototyping an Earth System Grid" (ESG-I) funded under the auspices of DOE's Next Generation Internet program (NGI) to cater the needs of climate scientists and to fulfil the emerging challenge of climate data [15]. The contributing institutes in ESG were Argonne National Laboratory (ANL), Los Alamos National Laboratory (LANL), Lawrence Berkley National Laboratory (LBNL), Lawrence Livermore National Laboratory (LLNL), National Centre for Academic Research (NCAR) and University of Southern California's Information Sciences Institute (USC/ISI).

In this initial phase, ESG was able to achieve not only the goals of large data-set movement and replication between participating institutes via data grid technologies developed by ESG, but also ESG was able to develop a prototype of climate data browser. As a result of this achievement ESG got the hottest infrastructure award at a Supercomputing Conference (SC) in year 2000. ESG though demonstrated the potential for remotely accessing and analyzing climate data scattered across different sites within a country with the data transfer rate of 500 MB per second; however, it was still a prototype with few real users. Therefore, it was a technical demonstration of future "to be" collective data platform for climate researchers. It is important to note that before the initiation of ESG-I there was no central archive system to serve the stored climate data. At this stage since the system was a prototype, user support considerations were not made. The success of ESG opened ways to start ESG-II described in the following sub-section.

4.2   ESG-II Phase 2 (2001–2006)

The success of ESG prototype encouraged DOE to fund another phase of ESG project, known as ESG II whose major aim was to "turn the climate data sets into community resources" under Scientific Discovery through Advanced Computing (SciDAC) program. Since the ESG prototype was ready, it was important to put it into practice to encourage users to use the system by offering some data holdings to the users. Therefore, ESG II started to dispense Community Climate System Model (CCSM), the Parallel Climate Model (PCM) and the phase 3 of the Coupled Model Inter-comparison Project (CMIP3) model data archived at PCMDI. "This first production system led to major advances in model archiving, data management and sharing of distributed data" [16].

Subsequently, ESG II efforts focused on developing technologies to offer the user access to the ESG II system through a web-based security for user registration via a web portal. In addition, the technologies included extracting meta-data from catalogue files and distributed data transport capabilities via OPeNDAP-g[1] protocol. As a result, the system started supporting 10,000 registered international users and managed some 200 terra-bytes (TB) of data [16]. At this point, at least an informal user support need came into being to serve the registered users to cater their technical needs.

In this phase, one can observe that the e-Science infrastructure *prototype* engineered in the first phase of ESG I, was evolving with the inclusion of end-users and an addition of another participating institution i.e. a stakeholder, Oak Ridge National Laboratory (ORNL). The product was the ESG II e-Science infrastructure with more data sets added to PCM data model archive and the inclusion of two new data model archives namely: CCSM and CMIP3. Therefore, ESG II was the service provider of the above mentioned products which are the scientific products in this case. CMIP3 was used to produce IPCC's AR4 report. In this regard, CMIP3 data users used ESG II communication channels to provide suggestions to enhance portability, accuracy and

---

[1] Open-source Project for a Network Data Access Protocol, an architecture for data transport including standards for encapsulating structured data and describing data attributes implemented in a distributed computing environment (www.opendap.org/).

performance issues about climate models. This was the first instance where end-users of the product interacted with the developers; it is interesting to note that there were no considerations of formal user support about the usage of the ESG II. The further evolution of ESG is given in the next section.

4.3 ESG-CET Phase 3 (2006–2011)

ESG entered a new structural and organizational form with the name of Earth System Grid - Centre for Enabling Technologies (ESG-CET) phase 3, after funding for another phase from DOE's Offices of Advanced Scientific Computing Research (OASCR) and Biological Environmental Research (OBER). The primary goal was to extrapolate the existing system to be compatible to incorporate more data types and data archives at different sites that are further distributed and diverse in nature, even beyond national boundaries [16]. Hence, this phase was geared towards fulfilling demands of users i.e. climate researchers, around the globe, to provide them access to: Data, information, models, analysis tools, and computational resources required making sense of enormous climate simulation and observational data sets for their research. Another challenge of ESG-CET was to extend the capabilities of the infrastructure, so that a user can conduct initial data analysis where data physically resides, thus reducing network over-head to transfer data. As a result, the extension of ESG-CET e-Science infrastructure to slot in these additional features was commended by American Meteorological Society (AMS) for leadership, which led to a new era in climate system analysis and understanding.

ESG-CET joined the Global Organization for Earth System Science Portals (GO-ESSP) consortium to have collaboration with other institutions. All institutions in GO-ESSP share common data-management interests thus building a community. Another institute, Pacific Marine Environmental Laboratory (PMEL), which is part of National Oceanic and Atmospheric Administration (NOAA), joined in 2010. Therefore, there was also a surge of data-holdings from different climate institutions, offered by ESG-CET to users. It included phases 3 and 5 of the Coupled Model Inter-comparison (CMIP3, CMIP5), Climate Science for a Sustainable Energy Future (CSSEF), Community Climate System Model (CCSM), Parallel Ocean Program (POP), North American Regional Climate Change Assessment Program (NARCCAP), Carbon Land Model Inter-comparison Project (C-LAMP), Atmospheric Infrared Sounder (AIS), Microwave Limb Sounder (MLS), Cloudsat and others in ESG-CET data archive system. Thus, ESG-CET data archive system got bigger and it served over 1 Peta-Bytes (PB) of climate data to 25,000 registered users with 500 users active per month.

As a consequence, this was a gigantic development that pulled users to use ESG-CET infrastructure, to get access to the data-holdings, especially for the generation of IPCC AR4 and IPCC AR5 reports. The interaction of users with the ESG-CET system to access data-holdings led to the necessity of user support. The users were beyond national boundaries thus user support was needed round the clock. For the users to get their problems solved, an effective and efficient user support system was needed, which was not formally present. Keeping this in view, communication channels between users, the developers of the ESG-CET technical system and data managers of concerned data projects were established. The most used channel of communication was via e-mail. In later years, multiple mailing-lists were established to cater the needs of different stakeholders.

In this phase, the main problem was a lack of stakeholders to realize the set-up of formalized user support system. Since the development and evolution of ESG-CET e-Science infrastructure was the primary concern, direct funding was not dedicated for the development of user support activities. It was in 2011 that an initiative was taken by one of the researchers i.e. the first author, who was working on C3Grid, a collaborative project of the ESG; to investigate the user support process, usability as well as user experience aspects in e-Research infrastructure and ESG-CET (now known as ESGF) was chosen as a case study.

4.4   ESGF P2P: The Current Phase (from 2011 Onwards)

The developments in the previous phase of ESG-CET continued with most of the funding under the DOE's OBER. Additional funding institutes within the US included NASA, NOAA and NSF; most of them are maintaining and taking care of their concerned administrative jurisdictions including node(s). In the European Union (EU), large funding for ESGF is being provided by IS-ENES project [17]. This phase was formally initiated in 2011 and is the current phase. Since then, ESGF-P2P has become an open consortium of institutions, laboratories and centers around the world, that are dedicated to supporting research of climate change, and its environmental and societal impact. With the inclusion of international institutions on board as stakeholders and inclusion of even more data-holdings, the need was felt to generalize the system in the form of a federation to encourage and attract climate data providers worldwide. Consequently, the system architecture of ESGF P2P data archive system evolved in the form, what now the current ESGF peer-to-peer (P2P) looks like.

The federation includes multiple universities and institutional partners in the US, Europe, Asia, and Australia, thus making it one of the outstanding e-Science infra-structures in the domain of climate science. This was the reason that during this phase, ESGF grew out of the larger Global Organization for Earth System Science Portals (GO-ESSP) community [18]. It now reflects a broad array of contributions from the collaborating partners.

It is interesting to note that with the enormous growth in the organizational structure of ESGF, an upward trend of registered users was recorded [19]. The registered users reached almost 27,000 in number, from different parts of the world, with almost 700 to 800 active users per month. With this rapid development in the ESGF organization, there is an ever-increasing need to meet long-term user-support requirements, as the number of data-holdings and number of users rise. One can infer that the development of ESGF P2P network is a trend setter for open data sharing in an environment of multi-institute and global collaboration, where beneficiaries of the whole set-up are users i.e. climate researchers. Therefore, user support services cannot be ignored.

The developmental collaboration of various institutes around the globe has contributed socially, technically and politically to introduce a global data connectivity for the users. However, though certain improvements were made with the passage of time to service users by introducing an ad hoc user support system. Yet, the full potential in delivering user support services was not achieved as the current user-support system lacks a directed and dedicated effort, as well as funding, to develop a long-term user support process (as it is evident from interviews with the stakeholders). Looking at the history of ESGF data archive system, the need to have a long-term, robust and scalable data archive system was sensed and fulfilled to some extent. However, the need to have long-term user support services was not highlighted in the policy of ESGF consortium. This was the reason that the funding was more or less oriented towards developing ESGF technically (to serve data holdings to the users), and efforts to support users were though present but insignificant. From the history of ESGF, it is evident that the data and computational resources are always increasing with the passage of time. There have always been new ways of organizing the ESGF system, i.e. revising the system architecture following new collaborative and organizational reforms to develop new methods of data access and discovery for users. This implies that ESGF is going through a continuous evolution of social, cultural, organizational, legal, institutional and technical re-structuring. Consequently, the users need a dynamic user support process which is adaptable to the changing needs of the system.

5 Discussion and Future Work

Looking at the history of ESGF, one can conclude that the architecture and organization of the e-Science infrastructure has a well-set trajectory or momentum of offering more scalability, more data holdings, international collaborations of institutions and more users. Historians who have studied e-Science infrastructures have referred to this as "momentum" of an infrastructure and argued that once a particular "path" or momentum has established and tend to continue in a particular direction, making reversals or alteration become costly, difficult and in some cases impossible [20]. Therefore, it is the right time to study processes behind user support services as at this stage ESGF has achieved maturity in its infrastructural trend. If this is not done at the earliest, efforts of the developers and scientists may get wasted. Thus, as a consequence the full potential of this e-Science infrastructure and collaboration of global institutes may not be fully realized until or unless user support services are not streamlined.

ESGF is stated as: "The Earth System Grid Federation (ESGF) is a multi-agency, international collaboration of people and institutions working together to build an open source software infrastructure for the management and analysis of Earth Science data on a global scale" [21]. However, in this ESGF definition user support services are not explicitly made part of the definition of ESGF. Keeping the anatomy of ESGF P2P data archive system in view, the user support system of ESGF has its sub-units. Though these sub-units are not formally designated as support units within administrative

Fig. 1. Distribution of administrative units of ESGF

bodies, the support units are implicitly part of administrative bodies. Consequently, from the geographically distributed organization of ESGF P2P network, it is understandable that each and every administrative domain have their own practices of handling user-requests. This observation is also evident from the qualitative cum quantitative inquiry into the support practices of ESGF undertaken by the authors. The diversity of practices in handling user queries by the user support staff, who themselves are developers of the ESGF system, form different support structures and models followed in each of the administrative domains that tend to make a heterogeneous user support process. Subsequently, the user support system in ESGF does not comply with any set standards of processing user support requests.

From the Fig. 1 one can anticipate that the numbers of administrative bodies (principal investigation institutions plus developing teams of ESGF), data holdings, ESGF users, and ESGF staffs participating in ESGF P2P system are subject to increase. Additionally, the role of an administrative body and its attached components such as nodes are subject to change, therefore this whole ESGF set-up is a complex, dynamic and evolving in nature. In ESGF system there is a continuous architecture re-designs activities, software development, hardware changes, data publishing, data curation, data quality check and other activities. Attached to these core operational activities is the necessity of the user support activities that cannot be ignored. A dynamic and an ever-evolving infrastructure need a dynamic user support "service desk." Therefore, e-Science is likely to be confronted with demanding issues of long-term and continuity of service, particularly related to user support services which is quite similar to data curation and software development.

In the future, ESGF will cover other scientific domains such as health sciences, biology, chemistry, energy as well radio-astronomy. With these additions of domains more users will be using the ESGF e-Research facility, consequently making usability and user experience very important. Therefore, there is a need to measure the user experience and usability of the interfaces provided by ESGF to the actors who interact with the ESGF system. Moreover, the current user interfaces of ESGF are needed to be evaluated and based on the findings of the investigation, recommendations can be made in future to enhance the usability and user experience.

6 Conclusion

In this paper a historical overview of the organizational and structural advances achieved in ESGF e-Research facility of climate science domain is presented. Furthermore, in this study, the evolution of ESGF e-Research infrastructure is observed with the help of research techniques such as participant observation, archival analysis and informal meetings. ESGF has evolved from a non-user oriented research experimental testbed towards a user-oriented environment. Currently, it is evident from the observations that the aspects of usability and user experience within e-Research facilities especially in climate science need improvement. Attention of sponsors, operational and executive staff members of e-Research facilities in climate science such as ESGF is required to improve the usability needs of users. Further studies are needed to be conducted with the users of ESGF to capture the user experience and restructure the complex and dynamic interfaces provided to different types of users of the e-Research facility. Currently, the authors are working on a conceptual model to improve the user experience and usability standards in e-Research interfaces within the climate science and other domain. In the future, the authors will observe the effectiveness of transferring front line user support units to various institutes in developing countries.

Acknowledgement. We appreciate the sincere participation and support of our all colleagues and the users of ESGF.

References

1. Chunpir, H.I., Badewi, A.A., Ludwig, T.: User support system in the complex environment. In: Marcus, A. (ed.) Design, User Experience, and Usability. User Experience Design Practice. Lecture Notes in Computer Science, vol. 8520, pp. 392–402. Springer International Publishing, Cham (2014)
2. Chunpir, H.I., Ludwig, T.: Reviewing the governance structure of end-user support in e-science infrastructures. In: Informatik 2014 Proceedings of Mastering Big Data Complexity. Lecture Notes in Informatics (LNI), vol. 232 (2014)
3. Chunpir, H.I., Ludwig, T., Badewi, A.: A snap-shot of user support services in earth system grid federation (ESGF): a use case of climate cyber-infrastructures. In: Proceedings of the 5th Applied Human Factors and Ergonomics (AHFE) Conference, July 2014

4. Hey, T., Trefethen, A.E.: Cyberinfrastructure for e-science. Science **308**(5723), 817–821 (2005)
5. Cinquini, L., Crichton, D., Mattmann, C., Bell, G.M., Drach, B., Williams, D., Harney, J., Denvil, S., Schweitzer, R.: The earth system grid federation (ESGF): an open infrastructure for access to distributed geospatial data. In: 8th IEEE International Conference on E-Science, pp. 1–10 (2012)
6. Chunpir, H.I., Ludwig, T., Badewi, A.A.: Using soft systems methodology (SSM) in understanding current user-support scenario in the climate science domain of cyber-infrastructures. In: Marcus, A. (ed.) DUXU 2014, Part III. LNCS, vol. 8519, pp. 495–506. Springer, Heidelberg (2014)
7. Leung, N., Lau, S.: Information technology help desk survey: to identify the classification of simple and routine enquiries. J. Comput. Inf. Syst. **47**(1), 70–81 (2007)
8. Leung, N.K.Y.: University of Wollongong Thesis Collection Turning user into first level support in help desk : development of web-based user self-help knowledge management system (2006)
9. Jäntti, M.: Improving IT service desk and service management processes in finnish tax administration: a case study on service engineering. In: Dieste, O., Jedlitschka, A., Juristo, N. (eds.) PROFES 2012. LNCS, vol. 7343, pp. 218–232. Springer, Heidelberg (2012)
10. Jäntti, M.: Lessons learnt from the improvement of customer support processes: a case study on incident management. In: Bomarius, F., Oivo, M., Jaring, P., Abrahamsson, P. (eds.) PROFES 2009. LNBIP, vol. 32, pp. 317–331. Springer, Heidelberg (2009)
11. Jäntti, M.: Examining challenges in IT service desk system and processes: a case study. In: Seventh International Conference on Systems, ICONS 2012, pp. 105–108 (2012)
12. Yin, R.: Case Study Research Design and Methods, 5th edn, p. 240. Sage Publishing, Thousand Oaks (2013)
13. Eisenhardt, K.: Building theories from case study research. Acad. Manag. Rev. **14**(4), 532–550 (1989)
14. Buchanan, D.A.: Case studies in organisational research. In: Symon, G., Cassel, C. (eds.) The Practice of Qualitative Organisational Research: Core Methods and Current Challenges, pp. 373–392. Sage Publishing, London (2012)
15. Bernholdt, D., Bharathi, S., Brown, D., Chanchio, K., Chen, M., Chervenak, A., Cinquini, L., Drach, B., Foster, I., Fox, P., Garcia, J., Kesselman, C., Markel, R., Middleton, D., Nefedova, V., Pouchard, L., Shoshani, A., Sim, A., Strand, G., Williams, D.: The earth system grid: supporting the next generation of climate modeling research. Proc. IEEE **93**(3), 485–495 (2005)
16. Williams, D.N., Drach, R., Ananthakrishnan, R., Foster, I.T., Fraser, D., Siebenlist, F., Bernholdt, D.E., Chen, M., Schwidder, J., Bharathi, S., Chervenak, A.L., Schuler, R., Su, M., Brown, D., Cinquini, L., Fox, P., Garcia, J., Middleton, D.E., Strand, W.G., Wilhelmi, N., Hankin, S., Schweitzer, R., Jones, P., Shoshani, A., Sim, A.: The earth system grid: enabling access to multimodel climate simulation data. Bull. Am. Meteorol. Soc. **90**(2), 195–205 (2009)
17. ENES: The ENES portal: European network for earth system modelling (2013). https://verc.enes.org/. Accessed 02 December 2014
18. ESGF: ESG: Earth system grid. ESGF (2010). https://www.earthsystemgrid.org/about/overview.htm. Accessed 13 May 2014

19. ESGF: ESGF use statistics for CMIP5 data sets (2015)
20. Jackson, S.J., Edwards, P.N., Bowker, G.C., Knobel, C.P.: Understanding infrastructure: history, heuristics and cyber infrastructure policy. First Monday **12**(6) (2007). http://pear. accc.uic.edu/ojs/index.php/fm/article/view/1904/1786
21. Williams, D.N.: Earth system grid federation (ESGF): future and governance, Livermore, CA, USA (2012)

Visualizing Group User Behaviors for Social Network Interaction Design Iteration

Zhenyu Gu[✉], Jia Ming Yu, Zhanwei Wu, and Zhan Xun Dong

Shanghai Jiao Tong University, Shanghai, China
zygu@sjtu.edu.cn

Abstract. Considering the popularity of UCD methods in recent years, it's no surprise that User behavior data analysis has become an important tool in design process. Behavior tools based on data mining technology, such as Flurry and Google Analytics, is widely used in web-based applications to support quantitative user research. However, information visualization provided by those tools is usually adapted to business other than design needs, which could be hardly used by designers. In this paper, successful experience from CRM system is analyzed, relations between user behavior and pattern is studied according to design factors. A prototype visualizing user data gathered from a social photo app is developed to integrate user behavior visualization into interaction design iteration process. User experiments are conducted to evaluate the prototype system. Results shown, interactive visualization on real-time user data could help to promote design iteration.

Keywords: Quantitative analysis · Information visualization · Design iteration

1 Introduction

With the development of social network and pervasive computing technology, social products that integrate social networking functions into daily activities are becoming more and more popular. However, in the initial design investigation or later design iterations of these products, traditional small-scale user test is usually problematic, including biased sample, difficulty in surveys for massive data or incapability of static questionnaires to reflect dynamic changes in social networking activities. Thus, big data processing techniques are introduced by some researchers and developers, to optimize interaction procedure through the analysis of social behavior data [1]. In addition, Cloud Computing technology is adopted to collect large-scale user behavior data and preference [2].

However, it is extremely difficult to find out the correlation between user behavior patterns and the design variations in the massive user data, which hinders the development of these applications. Research has shown that proper visualization enables designers to find the implicit correlations in big data and understand the trends for further design improvements [3].

In this paper, we take the interaction design of a social digital photo frame as an example to show how to perform visualization analysis on collected large-scale user

© Springer International Publishing Switzerland 2015
A. Marcus (Ed.): DUXU 2015, Part III, LNCS 9188, pp. 36–45, 2015.
DOI: 10.1007/978-3-319-20889-3_4

data and apply the results to the interface optimization. In the end, we testified the effectiveness of the method through the designers' practical real use.

2 Data Definition and Preprocess

The loading capacity of social applications can be evaluated through the number of hits of users captured by the server side. For user behavior analysis, the interaction activeness among users can also be evaluated with the user access behavior. Through the analysis of the user behavior data, social habits in different dimensions can be revealed, including daily online time and access frequency. In addition, these data can be used to enrich the node graph visualizing the social connections among the users with extra dimensions.

2.1 Definition of Dataset

Based on graph theory, user behavior data in social network can be divided into nodes set U and links set L. The nodes set is user information $u_i \in U$, which can be described as $\{N_u, N_a, T, A\}$. Wherein, N_u is the ID number assigned in the social network, T is the device type used by the user, N is the nickname of the user and A is the activation time of the user. The detail definition of nodes set is given as followed:

- User ID in social network (N_u) is unique number of every user, which is the identification of each user.
- User Device type (T) is the device which user login the social network, for example mobile, tablet and PC.
- User nickname (N_a) is a kind of text tag, which may imply the relationship between users.
- User Activation time (A) is the first time of user to login this social network.

Links set $l_{ij} = (u_i, u_j)$ describes the relation between user u_i and user u_j. The relation here can be divided into two layers f_{ij} and s_{ij}. The f_{ij} is relation in static data layer, while s_{ij} is the one in dynamic data layer. The difference between these two data layers is described as followed (in Fig. 1):

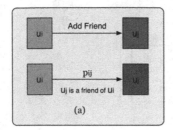 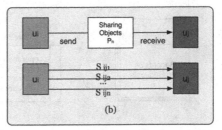

Fig. 1. Links based on contact layout; Links based on share action

- The link f_{ij} in static data layer is mainly based on the followers and friend list of users. In social network, the f_{ij} indicates the only directed line from u_i to u_j which means u_i add u_j as friend and the only value of f_{ij} is the create time of relation.
- The link s_{ij} in dynamic data layer makes share resources as primary key. Since some users will allow strangers to get their sharing content, through mining the commend records and related operation records of the same content, s_{ij} can indicate the content P shared from user u_i to user u_j. The P can be described as a collection of resources $\{p_1, p_2, p_3 \cdots p_n\}$. Wherein, p_i can be described as $\{P_N, P_T, U_T, N_F, N_T, T_G\}$, in which P_N is the name of the resource, P_T is the created time of the resource, U_T is upload time, N_F is the ID of user who shares the resource, N_T is the ID of user who receives the resource and TG is the tag added while sharing.

2.2 Data Preparation

Since social applications interact with server frequently, most of the user operation records can be analyzed from server log files. According to the data structure defined above, the raw data need to be got should contain user information, user relations and operation records. Among those, user information and user relations are both synchronized to the server. And the user operation records can be analyzed from the server log files of HTTP requests, since the parameters carried in the web request package may indicate the operator, operation time as well as other key elements.

In the visualization module, the target data is divided into relational data and line items. For efficient analysis, database is combined by line database and graph database. The line database stores user operations records, which are sorted by operation time, and the graph database stores user basic information as well as friend relations (in Fig. 2).

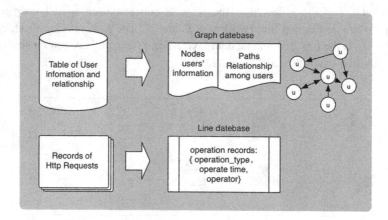

Fig. 2. The workflow of data preprocess

3 Visualization Solutions for User Behavior Data

It has been proved that the information visualization is an effective way of perception, because it can complement and strengthen the psychological perception with visual factors [5]. In prediction of intelligent transportation, the visualization techniques are applied to display the real-time status of traffic so as to identify potential congested roads quickly and make scheduling decisions timely [6]. In design process, in order to plan specific design goal, the designer will define an abstract character (Persona) from user research as well as depict the storyboard to describe the scenarios [7]. Then the interaction process will be defined clearly based on them.

The three processes above are familiar to designers. In many research, it is shown that association fresh knowledge to familiar things can improve the ability of understanding new knowledge. Next paragraph will mention a classification process of user data according to the design factors above.

To reflect the importance of the user behavior analysis of application, the sample data is from a family photo sharing social network whose online users are 4773. Different from stand-alone applications, the user behavior data not only contains line operation records of single user, but also involves associated operation records between users.

3.1 Frequency-of-Using Visualized by Heat-Map Matrix Diagram

Heat-map usually labels the weight in graphic by using different markers, such as attractiveness and click times. In the diagram, the weight is usually preformed by the brightness and hue of color.

In social network applications, frequency of accesses to SNS (social network sites), total time spent on SNS per user and number of online users over time are major variables of statistics. These variables can reflect user viscosity of the application, peak period of online users and etc. To designers, these variables can be linked to the user habits as defined in the model of persona.

In order to adapt to the visualization of complex multi-dimension data, we learn from heat matrix [8] to visual the interrelation among short-time distance, long-time distance and amount of information. This form was indicated helpful for designers to understand data from the macroscopic point of view through user interviews.

3.2 Connections Among Multi-devices Visualized with Bipartite Diagram

Bipartite graph, also known as bigraph, is a kind of special model in graph theory. Bipartite graph is a graph whose undirected vertices can be split into two disjoint sets (A, B) and two vertices i and j associated in same edge are in each of the two different vertex set A and B in figure [9].

For multi-terminal applications, understanding the proportion and correlation ratio of different terminals can help people to judge the trend of product in the market. The distribution and active number of all the members in social application are both important for analysis, which can assist marketing to make better decisions and can also provide information to enrich the usage scenarios (Fig. 3).

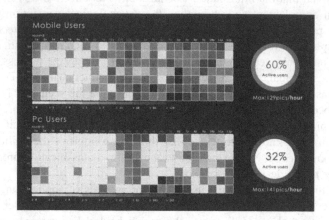

Fig. 3. User sharing frequency (The top is the mobile user and the bottom is PC user)

In the visualization, in order to describe relevance of terminal connections and photo-sharing amount, these are all visualized in the form of bipartite graph and added interactive mode to display association between two datasets (in Fig. 4). In the interview, some designers said that they could find correlation among data much more easily by combining interactive animation.

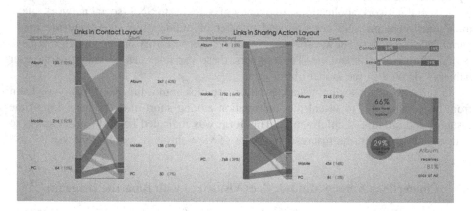

Fig. 4. Connections among multi-terminals

3.3   Using Paths and Interests of the Users

User traffic is usually used as a judgment standard of page attractiveness in Web site design such as conversion rate measuring the attraction of webpage content. In design, frequency of every operation can be mapped into the step defined in interaction process model. In order to get better express of interrelation between operation depth and usage frequency, the design of visualization combines the Sankey diagram [10], flow diagrams and tree diagram into it in order to display the usage amount of each operation and user difference between two operations (in Fig. 5).

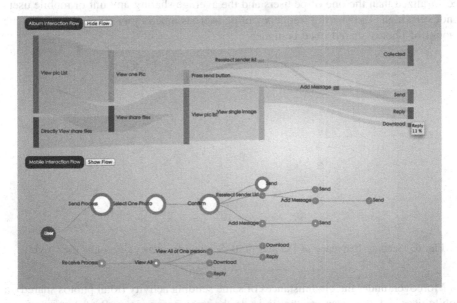

Fig. 5. Tree diagram and flow diagram of operations

Flow diagram is usually used to display quantity change. The connections in flow diagram are described as strip graphics whose height infers the value of weight. Tree diagram has strong meaning of levels, which can describe the sequence of operations directly. Sankey diagram, also called sankey energy split graph or Sankey energy balance diagram, belongs to a specific type of flow diagram. The width of branches in the diagram corresponds to the size of data flow and the width of beginning branches equals to the width of end branches, which performs the balance of energy. Interviews of users shows that the form of tree diagram is much more fit to display the unidirectional and hierarchy of operations directly and the flow diagram combining the Sankey diagram is conductive for users to understand the variation of user amount between different levels, which makes the diagram hold context properties.

4 Applying the Visualization Solutions

Based on the analysis of the three visualization diagrams above, the following will associate UI elements in actual App with user elements. The target application is a family photo-sharing platform, which contains three different devices (mobile, digital albums and pc). There are 4773 online users using this application currently, and the earliest user started to use the app since September 2013.

4.1 Comparing Behavioral Characteristics Among Multi-terminals

In Fig. 6, the proportion of mobile users and pc users is 2:1, while the sharing peak of pc users is higher than the one of mobile users. Through the distribution of the nodes in diagram, it can be inferred that the sharing frequency of mobile users is much more decentralized than the one of pc users and the average sharing amount of mobile users is not very high. The sharing frequency of pc users is much more concentrated and the amount of photos shared once is higher.

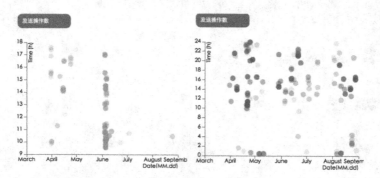

Fig. 6. Sending frequency of PC user (left), Sending frequency of mobile user (right)

Moreover, under the circumstances of same sending activity (total photos shared), a mobile user and a pc user are chosen to do the track comparison. By the comparison, we found that:

(1) Mobile users usually share pictures instantly and single sharing amount is lower, but the frequency of sharing is higher.
(2) The frequency of pc users is lower, but the sharing strength is higher, which means pc users have strong demand of batch sharing.

4.2 The Flow of Content Sharing Among Multi-terminals

In Fig. 4, contrast to the ratio of user connections and photo sharing amount, we can find that the largest number of connections exist between mobile user and album users, and the second largest number of connections exist between album user and mobile user in user relations layer. And in sending action layer, most of the photos are sent from mobile users, and album users receive 80 % of those photos, so most of feedback design should be applied between mobile users and album users.

4.3 Conversion Rate of Operations

Conversion rate is mainly used to evaluate the attractiveness of web-page design currently and in app design it can also be used to measure usability. Compared to the statistics of single operating amount, conversion rate can reflect the characteristics of process better. In interaction process diagram (Fig. 5), the operations with lower conversion rate are: replying messages when receiving photos, collecting photos and downloading photos. Among those, the low conversion rate of downloading photos is caused by automatic downloading function, so it cannot be optimized as target operation necessarily. Besides, although replying message and collecting photos do not affect the process of photo previewing and playing, these two operations belong to feedback design, which means the single operation may involve multi-users.

The feedback design mentioned above is mostly applied between mobile users and album users. The status of low feedback causes the problem that implementation rate of related operations in different devices is also lower. By the flow chart of users, we found that the depth of feedback operations is all 3 or 3 above, which means users have to go through at least 3 pages to read or commend a photo since they see the notification of new photos. Such design is obviously not conducive for the high feedback from users.

5 Test and the Efficacy

In order to verify the helpfulness of the solution, six students with design education background are invited to use this visualization tool. After a certain learning period to understand these visualization diagrams above, they all gave some solutions to improve the interaction design of this application. The main improvement advices given are:

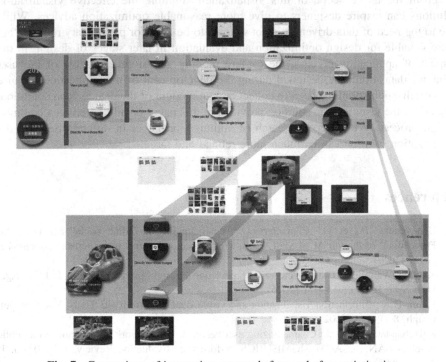

Fig. 7. Comparison of interaction process before and after optimization

(1) On the basis of original user habits, the feedback design in the process should be simplified. In order to allow album users to make high feedback to others, such operations such as photos commending and collecting should be migrated from the current depth that is deeper than level 3 to the position of level 1.
(2) In order to stimulate the album users user feedback operations, the messages caused by such operations are all displayed in the font-page automatically.

According to the advices above, the app for album users is redesigned, and some of the users were invited to use the new version. The new user behavior data collected from these test users are visualized by the same solution in paragraph 3. Compared to the diagrams driven by the old user data, the conversion rate of feedback operations is obviously higher than before (in Fig. 7).

6 Conclusion

Visualizing data by the demands of target users is one of the measurements to enhance the readability of diagrams. In this paper, the target demands of visualization are found from the design elements in the model of persona, scenario and interactive process and the demo was developed on the basis of an online photo social application. Then, students with design education background were invited to give improvement advices about interaction design by reading the visualization graph. And the data collected from small test sample is used to evaluate the effectiveness of the improvement advices.

From the usage scope of this visualization solution, the effective visualization solutions can inspire designers to give more reasonable optimization advices. While due to the need of data-driven, it is not suitable to be used for preliminary research but more suitable for design optimization and evaluation in later stages of design. In the respect of application process, the capture module and storage module of the user behavior data should be designed during the development of the application because the visualization solutions need to collect a large amount of the data as a precondition. Currently, the visualization solution provided in this paper is only based on a common design process. With deeper research of optimization target in different devices, the visualization solution can be much more refined and targeted.

References

1. Benevenuto, F., et al.: Characterizing user behavior in online social networks. In: Proceedings of the 9th ACM SIGCOMM Conference on Internet measurement Conference, ACM (2009)
2. Xu, M., Walton, J.: Gaining customer knowledge through analytical CRM. Ind. Manage. Data Syst. **105**(7), 955–971 (2005)
3. Keim, D.A.: Information visualization and visual data mining. IEEE Trans. Vis. Comput. Graph. **8**(1), 1–8 (2002)
4. Balachandran, A., et al.: Characterizing user behavior and network performance in a public wireless LAN. In: ACM SIGMETRICS Performance Evaluation Review, vol. 30, no. 1. ACM (2002)

5. Meirelles, I.: Design for Information: An Introduction to the Histories, Theories, and Best Practices Behind Effective Information Visualizations. Rockport Publishers, Beverly (2013)
6. Uchida, M., Shirayama, S.: Formation of patterns from complex networks. J. Vis. **10**(3), 253–255 (2007)
7. Kankainen, A.: UCPCD: user-centered product concept design. In: Proceedings of the 2003 Conference on Designing for User Experiences. ACM (2003)
8. Wilkinson, L., Friendly, M.: The history of the cluster heat map. Am. Stat. **63**(2), 179–184 (2009)
9. Dulmage, A., Mendelsohn, N.: A structure theory of bi-partite graphs. Trans. [8] Roy. Soc. Can. Sec. 3. **53**, 1–13 (1959)
10. Schmidt, M.: The Sankey diagram in energy and material flow management. J. Ind. Ecol. **12**(1), 82–94 (2008)

Understanding the Semantics of Web Interface Signs: A Set of Ontological Principals

Muhammad Nazrul Islam[1](✉) and A.K.M. Najmul Islam[2]

[1] Information Systems, Institute of Advanced Management Systems Research,
Åbo Akademi University, Turku, Finland
nislam@abo.fi

[2] Department of Information Systems Science, University of Turku,
Turku, Finland
najmul.islam@utu.fi

Abstract. Interface signs are the communication artifacts of web interfaces, with which users interact. Examples of interface signs are small images, navigational links, buttons and thumbnails. Although, intuitive interface signs are crucial elements of a good user interface (UI), prior research ignored these in UI design and usability evaluation process. This paper argues that ontology (the set of concepts and skills for understanding the referential meaning of an interface sign) mapping is critical for intuitive sign design. A light weighted experiment with six participants and twelve signs has been carried out in order to demonstrate the importance of ontology mapping in understanding the semantics of interface signs. The paper concludes with some practical implications and suggestions for future research.

Keywords: Ontology · Web interface sign · Web usability · User interface design · Usability evaluation

1 Introduction

Interface signs are the key elements of web user interface (UI). These signs act as the communication artifacts between the users and designers/systems. Examples of interface signs are navigational links, thumbnails, small images, command buttons, symbols, icons, etc. The semantic of interface signs refers to the meaning (referential or intrinsic) of an interface sign, i.e., for what purpose the sign stands in the UI. For example, the semantic of the 'HOME' sign in a webpage refers to 'getting the main/home page of the website'.

End users are required to interpret the web interfaces in order to interact with them. Interaction between users and web interfaces is mediated via interface signs since the content and functions of web systems are directed primarily through interface signs. Thus, at low level, users interpret the 'interface signs' of user interfaces (e.g., navigational links, symbols, icons, etc.) to understand the system's logic and to perform tasks [3]. It is thus important to design user-intuitive interface signs so that users can interpret the meaning (semantic) of the interface signs easily and accurately.

© Springer International Publishing Switzerland 2015
A. Marcus (Ed.): DUXU 2015, Part III, LNCS 9188, pp. 46–53, 2015.
DOI: 10.1007/978-3-319-20889-3_5

Understanding the semantics/meanings of interface signs properly allow users to go directly to the content of interest. For a user-intuitive interface sign, users do not need to click on the interface sign to see the referential content in order to understand the meaning of the sign in question. Thus, designing user-intuitive interface signs and evaluating the intuitiveness of interface signs become essential in UI design and usability evaluation process [2, 6]. Consequently, Bolchini et al. [1] suggested 'interface sign' as one of the major dimensions of web UI design and usability evaluation. However, very few studies explicitly focused on interface signs in UI design and evaluation [10]. In this paper, we describe a set of ontological principals that users use for understanding web interface signs.

The term *ontology* is defined as the set of concepts and skills for understanding the referential meaning of an interface sign [9]. From the users' perspective, ontology refers to the knowledge or concepts that users use to understand and interpret the meaning of an interface sign properly. From the designers' perspective, ontology refers to the knowledge or concepts presupposed and referred to by an interface sign. For example, an interface sign 'Junk' in an email application may be well designed in terms of color, layout, position, etc. but will not make any sense to the users who do not know what the concept of 'Junk' refers to.

2 Related Works

We have conducted a literature review on ontology in relation to interface signs in UI design and evaluation. The prior work carried out on ontology is briefly presented in Table 1.

Table 1. Related work

	Contributions
Speroni [9]	Introduces the concept of ontology and proposes seven ontologies for information intensive websites
Speroni et al. [10]	An expert inspection is carried out based on Speroni's [9] set of ontologies in order to evaluate the web interfaces
Bolchini et al. [1]	A number of heuristics to design and evaluate web interface signs grounded on Speroni's [9] ontology is proposed. The heuristics includes: avoid ontology conflict to design interface signs, and design interface signs based on the users' familiarity with ontologies
Islam et al. [5]	The interface signs of museum websites are analyzed to explore users' perceived difficulty in interpreting the meaning of interface signs that belong to different ontologies proposed by Speroni's [9]
Sharp [8]	Describes the importance of ontologies in information systems development based on Islam's [5] and Speroni's [9] work
Islam [4]	The interface signs of museum and university websites are analyzed to observe how interface sign re-design changes the ontology/ontologies referred to by an interface sign, and users' difficulty in interpreting the meaning of interface signs based on Speroni's [9] work

The literature review suggests that very few studies have been conducted on interface sign ontology. The studies have been carried out by considering the Speroni's [9] ontologies and focused on information intensive web interfaces. Speroni [9] proposed an example list of most common ontologies used in information intensive web UI. He further stated that the set of ontologies can be different depending on different websites. This suggests further research possibilities on (i) revealing a complete list of ontologies that goes beyond information intensive websites and is more general for web interfaces; and (ii) exploring the principles of ontologies in depth in order to design and evaluate user-intuitive web interface signs.

In response to the above research opportunities, Islam [7] proposed a list of twelve ontologies for web interface signs, and a set of principles for ontology mapping in interpreting the meaning of web interface signs. He conducted an extensive empirical study through semi-structured interviews and questionnaires for finding a list of ontologies and principles of ontology mapping for web interfaces. He identified the following set of ontologies to interpret the meaning of interfaces gins. Ontologies marked by * are also proposed by Speroni [9].

- *Internet Ontology (IO)*:* The knowledge of World Wide Web, web browsing and its concepts and conventions.
- *Real World Ontology (RWO):* The knowledge of the real world experiences and concepts.
- *System Ontology (SO):* The knowledge of the (studied) system, its functionalities and concepts.
- *Computer Ontology (CO):* The knowledge of computer and its use.
- *Mobile Ontology (MO):* The knowledge of mobile and mobile application use.
- *Current Web Domain Ontology (CWDO)*:* The knowledge concerning web interface signs, which are specific enough to the current web domain (e.g., educational web domain, email application domain).
- *Other Web Domain Ontology (OWDO):* The knowledge of web interface signs which are specific enough to a particular web domain other than the web domain where the sign is currently available.
- *Common-Sense Ontology (CSO)*:* The knowledge of concepts belonging to a common background of users and that uses common sense.
- *Topic Ontology (TO)*:* The knowledge of a particular subject or topic the website talks about.
- *Organization Ontology (OO)*:* The knowledge of web interface signs that refer to the institution or organization that owns a website.
- *Cultural Ontology (CuO):* The knowledge of interface signs which are specific to a particular cultural context.
- *Website Ontology (WO)*:* The knowledge of web interface signs which are specific to a particular website.

Islam [7] also found the following principles of ontology mapping in interpreting the meaning of interface signs:

I. Users use single or multiple ontologies to interpret the semantic of the interface sign. An interface sign may belong to a single or multiple ontologies.

II. A proper matching between ontology/ontologies referred to by an interface sign and one(s) owned by the participants leads users to interpret the semantic of interface sign correctly.

III. Ontology conflict (i.e., users are confused with ontology/ontologies that need to consider to interpret a sign) increases the users' perceived interpretation difficulty and decreases the accuracy of sign's interpretation.

IV. When multiple ontologies are referred to by an interface signs, a familiar ontology supports an unfamiliar ontology to understand the semantic of the interface sign.

This study is built on Islam's [7] work. In principle, this research carries out a light weighted experiment to investigate if the principles of ontology mapping are applicable to understand the meaning of web interface signs.

3 Study Design

A light weighted experiment was carried out in a usability testing lab and followed the followings procedure. First, 12 interface signs (see Fig. 1) were selected from home pages (English version) of two university websites (Universität Trier and RWTH Aachen University) and two museum websites (Drents Museum and Hunebed Centrum Museum). Second, 5 undergrads and 1 graduate student were recruited as test participants. They were aged 20–30 years (Mean = 25.33; standard deviation = 2.62). Third, a sign test was carried out with each participant via semi-structured interviews. The following activities were followed in each test session with each participant: (i) test subjects filled in pre-test questionnaires, that addressed their socio-biographical profile, experience with the use of computer, mobile and internet, and familiarity with the websites under investigation, (ii) a short introduction was given to inform the participants about the test in general: the test procedure, their role, etc., and (iii) the participants were asked to answer the following set of questions for each interface sign without clicking on the signs:

1. What could be the referential meaning of this sign?
2. Why do you think this is the meaning of this sign?
3. When interpreting this sign how intuitive it is to you (answer choices ranged from 1: not intuitive – 9: extremely intuitive)?

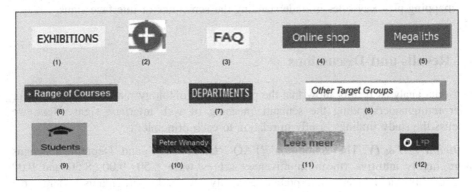

Fig. 1. Set of interface signs

Table 2. Model of the profiles of test-participants

Ontologies	Users familiarity with ontologies			
	Nil	*Less*	*Average*	*High*
IO				¤ #
RWO			¤ #	
SO		¤		#
CO				¤ #
MO				¤ #
CWDO		¤		#
OWDO			¤ #	
CSO			¤ #	
TO		¤	#	
OO			¤	#
CuO	¤ #			
WO	¤ #			

Context: ¤ - museum website and # - University website.

4. Do you have any suggestion for redesigning this sign that would make the sign more intuitive in terms of interpreting its meaning?

Each interview session lasted about 25–35 min and was audio-video recorded. Finally, the interview data was transcribed and then analyzed, using qualitative analysis and descriptive statistics.

We followed the following steps to analyze the study data:

- First, we modeled the users' profiles based on their familiarity with ontologies. The profiles are shown in Table 2. A set of pre-test questionnaires were used to understand users' familiarity with ontologies. For example, a question 'how long have you been using the internet?' gave an indication of users' familiarity with *Internet Ontology*.
- Second, we identified the ontology/ontologies referred to by the interface signs (i.e., designer ontology). For example, *Internet Ontology* is referred to by the 'FAQ' and 'Online shop' signs and *Website Ontology* is referred to by the 'L^{2}P' sign.
- Finally, we analyzed the data to observe whether the principles of ontology mapping play key roles in understanding the semantics of interface signs.

4   Results and Discussions

Our data analyses results show that the principles of ontology mapping are useful for interpreting/understanding the semantic/meaning of web interface signs. Next, we discuss the study findings briefly in relation to each principle:

Principle I, II & IV: The 'Exhibition', 'FAQ', 'Online shop', and 'Departments' signs were highly intuitive (mean intuitiveness scores were 8.50, 9.00, 8.50 and 9.00 respectively) and were interpreted correctly by all participants. Here, the ontology/ontologies referred to by these signs and the one(s) owned by the users were matched. For example, 'FAQ' and 'Online shop' signs point to *Internet Ontology* and all participates were highly familiar with this ontology (see Table 1).

The 'Exhibition' sign in a museum website and the 'Departments' sign in a university website are built on multiple ontologies such as *Current Web Domain Ontology, System Ontology,* and *Real World Ontology.* Participants interpreted the meaning of these signs accurately because of their familiarity with a few or all of these Ontologies. Here, a familiar ontology supports an unfamiliar ontology for understanding the meaning of the sign. One participant responded the following while interpreting the meaning of 'Exhibition' sign:

> "...I am familiar with this term [exhibition] from the outside world and also in museum visit...."

Principle III: Three participants found it difficult to interpret the meaning of the 'Students' sign in a university website. They thought that it could be either (i) for alumni students, because of the appended graduate hat icon, or (ii) for current students, because of the sign 'Prospective Students', which was placed to the left of this sign. One user responded the following in the regard:

> "...This sign may be for alumni or those who will graduate...Oh! It may be for local students, as the neighboring sign is for prospective students....I don't know! It may be for alumni due to the graduation hat sign...."

Here, the sign is built on the *Website Ontology*, since the 'Student' sign with the graduate hat is specific to this website for providing information for the current student. Three out of six participants treated this sign as built on *Current Web Domain Ontology, System Ontology,* and *Real World Ontology* to provide information for the alumni or for students who will graduate soon. They were familiar with this sign through the university, its websites, and real-world experience. As a result, an ontology conflict occurred that led them interpret the meaning of this sign inaccurately.

Ontology conflict occurred also in interpreting the meaning of the 'Range of Courses', 'Other Target Groups', 'plus icon' and 'Peter Winandy' signs in university websites. Participants reported higher level of difficulty in interpreting the meaning of these signs (mean intuitiveness scores were 5.67, 4.00, 1.00, and 3.21, respectively). For example, the sign 'Range of Course' actually stands for providing information of programs/degree offered (e.g., BSc and MSc in Psychology) in the university. But participants thought that the sign would provide the list of courses (e.g., object oriented programming language, data structure, etc.) offered in the university. They were also confused with the word 'range', as it could be used for different purposes like range of time or range of course fee. Here, this sign points to *Website Ontology*, since it is very specific to the website for this kind of information. However, participants treated the sign as built on *Current Web Domain Ontology, System Ontology,* and *Common Sense Ontology* to provide information about the list of courses offered in the university.

Principle V: The word 'Megaliths' means large stones. This sign in a museum website stands for providing its collection and exhibition information related to large stones.

This term is understandable only to a specific group of people who have familiarity with this Greek word. The 'Lees Meer' sign uses the Dutch language, and its meaning is 'Read More'. The Sign 'L^{2}P' is a very specific sign to navigate users to the university's learning and teaching portal. Thus, the sign 'Megaliths' and 'Lees Meer' in a museum website belong to *Website Ontology* and *Cultural Ontology* respectively; and the sign 'L^{2}P' in a university website belong to *Website Ontology*. Our study showed that the participants were not able to interpret the meaning of these signs properly and gave very low intuitiveness scores (mean intuitiveness scores of 'Megaliths', 'Lees Meer' and 'L^{2}P' signs were 1.67, 2.67 and 1.50, respectively), since they were not familiar with these ontologies. One participant responded the following when interpreting the 'Megaliths' sign:

"...*I do not know the meaning, without meaning how I judge it...*"

5 Implications and Conclusion

The paper discussed the interface sign ontologies and the principles of ontology mapping, and demonstrated these principles with a light weighted experiment. The findings of the study suggest practitioners follow the following ontological guidelines to design and evaluate the interface sign [7]:

(a) Design interface signs based on users' familiarity level with ontologies.
(b) Design interface signs that belong to multiple ontologies.
(c) Avoid ontology conflict when creating interface signs.
(d) (Re)design interface signs that belong to ontologies, with which user experienced lower level of perceived difficulty
(e) Avoid creating interface signs that belong only to the *Website Ontology*.

For example, the sign 'Megaliths' (points to *Website Ontology*) can be re-designed as 'Large Stones', 'Mega Stones', or 'Big Stones'. In this case, the sign will point to *Common Sense Ontology*, *Real World Ontology*, and *System Ontology*. This in turn may improve the interpretation accuracy and its perceived intuitiveness.

Additionally, the results of this study advance practitioners' knowledge on design and evaluate web interface signs. The results may assist practitioners: (i) to model the profiles of target users based on their level of familiarity with ontologies, (ii) to investigate the problems and intuitiveness of interface signs based on users' profiles, principles of ontology mapping, and ontological guidelines, and (iii) to apply the concept of ontologies as an integrated tool with other usability evaluation process (e.g., heuristic inspection, user tests, etc.) in order to improve the usability evaluation.

This paper has a number of limitations that may also serve as the avenue for future research. First, the current set of ontology and principles are derived for the desktop-based web interfaces. The ontologies and principles may not be directly applicable for mobile context. Thus, future work may focus on mobile interface, where signs have even more importance. Second, future research may integrate the concept of ontologies with other usability testing methods in order to assess its impact on improving the system usability.

Acknowledgments. The authors would like thank all the participants of this study. Finnish Economic Education Foundation and Nokia Foundation provided the grant that has made this research possible. For this, they are gratefully acknowledged.

References

1. Bolchini, D., Chatterji, R., Speroni, M.: Developing heuristics for the semiotics inspection of websites. In: Proceedings of SIGDOC 2009, pp. 67–72. ACM Press (2009)
2. de Souze, C.S.: The Semiotic Engineering of Human-Computer Interaction. MIT Press, Cambridge (2005)
3. Derboven, J., Geerts, D., Grooff, D.D.: Researching user interpretation beyond designer intentions. In: Extended Abstracts CHI 2013, pp. 367–372. ACM Press (2003)
4. Islam, M.N.: Semiotics perception towards designing users' intuitive web user interface: a study on interface signs. In: Rahman, H., Mesquita, A., Ramos, I., Pernici, B. (eds.) MCIS 2012. LNBIP, vol. 129, pp. 139–155. Springer, Heidelberg (2012)
5. Islam, M.N., Ali, M., Al-Mamun, A., Islam, M.: Semiotics explorations on designing the information intensive web interfaces. Int. Arab J. Inf. Technol. 7(1), 45–54 (2010)
6. Islam, M.N., Tétard, F.: Integrating semiotics perception in usability testing to improve usability evaluation. In: Garcia-Ruiz, M. (ed.) Cases on Usability Engineering: Design and Development of Digital Products, pp. 145–169. IGI Global, Hershey (2013)
7. Islam, M.N.: Exploring interface sign ontologies for web user interface design and evaluation: a user study. In: Liu, K., Gulliver, S.R., Li, W., Yu, C. (eds.) ICISO 2014. IFIP AICT, vol. 426, pp. 87–96. Springer, Heidelberg (2014)
8. Sharp, J.H.: Semiotics as a theoretical foundation of information design. In: Proceedings of CONISAR 2011, pp. 1–5 (2011)
9. Speroni, M.: Mastering the semiotics of information-intensive web interfaces. Ph.D. thesis, University of Lugano, Swizerland (2006)
10. Speroni, M., Bolchini, D., Paolini, P.: Interfaces: do users understand them? In: Proceedings of Museums and the Web (2006). http://www.archimuse.com/mw2006/papers

Cultural Reflections in Qatari Government Websites

Nouf Khashman[(✉)]

Independent Researcher, Ottawa, Canada
nouf.khashman@gmail.com

Abstract. Localizing a website by incorporating culturally appropriate design features arguably helps it become more functional and usable for its users. This paper seeks to explore cultural reflections in government websites from Qatar using the influential cultural model of Geert Hofstede. Through using systematic content analysis, the examination focused on Web design elements which have been proven to be good indicators of preferences within cultural groups. The results showed that Arab culture which Qatar belongs to is somewhat reflected in the design of Qatari websites.

Keywords: Web design · Usability · Qatar · Culture · Hofstede

1 Introduction

In recent years, the government of Qatar has demonstrated a strong commitment to making the Internet more accessible and affordable for people living in the country, something reflected in the number of people using the Internet in Qatar. According to Internet World Stats [9], there were almost 2 million (95 % of the population) Internet users in Qatar in 2014. Abdallah and Albadri [1] noted that these numbers are among the highest in the Arab world along with the United Arab Emirates and Bahrain, mainly due to the rich oil economy and attracting foreign Internet and Communication Technology (ICT) investment in these countries.

Qatar has a well-developed vision towards moving into knowledge society, along with a clear national ICT policies and strategies, with effective implementation plans supported by government and other stakeholders [1, 15]. Part of the strategy is to accelerate the nation's e-government efforts and increase the number of online government services to 100 % by 2020. The country is also looking into providing user-friendly "anytime, anywhere" access to government and its services to users, ensuring that they can complete online services through simplified and easy-to-use websites [15].

Culture is considered one of the attributes affecting the usefulness and usability of websites [5, 21]; therefore several studies have attempted to investigate it in relation to Web design [3, 4, 10, 13, 14]. The influential cultural model of Geert Hofstede [6, 7] has been utilized at length to examine cross-cultural Web design. In his model, Hofstede assigned comparative scores for 50 individual countries and three regions on five cultural dimensions. These dimensions comprise: Power Distance, Uncertainty Avoidance, Individualism/Collectivism, Masculinity/Femininity, and Long/Short-Term Orientation.

© Springer International Publishing Switzerland 2015
A. Marcus (Ed.): DUXU 2015, Part III, LNCS 9188, pp. 54–62, 2015.
DOI: 10.1007/978-3-319-20889-3_6

As one composite group, Arab countries scored 80 on Power Distance, 68 on Uncertainty Avoidance, 38 on Individualism (i.e. indicating a collectivist culture), 53 on the Masculinity dimension, and they had no score on Long-/Short-term Orientation dimension.

Qatar was not one of the seven countries Hofstede included in his model, which were Egypt, Lebanon, Saudi Arabia, United Arab Emirates, Iraq, Libya, and Kuwait. However, since it is considered an Arab state [12], this study looks into whether its websites actually reflect the cultural characteristics described by Hofstede's model.

2 Qatar in Cultural Web Design Studies

Arab countries, including Qatar, have received limited attention in cultural Web design research [10]. Studies that included these countries revealed that their websites reflected Arab culture described in Hofstede's model, but to different extent.

For example, national Web portals from Egypt had a strong focus on the Egyptian culture, reflecting a high Power Distance characteristic. While their counterparts from Morocco had a good presentation of women's issues and non-Islamic reference, relating to the Masculinity and Power Distance dimensions respectively [23].

In another study conducted by Callahan [4], university websites from Arab countries included in Hofstede's model reflected design characteristics that are inferred from the dimensions. This was also found in another study conducted by Marcus and Hamoodi [14] based on analysis of university websites from Jordan, Egypt, and the United Arab Emirates.

3 Methodology

3.1 Websites

The government websites chosen for analysis are primarily intended for the nation of Qatar, rather than the worldwide Internet community. Second, these websites can be expected to have as one design goal the reflection of the socio-cultural, technological and economic characteristics of their intended culture [23].

According to the Qatari e-government portal, Hukoomi [8], there are 17 ministries in the country, two of which have no websites while a third website was under construction at the time of the inspection and analysis between 24 and 26 October 2014. The website belonging to the Ministry of Development Planning and Statistics was divided into two units of analysis, as there were two websites available from the landing page, one for each section of this ministry. This leaves 15 websites in total for analysis; screenshots of three websites are provided in Figs. 1, 2 and 3.

3.2 Analysis

This study utilized content analysis, which is a valid method used to describe trends in communication context, allowing researchers to make inferences about the patterns and differences among similar components of that communication context [11].

Fig. 1. Ministry of energy and industry, 2014. http://www.mei.gov.qa

Fig. 2. Ministry of finance, 2014. http://www.mof.gov.qa

The components were the graphical, organizational, and navigational design elements (e.g. colors, images, graphics, spatial orientation, links) which had been identified as being culturally specific [3], and have been linked to Hofstede's model of cultural dimensions [2, 13, 19]. These elements were extracted from the home page of each of the selected websites, because it is argued to be the most important page on any website [17].

For categorical variables, such as entry page and menus, frequencies and percentages were used to describe the data. Non-parametric Chi-square test was also used to examine

Fig. 3. Ministry of foreign affairs, 2014. http://www.mofa.gov.qa

whether the presence of these elements is significant or not. Continuous variables, such as number of pictures and number of languages, do not have a fixed number of values thus were analyzed using descriptive statistics (mean and standard deviation).

4   Results

The content analysis of the 15 government websites from Qatar focused on design elements which are associated with Hofstede's dimensions: Power Distance, Uncertainty Avoidance, Individualism/Collectivism, Masculinity/Femininity, and Long-/Short-Term Orientation.

4.1   Power Distance

High power distance in Web design is manifested in the presence of social models (national and/or religious), structured page design through use of symmetrical pages, placing heavy focus on images of buildings rather than people, and using logos. When images of people are used rather than those of buildings, the focus would be more on images of officials rather than images of citizens.

The presence of social models on these interfaces was limited as only one website (7 %) had religious social models, probably due to the type of website (Ministry of Endowments). The results of the non-parametric Chi-square test confirmed the difference between those websites which had social models and those which did not ($\chi^2_{(1)} = 11.3$, $p = 0.001$). The same case was for the symmetrical design of the pages, as 10 of these pages (67 %) had non-symmetrical design, compared to semi-symmetrical (27 %) and ideally design (7 %).

Logos were present on all 15 homepages, with a total of 27 logos ($M = 1.8$, $SD = 1.6$). Additionally, there were a total of 98 images of people on these homepages ($M = 6.5$, $SD = 7.5$), compared to 54 images of buildings ($M = 3.6$, $SD = 10.7$). Of these 98 images, there were 38 for officials ($M = 2.5$, $SD = 2.8$), 28 for citizens ($M = 1.9$, $SD = 2.6$), 24 for mixed status ($M = 1.6$, $SD = 4.5$), and 8 unidentified status ($M = 0.5$, $SD = 1.1$).

After averaging all design elements associated with power distance, the score (21) was not even close to that which was collectively assigned by Hofstede to Arabic-speaking countries (80).

4.2   Uncertainty Avoidance

Web interfaces with high uncertainty avoidance are described as being simple with limited choices and a restricted amount of data. This dimension is reflected in the menu structure, number of links, and presence of news.

The analysis showed that 80 % of the homepages had complex menus (i.e. having sub-menus), and the difference between simple and complex menus was significant ($\chi^2_{(1)} = 5.4$, $p = 0.02$). As for the presence of news, all websites had news items on their interfaces. The mean for the number of links on the 15 homepages was 81 ($SD = 26.4$), the highest was for the Ministry of Labor and Social Affairs (122), while the lowest was for the Ministry of Youth and Sports (13).

After averaging the design elements associated with this dimension, the score (73) was higher than that assigned by Hofstede to Arabic-speaking countries (68).

4.3   Individualism/Collectivism

In Web design, interfaces with high individualism will depict more images of individuals rather than groups, provide provisions of user protection through privacy policy statements and site registration, and provide site customization for the users.

Of the 98 images of people, 21 were images of individuals ($M = 1.4$, $SD = 1.9$), 16 images of couples ($M = 1$, $SD = 1.2$), and 61 images of groups ($M = 4.1$, $SD = 6.5$).

The privacy policy, which is a statement provided to indicate to the user how the information could be used and shared, was available on 53 % of the home pages. While the rights reserved statement, which is used to indicate the ownership of the information provided on the website, is available on 73 % of the sampled home pages.

The customization variable refers to the ability to adjust some features of the interface such as changing the font size or the background color. The results showed only 20 % of the homepages providing some kind of customization for the users, such as changing the font size.

After averaging the design elements associated with Individualism/Collectivism, the score (42) was slightly higher than that assigned by Hofstede to Arabic-speaking countries (38), but still indicating a collectivist culture rather than an individualistic one.

4.4   Masculinity/Femininity

Masculinity in interfaces is depicted through traditional gender distinctions between users, and through animation and games. This is reflected in using images of men verses images of women, using animated images, and keeping a count of site visitors by using a visitor counter.

Of the 98 images of people on the 15 homepages, there were 66 of men ($M = 4.4$, $SD = 4.7$), 4 of women ($M = 0.3$, $SD = 0.5$), 25 of mixed gender ($M = 1.7$, $SD = 3.2$), and 3 of unidentified gender ($M = 0.2$, $SD = 0.8$).

Animated images were available on 14 websites (93 %), with a total number of 219 images ($M = 14.6$, $SD = 23.7$). The highest number was for the Ministry of Culture, Arts and Heritage with 97 animated images, while the lowest was for the Ministry of Foreign Affairs with no animated images at all. The results showed that only one website had a visitor counter.

After averaging the design elements associated with Masculinity/Femininity, the score (48) was slightly lower than that assigned by Hofstede to Arabic-speaking countries (53), which indicates slightly a feminine culture.

4.5   Long-/Short-Term Orientation

The content of Web interfaces with long-term orientation focuses on patience in achieving results, and on using cultural markers such as national colors. Web design elements that reflect this dimension are site searching tools such as search engines and site maps, frequently asked questions, and national colors.

The results showed that 80 % of the homepages had search engines, while the site map was less popular with only 53 %. Those results were further confirmed with the Chi-square test, as there were differences between those websites in terms of using search engines ($\chi^2_{(1)} = 5.4$, $p = 0.02$), but not of using site maps ($\chi^2_{(1)} = 0.07$, $p =$ ns). As for the frequently asked questions feature, it was available on 13 % of these websites. Averaging the design elements associated with long-/short-term orientation gave a score of 49. While Arabic-speaking countries have no score on this dimension, Qatar's score slightly indicates a short-term orientation.

5   Discussion and Conclusion

Users' needs and expectations are partly influenced by their cultural background [5, 16, 21], therefore many researchers have investigated cultural presence and reflection on the Web [3, 4, 13, 14]. In doing so, usability experts have heavily used and cited the influential cultural model of Geert Hofstede [6, 7] in understanding user interfaces from different cultures. This exploratory study also utilized Hofstede's model of cultural dimensions to examine 15 government websites from Qatar. The main purpose of the study is to shed light on cultural reflections in the design of these websites, paving the way for user-friendly and culturally adapted websites for local users in the country.

Generally, the sampled websites demonstrated consistency in the "feel and look" of the design by regularly using a traditional logo while using colors from the Qatari flag, maroon and white. There was also consistency in the URLs for these websites, as all but one indicated that these websites are for government bodies in Qatar by using gov. qa in the Web address. They also provide contact information such as telephone number and email address, along with social media tools such as Facebook and Twitter. Additionally, three homepages were available only in Arabic, 11 had two linguistic versions (Arabic and English), while the final homepage had three languages (Arabic, English, and French).

The results showed that Qatar matched the description of Arabic-speaking countries on two of the four of Hofstede's dimensions on which Arab countries had a score. While the collective score for Arab countries on the Power Distance dimension is 80, Qatar got a score of 21 in this study. This low score represented the low number of social models, symmetrical design, and images of buildings (compared to images of people). On the other hand, most of the logos available on the interfaces had traditional design using the Qatari national emblem with the name of the ministry in question. As for the status of people in images, the majority of these images depicted officials rather than citizens or mixed status.

The collective score on the Uncertainty Avoidance was also relatively high for Arab countries, with 68. Qatar on the other hand had a higher score than Hofstede's, with 73. This score is represented in the relatively low number of links (i.e. restricted amount of data), and presence of news items on all websites, providing information about the activities each ministry is involved in, as well as news about Qatar in general.

As a group, Arab countries scored 38 on the Collectivism/Individualism dimension, reflecting a culture oriented towards being in groups. While not perfectly matching this score, Qatar also showed a collectivist culture with a score of 42. This was reflected in the heavy use of images of groups (compared to images of individuals), and low number of customization options (e.g. font size, background color, etc.).

Arab countries are described as having a relatively masculine culture based on the collective score of 53 on Hofstede's Masculinity/Femininity dimension. Not far off from this score, Qatar scored 48 based on the high number of images of men (compared to images of women or mixed gender images) and the high number of animated images.

While Arab countries have no score on Hofstede's fifth dimension, Long-/Short-Term Orientation, the analysis focused on design elements associated with it. The results showed that with the score of 49, Qatar fell almost in the midpoint, slightly leaning towards short-term orientation. This is reflected in the use of search engines and site maps, but not for the frequently asked questions.

This small study has demonstrated that Arabic culture is somewhat reflected in Qatari government websites. While the results of this study confirm the results of other studies that included Arab countries [3] in regard to the use of culturally favored colors and images of people, they also refute the results of other studies [4] in regards to the presence of search engines. Designers would potentially benefit from this kind of research when it comes to incorporating cultural considerations in the design of websites, especially as the Web is becoming more global and more sophisticated in its design [20, 22].

The wider questions remain as: (a) whether the usability of an Arabic website is enhanced by designing it in accordance with these cultural markers; and (b) whether cultural background of Qatari users is reflected in the attitudes toward Web design elements. This would require further examination of user satisfaction [18], efficiency, and effectiveness of Qatari websites through subjective and objective usability testing, as usability is important for successful implementation of e-government.

References

1. Abdallah, S., Albadri, F.: A perspective on ICT diffusion in the Arab region. In: Abdallah, S., Albadri, F. (eds.) ICT Acceptance Investment and Organization Cultural Practices and Values in the Arab World, pp. 1–15. Information Science Reference, Hershey (2011)
2. Ackerman, S.: Mapping user interface design to culture dimensions. Paper presented at the International Workshop on Internationalization of Products and Systems, Austin TX (2002). http://www.usj.edu.lb/moodle/stephane.bazan/obs_interculturelle/culture%20dimensions%20in%20WS.pdf
3. Barber, W., Badre, A.: Culturability: the merging of culture and usability. In: 4th Conference on Human Factors and the Web (1998). Accessed from http://research.microsoft.com/users/marycz/hfweb98/barber/
4. Callahan, E.: Cultural differences in the design of human-computer interfaces: a multinational study of university websites. Published thesis, Indiana University (2007)
5. Fernandes, T.: Global interface design: a guide to designing international user interfaces. AP Professional, Boston (1995)
6. Hofstede, G.: Culture's Consequences: International Differences in Work-Related Values. Sage Publications, Beverly Hills (1980)
7. Hofstede, G.: Culture's Consequences: Comparing Values, Behaviors, Institutions, and Organizations Across Nations. Sage Publications, Thousand Oaks (2001)
8. Hukoomi- Qatar e-Government Portal. http://portal.www.gov.qa/wps/portal/directory/ministries
9. Internet World Stats (2014) http://www.internetworldstats.com/stats5.htm
10. Khashman, N., Large, A.: Measuring cultural markers in Arabic government websites using Hofstede's cultural dimensions. In: Marcus, A. (ed.) HCII 2011 and DUXU 2011, Part II. LNCS, vol. 6770, pp. 431–439. Springer, Heidelberg (2011)
11. Krippendorff, K.: Content analysis: an introduction to its methodology. Sage Publications, Beverly Hills (2004)
12. League of Arab States (2014). http://www.lasportal.org
13. Marcus, A., Gould, E.: Cultural dimensions and global web user-interface design: what? So what? Now what? In: Proceedings of the 6th Conference on Human Factors and the Web, Austin, Texas, June 2000. http://www.amanda.com/resources/hfweb2000/hfweb00.marcus.html. Accessed 25 September 2008
14. Marcus, A., Hamoodi, S.: The impact of culture on the design of Arabic websites. In: Aykin, N. (ed.) IDGD 2009. LNCS, vol. 5623, pp. 386–394. Springer, Heidelberg (2009)
15. Ministry of Information and Communication Technologies, Qatar (ictQatar). http://www.ictqatar.qa/en
16. Nielsen, J.: International use: serving a global audience. In: Designing Web Usability, pp. 315–344. New Riders, Indianapolis (2000)
17. Nielsen, J., Tahir, M.: Home page usability: 50 websites deconstructed. New Riders, Indianapolis (2002)

18. O'Connell, T., Murphy, E.: The usability engineering behind user-centered processes for website development lifecycles. In: Zaphiris, P., Kurniawan, S. (eds.) Human Computer Interaction Research in Web Design and Evaluation. Idea Group Publilsher, Hershey (2007)
19. Robbins, S., Stylianou, A.: Global corporate web sites: an empirical investigation of content and design. Inf. Manag. **40**(3), 205–212 (2003). doi:10.1016/S0378-7206(02)00002-2
20. Röse, K.: Globalization culture and usability. In: Ghaoui, C. (ed.) Encyclopedia of Human Computer Interaction, pp. 253–256. IGI Global, Hershey (2006). doi:10.4018/978-1-59140-562-7
21. Shneiderman, B.: Universal usability: pushing human-computer interaction research to empower every citizen. Commun. ACM **43**(5), 84–91 (2000)
22. Warf, B.: Global geographies of the Internet. Springer, Dordrecht (2013). doi:10.1007/978-94-007-1245-4_1
23. Zahir, S., Dobing, B., Hunter, G.: Cross-cultural dimensions of Internet portals. Internet Res. **12**(3), 210–220 (2002)

Usability Analysis of IxDA.org

Julija Naskova[✉]

Hong Kong Polytechnic University School of Design,
Hong Kong SAR, People's Republic of China
Naskova_productions@hotmail.com

Abstract. The International Standards Organization definition of usability as documented in ISO 9241-11 is for "...specified users... specified goals... particular environments" which implies that usability varies based on those three factors. The System Usability Scale (SUS) is a ten item questionnaire developed to evaluate systems' usability. Consequently, SUS became the scale of choice for measuring usability, broadly applied to various systems including websites. Contemporary websites are visited by a wide range of users for different reasons and from all kinds of environments - can SUS still effectively measure their usability? For a professional organization such as IxDA whose focus is user interface design a heuristic evaluation aided by the Expert Review Checkpoints provides detailed feedback on its website's compliance with contemporary design standards that affect usability.

Keywords: ISO · SUS · UX · Expert Review Checkpoint · Usability · IxDA

1   Introduction

The purpose of this study is to analyze the usability of Interaction Design Association's website ixda.org [1]. IxDA is a free membership based group for professionals and enthusiasts in the field of interaction design. Two methods were applied; first one being the System Usability Scale (SUS) and the second one is an expert review guided by the Expert Review Checkpoint workbook. SUS consists of ten questions that cover different aspects of a system's usability as perceived by the user with a possibility of five answers from strongly disagree to strongly agree. It was developed 29 years ago and since it has become the questionnaire of choice for various software, hardware, websites and other "systems"[2].

The SUS test can be customized for a specific task within the system, where the user fills out the questionnaire and is then interviewed about his experience. Since this simple test is meant to evaluate the system's overall usability, giving instructions to the user interferes with the goal that John Brooke, the SUS creator had in mind when labeling it "quick and dirty". This kind of adjustment is more applicable during agile website development, where specific functions of the website are tested as they are coded. This method protects against major mishaps during development but in most cases doesn't replace usability testing of the website as a finished product.

Another type of traditional or discount usability test [3] is the Rapid Iterative Testing and Evaluation (RITE) method that was championed by Dennis Wixon and used on PC games. During this iterative usability method changes to the system occur

© Springer International Publishing Switzerland 2015
A. Marcus (Ed.): DUXU 2015, Part III, LNCS 9188, pp. 63–73, 2015.
DOI: 10.1007/978-3-319-20889-3_7

as soon as issues are reported by a participant and a solution has been identified by the usability research team. The now updated prototype is being tested by the next participant until the system is deemed usable. These newer tests are meant not just to assess usability of a system but also to discover specific problems [4].

Other types of tests that discover specific problems are the expert review and heuristic usability evaluation. These tests use guidelines about user interface design based on principles established by usability authorities such as ISO, Jakob Nielsen and Don Norman. There are quite a few collections of guidelines for user interface design in existence that contain anywhere from few to 944 guidelines. To ease evaluation, sometimes the guidelines are presented as sets of questions grouped under specific usability theme. One such set of web usability guidelines was created by David Travis of Userfocus under the name of Expert Review Checkpoint [5]. These guidelines are to be used by an expert reviewer during the evaluation of a website's usability to discover specific problems and offer tangible solutions.

2 Analysis

2.1 SUS Method Analysis

Five PhD students at The Hong Kong Polytechnic University School of Design browsed ixda.org for on average fifteen minutes and then filled out the System Usability Scale (SUS) test. This number of study participants meets the ideal number of five test users as established by Jacob Nielsen [6]. According to him, testing more people will just yield similar results at a significant loss of time. There was no specific goal presented to the test subjects. They were just to look up an informational website of a professional group meant at promoting the field of interaction design. Most users will browse ixda.org for usability information to add to their current knowledge, search for conference opportunities, look up professionals who might become a potential contact, or search job leads if in the market.

Each of the user's response on the SUS questionnaire is valued from 1 to 5. Every odd question is graded at user's response minus 1 and every even question gets the score of 5 minus user response. So each answer can get the score from 0 to 4. Once all scores are added they are multiplied by 2.5 in order to have a range compatible with from 0 to 100. This doesn't create a percentile scale, where 100 presents the best. Interpretation of the score is based on mass studies that suggest a score of 68 to be an average, meaning 50 % of all websites are at this level of usability [7]. Without any gouging, the result of this SUS test was exactly 68 points (Fig. 1). According to the above references study by Sauro J., the conclusion is that ixda.org doesn't set up an example of good usability nor it is severely unusable. Other researchers such as Tullis T. and Albert B. report a larger variation in the SUS results and suggest interpretation for a score of below 60 % as relatively poor usability and for a score above 80 % as a pretty good usability [8].

The SUS test contains questions that imply use of a system for a specific purpose, where the user is performing an on the job task with its help. When browsing websites, especially ones set up by volunteer base professional associations there is no specific task at hand. Therefore the user cannot "feel very confident using the system" (question 9) when she doesn't know what to expect from the system. A professional website is to incite interest in its content, prolong browsing by clicking on its tabs and links, and eventually create desire to join the group or to contribute to its content by commenting on a post. Therefore, a more sophisticated design and engaging content is necessary in order to render this kind of a website "sticky" [9].

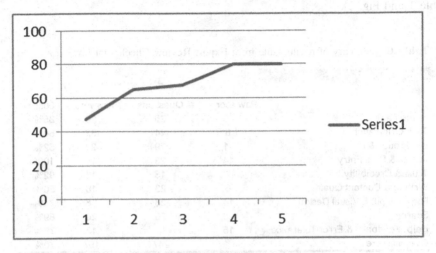

Fig. 1. Line chart of SUS scores for `ixda.org`

2.2 Expert Review Checkpoint

The Expert Review Checkpoint test is an expert usability test consisting of 247 questions subdivided into nine themes or categories that are indicative of a certain aspect of a webpage's usability. The first theme addresses the website's Home Page and consists of 20 questions, while the last one is about Help, Feedback and Error Tolerance and contains 37 questions. The expert reviewer starts by filling in the fields next to the statements about specific website characteristics with 1 for yes, 0 if it is met half way and −1 if the characteristic is not there. If some criteria don't apply to that specific website the reviewer should not grade it. There is also a comment section to the right of the checkpoints for noting specific issues. This section comes in handy later on when writing the actual usability review. The results are then automatically calculated and summarized in a table by categories with scores listed for each category including the overall score. Both the table and a spider web graph of the results are created on the Results Page.

The overall usability score was calculated at 70 %, which is close to the 68 % derived from the SUS test. The Expert Review Checkpoint creator Travis D. in our e-mail conversation from February 13, 2015 expressed skepticism about the proximity of the two results stating: "the margin of error on each score is probably larger than 2 %". He further stated: "I think you should use the scores only as a comparative measure, not as an absolute statistic. A web site that scores 80 % will probably be better than one that scores 60 % (assuming the same reviewer)." The Expert Review

Checkpoint overall score can be validated by having few expert reviewers fill in the checkpoint for the same website. But this is also very costly and contradictory since the main purpose of The Expert Review Checkpoint is to assist with an expert review and not as a freestanding test. It is up to the expert reviewer to determine the checkpoint's shortcomings and to alter and interpret this test according to the website's specifics (Table 1 and Fig. 2).

Table 1. Summary of results table from Expert Review Checkpoint for `ixda.org`

Summary of results	Raw score	# Questions	# Answers	Score
Home Page	-6	20	20	35%
Task Orientation	6	44	32	60%
Navigation & IA	-1	29	26	52%
Forms & Data Entry	14	23	14	100%
Trust & Credibility	7	13	13	92%
Writing & Content Quality	6	23	16	50%
Page Layout & Visual Design	14	38	38	74%
Search	18	20	20	89%
Help, Feedback & Error Tolerance	15	37	18	79%
Overall score		247	197	70%

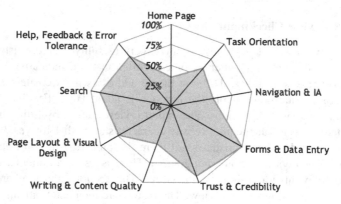

Fig. 2. Summary of results chart from Expert Review Checkpoint for `ixda.org`

2.3 Expert Review

The Expert Review Checkpoint starts with 20 questions about `ixda.org`'s Home Page and this theme received the lowest score of 35%. Two questions are in regards to its value proposition, one about it being clearly stated with a welcome blurb and another about the user understanding how valuable this website is. While the value proposition is well written and follows a standard template [10], one can only get so impressed with the home page considering there is a broken picture link underneath the value statement. The link does take you to the local leader spotlight as stated in the alternate text but the picture isn't viewable. In its center, the homepage streamlines user experience by dividing users into two categories: those that are new to design and seasoned IxDA pro users. Left column contains links to jobs, school, tool and design techniques and a right column contains info about keynote speeches and awards.

The left column content is from 2007, what gives an impression that this website isn't maintained on a regular basis. The right column content is recent, from 2014 and suggests the opposite. Nevertheless, the content under both categories fails to represent the wealth of information that one can access within this website's ornate structure. Ixda.org's homepage contains six menus, most of them cascading into few more submenus and sub submenus. The latter are not accessible unless we are on the corresponding page. Use of dropdown menus would have made it possible to see all the pages from the main menu [11]. On most pages there are hyperlinks that lead to pages with even more hyperlinks that can take the user to a very remote place.

The Checkpoint statement sometimes isn't site specific and the reviewer is puzzled about how to mark it. For example "the home page contains a search input box" received a 1, even though two search boxes on the homepage speak of bad design. Same rule against repetitive content applies to having a job board menu item and IxD jobs tile on the homepage where both link to the same content. The issue repeats with having a discussions menu in addition to IxDA Discussions tile. Another quality criteria that's not met is "navigation choices are ordered in the most logical or task-oriented manner (with the less important corporate information at the bottom)". IxDA.org's menus are not in a logical order. Discussions usually don't get a menu tab and especially not one right next to the logo. All items under this tab have the discussions.ixda.org web address, whereas ixda.org/discussions follows the right naming convention. On the discussions page the search box at the top right corner is now replaced with a loupe symbol under the header right. The resources menu item was left out from the discussions page, making it inconsistent with the homepage.

Next to Home Page is the Task Orientation theme structured around the task of purchasing products on ixda.org. Even though e-commerce is not its business model, ixda.org has few products to sell. As per this quality "when graphs are shown, users have access to the actual data (e.g. numeric annotation on bar charts)" it is only partially met. Under the Local menu there is a Network submenu containing a Google world map with electronic pins. Clicking on a pin corresponding to a local chapter is not very intuitive and the small pin size makes it difficult to pick the correct location. There is also an option to use the local directory filter placed in the right sidebar. One discovers that most chapters have been inactive for few years and their organizers don't have a contact e-mail address listed. Next to the Network submenu there is a Directory submenu with all local groups listed and Events submenu with only one future event listed. The same information repeats under each of the sub menus, in different parts of the page. Inclusion of three submenus under Local is unnecessary and confusing to the user. Therefore the guideline of "information is presented in a simple, natural and logical order" received a minus one, for the inclusion of unnecessary and poorly executed submenus. Obviously, the "less is more" principle established by Nielsen J. was not applied during this website design [12].

Under the Navigation and IA theme, few questions address the existence of a sitemap. A forum on www.ixda.org questions the need of a sitemap inclusion on a webpage but this important debate wasn't on the discussions page but on this page http://www.ixda.org/node/24433 accessible only through a hyperlink. Opinions are divided on this issue and some suggest that a sitemap only helps SE indexing. However, when analyzing a website a sitemap is very helpful. Otherwise one will assume that ixda.org was built and maintained from multiple sources and this made it impossible to have a sitemap. The Conan Design document accessible from page http://www.ixda.org/node/21287 contains a collection of wireframes and a sitemap at the end of the proposed improvements for ixda.org. In the words of Elizabeth Bacon, IxDA's Vice President and Conan lead from 2009: "This material represents the fruits of over 10 months of work from the all-volunteer IxDA Conan team. We investigated our community's needs, developed user experience requirements, conceived interaction design and visual design solutions, and conducted a concept feedback round" [13]. The Conan document features the principal design as a foundation for the expected iterative and collaborative future development. Growing Venture Solutions did the ixda.org coding in Drupal.

The statement "there is a site map that provides an overview of the site's content" received a score of zero, because the sitemap doesn't correspond exactly to the current layout of this website. The next statement "the sitemap is linked to from every page" received a score of minus one since the sitemap is hidden inside a .pdf document and not as a separate page linkable within the website. Finally, the question "the sitemap provides a concise overview of the site, not a rehash of the main navigation or a list of every single topic" received a minus one, due to its inconsistency as compared to the actually website.

Navigation and IA received a somewhat low score of 52 %, mostly due to slight inconsistencies in the visual design, which according to the sitemap appears to be a deliberate choice of the design team. Page two of the Conan document states: "On the home page, the colored triangles in the upper-left corners are hard-coded as special panel styles. Throughout the rest of the site except for Local, they are the IxDA Aqua. On the Local page, they are the IxDA Orange. There's a striped background image throughout the whole site" [14]. The aqua and orange colors don't mix well and interchanging them for buttons and links in an inconsistent manner creates confusion for the user. The striped background image is missing from the discussions page, and the logo here is also smaller than on the other pages.

There is not much discussion on the website after the Conan Design document was made available some five years ago and the call for reviewers went out. Looking for documentation on website updates is the next logical step, since this was a joint project and one would assume through communication was in place. Bugs database is mentioned with an inactive webpage link http://tracker.ixda.org/. A collaboration forum created on www.getsatisfaction.com has a last update from two years ago. Link to a blog specific to the implementation phase leads to page not found: http://www.ixda.org/blog/2009/09/conan-project-update-implementation-phase-begins. An effort was made at crowdsourcing design, with no documentation to support the fact that this actually took place. The slight deviations from this document to how this website looks today therefore cannot be explained.

On the bright side, the Forms and Data Entry theme received 100 % with fourteen out of 23 questions found relevant to this website. There are only few forms to fill out on this webpage and the process is smooth and error free. Chrome Autofill provided for most of the automated data input, so the question "users can complete simple tasks by entering just essential information (with the system supplying the non-essential information by default") was a function delegated to the browser. Google forms were used to create application to start a local group as well as to apply for the speaker network. The first form opened in another window but the second one opened in the same window.

When done applying for speaker engagements, the only return option is by clicking on the back arrow, where a return button would serve the purpose better. Another statement under this theme makes one ponder for a while "forms allow users to stay with a single interaction method for as long as possible (i.e. users do not need to make numerous shifts from keyboard to mouse to keyboard)." Some explanation on why this is important and what functions is this statement referring to would have been helpful. But the author only shared a numbered checklist of the guidelines under each theme instead of more specific explanation under: http://www.userfocus.co.uk/resources/formschecklist.html.

Trust and Credibility is an important theme in the Expert Review Checkpoint, especially since this is a voluntary membership based organization website. It received 92 % due to the fact that some of its content has not been updated for the last few years. This issue is brought up twice, question number one "the content is up-to-date, authoritative and trustworthy" and question number ten "the content is fresh: it is updated frequently and the site includes recent content". As per "the visual design complements the brand and any offline marketing messages" the branding is there but the visual shift between pages makes the user feel like she is drifting away from the original website. "The site is free of typographic errors and spelling mistakes" received a minus one due to few minor spelling mistakes. The site offers contact information but the feedback is inconsistent, therefore the zero grade for this quality staple.

A very strong one was given to the statement "the site avoids marketing waffle" and "the site avoids advertisements, especially pop-ups", a rather refreshing quality in this age of constant bombardment with online ads. "Delivery costs are highlighted at the very beginning of checkout" received one as well, since no delivery costs apply to the purchase of the IxDA logo embossed notebook.

In the Writing and Content Quality theme many checkpoints aren't that important. For example "pages use bulleted and numbered lists in preference to narrative text" is not a quality criteria since there are instances when bulleted and numbered lists cannot replace narrative text. It all depends on the context, which also defeats the purpose of "each content page begins with conclusion or implications and the text is written with an inverted pyramid style." All of these questions don't get grades due to being irrelevant or simply outdated in terms of responsive content organization. This site "avoids cute, clever or cryptic headings" is relevant in the context of IxDA and thus received a grade of 1. But this kind of headings can be useful for a more informal website, or one intended for kids.

"Text links are long enough to be understood, but short enough to minimize wrapping (especially when used as a navigation list)" – there are instances on the home page when entire question is made into a link to a page that contains the answer, and also an image and its title both being linked. The image title links to a Vimeo streamed videotaped conference presentation and the actual image links to a separate page with a blurb and the same video now streamed on `ixda.org`. It would have been equally effective if only the image was set as a link to one unique place. The most striking deviation is from the question "link names match the title of destination pages, so users will know when they have reached the intended page." "Node" and "page" placed after `ixda.org` with forward slash and a random number create addresses usually for pages that cannot be accessed from the menu but from hyperlinks within other pages. It would have been more effective to name these pages according to the page they derive from and an actual description of their content. Instead of `ixda.org/page/interaction` it should be `ixda.org/conference/interaction`.

Page Layout and Visual Design is a theme covered in the Expert Review Check-point and the website received an unexpectedly high score of 74 %. The reason for the high score is that the questions didn't address issues relevant to this website. For example "clickable images include redundant text labels" received a one, even though the fact that there is a broken image link on the home page can prompt some other reviewer to give this question a minus one. "Fonts are readable" received a zero because a similar if not the same san-serif font type is used for all of the text throughout this website. Headings are sized much bigger in comparison to paragraph text, the logo and menu items. "The organization's logo is placed in the same location on every page, and clicking the logo returns the user to the most logical page (e.g. the homepage)" is accomplished on this website. However, the header and the footer on the discussions page differ from the homepage, the logo is smaller and the aqua blue diagonal stripes across the header are missing. Use of bright orange color for the paragraph headings and hypertext under the local menu feels unpleasant next to the pastel blue color of the logo and the background stripes.

The Search theme is at 89 % with twenty out of twenty statements found relevant. Several searches were conducted and the obtained results were satisfactory. The "templates, examples or hints on how to use it effectively" appeared as soon as the search didn't yield any results. There were always options presented in tiled windows in the right sidebar to "sort by", "filter by author" and "filter by title" with different options and categories listed, so this question scored a 1. The only negative point went to "the search box and its controls are clearly labelled (multiple search boxes can be confusing)" due to the existence of two search boxes on the main page, one in the top right corner and one in a tiled window. While on the discussions page, search is presented just by the loupe symbol below the header on right.

The last theme is dedicated to Help, Feedback and Error Tolerance. The "FAQ and forum guidelines" in the footer links to guidelines on how to conduct itself in the discussion forum but it does not contain a "step by step instruction" as expected by the expert review checkpoint. It is not clear what kind of instructions should be included since there are no specific tasks to be performed by the user. Out of thirty-six questions under this theme only nine were relevant to this website. This theme received a score of 79%, which is due to the fact that most questions are for a website where the user has a specific goal, like buying a computer, or filling out a form. "The site uses a customized 404 page", which includes tips on how to find the missing page and links to "Home and

Search" – this guideline received a score of one due to a uniformly designed "page not found" that contains a search box and logo linked to the home page. This 404 page is accessed by searching `ixda.org/two`. But searching `disque.ixda.org` leads to a browser generic "this webpage is not available" webpage. Again, http://discussions. ixda.org/ doesn't follow the naming convention and the server won't associate it with www.ixda.org if the address is mistyped. Half of the questions under this theme are outdated since contemporary websites are expected to function smoothly and any error messages or extensive feedback interfering with the browsing will prompt the user to leave the website.

3   Discussion

The difference between SUS and Expert Review Checkpoint is that the first one is testing the user experience where the second one is used for a website review by an expert. In both cases the results are subjective and they can be made more reliable by adding more participant. This can easily be done with SUS since it is a rather inexpensive test. This test can also be applied during agile website development to test user experience for specific functions of the system [16]. The Checkpoint can also be taken by few experts and then the results compared but this is a more expensive process. Both tests give us a rough usability score but the Checkpoint review also provides a list of issues that can later be addressed during website improvement. The Checkpoint also has shortcomings, such as the same issue being repeated in statements from different themes.

The Checkpoint is obviously designed with an e-commerce website in mind, since an emphasis is placed on the existence of a shopping basket, product information, checking out and payment processes, searching etc. Some of the statements can be rephrased to better suit the business model of a professional group website. It is good to have the option of not answering statements that don't apply to the website, and they are consequently omitted in the scoring process. Using the Expert Review Checkpoint during an expert review is more helpful than just making a laundry list of issues. An expert with a background in graphic design would probably focus on the page layout and visual design and forget to test some of its functional characteristics. If another expert with an engineering background also reviews the website the average overall score derived from both reviews will be considered more valid.

4   Conclusion

The overall impression is that `ixda.org` is functional but still needs work to improve esthetic and navigational issues. This website's average usability was implied by the SUS score of 68% it received, but this score can also suggest that users are more tolerant when it comes to esthetic and navigational issues. The similar score of 70% for the Expert Review Checkpoint also tells us that this website is as functional as most others. If there was a continuation in testing Heuristic Walkthrough will be the next test. However, enough issues have been identified with the Expert Review Checkpoint and the accompanying expert review. Instead of assigning more assets to testing it will be more effective to assign assets to fixing the existing issues. Even though tests have been developed to prove the objective character of usability, the decision on what issues need fixing and what is the best way to do it still remains subjective.

In order to consolidate all the content and improve usability for this webpage one needs to start from adjusting the old sitemap to match the current website. Making changes and improvements to the updated sitemap according to the research findings will be the next step. It is one of the principles of heuristic research as stated by (Pólya, G., 1957) – "if you are having difficulty understanding a problem, try drawing a picture" [15]. Final step will be to change the code and transform ixda.org where it meets all of the standard website requirements as established by usability.gov [16]. In order to best reflects the Interaction Design Association's value proposition, attract more members and energize participation ixda.org should be transform into an exemplary website.

Acknowledgements. Thanks to David Travis of Userfocus for sharing his Expert Review Checkpoint and providing invaluable feedback and to Tim Schneidermeier for inspiring this paper's study design and mostly to IxDa.org for providing the research content.

References

1. Interaction Design Association. Welcome to Interaction Design Association. http://www.ixda.org/ (2014). Accessed 26 Dec 2014
2. Brooke, J.: SUS: A Retrospective (2009). http://uxpajournal.org/sus-a-retrospective/
3. Nielsen, J.: Usability engineering at a discount. In: Salvendy, G., Smith, M.J. (eds.) Designing and Using Human-Computer Interfaces and Knowledge Based Systems, pp. 394–401. Elsevier Science Publishers, Amsterdam (1989)
4. Medlock, M.C., Wixon, D., Terrano, M., Romero, R., Fulton, B.: Using the RITE method to improve products: A definition and a case study. Presented at the Usability Professionals Association 2002, Orlando Florida (2002)
5. Travis, D.: Expert Review Checklist (n.d.). http://www.userfocus.co.uk/resources/guidelines.html
6. Nielsen, J.: Why You Only Need to Test with 5 Users, 19 March 2000. http://www.nngroup.com/articles/why-you-only-need-to-test-with-5-users/. Sauro, J:. Measuring Usability With The System Usability Scale (SUS), 2 February 2011. http://www.measuringu.com/sus.php
7. Tullis, T., Albert, B.: Measuring the user experience: collecting, analyzing, and presenting usability metrics, p. c2008. Elsevier/Morgan Kaufmann, Amsterdam/Boston (2008)
8. Schneider, G.P.: Electronic Commerce. Course Technology. Cengage Learning, Boston (2015)
9. Gronsund, T.: 7 Proven Templates for Creating Value Propositions That Work, 29 November 2011. http://torgronsund.com/2011/11/29/7-proven-templates-for-creating-value-propositions-that-work/?utm_content=buffer3cc24&utm_medium=social&utm_source=twitter.com&utm_campaign=buffer
10. Plumley, G., Wyrostek, W.E., Books24x7, I., Plumley, G., Wyrostek, W.E.: Website Design and Development 100 Questions to Ask Before Building a Website, p. c2011. Wiley, Indianapolis (2011)

11. Nielsen, J.: Usability Engineering, p. c1993. AP Professional, Boston (1993)
12. Bacon, E., et al.: Conan Update and Design Document, 4 November 2009. http://www.ixda.org/blog/entry/conan-update-design-doc-0
13. Bacon, E., et al.: IxDA.org Conan Interaction Design, 4 November 2009. https://docs.google.com/file/d/0ByUefdff4crxYjI3ZWIzYjYtMjA0OS00NzE1LWI4NDgtZjhlOWY4OTVjZjg0/edit?ddrp=1&hl=en#
14. Morkes, J., Pausic L.: Agile Development and User Experience (n.d.). http://www.nngroup.com/courses/agile-development-and-user-experience/
15. Poilya, G.: 1887–1985: How to Solve it: A New Aspect of Mathematical Method, 2nd edn. Princeton University Press, Princeton (1957)
16. Website Requirements (n.d.). http://www.usability.gov/how-to-and-tools/methods/requirements.html

How We Perceive Search Engines

Leonardo Penna[(⊠)] and Manuela Quaresma

LEUI - Laboratory of Ergodesign and Usability of Interfaces,
PUC-Rio University, Rio de Janeiro, Brazil
leo.mep@gmail.com, mquaresma@puc-rio.br

Abstract. This article presents a literature review related to users' perceptions about search engines. Its motivation was establish an information source upon a topic that directly affects people's interactions with these tools and currently is scattered in the literature. It was discussed impact generated in users' behavior by the confidence degree in the companies producing search engines and by credit given to algorithms responsible for selection and ordering of results. It was also analyzed the public view about impartiality, accuracy and reliability of these tools.

Keywords: Search engines · Search · Perception · Users · Results · Ordering · Ranking

1 Introduction

The rapid growth of Internet in early years of the 90s served as a catalyst for the development of tools that aggregate content, allowing people to move in a more orderly way in the virtual space. The increase from 130 to 23.500 websites between 1993 and 1995 [1] attested to the Web expansion potential and showed that the manual recovery of information would become unviable in a short time. The search engines have become the most successful response to this demand for support systems, by allowing users to find documents related to an interest group of keywords. Currently, they are the basis for experimentation and transit at virtual spaces, playing an equivalent role of an expert [2], which makes content indications that are relevant to subjects' questions. Google, for example, became the main starting point for students, both for searches of everyday life, as for academic researches [3].

Inserted in this context, this article presents a literature review related to users' perceptions about search engines. Its motivation was establish an information source upon a topic that directly affects people's interactions with these tools and currently is scattered in the literature. Using Google Scholar as search system of academic articles, it was sought in November 2014 publications with the term "search engines" or "google", associated with one or more of the following keywords: "users", "evaluation", "assess", "perceive", "perception" and "interpret". After review of the abstracts of the documents found, it was defined a first set of items relevant to the study. The second stage of the literature review was to search for all articles quoting one of the selected publications. This process of selecting documents and subsequent evaluation of quotes was performed iteratively until there were no new items related to the subject

© Springer International Publishing Switzerland 2015
A. Marcus (Ed.): DUXU 2015, Part III, LNCS 9188, pp. 74–81, 2015.
DOI: 10.1007/978-3-319-20889-3_8

researched. Finally, it was performed a content analysis of the main issues addressed in the informational mass found.

2 Confidence at Systemic Ordering

The essence behind how the search engines work lies within the selection algorithm and the results ordering related to the searches done by the user. Through this operation set, invisible to those who use the tool, the relevance concept adopted by these systems come to life. "As there is no independent metric for what actually are the most relevant search results for any given query, engineers must decide what results look 'right' and tweak their algorithm to attain that result (...)" [4].

An aspect related to how we perceive the search engines is the belief we have in their proper functioning. Through a survey conducted by Purcell et al. [5], it was observed that most users understand these tools as fair and unbiased information sources, especially among young people. The prevailing view is that the informational clipping performed by search engines is reliable and accurate. Added to this, the vast people majority are satisfied with services offered and more than half of respondents believe that these systems are improving over time.

This positive view associated to the search tools becomes clear when we analyze the people behavior facing the computational processes responsible for results. Several studies show us that users trust the sorting done by the tools and are willing to click at the first results [6–12], in addition to possessing a distinct evaluative look for items in listing's lower positions [9, 10].

In an experiment conducted by Pan et al. [6], 16 individuals — graduating students which highly trusted Google (7.9/10) and had vast experience using the tool (10 out of 10) — completed ten tasks comprising navigational and informational searches, while their eyes were recorded by an eye tracking device. In order to understand the ordering influence at the decision-making process, the results were manipulated. Each individual was given one of the three possible scenarios: normal, where the results page was the same as Google's; swapped, where the first item changed places with the second one; reversed, where the results were changed to be displayed from last to first. Aiming to contribute with the interpretation of the output data during the experiment, the researchers asked five people to decide the relevance of the search results. All the items found in two of the tasks were randomly evaluated.

The data gathered indicates that the ordering has a strong influence over how the user interacts with the results page. In general, the individuals viewed the top position more frequently and clicked at the first result most of the times. When exposed to the scenario where the first two results were swapped, the click count for the first item was, nonetheless, three times higher than the second one. Besides that, the top item from Google's ranking — shown as first place for the normal scenario, as second for the swapped scenario and as tenth for the reverse scenario — had a decreasing eye fixations number the lower it was displayed.

Despite the overwhelming trust in the results sorting, according to the authors, the consumption of the content presented by the search tool is not passive. When exposed to the reversed scenario, the users took longer to interact with the pages (10.9 s for reversed, 6.5 s for normal, 5.8 s for swapped, $p < .05$), and the number of clicks was significantly lower compared to the other scenarios. It was also possible to notice an increased eye fixations number (30.0 reversed, 18.3 normal and 17.9 swapped, $p < .05$), a higher count of checked results (3.8 descriptions for reversed, 2.5 for normal and 2.7 for swapped, $p < .05$), and a larger quantity of description reevaluation (3.4 reversed, 2.2 normal and 1.9 swapped, $p < .05$). The interaction with results pages sorted inconsistently with the items' inherent relevance led to a higher awareness and caution by the individuals.

Statically foreseeing the different variables influence over the number of clicks among the viewed results, the list position had a slightly higher performance than the item's intrinsic relevance.

To assess whether data obtained in study performed by Pan et al. [6] would extend to other search engines or were exclusively related to Google, Lorigo et al. [7] conducted an experiment with very similar format to that used previously, replacing only the analysis target by Yahoo's tool. The reported results showed that both tools' behaviors is very similar, occurring a persistence of dependency on the result's ordering.

This relationship of trust between the users and the search engines can also be observed in a study by Balatsoukas and Ruthven [10], in which 24 college students (17–36 years of age, frequent or very frequent search engines' users) sought to satisfy a real informational need. Free to use any resource available on Internet, students had as restriction only a maximum time of 25 min to complete task. Their statements were analyzed, eye movements data were recorded (number of fixations and types of visualized components - titles, abstracts, url, etc.), and the displayed results' evaluations are stored (relevant, partially relevant and irrelevant). To complement information obtained during tasks execution, it was also conducted an interview at activity end. The researchers found that all participants used Google and during their interaction with the tool, tended to fix eyes longer on items at top of first results page, especially in the two highest positions. The influence of search engine's ordering was evidenced by variation in the relevance criteria used for evaluating results. On the first two items 11 criteria were used (e.g., topicality, quality and recency), while for the result in the page's last position (tenth) only four parameters were considered. In some intermediate positions, result's relation with the topic ceased to be the most important element in assessment, giving way to criteria such as the information and source quality (see Fig. 1).

One hypothesis to this behavior is the need for an extra incentive which compensates the inferior value attributed to lower listing's positions. In other words, to click on results that are not at top, individuals needs to know the source of information, consider it a good reference or have other evidences about displayed item quality.

Importantly, despite the evident favoring of results that appear in search engines' top positions, there isn't necessarily an extension of this behavior to selection process of reliable and quality contents. Salmerón et al. [12] conducted an experiment with 67 college students (average age of 22.27 years and with extensive experience in internet usage), in which they needed to research the topic "Reduction of greenhouse gas emissions" and point out the two most relevant pages in terms of information. All

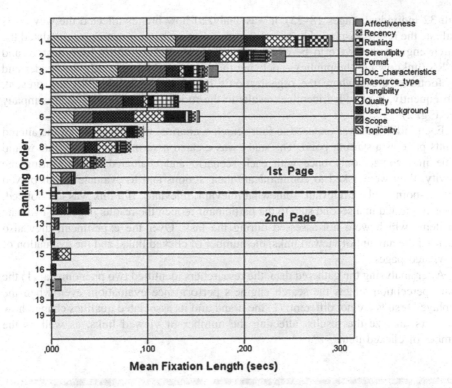

Fig. 1. Fixation in the selection criteria, according to the position (Source: [10], p. 1739)

participants received a list of 10 results that should be used in task. For half of them, items were showed in decreasing relevance order (default behavior at major search engines). The other half received an inverted list, that is, in ascending order. Although the subjects have clicked more over results at the top positions, the relevance and completeness assessment of content was similar in the two groups. Both chose an equivalent ratio of pages relevant/complete, relevant/incomplete and irrelevant.

3 Brands' Influence

As a comprehensive overview, we can classify brand as being the group of tangible representative elements — name, visual design, symbol — and the intangible components — values, concepts and personality — associated to an organization [13]. Its depiction is capable of inducting strong behavioral changes over consumers. Park, Harada, and Igarashi [14], for example, state that the brand perception of a product affected the user evaluation of the mental demand related to its use.

By directing attention to the search segment in internet environment, we can find data at literature that point out a strong relationship between brands and the information acquisition process. In an experiment conducted by Jansen, Zhang and Schultz [13] with 32 individuals (ages 18–25), it was analyzed how brands affected the way users evaluate the results displayed by search engines. For such, the researchers simulated the search engines that were to be evaluated – Google, Yahoo! MSN Live Search, and AI^{2}RS (unknown to the public) –, deleting the results and leaving only the header and the footnote, areas where the organization's brand and visual identity are present. Subsequently, they added identical results to the modified versions for each company (see Fig. 2).

Each individual was exposed to four search scenarios, which had one of the altered results page as a starting point. The study was created assuring the participants would come into contact only once with each scenario and evaluated brand. During the activity, they were asked to communicate their actions and to evaluate the displayed links (3-point scale: irrelevant, somewhat relevant, relevant). If a link was not noticed, it was requested in a second step to the participant reopen the results page and evaluate the items which were not assessed during the task. Over the experiment, they also recorded the amount of viewed links, the number of clicked links, and the evaluation of the visited pages.

After analyzing the gathered data, the researchers identified two phenomena: (1) the brand perception affects the search engine's performance evaluation, even when the displayed results are not different; (2) the brand and its associated qualities change how the users analyze the results, affecting the number of viewed links, as well as the number of clicked items.

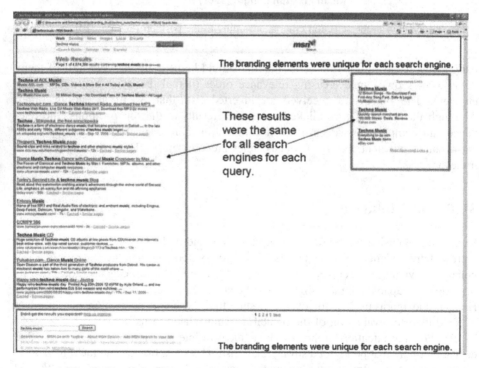

Fig. 2. Example of an experiment results page. (Source: [13], p. 1577)

3.1   Influence Over Performance Evaluation

Jansen et al. [13] gathered data showing that, although the results viewed by the individuals were constants, the link evaluation in each of the search engines presented significant differences. (Factorial ANOVA, p = 0.071). Judging the set of viewed links (organic and sponsored), Google had a higher rating than MSN Live Search, being considered 17 % more relevant than it competitor. Yahoo! and AI^{2}RS had 12 % higher evaluation than MSN Live Search. The fact that a tool without any public projection was superior than other belonging to a large company like Microsoft may indicate a negative brand view by consumers.

Although the study did not established which factors associated with brand are responsible for results evaluation differences, the relationship establishment between their findings and a later work by Jansen et al. [15] suggests that, since the tools have positive images, their performance will be better evaluated. This time, the researchers prepared a survey to understand the thoughts related to the brands of different search engines. With 207 respondents, the research asked participants to view 10 search engine logos – A9, AI^{2}RS (fake), Alltheweb, AOL Search, Ask.com, Dogpile, Google, MSN Live Search, Mahalo, and Yahoo! – and inform if they have ever used them, if they still used them, and what were their thoughts about them.

They verified that "Google has far and away the highest positive brand perception (...). Additionally, the depth of the positive sentiment is amazing (...). The term love was used by several participants to describe [it]" [15]. From all the participants, 87 % had a positive feedback, 12.6 % did not express any opinion, and only 0.5 % had a negative comments. There were no mixed or neutral perceptions about the tool. Only Yahoo! and Ask.com were also highly well rated, the former with 59.4 % of positive feedback and the latter with 52.7 %. MSN Live Search, despite being previously used by 54 % of the participants, got no good results. Microsoft's old engine received a number of bad reviews (27.1 %) higher than positive ones (22.2 %).

In the first experiment [13], evaluations of identical results by users was much more positive for Google and Yahoo!, especially when compared to MSN Live Search, which got a rating worse than the unknown search tool. In the 2012 research [15], similar results were found: Google and Yahoo! had a highly positive perception, whereas MSN Live Search got a very negative one. While it cannot establish a causal link between those two variables (i.e., a good perception implies a better feedback for the search engine), the data gathered in both studies seem compatible and encourage further investigation.

3.2   Influence Over How the Results are Analyzed

By statistically analyzing raw data about the links that were viewed and those clicked, Jansen et al. [13] were able to determine the interference exerted by changing brands of search engines. A significant difference was found regarding the number of viewed links (Factorial ANOVA, p = 0.022), with a prevalence of Yahoo! (40 % over AI^{2}RS) and Google (20 % over AI^{2}RS). "(...) When participants were viewing links, they favored the mainstream search engines (...) relative to the non-mainstream search engines. This may be because the participants were more trusting [in them]" [13]. In addition, was identified a possible value difference related to each engine's results ordering. MSN Live Search and AI^{2}RS got a higher number of viewed links at the top positions, meaning that the users were cautious when they faced the displayed rankings from these tools.

As well as the link visualization, the search engine brands affected the number of clicked links (Factorial ANOVA, p = 0.045). The total from Yahoo! was 27 % higher than Google, 46 % superior than MSN, and 11 % larger than AI^{2}RS. When using the dominant tools, users seemed to delegate the task of finding relevant sites to system, relying little in the results evaluation and assigning high value to its positioning. This behavior leads to a higher number of less quality clicks. In less known search engines, the lack of trust makes the users more discerning about the results: they click less, choosing more relevant links.

4 Conclusions

The literature analysis related to uniqueness of our search engines perception showed that people have a wide confidence in systemic ordering. It was found that they consider these tools accurate and unbiased information sources [5] and they are predisposed to click in the first items of pages shown [6–12]. The ranking proposed by search engines exerts an influence on the links clicked slightly higher than result's relevance [6]. Furthermore, the number of criteria used in results evaluation at the top of page is greater than those considered for items in lower positions [9, 10].

It was also realized that individuals change their analysis and evaluation of results according to search tool, even if results are identical [13]. The judgment that they make about search engines performance, the number of links examined and the amount of clicks in results are dependent on their perception of search engines' brand [13]. In general, the dominants tools have higher rates for all mentioned variables. Apparently, in unfamiliar tools, the lack of trust decreases users' general interest in the results, but encourages a closer evaluative behavior in which users click less often and choose more relevant links [13].

It is necessary to point out that few academic publications mainly focuses on the topic covered by the article. Data relating to users' perception about search engines is often located in articles dealing with distinct topics, that make brief observations on the subject. Thus, the extensive sample space of available documents makes impossible a complete literature review and creates need for data selection to be explored. As a result, it was given an important step towards concatenation of scattered data in literature and it was obtained a research dealing with major issues related to subject, although it isn't a complete reflection of the existing production.

References

1. Gray, M.: Measuring the Growth of the Web (1995). Accessed from http://www.mit.edu/people/mkgray/growth/
2. Simpson, T.W.: Evaluating Google as an epistemic tool. Metaphilosophy **43**(4), 426–445 (2012). Accessed from http://onlinelibrary.wiley.com/doi/10.1111/j.1467-9973.2012.01759.x/full

3. Asher, A.D.: Search magic. discovering how undergraduates find information. In: American Anthropological Association, Annual Meeting (2011). Accessed from http://www. erialproject.org/wp-content/uploads/2011/11/Asher_AAA2011_Search-magic.pdf
4. Gillespie, T.: The relevance of algorithms. In: Gillespie, T., Boczkowski, P., Foot, K. (eds.) Media Technologies: Essays on Communication, Materiality, and Society, pp. 167–194. MIT Press, Cambridge (2014). Accessed from http://www.tarletongillespie.org/essays/ Gillespie%20-%20The%20Relevance%20of%20Algorithms.pdf
5. Purcell, K., Brenner, J., Rainie, L.: Search engine use 2012 (2012). Accessed from http://www. pewinternet.org/files/old-media//Files/Reports/2012/PIP_Search_Engine_Use_2012.pdf
6. Pan, B., Hembrooke, H., Joachims, T., Lorigo, L., Gay, G., Granka, L.: In Google we trust: users' decisions on rank, position, and relevance. J. Comput. Med. Commun. 12, 801–823 (2007). doi:10.1111/j.1083-6101.2007.00351.x. Accessed from http://onlinelibrary.wiley. com/enhanced/doi/10.1111/j.1083-6101.2007.00351.x/
7. Lorigo, L., Haridasan, M., Brynjarsdóttir, H., Xia, L., Joachims, T., Gay, G., Granka, L., Pellacini, F., Pan, B.: Eye tracking and online search: lessons learned and challenges ahead. J. Am. Soc. Inf. Sci. 59, 1041–1052 (2008). doi:10.1002/asi.20794. Accessed from http:// onlinelibrary.wiley.com/enhanced/doi/10.1002/asi.20794/
8. Bar-Ilan, J., Keenoy, K., Levene, M., Yaari, E.: Presentation bias is significant in determining user preference for search results—a user study. J. Am. Soc. Inf. Sci. 60, 135–149 (2009). doi:10.1002/asi.20941. Accessed from http://onlinelibrary.wiley.com/ enhanced/doi/10.1002/asi.20941/
9. Balatsoukas, P. and Ruthven, I. (2010), The use of relevance criteria during predictive judgment: An eye tracking approach. Proc. Am. Soc. Info. Sci. Tech., 47: 1–10. doi:10. 1002/meet.14504701145. Retrieved from http://onlinelibrary.wiley.com/enhanced/doi/10. 1002/meet.14504701145/
10. Balatsoukas, P., Ruthven, I.: An eye-tracking approach to the analysis of relevance judgments on the Web: the case of Google search engine. J Am. Soc. Inf. Sci. Tech. 63, 1728–1746 (2012). doi:10.1002/asi.22707. Accessed from http://onlinelibrary.wiley.com/ enhanced/doi/10.1002/asi.22707/
11. Kammerer, Y., Gerjets, P.: How search engine users evaluate and select Web search results: the impact of the search engine interface on credibility assessments. Libr. Inf. Sci. 4, 251–279 (2012). Accessed from http://www.emeraldinsight.com/doi/abs/10.1108/S1876-0562%282012%29002012a012
12. Salmerón, L., Kammerer, Y., García-Carrión, P.: Searching the Web for conflicting topics: page and user factors. Comput. Hum. Behav. 29(6), 2161–2171 (2013). Accessed from http://www.sciencedirect.com/science/article/pii/S0747563213001465
13. Jansen, B.J., Zhang, M., Schultz, C.D.: Brand and its effect on user perception of search engine performance. J. Am. Soc. Inf. Sci. 60, 1572–1595 (2009). doi:10.1002/asi.21081. Accessed from http://onlinelibrary.wiley.com/enhanced/doi/10.1002/asi.21081/
14. Park, S., Harada, A., Igarashi, H.: Influences of personal preference on product usability. In: CHI 2006 Extended Abstracts on Human Factors in Computing Systems, pp. 87–92. ACM, April 2006. Accessed from http://dl.acm.org/citation.cfm?id=1125475
15. Jansen, B.J., Zhang, L., Mattila, A.S.: User reactions to search engines logos: investigating brand knowledge of web search engines. Electron. Commer. Res. 12(4), 429–454 (2012). Accessed from http://link.springer.com/article/10.1007%2Fs10660-012-9101-0#

Clicking Through Endless Seas: Understanding User Experience in the Design of Journalistic Websites

Ben Posetti[✉]

Department of Media Cognition and Communication, University of Copenhagen,
Copenhagen, Denmark
ben.posetti@gmail.com

Abstract. The research explores the visual design of journalistic content websites, from a producer and user perspective, to understand the forces underlying the design. A genre analysis approach is combined with an understanding of user experience (UX) in interaction design to investigate the meaning embedded in the design features of three websites. Ethnographic Content Analysis (ECA), observation tasks, and in-depth interviews reveal a negotiation process between users and producers in achieving their purposes through the website product.

Keywords: User experience · Website design · Ethnographic content analysis

1 Introduction

Media content today is produced in an environment of media convergence, characterized by the tendency for media products to become less segmented and distinguished by form and function, or production and consumption, as content flows across multiple media platforms [1]. The convergence process characterizes a rapidly changing paradigm of editorial and journalistic content production and consumption. This shift has altered not just where content is consumed, and in which media, but has also fundamentally changed the nature of content consumption to being less committed and more intermittent [2].

In this media environment, website design has played an influential role in how content consumers access and navigate online media. The multimodality and hypertextuality, inherent in online media, changes the way journalistic products are produced and consumed. The evolution of content production and consumption in new media has instigated a closer connection of multimedia design with the production of online content, and has increased the importance of website design for audience access, reception and understanding of content.

The present research explores the nature of website design for three journalistic content publishers. In particular, the research approach aims to incorporate both the user and the producer perspective of UX, as manifest in the visual website design. In studies of journalism and editorial content in new media, a focus on the social aspects of web-based communication and information, as well as the structural and

© Springer International Publishing Switzerland 2015
A. Marcus (Ed.): DUXU 2015, Part III, LNCS 9188, pp. 82–93, 2015.
DOI: 10.1007/978-3-319-20889-3_9

organizational changes in production have left a crevasse of knowledge where these two forces collide – namely, the website product itself.

This paper aims to incorporate a UX perspective into established media research approaches. The research employs genre analysis, applied within an interaction design paradigm, with the objective of understanding the website design of journalistic content websites. Genre analysis identifies meaning embedded in media artifacts, established through convention [3]. Since the media artifacts in question are digital interactive products, the interaction design worldview specifically deals with examining UX in these environments.

Research Question. How can the website design of online journalistic content be understood through a producer-oriented and user-oriented analysis of the website product and its use?

Note that this research question is exploratory in nature. The approach developed aims to understand website design in the context-rich environment of media production and consumption. Bargas-Avila and Hornbæk [4] note that researchers of UX emphasize the heavy influence that context of use has on the concept. They explain that when, where and with whom a product is used influences the type and quality of experiences triggered. In addition, questions of why a website is produced, for whom, and how (with which technologies) introduces another level of context to be understood in website design. The present research therefore aims to develop a more holistic approach to understanding the nature and influence of visual website design within the contexts of social, cultural, economic, and technological forces surrounding its production and consumption.

The research conducted is based around ECA from a producer perspective with a designer as expert coder. A user analysis including open-use observation and in-depth interviews with 10 online news consumers contribute a unique view of user motivations and behavior that is examined relative to the content analysis data.

2   Approach

Law et al. [5] surveyed UX researchers and practitioners to determine commonalities in a collective understanding of UX. Professional consensus converged on the dynamic, context-dependent, and subjective nature of UX. Hassenzahl et al.'s operationalization of such an understanding separates perception of product attributes, from their evaluation [6–8]. Three classes of attribute perception are described [7]:

Pragmatic Quality – Synonymous with usability, these attributes are connected to users' need to achieve behavioral goals. Hedonic Quality (Identification) – Referring to the self-oriented human need to express oneself through objects. Hedonic Quality (Stimulation) – Another self-oriented need for stimulation, novelty, and challenge as a prerequisite for personal development.

The independence of attribute perceptions and product evaluations means that the model can be applied to different contexts without assuming conceptual relationships. The model captures holistic product attributions, which can be related to various consequences such as emotions, evaluations, or behavior. With this understanding of UX, the present aim is to develop an evaluative framework for analyzing UX through website design, tied to the contexts in which the product is designed and interacted with.

Genre analysis similarly seeks to understand media products, through a context-sensitive analysis of the attributes of a designed product, relative to the community of producers, designers and users. Genre analysis has been utilized widely in media and communications research to analyze the conventions of form and function within a text and how those conventions shape discursive meanings ascertained from a media product. Genre analysis recognizes that documents contain styles and conventions, which can be interpreted as forming the social realities of the actors involved [3]. Frow [9] refers to this process as a cognitive organization of knowledge by schema, "making patterns of meaning relative to particular communicative functions and situations" (p. 133).

For the purposes of developing the present approach for studying website design as a text, a Swalesian understanding of genre is invoked. Swales [10] studies genre as an epistemological discipline, rather than a realist phenomenon. In this understanding, mutually understood communicative purposes characterize genre and are treated as the privileged criterion for genre analysis. Furthermore, it is recognized that the conventionalized constraints of genre are often exploited to achieve private intentions [11].

Digital genre. Askehave and Nielsen [12] suggest that the media and genre distinction is confounded when analyzing digital texts because of the nature of information interaction. Applying the Swalesian model of genre analysis, Askehave and Nielsen [12] propose that analysis of internet genres should consider the user's movements between the traditional sense of textual generic conventions, and the conventions surrounding hypertextual media characteristics. That is conceptualized as two user modes: Reading mode, represented by the traditional reception of texts, and navigating mode, represented by personal construction of a path through one or several sites [12, 13]. A key upshot of this model for the methodological approach being developed here is that the analyst considers the roles of both text producer and text receiver in the construction of meaning from generic artifacts.

2.1 A Framework for Website Design Evaluation

In order to examine communicative purposes in website design a framework is developed to structure methodologies from a user and producer orientation. Figure 1 represents the phenomenon of interest in each orientation – product design and product use. These are analyzed through the lens of three modalities which focus analysis on the central concepts of UX and communicative purpose in the website design.

Producer Orientation. The producer orientation incorporates a systematic and inductive analysis of the product design. According to Thorlacius' [14] model of visual communication focusing on web design, the implicit addresser (the designer or producer) can be analyzed via the expressive function of the product – the attitudes,

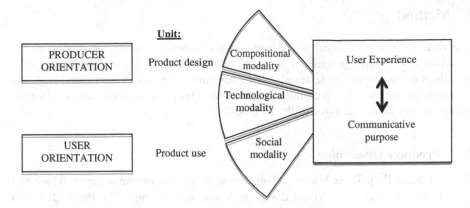

Fig. 1. A framework for website visual design evaluation

feelings and opinions expressed in the product. This view echoes the perspective in genre analysis that a text, is not just a neutral reflection of content placed by the publisher. But the website constructs the socio-cultural relationship between producer and user, and that reality is produced through conventions in the product [4].

Rose's [15] visual methodologies framework guides methodological procedures for analysis of visual texts based on three modalities which denote the meanings in an image. The model is adapted here to suit a visual analysis of website design focused on user interaction. *Compositional modality:* Referring to the actual visual elements and their material properties e.g. layout, typography, symbols and icons, color, and size. *Technological modality:* The technological aspects of the internet such as hypertext and multimedia, which guide navigation, structure information, and influence attention and perception processes. *Social modality:* The organizational context in which the websites are produced including the motivations and strategies of the producer, relative to social, economic and technological contexts of production.

In the present research, a qualitative media analysis approach was pursued to explore the design of journalistic content websites. This adapted Altheide's [16] method of ECA to the context of web design, coding components in websites based on the producer-oriented modality framework.

User Orientation. Product use is the phenomenon to be analyzed in the user-oriented aspect of the approach. This is also scrutinized through the lens of compositional, technological and social modalities, which characterize the contextual meanings of the website design from the user perspective. *Compositional modality:* User perception of the website's design features. *Technological modality:* How those features are attributed hedonic and pragmatic value, and influence user evaluations and behavior. *Social modality:* How the website design reflects on the evaluation of website content and the relationship between the user and the producer.

The present research supports the ECA of visual website design through a qualitative analysis of observed user interaction on the websites studied, and semi-structured interviews. The procedure is described below.

3   Method

The method revolves around a systematic and comprehensive deconstruction of the visual design of three journalistic content websites. This examines context-sensitive meanings in website design features, that are relevant for producers and users. With this overview of the product, preliminary user observation and in-depth interviews contribute further analytical rigor to the methodology.

3.1   Producer Orientation

Website Sampling. Three US-based websites were chosen for the research, which had a range of variation in the visual design style and components. The Huffington Post (www.huffingtonpost.com), Upworthy (www.upworthy.com), and Matter (www. medium.com/matter/). These websites were purposively sampled to represent a variation in producer motivations for content delivery, variation in user reception motivations, and for the diversity of visual design features. Palys [17] explains that implicit in purposive sampling is that the sampling strategy is tied to the research objectives. In this case, the research aims to understand website design relative to different contexts of production and use. Each of the websites is a 'digital native' content producer. That is, they produce journalistic content that is only published and distributed online. Critically, the sampled websites each project editorial values, in that the content is published and mass distributed under the overall publication brand, and attributed to individual authors and journalists.

ECA. Qualitative coding of the websites focused on the article webpage layouts on each website to limit the study to analyzing the design of content pages. The coding procedure followed prescriptions of ECA, moving reflexively between data, analysis and interpretation in a process of constant comparison and refinement [16].

An initial survey of the three websites served to identify and familiarize with the visual elements to be analyzed. This informed the development of a coding protocol, structured around Rose's [15] modalities previously outlined. Individual design components of each website were listed and described, identifying a total of 40 components in The Huffington Post (HP), 24 in Upworthy, and 19 in Matter.

In the initial phase of coding the lead researcher assigned codes to each component, in all three modalities. Questions were formulated to characterize the coding frame, ensuring that all codes flow from a single principle in each modality [18].

- *Compositional modality.* "What kind of information and/or information structure was this element designed to represent?"
- *Technological modality.* "In what ways might the component influence how the website is processed, consumed, or navigated?"
- *Social modality.* "What is the producer's apparent motive and purpose in how the component is represented on the website?"

Codes were defined and redefined by analytic memos in this first phase. Multiple codes were simultaneously applied to each component in each modality since multiple meaning descriptions and inferences were justified [19]. Codes were gradually added, deleted, combined and conceptualized during the process of coding, across each of the websites. With a list of the initial defined codes, and an empty coding sheet, a second coder went through the same coding process. The second coder is an experienced graphic design professional who has worked extensively on website design projects.

At a point when both coders felt that they had comprehensively accounted for each component across the three modalities they compared worksheets. Code-by-code and, component-by-component the coding protocol was discussed and refined. Areas of difference were collaboratively deliberated and reconceptualized to achieve 'interpretive convergence' in describing the design phenomena across the websites [19]. The function, purpose and design principles guiding each component's scheme within the layout were discussed to arrive at that description.

3.2 User Orientation: Data Collection and Analysis

Participants. Participants for the experimental and interview component of the study were selected as a convenience sample. All participants were consumers of online journalistic content. 10 participants were sampled, 5 males and 5 females, with ages ranging from 24-38. Surveys identified some key factors of the participants' internet use. 90 % of participants reported to spend more than 10 h per week surfing the internet. On average, 66.5 % of the time spent surfing the internet was on a desktop computer or laptop, the remainder spread across mobile phone and tablet devices. All participants reported that they source daily news from online news sources. 7 out of 10 reported online as their only news source. This data depicts the participants as accustomed internet and online content consumers.

Observation and Interview. The sessions were conducted with all participants in a familiar, comfortable location − either their own home or workspace. Participants started their website interaction on the homepage for each publication and had 15 min to freely browse the content. The open-use task was employed to overcome the pitfalls of tightly controlled tasks that do not emulate real-world interactions [4]. All observations were conducted on the same MacBook Pro 15" laptop computer and the screen was recorded using ScreenFlow software. The order of presentation of the three websites was rotated for each participant.

Videos of each participant's interaction on each website were analyzed by notation to track the user's activity within and between pages. Interactions were noted by time elapsed, description of the website feature interacted with, and outcome of the interaction. Observation notes also recorded a description of the participant's activity, focusing on the article pages. The URL of all articles pages visited was recorded and the researcher visited those pages and listed the design features particular to that page.

30−60 min interviews were conducted after participants had finished all observation tasks and surveys. All three websites were opened on a computer so that the participant could refer to particular design elements when necessary. Discussion was structured around the same modalities that drove the website content analysis. Interviews were partially transcribed and annotated with researcher notes and analytic memos, drawing attention to particular salient concepts.

4 Results and Analysis

4.1 Producer Orientation

Producer Rationales in Website Design. Figure 2 depicts the formalized concepts that were identified by ECA. Review of the final coding scheme structured the analysis into distinct rationales that describe the communicative purpose of design features in each of the three modalities. The model includes representational goals, user focuses, and organizational motivations. Organizations may place higher importance on particular rationales when designing the website, however all surveyed websites showed some influence for each of the rationales. Since a particular visual feature may be able to actualize more than one of the concepts within a modality, the rationales overlap.

Five Representational Goals. These goals explain the kind of information or information structure that individual graphic features represented.

'Content goal'[1] – The goal to represent the primary journalistic content of any given page. 'Structure goal' – Many elements had the goal to structure information, either by visually segmenting the page, or representing categorized information. 'Navigation goal' – The goal to represent a possibility for navigation to another page. 'Promotion goal' – A goal related to representing a feature in a way so as to promote that function or feature. 'Relational goal' – A goal in the website design to represent hedonic aspects of the publication and the content.

These goals were observed through the design features on all of the surveyed websites. Matter was dominant on the content and relational goals, since most of the design was centered on representing the content with a pleasing aesthetic. HP had features pursuing each of these goals, due to the comprehensiveness of the content and navigation options on that website. The promotional goal was evident in the crowding of content suggestions, and dedicated advertising units on article layouts. Upworthy design features exhibited the content and promotion goals.

Two User Focuses. The codes in the technological modality describe how the features were purposively designed in relation to user interaction.

'User-centered focus' – Design features which aided users in their core motive of content consumption. 'User-influence focus' – Design features intended to influence user interaction in pursuance of the producer's goals.

The user-centered focus and the user-influence focus may operate in parallel through different features on a web page. These concepts are a means to define the functional and technological purpose of the visuals in a website. Advertising units on HP could be considered 'user-influence' since it is designed to be prominent and not related to the user's primary purpose. In this case the user-influence focus is in contradistinction to the user-centered focus. The social media share buttons on the same layout invoke both focuses. The buttons are presented to make sharing easy for the user and communicate social proof for the content quality. However they also serve to influence users to share the content to increase the potential audience for the website.

---

[1] Individual codes and rationales from the model indicated by single quotation marks.

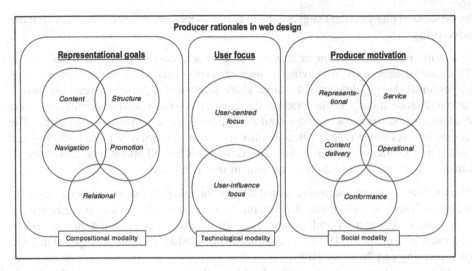

Fig. 2. Producer rationales in web design

Five Producer Motivations. Analyzing producer motivations in the design entailed looking at the wider context of the space in which the publication operated.

'Identification motivation' − The producer's motivation to develop a brand identity for the publication. 'Service motivation' − Features which provide a functional (pragmatic) or emotional (hedonic) service to the user. 'Content delivery motivation' − The design activities with a primary function of displaying content. 'Operational motivation' − Some design elements depict the producer's broader motivations for publishing journalistic content, such as advertising. 'Conformance' − Some design features conform to design standards for websites, or from offline media.

These producer motivations can also be pursued in parallel or in opposition. For example −Matter has an identification motivation in removing dis'tractions from their article layouts, in that their brand is based around appealing and dedicated content publishing. That might be in opposition to an operational motivation to promote other content or social media sharing. The result is that these forces play out in the design decision-making, defining the communicative purpose of the producer.

The following section further interprets the model with respect to the three analyzed website designs, and the unifying concepts of UX and communicative purpose.

The Huffington Post. The size and diversity of HP as a publication means that structure and navigation are important representational goals in their design. They are focused on both 'user-centered' features and 'user-influence'. They have an operational motivation to encourage users to stay on the website and view as many pages as possible, in order to earn advertising revenue. But this is balanced against a motivation to deliver content and a service to users who wish to be entertained or informed by the content. Data from the user-orientation revealed that participants found the design confusing and over-whelming, and they would visit this kind of news site when they were distracting themselves. The HP design plays a role in this, with features supporting user distraction by promoting many content suggestions to entice users to view −more pages with more advertising.

Upworthy represents content as easy to consume and easy to share on social media. This can be interpreted as having a 'user-centered focus'. But prominent, intrusive promotional design elements like large share buttons and popup boxes also have a 'user-influence focus'. Understanding the context of social media sharing in online content distribution helps to understand the communicative purpose in the design. The design features come together in a distinct style that aggressively pushes sharing and makes user interaction simple. This supports the site's overall operational motivation to build an audience, and to deliver the content that is curated.

Matter. Matter has an alternative layout design compared to many journalistic content websites. There is a clear visual focus on the content itself and less prominence for social media connection and content suggestion. That was reflected in the coding process with 8 out of the 19 (42 %) components labeled as 'content' (compared to 25 % on Upworthy and 28 % on HP).

Many visual components within the Matter layout emphasize classical aesthetic qualities in design − those focused on ordered structure and clarity [20]. Dominant rationales in the design were the representational 'content goal', and the 'content delivery' motivation. Many of the design features on Matter have a 'user-centered focus'. This reflects that Matter does not have a dominant operational motive evident in the design. This harmony between the producer's and user's communicative purpose explains participants' favorable user evaluations of Matter.

4.2 User Orientation

Interview and observation data supported the ECA examination of rationales that play out in website design. Navigation strategies and level of content immersion of participants indicated design influences on user modes of reception.

Reading mode and navigating mode. Askehave and Nielsen [12] proposed that the distinction between a user reading mode and navigating mode is pertinent in genre analysis because two different cognitive capacities and behavior patterns define interaction with the document. The results from the current research support this assessment. Participants had different approaches for finding content, and then different levels of engagement with that content. Some would browse for a long time with no observable strategy in finding content they were interested in. Particularly on Matter, participants spent more overall time searching for an interesting article, possibly because of the greater commitment involved for the longer, more in-depth content.

Some participants were very influenced by content suggestions where little time was spent searching, and enticing content was accessed without delay. These observed navigation strategies were mostly seen within a particular website interaction with a particular user. That is, users did not exhibit stable strategies across the three websites. Therefore, design features such as content suggestion influenced user interaction differently depending on the navigation strategy of the user.

Conversely, content immersion could be unstable within a single website session. Low content immersion is characterized by short time on an article page, skim reading, skipping ahead, and scanning images and headings. High immersion entails greater focus on the content and higher likelihood to read or watch from start to finish. Participants tended to have greater content immersion on Matter. They would scroll slower through article pages and stay longer before leaving a page, regardless of article length. On Upworthy users would often skip ahead in a video to see the content faster and move on.

The harmony of producer and user motivations on Matter was also evident in the user data. Participants recognized a context for consuming content on Matter that is more focused and purposeful. The design on Matter supports the reading mode by leaving out elements that encourage a navigation mode.

On Upworthy, simple presentation of visual features allows the user to focus on the content, with clear enticement to navigate or share on social media. Users commonly described the design as simple and easy to understand. On HP, reading and navigating modes can be seen as more interconnected in the design. The profusion of navigation options in the web page layouts makes a navigating mode of interaction constantly accessible in many forms. In this way, HP pursues their producer rationale for navigation, promotion, and an operational motivation based on advertising revenue.

The producer rationales play a role in shaping the design to move users between reading mode and navigating mode, which affects the overall UX for the website. This balances the user motivations for accessing content against the producer motivations for navigation, marketing, and content delivery.

5   Discussion

Interrelation of website design and content perceptions. Participants identified areas where the visual website design specifically contributed to their UX. This was commonly expressed in terms of their perception of the content itself. It was evident from these connections between design and content that the visual representation of content is closely related to evaluations of the content itself. On HP many participants commented that the crowding of content suggestions from all over the website, and also advertising, degraded their perception of the content they accessed.

"I liked the page, but I think it kind of ruined my experience that content that it links to out here [content suggestions column] is of such a different character... It kind of ruins my impression of, not the trustworthiness of the articles... well maybe a bit. The seriousness of this business." (Participant 8)

User content motivations interact with their experience in navigating and immersing themselves in content, and with their preconceptions. These findings indicate an inextricable link between how an online publication distinguishes itself in the mind of the user, and the visual design of the content. The visual design of the website influences the user perception of the content style and quality, and also indicates to the user what experience they should expect out of their interaction with the website.

Perceived value of the UX. This concept emerged relative to the contexts and motivation states in which users accessed the websites The perceived value concerns a personal evaluation made by the user regarding how they spend their time online, and an assessment of the quality of the content they receive in that time.

In reference to the visual website design, participants often discussed the journalistic quality of the content, difficulty in finding desired content, being enticed into content, distraction, and time wasting. This collectively contributes to how the user feels about the whole website experience, whether the website is valued and worthy of time and effort, and how the content should be engaged with.

The influence of web design on UX operates through these myriad perceptions in the context of the interaction. A confusing layout on HP might decrease perceptions of the quality of content, but it supports a distracted mode of navigation to more pieces of content. The perceived value of the experience inputs back into user decisions and assessments of what content is worthy in what situations and to what extent they should interact with the website. By this process, the producer constructs the design to balance their rationales against UX perceptions and associated user interaction that they seek.

6 Conclusion

In Hassenzahl's [6, 7] conceptualization of UX, the analysis here points to links between perceptions of hedonic and pragmatic quality in navigation and content immersion, and overall quality evaluations. The evaluations are played out in user interaction, which is fed back to the producer so that design is optimized to pursue producer rationales, and the desired UX effects. By this process the communicative purposes of producers and users are negotiated and become evident in the website design.

Analyzing the user and producer perspectives of the meanings ascertained from website design features allowed a context-rich view of the forces underlying website design of journalistic content websites. Future research could further explore this approach in more tightly controlled user and website design scenarios.

References

1. Jenkins, H.: Convergence Culture: Where Old and New Media Collide. NYU press, New York (2006)
2. Siapera, E., Veglis, A. (eds.): The Handbook of Global Online Journalism. Wiley, New York (2012)
3. Atkinson, P., Coffey, A.: Analysing documentary realities. In: Silverman, D. (ed.) Qualitative Research. Sage, London (2010)
4. Bargas-Avila, J., Hornbæk, K.: Foci and blind spots in user experience research. Interactions 19, 24–27 (2012)
5. Law, E.L.C., Roto, V., Hassenzahl, M., Vermeeren, A.P., Kort, J.: Understanding, scoping and defining user experience: a survey approach. In: Proceedings of the SIGCHI Conference on Human Factors in Computing Systems, pp. 719–728. ACM (2009)
6. Hassenzahl, M., Burmester, M., Koller, F.: AttrakDiff: Ein Fragebogen zur Messung wahrgenommener hedonischer und pragmatischer Qualität (in German). In: Mensch & Computer, pp. 187–196. Vieweg + Teubner Verlag, Berlin (2003)

7. Hassenzahl, M.: The interplay of beauty, goodness, and usability in interactive products. Hum.-Comput. Interact. **19**, 319–349 (2004)
8. Hassenzahl, M., Diefenbach, S., Göritz, A.: Needs, affect, and interactive products–facets of user experience. Interact. Comput. **22**, 353–362 (2010)
9. Frow, J.: Genre. Routledge, Abingdon (2006)
10. Swales, J.: Genre Analysis: English in Academic and Research Settings. Cambridge University Press, Cambridge (1990)
11. Bhatia, V.K.: Analysing Genre Language use in Professional Settings. Routledge, Abingdon (1993)
12. Askehave, I., Nielsen, A.E.: Digital genres: a challenge to traditional genre theory. Inf. Technol. People **18**, 120–141 (2005)
13. Finnemann, N.O.: Hypertext and the Representational Capacities of the Binary Alphabet. Center for Kulturforskning, Aarhus Universitet, Aarhus (1999)
14. Thorlacius, L.: Visual communication in web design–analyzing visual communication in web design. In: Hunsinger, J., Klastrup, L., Allen, M. (eds.) International Handbook of Internet Research, pp. 455–476. Springer Netherlands, Amsterdam (2010)
15. Rose, G.: Visual Methodologies: An Introduction to Researching with Visual Materials. Sage, London (2012)
16. Altheide, D.L., Schneider, C.J.: Qualitative Media Analysis, vol. 38. Sage Publications, London (2013)
17. Palys, T.: Purposive sampling. In: The Sage Encyclopedia of Qualitative Research Methods, 697–698. Sage, London (2008)
18. Bauer, M.W., Gaskell, G. (eds.): Qualitative Researching with Text, Image and Sound: A Practical Handbook for Social Research. Sage, London (2000)
19. Saldaña, J.: The Coding Manual for Qualitative Researchers. Sage, London (2013)
20. Lavie, T., Tractinsky, N.: Assessing dimensions of perceived visual aesthetics of web sites. Int. J. Hum Comput. Stud. **60**, 269–298 (2004)

Origins and Perspectives on Designing Virtual Communities of Practice for Permanent Education: A Case Study in the Collective Health Sector

Carlos Eduardo Ribeiro$^{(\boxtimes)}$ and Cláudia Renata Mont'Alvão$^{(\boxtimes)}$

LEUI, Laboratory of Ergodesign and Usability Interfaces, Pontifical Catholic
University – Rio de Janeiro, Rio de Janeiro, Brazil
cadu@focar.com.br, cmontalvao@puc-rio.br

Abstract. With the advance of Information and Communication Technologies (ICTs), information sharing is getting faster. The use of ICTs facilitates the circulation of information and knowledge, but the cognitive ability and the capacity for innovation are not affected by the technology. By this mean, the communities of practice using traditional technological tools used in corporate, personal or relationship websites, only change their goals and forms of use. This paper describes the development of a conceptual interface to the community of practice platform used as support for Brazilian National Policy of Permanent Education in Health, of the Ministry of Health.

Keywords: Online communities · Telemedicine · Education in health · Interface design

1 Context: The Necessity of Permanent Education in Health

According to the Ordinance 198GMMS (BRAZIL, 2004), Permanent Education is work training, where learning and teaching are incorporated to daily organizations and work. It is proposed that the procedures for training of health workers take as a health reference, needs of individuals and populations, from sector management and social control in health, having as goals, the transformation of professional practices and the organization of work and being structured from the issues of work process.

According to Ceccim and Ferla (2014), Permanent Education in Health as "teaching-learning practice" means the production of knowledge in everyday health institutions, from the reality experienced by the actors involved, and the problems found in daily work and the experiences of these actors as the basis of questioning and change.

The work in health is a job of listening, in which the interaction between health professional and user is determinant in the quality of healthcare response. The incorporation of updated technology is urgent and constant, and new processes of decision-making have an effect on technological, scientific, social and ethic care responsibility on treatment or health monitoring. Healthcare requires permanent education (Ceccim and Feerwerker, 2004).

© Springer International Publishing Switzerland 2015
A. Marcus (Ed.): DUXU 2015, Part III, LNCS 9188, pp. 94–103, 2015.
DOI: 10.1007/978-3-319-20889-3_10

The Ministry of Health of Brazil (MS), created the National Policy of Permanent Education in Health (Ordinance No. 1,996 GMMS) in which determines that the health education issues become part of the many system assignments. Observing and carrying it out, the Ministry of Health has created and introduced several strategies and policies towards the adequacy of training and qualification of health workers to the needs of the population and development of Centralized Health System (*Sistema Unico de Saude* – SUS).

Thus, the Brazilian Government has invested in the construction of collaborative virtual learning environments for permanent education in health through community practices.

The communities of practice allow healthcare professionals to expand their knowledge through the formation of a collaborative network with focus on the improvement of the work. The exchange of experiences in virtual environments generates a multiplier effect that contributes to its training and mainly for the quality of service to the citizen.

In a country of continental dimensions such as Brazil, proper development and good use of virtual platforms facilitates the spread of information and promotes shared knowledge, rapidly and undeniable resources saving. In this way, virtual spaces create benefits for the whole of society, since professionals are linked to one of the rare single health systems all over the world and the coverage is a constitutionally guaranteed right to the entire population.

2 Learning in an e-Health Platform: Users and Roles

Social theory of learning is not exclusively an academic approach. A new framework about learning is important not only to those dedicated to study the theory, but also for all of us – teachers, students, parents, young people, health professionals, patients, managers, workers, citizens, politicians –that indifferent ways need to follow the phases of learning (to ourselves or to others) in our communities and organizations. (Wenger, 2008, p. 11)

Lacerda (2013) refers Sarangi (2010), that offers a new vision about the notion of activities and roles. Using as example a medical appointment, we expect some participation of these speakers. When the doctor asks `How are you?´ the meaning of this activity comes from the type of activity in which this dialogue belongs. In the same way, this question can be answered in many different ways to (re) define the role of patient and doctor in this relation (Sarangi, 2010, p. 2).

Completing this reflection about social interaction the authors cite that leaning must be understood as a social relation, as a process in which ' people are not only active participants in the practice of a community, but also develop their own identities when in that community.' (Hildreth e Kimble, 2002, p. 23 apud Albagli, 2007).

The usage of information and communication technology turns easy the circulation of information and knowledge, but the cognitive and innovative capacities are not affected by technology (Albagli, 2007). In this way, communities of practice use traditional technological tools, used in personal, corporate or social websites, changing only their objective and ways of utilization (Fiorio, 2011).

The interfaces required by communities of practice are identified by Wenger et al. (2005) considering the tensions in the relations among members and community (Fig. 1) generating three kind of necessities that define technological possibilities, that aim to attend the community members necessity: *Interaction* (synchronous and asynchronous), *Publication* and *Tendencies* (individual engagement and community growing). (Tavares; Ribeiro; Fiorio, 2011).

3 A Case Study of CoPPLA System

The system Communities of Practice Platform - CoPPla is a generic platform for construction of virtual communities of practice, providing a range of integrated communication and collaboration tools in an environment focused on knowledge sharing, where content creation and manipulation of objects is flexible and intuitive.

CoPPla is developed with Plone, a Content Management System (CMS) free and open source, written in Python language. Plone is among the top 2 of all open-source projects in the world, with more than 300 consultants in 57 countries. The project is actively developed since 2001. It is available for more than 40 languages and has the best safety record among the great CMS. (Plone, 2015).

CoPPLA platform provides resources for the management of the community, allowing the creation, storage, and access to its content and participants. The set of management tools, communication and publishing are configurable and involve the manipulation of texts, images, web pages, links, events, discussion forums and spaces for learning experiences. Users have the ability to create and manage their communities as a space for sharing knowledge, involving learning activities. The platform offers spaces for the creation of content and interaction between participants through:

a. Calendar: Where events can be created by participants and moderators
b. Collection: Storage of the general content of the community. Files and images can be inserted, links, pages and folders. Used for publishing collective productions;
c. Portfolio: Used for publishing individual productions, provides the creation of files, images and pages;
d. Tasks: Space for delivery of tasks (in educational contexts);
e. Discussion forum: In the communities, discussions may arise in comments of published items or through an environment of conversation that uses the Ploneboard product;
f. Notifications: Two forms of notification in communities are used. The first is a mechanism that allows moderators to send messages direct to the participants, and the second is through a daily summary of activities of the community sent by e-mail;
g. Users Profile: It displays information concerning the user as well as shared content;
h. List of participants: It displays the participants and moderators of the community. It is possible to research and access the profile of everyone;
i. Activity level: A tool designed to check the level of interaction in the community, both collective and individual;

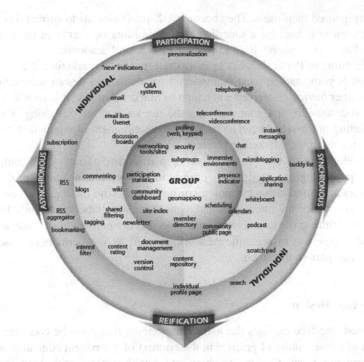

Fig. 1. Relation between activities and technological tools in communities of practice (WENGER, 2013)

j. History: It stores all content produced by the participants, it allows to search for specific content by using filters such as, name, date of creation, who published it, among other issues.

k. Invitation: A tool for sending invitations via e-mail, where you can attach customized messages.

l. Community profile: Through the home page of a community you can find your name, image, description, list of participants and history.

3.1 User Experience (UX)

UX professionals want to create great experiences for users, therefore, they need to know something about them. This phrase, "meet your users" can be easily found in a quick study on literatures about use, ergonomics and throughout the universe of design concepts centered in the user. However, long before the term "user experience-UX" had become known, traders and the Marketing market were already concerned on meeting their users.

Porter (2014) describes that UX professionals are more focused on design than traders. People begin to consider the user experience, often as a response to a design process that ignored their users. They become UX professionals to correct this mistake. They have seen how harmful a superficial understanding of users can be. That's why the phrase "meet your users" is so important to UX professionals.

Still according to Porter, UX can be compared to a good marketing. It is intended to know which is your market, what is important for them, and design accordingly. It is also to hear after having conceived and adjust to market changes. It is easy to recognize that when you consider that your users are the market you are designing. That's why good Marketing professionals can be part of the development of interaction design and UX professionals in the Marketing projects.

The development of CoPPLA consists of a multidisciplinary team composed of educators, psychologists, designers, programmers, communication professionals, administrators and information technology professionals who use their own community of practice to enhance the interaction and system tools collaboratively in a horizontal cooperation. Health professionals who promote the dissemination of knowledge and technological expertise in scientific network as well as the permanent education in health, are also part of this team.

3.2   Interface Design

The proposed interface exposes the main components that must be considered in the interaction of a community of practice in the context of permanent education in health. The platform has a set of users, teachers and health professionals who share their knowledge by ensuring the dynamics and functioning of the tool. To make sure that the tools used on the platform are intuitive is the aim of this work, in which shows the influence of design on the proactive participation of the user.

As illustrated in Fig. 2 a template that can be adapted to any content generated by the tools of the community, separated into three columns for easy adaptation to mobile devices. On the left are the tools of interaction, in the Center the latest posts or activities of the community and on the right the supporting information, such as monitoring of events and courses, just below, the preview of the participants of the community. All Visual elements compose modules that work in contrast with the background, enabling perception of visual hierarchy intuitively. In addition, the use of modules overlapped to each other, allows easy visual adaptation for applying sub-groups of communities to the system, if necessary.

4   Beyond the Interface: An Interaction Is Really Happening?

Distance Education (DE) explore certain techniques of distance learning, including hypermedia, interactive nets and all intellectual technologies of cyber culture. However, the essential is the new style of pedagogy that favor at same time personalized and collective learning in the same net. In this context, the teacher is an animator of the collective intelligence of their students instead of a direct provider of knowledge (LÉVY, 2008, p. 158)

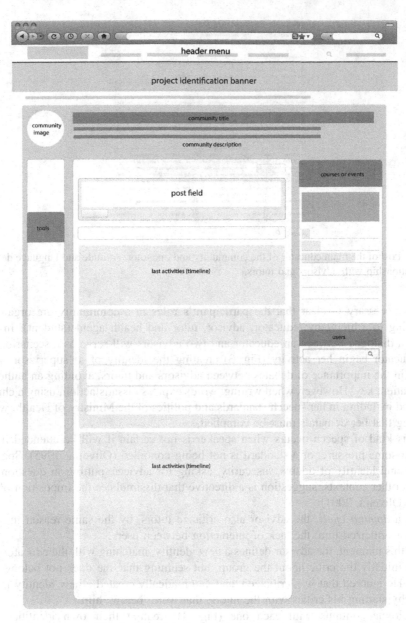

Fig. 2. Template for community of practices

Nevertheless even using so many resources can be questioned if the teacher or supervisor can act as a facilitator of the group knowledge and students as agents of the collective intelligence.

Fig. 3. Post of the main educator of the community and one tutor. Attitude and language defines the relationship with advisors and tutors.

It´s necessary to clear that the participant's roles in a community are organized according to a hierarchy: educator, advisor, tutor and health agent (student). In this paper, a dialogue between an educator and two advisors will serve as a scenario.

Educator begin her activity (Fig. 3) creating the identity of a 'supervisor'. She insists in the importance of debates between advisors and tutors, avoiding an authority or impatient key. However, when writing, words express dissatisfaction, using a charge key, and including in her speech standards and politics of the Ministry of Health, while insisting that her demands must be complied.

This kind of speech occurs when speaker is not certain if will be attended if not making some pressure, or a standard is not being complied (Oliveira, 1995). Speaker creates and identity of doubts, insecurity, asking for advices, putting in question her role. In other contexts, suggestion is a directive that dissimulates the imposition of the force. (Oliveira, 2001).

As a *domino effect*, the advisor also criticize tutors, by the same reason that the educator criticized him: the lack of interaction between users.

At this moment, the advisor defines a new identity, matching with the educator that posted initially the critic about the group, but seeming that she does not belong that group. He ignored that was criticized, and automatically created a new identity in the hierarchy starting his critics with the tutors, that were ´below´ him.

Dialogue continue with each one (Fig. 4) creating their own identities and strengthen the critic about the other professionals.

It is not a formal text. It´s not a conversation. It is an artificial text. Again, an identity is created to him, and to the other one, that is a subordinated. Speech is polite and professional. He gives some clues doing vague references about alternatives to increase system interaction. However, he uses words as 'I believe that' to give suggestions, but not any real or specific action.

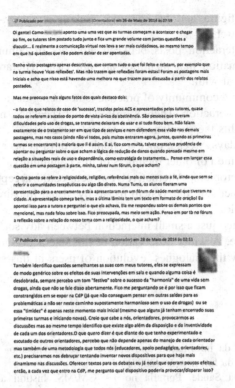

Fig. 4. (on the left) and 5 (on the right) – Posts of the tutors, answering the educator.

"What I want to say is that once considering the experience and the speech of other advisors, I believe that it depends not only on each advisor, but also on a methodology including all of us (educators, pedagogic staff, advisors, etc.) "

In addition, quoting somebody else, he uses the comments of another person to exemplify his critique, and in the end, he mentions:

"we need to invent new devices that can put some dynamism into the discussions".

Willingly statements are weaker than the ones related to the necessity, once the will of a real action is expressed using an affirmative of sincerity. In this case, he´s in the middle, his post is a hint, but without being committed to it. In the end, he affirms that the problem exists but the responsible are the tutors.

5 Final Comments and Future Work

A study of interface design based on the needs of the community of practice platform for permanent education in health and in the specifications of the tools that make up the system was presented in this work.

The interface design presented, offers a modular structure easily adaptable to the tools and functionalities of the platform through a set of visual solutions using contrast techniques between figure and background, making the hierarchy of information intuitive for the end user.

Analyzing the interaction posts between advisors in communities of practices comes out the information that identities are not clear. Hierarchy is confused and difficult to them to deal with.

The proposition of a community of practice is not being developed as the proposed concept. There's no interaction. There's professional speeches, no commitments. The lack of interaction tights the permanent system of education.

Discussions take days, weeks, once a couple of days is necessary between a post (question) and the opinion of other members of this community. Using a real-time chat could minimize this problem. Alternatively, system could accept voice records. This resource could also facilitate the system usage by visual impaired users, making the system more accessible.

This paper presented just a small interaction between advisors and in a determined community of practice. A wider observation of this interaction must be carried out to understand and follow the dialogues' evolution of users in this system.

References

Albagli, S.:Tecnologias da informação, inovação e desenvolvimento. VII Cinform Encontro Nacional de Ciência da Informação (2007)

BRASIL. Ministério Da Saúde. Portaria no 198/GM/MS. Institui a Política Nacional de Educação Permanente em Saúde como estratégia do Sistema Único de Saúde para a formação e o desenvolvimento de trabalhadores para o setor. Brasília (DF): MS, p.14 (2004). http://dtr2001.saude.gov.br/sas/PORTARIAS/Port2004/GM/GM-198.htm. Accessed

BRASIL. Ministério Da Saúde. Secretaria de Gestão do Trabalho e da Educação na Saúde. Departamento de Gestão da Educação em Saúde. Política Nacional de Educação Permanente em Saúde / Ministério da Saúde, Secretaria de Gestão do Trabalho e da Educação na Saúde, Departamento de Gestão da Educação em Saúde. – Brasília: Ministério da Saúde, p. 64 (2009). http://bvsms.saude.gov.br/bvs/publicacoes/politica_nacional_educacao_permanente_saude.pdf. Accessed

Ceccim, R.B.: FERLA, Alcindo Antônio. Educação Permanente em Saúde. Dicionário da educação profissional em saúde (2014). http://www.epsjv.fiocruz.br/dicionario/verbetes/edupersau.html

Ceccim, R.B., FEUERWERKER, L.C.M.: O quadrilátero da formação para a área da saúde: ensino, gestão, atenção e controle social. Physis, vol. 14, issue no. 1, pp. 41–65 (2004)

Fiorio, M., da Silva, J., Ribeiro, A.: Um framework de comunidades de prática em ambientes virtuais de aprendizagem.RENOTE, vol. 9, issue no. 1 (2011)

Lacerda, D.: A interação tutor-aluno no ambiente de educação a distancia: um estudo de caso. Dissertação de mestrado. PUC-Rio / DepLetras (2013)

Lave, J., Wenger, E.: Communities of practice, vol. 9, p. 2008 (1998). Accessed June

Lévy, P.: O que é o virtual? Tradução de Paulo Neves – São Paulo: Ed.34, 2011

Oliveira, Maria do Carmo Leite de et al.: Saúde, doença e burocracia: pessoas e dramas no atendimento de um seguro saúde. Narrativa, identidade e clínica, pp. 162–187 (2001)

Plone. CMS/WCM (2015). http://www.plone.org. Accessed

Porter, J.: Why UX is really just good marketing. http://52weeksofux.com

Tavares, J.L., Ribeiro, A.M., Fiorio, M.: Um estudo de implantação de comunidades de prática em um portal institucional-doi:10.3395/reciis. v5i3. 460pt. RECIIS, vol. 5, issue no. 3 (2011)
Wenger, E.: Communities of practice: a brief introduction (2013). http://wenger-trayner.com/wp-content/uploads/2013/10/06-Brief-introduction-to-communities-of-practice.pdf
Wenger, E., White, N., Smith, J.D.: Technology for Communities (2005). http://www.scribd.com/doc/2531741/Technology-for-communities-Wenger-CEFRIO-Book-Chapter-v-5–2
Wenger, E.: Communities of practice: learning as a social system. Systems thinker 9(5), 2–3 (2008)

The Challenges and Opportunities of Designing National Digital Services for Cross-Border Use

Molly Schwartz[1(✉)] and Heli Kautonen[2]

[1] Aalto University, Helsinki, Finland
molly.schwartz@aalto.fi
[2] The National Library of Finland, Helsinki, Finland
heli.kautonen@helsinki.fi

Abstract. By creating a centralized online access points for Finnish library, archives, and museum materials, the National Library of Finland's web portal, called Finna, is playing an active role in the wider movement to open and expand access to cultural content. But as its ever-expanding online audience is no longer constricted by physical or national borders, the National Library must cope with the challenges of designing personalized user experiences for diverse users. This study contains data from a survey and interviews of users accessing Finnish materials from abroad to determine the nature of potential target audiences for Finna outside of Finland and determine the major usability barriers for this group.

Keywords: Digital library · User studies · Open knowledge

1 Introduction

We live in a world connected by a global internet but ruled by local laws [15]. Although digital platforms are providing widespread access to the cultural heritage products that libraries, archives, and museums hold, publicly funded digital access portals are inherently tied to locally situated governing bodies. Therefore, while the potential end-users accessing digital cultural heritage materials are heterogeneous and geographically dispersed, the bodies that administer the platforms and services are generally location-based and more culturally, linguistically, and legally homogenous. As public services sectors try to shift to an increasingly user-centric digital model, it will be necessary to grapple with the fundamental differences between the administrators and users of public services in the digital space. By addressing these differences it may be possible to improve, circumvent, or mitigate poor user experiences in the public service sector.

In this paper we address the challenge of providing public services for heterogeneous audiences by presenting a study, in which we test the service concept for a national digital library service, namely the Finnish Digital Library called Finna. The National Library of Finland is responsible for the development and maintenance of the service. Finna is one of the ambitious digital library enterprises that have been launched all over the globe in order to unite the vast repositories of cultural heritage hosted by libraries, archives, and museums. The investments on these digital libraries are noteworthy, and

© Springer International Publishing Switzerland 2015
A. Marcus (Ed.): DUXU 2015, Part III, LNCS 9188, pp. 104–115, 2015.
DOI: 10.1007/978-3-319-20889-3_11

most of the funding comes usually from the public sector. The stakeholders have a keen interest in the usability of these services, and they require that their audiences' needs be met. There is a general aim that new technologies attract new users to use and engage with cultural heritage. Digital library user studies, however, still seem to define end-users based on the pre-existing user pool, and categorize the users based on the perspective of how they fit into the management of digital library content [5].

The digitalization has, on the one hand, enabled the construction of newer and better services for accessing and interacting with cultural heritage. On the other hand, it has increased the feeling of inadequacy among organizations maintaining the collections of culture and science, because digital technologies and the preservation of digital repositories require wider competencies and resources than one organization can hold. Open solutions, i.e., open access, open data, and open source, have been considered as an opportunity to preserve public services [8]. The term "open knowledge" refers to data and content that is free to access, use, modify, and share. Digital information formats have made it possible for an increasingly large segment of humanity to access and use content that contributes to knowledge creation, but national borders and linguistic differences still act as barriers to access in the digital cultural heritage space. In 2014, of the approximately 756,000 visits to Finna, 92.9 % came from Finland. The concept of open knowledge seeks take advantage of the opportunities provided by digital platforms for cultural heritage by opening up processes to the public's diverse skills and interpretations and involving audiences in the design and development of cultural heritage processes [12].

The purpose of our work was to elaborate upon these challenges that reflect on the design, development, and use of Finna. Our first research question was: *How can open digital cultural heritage platforms create a positive user experience for audiences that are diverse, geographically dispersed, and sometimes undefined?* We also wanted to know, *how audiences perceive the possibilities of open knowledge.* To study these questions, we tested the service concept of Finna on a target audience outside of Finland: Finnish studies students and professors at universities across the United States. Finna consolidates access to all of the library, archives, and museum materials in Finland through one centralized web service and platform. Thus, it could attract our target group, but there also may be points at which national, cultural, or linguistic barriers exist.

The paper begins with some relevant concepts and research on the subject, then describes the methods of conducting the test and some key results. We end the paper with a brief discussion on the value of opening cultural heritage materials to wider audiences.

2 Background

2.1 Digital Libraries as Open Knowledge Platforms

The Finna portal is one initiative within a wider movement to open up access to cultural heritage content in ways that increase accessibility, expand audiences, and improve the user experience by taking advantage of technological innovations, such as the Web and sophisticated search engine mechanisms. As a type of digital library, Finna is operating as an open knowledge platform that has the potential to increase accessibility to Finland's cultural heritage content and innovate the information-gathering experience.

Created and funded by the European Commission's Information Society and Media project, the DELOS Network of Excellence on Digital Libraries created a report [1] that contains background research, overarching theory, and long-term initiatives on the policy level for digital libraries. The DELOS report sees the role of the library as shifting its role from an institution that stores and retrieves information to one that facilitates collaboration and interaction. This shift is a move from a content-centric system to person-centric systems with the aim of providing users with personalized experiences. While the new digital library model is intended to evolve toward a more participatory user-centric focus across the European Union, the report also explains that in the digital space there are no physical or temporal barriers defining end-user groups. Therefore, it is increasingly important that studies such as this one explore the ways that libraries and information are engaging end-users across borders and draw findings that can create an optimal user experience for diverse user communities.

A collaborative study conducted by Jaeger et al. [6] investigated the role that information intermediaries, and specifically public libraries, play in the relationship between citizens and public services, with a specific emphasis on the importance of facilitating digital inclusion. The authors acknowledge the challenges of reaching across language barriers, attitudes toward technology, and education about government services to reach a wide user base and deliver inclusive services. Using a combination of quantitative and qualitative data gathered through surveys, case studies, interview, site visits, and usability and accessibility testing, the authors measured the role that libraries play in delivering e-services as end-users operating in local, intermediate, and high-level world of information flow. Based on the ways that the study found that the Internet and online social networks can bridge small information worlds, the authors found that at the macro level public services should make information available in the different formats, languages, and venues that smaller worlds of user groups require.

According to Salgado and Marttila [12], strategies for increasing the general public's engagement with cultural heritage professionals, processes, and practices should be based on principles of social inclusion, accessibility, participation, and openness. As Salgado and Marttila address in their study, one purpose for openness in cultural heritage is to engage with new audiences and widening cultural heritage communities "using alternative means" that the cultural heritage professionals may not have foreseen. The principle of facilitating openness and audience participation is one solution within the cultural heritage field for designing positive user experiences for new or unknown audiences and widening the impact of cultural heritage in society.

2.2 Design for Diverse Audiences

Past research relating to user-centered design for public services and heterogeneous populations has cut across fields of anthropology, human-computer interaction, inter-action design, e-government, information science, and social networks. As such a broad and encompassing topic, there has been ample research done using both qualitative and quantitative techniques in the public, private, and third sectors related to how digital platforms can respond to diverse user groups in user-centered design practices.

The principles of universal design have guided the development of public services for all types of audiences. Erlandson [3] draws upon the joint principles of accessible and universal design: Instead of addressing products, services, and processes to mainstream audiences alone, our society should recognize the needs of everyone regardless of his/her abilities. The origins of universal design lie in educational settings, where equal access to information was recognized as a necessity. Although universal design focuses on recommendations for how to enable interaction with technology for people with different disabilities, some universal design concepts, e.g. design for adaptation, can be useful in other contexts. Gassman and Reepmeyer [4] also emphasize the economical potential of universal design approach. They argue that new products and innovations should be designed and marketed with all age groups in mind, because that substantially increases the target markets.

There has been more extensive research conducted on how to account for diverse audiences in user-experience design in the private sector. As companies find unexpected audiences around the world in an increasingly globalized economy, there is a strong commercial use case for accommodating for diverse user needs in the design process. Marcus and Gould [9] argue that by incorporating globalization and localization concepts into design processes, it is possible to tailor user interfaces to meet the needs of diverse audiences across the globe. They encourage designers to acquaint themselves with cultural dimension, i.e., culture-dependent patterns of thinking, feeling, and acting, and adjust their design to them.

Shah [13] has outlined the constant tension between designing for localized versus globalized audiences. She has acknowledged that online culture may become increasingly more homogenous. Cyr [2] also argues that users prefer to interact with products services that seem to be designed specifically for them. Shah [13] concludes that globalization and localization of digital services must work in tandem and separates the two concepts into two separate functions: First, internationalization refers to the back-end processes of creating modular and accessible global website templates. Second, localization refers to the front-end customization where websites are adapted to meet expectations of a culturally diverse user group.

Quesenbery and Szuc [11] led a series of 65 interviews with user experience professionals around the world to study how national and cultural differences shape the practice of user experience design. Their findings reveal the way that products and services that are originally developed for a local market find unexpected user bases and target audiences around the world facilitated by new communication technologies and providing businesses and organizations with unforeseen opportunities. Quesenbery and Szuc found that the companies with the strongest global strategies were constantly researching and watching market information across border s and ensuring that they experiences they delivered worked for many places and cultures.

3 Methods and Data

3.1 Approach: From Usability to Testing of Service Concept

Usability is one of the leading principles of Finna's development, which means that user-centered design methodology has been applied in the development process. From the beginning of the project in 2008, resources have been assigned to usability work. In 2009 the Usability Working Group made a Usability Plan, which has been updated annually. Different kinds of user-centered activities have been conducted throughout the development of the service. E.g., target user groups have been involved in iterative testing of the service [7]. Thus, we had a foundation of usability as a core institutional value and data from which to build our study.

Our aim was to reach students and professors of Finnish studies across the United States. Due to the uncertainty of reaching a large enough sample for a single survey, we decided to combine two methods: we planned a questionnaire to all potential respondents and an interview to selected key informants.

In this study we were targeting cultural heritage users who probably were not familiar with Finna beforehand. By asking them about their expectations and gathering feedback on the current service concept, our work actually bordered on the field of marketing research. In marketing, users' response to an idea can be tested before or after the product or service is introduced to the market. Evolving services, and participatory methods of design and development, known as co-design or co-creation, have also gained popularity in service marketing [10]. Our priority, however, was to get input for further development of the service.

3.2 Survey to Finnish Students and Professors in the United States

The original motivation for creating this survey was to identify points at which national, cultural, and linguistic barriers exist in digital cultural heritage portals. It started with the research questions: *Are there potential target audiences for Finna outside of Finland? If so, what is deterring this audience from using Finna?* Therefore, we planned to create a survey that investigates how non-Finnish people use and experience Finna by asking non-Finns about their awareness of Finna, possible use cases or motivations for the use of Finna, and how they currently access Finnish cultural heritage materials. During this study, we sought opportunities for collaboration with the Digital Public Library of America (DPLA), and thought that there might be increased opportunities for further synergy if we chose our target groups from the United States.

We created the questionnaire to target students engaged in the study of Finnish language, culture, history, literature, politics, or any other field that might benefit from the use of materials from Finnish libraries, archives, museums, or other cultural heritage institution at colleges or universities located across the United States.

The survey included a total of 14 questions, 11 of which were multiple-choice questions with a range of answer options and three of which were open-ended.

We divided the questions into three sections. The first section addressed how students access information and different formats. The second section addressed prior knowledge of concepts related to open knowledge. The third and final section addressed current and potential future use of social and collaborative media. One final question asked about prior awareness of the Finna web portal.

We contacted survey participants via their Finnish studies professors. The Fulbright Finland Center provided a list of the universities in the United States that provide Finnish studies courses. The list included 11 universities and the names and contact information of the individual professors who teach the courses. We contacted each of the 28 professors and received responses from 25 professors, nine of whom agreed to participate in the survey. We estimated that a pool of about 70 students would receive the link to the survey. Of the nine original professors who agreed to participate, four confirmed that they distributed it to their students.

After two rounds of pre-testing with 12 participants representative of the survey's target audience, we distributed the survey and kept it open for one month. A total of 11 students completed the survey. 24 students started the survey but did not complete it and 9 students opened the survey without responding to any questions. We administered the survey using an online questionnaire hosted on a subscription-based survey tool and professors distributed the to his/her students through via a link sent over email.

3.3 Interviews of Key Informants

Based on the findings from the survey, we conducted follow-up interviews with the purpose of speaking to real potential users in our target audience and gather the detailed use cases for their use of Finna. We composed two sets of nine interview questions, one for students and one for professors, to be conducted in a semi-structured style.

We recruited participants for the interviews by contacting the four professors who confirmed that they distributed the survey and asking them to send around an email asking students to participate in the interview. Students who were interested in participating in the interview contacted us via email. We also asked the professors if they would be willing to participate in an interview.

We conducted interviews with four students at the same university who had completed varying levels of Finnish language courses and had not participated in the survey. We interviewed three professors at three different universities: one a professor of Finnish language, one of Finnish culture and literature with more of a anthropological focus, and one of Finish theater studies. We conducted the interviews over video chatting software, asking follow-up questions when appropriate. At the end of the interview, we requested that the interviewees navigate to the National View of Finna at the URL finna.fi and we asked them to speak aloud during their initial experience with the service. We asked probing questions based on their observations and provided basic instructions on how to use the interface if they seemed to need help (Fig. 1).

Fig. 1. The National View of Finna on a mobile browser at the time of this study

4 Results and Conclusions

4.1 The Survey: Access Formats and Barriers

While the results from the survey were too few to be conclusive, they did suggest trends in how university students in the United States are accessing information in general and in Finnish. The results also revealed clear patterns in the types of barriers that students encounter when trying to access cultural heritage materials.

The open-ended question about the most common or significant barriers that the participants encounter when trying to access content revealed that the most common barriers are: content that is not accessible online, content that is restricted based on rights management or pay walls, language barriers, and format inaccessibility.

The survey results showed that clear majorities of students access books in physical building while clear majorities access pictures, photographs, journals, articles, newspapers, music, sound recordings, and videos on digital platforms. Of the survey responses to the open-ended question about how students find out where to look for materials that they want or need to access from libraries, archives, or museums, seven responded that they would start with an online search either in a general search engine or on the library's webpage while four responded that they would make inquiries at the library building.

Survey respondents also accessed materials in Finnish language in most of the formats covered on the survey, including books, pictures, journals, articles, newspapers, music, video, and archives, either for studies or hobbies and leisure, in large majorities. Studies was the most popular reason for accessing materials in Finnish in each category, suggesting that students of Finnish studies would be a more likely audience for Finna than other members of the US population with an interest in Finland.

Of the open knowledge concepts, participants were the most familiar with the concepts of digitization, public domain, and crowdsourcing. Responses showed the participants were the least familiar with the concepts of "Creative Commons" and metadata. They were at least comfortably familiar with the concepts of open access, open data, and open content, but less familiar with the concept of linked data or the semantic web. No participant was familiar with the term "OpenGLAM," suggesting that the term is not clear or descriptive of the movement to audiences outside of it. While these results would contain more validity with more responses, they reveal a general trend toward familiarity with open knowledge terms that are descriptive in language that the layperson understands and less familiarity with technical concepts or names of concepts that are not descriptive.

Although these findings would also need further research to be conclusive, they show a general trend that participants found open content to be most useful to the degree that it makes it easier for them to engage in their work as individuals by making content easier to find and reducing legal complexities. For these respondents, community-building or institutional accountability were less obvious advantages to open content. One of the most conclusive results of the survey was that 9 of the 11 respondents were not familiar with Finna.

4.2 The Interviews with Students: Curiosity Meets Contextual Barriers

Two of the four students we interviewed were motivated to study Finnish because they have Finnish ancestry, one has a close friend who is Finnish, and the fourth was attracted to Finnish by its exoticism and an interest in studies that are strong in Finland, such as digital media and sustainability. The two students with ancestry were more advanced in their Finnish language studies and the other two were in their second semester of beginning Finnish.

All four students had trouble understanding the full range of content types included under the umbrella term "cultural heritage." For example, students would say that they rarely access cultural heritage after hearing an explanation of what the term means, but then go on to talk about frequently accessing Finnish materials or information that would be categorized as cultural heritage on YouTube or Wikipedia. When they do interact with materials on any subject that they think of as cultural heritage it is usually through the university library or for specific courses on a learning management system. Although one student expressed a preference for accessing books and articles in analog format, the students generally access materials online because there are many Finnish materials available and, as one said, "it's just quicker."

Due to an interest in their Finnish ancestry, both students with Finnish heritage had accessed Finnish parish records as part of personal genealogy projects. One of them also likes to find fun articles and resources about Finland in English through groups that she follows on Facebook, such as a Finnish language summer school program and government-sponsored tourism information. These two students also look to local cultural institutions, such as the Finnish-American Chamber of Commerce or the American Swedish Institute, to find information about local Finnish cultural events and resources.

Barriers to accessing Finnish materials that multiple students encountered in the past were videos or articles that were inaccessible or stored behind a pay wall for visitors coming from an IP address outside of Finland. One student described her inability to find podcasts in simple Finnish language after multiple attempts starting from search engines.

When we asked him to navigate to finna.fi, three students used a web browser on their computers and one student opted to open the website on his smartphone. Most of the initial reactions were in regards to the fact that the website is in Finnish. When one student, who is a Finnish language beginner, came to the website his initial reaction was "Ahh, all Finnish, scary!" After about 10 s he noticed that there is also an English language option on the website. The other beginner was also deterred from navigating the website from the language barrier and was relying on Google Chrome to automatically convert the site using Google's embedded translating services, which was not happening on the home page. She never found Finna's English language option. The two more advanced students began navigating the site in Finnish and both saw it as a good opportunity to practice their Finnish. One took about 20 s to notice that there was an English language option, and once she did she switched to the English version of the site. The other advanced Finnish student expressed the opinion that most other students taking Finnish would prefer to access the site in English because Finnish is very dissimilar to English so it is hard to understand unknown words. The language barrier seemed like a significant barrier for students, especially because the link to the English-language option was not in a location that they found intuitive. They were not experienced, as many foreigners are who live in Finland, with the fact that many Finnish websites are also available in both English and Swedish.

Every student enjoyed the visual design of the user interface and enjoyed the photographs on the homepage. When asked, every student expressed the opinion that the site could be useful for their studies and a resource for leisure time pursuits. Based on their normal practice of accessing materials online and their perception that it can be difficult to find the types of Finnish materials that they are looking for, every student had a clear use case for the Finna website.

4.3 The Interviews with Professors: It's About Knowing Where to Look

According to the three professors we interviewed, the largest barrier to access for Finnish materials outside of the traditional course materials is not knowing where to look, not knowing which keywords to use to find materials of interest, and a lack of financial resources for materials that are not freely available. A typical discovery process for both the professor and students involves unstructured searching online, usually beginning with a search engine, that both depends on and falls prey to the haphazard and serendipitous search process that is typical of unstructured knowledge discovery online.

The professors rely on authoritative sources and channels, such as the CIMO community of Finnish teachers abroad that is active both online and at an annual conference, lists that groups such as Finn Lectura and Akateeminen kirjakauppa curate, the Journal of Finnish studies, and knowledgeable colleagues and friends.

Although currently all three professors use creative and resourceful methods for finding Finnish cultural heritage materials to use in their courses, sometimes lending out items from their personal libraries or finding content on platforms such as YouTube, there was a strong interest in finding authoritative, curated resources, especially ones geared for teaching Finnish studies abroad.

The professors all found that the most consistent motivation for their students to study Finnish language is some kind of personal connection to Finland, usually because they have ancestry or heritage from Finland. Others have a close personal connection through spouses, partners, or friends that motivates them to want to learn the Finnish language.

Upon interacting with the Finna interface, the professors all remarked that they liked the visual layout and quickly commented on the site's rich content. The Finnish language professor's main question was exactly what content the site provides access to. He expressed the opinion that when visiting an institution's digital repository it is evident that all of the content comes from that one institution, but in the case of an aggregation like Finna, he wanted more clarity as to exactly which institutions contribute content and how comprehensive the collections are. Two of the professors explained that they would use the website in Finnish because, in past experience, even websites that offer language translations are not as fully functional in secondary languages, so the assumption is that it would be the same for Finna.

4.4 Lessons Learned

In evaluating our methods for this study, there were several areas that could be improved. Given our limited sample set for the survey, it would have been wiser to take a more active role in recruiting students to participate in the survey or gone with a more qualitative approach by conducting interviews from the outset. We could have used more innovative methods to recruit participants, such as via social media.

5 Discussion

The aim of this study was to fill in a dearth of research in terms of the specific issues that public digital library services may encounter as they serve patrons across national borders and cultures on a large scale. Through concept testing that involved a survey and an interview of a key informant, the study of potential users outside of Finland was supposed to reveal whether there is target audience for Finna outside of Finland.

The results provided information for evaluating how Finna could be improved for external audiences by proactively researching the nature of Finna's potentially heterogeneous user base. On the basis of the results, this paper discussed the questions: *Do public services have an obligation to prioritize the user experiences of users within their national borders? What are the advantages and disadvantages of running digital cultural heritage portals through centralized, public institutions?*

Based on the results of this study, restrictions to patrons trying to use Finna from outside of Finland remain. As confirmed in the survey results, there are certain cultural heritage materials that patrons still access primarily in physical or analog formats, either by choice or necessity. For content that is only available in a physical format or is subject to certain licenses or restrictions, Finna still plays a role in the information ecosystem by serving as a portal. Users can discover analog materials on Finna and find details about where the physical materials are located, and potentially even reserve the materials at a physical site. There are certain licensed materials that require payments to access online but are fully available at physical locations, but this is only useful to users who can travel to or within Finland.

Public cultural heritage institutions have an especially strong professional mandate to serve the entire public, not just cater to the majority population [6, 14]. Via new digital platforms, users can potentially discover, view, and interact with all of the libraries, archives, and museum materials in public holdings anywhere they have access to the internet. Such widespread and distributed access offers an opportunity for breaking down traditional barriers to knowledge and opening content to a dispersed, heterogeneous population. This is, in itself, a major triumph for the accessibility and usability of public services.

It is in the interest of cultural heritage institutions to provide broader access to their materials. The institutions are already acquiring, organizing, and preserving cultural heritage materials. The impact value comes from the use of the materials, which institutions are increasingly being required to prove through analytics and evaluations. Therefore, it is to the benefit of the public cultural heritage sector to provide a positive user experience for as large and heterogeneous audience as possible.

In the future, it would be important to do further user research and outreach with professors of Finnish studies and active participants in Finnish cultural societies abroad. Based on the results of this study, it is clear that there is an audience outside of Finland that would benefit from using Finna. Everyone who participated in our study seemed to engage with Finland through a gateway composed of educational institutions, cultural institutions, or friends and family. By targeting these gatekeepers, or facilitators, we could reach a large target audience with a more focused and effective initial approach. It would also be valuable to expand the reaches of our study by conducting subsequent studies on how Finnish students of, e.g., history and English language, can utilize the materials on a foreign cultural heritage portal, such as the Digital Library of America. Such a study could provide interesting information for the development of digital libraries in general, and an opportunity to compare the results to the ones of this study.

Acknowledgments. We would like to thank the Fulbright Center Finland, the University of Minnesota, Brigham Young University, and Finlandia University for their help in facilitating this study. We would also like to thank the Finna team, who worked extensively with Molly to make this study possible.

References

1. Candela, L. (Ed.): The Digital Library Reference Model. DL.org Project Deliverable (2010)
2. Cyr, D.: Modeling Web Site Design Across Cultures: Relationships to Trust, Satisfaction, and E-Loyalty. J. Manage. Inf. Syst. 24(4), 47–72 (2008)
3. Erlandson, R.F.: Universal and Accessible Design for Products, Services, and Processes. Taylor & Francis, Boca Raton (2008)

4. Gassmann, O., Reepmeyer, G.: Universal design - innovations for all ages. In: Kohlbacher, F., Herstatt, C. (eds.) The Silver Market Phenomenon. Marketing and Innovation in the Aging Society, 2nd edn, pp. 125–140. Springer, Heidelberg (2011)

5. Heraldio, R., Fernández-Amorós, D., Caberizo, F.J., Herrera-Viedma, E.: A review of quality evaluation of digital libraries based on users perceptions. J. Inf. Sci. **38**(3), 269–283 (2012)

6. Jaeger, J., Gorham, U., Bertot, J., Greene Taylor, H., Larson, E., Lincoln, R., Lazar, J., Wentz, B.: Connecting government, libraries and communities: Information behavior theory and information intermediaries in the design of LibEGov.org. First Monday 19 (11). (2014)

7. Kautonen, H.: Evaluating digital library's service concept and pre-launch implementation.In: Proceedings of AFHE, pp. 111–122. AHFE, USA (2014)

8. Kruse, F., Thestrup, J.B.: Research libraries new role in research data management, current trends and visions in denmark. Liber Q. **23**(4), 336–357 (2014). URN:NBN:NL: UI:10-1-116068 (2014)

9. Marcus, A., Gould, E.W.: Globalization, localization, and cross-cultural user interface design. In: Jacko, J.A. (ed.) The Human-Computer Interaction Handbook Fundamentals, Evolving Technologies, and Emerging Applications, 3rd edn, pp. 341–366. Taylor & Francis, Boca Raton (2012)

10. Rust, R.T., Huang, M.-H.: Handbook Of Service Marketing Research. Edward Elgar Publishing, Cheltenham (2014)

11. Quesenbery, W., Szuc, D.: Global UX: Design and Research in a Connected World. Elsevier, Waltham (2012)

12. Salgado, M., Marttila, S.: Discussions on inclusive, participative and open museums. In: NODEM 2013 Conference Proceedings. Interactive Institute Swedish ICT, Sweden (2013)

13. Shah, N.: Cross cultural considerations for user interface design. Hum. Factors Int. Newsl. **5**(3), 299–305 (2013)

14. Wigell-Ryynänen, B.: Supporting societies needs: a model framework for developing a policy for libraries.In: National Public Library Policy in Finland - A Case Study. Network for Information and Digital Access (NIDA), Helsinki, Finland (2011)

15. Zittrain, J.: Be Careful What You Ask For: Reconciling a Global Internet and Local Law. Who Rules The Net?: Internet Governance and Jurisdiction. pp. 13–29. The Cato Institute, Washington (2003)

Designing the Learning Experience

Heuristic Evaluation of University Institutional Repositories Based on DSpace

Maha Aljohani$^{(\boxtimes)}$ and James Blustein

Faculty of Computer Science, Dalhousie University, Halifax, Canada
mh578194@dal.ca, jamie@cs.dal.ca

Abstract. The number of Institutional Repositories (IRs) as part of universities' Digital Libraries (DLs) has been growing in the past few years. However, most IRs are not widely used by the intended end users. To increase users' accept-ability, evaluating IRs interface is essential. In this research, the main focus is to evaluate the usability of one type of IR's interface following the method of Nielsen's heuristics to uncover usability problems for development purposes. To produce a reliable list of usability problems by applying the heuristic evaluation approach, we examine the impact of experts and novices on the reliability of the results. From the individual heuristic analyses (by both experts and novices), we distilled 66 usability problems. Those problems are classified by their severity. The results of applying the heuristic evaluation show that both experts and non-experts can uncover usability problems. We analyzed the differences between these types of assessors in this paper. Experts tend to reveal more serious problems while novices uncover less severe problems. Interestingly, the best evaluator is a novice who found 21 % of the total number of problems. The ability to find difficult and easy problems are recorded with both types of evaluators. Therefore, we cannot rely on one evaluator even if the evaluator is an expert. Also, the frequency of each violated heuristic is used to assigned priority to the uncovered usability problems as well as the severity level. The result of the heuristic evaluation will benefit the university through improving the user interface and encouraging users to use the library services.

Keywords: Human computer interaction · Heuristic evaluation · Digital libraries · Digital repositories · Institutional repositories · Usability problems · Scholarly output · Dspace

1 Introduction

The user interface of Open Access (OA) repositories has an effect on their users' performance and satisfaction. To add to the ongoing development of these types of repositories, usability evaluations need to be implemented on the user interface. There are two foci of this research: to evaluate the usability of Institutional Repositories as part of universities' digital libraries interface using Nielsen's heuristics to uncover usability problems and to examine the differences between user-interface experts and non-experts in uncovering problems with the interface.

© Springer International Publishing Switzerland 2015
A. Marcus (Ed.): DUXU 2015, Part III, LNCS 9188, pp. 119–130, 2015.
DOI: 10.1007/978-3-319-20889-3_12

1.1   What Is Usability?

In 1998, the term "user friendly" reached a level of vagueness and subjective definitions, which led to the start of the use of the term "usability" instead [1]. The International Standards Organization (ISO) [26] defines usability as "the extent to which a product can be used by specified users to achieve specified goals with effectiveness, efficiency and satisfaction in a specified context of use.

Nielsen [2] suggests that usability cannot be measured by one dimension; these five attributes are associated with the usability components, which include learnability, memorability, efficiency, error recovery, and satisfaction. While Hix and Hartson [3] suggest that usability relies on the following factors, which include first impression, initial performance, long-term performance, and user satisfaction. Also, Booth [4], Brink et al. [5] share similar viewpoints that define usability as the effectiveness, efficiency, ease to learn, low error rate and pleasing. Nielsen's and ISO's usability definitions are the most widely used [6, 27, 28].

1.2   Usability Evaluations

Evaluation is considered as a basic step in the iterative design process. There are varieties of approaches to follow in evaluating the usability, which include formal usability inspection by Kahn and Prail [7], the cognitive walkthrough by Wharton et al. [8], heuristic evaluation by Nielsen [2, 9, 10], Contextual Task Analysis [11], paper prototyping by Lancaster [12].

1.3   What Are Institutional Repositories?

Institutional repositories are popular among universities worldwide [13]. IR as a channel allowing the university structuring its contribution to the global community, there exists the responsibility for reassessment of both culture and policy and their relationship to one another [14].

Over the past fifteen to twenty years, research libraries have been used to create, store, manage, and preserve scholarly documents in digital forms and make these documents available online via digital Institutional Repositories [15]. IRs host various types of documents [15]. An Example of IRs is DSpace [16]. In 2000, the Hewlett-Packard Company (HP) at MIT Libraries was authorized to, cooperatively, build DSpace, which is as Institutional Repository for hosting the intellectual output of "multi-disciplinary" organizations in digital formats [17].

1.4   Nielsen's List of Heuristics

The set of heuristics was constructed from some usability aspects and interface guidelines [18]. The heuristics include visibility of the system status, match between system and the real world, user control and freedom, consistency and standards, error prevention, recognition rather than recall, flexibility and efficiency of use, aesthetic and minimalist design, help users recover from errors and help and documentation [9].

2 Related Work

Ping, Ramaiah, and Foo [19] tested the user interface of the Gateway to Electronic Media Services system at the Nanyang Technological University. The researchers' goal was to apply Nielsen's Heuristics to find strengths and weaknesses of the system. In their findings, they determined that the heuristic evaluation helped to uncover major problems such as being not able to have search results as desired. Researchers suggested that the uncovering of these problems ensures that the GEMS system needs development.

Qing and Ruhua [20] point out that the usability evaluation of Discipline Repositories offers the digital library developers a critical understanding of four areas: understanding the target users' needs, finding design problems, create a focus for development, and the importance in doing so to establish a valid acceptability of such educational interactive technological tool. Three DRs were evaluated include arXiv,[1] PMC[2](PubMed Central) and E-LIS.[3] The three DRs are different in the subject domain and their design structures. The findings show that DRs inherit some of the already successful features form DLs. The three digital repositories provide limited ways, regarding the advanced search tools, to display and refine the search results.

Hovater et al. [21] examined the Virtual Data Center (VDC) interface that is classified as an open access web-based digital library. VDC collects and manages the research in the social science field. The researchers conducted a usability evaluation followed by a user testing. They found minor and major problems that included "lack of documentation, unfamiliar language, and inefficient search functionality".

Zimmerman and Paschal [15] examined the digital collection of Colorado State University by completing some tasks that focused only on the search functions of the website. The talk-aloud approach was used to observe participants. Researchers found that two-fifths of users had problems downloading documents, which would discourage them from using the service. The findings suggest that the interface should be evaluated periodically to ensure the usability of the features.

Zhang et al. [22] evaluated three operational digital libraries, which include the ACM DL, the IEEE Computer Society DL, and the IEEE Xplore DL. Heery and Anderson's [23] conducted a review to form a report on Digital Repositories sent to repository software developers. Heery and Anderson [23] impart, that engaging users is vital during developing open access repositories.

3 Heuristic Evaluation Study

The heuristic Evaluation study was conducted on a DSpace as an extension of university library services that enables users to browse the university's collections and academic scholarly output. Our focus on evaluating Institutional Repositories (IRs) is

---

[1] http://arxiv.org/.

[2] http://www.pubmedcentral.nih.gov/index.html.

[3] http://eprints.rclis.org/.

motivated by the need to focus on the usability of the interface while the concept of usability evaluation implemented on IRs is fairly new. The research objectives of evaluating the university repository interface include:

- To determine the usability problems of the University Repository Interface
- To provide solutions and guidelines regarding the uncovered problems.
- To provide the development team in the University with the suggested solutions to be used in the iterative design process for development purposes

Two key aspects are investigated: Does the expertise and number of evaluators affect the reliability of the results from applying the heuristic evaluation to the user interface? To answer the first of those general questions, we consider the following hypotheses:

- Severe problems will be uncovered by experts while the minor problems will be uncovered by novices
- Difficult problems can only be uncovered by experts and easy problems can be uncovered by both experts and novices
- The best evaluator will be an expert
- As Nielsen and Mack [24] reported for the traditional heuristic evaluation, experts will tend to produce better results than novices
- The average of number of problems uncovered by experts and novices will differ. Experts are expected to find more problems than novices

To answer the second of those general questions, does the number of evaluators affect the reliability of the results? we consider the following hypotheses:

- A small set of evaluators (experts) can find about 75 % of the problems in the user interface as Nielsen and Mack [24] suggest.
- More of the serious problems will be uncovered by the group (experts or non-experts) with the most members

3.1 Participants

To produce a reliable list of usability problems, having multiple evaluators is better than only one because different people uncover different problems from different perspectives. A total of 16 participants were recruited and were university students who were divided into three groups 9 regular experts, four amateur and 2 novices.

3.2 Tasks

The tasks were designed according to most important elements in the interface that should be examined according to the result from previous study called user personas [29]. Each task is designed to describe the following:

- The goal of the task;
- The type of the task, is it regular, important, critical task;
- The actual steps that a typical user would follow to perform the task;
- The possible problems that users might face during performing the task;
- Time for expert to reach the goal;
- And the scenario.

3.3 Methodology

We started with conducting a tutorial lecture about the heuristics and how evaluators should apply them on the interface dialogs during the evaluation session. Examples usually are better than just lecturing. The researcher explained each heuristic's main concept and gave examples. This was meant to help in carrying out the evaluations without having problems while referring to the heuristics. Evaluators who have not performed a heuristic evaluation before were required to attend the lecture to increase their knowledge about heuristics and the overall method. Other evaluators, who have experience in heuristic evaluation, would not need to review the heuristics, but they would need to be trained in using the interface. Therefore, the objective of this lecture is to increase evaluators' knowledge about how to applying the heuristics.

The study lasted for 120 min. Participants started with the training session followed by the evaluation session. Then the severity rating was assigned for each uncovered usability problem. Finally, the solutions session was conducted to discuss problems and propose guidelines for the uncovered problems.

4 Results and Discussion

4.1 Problems Report

A report that describes each uncovered problem was delivered to the developers of the University DSpace for development purposes. We believe that uncovering these problems would benefit any university that utilizes a DSpace Repository as part of the digital library to maintain its scholarly output.

4.2 Number of Problems

For each problem and evaluator, data were coded as 1 for detected and 0 for not detected. Table 1 shows that the average number of problems found by experts was 6.8 while the average number of problems found by amateurs and novices were 3.5 and 2.5 respectively. 4.57. There is no significant difference between the means ($F(2,13) = 3.205$, $p < .075$) with an effect size of $\eta^2 = .330$. Some would say that it the effect is marginal. The lack of significance combined with the reasonable effect size, is likely due to the small sample sizes.

Table 1. Evaluators' performance

Evaluator type	Total number of problems	Best evaluator	Worst evaluator	Average number of problems	SD
9 Regular experts	66	14 (21.2 %)	2 (3.0 %)	6.80	3.29
4 Amateurs	66	5 (7.6 %)	2 (3.0 %)	3.50	1.29
2 Novices	66	3 (4.5 %)	2 (3.0 %)	2.50	0.71

As would be expected, the largest differences were found between Experts and Novices. However, further analyses indicated that Experts were not different from Amateurs ($F(1,12) = 3.639$, $p < .081$, $\eta^2 = .233$), that Experts were not different from Novices ($F(1,10) = 3.141$, $p < .107$, $\eta^2 = .239$) and that Amateurs were not different from Novices ($F(1,4) = 1.333$, $p < .970$, $\eta^2 = .195$)

Not surprisingly, the best evaluator was an expert, (evaluator ID 10) with a total of 21 % of the all problems (note, the total number of problems is the final number after applying the aggregation process, not including the "non-issues"). However, the best amateur found only 7.6 % of the total and the best novice only found 4.5 % of the total. The worst expert, amateur, and the novice found just 3 % of the total.

4.3   The Severity of Uncovered Problems

Of that 66, 17 were classified as Catastrophic (Level 4), 17 as Major (Level 3), 21 as Minor (Level 2) and 11 as Cosmetic (Level 1). Minor problems were the most common, but this difference was not significant using a chi-square analysis ($\chi2(3) = 3.09$, $p < .377$). The lack of more severe (catastrophic or more) problems is likely attributable to the fact that the DSpace website has been in use for a number of years. It is likely that the majority of major and catastrophic problems have been uncovered and fixed.

4.4   The Severity by Expertise Interaction

Nielsen [18] suggested that usability specialists are better in uncovering problems than novices. To examine that, I compared the type of usability problems that were uncovered by both experts and novices. Each level of severity (Catastrophic, Major, Minor, Cosmetic, not including Non-Issues) was considered in isolation. The full analysis is a mixed ANOVA with one between subjects factor (Groups) and one within subjects factor (Severity). This analysis indicated that there were no differences for groups ($F(2,13) = 3.205$, $p < .075$, $\eta^2 = .330$, as noted above), no differences for Severity ($F(3,39) = 1.375$, $p < .698$, $\eta^2 = .051$) and no interaction ($F(3,39) = 0.521$, $p < .265$, $\eta^2 = .039$) . However, one must again be mindful of the small sample sizes. The means are provided in Table 2 and Fig. 1.

Because we were more concerned about the severity of the problems found by each group of evaluators, specific tests for each level of severity were computed. For Catastrophic problems (Level 4), the number of problems detected by Experts was higher than the number of problems detected by Amateur and Novices, but the difference was not significant. Further analyses revealed that Experts were not different from Amateurs ($F(1,12) = 3.377$, $p < .091$, $\eta^2 = .220$), that Experts were not different from Novices ($F(1,10) = 0.714$, $p < .418$, $\eta^2 = .067$) and that Amateurs were not different from Novices ($F(1,4) = 1.333$, $p < .312$, $\eta^2 = .250$). The same results held for Major (Level 3), Minor (Level 2) and Cosmetic (Level 1) problems. For Major problems, Experts were not different from Amateurs ($F(1,12) = 2.455$, $p < .143$, $\eta^2 = .170$), Experts were not different from Novices ($F(1,10) = 4.276$, $p < ..127$, $\eta^2 = .217$), and Amateurs were not different from Novices ($F(1,4) = 0.333$, $p < .506$, $\eta^2 = .118$). For Minor problems, Experts were not different from Amateurs ($F(1,12) = 0.489$, $p < .498$, $\eta^2 = .039$), Experts were not different from Novices ($F(1,10) = 0.542$, $p < .478$, $\eta^2 = .051$) and Amateurs were not different from Novices ($F(1,4) = 0.038$, $p < .855$, $\eta^2 = .009$). Finally, for Cosmetic problems, Experts were not different from Amateurs ($F(1,12) = 0.023$, $p < .822$, $\eta^2 = .002$), Experts were not different from Novices ($F(1,10) = 0.437$, $p < .524$, $\eta^2 = .042$), and Amateurs were not different from Novices ($F(1,4) = 1.091$, $p < .355$, $\eta^2 = .214$).

Table 2. Evaluators' performance within each level of severity

Severity	Expert (n = 10)	Amateur (n = 4)	Novice (n = 2)	F	p(F)	η2
4:Catastrophic	1.90 (1.45)	0.50 (0.58)	1.00 (0.00)	3.019	.179	.233
3: Major	2.10 (1.28)	1.00 (0.81)	0.50 (0.71)	2.372	.132	.267
2: Minor	1.90 (1.59)	1.25 (1.50)	1.00 (1.41)	0.421	.669	.062
1: Cosmetic	0.90 (1.85)	0.75 (0.96)	0.00 (0.00)	0.261	.774	.039

4.5   Does One Need Experts Amateurs and Novices?

Even though the differences were not significant, Experts consistently found more problems than Amateurs, and Amateurs consistently (excepting catastrophic) found more problems than Novices.

Clearly, it would seem that experts will find "most" of the problems, and experts will find more of the serious problems. However, the simple presentation of Table 3 confounds the fact that there were more Experts (n = 10) than Amateurs (n = 4) or novices (n = 2). That is, more people imply that more problems can be found. As such, the analysis presented in Table 7 is a better measure of the capabilities of a single evaluator. However, this data does provide the opportunity to estimate the number of each category that would be required to find all problems. That is, using simple linear extrapolation (i.e., ratio), as shown in Table 4, one could conclude that it would require 17 Novices, or 24 Amateurs or 12 Experts to find all the Catastrophic problems.

Implications: This is consistent with the notions of Nielsen [25]. The severity of problems uncovered by experts is higher than the severity of problems uncovered by the novices. Hence, one could conclude that a small set of expert evaluators is needed to find severe usability problems.

Table 3. Severity of problems uncovered by evaluators

Severity	Total	Novice	Amateur	Expert
1: Cosmetic	11	0 (0.0 %)	3 (27.3 %)	9 (81.82 %)
2: Minor	21	2 (9.5 %)	5 (23.8 %)	16 (76.2 %)
3: Major	17	1 (5.9 %)	3 (17.7 %)	17 (100.0 %)
4: Catastrophic	17	2 (11.8 %)	2 (11.8 %)	15 (88.2 %)

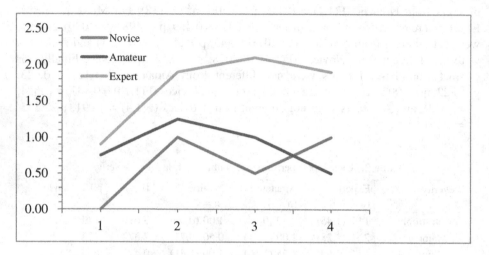

Fig. 1. Evaluators mean performance as a function of problem severity

Table 4. Number of evaluators who would be required to find all problems

Severity	Total	Novice	Amateur	Expert
1: Cosmetic	11	∞	15	13
2: Minor	21	21	17	14
3: Major	17	34	23	10
4: Catastrophic	17	17	34	12

4.6 Difficulty of Uncovering Problems

The performance of evaluators can be rated according to the difficulty of uncovering problems in the DSpace interface. We mean that an Easy problem is one that is found by many evaluators, whereas a Hard problem is one that is found by a few evaluators, or even just one evaluator.

One can also rate the ability of each evaluator to find usability problems from Good to Poor. An evaluator who found many problems would have high ability whereas an evaluator who found few problems would have low ability. These two factors were investigated.

Some might think that experts can only uncover difficult problems and both experts and novices can uncover easy problems. This raises three questions: do experts, who are presumed to have a high ability to uncover problems, find only difficult problems? Do novices uncover only easy problems? Most importantly, can novices, who have presumed to have lower ability, find difficult problems? To address these questions, Fig. 2 summarizes the ability of evaluators to uncover problems. The blue diamonds represent the Novices, the red squares represent the Amateurs and the green triangles represent the Experts. Red Xs represents experts. Each row represents one of the 66 problems, and the column represents one of the 16 evaluators.

We can see from Fig. 2 that the two types of evaluators are fairly interspersed. In this, one must be mindful of the fact that there are ties (e.g., three evaluators found 2 problems, two found 3, 4 and 5, three found 6, and one found 7, 9, 10 and 16). However, in the top rows, one can see that both Amateurs and Experts found the hardest problems, and both all groups found the easiest (lowest rows) problems. Generally, the Experts cluster to the upper right while the Novices and Amateurs cluster to the lower left.

4.7   The Violated Heuristics and Type of Problems

It was essential to investigate the number of times each heuristic was violated. Figure 2 provides the same information graphically.

Figure 3 shows the recommended priority levels for violated heuristics starting by problems associated with heuristic 4, 8, 3, 5, and 7 respectively (Fig. 4).

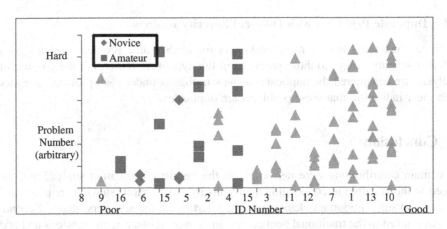

Fig. 2. Problems found by evaluators

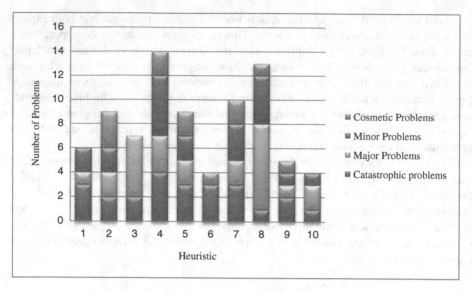

Fig. 3. Heuristics violated and type of problems

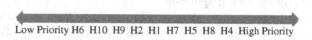

Low Priority H6 H10 H9 H2 H1 H7 H5 H8 H4 High Priority

Fig. 4. Suggested priorities according to the violated heuristics and problems severity

4.8 Duplicate Problems with Different Severity Ratings

In some conditions, two or more evaluators found the same problems but assigned different severity ratings to those problems of this type were found. For the purpose of analysis, we considered the duplicates as new problems under each problem category with clear indication that these problems are duplicates.

5 Conclusion

Two main contributions were derived from the heuristic evaluation study. First, we added to the literature in cooperating the results from a previous study "user personas" to focus on some important elements on the interface and study users' needs. Second, we have added to the traditional heuristic evaluation by separating the sessions and add a new session, which is the proposed solutions session. The results from the study show that applying the heuristic evaluation on DSpace produced a large number of usability problems that will improve the service if fixed. The findings from the heuristic evaluations study suggest a list of usability problems classified depending on their severity ratings. Two key aspects are investigated: Does the expertise and number of evaluators affect the reliability of the results from applying the heuristic evaluation to University DSpace user interface? To communicate the initial hypotheses with the findings, I examined the evaluators' performance according to three factors: the number of problems found by each evaluator and the severity of the uncovered problems. The best evaluator among the group of evaluators (both experts and novices) is an amateur who found 21 % of the total number of problems. The best expert found 13 %. This contradicts the initial hypothesis that the best evaluator will be an expert. From this point, I conclude that only one evaluator cannot find all the usability problems even if this evaluator is an expert, which agrees with Nielsen suggestion (1994) that it is advisable to have more than one evaluator to inspect the interface. Compared to Nielsen's finding, one evaluator can find 35 % of the usability problems in the user interface while, from the study findings, 21 % of the total number of problems was uncovered by the best evaluator. We conclude that the majority of the problems found by experts were serious (catastrophic and major). Finally, we believe that applying the heuristic evaluation methodology to Institutional Repositories as apart of the Digital Libraries and based on Dspaces would uncover usability problems and, if fixed, increase the libraries' usability.

Acknowledgment. This research was supported and funded by the Saudi Cultural Bureau in Ottawa-Saudi Royal Embassy. Special thanks to the supervisor Dr. J. Blustein, for the valuable comments

References

1. Bevan, N., Kirakowskib, J., & Maissela, J.: What is usability? In: Proceedings of the 4th International Conference on HCI, September 1991
2. Nielsen, J.: Usability Engineering. Academic Press, Boston (1993)
3. Hix, D., Hartson, H.R.: Developing user interfaces: ensuring usability through product & process. Wiley, New York (1993)
4. Booth, P.A.: An Introduction To Human-Computer Interaction. Psychology Press, Hove (1989)
5. Brink, T., Gergle, D., Wood, S.D.: Design Web Sites That Work: Usability for the Web. Morgan-Kaufman, San Francisco (2002)
6. Jeng, J.: What is usability in the context of the digital library and how can it be measured? Inf. Technol. Libr. **24**(2), 47–56 (2005)
7. Kahn, M.J., Prail, A.: Formal usability inspections. In: Nielsen, J., Mack, R.L. (eds.) Usability Inspection Methods, pp. 141–172. Wiley, New York (1994)
8. Wharton, C., Rieman, J., Lewis, C., Polson, P.: The cognitive walkthrough method: a practitioners guide. In: Nielsen, J., Mack, R. (eds.) Usability inspection methods, pp. 105–140. Wiley, New York (1994)
9. Nielsen, J.: How to conduct a heuristic evaluation (1994). http://www.useit.com/papers/heuristic/heuristic_evaluation.html
10. Nielsen, J.: The Usability Engineering Lifecycle. Academic Press, Boston (1993)
11. Usability Methods: Contextual Task Analysis: Usability First (Accessed 2 April 2013). http://www.usabilityfirst.com/usability-methods/contextual-task-analysis

12. Lancaster, A.: Paper prototyping: the fast and easy way to design and refine user interfaces. IEEE Trans. Prof. Commun. **47**(4), 335–336 (2004)

13. Bailey Jr., C.W.: Institutional repositories, tout de suite (2008)

14. Lynch, C.A.: "Institutional Repositories: Essential Infrastructure for Scholarship in the Digital Age." ARL no. 226, pp. 1–7 February 2003. http://www.arl.org/resources/pubs/br/br226/br226ir.shtml

15. Zimmerman, D., Paschal, D.B.: An exploratory usability evaluation of Colorado State University Libraries digital collections and the Western Waters Digital Library web sites. J. Acad. Librarianship **35**(3), 227–240 (2009)

16. DSpace (2012). <http://dspace.org>

17. Smith, M., Barton, M., Bass, M., Branschofsky, M., McClellan, G., Stuve, D., Walker, J.H.: DSpace: an open source dynamic digital repository (2003). http://www.dlib.org/dlib/january03/smith/01smith.html

18. Nielsen, J. Molich, R.: Heuristic evaluation of user interfaces. In: Proceedings of the SIGCHI Conference on Human Factors in Computing Systems, pp. 249–256. ACM (1990). http://doi.acm.org/10.1145/97243.97281

19. Ping, L.K., Ramaiah, C.K., Foo, S.: Heuristic-based User interface evaluation at Nanyang Technological University in Singapore. Program **38**(1), 42–59 (2004)

20. Qing, F., Ruhua, H.: Evaluating the usability of discipline repositories. In: 2008 IEEE International Symposium on IT in Medicine and Education, ITME 2008, pp. 385–390. IEEE, December 2008

21. Hovater, J., Krot, M., Kiskis, D.L., Holland, I., Altman, M.: Usability testing of the virtual data center. Ann Arbor 1001, 48109–2122 (2002)

22. Zhang, X., Liu, J., Li, Y., Zhang, Y.: How usable are operational digital libraries: a usability evaluation of system interactions. In: Proceedings of the 1st ACM SIGCHI Symposium on Engineering Interactive Computing Systems, pp. 177–186. ACM, July 2009

23. Heery, R., Anderson, S.: Digital Repositories Review (2005). http://www.jisc.ac.uk/uploaded_documents/digitalrepositories

24. Nielsen, J., Mack, R.L. (eds.): Usability Inspection Methods, pp. 203–233. Wiley, New York (1994)

25. Nielsen, J., Hackos, J.T.: Usability Engineering, vol. 125184069. Academic Press, Boston (1993)

26. Nielsen, J.: Enhancing the explanatory power of usability heuristics. In: Proceedings of the SIGCHI Conference On Human Factors In Computing Systems: Celebrating Interdependence, pp. 152–158. ACM, April 1994

27. Jeng, J.: Usability assessment of academic digital libraries: effectiveness, efficiency, satisfaction, and learnability. LIBRI **55**(2–3), 96–121 (2005)

28. International Standards Organization ISO 9001: 1994 (E): Quality systems: Model for quality assurance in design, development, production, installation and servicing. ISO, Geneva (1994)

29. Aljohani, M., Blustein, J.: "Personas help understand users' needs, goals and desires in an online institutional repository". Int. Sci. 9(1) (2014)

Building Information Architecture
Criteria for Assessing and Evaluating
Universities' Web Portals

Hamad Ibrahim Alomran[(✉)]

Department of Information Studies, College of Computer
and Information Sciences, Al-Imam Muhammad Ibn Saud Islamic University,
Riyadh, Saudi Arabia
alomran@imamu.edu.sa

Abstract. Information architecture (IA) or web information design is the art
and science of organizing information on web pages. It creates ways for people
to find, understand, exchange, and manage information.

This paper aims to highlight the development of IA evaluation by proposing
and explaining its main features, and by providing IA stakeholders with the
necessary tools for assessing IA qualities, ensuring their suitability for business
needs. This research will contribute to a greater understanding of building web
IA criteria for assessing and evaluating universities' web portals.

This paper uses the Delphi technique to identify the most important questions
to build these criteria. Input from three disparate professional areas, each with a
specialized area of expertise: web designers, web masters, researchers and
faculty members in web design. Data collected over a three-month period.

This paper illustrates 45 criteria and types of evidence, which are divided into
seven sections: users, content, content management, structure, design and build,
navigation, and security.

Keywords: Information architecture · IA criteria · Web page evaluation ·
Academic websites

1 Introduction

Pure research into information architecture (IA) is rare; the field borrows from external
research as needed, rather than tackling research questions directly. However, as IA has
become more structured and recognized, dedicated IA-related research has resulted.
This research is based on design problems, and the drive to find answers.

Navigation is the method by which users investigate a web page or other mode of
information. Navigation is a major research theme in IA. It encompasses labeling and
menu structures, as well as navigation behavior models. Many research publications
now deal with IA-related topics [1]. As research progresses, the reliance on external
models or methodologies will diminish.

IA for the internet is concerned with applying the principles of architecture and
library science to website design. Each website is like a public building: it is available
for tourists and regulars alike to browse through at their leisure. The job of the architect

© Springer International Publishing Switzerland 2015
A. Marcus (Ed.): DUXU 2015, Part III, LNCS 9188, pp. 131–141, 2015.
DOI: 10.1007/978-3-319-20889-3_13

is to set up the site's framework, making it comfortable and inviting to visit, relax in, and perhaps even return to [2].

In 1976, Richard Saul Wurman first coined the term "information architecture" [3]. He was a trained architect who became interested in urban environments. Wurman examined the ways in which urban environmental data interacted meaningfully with architects, urban planners, utility and transport engineers, and urban-dwelling people [3]. His initial definition of information architecture was "organizing the patterns in data, making the complex clear" [4]. He sees that the problems of gathering, organizing, and presenting information have many parallels with those faced by architects in designing buildings to serve occupants' needs [4].

IA encompasses structuring web page content to make it easily accessible for users. When designing IA for a website, the designer is concerned with navigation, labeling, and content organization: the elements help people understand and find what they are looking for. This practice draws on library science, cognitive psychology, semiotics, cybernetics, discrete mathematics, and architecture itself.

IA is essential to the process of building websites aligned with business needs. Some IA stakeholders with limited knowledge of IA matters—such business owners, web designers, information management specialists, and web programmers—do not have simple methods to evaluate IA regarding contextually derived desired qualities.

Recognizing the need for a coherent way to represent IA, Vasconcelos et al. [5] proposed a set of enterprise-modeling primitives (later extended to IA modeling) regarding information, application, and technological information. Subsequently, the IA modeling framework tested on real world case studies. This research step confirmed the need for tools capable of supporting the architect, while building IA and quickly accessing users' choices.

As the evaluation topic is a mature issue in software engineering, there is several software evaluation approaches to consider their applicability for IA evaluation. In addition, they adapted some software metrics to the IS context. This paper aims to highlight the development of IA evaluation by proposing and explaining the main features of IA evaluation and providing stakeholders with the tools for assessing IA qualities to ensure their business suitability.

2 Overview

2.1 Defining IA

IA describes both the information design process and its outcomes. Hence, the relationship between architecture, information, and IA can be viewed from an architectural history perspective. Initially, architecture may not reference a built structure: it may be conceptual; this is, information. Early digital design was visual, incorporating images of buildings and cities. Gradually, similarities to physical realities like buildings have disappeared in IA; but users still interact with abstract and multiple IA spaces using navigation techniques. Users relate with information in semantic space, screen space, and interaction space. An information architect must address each of these spaces. The pervasiveness of contemporary computing might disrupt these navigation concepts, leaving only abstracted links between users and information. This new interaction may shape IA spaces.

IA is the term used to describe the structure of a system: how information clusters, the navigation methods, and the terminology used within the system. Effective IA enables people to step logically through a system and be confident they are reaching the required information. Most people only notice IA when it is inadequate and stops them from finding information. IA is most commonly associated with websites and intranets; however, it can be used in the context of any information structure or computer system [4].

IA is critical to information delivery and communication between clients and organizations. IA is a relatively recent phenomenon, with its own characteristics and contexts. The information structures of organizations' websites are contributed to by multiple and diverse people, using IA [6].

IA is neither an information technology (IT) implementation end in itself, nor the solution to all information problems. Rather, it is an iterative process, a team activity, part of a solution, and an approach to solving issues around storing and finding information [7].

Dillon has offered a broad definition that attempts to accommodate the diversity of approaches. Dillon defines IA as "the process of designing, implementing, and evaluating information spaces that are humanly and socially acceptable to their intended stakeholders" [8]. This is an inclusive definition, despite not referencing IA as a discrete discipline. Instead, here IA is aligned to human activities such as design or creative writing. Further, Dillon advocates a view of IA as craft rather than engineering—a distinction based on the lack of separation within IA between the design and manufacture of the resulting application [8]. As craft, IA creates as it produces, often reacting to emerging elements of its own design to drive subsequent modification. Craft-based disciplines are less amenable to formal methodological abstraction for management and instructional purposes. This can result in them shifting or being altered by outside forces. IA organizes and simplifies information, as well as the design, integration, and aggregation of information spaces and systems. IA facilitates the finding, understanding, exchange, and management of information, allowing users to navigate complex information structures [8].

From the above we can identify the most important elements of IA: users, content, content management, structure, design and build, navigation, and security (Fig. 1).

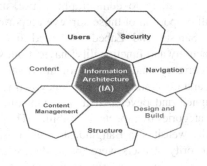

Fig. 1. The main elements of IA.

2.2 A Brief History of IA

IA started with Argus Associates, a consulting company set up in 1994 by Joseph Janes and Louis Rosenfeld, from the School of Information and Library Studies at the University of Michigan. The company was involved in a range of internet and web developments, and began to use the architecture metaphor with clients to highlight the importance of structure and organization in web design. *Web Review* magazine started a column entitled "Web Architect", authored by Rosenfeld. Peter Morville, also a graduate of the School, later joined Rosenfeld and became the first employee of Argus Associates [9].

In 1996, Wurman published a book entitled *Information Architects*, in which he claimed to have invented the expression "information architect" in 1975. This book took an information design approach to IA [10].

IA dates from 1998. By this time, Argus Associates had built a considerable reputation for IA expertise. O'Reilly Publishing commissioned Rosenfeld and Morville to write a book: *Information Architecture for the World Wide Web* (also known as the "polar bear book", owing to the distinctive line-drawn polar bear on its cover) [9]. Rosenfeld and Morville approached the issues from a library and information science perspective.

In 2000, the American Society for Information Science and Technology organized the first in a series of IA summits. This event further catalyzed the development and visibility of IA. Argus Associates folded during the dot-com bust of 2001; however, by then IA had moved into mainstream web design. In 2002, a number of books were published that shed new light on the emerging discipline.

In Europe, IA is starting to become the subject of conferences and workshops. IA sessions at the 2003 Online Information Conference in London were well attended. In 2004, an IA conference in Denmark attracted 150 delegates. In March 2004, the United Kingdom (UK) Online User Group ran a seminar in London. In June 2004, Information Today Inc. launched an IA conference in Paris (www.infotoday.com/iaparis/).

3 Literature Review

Samsur and Zabed have reviewed definitions of website usability from the 1990 s until now and examined several approaches toward evaluating university websites [11]. This led them to develop a survey instrument that they used to explore students' views of the website of the University of Dhaka (their own institution). Student population responses were analyzed according to demographics, use, and website usefulness, revealing that only a small proportion of those surveyed reported always being able to find what they needed. Samsur and Zabed identified five important factors for achieving usability: interactivity and functionality; navigation, searching, and interface attractiveness; accuracy, currency, and authority of information; accessibility, understandability, learnability, and operability; and efficiency and reliability [11].

Islam and Tsuji designed and developed a questionnaire based on 23 usability criteria divided into five categories by aspects of usability. They used this instrument to evaluate selected university websites in Bangladesh from a usability perspective [12] and found that a large majority of users were dissatisfied with the usability of these websites [12]. Weaknesses were found in terms of design, interface, and performance, and the websites' internal features were identified, with suggestions to enhance website usability [12].

Mustafa and Al-Zoua'bi studied Jordanian university websites, using tools to measure internal website attributes not perceptible by users, such as html code errors, download times, and the size of html pages [13].

In his study of website usability and search issues involving 13 Australian and two overseas universities, Alexander concluded with five action-oriented recommendations:

- to design an IA that meets prospective students' needs
- to create content that meets prospective students' needs
- to improve search performance
- to not assume that prospective students have relevant domain knowledge
- to not use PDFs (the primary format for web content) [14].

Ruwoldt and Spencer examined homepage screenshots to develop a questionnaire involving 68 Australian and overseas universities [15]. They sorted comments into specific content aspects, labeling and navigation, design, and branding, and concluded that IA best practice provides multiple navigation paths [15]. They made the following suggestions:

- static links should be grouped according to audience or topic and labeled "for" and "about"
- two or more links should be provided from the homepage to a key content page (as appropriate), with the links given different titles
- links to key content should be emphasized visually
- users should be allowed to choose between a search engine or browsing a site map or index/directory [15].

In her study on web standards and navigation structures, Nichani surveyed 25 universities, mostly from Australia, the UK, and the United States (US) [16]. She concluded that website re-design projects foregrounded considerable experimentation [16].

DeWeaver and Ellis surveyed a representative sample of nine universities in New South Wales and Queensland on 28 marketing parameters [17]. They concluded that, despite lengthy experience in web marketing, some universities still rated very low in this category [17]. DeWeaver and Ellis suggested that effective web marketing for universities requires greater integration of design and content. This relates to recognizing how visitors navigate websites [17].

Bao and Ellis conducted a pilot study with 31 institutions (21 universities [general curricula] and 10 business schools) across the US, Australia, the UK, Asia and France [18]. British and Australian institutions were found to appear more compliant with web standards and usability issues [18], while significant variation was found between other institutions in their organization of their homepage information. Scope for significant improvement was found for most institutions [18].

Powell recounted usability guidelines relating to website use:

- learnability
- memorability

- efficiency
- reliability
- satisfaction [19].

McLaughin and Skinner identified six related but distinct components of usability:

- checkability
- confidence
- control
- ease of use
- speed
- understanding [20].

Aziz and Kamaludin used web evaluation to validate websites to determine how they perform. When analyzing a website, typical factors to be considered include: how the information is organized and presented, and how to access and navigate informative structure [21].

Morville described the interrelationship between the world and the Web [2]. He asked, "How do we rise to the new challenges of creating paths and places that bridge physical, digital, and cognitive spaces?" [2]. Viewed from this angle, information architects are at least partly responsible for creating these bridging paths. We might ask how user experience of similar paths, spaces, and usability models differs. Morville proposed guidelines to determine design and usability [2].

Rosenfeld and Morville stipulated that users, content, and context inform good IA [9]. Although conceding that the basic model was oversimplified, they did note that concepts intertwined "within a complex, adaptive information ecology" [9]. Rosenfeld and Morville also stressed the "dynamic, organic nature to both the information systems and the broader environments in which they exist" [9]; continuing with "we're talking complex, adaptive systems with emergent qualities" [9]. These statements make a clear connection between IA and context-aware adaptive systems, as described above. However, these fields do not interact very much [9].

4 Research Design

4.1 Research Problem

One problem facing the IA community, in its drive for professional status, is the need to overcome abstraction and education problems. This will provide the legitimacy accorded to related fields within information science. There are no clear criteria to assess and evaluate universities' web portals.

4.2 Methodology

The purpose of this study is to build IA criteria for assessing and evaluating universities' web portals. Thus, this study uses the Delphi technique to identify the most important questions to build these criteria, because the Delphi method is described as a group process used to solicit, collate, and direct expert responses to reach consensus [22]. The methodology behind the current study is based on exploratory research by Farrokhi, Chizari and Mirdamadi [23], who used the Delphi method when examining the development of web-based distance education in Iran's higher education system.

Therefore, to encourage a broad range of potential priorities, this study sought input from three disparate professional areas, each with a specialized area of expertise.

- web designers (n = 10)
- web masters (n = 10)
- researchers and faculty members in web design (n = 10).

Data collected over a three-month period (January, February, and March) 2014. A letter of invitation to participate in this study was sent by e-mail to 30 potential participants around the world. They were identified through a search of technology administration websites, university websites, websites associated with web design, and a thorough literature review.

The researcher applied the Kendal coefficient to determine the consensus scale, using the following formula:

$$s = \sum \left[R_J \frac{\sum R_J}{N} \right]$$

This coefficient determines the degree of agreement between priorities related to N people or things.

In total, six of the 30 selected people chose not to participate, or did not reply. The number of participants was thus reduced to 24. Dalkey [24] stated that for a study to be reliable, greater than 80 percent participation is needed.

This study used a series of four mailed questionnaires; a methodology that Moore and Kearsley [25] note is typical of the Delphi technique. A wide range of responses was collected using an open-ended question. These responses were then categorized to produce the items for the subsequent three rounds of the questionnaire, which required respondents to rate items on a five-point Likert-type scale (1–1.79 = strongly disagree, 1.80–2.59 = disagree, 2.60–3.39 = uncertain, 3.40–4.19 = agree, 4.20–5 = strongly agree). A panel of experts from outside the study validated the questionnaire. The four questionnaire rounds ran as follows:

- The first round used the open-ended question: what are the most important things to consider before starting to design a website? This elicited a wide range of responses, which were categorized to produce the items for the second-round questionnaire.
- In the second round, respondents were asked to rate the items identified in round one on a five-level Likert-type scale regarding the agreement level (from 1 = strongly disagree to 2 = strongly agree). From this second round of responses, the category list was reduced to 62.
- The third round aimed at achieving consensus. Participants were asked to indicate their agreement using the Likert scale, and to provide comments if they did not agree with the summary findings. Consensus was reached on 54 of 62 items in this

round. These items were divided into seven categories: users, content, content management, structure, design and build, navigation, and security.

- A fourth round sought to reach consensus on the remaining items. This questionnaire asked respondents to indicate whether questions were the same as the modified ones from round three. Consensus was reached on 48 of the questions in this round.

5 Analysis of Data

The collected data were treated as interval data and reported using descriptive statistics, including means and standard deviations.

6 Results

This paper proposes criteria for assessing and evaluating web pages. The first draft of these criteria were based on an extensive literature review and experts' opinions, expressed by web designers, web masters, researchers, and faculty using the Delphi method. The final proposed criteria displayed in Table 1.

Table 1. IA Criteria for Assessing and Evaluating Universities' Web Portals

Users
The intended audiences are clear.
The website describes the intended audiences (i.e., interests, needs, skills, capabilities, and assumptions).
The website is easy to use and easy to understand.
The website works anytime, anywhere.
The GUI is friendly.
Content
The website provides the content required to support the services.
The goals of the website are clear.
The content is well written in a style suitable for the intended audience.
The content has been optimized for search engines.
The content remains human-readable and user-friendly even after search engine optimization.
Any in-page tools or other functionalities are easy to use, intuitive, and/or clearly explained with supporting content as needed.
Content management
Current behavior and popular content are identified.
There is a monitor that evaluates the use of the website.
There are processes that standardize the management and use of data.
There is a process for entry validation of the data.
The tier data server been identified for storing critical operational data.

(*Continued*)

Table 1. (*Continued*)

There is a discipline for website back-ups in case of failures.

There are mirror sites to increase website availability in case of failures and to do load-balancing at peak times.

Structure

The content is organized into an appropriate and logical site structure.

There is an information classification strategy.

The use of any metadata/classification schema is appropriate to the needs of both content managers and front-end users.

There are data entity and attribute access rules.

Governance policies and procedures are correctly implemented in the site administration system.

The website determines which classification schemes are implemented for the content.

The above choices will support the website's content in the future.

Design and build

The site is built using standards-compliant HTML and CSS.

The website's proposed structure has been tested with users.

The website will consume information made available by other data sources.

There is a method to aggregate information based on modeling, classification, and semantics.

The website is compatible with social networking technology.

The website supports publish-subscribe features (e.g., to notify subscribers in case of updates).

Navigation

The website creates labels to represent information to the users.

The site navigation system accurately reflects the site's structure.

The site's navigation is clear, intuitive, and consistent.

The site has a clearly defined section for global navigation, which is the same on every page.

The use of metadata-based navigation (e.g., facets, tags) supports the users' needs.

The navigation systems support users' information needs.

Security

Security needs for accessing the information have been determined.

Information access is compliant with FOI and privacy legislation.

There is an authorization scheme to protect tagging based on user roles.

There are data protection mechanisms to protect data from unauthorized external access.

The website provides secure protocols and communication mechanisms when handling user passwords and user accounts.

User passwords are stored in an encrypted format so that even site administrators do not have access to them.

Users have protection against excessive outsider crawling.

The list has seen several significant changes from one round to another. In the round, two of the panelists added many phrases and changed the formulation of some. Context in the first round increased from five to sixteen, users increased from five to nine phrases. All phrases of component design are found in the uncertain response.

Panelists suggested deleting context, documenting IA and implementation and testing IA. They proposed changing some addresses.

The third round also has many changes. The number of context phrases has decreased to six, although most were in the category of uncertain response. Users decreased to four phrases, with the recommendation to redistribute some phrases and transfer to other subjects. Panelists suggested add new subjects, such as security, navigation, and evaluation, and proposed many phrases that fall under these new themes.

The final list also saw some important changes. The large number of panelists suggested deleting context and the distribution some of phrases. A new proposal was to structure and determine the number of phrases. Some subject addresses were changed or shortened, the title 'design component' has been changed to 'design and build'. Then came the final list, including seven subjects described in the final list.

7   Conclusion

IA plays a vital role in organizing and simplifying information on web pages. It creates ways for people to find, understand, exchange, and manage information.

Within the framework of this study, the objective was to develop IA criteria for assessing and evaluating universities' web portals. Thus, this paper illustrates 45 criteria and types of evidence, which are divided into seven sections: users, content, content management, structure, design and build, navigation, and security.

References

1. Pirolli, P.: Powers of 10: Modeling complex information-seeking systems at multiple scales. IEEE Comput. **42**(3), 33–40 (2009)
2. Morville, P.: Information architecture for the World Wide Web, 1st edn. O'Reilly & Associates, Sebastopol, CA (1998)
3. Wyllys, R.: Information Architecture, Graduate School of Library and Information Science (2000)
4. Barker, I. What is information architecture? 2 May 2005 (Accessed on 15 october 2013). http://www.steptwo.com.au/papers/kmc_whatisinfoarch. 2005
5. Vasconcelos, A., Caetano, A., Neves, J., Sinogas, P., Mendes, R., Tribolet, J.: A framework for modeling strategy, business processes and information systems. In: Fifth International Enterprise Distributed Object Computing Conference pp. 4–7, Seattle, US (2001)
6. Burford, S.: Web information architecture: A very inclusive practice. J. Inf. Archit. **3**(1), 11–40 (2011)
7. Hourican, R.: Information architectures - what are they? Bus. Inf. Rev. **19**(3), 16–22 (2002)
8. Dillon, A.: Information architecture in JASIST. Just where did we come from? J. Assoc. Inf. Sci. Technol. **53**(10), 821–823 (2002)
9. Rosenfeld, L., Morville, P.: Information Architecture for the World Wide Web: Designing Large Scale Web Sites, Sebastopol. O'Reilly & Associates Inc, CA (2006)
10. Wurman, R., Bradford, P.: Information Architects. Graphis Press, Zurich, Switzerland (1996)

11. Samsur, R., Zabed, A.: Exploring the factors influencing the usability of academic websites: A case study in a university setting. Bus. Inf. Rev. **30**(1), 40–47 (2013)

12. Islam, A., Tsuji, K.: Evaluation of usage of university websites in Bangladesh. DESIDOC J. Libr. Inf. Technol. **31**(6), 469–479 (2011)

13. Mustafa, S.H., Al-Zoua'bi, Loai, F.S.: Usability of the academic websites of Jordan's universities: An evaluation study. Accepted for presentation In: the Ninth International Arab Conference on Information Technology, Tunisia, Sfax University 16–18 December 2008

14. Alexander, D.: How usable are university websites? A report on a study of the prospective student experience, AusWeb05 In: Proceedings of the 11th Australasian World Wide Web Conference, Southern Cross University, Lismore, pp. 303–320 (2005)

15. Ruwoldt, M.L., Spencer, C.: Navigation and content on university home pages. AusWeb05. In: Proceedings of the 11th Australasian World Wide Web Conference, Ausweb2005. Southern Cross University, Lismore, pp. 431–434 (2005)

16. Nichani, M.: The changing face of university websites. 17 August 2006 (Accessed on 10 September 2013). http://www.pebbleroad.com/perspectives/The-Changing-Face-of-University-Websites/

17. DeWeaver, L., Ellis, A.: University Web-Marketing: A Report Card. In: Treloar, A., Ellis, A. (Eds.) AusWeb06. In: Proceedings of the 12th Australasian World Wide Web Conference, pp. 9–14. Southern Cross University, Lismore (2006)

18. Bao, T., Ellis, A.: Assessing university homepages from Web standard and usability perspectives. In: Proceedings of the 13th Australasian World Wide Web Conference Ausweb07, Coffs Harbour, NSW, Australia (2007)

19. Powell, T.A.: Web Design: The Complete Reference. McGraw-Hill Osborne Media, Berkeley (2000)

20. McLaughlin, J., Skinner, D.: Developing usability and utility: a comparative study of the users of new it. Technol. Anal. Strateg. Manag. **12**(3), 413–423 (2000)

21. Aziz, N.-S., Kamaludin, A.: Assessing website usability attributes using partial least squares. Int. J. Inf. Electron. Eng. **4**(2), 137–144 (2014)

22. Dyer, J., Breja, L., Ball, A.: A Delpi study of agricultural teacher perceptions of problems in students retention. J. Agric. Educ. **44**(2), 86–95 (2003)

23. Farrokhi, S., Chizari, M., Mirdamadi, M.: Web-based distance education: opportunities and threats. Int. Res. J. Appl. Basic Sci. **2**(7), 254–262 (2011)

24. Dalkey, N.C.: The Delphi Method: An Experimental Study of Group Opinion. The Rand Corporation, Santa Monica, CA (1969)

25. Moore, M., Kearsley, G.: Distance Education: A Systems View, 2nd edn. Thomson Wadsworth, Belmont, CA (2005)

Designing with Young Children: Lessons Learned from a Co-creation of a Technology-Enhanced Playful Learning Environment

Nanna Borum$^{(\boxtimes)}$, Eva Petersson Brooks, and Anthony Lewis Brooks

Department of Architecture, Design and Media Technology,
Aalborg University, Aalborg, Denmark
{nb,ep,tb}@create.aau.dk

Abstract. This paper reports on the lessons learned from working with creative visual methods with young children between the ages of 3 to 5 years-of-age in an early years educational setting in Southern Denmark as part of an 18-month project on Digital Playful Learning. The overarching goal of the study was to create a practice-based technology-enhanced playful learning environment. Collaboration was with the pedagogical education University College Syd-Danmark, the preschool teachers and the children. 55 children took part in the sessions. The study investigated a selection of methods developed for children, but not necessarily young children, such as the Bags of Stuff technique and the Mixing Ideas technique. This paper will discuss the advantages and challenges of these when applying them together with young children. The findings suggest that when working with younger children researchers should make efforts into understanding the children and their conceptual framework before engaging in design activities. In addition, young children need support in their creative expression.

Keywords: Early years education · Creative visual methods · Designing with young children

1 Introduction

With the rapid development of technology, traditional resources for children's play and learning have undergone major changes [1, 2, 3]. In Denmark 97 % of children of 3-5 years-of-age attend a preschool, and the municipalities, who govern 72 % of the preschools, are increasingly putting a focus on digitalising play and learning for young children [4]. In the context of this paper, all preschools in the present study have been equipped with an array of digital technology and playware as part of this effort.

Generally, the Danish children are quite familiar with technologies given that 99 % of families with children have a computer with Internet access at home, one third of the families have a tablet, and two thirds have a smartphone [4]. In addition, the parents of the children are generally positive towards children's access to technology with 94 % stating that technology should be a natural part of the every day lives of children [5].

© Springer International Publishing Switzerland 2015
A. Marcus (Ed.): DUXU 2015, Part III, LNCS 9188, pp. 142–152, 2015.
DOI: 10.1007/978-3-319-20889-3_14

The positive attitude towards technology is also reflected in numbers saying that families use different technological platforms more often compared to couples without children and people living alone [4].

In continuation of these numbers, this paper presents the lessons learned from a study where the overarching purpose was firstly to investigate how children in early years education in Denmark explore and play with digital technology and electronic playware. Secondly, the gathered information should feed into a practice-based design of a technology-enhanced playful learning environment created together with the children.

The study has been carried out following a Design-Based Research framework (DBR). DBR, originally coined by Brown [6] as design experiments, emphasises a merging of research, practice and design into one entity aimed towards extending current methodologies and theories in educational science [7, 8]. DBR underlines an iterative design process and allows for flexible and mixed methods [9].

In this paper we will draw on experience from the methods utilised in the field of interaction design, which bear commonalities with DBR when it comes to the design process [10]. In interaction design there is an emphasis on a user-centred design approach including methods such as design metaphors, interview with users, usability testing, video ethnography, use of focus groups, think aloud sessions and development of user personas (c.f. [11, 12]), all of which the results intend to inform the iterative design process. A challenge of these methods is that they are designed for adults and do not necessarily lend themselves to inquiries with young children [13]. The conceptual framework and terminology of children is inherently different than those of adults (cf. [14]).

Interaction design with children (IDC) and child-computer interaction (CCI) are emerging fields (cf. [12, 14, 15, 16]) where design researchers strive to meet some of the challenges of designing for and with children [13]. In their study, Read and Markopoulos highlight that current literature often neglects to consider the importance of the gatekeepers and the context and space of the inquiries that is unique to CCI. Moreover, researchers only seldom work with preschool children. This paper will try to meet some of these challenges.

2 Related Works

When including children in a design process Druin [14] differs between four roles the children can employ: *user*, *tester*, *informant*, and *design partner*. The main difference is the distribution of power between the children and the researchers. The first two terms, Druin [17] constitutes as reactive users. It includes methods such as video probes [18], children observing other children [14], play sessions [19], peer tutoring [20], co-discovery [21], and post-task interviews [22].

The last two terms, *informant* and *design partner*, Druin [17] categorises as participative users. The design process from this perspective includes techniques such as cooperative low-tech prototyping [17], drawings [15], technology immersion [14], and mixing ideas [23].

Iversen and Dindler [16] emphasise that participation is not necessarily equal to actual generation of knowledge but the term also covers "a means to end of exchanging and negotiating values among participants in a highly dialogic and iterative process facilitated by designers".As advised by the preschool ([16] p. 26). In this sense children come to understand not only their own values, but also the values of their peers. Similarly Bødker, Ehn, Sjögren and Sundblad [24] pointed out that participation in itself could be considered as a way of learning.

3   Participants and Methods for Data Gathering

This project included children and their teachers as testers, informants, and design partners depending on the stage of the development process. In this paper we will however only cover the first stage of design process where the ideas were generated and hence the participants were:

- Preschool Teachers: 9 (7 female, 2 male) who came from five different preschools across Southern Jutland, Denmark. The teachers volunteered to participate.
- Students from preschool teacher education: 25, (13 female and 12 male) who came from the pedagogical educations at University College SydDanmark across Southern Jutland, Denmark. The students functioned as facilitators of the sessions with the children.
- Children: 55 boys and girls between 3-5 years-of-age came from five different preschools in Southern Jutland, Denmark. The children were selected to participate by the preschool teachers on the criteria that the children should neither be shy or over active.

3.1   Procedure

The study has utilised a number of creative participatory methods to inform the design of the technology-enhanced playful learning environment. In the context of this paper, the product of the process, i.e. the virtual environment, will not be treated, but merely the lessons learned from the methods utilised to create the environment.

3.2   Data Gathering

All sessions except the Ice Breaking sessions were video recorded, photographed and the creative contributions were archived for later analysis.

4   Setting the Scene

When working with young children there are a lot of considerations to take into account. First of all, ethical considerations, which will however not be covered in this paper (see [2, 25] on the ethical directions this project has followed). Secondly, preparations have to be put into how to get to know the children and hence be able to design together with them. An emphasis was on enabling the researchers' understanding of the children's conceptual frameworks. Even though efforts were put into ensuring this coherency, when working with children surprises always happen. As noted by Veale [15], working with younger children calls for equal amounts of preparation and flexibility.

4.1 Breaking the Ice

Background. Before engaging in the actual design process with the children, this project worked with a set of techniques in order to ensure an equal distribution of power between the researchers and the children. Fails, Druin, Bederson, Weeks and Rose [26] describe that a means to equalise the power is by only using first names, wearing informal clothes, sitting on the floor, and not using a raise of hand when speaking. In Denmark, the three former would be how teaching naturally is conducted in preschools, so instead the efforts were put into ensuring good communications between children and adults. Different methods for getting-to-know-each other are common when bringing groups together for e.g. teamwork and creative work especially in the fields of team building and Human Resources (cf. [27]).

How It Was Used. As advised by the preschool teachers, the first day in the different preschools had sessions that were dedicated to breaking the ice. The sessions were aimed towards building trust and friendship between the preschool teacher students, who functioned as facilitators of all the sessions, and the children. In order to do so, the preschool teacher students did two things; (a) they played and sang with the children and (b) the children took the preschools teacher students out on a tour in the preschool to present their favourite spots. The children were handed a set of stickers that allowed them to categorise the different spots in e.g. "best place to play wild" and "best spot to fantasise" in order to trigger the conversation.

Lessons Learned. The activities were intended for the children to build ownership of the process. The experience was that neither of the methods should stand alone. The playing and singing were beneficial for building a relationship between the children and the preschools teacher students. The children quickly seemed to feel comfortable with the new adults present in the preschool. The sticker tour proved efficient in two ways; (a) it gave the children initiative and a "voice" and hence sparked communication, and (b) it helped clarifying to the children that the preschool teacher students did not have the same role as the children could expect from their regular teachers. The children understood that there was a task at hand that they could help solving, which in return again supported a sense of ownership and empowerment through the process. The experience was supported by feedback from the parents of the children, who expressed that the children were very proud of their participation and that they talked a lot about the process at home.

As a means to not be invasive in the icebreaking process, these sessions were not video recorded and data from the sessions consisted only of verbal feedback from the preschool teacher students, the preschools teachers, the verbal feedback from the parents, and field notes.

4.2 Establishing a Common Ground

Background. "All collective actions are built on common ground and its accumulations." ([28], p. 127). From the basics of communication theory it is evident that when two people communicate the process it contains more than just planning when to speak and listen. It is merely an on-going process where both parties constantly update their models of what the counterpart know and together they create a shared base to converse from. When working with children Clark [29] found that infants down to age of 14 months are able to establish a common ground with adults and are able to build on the shared knowledge in the further communication.

How It Was Used. The researchers spent time watching children's television, reading children's books, learning children's songs and scouted out what was trending in the toy and app industry. This was done in order to ease the establishment of a common ground when talking with the children and also to aid the analysis and understanding of children talking with children.

Lessons Learned. The experience was that when the children realised that the researchers were aware of their universe they more easily opened up and discussed. In the sessions where the children played freely with technology, it was key to understand their frameworks in order to understand their play. The children's play was often bound in the physical world meaning that it was initiated from the objects at hand, but the play frame the children engaged in was not spontaneous, but merely initiated from existing frames of the children. The children would evolve their stories around existing characters from children's literature and television (cf. [30]). In one example, a group of children were playing in a Kinect-based system developed for the project where the children were able to draw interactive objects on the wall. The children stated that their creation was a character from a Danish children's novel. In the book a boy is able to draw with crayon on the wall and everything he draws comes to life. The association between the system and the book was not far reached and if the researcher had failed to recognise the child's association we would also have failed to recognise that the young child actually had a good understanding of the system features.

4.3 Framing the Sessions

Background. As emphasised by Veale [15] and Markopoulos et al. [2] when working with children and perhaps even more when working with young children, planning and preparations are crucial to create a good experience for the children and also to strengthen the results of the design process. Not only following the ethical guidelines for working with children, which state that children should not be put in distress by being put into unfamiliar settings (cf. [2]), the use of field studies and in situ interviews also gives richer data, in comparison to a controlled lab setting, when the scope is to understand how young children use technology in their everyday lives.

How It Was Used. Since the sessions were carried out in five different preschools, naturally the type of rooms and décor differed from place to place. The aim was that the use of the room should feel natural to the children but also not cause any organisational problems for the preschool. In some of the preschools the preschool teachers intentionally selected the rooms for the purpose (a play room for an active session, a creative workshop for a creative session, and so on) and in others the rooms were selected out of convenience by the preschool leaders. In all sessions the researchers, the preschool teacher students and the children made flexible use of the objects available in the room such as a mattress on the floor, a stereo system to play music, and costumes to act out. **Lessons Learned.** A tendency was clear from the different settings; the children would carry with them the perceived and interpreted affordance of the space into the design activities. This meant that when the activities were carried out in a room regularly used as a creative workshop, the children sat down and focused mainly at the task at hand in contrast to when the creative activities were carried out in a room utilised for physical play. Here the children would be more physically active, use the whole space, bring in other objects for their creations and have more difficulty in staying focused.

Another experience from the field studies was that, in the instances where the preschool teacher students wanted to interview the children about their opinions on different technologies and digital playware, it was of benefit to physically frame the setting. In one session the frame was a big mattress on the floor, in another it was lines one the floor surrounding the children and preschool teacher students. It signalled to the children that this is where the action takes place and the sessions where this was applicable were more successful in regards to letting the student preschools teachers connect with the children.

5   Creative Design Methods

In this section we present two different visual creative methods for designing with children that were utilised in the project. These were used in the initial phase of the project and hence helped inform the requirements and design guidelines for the concept development.

5.1   Drawings

Background. The use of children's drawings as a means for investigating children's experiences is not of new date. As cited in Veale [15] the use can be dated back to early 1900 s in psychology as a tool for assessment of cognitive and emotional functioning. Veale has experimented with using drawings as a method for understanding children's experience in different ways, e.g. free drawings, commenting on generic drawings, and interpreting other children's drawings. Not all methods were equally successful in obtaining the interest of the children. The author stressed that even though drawings contain visual data, it was the children's interpretations of the drawings that yielded more rich data for interpretation.

Developed from the Cooperative Inquiry approach, another drawing technique that inspired the work in this project was the Mixing Ideas technique [31, 32]. The technique was developed for design work with younger children and hence takes into account the extra support needed for interpreting the drawings together with the children. The work is centred on the metaphor of baking cookies meaning that the ideas of the children become "tastier" and richer when mixed together.

How It Was Used. In the Mixing Ideas technique the children's ideas are mixed together using scissors and glue, which enabled the children to, by guidance of adults, stick together ideas as they see them fit. In the context of this project, the children worked with drawings in two different ways. In one preschool the children, in groups of 4-6 children, collaboratively worked to create universes and stories together using a large piece of paper that was rolled across the floor (see Fig. 1). Adults annotated the drawings in order to keep track of the story that emerged from the drawings. In other preschools the children worked in pairs together with a preschool teacher student to produce drawings on postcards that then afterwards could be mixed, matched and rearranged to form the stories of the children's likings.

Fig. 1. Children and adults drawing together

Lessons Learned. Originally the Mixing Ideas technique was grounded from Cooperative Inquiry based on the experience that younger children need more assistance in combining the ideas of each other [32]. In the sessions where children were drawing together in groups of 4-6 people this was a challenge. The researchers experienced that, in spite of trying to accommodate the knowledge from Guha et al. [31] by assisting the children, it still proved difficult to let ideas spark from each other without having some children feeling left behind. The group was too big for the children to be able to still see their ideas in play. This was only a minor problem in the groups where two children drew together.

Another challenge, which was evident in both types of drawing sessions, was that when the young children were asked to make up a story and draw it, it was too abstract for them. The intention with the task was to see what types of story world they would create and to let this knowledge inform the design of the interactive environment. The children would either draw stories related to e.g. famous fairy tales or their favourite TV-shows. In one session one preschool teacher tried to spark the imagination of children by introducing different play figurines such as dragon or a knight, which helped bring depth into the children's stories and make them develop more to the story line. Unfortunately it also streamlined the stories so that the general concept of the stories was basically the same.

5.2 The Magical Suitcase

Background. The Magical Suitcase as it was called in this project, draws heavily on the brainstorming technique from Cooperative Inquiry [17] often refereed to as the Bags of Stuff technique. Originally adapted from Bjerknes, Ehn and Kyng [33] the technique aims towards creating lo-fi prototypes in teams; children and adults together. The goal is to get as many solutions as possible. The groups are provided with several types of art supplies and presented to a problem that needs solving. Typically the technique has been used with children between 7 to 11 years of age.

How It Was Used. Given that the participants who took part in this project were younger children, the use of the Bags of Stuff technique was accommodated accordingly. The Magical Suitcase was a suitcase filled with not only art supplies but also different objects with assigned meaning (see Fig. 2), e.g. a couple of glasses were told to be magical which would allow the children to see everything they wanted to see. The intention was that instead of focusing on building actual lo-fi prototypes, instead the materials provided should open up for different types of play than the children would not usually engage in. In addition, the hope was that the material would open discussions between the children and preschool teacher students on the possibilities and limitations with technology. Each group consisted of 5-6 children and 2-3 preschool teacher students that together engaged with the different materials.

Fig. 2. The magical suitcase with a selection of the content

Lessons Learned. A challenge was that the stories built around the different objects did not have enough depth to engage the children. It was wrongfully anticipated that when young children were told that e.g. a potion or a set of glasses were magical, it would spur enough interest for them to start exploring and playing with the objects. Instead they most often wanted the background story on how these object became magical and similar questions before being intrigued into the play.

6   Conclusion

The overarching goal of the study presented in this paper was to investigate how young children make use of digital technology in their everyday lives in a preschool setting and to let these experiences inform the design of a technology-enhanced playful learning environment. The information was provided through a set of field studies, which was derived into design requirements and design guidelines in an iterative design process. The children were included in the design through a number of creative methods for designing with children adapted from Cooperative Inquiry [17]. Moreover, efforts were put into setting the scene for the following design sessions.

The work focused around adapting design methods designed for children, but not necessarily young children, and applying these on a target group of children between 3-5 years-of-age. The findings suggest that when working with young children preparations have to be carefully considered in order to engage the children in the design process. Creating a common ground was essential to communication. Techniques for breaking the ice were beneficial for building trust between the children and the facilitators of the sessions. In addition, setting the right physical frame for the sessions improved the quality of the design solutions.

The creative methods utilised for the cooperative design process was transferred to the younger target group with difficulty. Adding objects that intentionally should open up for playful creations of new play scenarios modified the Bags of Stuff technique [26]. The results indicate that such a modification of the technique can potentially add value to the design process, however more work has to be put into the stories behind the objects in order to engage the children.

Some sessions included drawing techniques inspired from the Mixing Ideas technique [31], which also presented itself with challenges. The children's ability to communicate through drawings differs and hence the sense of skill and ability change the motivation the children have towards the task. Moreover, the children find it hard to draw something from free imagination and the help of adults can easily affect the direction of the children's drawings.

The findings imply that further development of design methods for young children are needed.

Acknowledgements. University College SydDanmark supported the study presented in this paper.

References

1. Buckingham, D.: After the Death of Childhood: Growing Up in the Age of Electronic Media. Polity Press, Oxford (2000)
2. Markopoulos, P., Read, J.C., MacFarlane, S., Höysniemi, J.: Evaluating Children's Interactive Products: Principles and Practices for Interaction Designers. Morgan Kaufmann Publishers, Burlington (2008)
3. Rogers, Y., Price, S.: How mobile technologies are changing the way children learn. In: Druin, A. (ed.) Mobile Technology for Children: Designing for Interaction and Learning. Morgan Kaufmann Publishers, Burlington (2009)
4. Rambøll Management Consulting & Implement Consulting Group.: IT og digitale medier er kommet for at blive: Kortlægning af digitale redskaber på dagtilbudsområdet. Rambøl, Copenhagen (2014)
5. Analyse, K.M.D.: Den digitale daginstitution: En temperaturmåling af daginstitutionernes digitale tilstand og potentiale. KMD, Copenhagen (2013)
6. Brown, A.L.: Design experiments: theoretical and methodological challenges in creating complex interventions in classroom settings. J. Learn. Sci. 2(2), 141–178 (1992)
7. Barab, S., Squire, K.: Design-based research: putting a stake in the ground. J. Learn. Sci. 13(1), 1–14 (2004)
8. Wang, F., Hannafin, M.J.: Design-based research and technology-enhanced learning environments. Educ. Tech. Res. Dev. 53(4), 5–23 (2005)
9. Andersson, T., Shattuck, J.: Design-based research: a decade of progress in education research? Educ. Res. 41(1), 16–25 (2012)
10. Zimmerman, J., Forlizzi, J., Evenson, S.: Research through design as a method for interaction design research in HCI. In: Proceedings of the SIGCHI Conference on Human Factors in Computing Systems, pp. 493–502 (2007)
11. Sharp, H., Rogers, Y., Preece, J.: Interaction Design: Beyond Human-Computer Interaction, 2nd cdn. Wiley, New York (2007)
12. Antle, A.N.: Child-based personas: need, ability and experience. Cogn. Technol. Work 10(2), 155–166 (2008)
13. Read, J.C., Markopoulos, P.: Child-computer interaction. Int. J. Child-Computer Interaction 1(1), 2–6 (2013)
14. Druin, A.: The role of children in the design of new technology. Behav. Inf. Technol. 21(1), 1–25 (2002)
15. Veale, A.: Creative methodologies in participatory research with children. In: Greene, S., Hogan, D. (eds.) Researching Children's Experience: Approaches and Methods, pp. 253–272. Sage, London (2005)
16. Iversen, O.S., Dindler, C.: A utopian agenda in child-computer interaction. Int. J. Child-Comput. Interact. 1(1), 24–29 (2013)
17. Druin, A.: Cooperative inquiry: developing new technologies for children with children. In: Proceedings of the SIGCHI Conference on Human Factors in Computing Systems: The CHI is the Limit, pp. 592–599 (1999)
18. Hutchinson, H., Mackay, W., Westerlund, B., Bederson, B.B., Druin, A., Plaisant, C., et al.: Technology probes: inspiring design for and with families. In: Proceedings of the SIGCHI Conference on Human Factors in Computing Systems, pp. 17–24 (2003)
19. Marco, J., Cerezo, E., Baldassarri, S., Mazzone, E., Read, J.C.: Bringing tabletop technologies to kindergarten children. In: Proceedings of the 23rd British HCI Group Annual Conference on People and Computers: Celebrating People and Technology, pp. 103–111 (2009)

20. Labrune, J.B., Mackay, W.: Tangicam: exploring observation tools for children. In: Proceedings of the 2005 Conference on Interaction Design and Children, pp. 95–102 (2005)
21. Bruckman, A., Brandlow, A.: HCI for Kids. In: Jacko, J., Sears, A. (eds.) Human Computer Interaction Handbook. Lawrence Erlbaum, Hillsdale (2003)
22. Baauw, E., Markopoulous, P.: A comparison of think-aloud and post-task interview for usability testing with children. In: Proceedings of the 2004 Conference on Interaction Design and Children: Building a Community, pp. 115–116 (2004)
23. Guha, M.L., Druin, A., Chipman, G., Fails, J.A., Simms, S., Farber, A.: Working with young children as technology design partners. Commun. ACM **48**(1), 39–42 (2005)
24. Bødker, S., Ehn, P., Sjögren, D., Sundblad, Y.: Co-operative design: perspectives on 20 years with "the Scandinavian IT Design Model". In: Proceedings of NordiCHI 2000, pp. 1–9 (2000)
25. Pink, S.: Doing Visual Ethnography, 2nd edn. Sage, Thousand Oaks (2007)
26. Fails, J.A., Druin, A., Bederson, B.B., Weeks, A., Rose, A.: A child's mobile digital library: collaboration, community, and change. In: Druin, A. (ed.) Mobile Technology for Children: Designing for Interaction and Learning. Morgan Kaufmann Publishers, Burlington (2009)
27. Midura, D.W., Glover, D.R.: Essentials of team building: principles and practices. Human Kinetics, Champaign (2005)
28. Clark, H.H., Brennan, S.E.: Grounding in communication. Perspect. Socially Shared Cogn. **13**, 127–149 (1991)
29. Clark, H.H.: Using language. Cambridge University Press, Cambridge (1996)
30. Johansen, L.S.: Medier i hele kroppen: Når små børn bruger medier. Barn **1**, 63–78 (2010)
31. Guha, M.L., Druin, A., Chipman, G., Fails, J.A., Simms, S., Farber, A.: Mixing ideas: a new technique for working with children as design partners. In: Proceedings of Interaction Design and Children 2004: Building a Community, pp. 35–42 (2004)
32. Fails, J.A., Guha, M.L., Druin, A.: Methods and techniques for involving children in the design of new technology for children. Found. Trends ® Hum.-Comput. Inter. **6**(2), 85–166 (2012)
33. Bjerknes, G., Ehn, P., Kyng, M.: Computers and Democracy: A Scandinavian Challenge. Alebury, Aldersho (1987)

Application of Dashboards and Scorecards for Learning Models IT Risk Management: A User Experience

Ernesto Celi[✉]

Escuela Profesional de Ingeniería de Sistemas,
Universidad Nacional Pedro Ruiz Gallo, Juan XXIII 391, Lambayeque, Perú
eceli@unprg.edu.pe

Abstract. The process of education of students and professional training in themes such as IT Risk Management entails use frameworks such as Magerit or Octave. The understanding of these frameworks becomes difficult when learning sessions are short, even if we use specific software, due to the large number of elements to identify, understand, relate and apply. Using dashboards and scorecards prepared in tools like Excel helps enhance this learning. The purpose of this study was to measure the usability and effectiveness in achieving the expected outcomes, evaluating the experience of users through questionnaires type System Usability Usability Scale (SUS); and to examine the needs and expectations of users. The results show that participants learn faster the practical application of the frameworks studied, because the dashboards and scorecards allows them easier to identify its elements and its practical application.

Keywords: User experience · Ease of use · Usability · Learning · Dashboard · IT risk management

1 Introduction

Effective pedagogical practices are what create the effectiveness of learning, rather than the particular medium with which information is transmitted. This observation is often overlooked in research on technology-based courses. The designs of the studies comparing learning media are not likely to improve, and researchers should not assume that students learn best means most technologically advanced learning. They pose a question for researchers, "What combination of instructional strategies and delivery media will best produce the desired learning outcome for the intended audience?" [1].

Typically, dashboards display data integrated from multiple sources and exhibited in an easy-to-comprehend, informative graphic representation with explanatory text. This allows a reader to understand complex information in less time than it would take to read a full report... Dashboards offer convenient tools for the principal officers (typically, CEOs, CFOs, and CIOs) to track the key performance measures [2]. In a business community, a dashboard is recognized as an emerging performance management system, for example, to monitor productivity, analyze cost-effectiveness and

© Springer International Publishing Switzerland 2015
A. Marcus (Ed.): DUXU 2015, Part III, LNCS 9188, pp. 153–165, 2015.
DOI: 10.1007/978-3-319-20889-3_15

improve customer satisfaction [3]. Managing strategic risk is one of the most challenging aspects of an executive's job [4].

Education level seems to be a factor in the likelihood of trainees to excel when using computer technology in their respective training programs. However, education may or may not be a factor in the success of trainees when using a computer-based dashboard. Scorecards and dashboards are meant to be tools that help maintain data, identify trends, predict outcomes and strategize, but there exist very few empirical studies regarding the usability of a dashboard [5].

Usability relates to how easily a user is able to use a system or tool, how easy it is for the user to effectively and efficiently achieves goals with the system or tool and how satisfied the user feels while using the system or tool [6, 7]. In regard to how educated a user is, education level may either positively or negatively affect the usability that a user perceives [5].

In learning IT Governance issues, especially IT Risk Management, to understand its practical application, involves knowing frameworks like COBIT, Magerit, Octave, etc., which abound in concepts, catalog items, controls, formulas and other theoretical dimensions. This means that often understand the practical application of these frameworks is not an easy task. Use specific software can also lead to complicate their practical learning.

This study aims to demonstrate that the use of dashboards and scorecards developed for educational purposes, in simple tools such as Excel, allow us to understand more easily the applicability of reference models, in this case related to IT Risk Management.

2 Model Risk Management IT Used

Risk governance includes the totality of actors, rules, conventions, processes, and mechanisms concerned with how relevant risk information is collected, analyzed and communicated and with how management decisions are made... Risk governance does not rely on rigid adherence to a set of strict rules, but calls for the consideration of contextual factors such as: (a) institutional arrangements (e.g., regulatory and legal framework and coordination mechanisms such as markets, incentives, or self-imposed norms); and (b) sociopolitical culture and perceptions [8].

The risk factors of converging technologies can be grouped into four categories, according to their sources: Technological (such as wireless communications, hybrid nanobiodevices, engineered and byproduct nanoparticles); Environmental (such as new viruses and bacteria, and ultrafine sand storms); Societal (such as management and communication, and emotional response); and Dynamic evolution and interactions in the societal system (including reaction of interdependent networks, and government's corrective actions through norms and regulations) [8].

The typical information-security risk assessment process commonly includes the phases of context establishment, risk identification and risk analysis. Each of these phases is usually made up of a number of activities and sub-processes. There exist a number of popular information-security risk assessment methodologies including

FRAP, CRAMM, COBRA, OCTAVE, OCTAVE-S and CORAS in use in Europe, the US and Australasia. These methodologies are widely used by industry. Though these risk-assessment methods range in their underlying activities, order and depth, they generally apply a methodology consistent with context establishment, risk identification and risk analysis [9].

OCTAVE-S was selected as an ISRA[1] methodology for study. Developed by Carnegie Mellon University and applied throughout industry, OCTAVE-S is a variant of the OCTAVE (Operationally Critical Threat and Vulnerability Evaluation) method, geared specifically for small-medium enterprises. Consistent with our literature review, the OCTAVE-S risk assessment model flows through the three phases of context establishment, risk identification and a risk evaluation coupled with an analysis of the desired risk treatment plans [9].

Magerit is a methodology promoted by the Spanish Ministry for Public Administrations. It must be used by Spanish public administrations, but it can also be used by public and private corporations [10, 11].

For this study, a model of IT Risk Management was designed with reference methodologies MAGERIT and OCTAVE-S. Figure 1 shows the model of IT Risk Management which was built as a basis for the development of dashboard.

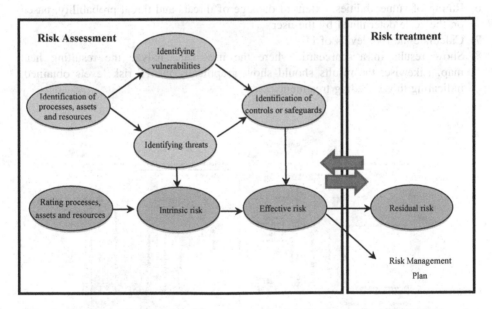

Fig. 1. Model Risk Management IT used as a reference for the construction of dashboard

---

[1] Information security risk assessment.

3 Dashboard Prototype

There is no standard design for a given computer-based performance dashboard. Because dashboards are typically designed for the sole use of only one corporation, a great variety of characteristics among dashboards is possible, and there are no formal guidelines in place for dashboard development. General principles from usability and Human-Computer Interaction can be applied to dashboards, at the discretion of their creators; however, there is no specific recommendation applicable to all varieties of dashboards that are commercially available [5] (Fig. 2).

The functionality required for the prototype dashboard was:

1. Allow selecting IT assets that will be evaluated according to their type or classification
2. Define assessment scales for IT assets, vulnerabilities, extent of damage of threats and threat probability.
3. Determine the classification of risk levels, determining from that level are not tolerable
4. Determine the criticality of IT assets selected
5. Allow selecting the threats and vulnerabilities that are related to each asset selected IT
6. Rating of vulnerabilities, extent of damage of threats and threat probability, based on the scale determined by the user
7. Calculate the risk levels of IT
8. Show results in a scorecard, where the user can analyze the resulting heat map. Likewise, the results should show graphically the IT risk levels obtained, indicating those needing treatment

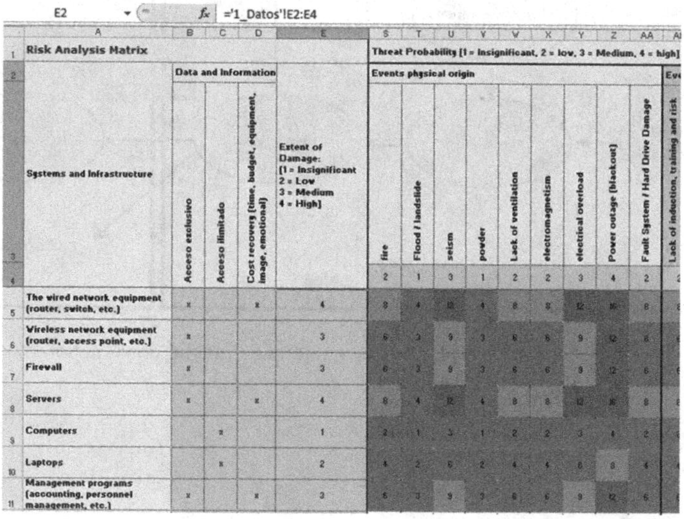

Fig. 2. View of the risk assessment through the heatmap

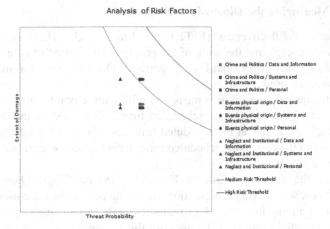

Fig. 3. Risk appetite: acceptable risks and unacceptable risks

4 Methodology

The evaluation is a metric comparison of the use of dashboards with scorecard in learning models for IT Risk Management. To this end, participants were previously trained in the theoretical framework of Model IT Risk Management used. At the time of using the dashboard, participants would have the role of users "IT Risk Evaluator" (Fig. 3).

To measure the effectiveness of construct "Use of dashboards with scorecard", it was considered the following dimensions, as relevant evaluation criteria: [D1] Ease of use (positive relationship), [D2] Effectiveness (positive relationship), [D3] Usability (positive relationship) and [D4] User experience (positive relationship). Also considered the moderating variables [M1] user education level (positive relationship) and [M2] Complexity of assessment task (negative relationship), in the relationship effectiveness of using dashboards with scorecard in learning models for IT Risk Management.

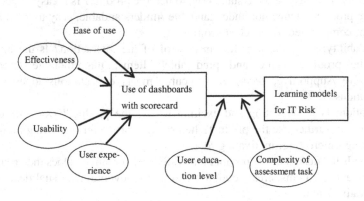

Fig. 4. The conceptual model of study

4.1 Scales Measuring the Dimensions Evaluated

The dimensions of Effectiveness (EFFE) and Ease of Use (EU) were measured immediately after completing the work of the practical application of case studies. The dimensions of Usability (USA) and User Experience (XU) were used as metrics of the prototype dashboard used.

The Effectiveness dimension was measured with a three-point scale: (1) completed the development of the case at the scheduled time, (2) needed of the assistance of teacher to complete the task at the scheduled time and (3) not successfully completed the development of the case at the scheduled time. Effectiveness was measured for each of the three case studies.

To measure the dimension Ease of Use was used the Single Question (SEQ): "Overall, This task was?". SEQ is a question that could be used to ask a user to respond immediately after attempting a task. It provides a simple and reliable way of measuring task-performance satisfaction [12]. To measure the perception of users on the domain "Ease of Use" dashboard, the question was changed to: "Overall, Using dashboard, the task of IT risk assessment was?". The Ease of Use was measured for each of the three case studies. A measuring 7-point scale was used.

Usability dimension was measured using the System Usability Scale (SUS) questionnaire [13]. The questionnaire consists of 10 items that are answered using a 5-step Likert scale reaching from "strongly disagree" to "strongly agree". It was chosen, because it is a reliable and valid measure of perceived usability [14]. The questionnaire was answered once was completed the time for each case study.

User experience dimension was measured using User Experience Questionnaire (UEQ) [15]. The user experience questionnaire contains 6 scales with 26 items in total:

1. Attractiveness: General impression towards the product. Do users like or dislike the product? This scale is a pure valence dimension. Items: annoying /enjoyable, good / bad, unlikable /pleasing, unpleasant /pleasant, attractive /unattractive, friendly / unfriendly
2. Efficiency: Is it possible to use the product fast and efficient? Does the user interface looks organized? Items: fast /slow, inefficient /efficient, impractical /practical, organized /cluttered
3. Perspicuity: Is it easy to understand how to use the product? Is it easy to get familiar with the product? Items: not understandable /understandable, easy to learn /difficult to learn, complicated /easy, clear /confusing
4. Dependability: Does the user feel in control of the interaction? Is the interaction with the product secure and predicable? Items: unpredictable /predictable, obstructive /supportive, secure /not secure, meets expectations /does not meet expectations
5. Stimulation: Is it interesting and exciting to use the product? Does the user feel motivated to further use the product? Items: valuable /inferior, boring /exiting, not interesting /interesting, motivating /demotivating
6. Novelty: Is the design of the product innovative and creative? Does the product grab user's attention? Items: creative /dull, inventive /conventional, usual /leading edge, conservative /innovative

The items are scaled from -3 to +3. Thus, 3 represents the most negative answer, 0 a neutral answer, and +3 the most positive answer... Scale values above +1 indicate a positive impression of the users concerning this scale, values below -1 a negative impression [15].

A 3-category scale was used to measure the moderating variable User Education Level: (1) student, (2) bachelor and (3) professional.

For the variable Assessment Task Complexity three case studies were developed, which were applied in the last learning session when the dashboard was used for risk assessment. Each case study had different level of complexity. The first case was of a low complexity and the third case was more complex.

4.2 Application of the Survey

The surveys were applied to finalize the development of the theme of IT Risk Management, including using the dashboard, during last session of learning (duration 3 h). In the last session of learning, 3 case studies of different complexity were assessed using the dashboard.

The surveys were applied as follows:

- 32 students in the last academic year of the Professional School of Systems Engineering - Semester 2013-II
- 37 students in the last academic year of the Professional School of Systems Engineering - Semester 2014-I
- 23 participants of the course "IT Risk Management" developed in the School of Engineers of Peru, Departmental Council of Lambayeque, developed during the months of September and October 2014
- 19 participants of the course "Audit and Risk Management IT" developed in the School of Engineers of Peru, Departmental Council of Lambayeque, developed during the months of November and December 2014

5 Results and Discussion

The information obtained in the surveys was processed with SPSS software. The results of measurements of selected variables are shown below:

For the evaluation of the dimension "Ease of Use", a survey for each case study developed was applied, using a measuring 7-point scale, where 1 - means the dashboard made them difficult task and 7 - means that the dashboard provided them work. Three case studies were developed. Each case study had different level of complexity as it rises. The first case was of a low complexity and the third case was more complex (Fig. 5).

The Table 1 shows that the dashboard facilitated the task of assessing the risks in each case. Although, increasing the complexity of the case study, the mean and median declined, but always obtained values superiors to 3.5, which is the midpoint of the metric evaluation scale used.

The Fig. 4 displays the comparative results of the means obtained for each case study evaluated with the dashboard, by User education level. It can be seen that there is more easily use the dashboard for professional.

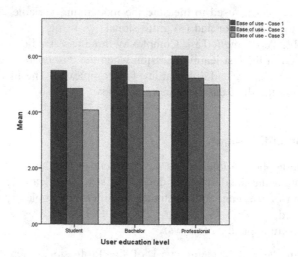

Fig. 5. Comparison of means for each case study developed by User education level

Table 1. Results of the evaluation of the dimension "Ease of Use" dashboard, for every case of studio developed.

		Ease of use - Case 1	Ease of use - Case 2	Ease of use - Case 3
N	Valid	111	111	111
	Lost	0	0	0
Mean		5.6577	4.9730	4.4054
Median		6.0000	5.0000	4.0000
Mode		6.00	5.00	4.00
Standard dev.		.75673	.59482	.83534
Variance		.573	.354	.698

Regarding the Effectiveness dimension, the processed data of the survey are shown in Tables 2 and 3. Whereas the surveyed population was 111 participants, the results show that the percentage of participants who successfully completed the task of IT risk assessment, using the dashboard, decreases when increased complexity of the case, from 73 % in the simplest case to 53.5 % in the more complex case. The opposite happened to participants who needed help the teacher, from 23.4 % in the simplest case, to 55.9 % in the more complex case.

The Table 3 shows that users with level of professional education need less help from the teacher to complete the task of assessing the risks of IT with the dashboard. The opposite happens with users with level of student education.

Table 2. Results of the evaluation of the dimension "Effectiveness" of the dashboard

		Frequency	Percentage	Valid percentage	Cumulative percentage
Effectiveness - Case 1					
Valid	completed the development	81	73.0	73.0	73.0
	needed of the assistance	26	23.4	23.4	96.4
	not successfully completed	4	3.6	3.6	100.0
	Total	111	100.0	100.0	
Effectiveness - Case 2					
Valid	completed the development	59	53.2	53.2	53.2
	needed of the assistance	48	43.2	43.2	96.4
	not successfully completed	4	3.6	3.6	100.0
	Total	111	100.0	100.0	
Effectiveness - Case 3					
Valid	completed the development	35	31.5	31.5	31.5
	needed of the assistance	62	55.9	55.9	87.4
	not successfully completed	14	12.6	12.6	100.0
	Total	111	100.0	100.0	

Table 3. Results of the evaluation of the dimension "Effectiveness" of the dashboard by User education level

		User education level		
		Bachelor	Professional	Student
		Total	Total	Total
Effectiveness - Case 1	completed the development	12	24	45
	needed of the assistance	1	5	20
	not successfully completed	0	0	4
Effectiveness - Case 2	completed the development	10	20	29
	needed of the assistance	3	8	37
	not successfully completed	0	1	3
Effectiveness - Case 3	completed the development	6	15	14
	needed of the assistance	7	13	42
	not successfully completed	0	1	13

System Usability Scale (SUS) questionnaire was used to measure the dimension Usability. In the reliability test is reached a Cronbach's alpha of .720. The 10 items of the questionnaire are stable and consistent, with an acceptable level of correlation between them, as shown in Table 4.

Table 4. Results of the reliability test of the SUS questionnaire to evaluate the Usability dimension.

Cronbach's alpha	N elements
.720	10

	Half of the scale if the item is deleted	Variance of the scale if the item is deleted	Correlation corrected item-full	Cronbach's alpha if item deleted
I think that I would like to use this dashboard frequently	29.9279	14.977	.387	.697
I found this dashboard unnecessarily complex	30.6577	13.227	.434	.689
I thought this dashboard was easy to use	30.2793	14.949	.406	.695
I think that I would need assistance to be able to use this dashboard	30.8288	12.743	.536	.667
I found the various functions in this dashboard were well integrated	29.7928	15.820	.272	.713
I thought there was too much inconsistency in this dashboard	30.6937	13.578	.524	.672
I would imagine that most people would learn to use this dashboard very quickly	29.8198	15.985	.226	.718
I found this dashboard very cumbersome/awkward to use	30.8108	13.264	.444	.687
I felt very confident using this dashboard	29.8378	15.992	.227	.718
I needed to learn a lot of things before I could get going with this dashboard	30.4324	15.429	.298	.709

The results of the evaluation of perceived usability of the dashboard are shown in Table 5. The mean total equals 3.368, equivalent to 67.35 %.

For the evaluation of the "User Experience" dimension used the User Experience Questionnaire (UEQ). The UEQ questionnaire assesses 26 items, grouped into 6 factors: Attractiveness (6 items), Efficiency (4 items), Perspicuity (4 items), Dependability (4 items), Stimulation (4 items) and Novelty (4 items). In Table 6 are shown the results the reliability tests, proving that in each factor, here stability and consistence between their items. Were obtained Cronbach's alpha greater than 0.7.

Table 5. Results of the evaluation of the perception of usability of the dashboard

	Strongly Disagree				Strongly Agree	
	1	2	3	4	5	Mean
I think that I would like to use this dashboard frequently	0	2	37	59	13	3.748
I found this dashboard unnecessarily complex	14	14	39	44	0	3.018
I thought this dashboard was easy to use	0	7	57	43	4	3.396
I think that I would need assistance to be able to use this dashboard	14	21	44	32	0	2.847
I found the various functions in this dashboard were well integrated	0	1	24	73	13	3.883
I thought there was too much inconsistency in this dashboard	2	33	41	35	0	2.982
I would imagine that most people would learn to use this dashboard very quickly	0	2	24	73	12	3.856
I found this dashboard very cumbersome/awkward to use	9	36	27	39	0	2.865
I felt very confident using this dashboard	0	2	25	73	11	3.838
I needed to learn a lot of things before I could get going with this dashboard	0	15	54	42	0	3.243

Table 6. Results of the reliability test of the user experience questionnaire (UEQ) to evaluate the User Experience dimension.

Factor	Cronbach's alpha	N elements
Attractiveness	.711	6
Efficiency	.713	4
Perspicuity	.746	4
Dependability	.702	4
Stimulation	.725	4
Novelty	.872	4

The measurement scale to evaluate the items of User Experience dimension is 7 points from −3 to +3. Table 7 shows the means obtained for each factor, showing that exceed the average of the scale used. As shown, all have been measured item greater than 0, are positive.

Table 7. Results of the evaluation of the user experience dimension

Item	Mean	Item	Mean
annoying /enjoyable	1.98	confusing /clear	2.22
bad /good	2.02	unpredictable /predictable	1.41
unlikable /pleasing	2.00	obstructive /supportive	1.28
unpleasant /pleasant	1.97	not secure /secure	1.20
unattractive /attractive	2.03	does not meets expectations /meet expectations	1.40
unfriendly /friendly	2.09	inferior /valuable	1.68
slow /fast	2.25	boring /exiting	1.67
inefficient /efficient	2.26	not interesting /interesting	1.92
impractical /practical	2.27	demotivating /motivating	1.89
cluttered /organized	2.30	dull /creative	1.18
not understandable / understandable	2.43	conventional /inventive	1.23
difficult to learn /easy to learn	2.32	usual /leading edge	1.21
complicated /easy	2.31	conservative /innovative	1.16

6 Conclusions

The results show that the process of learning methodologies, methods and tools to manage IT risk, improves with the use of dashboard with scorecard. These tools enable users to identify the model elements and, as are structured and organized, above all, allow the user to practice the theory through case study, from a perspective of prior training.

The evaluations of dimensions, "Effectiveness" and "Ease of use" of dashboard, shows that are related to the degree of knowledge that the user has the model of IT risk management, developed in the dashboard (level of education user) and with the complexity of the cases evaluated. This means that the previous user experiences about IT Risk Management improves training using dashboard.

With regard to the evaluation of the product itself, by the dimensions Usability and User Experience, shows that the dashboard generates a user-machine interaction easy to understand, friendly and efficient to support the work of IT risk assessment. However, it is pending, the development of future research to evaluate other caracterísiticas the dashboard, through the User Experience Questionnaire (UEQ), trying to improve and adapt these products to other scenarios, models and types of user. I believe that the UEQ is a tool that can still be explored to achieve these possibilities.

References

1. Joy, E., Garcia, F.: Measuring learning effectiveness: a new look at no-significant-difference findings. J. Asynchronous Learn. Netw. **4**, 33–39 (2000)

2. Ganapati, Sukumar. Use of Dashboards in Government. Fostering Transparency and Democracy Series. (2011)
3. Eckerson, W.W.: Performance Dashboards: Measuring, Monitoring, and Managing Your Business, 2nd edn. Wiley, Hoboken (2010)
4. Ballou, B., Heitger, D., Donnell, L.: Creating effective dashboards. Financ. Strateg. **91**, 27–32 (2010)
5. Grant, A., Moshyk, A., Diab, H., Caron, P., Lorenzi, F.D., Bisson, G.: Integrating feedback from a clinical data warehouse into practice organization. Int. J. Med. Inform. **75**(3–4), 232–239 (2006)
6. Hartson, H., Andre, T., Williges, R.: Criteria for evaluating usability evaluation methods. Inter. J. Hum. Comput. **15**, 145–181 (2003)
7. ISO: Ergonomic requirements for office work with visual display terminals - Part 11: Guidance on usability (1988)
8. Roco, M.: Possibilities for global governance of converging technologies. J. Nanopart. Res. **10**, 11–29 (2008)
9. Shedden, P., Smith, W., Scheepers, R., Ahmad, A.: Towards a knowledge perspective in information security risk assessments – an illustrative case study. In: ACIS 2009 Proceedings. Paper 96. In 20th Australasian Conference on Information Systems. Melbourne. (2009)
10. García, D. Fernández, A.: Effective methodology for security risk assessment of computer systems. Int. J. Comput. Inf. **7**(8), 440–447 (2013). http://waset.org/Publication/16113
11. MAGERIT – versión 3.0 - Methods of Analysis and Risk Management Information Systems. Ministry of Finance and Public Administration: Madrid (2012)
12. Gong, L. Adding software downloading tasks to LEGO-based assembly simulators for on-site training (2014)
13. Brooke, J.: SUS - A quick and dirty usability scale. In: Jordan, P.W., Thomas, B., Weerdmeester, B.A., McClelland, A.L. (eds.) Usability Evaluation in Industry, pp. 189–194. Taylor and Francis, London (1996)
14. Bangor, A., Kortum, P.T., Miller, J.T.: Determining what individual SUS scores mean: adding an adjective rating scale. J. Usability Stud. **4**(3), 114–123 (2009)
15. Rauschenberger, M., Schrepp, M., Pérez Cota, M., Olschner, S., Thomaschewski, J.: Efficient measurement of the user experience of interactive products. How to use the user experience questionnaire (UEQ). Example spanish language version. Int. J. Artif. Intell. Interact. Multimed **2**(1), 39–45 (2013)

Mapping Metaphors for the Design of Academic Library Websites

Ming-Hsin Phoebe Chiu(⌧)

Graduate Institute of Library and Information Studies,
National Taiwan Normal University, Taipei, Taiwan
phoebechiu@ntnu.edu.tw

Abstract. Internet has changed the way people acquire and consume information. In the academic setting, students turn to the library websites in the stead of visiting the library for their information needs. Using metaphor in the design of library website creates a resemblance that is grounded sensorily, psychologically, and conceptually on the physical library. This study aims to identify the analogies that connect the library website elements to the real-life library experience. Organizational, functional, visual, and textual metaphors elicited from the participating library users may provide an integrative design construct that incorporates real-life library experience into the design of library website.

Keywords: Metaphor design · Metaphor · Academic library website · Usability

1 Background

Most library users perceive library as an authority in hosting and providing intellectual and cultural enrichment. They have already developed a conceptualization of what a library is like. The Reading-For-All civic engagement effort, further elaborates the concept of a "place for reading". Independent bookstores, cozy coffee shops, restaurants, are all becoming favorite places to read, in addition to the libraries. This change inevitably increases general public standards and attitudes toward reading places and the atmosphere.

Internet has changed the way people acquire and consume information. In the academic setting, students turn to the library website in the stead of visiting the library for their information needs. Library website, thus, becomes an one-stop-shop for university students when it comes to information needs for academic purposes. The usability and user experience of the library website therefore become a top priority in achieving quality information services. Using metaphor in the design of library website creates a resemblance that is grounded visually, sensorily, psychologically, and conceptually on the physical library. It is a useful technic of design, especially for those who may be frequent library users, but are novice website users.

Metaphor is a fundamental cognitive competence and is pervasive in everyday life [1], which can also be regarded as the concepts, terms, and images by which and through which information is easily recognized, understood, and remembered [2]. In this study, metaphor is reasoned as conceptual rather than linguistic metaphor, with

A. Marcus (Ed.): DUXU 2015, Part III, LNCS 9188, 166–172, 2015.
DOI: 10.1007/978-3-319-20889-3_16

which mapping from a source domain to the target domain represents the interaction between two domains [3]. It has been widely discussed and utilized in the design of user interface in the Web environment. It is proved to be effective when designer take an unfamiliar domain and utilize its characteristics to find similarities and differences between it and the unfamiliar domain, so that an analogy can be created to minimize the sense of unfamiliarity and unknown. This study aims to identify the analogies that connect the library website elements to the real-life library experience. Organizational, functional, visual, and textual metaphors elicited from the participating library users may provide an integrative design construct that incorporates real-life library experience into the design of library website.

2 Study Design

In this study, a series of search tasks were designed to engage 14 undergraduate and 16 graduate students, to interact with various library services. These students, all frequent library service users who went to the university library or used the library services at least three times a week, were solicited into the study through research team members' social network as well as a call-for-participation invitation posted on several universities' bulletin board systems (BBS) based in Taiwan. Information on the participants' academic background, degree status, and frequent use of library services are provided in Table 1.

Table 1. Research participant's academic ground, degree status, and frequent use of library services.

#	Academic Background	Degree Status	Frequent Use of Library Services
1	Politics	Graduate	Study, borrow/renew/reserve
2	Electrical Engineering	Graduate	Study
3	Physics	Undergraduate	E-journals, borrow/renew/reserve
4	Chinese Literature	Undergraduate	borrow/renew/reserve, multimedia resources
5	Linguistics	Graduate	borrow/renew/reserve, WebPAC, E-books, E-journals
6	Business Administration	Undergraduate	Multimedia resources, newspapers & magazines, study
7	Dental Technology	Undergraduate	Compter access
8	Dentistry	Undergraduate	E-journals
9	Dentistry	Undergraduate	E-journals, WebPAC
10	Industrial Design	Graduate	Multimedia resources, borrow/renew/reserve
11	Industrial Design	Graduate	Multimedia resources, borrow/renew/reserve
12	Industrial Design	Graduate	Multimedia resources, newspapers & magazines

(Continued)

Table 1. (*Continued*)

#	Academic Background	Degree Status	Frequent Use of Library Services
13	Information Management	Undergraduate	Multimedia resources, study
14	Chemical Engineering	Undergraduate	borrow/renew/reserve
15	Library and Information Science	Graduate	Study, borrow/renew/reserve
16	Library and Information Science	Undergraduate	Study, borrow/renew/reserve, group study room
17	Library and Information Science	Undergraduate	Study, borrow/renew/reserve, WebPAC
18	Library and Information Science	Undergraduate	Study
19	Psychology	Undergraduate	borrow/renew/reserve, WebPAC
20	Library and Information Science	Graduate	Multimedia resources, borrow/renew/reserve
21	Library and Information Science	Graduate	E-journals, WebPAC
22	Library and Information Science	Graduate	borrow/renew/reserve
23	Library and Information Science	Undergraduate	Study, study room, borrow/renew/reserve
24	Library and Information Science	Graduate	WebPAC
25	Library and Information Science	Graduate	borrow/renew/reserve
26	Ethnology	Undergraduate	Computer access
27	Library and Information Science	Graduate	Study
28	Library and Information Science	Graduate	Computer access
29	Library and Information Science	Graduate	Study
30	Library and Information Science	Graduate	Study, group study room

The search task was conducted in the academic libraries of the participants' university. The participants were first asked to observe the library designs and environment, specifically on the public use areas, such as the circulation desk, reference desk, reading room, bookshelves and collection, and overall functional layout. Then they were instructed to navigate the library website, with focus on website's looks and feel, functions, navigation, accessibility, and multimedia use. The observation activity was a critical element in the search task so that the participants were able to socialize into and experience the library and its services. Each participant was later given a list of six items to be obtained, three for physical collections, and another three for digital collections or online services. The participant was asked to search and locate the items in order to complete the tasks.

After the search tasks session, in-depth interview was followed by. Three research themes were probed: (1) What characterizes a physical space as a library? (2) What characterizes an online space as an academic library website? (3) What elements of a library website and a physical library can be related to each other? During the interview, the participants were asked to recall their library and library website experiences and describe what they found most appealing and representative in the aspects of design and atmosphere. The metaphor elicitation process allowed the participants to recall what they just experienced in the search tasks and to offer analogies to connect the website materials to the real world. Meanwhile, the researchers were able to establish mapped relationship between the sources and targets of the metaphor.

All 30 interview sessions were recorded and transcribed for data analysis. Analysis was organized around three themes: characteristics of an academic library as a physical place, characteristics of an academic library website as a virtual place, and the metaphorical linkage of the physician library that can be applied to the design of library website. Data was analyzed qualitatively with constant comparison method, by which the concepts mentioned by the participants were compared, added to, and refined into the coding schemes. For example, the concept of "consulting a research librarian" was constantly found in the interview transcripts, it was then coded as "reference interview" as one of a common activities that characterized library as a place.

3 Research Findings

This study found that most library users have already developed mental models of what a library and a library website is like. What characterizes a physical library and a library website can be perceived from social, physical, behavioral, and sensory perspectives. Table 2 lists the selected findings regarding how both entities were perceived by users of academic libraries.

Table 2. Characteristics of physical libraries and library Website

	Physical library	Library website
Social perspective	Consulting librarians; discussing with friends,	Facebook, virtual reference, welcome messages
Physical perspective	Books; Bookshelves; Computers; desks and tables	Library logo; image of the library; use of table; words of "books," "libraries," and "Information
Behavioral perspective	Reading books; using computers; finding collections	Search box; RSS
Sensory perspective	Hear (quietness); smell (smell of books)	Color schemes and color combination

The physical perspective of a library can be best represented by books, book-shelves, library furnitures (tables and chairs), and electronic security systems (gates). Students commented that the university libraries and the dorms are few places on campus where ID is checked and granted for access. Other students also mentioned the carpet and poster on the wall.

The behavioral perspective can be observed from the activities that the library users are engaged in. The most common activities are reading, using computers, searching for collections, and borrowing or returning books/collections. Students further indicated that while these activities were major reasons people went to the libraries, the surroundings remained quiet and orderly. However, these activities created a visually engaging and dynamic form of image of the library, as a place with people who were focused and with a particular purpose.

The social perspectives is best examplified by the interaction between users and librarians. The interaction is primarily non-technical and non-academic. During the interview, the participants constantly mentioned the kindness generosity, and trust-worthiness they felt when interacting with librarians. The library was also a place that provided a sense of fulfillment after leaving the libraries with some academic goals achieved. Diversity, was another concept frequently mentioned by the participants as library was one of the few places on campus where diversity was acknowledged and considered.

Lastly, the sensory perspective incorporated four out of all five senses, and they were sight, hearing, smell and touch. To the participants, a library was a place where it was quiet and respectful in conversation and interaction. Voice and sounds were managed to be minimal. The color was predominantly white with wood color furniture, creating a yellow-brown tone in interior decoration. What also distinguished a library from other types of architectural buildings was the musty smell of books, along with a light scent of wood. As to the sense of touch, the participants tended to focus on the texture of the books and the furniture, which they found smooth due to frequent use.

In this study, what the library users saw in the physical library was served as the source of the metaphor, and their perception of the library website was interpreted as the target of the metaphor. The findings identified four types of library metaphors that may be applied to library website design. Organizational metaphor, like elevator or signs in the physician library, can be applied as navigation guides or a drop-down menu in the library homepage. It is used to better organize the information on the website to facilitate efficient flow, similarly to the installation of the elevator or escalator in the libraries in order to support rapid services to the users. Another popular example of the organizational metaphor and its analogy would be the use of bookshelves in the library and the use of tables in organizing the content (See Table 3).

Functional metaphor, such as browsing the collection through bookshelves with friends, can be designed as browsing the digital items checked out by users with similar reading interests. Visual metaphor, such as color of the furniture, can be coordinated with color scheme of the library website. For example, a student mentioned the con-nection between the color of library wall and the background color of the library website, as well as the color of the furniture and bookshelves and the main color used

Table 3. Example of the source and target of organizational metaphor

Source- Bookshelves (Shih-Chien University Library)	Target- Use of Table (National Taiwan Normal University Library Website)

in the website. The student further commented that academic library websites tend to use white or light color for the background, and earth tone colors for the main scheme as this color combination blends well with the white wall and wood-framed shelves and furniture (See Table 4 for example).

Table 4. Example of the source and target of the visual metaphor

Source- White Wall (National Taiwan Normal University Library)	Target- White Background (National Taiwan University Library Website)

Textual metaphor is primarily verbal and graphical in nature, for example, the words "book," "collection," "library", and the images of "library" are found all over the website. The use of these words in the Website homepage, creates a direct linkage to the actual artifacts found in the physical libraries.

4 Implications of the Study

The results of the study suggests that library users are seeking real-life experiences in the library website, and the sensory representation that a website displays greatly influences the user experience. University students of younger generation grow up with libraries, and many of them with regular visits to browse collections. However, an academic library website is one of the most complex types of websites, as it hosts countless data in both downloadable and networked forms. To facilitate users' ability to search and retrieve information, this study suggests the strategic use metaphor in the design of the library presence in the virtual world.

The findings of the study can be developed into library website design guidelines. Findings of what characterizes a library space may be translated into the essential elements of the library website. These characteristics of what is familiar may provide an orientation and structure for users unfamiliar with the library websites. For example, the social aspects of the physical library may inspire the interactive experience by social networking and instant messaging capabilities. Quietness in the library suggests the need to avoid complicated use of sound effects in designing library website. Four types of library metaphors identify the linkage types between the sources and targets of the metaphor. Organizational, functional, visual, and textual metaphors elicited from the participating library users may provide an integrative design construct that incorporates real-life library experience into the design of library website. Some examples could be the use of white or light-color as the predominant color for Website background to mimic the wall color of the library. Also, effective alignment of the Web content and the organizational strategy can be best arranged with the use of tables, because according to the results of the study, the concept of bookshelves in the physical library can be translated into tables in the Web content design. In this case, both source domain and target domain represent a means of organizational artifacts for physical or virtual collection.

References

1. Lakeoff, G., Johnson, M.: Metaphors We Live by. University of Chicago Press, Chicago (1980)
2. Marcus, A.: Principles of effective visual communication for human-computer interfaces. In: Buxton, B., et al. (eds.) HCI-2000. Morgan Kaufman Publishers, Palo Alto (2000)
3. Lakeoff, G.: The contemporary theory of metaphor. In: Ortony, A. (ed.) Metaphor and Thought (2nd edition), pp. 202–251. CUP, Cambridge (1993)

A Holistic Approach to User Experience in the Context of an Academic Library Interactive System

Andrea Alessandro Gasparini[✉]

Department of Informatics and University of Oslo Library, Oslo, Norway
a.a.gasparini@ub.uio.no

Abstract. This paper addresses the impact the user perspective has on an interactive system, when designing for experience. The context is the introduction of a discovery tool in an academic library, where the effects of addressing the users experience (UX) are gathered in the digital and the physical space. How the UX was addressed before the introduction of this new discovery tool and how the users experience was tested afterward, will be discussed. The paper analyzes the results of a multi-folded testing of the discovery tool, including a large survey, focus groups, observations and usability testing. The main focus of this paper is on how the results may support the re-design of this system, and how the library staff made sense of the new insight gained by this approach. This new insight is also a point of entrance to look at those usability and design processes, both intensive and somehow chaotic, that influence the design for the user experiences. This holistic approach will give new insight both to the research community and to the academic libraries.

Keywords: User experience · Usability testing · Academic library search tool

1 Introduction

Addressing interactive systems is no longer only a matter of web interfaces or interacting with products [1]. Consequently it requires a holistic view of the complex ecology of users, spaces, and technologies used on a variety of platforms [2]. From interactions with products and small ubiquitous services in the world of the internet of things, to large interactive system, the user and his way of experiencing the interaction, has been the focus for the Human Computer Interaction (HCI) research milieu. Nevertheless understanding user experience in a theoretical valid way has proved to be a difficult task [3]. Some of the attributes given to this interaction range from a dynamic, contextual and personal experience [4] to more emotional perspectives [5]. A holistic approach may give a foundation to understand and address the experience users have within a complex ecology. This complexity also requires the use of multiple methods to discover tensions and synergies between the anticipated use of an interactive system and the actual user experience. Tensions may address the usual problem of the mismatch between designer's plans and ideas, and how users actually experience the results of the design process [5]. Synergies, on the other hand, address how designers

© Springer International Publishing Switzerland 2015
A. Marcus (Ed.): DUXU 2015, Part III, LNCS 9188, pp. 173–184, 2015.
DOI: 10.1007/978-3-319-20889-3_17

and staff can use the positive effects of the new insight on user needs to achieve a well-functioning interactive system. Values like empathy [6] and sense-making of this gained competence can generate more radical changes and not incremental ones [7]. The context of this research effort is an academic library, and the addressed interactive system is a discovery tool used to find and read resources the library pay for. The academic library also offers an interesting context with specific user groups and specific tasks to be performed, resulting in a unique platform to observe and understand effects in the library when changes are made in an interactive system. The ecology consists of different and well defined types of stakeholders (e.g., students, academic and library staff), and with services existing in a constraint arena (digital and physical space).

In fact libraries are often used as an arena for testing and case analysis [2, 8], and especially academic libraries are relevant, since they have to stay up to date both in regards to technology and service offered [9, 10]. When it comes to large interactive systems in libraries a change in the type of software used has occurred during the last decades, from an in-house development to purchasing off-the-shelf software or adopting Open Source software like Koha [11]. The process itself of purchasing is similar between among academic libraries [12, 13]. The process of acquiring large systems is usually performed without performing various tests with real users in advance, and is based on Request for Information (RFI) produced by committees, visiting other institutions and finally ending in a Request for Proposal (RFP), while the user experience is still not addressed. When an interactive system is introduced in the ecology of the library, the majority of user experience and usability testing are focused on the web-interfaces using different usability methods [14–21]. The holistic perspective of the user experience is often neglected, as the use of the system are performed in different contexts, both inside and outside the library, using a variety of platforms and influences other library services. In this scenario, actions derived from usability testing and usability metrics (e.g. efficiency, effectiveness, satisfaction) [22], are small adjustments of cosmetic art or functional issues of the interactive system. This paper presents a more holistic approach to the user experience where the introduction of an interactive system, is followed by a multi-folded testing, including a large survey, focus groups, observations and usability testing, and show how the library staff gained new insight, and further supported the re-design of this system taking into account both the physical and the digital space.

2 User Experience in Interactive Systems

User experience is a fluid field of research, gaining momentum from a variety of scopes, and therefore pointing out a theoretical foundation is difficult [23]. To describe the UX between users and products or services, it is possible to use attributes ranging from dynamic, contextual and subjective [4], to more emotional perspectives [5]. The latter can be described as a dimension including affect, aesthetics and enjoyments, and additional new values are among others relevance and engagement [22]. As part of this complex scene, some voices argue for and against the possibility to use metrics and values from usability to enrich UX analysis [24]. Usability metrics address values like efficiency, effectiveness, and satisfaction (ISO 9241-11), where the latter is also suggested, as a possible common value for a "person perceptions and responses"(ISO FDIS 9241-210 definition of user experience) [24].

When using a system, the interaction can be described as fluent, cognitive or expressive [1]. Fluent interaction is when the user does not need to reflect upon the task to be executed, cognitive interaction requires a learning process, while the expressive interaction emphasize the construction of a common ground where bonds are made [1]. The aforementioned values contribute to address some of the less researched factors affecting experience, like context, situation and temporality of the act [5]. The temporality of the act can then be discuss in regard to how it is consumed in time, where "an experience" is one occasion of, for instance using an emergency system, while the "experience" of login on a computer at work gives a completely different experience of interaction [1]. The "perceptions and responses" [24] of the experience changes over time as the user learn and embodies how to use an interactive system. Context and situation influences the learnability of the system. In regard to interactive systems, the effects of interaction and experience over a longer period of time probably have an impact as the user learn to use the system better and better, with or without help. This situation is assumed to influence task achievement and satisfaction of the experience [25]. Few longitudinal studies on UX have been done [22], reducing the possibility to analyze how the user experience may evolve over a longer period of time. An academic library may give a fruitful arena to conduct this type of study.

3 User Experience in a Library Interactive System

A shift has occurred in the type of services provided by libraries, from an "institutions" of knowledge with loan of paper books and helpdesk to find information as the primary task, to a place where users learn about access to quality assured information and a place to stay and work together with other students. New technologies and new forms of knowledge-based items like e-books and online databases, have made the libraries more important than before, on the other hand requiring them to be more pro-active to season based technologies [9, 10]. The use of services everywhere, has posed the library in the dilemma between either cannibalize their existing services in the physical space by moving them in to the digital one, or try to combine services from the two spaces using a UX perspective. A holistic approach that includes the two spaces, may inform how this process can be addressed, and evaluating the user experience of an interactive system may generate new insight for the library staff.

An holistic perspective on UX is usually not addressed by libraries [26], and as mentioned in the introduction the majority of the attempts has been in regards to web-interfaces (digital space), or library interiors, like signs and way finding [27] (physical space), but lack of good combination between the two spaces [28]. This article argues for an approach including both the physical and the digital space at the same time, and in doing so, combining what users do, and what users feel and expect [29].

4 The Study

4.1 Context of the Study

The context of this study is an academic library situated in a Scandinavian country. Since the beginning of the'90 this library was part of a consortia consisting of 108 research libraries sharing a large Integrated Library System (ILS). This system was a self-made solution, but failed over the years to migrate to platforms that could sustain new requirement from library users. The process of acquiring and implement to a new front-end system in 2013 was the first step toward the migration of a new ILS. The front-end system used in this study was adopted by all the libraries in the consortia, but each one had a local plan in regards in how and when implement the system. The system had a new discovery tool and similar features as the previous such as login for users where it was possible to renew book loans. Another difference between the old system and the new one was the process of ordering books and articles. In the old system the ordering form was a web page while now a login is required. Since the system was renowned cloud-based off-the-shelf software, it was only partly possible to change. Unfortunately, in this library the migration was done with little regard to the *user experience* perspective. In the physical space this academic library has different type of services, ranging from courses about information literacy, or use of library resources, to the possibility to order books from other libraries. The discovery tool, as part of the library ecology, addresses directly some of those services, affecting how users experience library services.

4.2 Methodology

After four months of use of the new discovery tool, the planning and effort of collecting UX data started. In approximately four weeks, survey, usability tests, and focus group interviews were done, while observation about the use of the physical library was gathered in two different occasions and not only during the intensive four weeks period. While the author had the overall responsibility for the theoretical anchoring, seven persons from different departments within the library, like management, web publishing, help-desk and so on, were the core project group. The project generated discussions in the library in regards to the methods used, giving a better understanding of the necessity of various efforts to gain better understanding of the user needs. Some observations of how users approached the physical library were done before and during the four weeks tests were underway. The mobile platform, often forgotten as part of the library ecology, was in this case addressed as one of the last points in the migration plan. The use of survey (quantitative data) and focus groups (qualitative data) are common in sociology studies [30], but seldom found in combination with usability test and observations.

In this study the result from the survey and the focus groups helped to inform a first re-design of the search tool and the library main web page, where the discovery tool search box was placed. Together the four methods provide a broad and deep insight and complement each other. The participant of the focus group and the usability test had to sign a consent form about the use of the collected data, while information about the use of the results was provided on the questionnaire.

4.3 User Survey

An overall of 727 answers was gathered during 3 h of work in the library departments of medicine, law, science, and humanities. The survey was short, with 3 questions, presented on paper. Library users were invited to participate in the survey when entering the library. As a motivation to participate, we announced the possibility to win an iPad mini. The questions were as follow:

1. Are you a : (a) Researcher, (b) Student, (c) University staff, (d) Other
2. Have you:

   (a) Not tested the new discovery tool
   (b) Tested the new discovery tool and still using it
   (c) Tested the new discovery tool, but using only the old one
   (d) Tested the new discovery tool and using it, but use also other search services as well
3. If you have tested the new discovery tool, how pleased are you?

The first and second questions were possible to answer with a check mark while the third was a Likert scale with a 5-point scale, from very satisfied to very unsatisfied with the discovery tool. Although the test was done during the exam period, the amount of users that had participated was adequate for our test. On the other side, the library was visited by students from other institutions and college in the city since the service declaration ensure anyone above eighteen years to be a user of this library.

4.4 Usability Tests

Using data from the questionnaire, we managed to get in contact with 10 respondents. The respondents had a good distribution of age, gender, and subjects. They were in a different stage of their study, from bachelor to Ph.D. students. The method used to gather data from the respondents were to let them "*speak aloud*" while two observers made notes of what was said and done, and a moderator was asking the questions. Been three persons could be a problem, but we saw gains by doing the test this way. Additional questions were also added, when needed, by the other observers to clarify the user comments. Usability tests have usual effectiveness, efficiency, and satisfaction as quantifiable values. The approach in this part of the study assesses satisfaction, based on how the users reacted when performing the tasks, and efficiency, if they managed to complete them. The data analysis was based on observations of what users did, and their comments. Avoiding a statically approach to the data, the focus was no longer on the instrumental value of the tested system [5].

The goal of this usability test was not only to test the efficiency and satisfaction of the discovery tool, but also if the library main web page, where the discovery tool search box was, did help the user in performing the tasks in a satisfactory manner. Using two different interfaces, with five respondents each, we expected to gain fruitful results. The first interface for the discovery tool on the library web page had various information (see Fig. 1), while the second was inspired by Google with one search field and 5 small link to other services and customized with the findings from the survey and the focus groups.

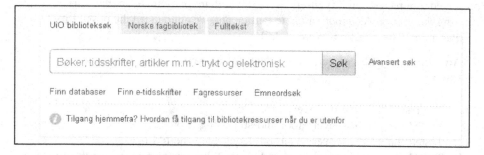

Fig. 1. First interface to the discovery tool on the library website

As a motivation for participants to enroll to the test, a reward of approximately 25$ was previously announced in the questionnaire from the aforementioned user survey, where the respondent could write an email address. The time spent was approximately 45 min, where twelve questions about how they approached our services to execute different type of tasks were used. The tasks had a clear intersection with the physical library. For instance, one of the tasks was about finding an item that we had not access at all, the results should show what they usually do, but also expectation they had in regards to the library services. Other question could be a crossover between the digital and the physical library, like finding a book and choose to get the paper version. Also access to databases or using other library resources was part of the tasks given to them. This type of questions had both effectiveness and utility in mind, while additional questions were especially focused on how the use of the discovery tool affected the use of other services, both in the physical and the digital space.

4.5   Focus Groups

The project managed to organize three focus groups with research groups from Department of Informatics (Design of Information System) with four participants, the Faculty of Law (Center for European Law) with three participants and Humanities (Greek and Latin) with five participants. As a sign of gratitude for their time, we offered a lunch. After a short introduction about the goal of the meeting, they tested the system for about 15 to 20 min, and could ask us about different functionality of the interactive system or other questions about services the library had. The whole session lasted about 2 h, which was concluded with the lunch. In addition to one questioner, two other observers were taking notes. The content of the notes was then discussed afterward, resulting in one report. We had eight open-ended questions to ensure all the topics should be covered. Even though the questions were not mandatory to follow, the discussions often touched almost all the topics using fewer. The questions dealt with issues regarding how the discovery tool was presented on the library web pages, and how the information there helped the experience and expectation of using this system. Other questions were more specific about the functionality and relevance of the results, and also addressed the intersection between the physical and digital space.

4.6   Observations

Observations were made in two phases. First in the science library, two different efforts of one hour each were made during a prior occasion [31], while the second phase was made in the Humanities and Social Sciences Library. During the sessions, observations were made of what user did when they were approaching and using the physical library. Notes and photos were taken of actions the users did. The last observation was done during the same period as the other test of this study was performed while the first two were done in conjunction with data gathering for a master thesis [31]. Results of the observations were more sensible to changes in the context than the other methods used. The last observation was done in November, a period where students are preparing for exams and the library is often overcrowded. This type of observations may have a constrained value, emphasizing the need to be triangulated with other evaluations effort.

5   Findings

5.1   User Survey

Out of 727 participants, the majority (88 %) were students. On the second question, about their use of library resources 39 % had not yet tested the new discovery tool, and only 11 % did not use or used other search services. On the last question the majority of the users of the new system were satisfied (17 % very pleased, 50 % pleased, 30 % middle), where only 3 % was partially unsatisfied and 0 % completely unsatisfied. Even the users aware of the new system were pleased with it, when 39 % had not yet tested it out after four months it went live, is a relevant observation. On the other hand, we observed a willingness explore the new discovery tool among nonusers. One of them said to us: "*I will go right away and test it*". Those findings address how the library brands and does market its services. Another relevant feedback was the naming of the interactive system, where, although the library had chosen a new name, the majority of the users opted to use in their conversations the original name of the software. A consequence of this misconception affected the possibility the library had to help users in a fruitful way since information and support web-pages used the new name. A positive side effect was the involvement of the library staff as they were given the possibility to have direct contact with the users in another context. Asking users for information was a new experience and as some of the library staff commented: "*We should do this more often*", or "*What I heard was that your colleague was happy and that this was good advertising for the tool*". As far as we know, the staff had only positive feedback from users when they were asked to participate in the survey, and using only three hours to carry out the test, the overall cost was very low.

5.2 Usability Testing

As mentioned this part of the study was focused on satisfaction and efficiency. The majority of the users fulfilled the tasks, in a similar manner. For instance, in the first interface (see Fig. 1) the tabs in the search box were not used, or very little, since they opted to use the first one, and then deal with the results. They also commented about too much information in the same search interface (see Fig. 1), and used google simple search box as an example of how a starting point for their tasks should look like. The usability testing also revealed some assumptions the library had about user behaviors, later on confirmed by the focus group. From a holistic point of view, a relevant task in the usability test was when they should find an item the library had no information about or access to. Their prompt reaction was to move theirs search into Google Scholar. From our observations during usability testing, the interaction with the system was not cognitive but had a fluent value [1]. In a more descriptive way, we can say the impression we had of their behavior was of users using the interactive system so often, so they did not reflect so much upon their action. Some of them said, in fact, that they did not need to get help or go to courses to learn how to use it. Since some of the questions were specific task to be completed the results could also be constrained to address usability problems of the service from a heuristic perspective [32], and help the further development of the service.

5.3 Focus Groups

The results from the focus groups were the richest about data and revealed the need for a clear holistic approach to the use of the interactive system and the physical library. Some participants did not know about other services the library had, like the possibility to order books or articles from other libraries in the country or abroad. Also services like library courses to learn how to use in an effective way the interactive system was unknown by some of them. Several participants stressed that their next step was to search Google if they did not find the book or articles using the library system. The discussions showed also a practice among researchers about sharing literature resources and search strategies, giving possibility of the nurture of myths about how to find relevant literature.

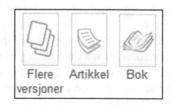

Fig. 2. Icons for book, articles and multiple versions of an item

Some of the comments had also a clear impact on the user experience even those could be characterized as usability issues. For instance the discovery tool lack of image for book covers or good icons to describe different type of materials (i.e.g. books, articles and multiple versions of an item, see Fig. 2), from a usability point of view the effectiveness is affected since a visual recognition is lacking, and in regard to experience the aesthetics of the icons gives a poor impression.

5.4   Observations

All three observations showed tasks focused users. The foremost of the users did go directly to find a computer to work on it, others to meet other students to work together. Very few did go directly to the bookshelves. Other observations confirm [9] that student start their search for literature from the digital space. During the observations we also realized that this type of information shows only users outside the entrance of the library and their behavior inside. This type of observations does not give insight in why other users do not visit the library at all. Since one of the periods was during exams, the queue outside the library before opening hours was quite long, making the library very crowd for the rest of the day, and causing students to sit in every corner, and also outside the main door (see Fig. 3).

Fig. 3. Students outside the library during exams period

6   Discussion

The findings support an understanding were the library users had a clear idea of the task they had to do when using the interactive system. In the same way users are using the physical library and know they will get help to find any type of resources, they have the same expectation when using the library interactive system. This anticipation has an impact on how the experience will unfold when the discovery system is used. To grasp this dislocated experience, an holistic approach is needed, and factors like context, situation and temporality of the act [5] can be addressed and gives then an added value when the interactive system is designed, or needs to be re-designed, as in this case. The temporality of the user experience in the library is represented by an antecedent expectation of using the system, then an experience of using it, and finally the experience afterward. Our findings also show that users do not reflect upon the use of the library interactive system, this is in line with a description of a fluent interaction [1]. In doing so, the cognitive interaction is absent reducing the possibility to learn how to use the system in a better way. We have also denoted in our case the difficulty the interactive system has to help the user further to find their way to the physical space to solve their unsolved tasks. The consequences may be "an experience" perceived negatively, an antecedent expectation of the system not accomplished, resulting in users migrating to other systems, where an opposite experience could give loyal users.

The result from the survey describe a picture where users say they are pleased with the system, while the experience is more nuanced when we take into account the feedbacks from the participants of the usability test and focus group, where they had problems to find other services the library had and could then solve theirs tasks. This dichotomy implies some difficult questions, like how to communicate to the user in a holistic way the services the library provide, or how to visualize services starting in the digital space and ends in the physical, like realizing the need for help when using the discovery tool and then participating in courses provided by the library. This view of experience may have the potential to impose a non-instrumental understanding of the interactive system, and prevent us from characterizing the experience as based on product features [33].

For the Academic libraries an issue affecting the user experience is the tension between the willingness the library has to develop and adopt a user friendly system and the complexity of giving an arena where users can learn how to use and search quality checked literature. This tension is best illustrated by a comment from one participant of the focus group: "If I can't find it using the library systems, the next step is Google Scholar". While the library has several different services that may help the user solve a task in an easy way, the question then is how the library shall inform the users in a proper way. When 39 % of the respondents had never tested the system, the library should address how the services are branded both in the physical and digital space.

7   Conclusion

In this paper, we have argued for a holistic view when designing for experience in an interactive system, where the digital and physical space has to be taken into account. This approach seems to avoid an instrumental understanding of the service, focusing more on the experience the user has when using the system. Antecedent expectations are also relevant for how the users experience unfold and will affect future behaviors. To achieve this holistic insight scholar need to investigate both the digital and the physical space using multi-folded testing methods. Better visibility of library services and a tactful branding are necessary but have to be addressed as part of the complex ecology the library is. A knowledge-based development of services is mandatory, where the library has to react to findings on the behavior of their primary users. This effort may help introduce a culture in the library in regards to performing multi-folded tests to discover user needs and at the same time give library staff insight and new knowledge.

References

1. Forlizzi, J., Battarbee, K.: Understanding experience in interactive systems. In: Proceedings of the 5th Conference on Designing Interactive Systems: Processes, Practices, Methods, and Techniques, pp. 261–268, New York, USA (2004)
2. Nardi, B.A., O'Day, V.L.: Information Ecologies: Using Technology with Heart. MIT Press, Cambridge (1999)
3. Forlizzi, J., Ford, S.: The building blocks of experience: an early framework for interaction designers. In: Proceedings of the 3rd Conference on Designing Interactive Systems: Processes, Practices, Methods, and Techniques, pp. 419–423, New York, USA (2000)
4. Law, E.L.-C., Roto, V., Hassenzahl, M., Vermeeren, A.P.O.S., Kort, J.: Understanding, scoping and defining user experience: a survey approach. In: Proceedings of the SIGCHI Conference on Human Factors in Computing Systems, pp. 719–728, New York, USA (2009)
5. Hassenzahl, M., Tractinsky, N.: User experience - a research agenda. Behav. Inf. Technol. 25(2), 91–97 (2006)
6. Gasparini, A.: Perspective and use of empathy in design thinking. In: ACHI, The Eight International Conference on Advances in Computer-Human Interactions, pp. 49–54 (2015)
7. McQuaid, H.L., Goel, A., McManus, M.: When you can't talk to customers: using storyboards and narratives to elicit empathy for users. In: Proceedings of the 2003 International Conference on Designing Pleasurable Products and Interfaces, pp. 120–125, New York, USA (2003)
8. Sharp, H., Rogers, Y., Preece, J.: Interaction Design : Beyond Human-Computer Interaction. Wiley, Chichester (2007)
9. Culén, A., Gasparini, A.A.: Find a book! unpacking customer journeys at academic library. In: ACHI 2014, The Seventh International Conference on Advances in Computer-Human Interactions, pp. 89–95 (2014)
10. Culén, A.L., Gasparini, A.A.: Student driven innovation: designing university library services. In: CENTRIC 2013, The Sixth International Conference on Advances in Human oriented and Personalized Mechanisms, Technologies, Services, pp. 12–17 (2013)
11. Breeding, M.: Open source ILS gains ground with academic libraries. Smart Libr. Newsl. 28, 2 (2008)
12. Breeding, M.: The elusive cost of library software. Comput. Libr. 29(8), 28–30 (2009)
13. Breeding, M.: Helping you buy: electronic resource management systems, Comput. Libr., vol. 28, no. 7, pp. 6–8,10,12–14,16–18,94,96, Aug 2008
14. Battleson, B., Booth, A., Weintrop, J.: Usability testing of an academic library Web site: a case study. J. Acad. Librariansh. 27(3), 188–198 (2001)
15. Fagan, J.C., Mandernach, M.A., Nelson, C.S., Paulo, J.R., Saunders, G.: Usability test results for a discovery tool in an academic library. Inf. Technol. Libr. 31(1), 83–112 (2012)

16. Foster, A.K., MacDonald, J.B.: a tale of two discoveries: comparing the usability of summon and EBSCO discovery service. J. Web Librariansh. **7**(1), 1–19 (2013)
17. Nichols, A., Billey, A., Spitzform, P., Stokes, A., Tran, C.: Kicking the tires: a usability study of the primo discovery tool. J. Web Librariansh. **8**(2), 172–195 (2014)
18. Buchanan, S., Salako, A.: Evaluating the usability and usefulness of a digital library. Libr. Rev. **58**(9), 638–651 (2009)
19. Hartson, H.R., Shivakumar, P., Pérez-Quiñones, M.A.: Usability inspection of digital libraries: a case study. Int. J. Digit. Libr. **4**(2), 108–123 (2004)
20. Jeng, J.: Usability assessment of academic digital libraries: effectiveness, efficiency, satisfaction, and learnability. Libri **55**(2–3), 96–121 (2008)
21. Lynema, E., Lown, C., Woodbury, D.: Virtual browse: designing user-oriented services for discovery of related resources. Libr. Trends **61**(1), 218–233 (2012)
22. Bargas-Avila, J.A., Hornbæk, K.: Old wine in new bottles or novel challenges: a critical analysis of empirical studies of user experience. In: Proceedings of the SIGCHI Conference on Human Factors in Computing Systems, pp. 2689–2698, New York, USA (2011)
23. Obrist, M., Roto, V., Vermeeren, A., Väänänen-Vainio-Mattila, K., Law, E.L-C., Kuutti, K.: In search of theoretical foundations for UX research and practice. In: CHI 2012 Extended Abstracts on Human Factors in Computing Systems, pp. 1979–1984, New York, USA (2012)
24. Bevan, N.: What is the difference between the purpose of usability and user experience evaluation methods. In: Proceedings of the Workshop UXEM 2009, Uppsala, Sweden (2009)
25. Finstad, K.: The usability metric for user experience. Interact. Comput. **22**(5), 323–327 (2010)
26. Bell, S.J.: staying true to the core: designing the future academic library experience. Portal Libr. Acad. **14**(3), 369–382 (2014)
27. Schmidt, A., Etches, A.: User Experience (UX) Design For Libraries. Facet Pub, London (2012)
28. Somaly Kim Wu and Donna Lanclos: Re-imagining the users' experience. Ref. Serv. Rev. **39**(3), 369–389 (2011)
29. Wright, P., McCarthy, J., Meekison, L.: Making sense of experience. In: Blythe, M.A., Overbeeke, K., Monk, A.F., Wright, P.C. (eds.) Funology, pp. 43–53. Kluwer Academic Publishers, Norwell, MA, USA (2004)
30. Morgan, D.L.: Focus groups. Annu. Rev. Sociol. **22**, 129–152 (1996)
31. Edvartsen, Y.: Kan jeg låne en bok med mobiltelefonen?. University of Oslo, Oslo (2013)
32. Nielsen, J., Molich, R.: Heuristic evaluation of user interfaces. In: Proceedings of the SIGCHI Conference on Human Factors in Computing Systems, pp. 249–256, New York, USA (1990)
33. McNamara, N., Kirakowski, J.: Functionality, usability, and user experience: three areas of concern. Interact. **13**(6), 26–28 (2006)

Antique School Furniture, New Technological Features Needs

Andreia Gomes[1(✉)], Ernesto Filgueiras[2,3], and Luís Lavin[2]

[1] University of Beira Interior UBI, Covilhã, Portugal
andreia.sofiagomes@hotmail.com
[2] LabCom - Laboratory of Online Communication UBI, Covilhã, Portugal
ernestovf@gmail.com, lavin@ubi.pt
[3] Centre for Architecture, Urban Planning and Design (CIAUD),
Lisbon, Portugal

Abstract. Question: Over the years the demands of teaching design contributed to the differentiation of school furniture, giving it a specific and distinctive character from the traditional classrooms. This fact is mainly due to the tools used by the students in the activities performed in this kind of classes. However, the material used by the students and the teaching methods have undergone significant changes over the years. A recent example is the replacement of traditional design methods by computer-aided ones as a consequence of the rapid evolution of technology. The generation of students now entering higher education, millennium generation, grew up with the presence of technology and the internet, so the pencil and paper are for previous generations as the computer is for millennial. Today's furniture does not show signs of this evolution, thus still features characteristics of the beginning of the twentieth century. This absence of modern adapted furniture forced schools to provide supplementary material to compensate the problems caused by constant changes. **Purpose:** It is part of this article's goals to perform a morphological and evolutionary analysis of the products with which the students interact directly. The analysis of some reference situations, such as the environment in school study rooms and in the classrooms, will allow students to identify their needs. In order to achieve our goal, data will be collected through observation techniques, surveys and morphological analysis of the current and antique furniture.

Keywords: School furniture · Observation method · Morphological product methodology analysis · Conceptual product design

1 Introduction

The present study aims at exposing the students' problems and needs in what design is concerned regarding the inadequate school furniture, taking into account the students' needs in terms of technological resources.

Assuming that there is an evident lack of scientific data, as well as of ergonomic studies that evaluate classroom activities and promote suggestions to the design of a more efficient and adequate furniture, both to the present and future realities, it is

© Springer International Publishing Switzerland 2015
A. Marcus (Ed.): DUXU 2015, Part III, LNCS 9188, pp. 185–196, 2015.
DOI: 10.1007/978-3-319-20889-3_18

necessary to evaluate the classroom environment so that it is possible to understand the main problems regarding the use of technology in the existing furniture.

Society's ability to adapt to the fast technological evolution é available and accepted in a natural way and laptops have invaded the market. In Portugal, in 2010, 97 % of the population with higher education uses the computer, which shows the importance that it has today in higher education [1]. The generation which is about to enter the higher education, millennial generation, grew up surrounded by technological equipments and with the internet in their daily life, thus making the computer an essential tool of study, as the pencil and the paper were to the previous generations. So, it is essential to adapt the personal computer to the academic environment as an essential work tool that leads to the need of change in many other school equipments, such as school furniture. Furniture equipments didn't follow this change and still present obsolete characteristics from the beginning of the XXth century, and so they don't assume the use of new work tools in higher education.

2 Morphological and Evolutionary Analysis of School Furniture

In order to make an adequate contextualization of the school furniture evolution, as well as the reasons why these changes occurred, a study was developed focusing on the analysis of morphological school furniture that presents a direct interaction with the students of design.

In the XIIth century, the Christian school appeared which main goal was to teach people, who wanted to follow a clerical path, to learn and write. The only necessary furniture was a beach and a table, so that they could rewrite the holy texts. Later, in public schools, students, that didn't have any school furniture available, could have access to benches if they paid for them.

Until the XIXth century, school furniture didn't suffer a significant evolution, when the architects, together with health and education professionals' worries regarding the well being and hygiene of students, developed new furniture ideas in which ergonomic cares, aesthetic and new materials were an obligatory request [2] A network including people from different areas of knowledge with the same goal, to change the school environment, against old ideologies, was born. The worries regarding the construction of school furniture suffered changes and demands, such as simple, easy and low-cost building, were no longer the most important. These changes were supported by the appearance of new manufacturing methods and materials, such as iron, which had a major industrial impact in the furniture field in the 1880's, and wood.

In the 1880's, in France, the instructions for the production of school furniture recommended the production of desks for one or two students, preferring individual ones.

The furniture was made of wood and iron, but this tendency changed throughout the XXth century, when the appearing of tubular steel and aluminium appeared. A resistant material and, as with iron, can be associated with wood and can be covered, this material allowed the creation of individual, independent and resistant desks with an objective, functional, light, convenient, hygienic and practical language [3], that rapidly reached schools throughout Europe. This way, furniture should be practical, light, washable, lifelong and with rounded edges, to avoid accidents, adapting to the anthropometry of the child and not on the other way around, characteristics sustained by Maurice Barret and Dr. Eitner [4, 5].

The same way the tubular steel in the 1930's decade changed the industry, in the beginning of the XXIst century plastic and polyester fibers invaded the markets and industries. The awakening of industries to recent technologies associated to the appearance of plastic and to the new production methods that it allows, meant a revolution, in what the creation of furniture components is concerned, considering aesthetic characteristics, keeping the functionality of the furniture of the end of the XXth century.

Concluding, we can confirm that, except for the materials, the evolution of school furniture is stagnated for several centuries, for it is still possible to find, in several schools, furniture from the XIX's century, with no worry regarding the technological evolution of the last years. We showed that during the last years the evolution is not significant and we are facing stagnation in the furniture build for schools.

3 Problems Associated with School Furniture

Children spend about 30 % of their day at school and consequently the time using school furniture is excessive. During this time, students between 13 and 16 years old are sat, on average 78,7 % of time, even though this data varies according to the different countries [6]. Children positioning during classes makes them be on the same position for long periods of time, several times inadequately, which causes headaches, throatlatches, less concentration, neck and back muscular contraction, back discomfort and pain (the last visible among 28 % to 50 % of teenagers), that are mainly caused by the inadequacy of school furniture which is not prepared to allow postural variation [7–15].

Several studies have identified poorly achieved school furniture projects, as a relevant aspect to the high incidence of muscular and skeleton injuries among the school aged community. These problems can be caused by the incompatibility between the furniture and anthropometrical attitudes from the users that lead to back pain and muscular and skeleton discomfort, which can bring about problems both in short and long term, taking into account that back pain is today a serious health problem [13, 16–18].

Linton et al. [19] designed schools taking into account Comfort and ergonomic worries, achieving a positive feedback in the experimental evaluation of furniture regarding muscular and skeleton symptoms and comfort. The result shows that furniture design is a multidimensional issues. It is also necessary that work environment is planned to promote changes of several positions, an adequate set of desk and chair is essential, with a plain ergonomically projected surface, considering the range of vision. In sedentary tasks, as working on the computer, there is a limited variation in posture and limited muscular activity, comparing the muscular activity required in tasks which involve paper and pen [20], both in children and adults.

Postural activities are more neutral and systematic in the use of computer than in the use of paper [21], so it is advisable to alternate between these two types of activities.

These problems can increase with the use of the computer that nowadays, has a strong influence in what cognitive and social levels of its users are concerned.

We can conclude that school furniture has a great influence in the appearance of pain symptoms in teenagers.

As Mandal [22], we recommend that the school furniture design project is reviewed and updated considering the increase of information technology in school context [23].

4   User Evaluation of Real Environment

Taking into account the already described needs, there is a need to evaluate the users' opinion as well as their interaction with the furniture in the classroom. There is also the essential need to adjust the furniture to the users, so it is important to make a rigorous and detailed observation of users regarding their activities and tasks and the time spent on them.

A study was developed through the inquiring of real users in order to identify the problems found in classrooms and work environments of design courses in higher education Portuguese institutions. So, to obtain data, it was necessary to use two methodological techniques, firstly to evaluate the design students' opinion, through questionnaires, secondly, to see and analyze the users' interaction with equipments and environments. The survey contained 5 groups of questions, the first one containing the characterization of the sample, the second regarding social questions, the third containing questions about the classroom environment, the fourth including questions about the interaction with equipments, and the last referring questions about available infrastructures. To answer the survey, present or previous students from the 1st or 2nd cycles of studies from Design courses, were selected. The study included 78 students, 54 female, aged between 19 and 47 years old (average age 24,28 and standard deviation 5,73). This number included answers from several Portuguese institutions, mainly from the University of Beira Interior, University de Lisbon e Polytechnic Institute of Castelo Branco, from the Industrial Design, fashion Design and Multimedia Design courses (Fig. 1).

Design courses lectured at Portuguese higher education institutions have different teaching methodologies. Curricular units included in the Study Plans are divided into

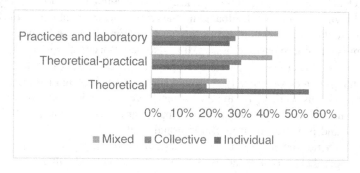

Fig. 1. Graphic 1- Work in different disciplines

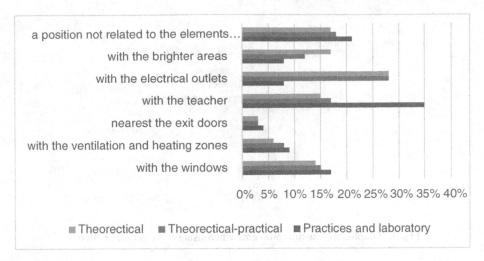

Fig. 2. Graphic 2 - Influence of the physical environment from the positioning in the classroom

theoretical (T), theoretical-practical (TP) and laboratory practice (LP). According to the type of classes, the work demanded is different. By analyzing the graph below representing the answers to the survey, we can see that in theoretical classes the individual work is significant and privileged, while in theoretical-practical and laboratory practice lessons the work focuses on both individual and group work.

Students' needs in theoretical classes are different from the needs that practical and laboratory lessons demand. Theoretical classes demand the student more attention during more time, while in practical classes the demands are associated with working elements in the classroom. Taking into account the analysis of the following graphic, we can say that in theoretical classes the physical environment does not interfere in the choice of the placement and that the teacher is, for the majority of the surveyed, the most important aspect in the what the choice of placement is concerned (Fig. 2).

In theoretical-practical and laboratory practice classes the demands are mainly connected with the elements within the classroom. The most important demands for the majority of the surveyed are to choose places near light, windows and electric plugs.

The reason that leads to the choice of positioning near electrical plugs is shown in the graphic below, in which the main problems in the use of this equipment are presented. The aspect that connects the previous graphic data and the following is evident when the surveyed agree that plugs available in the classrooms are not sufficient as the ones that exist are too far. The need to use electric plugs is related to the use of the computer in today's classes, as it has been referred throughout this study, devices that need refilling while on use.

These choices, made by the students, are a consequence of the activities demanded in each class. Many classes need a practical component in which the use of computers is essential, and even though some classrooms are prepared to CAD classes, students prefer to use their own laptop, 93 % of the surveyed claimed they used their own laptop / tablet, even when they have traditional computers available in the classroom. To use

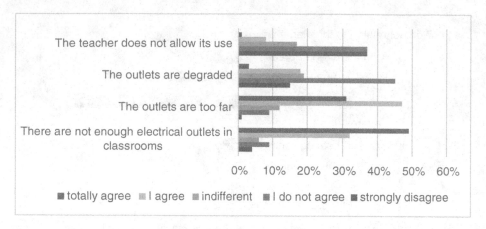

Fig. 3. Graphic 3- Existing problems when using the electrical outlets

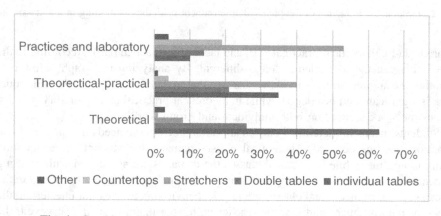

Fig. 4. Graphic 4- What kind of work tables are prevalent in classrooms?

their own computer, the possibilities of using a pointing device are relevant, because each student has its own working method that can influence the available desk space as well as the use of a laptop base (Fig. 3).

The differences between the type of classes are not just the ones referred previously, because the classrooms' furniture also varies according to the needs of each subject. The most important sets of school furniture in the classroom is the chair and desk on, and according to the analysis of the results obtained in the survey, related to the work desks, we can prove those differences.

The following graphic shows that in the classrooms where theoretical subjects are lectured the individual (68 %) and double (26 %) desks prevail, in theoretical-practical classes board desks (40 %) and individual desks (35 %) prevail, while in laboratory practice the board desks and the workbenches are the most used (Fig. 4).

The existence of different school desk models is related with the necessary space for each student in each subject. Although there are already school desks that allow

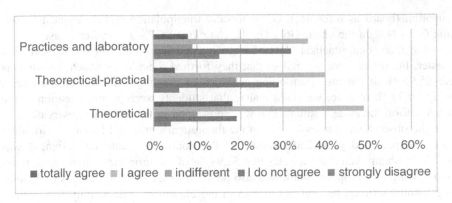

Fig. 5. Graphic 5 - The work surface has enough space?

students to have more space to fulfil their tasks, this is space is not always adequate to the activities to perform and to the necessary elements to the do them. When asked if the work surface has enough space to place the materials used during the class, the option with more answers was the one that indicates agreement, no matter the type of class. In what laboratory classes are concerned, 47 % answered "I don't agree" and "I totally disagree". In what theoretical-practical classes is concerned, to 35 % answered negatively (Fig. 5).

Regarding school furniture the main demands are related to mobility, transportation and lightness, but these are not always followed, and as a consequence school desks are not always movable due to their characteristics.

Classrooms do not always have the same layout, and it can vary according to the needs of each activity. To the question "Is it possible to change the disposal of the desks in the classrooms whenever that is necessary?", 19 % answered that it is possible in "all the classrooms", 35 % answered "in more than half of the classrooms", 47 % answered negatively: "in no classroom", "on less than half of the classrooms" and "on half of the classrooms".

So that the credibility of the answers is checked and to obtain data that can be used as a reference, regarding the use of study environments and classrooms by students, and to allow the identification of the needs and the components that need furniture adapting, indirect observation techniques were used, through the video recording of classes, in three different design schools in Portugal.

Recording took place in classes of the 1st cycle of studies, at the University of Lisbon – Architecture University (UL-AU), at the University of Beira Interior (UBI) and at the Superior Institute of Applied Arts of the Polytechnic Institute of Castelo Branco, in the courses of Design (UL-AU), Industrial Design (UBI) and Interior and Equipment Design (ESART-IPCB).

After obtaining all the images, indirect observation analysis took place with the help of a computer iSEE, so that the results obtained are more conclusive.

To obtain the data it was necessary to create a list of requirements that allowed the definition of the categories of observation that represent the patterns of interaction of the students in the classroom, that are: G1 – Mainly students' actions; G2 – Classroom occupation (board as reference); G3 – Specific manipulation; G4 – Atypical behaviours; G5 – Not on the chair; G6 – On the chair (sat); G7 – Computer in use.

In the theoretical-practical class of Drawing and representation II, 1st year, 2nd semester, the desks were ordered so that they formed a circle, in which the students were 45,95 % of the time performing activities of drawing while sat on the chairs. During 29,73 % of time, we could realize that students were paying attention to the teacher, sat on the same positions that were presented in the previous observation.

In the observation that took place in the theoretical - practical lesson of Moulding and Prototypes, 2nd year, 2nd semester of the course of Industrial design, it was possible to obtain data that indicates that 52,94 % of the time the students took notes without using the computer, but it was also possible to see that the students took notes using manual writing, but moving around in the classroom, this activity was seen in 11,76 % of the time. In the time corresponding to 23,53 % of class time, the students were seen talking among themselves, in selected places, once again, on the sides of the classroom.

In the observation of the recorded data collected in the theoretical-practical class of Product Design III, from the course of Industrial Design, with students from the 3rd, during the first semester, we saw that most of the time (15,79 %) the students are moving randomly. This behaviour was noticed in significant periods of time that occurred during the class activities when the use of the laptop was noticed on the desks near the sides of the classroom, the described observation was seen in 10,53 % of the time. The time that corresponds to 13,16 % of the class time was spent paying attention to the teacher, occupying the same places from the previous observation, that is to say on the sides.

In the observation of the recorded data collected in the theoretical-practical of systems of digital representation in design, with students from the 1st year, it was possible to see two types of different activities that occupied most of the time.

The first one that occupied students during 55 % of the time corresponds to the following selection of categories, in which we can notice that most part of the time the students are paying attention to the teacher while using the laptop. The second main activity, occupying more than 11 % of the class, in which the students talked among themselves, without changing their places in the classroom, using simultaneously the laptop.

In the observation of the theoretical-practical of Design IV, from the 2nd year, we noticed several main activities in the classroom. These include the following observation in iSEE software, that corresponds to 37,83 % of the class time, in which the students are in spread groups in the classroom, talking about the observations they are doing about the object they are manipulating. The same activity was verified, in 15,10 % of the class, but without the manipulation of objects. As well as the presence of the laptop being used by the majority of the students during the discussion activities. In some situations, it was noticed that the students from their places pay attention to the teacher.

The observation related to the theoretical-practical class of Design IV, from the 3rd year students, noticed that most of the class time students gathered in grouped desks, spread around the classroom, to talk among themselves, while manipulating personal objects, helped by the laptop. This activity was seen in 30,49 % of the class time. It was possible to observe that students keep at the same desks during the whole class, only changing their activity, while talking with colleagues and paying attention to the teacher.

5 Results

At this stage of the study, two methods of collecting were used.

The use of a second method helped to complete information from the surveys, because not always the collected data, using the questionnaire method correspond to the reality.

By comparing the already analyzed data of the two observation methods, allows us to achieve conclusions more accurately.

Concerning the areas of the classrooms that are preferred by the students, to attend classes, it was possible to see that in TP and LP classes the data is contradictory. In the questionnaires the questioned indicated a preference for the centre of the classroom, but in the observation (both direct and indirect) the values indicate a preference for the sides of the classrooms.

After analyzing the recorded data from some classes, it was possible to conclude that this situation happens because the students need access to electrical plugs, because in most of the classes the laptop is an essential work tool.

In what the space of work, in the desk surface, is concerned, it was possible to see that these are occupied by personal items, as schoolbags, coats, umbrellas, among others, that occupy a considerable space of the work surface. Those elements shouldn't be placed on that surface, but the lack of lockers to place personal objects in most of the classrooms makes this event a students' routine. Besides personal objects, it also necessary to have space to place working material, as the computer and its accessories (mouse, cooling devices, etc.), writing, drawing and painting material, as well as material used in the construction of moulds. There is a need to create areas in which students can place their personal things on the desk, so that it is possible to have a wider working area.

In theoretical classes, as referred throughout this document, the needs and the students' activities are very different from those that occur on TP and LP classes because there are different desks.

6 Conclusion

Nowadays technology is everywhere and suffers significant changes almost every day. This fast evolution requires a fast adaptation from society, in which the technological progress is accepted, understood and quickly adopted. This evolution brings about new needs, that weren't considered previously. An example to illustrate the changing of needs is the use of the computer. In the last decade, it was rare to see laptops in the classrooms. We only had desk computers and many time only in some classrooms. Today's superior education generations have the computer on their daily lives, but this always like this. Today the laptop is an essential element in teaching and we can find, at least, a laptop in every classroom. The needs demanded and adopted by teachings, that are present in the classrooms, also suffer changes. This adaptation is not always seen, as in the case of the demands of design teaching, in which new technological skills are demanded to the students, that result in the need of furniture adequate to the new instruments of work, as well as in the essential need of reorganizing the classrooms. These needs can change very quickly. But the consequence of the fast technological evolution is seen when we assume that the laptop, in many cases, is gradually being replaced by the use of the tablet. With this technological evolution, accepted and adopted by society, we will in the future see, in superior education, a technological generation, the millennium generation, in which technology is present since the first days of life. So, if the furniture was already out of date for the older generations, it will be more evident in the future, in which gradually paper is being replaced by electronic devices.

This way, the evolution of school furniture must follow the evolution of technological needs in the academic environment.

References

1. UMIC. Agência para a sociedade do conhecimento (21 de Julho de 2011). http://www.umic. pt/index.php?option=com_content&task=view&id=3680&Itemid=161. Citação: 20 de Novembro de 2013
2. Bencostt, M.L.: Mobiliário escolar francês e os projetos vanguardistas de Jean Prouvé e André LLurçat na primeira metade do século XX. Educar em Revista n° 49, 19–38, Julho/Setembro de 2013
3. Cobbers, A., Costa, D., Marcel, B.: 1902–1981: criador da forma do século vinte. (2008)
4. Architecture D'aujourd'hui. Revue Mensuelle, Paris, 9me Année (1938)
5. BATIR. Bruxelles, n. 16, mars 1934
6. Knight, Grenville e Noyes, Jan. Children's behaviour and the design of school furniture. Ergonomics, 10 de Novembro de 2010
7. Faassen, F.: Anatomische achtergronden van werkhoudingen, Ergonomie n°1 (1978)
8. Liebisch, R.: Bewegungspausen fur Schu ler sind zwingend erforderlich! Haltung und bewegung, 3/90, Mainz, S. 31–34. CEN/TC 207/WG 5/TG 1 – Educational seating and workstations N13 (1990)
9. Snijders, C.J., Nordin, M.E.V.H., FRANKEL, V.H.: Biomechanica van het spier-skeletstelsel. Lemma BV, Utrecht (1995)
10. Pascoe, D.D., et al.: Influence of carrying book bags on gait cycle and posture of youths. Ergonomics 40, 631–641 (1997)
11. Balague, F., Dutoit, G., Waldbuger, M.: Low back pain in schoolchildren. Scand. J. Rehabil. Med. Suppl. 20, 175–179 (1988)
12. Kujala, U.M., et al.: Subject characteristics and low back pain in young athletes and nonathletes. Med. Sci. Sports Exerc. 24, 627–632 (1992)
13. Olsen, T.L., et al.: The epidemiology of low back pain in an adolescent population. Am. J. Public Health 82(4), 606–608 (1992)
14. Salminen, J., Laine, M., Laine, M.E., Pentti, J.: Back disorders and nonneutral trunk postures of automobile assembly workers. Scand. J. Work Environ. Health 17, 337–346 (1995)

15. Burton, A.K., et al.: The natural history of low back pain in adolescents. Spine **21**, 2323–2328 (1996)
16. Diep, N.B.: Evaluation of fitness between school furniture and children body size in two primary schools in Haiphonh, Vietnam. Unpublished Master thesis, Department of HumanWork (2003)
17. Legg, S.J., et al.: Spinal musculoskeletal discomfort in New Zealand intermediate schools. In: Proceedings of the 15th Congress of the International Ergonomics Association. Ergonomics for Children Ergonomics for Children 6, Seoul, Korea, pp. 336–338 (2003)
18. Molenbroek, J.F.M., Kroon-Ramaekers e Snijders, C.J.: Revision of the design of a standard for the dimensions of school furniture. Ergonomics **47**(7), 681–694 (2003)
19. Linton, S.J., Halme, T.E., Akerstedt, K.: The effects of ergonomically designed school furniture on pupils' attitudes, symptoms and behaviour. Appl. Ergonomics **25**, 2304–2399 (1994)
20. Wærsted, M.E., Westgaard, R.H.: An experimental study of shoulder muscle activity and posture in a paper version versus a VDU version of a monotonous work task. Int. J. Ind. Ergon. **19**, 175–185 (1997)
21. Straker, L., Maslen, B., Burgess-Limerick, R., Johnson P., Dennerlein J.: Evidence-based guidelines for the wise use of computers by children: Physical development guidelines. Ergonomics, 22 Março 2010
22. Mandel, A.C.: Changing standards for school furniture. Ergonomics in Design **5**, 28–31 (1997)
23. Zandvliet, D.B., Straker, L.: Physical and psychosocial aspects of the learning environment in information technology rich classrooms. Ergonomics **44**, 838–857 (2001)
24. Wingrat, J.K., Exner, C.E.: The impact of school furniture on fourth grade children's on-task and sitting behavior in the classroom: A pilot study. Work **25**, 263–272 (2005)
25. Wilsonand, J.R., Corlett, E.N., Wilson, J.R.: A framework and a context for ergonomics methodology. Eval. Hum. Work **2**, 1–39 (1995)
26. Wheldall, K.: Seating arrangements and classroom behaviour. Assoc. Child Psychol. Phychiatry News **10**, 2–6 (1982)
27. van Wely, P.: Design and disease. Appl. Ergonomics **1**, 262–269 (1970)
28. Troussier, B., Davione, P., de Gaudemaries, R., Fauconnier, J., Phelip, X.: Back pain in school children; A case study among 1178 pupils. Scand. J. Rehabil. Med. **26**(3), 143–146 (1994)
29. Thompson, J.A., Davis, L.: Furniture design decision-making constructs. Home Econ. Res. J. **16**, 279–290 (1988)
30. Steenberkkers, L.P.A.: Child Development, Design Implications and Accident Prevention. Delft University Press, Delft (1993)
31. Silverstein, B.A., Fine, J.L., Armstrong, T.J.: Hand wrist cumulative disorders in industry. Br. J. Ind. Med. **43**, 779–784 (1986)
32. Schroder, I.: Variation of sitting posture and physical activity in different types of school furniture. Coll. Anthrop. **21**(2), 397–403 (1997)
33. Salminen, J.: The adolescent back. Acta Pediatrican. Scandinavica **315**, 1–12 (1984)
34. Roelofs, A., Straker, L.: The experience of musculoskeletal discomfort amongst bank tellers who just sit, just stand or sit and stand at work. Ergonomics J. South Africa **14**, 11–29 (2002)
35. Pynt, J., Higgs, J., Mackey, M.: Seeking the optimal posture of the seated lumbar spine. Physiotherapy Theory Pract. **17**, 5–21 (2001)
36. Oxford, H.W.: The probem of misfit forniture. In: 3rd Annual Conference of the Ergonomics Society of Australia and New Zealand. s.n., Sydney (1966)

37. Musa, A.I. et al.: Ergo-effects of designed school furniture and sitting positions on students' behaviour and musculo-skeletal disorder in Nigerian tertiary institutions (2010)
38. Murphy, S.: The Occurrence of Back Pain and Associated Risk Factors in Schoolchildren. Ph.D. dissertation, University of Surrey (2003)
39. Mucchielli, A.: Les réactions de défense dans les relations inter-personnelles. Entreprise moderne d'édition, França (1978)
40. Milanese, S., Grimmer, K.: School furniture and the user population- an anthropometric perspective. Ergonomics 47, 416–426 (2004)
41. Mierau, D., Cassidy, J.D., Young-Hing, H.: Low back pain and straight leg raising in children and adolescents. Spine 14, 526–528 (1989)
42. Mandel, A.C.: The correct height of school furniture. Hum. Factors 24, 257–269 (1982)
43. Mandel, A.C.: The Seated Man: Homo Sedens. Dafnia Publications, Klampenborg, Denmark (1985)
44. Laville, A.: Postural stress in high-speed precision work. Ergonomics 28, 229–236 (1985)
45. Kemper, H.C.G., Storm Van Essen, L., Verschuur, R.: Height, weight and height velocity. Medicine and Sport Science 20 (1985)
46. Karvonen, M.J., Koskela, A., Noro, L.: Preliminary report on the sitting postures of school children. Ergonomics 5, 417–477 (1962)
47. Mekhora, K., et al.: The effect of ergonomic intervention on discomfort in computer users with tension neck syndrome. Int. J. Ind. Ergon. 26, 367–379 (2000)
48. Hertzberg, H.T.E.: The Conference on Standardization of Anthropometric Techniques and Terminology. Am. J. Phys. Anthropol. 28, 1–15 (1968)
49. Grimmer, K.A., Williams, M.T.: Gender-age environmental associates of adolescent low back pain. Appl. Ergonomics 31, 343–360 (2000)
50. Garcet, P., Nisius: Catalogue de Mobilier Scolaire. Matériel d'Enseignement (1882)
51. Floyd, W.F., Ward, J.S.: Anthopometric and physiological considerations in school office and factory seating. Ergonomics 12, 132–139 (1969)
52. Filgueiras, E.V.: Desenvolvimento de um Método Para Avaliação da Interacção Homem/Cadeira de Escritório numa Perspectiva Sistémica e Ecológica(Tese de Doutoramento em Motricidade Humana na especialidade de Ergonomia). Faculdade de Motricidade Humana da, s.n. Universidade Técnica de Lisboa (2011)
53. Fairbank, J.C.T.: Influence of anthropometric factors and joint laxity in the incidence of adolescent back pain. Spine 9, 461–464 (1984)
54. Drury, C.G., Coury, B.G.: A methodology for chair evaluation. Ergonomics 13, 195–202 (1982)
55. Craven, J.: Backs for fututre. Times Educational Supplement, 3 (1993)
56. Barbosa, A.F.: Avaliação da Influência do Mobiliário Escolar na Postura Corporal em Alunos Adolescentes, Dissertação de Mestrado em Engenharia de Produção e Sistemas Área de Especialização Engenharia Humana. s.n., Universidade do Minho (2009)
57. Azevedo, L.P.: Design de Interiores e Espaços Escolare- Influências na aprendizagem, Dissertação para obtenção do Grau de Mestre em Design Industrial e Tecnológico. s.n., Universida da Beira Interior (2012)
58. Axelrod, S., Hall, R.V., Tains, A.: Comparison of two common seating arrangements. Acad. Ther. 15, 29–36 (1979)

Analysis of Usability and Information Architecture of the UFRN Institutional Repository

Débora Koshiyama[1,2], André Luís Santos de Pinho[1,3],
and José Guilherme Santa Rosa[1(✉)]

[1] Post-Graduate Program in Design,
Federal University of Rio Grande Do Norte, Natal, Brazil
jguilhermesantarosa@gmail.com
[2] Brain Institute, Federal University of Rio Grande Do Norte, Natal, Brazil
[3] Department of Statistics, Federal University of Rio Grande Do Norte,
Natal, Brazil
debora@neuro.ufrn.br, pinho@ccet.ufrn.br

Abstract. In order to identify the possible problems of usability and information architecture of the institutional repositories, the case study of the Institutional Repository of the Federal University of Rio Grande do Norte was chosen. As research hypothesis, it was established that the information architecture of the UFRN Institutional Repository interface, version 1.8.1, disadvantage usability in performing the tasks by system user groups. Data collection was carried out by applying the techniques of Cooperative Evaluation and Usability Testing of the UFRN/IR system. Problems of usability and information architecture were found in the Institutional Repository from the results obtained. The redesign of the UFRN Institutional Repository interface on areas related to the tasks presented in the research, and considering the aspects of usability and information architecture, mentioned above, we will contribute to access and visibility of information improvement.

Keywords: Design · Information ergonomics · Institutional Repository · Usability · Information architecture

1 Introduction

The amount of generated information becomes difficult to be measured and stored inasmuch as new knowledge arises. Thus, it is proven to be crucial to the countries development due the Internet advent and the disclosure of what is produced, especially between academics.

Therefore, universities have developed tools that allow the disclosure, storage and recovery of produced knowledge, such as digital repositories. According to Viana, Arellano and Shintaku [1] digital repository is "a form of storage for digital files that

© Springer International Publishing Switzerland 2015
A. Marcus (Ed.): DUXU 2015, Part III, LNCS 9188, pp. 197–207, 2015.
DOI: 10.1007/978-3-319-20889-3_19

have the ability to maintain and manage it over long periods and to provide its access". Then, the repository fulfills its role of storage, disclosure and preservation of digital documents.

In Brazil, the institutional repositories initiative has began in 2009 when the Brazilian Institute of Information, Science and Technology - IBICT (Instituto Brasileiro de Informação, Ciência e Tecnologia) published the Public Notice FINEP/PCAL/XBDB n° 003/2009, in order to encourage the implementation of repositories and periodicals in Brazilian public institutions of teaching and research. The public notice required, among others, the implantation of the repository system and the inclusion of scientific production of the last five years, within three months, and the team shall be formed by information and computer technicians.

Thus, we questioned if the information architecture and the interface design of the Institutional Repository of the Federal University of Rio Grande do Norte - UFRN, Brazil [2], DSpace software version 1.8.1, would provide interaction with suitable user's groups, achieving the institutional interest of promoting transparency and free access to produced information by the research developed at the university.

As a research hypothesis, it was established that the information architecture of UFRN Institutional Repository system, DSpace software version 1.8.1, discourages the usability when performing tasks by the system user groups.

2 Digital Information Repository

Digital repositories were created in the 90 s, and implemented at Los Alamos laboratory (New Mexico), USA, named virtual repositories (arXiv**) in computing, physics and mathematics areas [3]. Since then, a consensus was agreed among publishers and authors on the importance to provide its open scientific production with unrestricted access, providing large visibility to scientific research.

In 2004, the scientific experts' production of the Brazilian Institute of Information, Science and Technology - IBICT was released in repositories, in which the authors could publish their studies, ensuring open and continuous access to the information. In 2009, the IBICT published a public notice to encourage the implementation of repositories and periodicals in Brazilian public education and research. Thus, the institutions had three months to implement and include their documents helped by a team of information technology technician and librarian. The institutions covered by the public notice received the free DSpace software, version 1.8.1, to manage the repository with the responsibility to customize it.

The Federal University of Rio Grande do Norte - UFRN launched its repository in 2010, being its Institutional Repository RI/UFRN [2] (Fig. 1) responsible for gathering all the intellectual production of the university community (teachers, technicians and post-graduate students) with a mission to storage, preserve and make available on the Internet full texts with free access.

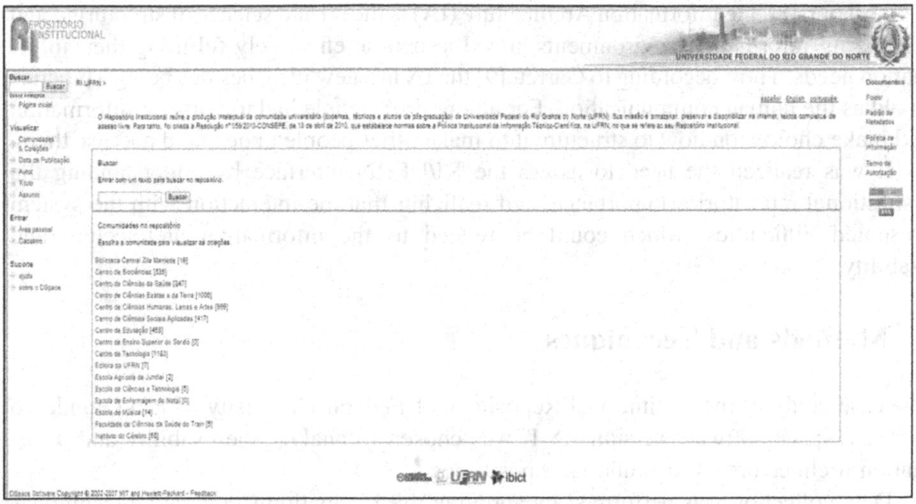

Fig. 1. UFRN institutional repository interface

By the Resolution nº 059/2010-CONSEPE, of April 13, 2010, standards were established on the Institutional Policy of Technical-Scientific Information, in UFRN, regarding your RI, which objectives: manage and disseminate technical-scientific production in digital media and make it visible; and preserve the intellectual memory of the university and serve as a tangible indicator of quality with scientific, economic and social relevance. According to the information policy of RI/UFRN, articles published in journals, complete papers presented at events, dissertations presented in other institutions, electronic books and book chapters were deposited in its collection. Thus, the authors provide to UFRN authorization under the Creative Commons 3.0 Unported license for deposit and disclosure of their documents in digital format.

2.1 Usability and Information Architecture

Usability is the quality that characterizes the use of programs and applications. Thus, it is not an intrinsic quality of a system, but depends on the relationship between its interface and users characteristics to pursue determined objectives in determined situations [4].

For Nielsen [5], the usability is not a single property of a system, but it is associated with 5 quality attributes: (1) Learnability; (2) Efficiency; (3) Memorability; (4) Errors and; (5) Satisfaction.

Shneiderman [6] also set attributes for projects involving graphical interfaces, called "The Eight Golden Rules": (1) Strive for consistency; (2) Enable to use short-cuts; (3) Offer informative feedback; (4) Design dialogues to yield closure; (5) Prevent errors; (6) Permit easy reversal of actions; (7) Support internal locus of control and; (8) Reduce short-term memory load.

Similarly, Norman [7] establishes 7 principles: (1) Use both knowledge in the world and knowledge in the head; (2) Simplify the structure of tasks; (3) Make things visible; (4) Get the mappings right; (5) Exploit the power of constraints, both natural and artificial; (6) Design for error, and (7) When all else fails, standardize.

To Toub [8], the Information Architecture (IA) is the art and science of structuring and organizing information environments aimed at people effectively fulfilling their information needs. Thus, according to Garrett [9] the IA is a new idea, besides being a practice as old as the human communication. For a long time people had to transmit information and make choices on how to structure it to make other people understand and use them.

It was realized the need to assess the RI/UFRN interface by understanding the institutional repositories importance, and realizing that the interaction with the system presented difficulties, which could be related to the information architecture and usability.

3 Methods and Techniques

The case study of the Institutional Repository of Federal University of Rio Grande do Norte, DSpace software version 1.8.1, was chosen to analyze the usability and information architecture of institutional repositories.

Data collection was performed by applying the Evaluation Cooperative techniques and Usability Testing of RI/UFRN system with a representative group of users (ten librarians, ten graduate students and ten post-graduate students) between February and March of the current year. Despite the teachers also be part of the system user universe, there was no opportunity to include them in the tests.

"Search" and "Submission" of a scientific article was the representative task selected. Besides the evaluation techniques, the participants answered a social-demographic and satisfaction questionnaire adapted from the Questionnaire for User Interaction Satisfaction - QUIS [10] applied after the usability testing.

Usability testing was performed individually, in a computer lab at the university, with the same equipment for all participants, following such configuration: AMD Athlon ™ II X2B22, Processor 2.8 GHz; 2.00 GB RAM; Windows Operating System of 32-bit. The Internet speed was, approximately, 23.8 Mbps for download and 42.28 Mbps for upload. Camtasia Studio software, Trial version, was utilized to analyze user navigation route in the system, allowing recording audio, video and images of screens browsed by the user, thus enabling the detailed analysis of the navigation. The free-license statistical software R, version 3.1.1, was utilized for producing graphs and statistical tests. Five percent (5 %) significance level for statistical tests performance was used in all cases.

The Cooperative Evaluation was performed in a place chosen by the participants. The user interaction and verbalization during the tasks were also recorded by Camtasia Studio software, Trial version.

3.1 Cooperative Assessment and Usability Testing

According to Monk et al. [11], cooperative evaluation is a low-cost technique utilized to identify usability problems in prototype products and processes. The technique encourages design teams and users to collaborate identifying usability problems and possible solutions. Users interact with a prototype in order to realize tasks defined by the design team.

After all, the preliminary results consist of users' comments and evaluation summary, and their experiences observed during the use of the system, allowing the development of recommendations aiming to improve the product.

Dumas and Redish [12] consider the usability testing as a method in which representative participants of a system user group identify problems or validate interface solutions, and this test shall be inserted as part of the project since the initial stage. Therefore, the participants shall represent real users and shall be submitted to typical system tasks.

After Usability Testing, the data was analyzed and the information may confirm the usability of a system or give recommendations for improvements.

4 Analysis and Discussion of Results

Comparing the problems highlighted by users and the usability attributes proposed by Nielsen [5], Shneiderman [6] and Norman [7] is required to identify who was committed during all tasks, as shown in Tables 1 and 2:

Table 1. Comparison among the problems highlighted by users of RI/UFRN, on "Search" task and usability attributes described by Nielsen [5], Shneiderman [6] and Norman [7].

TASK	PROBLEM	Committed attributes		
		Nielsen	Shneiderman	Norman
	Lack of texts standardization on the labels.		Strive for consistency	
	Small font		Strive for consistency	
	Two search fields on the main page are not necessary.		Reduce short-term memory load	Simplify the structure of tasks
	Excessive amount of information on the main page.		Reduce short-term memory load	Simplify the structure of tasks
	The "View/Open" button nomenclature does not indicate if the documents downloadwill be done.	Errors	Prevent errors	Design for error
	The *download* button (View/Open) shall be next to the title.		Strive for consistency	When all else fails, standardize
	"Show Full Registration" option is unnecessary and confusing.	Errors	Prevent errors	Design for error
	The button presenting the access statistics to the document is in English "*View Statistic.*"		Strive for consistency	When all else fails, standardize
SEARCH	In the results list, the "Preview" field is frustrating because does not present any information.	Satisfaction	Offer informative feedback	When all else fails, standardize
	There is no option to return to the search results list when the user chooses one of them.	Efficiency	Permit easy reversal of actions	Get the mappings right

Table 2. Comparison of the problems highlighted by users of RI/UFRN, in "Submission" task and the usability attributes described by Nielsen [5], Shneiderman [6] and Norman [7].

TASK	PROBLEM	Committed attributes		
		Nielsen	**Shneiderman**	**Norman**
SUBMISSION	The "Personal Area" *login* nomenclature is unclear.	Easelearning	Strive for consistency	Make things visible
	Small font		Strive for consistency	
	Login buttons are widely spaced.		Strive for consistency	When all else fails, standardize
	The options to be selected are unclear in the first step, "Describe" the information.	Learnability	Prevent errors	Design for error
	The submission form is not customized for each document type.	Efficiency	Reduce short-term memory load	Simplify the structure of tasks
	There is no information about success or failure when the actions are performed.		Offer informative feedback	Feedback
	The system does not indicate required fields.	Learnability	Prevent errors	Design for the error
	The introductory texts of the steps are not wording clear.		Offer informative feedback	Feedback
	There is no information procedure for filling the fields.			Simplify the structure of tasks
	The "access Right" button is not available with other disclosure document licenses.	Efficiency	Strive for consistency	When all else fails, standardize
	Form fields are centered on the page.	Satisfaction	Strive for consistency	
	The "Cancel/Save" button indicates ambiguous action, which shall be separated, leading the user to cancel the submission performed.	Errors	Prevent errors	Design for error
	When you select to add more fields, to include other authors and keywords, the system adds two fields at a time.		Strive for consistency	
	In "load" step, the system does not report if the document was attached to the system.		Design dialogues to yield closure	Feedback

(Continued)

Table 2. *(Continued)*

TASK	PROBLEM	Committed attributes		
		Nielsen	Shneiderman	Norman
	In "load" step, the information "Show *checksums*" is confusing and unnecessary.			When all else fails, standardize
	The help information is available in English.	Learnability	Strive for consistency	
	The help information appears in *pop-up* format, which may be blocked in some computers.	Efficiency		
	In "Check" button, the system does not return to this field when a correction of some information is required.	Efficiency	Shortcuts for heavy users	
	Some labels and information are presented in English.	Learnability	Strive for consistency	
	There is no explanation on the *Creative Commons* license.	Learnability		
	After selected the *Creative Commons* license, the "Continue" button appears in small font and in *link* format, inducing the user to select "Skip *Creative Commons*" to continue the submission.		Strive for consistency	
	The disclosure license text is available in English.	Learnability	Strive for consistency	
	In "Complete"buttom, the last task, show the return fields to "My Space" and "Communities and Collections" as links, which induces the user to select "*Submit another item to the same collection*"		Strive for consistency	

It was observed that, according to the authors, some usability attributes were committed during the tasks performance as: Feedback, Consistency, Learnability, among others. Thus, these attributes shall be considered for future redesign projects of RI/UFRN interface.

4.1 Application of Severity Level

According to Nielsen [13], severity of a usability problem is a combination of 3 factors: (1) the frequency with which the problem occurs; (2) the impact of the problem for users (difficult or easy to overcome) and (3) the persistence of the problem (is it a one-time problem that users can overcome once they know about it or will users repeatedly be bothered by the problem?). He also proposes a classification scale to achieve an overall assessment of each usability problem, in order to facilitate the prioritization and decision-making.

Severity	Description
0	I do not agree that this is a usability problem at all
1	Cosmetic problem only: need not be fixed unless extra time is available on project
2	Minor usability problem: fixing this should be given low priority
3	Major usability problem: important to fix, so should be given high priority
4	Usability catastrophe: imperative to fix this before product can be released

Fig. 2. Nielsen's usability problems severity level

Thus, after the evaluations and problems comparison highlighted individually by the users, with the usability attributes committed, its severity levels were attributed to the "Search" task (Table 3) and "Submission" task (Table 4) (Fig. 2).

Table 3. Severity Levels Application in errors identified in Search Task of RI/UFRN

TASK	PROBLEM	SEVERITY				
		0	1	2	3	4
SEARCH	Lack of texts standardization on the labels		X			
	Small font		X			
	Two search fields on the main page are not necessary			X		
	Excessive amount of information on the main page			X		
	The "View/Open" button nomenclature does not indicate if document *download* will be done	X				
	The *download* button (View/Open) shall be next to the title		X			
	"Show Full Registration" option is unnecessary and confusing				X	
	The button presenting the access statistics to the document is in English "*View Statistic*"				X	
	In the results list, the "Preview" field is frustrating because does not present any information.				X	
	There is no option to return to the search results list when the user chooses one of them.			X		

Table 4. Severity Levels Application in errors identified in Submission Task of RI/UFRN

TASK	PROBLEM	SEVERITY				
		0	1	2	3	4
	The "Personal Area" *login* nomenclature is unclear		X			
	Small font			X		
	Login buttons are widely spaced			X		
	The options to be selected are unclear in the first step, "Describe" the information				X	
	The submission form is not customized for each document type				X	
	There is no information about success or failure when the actions are performed			X		
	The system does not indicate the required fields				X	
	The introductory texts of the steps are not wording clear			X		
	There is no information procedure for filling the fields				X	
	The "access Right" field is not available with other disclosure document licenses			X		
	Form fields are centered on the page	X				
	The "Cancel/Save" button indicates ambiguous action, which shall be separated, leading the user to cancel the submission performed					X
	When you select to add more fields, to include other authors and keywords, the system adds two fields at a time			X		
	In "load" field, the system does not report if the document was attached to the system				X	
	In "load" field, the information "Show *checksums*" is confusing and unnecessary			X		
	The help information is available in English				X	
	The help information appears in *pop-up* format, which may be blocked in some computers				X	
	In "Check" step, the system does not return to this step when a correction of some information is required			X		
	Some labels and information are presented in English				X	
	There is no explanation on the *Creative Commons* license			X		
SUBMISSION	After selected the *Creative Commons* license, the "Continue" button appears in small font and in *link* format, inducing the user to select "Skip *Creative Commons*" to continue the submission.				X	
	The disclosure license text is available in English				X	
	In "Complete" bottom, the last task, show the return fields to "My Space" and "Communities and Collections" as links, which induces the user to select "*Submit another item to the same collection*"				X	

5   Recommendations

A list of design recommendations was elaborated for RI/UFRN from the obtained results analysis during the research, in areas of tasks as documents "Search" and "Submission" (Fig. 3). The recommendations list was organized by solving priority of the problems highlighted by the severity levels.

RECOMMENDATIONS LIST
High Resolution Priority
• Separate the options Cancel and Save found in the submission form, to avoid the submission induction exclusion started by the user.
Medium Resolution Priority
• Perform a revision throughout the layout and labeling/terminology text to make them simple, clear and consistent.
• Remove information from the page that is not necessary for the user.
• Customize the submission form according to the document type.
• Provide confirmation to the tasks performed by the user.
• Translate the labels and available texts in the system to Portuguese.
• Highlight important information and commands to perform the task.
• Highlight form fields that are filling required.
Low Resolution Priority
• Use text and fields of the form aligned on the left.
• Collect the access permissions and licenses in a single space.
• Provide more information about the *Creative Commons* license
• Limit the inclusion of additional fields in the form to one at a time.

Fig. 3. Recommendations List of RI/UFRN

The implementation of these recommendations, based on collected information from users, could help to develop a more efficient and satisfactory interface, favoring the system usability in tasks as "Search" and "Submission".

6   Conclusion

Usability problems and information architecture present in the Institutional Repository system, such as labeling, size of source, buttons nomenclature, lack of system feed-back, were found in the obtained results through the Cooperative Evaluation with post-graduate students and Usability Testing with graduate students and librarians. The participants would be unsatisfied with the problems and undermine their perception regarding the safety, as occurred with the post-graduate students.

Thus, the generated hypothesis at the beginning was confirmed, as the "information architecture of UFRN Institutional Repository system discourages the usability in tasks performing by the system user groups".

Despite this, the participants consider the institutional repository a significant value tool, since it allows free access to scientific publications and research developed by IES.

Finally, the UFRN Institutional Repository interface redesign for "Search" and "Submission" tasks, will consider the usability aspects and information architecture mentioned above, and will contribute for a change in access and information visibility [14], as well as promote a centered approach on the user, according to Santa Rosa [15], all based on the proposed amendment recommendations of this study. Additionally, the valuation techniques application is recommended to other tasks, which the repository users are submitted, in order to complete the study for the whole system.

References

1. Viana, C.L.M., Arellano, M.A., Shintaku, M.: Repositórios institucionais em ciência e tecnologia: uma experiência de customização do DSpace (2014)
2. Repositório Institucional da Universidade Federal do Rio Grande do Norte. http://repositorio.ufrn.br:8080/jspui/
3. Kuramoto, H.: Distinguindo os conceitos de repositórios e publicações eletrônicas. Blog do Kuramoto (2013)
4. Cybis, W., Betiol, A.H., Faust, R.: Ergonomia e Usabilidade: conhecimentos, métodos e aplicações, 2nd edn. Novatec, São Paulo (2010)
5. Nielsen, J.: Usability Engineering. Sunsoft, Montview (1993)
6. Shneiderman, B.: The Eight Golden Rules OS Interface Design. University of Maryland, Maryland (2010)
7. Norman, D.: O Design Do Dia A Dia. Rocco, Rio de Janeiro (2006)
8. Toub, S.: Evaluating Information Architecture: A Practical Guide To Assessing Web Site Organization. Argus Center for Information Architecture (2000)
9. Garrett, J.J.: The Elements of User Experience: User-Centered Design for the Web and Beyond. Peachpit Press, New York (2010)
10. Shneiderman, B.: Designing the User Interface Strategies for Effective Human-Computer-Interaction, 3rd edn. Addison Wesley Longman, Reading (1988)
11. Monk, A., Wright, P., Haber, J., Davenport, L.: Improving your Human-Computer Interface: A Practical Technique. Prentice Hall International, UK (1993)
12. Dumas, J.S., Redish, J.C.: A Pratical Guide To Usability Testing. Intellect, Portland (1999)
13. Nielsen, J.: Severity Ratings for Usability Problems, 1 January 1995
14. Koshiyama, D.A., Carvalho, M.F., Ramos, A.S.M.: Implantação de repositório digital em universidade: relato de duas experiências na UFRN. Natal, 2011. 30f. Artigo (Especialização). Universidade Federal do Rio Grande do Norte, Especialização em Gestão Universitária (2011)
15. Santa Rosa, J.G.: Em rumo ao paradigma Biblioteca Centrada no Leitor. In: Congresso Internacional de Usabilidade de Interfaces Humano-Computador, 9 2009, Curitiba. Anais... Curitiba: UFPR 2009. pp. 1–6 (2009)

Ergonomic and Usability Analysis of Interactive Whiteboards in the Academic Environment

Eduardo Oliveira, Erick Vasconcelos, Elzani Sobral[✉],
Sayonara Bittencourt, Tiago Ramos, and Marcelo M. Soares

Department of Design, Federal University of Pernambuco, Recife, Brazil
sobral.rafaela@hotmail.com

Abstract. This paper presents the usability analysis about the using of interactive whiteboards, specifically the EPSON Brightlink 475wi + model, evaluating its functionality for didactic purposes in classrooms. The research was done in CAC, the Centre of Arts and Communication of the Federal University of Pernambuco, where observations, interviews and questionnaires with potential users have been done. The aim of this research is to propose possible improvements that could be done in its hardware, software and interface, in addition to evaluate the educator's preparing in relation to all the tools that the interactive whiteboard disposes, and how its knowledge is shared to the students when using this equipment. The purpose of this investigation is to do an ergonomic analysis of this important educational tool, which is generally underused by the educators, and to bring the users possible solutions so they can explore its maximum resources in their classrooms.

Keywords: Technology in education · Ergonomics · Usability

1 Introducion

Usability is a term used to define the ease which people employ a tool or a certain object to perform a task. It's also the property of a system in making a user succeed when executing its tasks (1). Ergonomics is studied in order to improve, per example, the workspace of people, creating compatibility between the needs, abilities and the worker's comprehension capacities. When dealing with products and virtual interfaces, ergonomics studies the best way for an object, or information, successfully reach the user, thus achieve its own goal.

The digital interactive whiteboard mixes elements from a wide number of Technologies as well as typical educational utilities, as the computer, the traditional whiteboard, the touch function – formely present in tablets and smartphones – and the slide projector. Its board (or device) is connected to the computer and its image is projected by a multimedia projector. Until then, the datashow performed under the same procedure, however, the interactive board may have its projected screen directly manipulated by the user's finger or a special pen. In this aspect, everything that is

© Springer International Publishing Switzerland 2015
A. Marcus (Ed.): DUXU 2015, Part III, LNCS 9188, pp. 208–217, 2015.
DOI: 10.1007/978-3-319-20889-3_20

available in the form of computer resources, multimedia, image simulation and web surfing is possible through the user's interaction directly with the content.

The digital boards are available in a wide array of models in the Brazilian Market. Regardless of the utilization approach by the user, the interactive boards can be used in: companies, shows, events, schools, universities, etc. This research studies the digital board in the educational setting, focusing on its use in the undergraduate/graduate levels. It can be observed that, in the XXI century, technology is operating everywhere, reaching the classrooms. There are four models of digital board in Brazil, as follows:

1. **The electromagnetic board** is an equipment that allows interacting through the touch of specific pens on a surface, that being an electromagnetic field. Despite the high-quality writing recognition ability, it only works with specially designed pens, which are costly if lost. Furthermore, it does not tolerate two or more simultaneous users.

2. **The resistive digital board** allows interaction through finger touch on its surface, usually made of polyester, what makes it very soft. What makes this board different from the others is that the touch command will only be identified if the surface possesses a resistive membrane that refuses the use by more than one person at a time, since it recognizes pressure points on the membrane. By requiring a resistive membrane, the board may also need more constant and expensive technical repairs.

3. **The infrared digital board** has been evolving along the years, becoming capable of being produced without the necessity of special pens, however, most equipment still demands pens that, if lost, will prove to be expensive for the consumer. The infrared digital board has infrared light rays being directed on the board in a down and across pattern. When an object touches the board, it stops the light rays and through coordinates, the computer identifies the location where the stroke is being made.

4. **The optical digital board** possesses sensors that capture the movements of the user and also allow interaction through finger touch or simple pens. Depending on the model, up to four users can be recognized by the board.

According to Jeffrey Rubin, usability can also be defined as the group of four factors united in a single device:

1. Capability of being successfully used;
2. Ease of being used;
3. Capability of the user learning how to use the device in a simple, fast manner;
4. Provoking visual satisfaction to the user.

Following these four factors, this article has the objective of evaluating the Epson Brightlink 475 wi + digital board, currently installed in the Design Department of Universidade Federal de Pernambuco. Basing ourselves on the parameters established by Jeffrey Rubin, an experiment was developed and put to practice with the Design students and other potential users of the device, such as teachers of other departments of the university. The equipment is being used in both public and private schools of Recife, and is available in different models.

The research was prepared for the Ergonomia e Usabilidade class of the Bacharelado em Design course of Universidade Federal de Pernambuco, conducted by professor Marcelo Soares. The objective of this research is to evaluate the usability of the digital board, taking note of criticism, difficulties, observations and suggestions the users may want to make. The research, administered during the length of the discipline, is focused in the analysis of the digital board and its physical and interactive properties and, based on this, organize an experiment using surveys, observation sheets, functionality registration videos and thus, gather data for how to make best use of the equipment.

1.1   Selected Model: Epson Brighlink 475wi+

The digital board model was available for the research group in the Design Department office of UFPE, and was evaluated during the semester of the Ergonomia e Usabilidade discipline. To better understand the tools of the device, many assignments were done during the classes, summing up information about the digital board and its technical functions.

The box includes: one interactive projector (Fig. 1), two interactive pens (Fig. 3) and a remote controller (Fig. 2). This **infrared interactive projector** is usually permanently installed in a classroom, usually on the ceiling, what improves its short-distance function, avoiding the casting of shadows and visual disturbance caused by its light. The **interactive pens** can be used simultaneously by two users when the board is connected to an USB port, being a manually-operated device that can have its points and batteries (AA type) changed. The **remote control** takes care of two functions: projection and interactive configurations, besides controlling how the digital board must be activated (USB or VGA), and to control screens in real time.

Fig. 1.

Fig. 2.

Fig. 3.

Fig. 4.

There are many differences between using this model either with or without the help of a computer the main one is regarding the simultaneous use of pens. In the VGA mode (without the help of a computer) only a single pen works when touching the surface. On the USB mode (with the help of computers), two users can use pens simultaneously. Another major difference is in the "screen saving" function, available on the USB mode but not on VGA, due to the absence of internal memory. Moreover, the interactive toolbar for the VGA mode (Fig. 4) has less functions than that of the USB mode, which makes use of the **Easy Interactive Tools** (Fig. 5), software that can

Fig. 5.

be installed on the computers for more complex annotations. One of the functions of the Easy Interactive Tools is to adapt itself to different software, as Power Point, becoming even simpler for presentations. Furthermore, the Easy Interactive tools can be configured by the remote control, making the interaction between user, desktop and computer devices, such as a mouse, possible.

2 Methodological Procedures: Field Analysis in Conjunction with the Academic Community

After the data-gathering period about the Epson Brightlink 475 wi + digital board, a practical analysis was needed for the team to know, regarding ergonomics and usability points, gather data about improvements, experiments and critics about the product. The field analysis became necessary due to the lack of use by the professors and the whole of the academic community. Few students knew the equipment was interactive, so it was being used just for projections. The professors of the department who knew the equipment was interactive did not use the pens due to fear or lack of technical preparation.

We decided to use methods learned during the Ergonomia e Usabilidade course for the practical analysis. The Epson Brighlink 475 wi + digital board studied by us belongs to the auditorium of the Design course of UFPE. The users selected for test are part of the academic community of Centro de Artes e Comunicação, where the Design e Expressão Gráfica course keeps the device. We've evaluated Design students and professors from different areas, including Expressão Gráfica, Design and Engineering.

An analysis in which the final product is appraised for the gathering of critical information and possible improvements of the product was made. For the purpose of studying all the participants in a uniform manner, we proposed a task they could perform on a daily basis: a powerpoint slide presentation. With the objective of evaluating how the user behaves while using the tool, regardless of having used it before or not, we asked them to only use the interactive pen on the digital board, without using the mouse or keyboard for any task.

The interface of the digital board has two lateral interaction bars: one that can be used on any screen, and another that becomes simpler when a full screen powerpoint presentation is being shown. We asked the users to use only the simplified interface.

The research group developed exercises of different difficulty levels, selecting that one which all of the users would be capable of completing. We prepared a presentation with seven slides, aiming for the observation of the behavior of users when *passing a page*. On the seventh slide, we asked from the users to perform three tasks of the interactive board (Figs. 6, 7).

A - Highlighting a part of text with the *highlights* tool.
B - Writing two notes, with two distinct colors each.
C - Erasing what had been written.

All the tasks were documented in video so that the research group could register the opinions and progress of each user, as well as the time taken by each one of them to accomplish each task.

Fig. 6. Complete bar

Fig. 7. Simplified bar

The collecting of users' data was done through a semi-structured type interview survey developed by the group and given to the users at the end of the task, procedure that was also documented in video. We developed a survey on which the user would feel comfortable to take any notes about the product, and making use of questions that, if by any chance a user had forgotten to comment about at a given moment, they would be able to comment about moments later.

Semi-Structured Interview about the Use of the Digital Board:
Age: *Occupation:*

General	*About the interface*	*About the physical pen*
1. Have you ever used a digital board before?	9. What did you think about its digital interface?	15. Did you like the physical pen tool?
2. Do you use this device? If the answer is "yes", how frequently?	10. Was it easy to locate the writing tools?	16. Did you think it was easy to use?
3. What did you think about the experience with this digital board?	11. Was it easy to select the desired tool?	17. Is the physical pen comfortable? Why?
4. What did you like about it?	12. Was it easy to select the color of the pen?	18. What did you like about it?
5. What didn't you like about it?	13. Was it easy to highlight the text?	19. What didn't you like about the physical pen?
6. Would you use this device again? Why?	14. Could you erase what you wanted?	20. What did you think about the pen's sensitivity?
7. Which were your biggest difficulties with it?		
8. What would you suggest to be changed?		

An structured observation sheet with headings and pre-made, multiple-choice answers was developed, and in addition, open points for general observations and for the description of the environment, so that the observers could, as a unity, evaluate how each user behaved while using the digital board. The sheet used for this observation was based on a sheet used in a previous research, in which the professors (final users) of the public and private schools of Recife were appraised while using the digital boards that belonged to the schools (BITTENCOURT, 2014). Differently from this previous research, the observers could, this time, study how the Design department board works for the purpose of elaborating a sheet and tasks which are more accurate to the product.

Observation Sheet for the Classroom – Digital Board

Institution: Occupation: Age:

1. Description of the environment of the classroom being studied:

2. Physical complement of the digital board:

( ) pen ( ) 3D glasses ( ) projector ( ) Others: _____

3. How does the user relates to the digital board?

( ) Without difficulties   ( ) With little difficulty   ( ) With a lot of difficulty, presenting interruptions   ( ) With difficulty, requiring assistance of other people

4. How well could the user present the class making use of the slides?

( ) Without difficulties ( ) With little difficulty ( ) With difficulties, being helped by other people

5. How did the user passed from slide to slide?

( ) In one of the correct ways, by clicking on the screen ( ) In one of the correct ways, by clicking on the arrow located in the simplified tool bar ( ) Initially incorrectly, but later noticing his/her mistake and performing the correct operation ( ) In an incorrect way ( ) Could not pass the slides by him(her)self

6. Could the user highlight the text?( ) With no difficulties ( ) With little difficulties ( ) With difficulties, needing assistance of other people ( ) Could not perform the task

7. How did the user highlight the text? ( ) With the correct tool ( ) Initially with the incorrect tool, but changing to the correct one after noticing the mistake ( ) In the incorrect way

8. Could the user write? ( ) With no difficulties ( ) With little difficulty ( ) With difficulties, needing assistance of other people

9. How did the user write? ( ) With the correct tool ( ) Initially with the incorrect tool, but changing to the correct one moments later ( ) In the incorrect way

10. Did the user present difficulties while dealing with the pen? ( ) Yes ( ) No

11. Usually, which devices does the user – when a professor – uses during classes? ( ) Datashow ( ) White board ( ) Online researches ( ) Games and dynamics

12. General Observations:

The experiment was conducted during the course of two days, each day with students and professors of different age groups – precisely, six Design students and two Design professors, and the other two professors coming from Expressão Gráfica and Engineering.

As a result of the user experience, only three of them affirmed to have utilized some kind of digital board before, the first experience as user being with the interactive board of the Design department. All the interviewed users maintain contact with touch screen devices, making the task easier for some.

The task was analyzed since the first moment in which the user touches the pen on the slide for the first time, making it possible to observe if they would click on the screen – what happened to half of participants. The other half employed another correct way of passing a slide, although a more laborious one, which is to reach for the interactive toolbar and to press the arrow to get to the next screen. Four of five users who simply touched the screen in order to pass to the next slide had the intuition of *sliding* the tip of the pen to pass to the next page, linking the experience to the use of an average touch-device (tablet and smartphones).

Regarding the graphic interface of the interactive toolbar, a unanimous opinion surfaced: the pen and highlights icons should be easier to differentiate – some users selected the wrong tool for a determined task – what made the experience of identifying an icon a matter of luck or trial and error.

While performing the task (writing two notes, each one with different colors), some users found it hard to accomplish due to some technical issues of the product: in some moments, the user pulled the pen away but the magnetic recognition remained as if the pen were touching the surface, leading to the appearance of non-intentional strokes. Another problem that was observed is that, even when touching the surface, some pen strokes were not recognized, what made the users try to repeat the command once more or apply extra pressure on the tip of the pen.

Out of the ten selected users, two raised the issue of the inadequacy of the surface used for the projection: a shiny, translucent glass board. It was mentioned that during classes without the digital board, marker pen strokes become hard to be seen due to the glass board. Design students have claimed to feel difficulty while reading from the glass surface. Even though a removable sheet of white canvas had been provided, the surface makes the task of writing on the board even harder, due to its lack of stability.

As a conclusion to the analysis, the participants raised criticism and suggestions about the physical pen. Complaints as poor battery access positioning and lack of texture – the body of the pen is completely slick, what makes it easier to slide off or hurt a user's hand – were also made. The users felt that the task would have been more dynamic if shortcut buttons were added to the pen, such as forward/backward buttons or buttons that could change the function of the pen from regular pen to highlighter to an eraser or a color function. Out of the ten users, three suggested that one of the extremes of the pen could work as a *magnetic eraser,* eliminating the need of reaching for the eraser icon.

None of the users expressed dissatisfaction about stature, given that the object of the activity did not allow for them reaching for extreme points of the surface, thus, making it possible to keep the activity within eye level. Nevertheless, while interacting with other software, some users could find it uneasy to use icons or menus set too distant from their regular reach area.

3 Conclusion

It was possible to verify that many of the difficulties found during the tasks happened because of the lack of familiarity or non-adaptation of the users to the equipment, making it being used only as a *datashow*. This issue could have been solved with a brief training with professionals from the companies that sell the product, as a way to increase the use of the boards by the users.

During the tasks performed by the participants, we observed that text highlighting was done in the incorrect way: by making a circle around the text instead of choosing the appropriate marker. These mistakes lead us to a reflection about the term "highlight the text" used on our activity sheets, since the word used could have caused some confusing (being mistaken with "emphasize") or by the fact of some people having habit of making their texts more visible by using circles around the words. Yet, another determining factor for the problems found was choosing the incorrect tool, since the pen and marker icons look similar; what left users in doubt or even lead them to make mistakes. Some participants opted for the trial-and-error method in order to verify if the selected tool was the correct one. This also happened because of the equipment being feedback-deficient.

Consequently, we propose a redesign of the highlight marker icon, as well as offering feedback to the user when selecting this tool, along with a color-choice feedback function, thus, decreasing the chances of mistakes and increasing rates of successful use of the tool.

Regarding the interaction between user and physical pen, used during every moment of the experiment, we could verify a deficiency in sensitivity from the device, especially during the free-handwriting moments, what put obstacles in the way of the task and made the users disconcerted. The classroom were the users took the tests has a glass board, what may influence on the sensitivity of the pen, given its surface being translucent and reflective. The ideal surface for the digital board should have a smooth, dull white finish. Some participants informed that the pen was a somewhat thick and caused discomfort when being manipulated.

To make the experience more productive and pleasant, the pen could be redesigned, in order to improve its sensitivity and speed to answer to commands, besides including, on its laterals, shortcut buttons so that more dynamic actions could be performed, making an easier use of the most used commands, such as forward, backwards possible and changing from pen to highlight marker or eraser.

In face if the results, improvements on the interface of the digital board are necessary, as well as improvements on the physical attributes of the device, with the aim of decreasing chances of uneasiness by the users, turning it into an easier, more enjoyable task. For this reason, it's essential that the companies and professionals producing this type of device give more attention to the needs of the users, making sure the equipment is adequate for them. Moreover, it's indispensable that the user should be interested and familiar with the equipment, what will help him/her to make better use of it – even though the device may present some technical issues, it's still capable of helping to produce dynamic, playful classes for both professors and students. Ergonomics and usability provide a base to these studies, placing humans as the main focus, improving relations between people, machines and interfaces.

References

1. Cybis, W., Holtz, A., Faust, B.R.: Ergonomia e Usabilidade Conhecimentos, Métodos e Aplicações. Avaiable in: http://www.univasf.edu.br/~jorge.cavalcanti/cap1_livro_ergonomia_usabilidade.pdf. Accessed on 01 February 2015
2. Rubin, J., Chisnell, D., Handbook of Usability Testing. Available in: http://ccftp.scu.edu.cn:8090/Download/efa2417b-08ba-438a-b814-92db3dde0eb6.pdf
3. Nakashima, R.H.R.: A Linguagem Audiovisual Da Lousa Digital Interativa No Contexto Educacional. Available in: http://lantec.fae.unicamp.br/lantec/publicacoes/rosaria.pdf. Accessed on 15 june 2014
4. Twyman, M.L. A schema for the study of graphic language. In: Processing of visible language. Kolers, P.A., Wrolstad, M.E., Bouma, H. (eds.). Nova Iorque, pp.117–150 (1979)
5. Epson Brighlink 475 wi + - Manual do Usuário. Avaiable in: http://files.support.epson.com/pdf/bl475wipl/bl475wipluu7.pdf?utm_medium=Special-Content-Brasil&utm_source=Product-Manual&utm_campaign=Projectors&utm_content=BrightLink-475Wi. Accessed: 01 February 2015
6. Braox - Lousa Digital: Saiba todos os diferentes tipos antes de comprar uma. Available in: http://www.braox.com/blog/diferenca-lousa-digital/. Accessed on 01 February 2015
7. Bittencourt, S.P., Coutinho, S., Cadena, R.: Análise do uso da lousa digital na educação básica do Recife. Available in: https://www.dropbox.com/s/lhccuwfo812sjwr/O%20Uso%20da%20Lousa%20Digital%20nas%20Escolas%20do%20Recife%20-%20Sayonara%20Bittencourt.pdf?dl=0. Accessed: 01 Febraury 2015

E-Learning Platforms and Lacking Motivation in Students: Concept of Adaptable UI for Online Courses

Hana Oveslеová[✉]

Information Science and Librarianship, Charles University,
Prague, Czech Republic
hana.ovesleova@gmail.com

Abstract. Current trend of facilitating education for masses through MOOC (Massive Open Online Course) does not much respects different individual specifics influencing success rate of users during the learning process. This paper focuses on issues of MOOC user interfaces from the viewpoint of users' individual needs. It deals with the question of motivation of users depending on an interface, with the question of persuasive design and its potentials in a given context. The paper analyzes effects influencing the user along the learning process, the aim being to specify evaluation criteria for adaptable interface formulation. EdX, Coursera and user interfaces of e-learning courses of the largest Czech universities serve as examples.

Keywords: Persuasive technology · User interface · Motivation · Massive online open course · E-learning · Learning machine · Human computer interaction · Semiotic

1 Introduction

In face to face teaching, a lector has a number of possibilities of instructing and motivating her or his students. Classroom conditions make direct social connections possible. Methodical leadership and personality of the lector are foundations of motivation process. In online environment, it is necessary to delegate this supportive process on system processes and algorithms, whose aim it is to enable the lector to lead arbitrary number of students across time zones and cultures. User interface (UI) thus becomes a deputy of the teacher in relation to the student. This state of matter can be described with the help of semiotics [20]. In such a number of students and multitude of differences among them, maximal use of available tools and manners of UI customization becomes inevitable. Use of new media can be associated with creation of influential learning space. Acquiring of knowledge and skills and support of learning meaningfulness is possible there. New media is capable of supporting learning as an active and creative process, mediating realistic learning situations, and transforming of learning into an interactive process [1].

In recent years, learning has changed from a collection of procedural and factual knowledge into process that springs from what people already know and, according to

© Springer International Publishing Switzerland 2015
A. Marcus (Ed.): DUXU 2015, Part III, LNCS 9188, pp. 218–227, 2015.
DOI: 10.1007/978-3-319-20889-3_21

the context, expands their knowledge. It is therefore necessary to explore and get to understand users' behavior as to effectively exploit the learning process. Aaron Marcus's research and his Learning Machine are a good starting point for the requirements of teaching and the learning process. Using digital technologies, Marcus combines learning theories with user experience, information design, and persuasive techniques [4]. Research, which he carried out at the University of California at Berkeley, implies that majority of students have similar study habits: they have limited experience with online learning, but their relationship towards it and expectations are overall positive. The research has shown that the in the students' view the key part in the learning process is not only the social interaction "student – teacher" but "student – student" as well. An interesting indicator of their perception of the quality of online learning was information about approximately half the price students were willing to pay for online courses in comparison to face to face teaching [4]. Similar research was carried out by the Institute of System Engineering and Informatics, Faculty of Economics and Administration, University of Pardubice; it dealt with introduction of e-learning into the education process and its influence on the students' study outcomes. The results of the research showed quite clearly that introduction of electronic learning influences positively students' study scores and therefore can be a strong motivation factor for studies [10].

If we discover main motivation in a people and respect their individuality, we can effectively influence their behavior and coach them. Interactive technologies whose aim is to influence users' attitude and actions are known as persuasive technologies [2]. They can influence users' attitudes towards themselves as well as to others in a positive way. Being able to use positive characteristics of interpersonal and mass communication, these systems and applications purposively affect human behavior. Well known are applications that can indicate potential health issues as well as those that motivate a person towards better care of her or his physical condition (the application monitors person's physical activity, records physiological processes in the body, assesses results in a longer term, and finally compares the results with known facts). According to Oinas-Kukkonen et al., there are three basic processes of influence on human behavior that need to be taken in account when defining a persuasive system. In the first instance, we reinforce current behavior and make it more resistant towards changes. In the second case, we shape person's reaction to a common problem or a situation, and in the third case, we form a pattern for a new situation. Different aims thus mean use of different strategies and persuasive techniques [3].

2   Theory of Motivation

Motivation is an integral part of human behavior which influences the learning process. Strength and course of motivation are agents of decision making and orientation of every human being. The loss of motivation is the most occurring hindrance on the journey to success. If the term motivation is understood as process of actuation and organization of behavior in order to change positively the existing situation or state of matter, then it is necessary, in the research process, to comprehend especially the roots of human behavior. Over the course of history, attempts have been made to describe and classify the incentives of human behavior, e.g. Maslow [12] or Murray [11]. Human motivation can be generally divided according to the source that brings it about: internal and external motives or combination of both. Inner motives rise from basic biological or social needs. According to Weinschenk, people are generally more motivated by inner than outer rewards. Inner rewards are subconscious and less time dependent [7]. It is therefore necessary to weigh the effectivity of the reward system and other matters that influence the strength of motivation.

2.1 Learning Motivation

Combination of learner's internal and external motives is projected into the learning process. This combination depends on the learner's nature, health state, well-being, and current life situation. Intensity of motives changes along the course of study, and it is therefore necessary to confront them individually. Good example can be Self-Determination Theory (SDT) that focuses on free human decision making and conduct. Does Self-Determination Theory apply to e-Learning? According to Wroten, it is sufficient to satisfy a learner's need for competence, autonomy and relatedness. Learning content should be adequately demanding, allow for individual choice of solution, and should make possible the collaboration among students, which enhances contextual perception [6].

As already mentioned, social aspect of learning is one of the most important requirements in online environment. Social motives influencing interpersonal relationships and experience of these relationships come into play here. Good accomplishment might be therefore determined by effort to achieve success or avoid failure. The strength of achievement motivation effects the difficulty of exercise or ability of working in a team [5]. Another strong motive implemented in learning is the need for affiliation that makes the learner form necessary social contacts and become integrated into social groups. Earlier research has shown that effective management of the social presence in user interface design can improve user engagement and motivation. Enhancing social presence in an e-learning environment seems to instill the learner with an impression of a quality learning experience. One benefit is to induce and sustain the learners' motivation. The enhancement of social presence can create a successful learning experience in situations involving learners and instructors in online environments [4]. That is why is social network module is one of the main five pillars of information architecture in Marcus's Learning Machine.

2.2 Motivation in MOOC Students

In MOOC environment, meeting of large numbers of students from different cultures and with different motivations occurs. As observed in Frequently Asked Questions at Openculture.com, one of the prominent kinds of motivation for passing the course is a prospect of a better job or stronger position at the labor market. Although it is difficult to prove causal relationship between getting a new job and finishing an online course, passing of the course might be viewed in learners as a positive initiative to "update their skill set, acquire new skills, or simply extend their knowledge base" [13]. Character-istics of open courses is a broad offer of highly valuable content to a large audience together with high time and space flexibility. Their feature is connecting people from all parts of the world [8]. Whereas individual learning suits people who prefer their own learning pace, social aspect of MOOC gives opportunity of social interaction to those who need it for reaching their goal. According to Yesil, there are four basic groups of students, when it comes to observing their course participation: There are those who fulfill most of assignments in the course, those who watch videos only, students who fulfill all the assignments at the beginning of the course and resign after three weeks, and finally the occasional visitors, who view the videos only in the assessment period [8]. What might be an important finding is a fact, that the most social interaction and activity in the discussion forums is carried out by the first mentioned group. It is possible to stipulate that there is a certain connection between social interaction and passing of the course [8]. Thus it is appropriate to focus on the support of students' social motivation through external motivation agents, such as variable awards, contests, competition [7] or tools, which are commonly used in outside classroom sphere of social media, such as the option of sharing, approving comments and likes, that increase social presence [4].

3 Interface in Learning

"Everybody is a genius. But if you judge a fish by its ability to climb a tree, it will live its whole life believing that it is stupid." –Albert Einstein

User interface specifics for learning purposes are dealt with by Marcus. The Learning Machine's primary objectives are the following: Combine information design/visualization with persuasion design; persuade users to adapt their behavior and lifestyles to include better understanding of engagement, exploration, explanation, extension, and evaluation in the learning process; and apply user-centered design along with persuasive techniques to make the Learning Machine highly usable, useful, and appealing, thereby increasing the efficiency and effectiveness of users' efforts of knowledge-acquisition and retention behaviors [4]. Due to the fact that mental load on the user is considerable during the learning process, further load, caused by inappro-priately designed interface, is not desirable. From ergonomics point of view, mental load is much more demanding on the user than the motoric load, and that is why the key demand on the learning interface is intuitiveness and simplicity [7]. That way, it is not necessary to concentrate on absolute minimum of operations connected with certain action, but on agreement of the concept with mental model of the user. This is the reason why use of design patterns, that observe the cognitive consistency, is advisable.

From the point of view of content, it is important to realize in which way and form the information will be distributed. In this respect, asking the following questions is useful: Is arrangement of information linear or is it interconnected? Is information processed dynamically, as in case of simulation? Is it administered in a parallel way, is it possible to transform information of one type into another type of information? In this case, selection of solution, which well reflects student's preferences according to

How would you prefer to learn online?

Item	Score		Overall Rank
Video-recorded lecture	males	84	1
	females	91	
Online textual materials	males	35	2
	females	7	
Video conference	males	21	3
	females	35	
Textual chat/forum	males	14	4
	females	21	
Slides (PPT)	males	14	5
	females	21	
Conference call	males	7	6
	females	0	
Sound-recorded lecture	males	0	7
	females	0	

Fig. 1. Students' preferences in the learning form context (Brejcha et al. 2014)

learning typology, should be made [14]. Outcomes of 2014 research carried out by Brejcha et al. at Sino-European Usability Center can be used as an example [15] (Fig. 1).

User interface of e-learning systems must be, on the top of all the requirements mentioned above, highly motivational. Keeping to several general principles that influence users in a positive way is advisable, according to Weinschenk. She works on the assumption that the closer the users are to the goal, the more motivated they are, and that is why she suggests the goals be visualized and kept visible during the whole course of the learning process. Furthermore, she emphasized reward variability – with regard to the time interval as well as to the number of reactions –, progress monitoring, control over performed activity and last but not least adequate competition environment [7]. Apt example of implementation of plausible reward system is Open Badges Veriod system [9], independent platform for issuing and collecting of digital verification badges. They work as a certificate, universal manner of recognition, documentation, and sharing of life achievements.

4 Ergonomics of E-Learning User Interface

User interfaces of EdX and Coursera MOOC as well as the interfaces of online courses of the largest Czech universities (Charles University Prague, Technical University of Ostrava, Masaryk University of Brno, University of Pardubice, and University of West Bohemia Pilsen) are being analyzed within "Concept of Adaptable UI for Online Courses" framework. For the interfaces of above mentioned courses, highly specialized content is typical, which is being offered to the wide public. In case of MOOC, we speak about tens of thousands of users, in Czech environment, it is more likely thousands of users. Whereas e-learning environment of Czech universities is meant especially for Czech users (with the exception of several hundreds of foreign students who study at Czech universities within the frame of ERASMUS exchange program), which means quite homogenous group of users with low age variability, MOOC EdX a Coursera turn to users from all over the world, thus facilitating education to everyone, independently of age, previous education, age or nationality. The only precondition is adequate language knowledge (Figs. 2, 3).

Fig. 2. EdX University of Toronto (retrieved Feb 7, 2015)

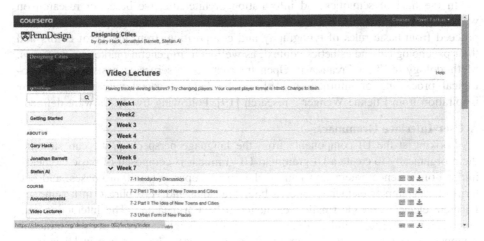

Fig. 3. Coursera University of Pennsylvania (retrieved January 23, 2015)

Outcome of the analysis will be definition of evaluation criteria for UI of online courses and putting together of methodology of UI design for e-learning platforms, furthermore concept of adaptable UI for MOOC e-learning platforms and comparative testing of users (Fig. 4).

Fig. 4. Moodle University of Pardubice (retrieved February 9, 2015)

4.1   Starting Points for UI MOOC Assessment

Main starting points for UI of e-learning courses examination rise loosely from general evaluation rules and are complemented with aspects related directly with learning process.

In the field of semiotics and information architecture, we base our research on works by Aaron Marcus and Jan Brejcha [16]. In the field of graphics design, we proceed from basic rules of typography and composition, from theory of colors and their psychological and esthetics context, as well as from general marketing strategies. Methodology for Text Creation in Open Internet Space serves as basis for methodological processing of information [18]. In the field of social networks, we draw inspiration from Etienne Wenger's research [19]. Following five fields were defined:

A User Interface Grammar.

Looking at the UI components from the language perspective, we can structure them organically to create a UI grammar. UI grammar is composed of basic elements: interaction sentence, interaction games, rhetorical tropes, interaction phases, and patterns. The grammar elements concern both the noun and verb phrase in a sentence. Discrete elements are the smallest elements to have a meaning. The interaction sentence is a meaningful unit describing a task in a user's interaction. A set of interaction sentences with the same goal form an interaction game. The narrative in UI is made both by the designer's metacommunication and the temporal aspect of perceiving UI elements. Rhetorical tropes are devices of persuasion and emphasis, often presented as metaphors. Patterns are typical configurations of UI language components in different settings [17].

B Information architecture.

Meaningful interconnection of all UI components maintains consistency and contributes to "making smarter decisions faster" [4]. These UI components are: metaphors (essential concepts in words, images, sounds, touch), mental models (organization of data, functions, tasks, roles of people at work or play, static or mobile), navigation (movement through mental models via windows, dialogue boxes, buttons, links, etc.), interaction (input/output techniques, feedback, overall behavior of systems and people) and appearance (visual-verbal, acoustic, tactile qualities) [4].

C Look and Feel.

Graphical design induces desirable positive emotions that support learning activity. Design includes respecting of typographical rules, use of suitable composition solutions for individual types of display, and use of appropriate graphical elements supporting understanding and amount of their simplification (ranging from simple pictograms to realistic images or 3D models). Furthermore it includes system of visual hierarchy of individual UI elements and also use of color schemes that respect sensory effects of colors and cover individual culture specifics. Global design must support visual comfort of the user – mental condition in user when visual tasks are being solved with minimal eye fatigue and the user feels pleasant.

D Methodology of information processing.

A form of mediated content depending on user styles typology - visual (spatial), aural (auditory-musical), verbal (linguistic), physical (kinesthetic), logical (mathematical), social (interpersonal) and solitary (intrapersonal) [21] - which respects the student's choice and supports new information contraction. Moreover inclusion of gamification elements that help reach users' goals through incentives, loyalty programs, collections, status strengthening, needs fulfillment etc.

E Social Network.

Social environment and the possibility of engagement (social environment, social media, virtual environment). For current users, social media is a natural environment, which supports teamwork and peer learning. Moreover, social media is connected to positive emotions and offers wide choices of motivation agents. Furthermore teaching support, role of the teacher or lector consisting of feedback provision, encouragement, and learner's support.

5 Conclusion

Current e-learning platforms of courses in Czech university environment propose to extend their role from mere support of full-time classes to fully-fledged online courses for wide public. To realize successfully their role, the courses must be prepared and created with great care. Inspiration can be drawn from current MOOC, even though user interfaces of these courses do not respect learners' individuality, their needs nor cultural manners, which play substantial part in the learning process. The aim of the project is a design of adaptable MOOC user interface, which will support the students in active work, motivate them to progress, influence them in a positive way and make the process of learning easy on them. A set of evaluation criteria for online courses UI creation will also be the result of the research.

References

1. Hartl, P.: Kompendium pedagogické psychologie dospělých. Praha: Karolinum, 231 s (1999). ISBN 80-7184-841-7
2. Fogg, B.J.: Persuasive Technlogy: Using Computers to Change What We Think and Do. Morgan Kaufmann Publishers, San Francisco (2003)
3. Oinas-Kukkonen, H., Harjumaa, M.: A systematic framework for designing and evaluating persuasive systems. In: Oinas-Kukkonen, H., Hasle, P., Harjumaa, M., Segerståhl, K., Øhrstrøm, P. (eds.) PERSUASIVE 2008. LNCS, vol. 5033, pp. 164–176. Springer, Heidelberg (2008)
4. Abdelnour-Nocera, J., Austin, A., Michaelides, M., Modi, S.: A Cross-cultural evaluation of HCI student performance – reflections for the curriculum. In: Marcus, A. (ed.) DUXU 2013, Part II. LNCS, vol. 8013, pp. 161–170. Springer, Heidelberg (2013)
5. Plháková, A.: Učebnice obecné psychologie. Academia Praha (2010). ISBN 978-80-200-1499-3
6. Wroten, C.: Motivate your learners! the self-determination theory for e-Learning. eLearning Industry (2014). http://elearningindustry.com/motivate-learners-self-determination-theory-e-learning
7. Weinschenk, S.: 100 Things Every Designer Needs to Know About People. New Riders Publishing, Berkeley (2011). ISBN 9780321767530
8. Yesil, D.: How To Motivate MOOC Learners. eLearning Industry (2014). http://elearningindustry.com/motivate-mooc-learners
9. http://www.veriod.com
10. Komárková, J., Hub, M., Sedlák, P.: Benefits of e-learning in the education of geoinformation technologies at the faculty of Economics and Administration University of Pardubice. In: DIVAI 2014 10th International Scientific Conference on Distance Learning in Applied Informatics Conference Proceedings. Štúrovo, Slovakia, pp. 93–103 (2014). ISBN: 978-80-7478-497-2
11. Murray, H.: A: Exploration in personality. Oxford University Press (1938). https://archive.org/details/explorationsinpe031973mbp
12. Maslow, A.H.: A theory of human motivation. Psychol. Rev. **50**(4), 370–396 (1943). http://psychclassics.yorku.ca/Maslow/motivation.html
13. Will MOOCs help you open career doors? http://edf.stanford.edu/readings/will-moocs-help-you-open-career-doors
14. Education Planner: What's Your Learning Style? http://www.educationplanner.org/students/self-assessments/learning-styles-quiz.s.html
15. Jan Brejcha et al.: Chinese UI Guidelines Revisited (2015)
16. Brejcha, J., Marcus, A.: Semiotics of Interaction: Towards a UI Alphabet. In: Kurosu, M. (ed.) HCII/HCI 2013, Part I. LNCS, vol. 8004, pp. 13–21. Springer, Heidelberg (2013)

17. Brejcha, J.: Cross-Cultural Human-Computer Interaction and User Experience Design: A Semiotic Perspective. CRC Press, Taylor & Francis Group, LLC, Boca Raton, London, New York (2015). ISBN 978-1-4987-0257-7
18. Dlouhá, J. et al.: Metodika tvorby textů v otevřeném internetovém prostoru. http://www.msmt.cz/file/25110/download/
19. Wenger, E.: Communities of practice and social learning systems: the career of a concept. In: Blackmore, C. (ed.) Social Learning Systems And Communities Of Practice. Springer and the Open University, London (2010)
20. De Souza, C.S.: The Semiotic Engineering of Human-computer Interaction. Acting with technology. MIT Press (2005)
21. http://learning-styles-online.com/overview/

A Usability Study with Children on an Online Educational Platform

Tuba Ugras[1(✉)] and Orhan Sener[2]

[1] Education Faculty, Yildiz Technical University, Istanbul, Turkey
tugras@yildiz.edu.tr
[2] Media and Communication Studies, Galatasaray University, Istanbul, Turkey
orhan.sener@ogr.gsu.edu.tr

Abstract. Online education has become widely popular in the last decade. Although there are various online educational portals for children in the World and in Turkey, the number of usability studies focusing on the needs of children is limited. This study aims to fill this gap. The study focuses on Vitamin online educational platform in Turkey and investigates the find and search strategies that child users employ when navigating in the web site. A qualitative usability test with a multi-method approach was conducted with a sample of 12 Turkish students between the ages of 9–13. Observations were made while the participants were executing the given tasks. Additional data was collected by using the retrospective think aloud procedure, pre-test survey and video recordings. The findings showed that several improvements can be made in terms of information architecture in order to improve the usability of the platform for children.

Keywords: Usability · Children · Educational platforms

1 Introduction

Online educational platforms have become widely popular in the last decade. There are several kinds of online educational platforms: Learning Management Systems (LMSs) such as Moodle (*moodle.com*), Massive Open Online Courses (MOOCs) such as Coursera (*coursera.org*), Learning Object Repositories (LORs) such as Khan Academy (*khanacademy.org*), Social Networking Sites (SNSs) such as Wikispaces Classroom (*wikispaces.com/content/classroom*), etc. These types of online educational platforms have not drawn sharp distinctions. Indeed, most of the time, an online educational platform shows the characteristics of more than one type. However, the main point here is to illustrate the platforms that support learning activities rather than making any categorization.

The most important online educational platform for children in Turkey is EBA (*eba.gov.tr*), the Educational IT Network, which is one of the outcomes of the national project named FATİH. It is a huge project supported by the government in order to provide technology integration in schools [6]. Vitamin (*vitaminegitim.com*) and Morpa Kampüs (*morpakampus.com*) are among the content suppliers of EBA. Vitamin and Morpa Kampüs both provide online learning contents in parallel to the national educational program for students -K12 and K8, respectively- as well as tracking their

© Springer International Publishing Switzerland 2015
A. Marcus (Ed.): DUXU 2015, Part III, LNCS 9188, 228–239, 2015.
DOI: 10.1007/978-3-319-20889-3_22

progress in the platform. These two are the most popular and the largest online educational platforms in Turkey. On the other hand, Khan Academy has started to publish its Turkish version but it is new and the size of its content is very limited.

LMS is *"a software application that automates the administration, tracking, and reporting of training events"* [5] and thus it is used for managing online educational environments. MOOC is *"an online course with the option of free and open registration, a publicly shared curriculum, and open-ended outcomes"* [12] and its main features are offering courses as free and targeting massive audience. LORs are the platforms that provide mechanisms to encourage learning objects' discovery, exchange, and reuse [16] and LORs are important for both students and teachers to share and utilize from learning objects. There are other types of online educational platforms, as well. However, the general benefit of online education platforms are summarized by Appana [1] as *"increased access, improved quality of learning, better preparation of students for a knowledge-based society, lifelong learning opportunity"*. In this context, it is important to examine on usability issues of online educational platforms in order to maximize the advantages of them. Additionally, considering children as one of the diverse user groups, examining on usability issues of the ones targeting children comes into prominence.

This study is planned to be a first step in a series of long-term research. The online educational platform, Vitamin, was investigated since it offers the richest content for children in Turkey. The study aims to offer insights to improve usability in online educational platforms. In order to fulfill the aim, a qualitative usability test, based on a multi-method approach, was designed and conducted with 12 participants who are between 9–13 years old.

2   Theoretical Background

Online educational platforms offered for children have been studied by several researchers in the frame of usability issues. Among those studies which are conducted with children, the recent ones that have employed user testing method are exemplified below.

Mohammad, Repass, and Mazarakis [13] published a report on usability of Khan Academy, which is based on a user testing study done with three children from 4th, 5th, and 7th grades. According to the report, task completion success rates were 100 % - with some minor errors- and the satisfaction level of children was found to be high. On the other hand, some participants stated that they had some trouble with, for example, locating the links which they were asked for.

Çetin and Özdemir [4] analyzed the usability issues of Morpa Kampüs via user testing with ten children aged 9–11, within the frame of satisfaction and ease of use. The results showed that the satisfaction level was very high although the participants rated the difficulty level as also very high. Some of the participants couldn't see the homepage link easily, which was on the top menu frame. All participants had difficulty in finding the menu item for the topic requested. Researchers commented on that the menu items should be rearranged. Participants could easily close the windows but it took longer for one participant because the close icon was near the arithmetical "x" symbol, which has the same representation of the close icon. In other words, there was a confusion with the symbols and/or the placements of the symbols. Some participants couldn't use easily the drop-down menu for the exam part. Researchers explained that it may be more difficult to use drop-down menus for children. Only one participant used the search bar. Some participants didn't try to the link for return back, instead, they used the "Undo" button while navigating between the pages. On the other hand, participants did not have any difficulty to complete the task of finding and playing the educational game.

Yılmaz and Tüfekci [17] identified usability problems for the ex-design of the Vitamin platform in their study with twelve 6th graders. Most participants had trouble with the tasks of finding the required topic and using the search bar for the required word. The researchers put some suggestions as the followings: the topic hierarchy should be revised according to the age groups' characteristics, search bar should get standardized in order for making sure of its consistency, and the exit button should be used on a standard position on the top right corner.

On the other hand, it should be noted that children are considered as a special user group in terms of user testing. As stated by Nielsen [14], children and adults are different in their user behaviors and their needs regarding web design issues. First of all, physical and mental abilities of children differ from adults. Additionally, children's expectations from web sites are towards entertainment whereas adults expect mainly to get things done and to provide communication. In other words, it is observed that children have different characteristics while navigating and searching the web.

As a result, the main concerns related to educational platforms targeting children are revealed as the issues on information architecture and satisfaction. Thus, there is a need for more studies with higher-quality, which have the power of especially revealing the weaknesses in information architecture of those web sites and perceiving the actual level of children's satisfaction. However, it is not easy to conduct a user testing with child users. The only way to accomplish this is to conduct the user testing sessions by considering the rules -as suggested by several researchers [2, 7, 8, 11] - on working with child users. Also, an appropriate framework for discussion should be drawn carefully. We tried to design a usability study by taking this kind of need into consideration. Our study has importance in terms of recommending implications to improve usability in online educational platforms targeting children.

3   Methodology

This study aims to explore the usability issues in online educational platforms offered primary and secondary students in Turkey concerning the navigation and information search strategies. Research question of the study is the following: What are the usability issues regarding the navigation and information search strategies for 9–13 years old children in Vitamin educational platform?

In order to fulfill the objectives of this study, Vitamin online educational platform was chosen since it has been commonly used in Turkey and has a variety of contents for different age groups.

In the studies concerning design for children, it is needed to target very narrow age groups [5]. Therefore, one of the narrow age groups, 9–12 aged children –named as *older children* by Nielsen [14] – was chosen as the target user group in this study. Because "*children younger than 7 years have difficulty in expressing themselves verbally and being self-reflective*" [3], in usability studies, it'd better to work with older children especially for novice researchers. On the other hand, the content of Vitamin platform is categorized under school subjects based on the grades in schools; and the age range of 9–12 correspond to 4th-7th graders. However, some children at the same age may be in different grades. For instance, one of 4th graders may be at the age of 9 and the other at the age of 10. Therefore, we chose the sample based on the grades. The sample then comprised 12 children (4 girls, 8 boys) aged between 9 years and 13 years, from different schools in Istanbul, Turkey. 3 participants were 4th graders, 2 were 5th graders, 4 were 6th graders, and 3 were 7th graders. In order to mention the participants, we used the codes like that "number, grade-gender-age", for example, "second, 4-M-10" refers to the second participant who is a 4th grader boy at the age of 10.

The tests were conducted in the places of the children, instead of a laboratory environment, in order not to let them be anxious. Indeed, several researchers [2, 8, 11] suggest to work with children in an appropriate environment which children can feel themselves comfort. Also some other precautions have been taken in order to execute the test process with children in an effective way, such as setting the test duration no more than 30 min, encouraging children by offering positive feedback, and using phrases like in the form of "*I need you to...*" instead of asking them if they want to do a task -as suggested by several researchers [2, 8, 11]. Most importantly, it should be asserted the child is not the one being tested, even if it is called as a test [8]. Accordingly, we carried out a protocol with each child.

This study is a qualitative study based on a multi-method approach consisted of pre-test, test, and post-test sessions. Pre-test is an interview carried out using a structured questionnaire, which is consisted of questions about the participant's background in computer, Internet, and educational platform usages. Test has two sub-sessions of task observation and retrospective think aloud. As Barendregt and Bekker [2] stated that thinking aloud is not easy for young children. Even though our participants are not young children, we did not want to impose them to think aloud, then we decided to use retrospective think aloud method. Post-test is again an interview carried out using another structured questionnaire, which is consisted of questions concerning overall impression of the participant for the platform.

In the beginning of the test process, we run the pre-test at first. Meanwhile, we made sure that the participant was comfortable with the computer setup, as suggested by Hanna, Risden, & Alexander [8]. Then, we asked their opinions about the sections on the homepage in order to get them practice the platform before the actual test for a while, -as suggested by Barendregt and Bekker [2].

After the pre-test and some warm-up with the computer and the platform, we conducted the test. The test scenario was written for the Vitamin platform with five tasks: (i) Finding a specific topic, (ii) playing the video for that topic, (iii) examining the video content, (iv) taking the test for that topic, (v) returning back to the main page. Although the structure of the tasks are the same for each grade, the topics differ according to the grades since the content of the courses differ for each grades. Task completion for each participant was directly observed and recorded on a structured observation sheet by the researchers, one moderator and one observer. It was also recorded through a screen-recorder software (Silverback 2.7). After completion of the tasks, we talked to the participant about the task, in the retrospective think aloud session. Then, the post-test was carried out.

In this study, a descriptive qualitative analysis, by using a framework, is conducted for the discussion of the findings. The analysis framework was derived by integrating the fundamental principles of usability [9] into the study of Nielsen [14] which summarizes some of the main similarities and differences observed in user behavior between children and adults. The framework includes the following parameters: Information Architecture, Visibility, Discoverability and Feedback, and User Satisfaction.

4 Results and Discussion

The results of the background questionnaire revealed that the participants were active Internet users with an average of 2 h Internet usage per weekdays and 3.5 h per weekend days. 8 of them have used Vitamin or a similar online educational platform before and 2 of them are current users of that platform.

During the test process, each session took approximately 13.5 min. All of the participants completed the tasks successfully, except 2 participants who had help in Task 2 which was about finding the required topic. It was observed that gender was not a distinctive parameter in task performances. On the other hand, older participants were more effective in task performance. This is an expected situation since Nielsen [14] says about child users that they get substantially more web-savvy as they get older.

4.1 Information Architecture

The major issues observed in terms of information architecture were related to navigation structure and labeling.

One of the most remarkable problems with navigation structure appeared in 3rd level vertical left-hand navigation menu. For some courses, there are two menu items with the same name in different levels, such as "Net Force" ("Bileşke Kuvvet") seen in Fig. 1. The ninth (6-F-11) and the sixth participant (6-M-12) could not find this sub-tab menu item, thus could not access its content. Although both participants clicked the main tab and saw the sub-tab with the same name, they could not see the content on the right pane, they got frustrated and then started looking for the content on other places within the page. Thus, they had to complete the related task by getting some help. They told that they had expected to see the content on the right pane when the sub-tab was clicked. Although this problem did not exist in each course -thus we observed it only with 6th graders-, it is an important one in terms of information architecture. As evidently seen, participants had some confusion because of the misleading navigation structure.

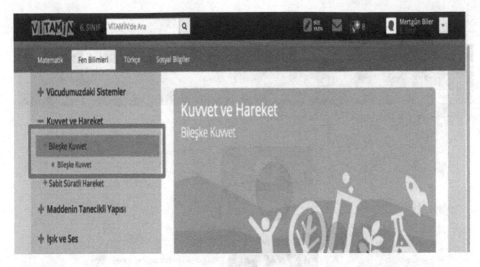

Fig. 1. 3rd level vertical left-hand navigation menu detail from content page of Vitamin

The reason behind this information architecture issue is the deep navigational structure of four-degree leveling -seen in Fig. 2. It seems that this deep structure made it difficult to navigate through the web site for children. As Nielsen [14] stated that multiple levelling in navigation is very confusing for children.

Labeling was the other major issue in terms of information architecture; the labels of menu items and buttons were found to be confusing. For example, on the content pane, there are two sub-sections of "Study Selectively" ("Seçerek Çalış") and "Study Sequentially" ("Sıralı Çalış") seen in Fig. 2. In fact, these two sub-sections comprise the same learning materials but in different ways, i.e. they offer different ways to study the materials. It was found to be difficult for participants to understand that these sub-sections had different functionalities (n = 5). Additionally, although one participant (third, 4-M-10) understood that they were different, he could not explain what the difference was.

As another example for the confusion related to labeling: The similarities and differences between "Exams" ("Sınavlar"), "Review Tests" ("Tarama Testleri"), and "Practices" ("Alıştırmalar") -seen in Fig. 2- were found to be difficult to understand (n = 2). For instance, eighth participant (6-M-11) could not understand that it was possible to access the "Review Tests" by clicking the "Exams" menu item. In fact, the "Review Tests" menu item on the 4th level menu navigates to the same page as the "Exams" menu item on the main menu does. On the other hand, the "Practices" menu item on the 4th level menu navigates to another page that also includes tests but in a different format. The reason behind these kind of confusions may be related to the common perception that any difference in the menu names implies to navigate different contents.

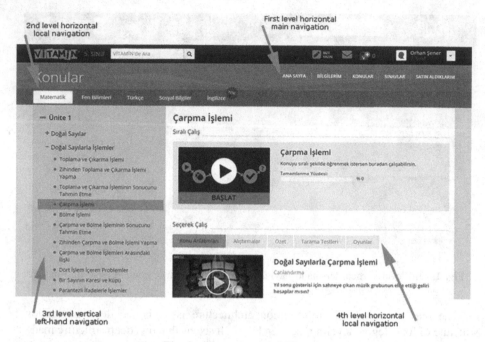

Fig. 2. Content page of Vitamin

As another example, the section of "My Info" ("Bilgilerim") -seen in Fig. 3- on the homepage contains information about the web site user, seventh participant (6-F-11) thought that it contained information about the Vitamin web site. This can be interpreted as children perceives the possessive pronouns used in the labels in a different way than adults. Another confusion observed with sixth participant (6-M-12) who said that *"it is the info about my courses"*, implying all the information was about his courses, not something else. Additionally, the function of "My Purchases" ("Satın Aldıklarım") -seen in Fig. 3- was found to be difficult to understand (n = 7). For instance, eleventh participant (7-F-12) thought this section contained books that she had and said *"There should be an explanation here"*. It is possible to argue that children may have trouble to understand abstract concepts, such as information and purchase.

4.2 Visibility

In terms of visibility, the major issues were found to be color contrast, location basis issues, size issues, and multiple levelling.

The most significant problems observed as the difficulty in seeing of menu items and buttons, such as "Review Tests" menu item, the play/pause buttons on the videos, the video navigation bar itself, the main menu itself, and the search bar. "Review Tests" menu item on the 4th level horizontal local navigation menu could not be seen (n = 7). Some difficulties were experienced with the visibility of play/pause buttons which are the learning materials presented on the sections of "Exercises" and "Tutorials"

("Konu Anlatımları") -seen in Fig. 2- (n = 5). As a unique but interesting case, one participant (twelfth, 7-F-13) could not see the 1st level horizontal main navigation menu. Additionally, the search box could not be seen in some cases (n = 4).

When asked why they could not see the search bar and the main menu, the participants stated that they could not identify the reason specifically but one (twelfth, 7-F-13) -the one who could not see the main menu- stated that it could be related to the resemblance of colors. Regarding color contrast issues, there were some suggestions stating that the color of the active (selected) sub-section of the 3rd level vertical left-hand navigation menu could be in a different color than the other sub-sections. For instance, twelfth participant (7-F-13) said *If this link (sub-section) was in a different color, I could better understand where I am.* It implies that there is an insufficiency in terms of breadcrumbs on the platform.

The video navigation bar which was placed in the top right on the video screen while it is normally common to place it in the bottom. For example, twelfth participant (7-F-13) said that the video navigation bar should have been bigger, since it was placed in a different position. This comment implies that there are both size and location basis issues with the video navigation bar. Indeed, it is suggested, by the conventional best practices for children, to add navigational elements as being large and easy to find [10].

Additionally, first participant (4-M-10), who could see the main menu, stated that the main menu would be really useful if the 4th level horizontal local navigation menu did not exist. Thus it seems there is a problem caused by multiple levelling in the navigation structure.

Location basis issues and multiple levelling issues can also be evaluated as an issue regarding the lack of consistency and standards. There is a four-degree levelling in navigation structure, three are horizontal and one is vertical. The main menu -which is horizontal- is on the right but another horizontal menu -the 2nd level navigation menu- on the left. There is also one more horizontal menu -4th level navigation- on the right. Therefore, regarding the lack of consistency and standards, there is a confusion with the locations of the menus due to multiple levelling.

4.3   Discoverability and Feedback

The major issues in terms of discoverability and feedback appeared to be related to navigational alternatives and visualization.

Most significant issue related to discoverability and feedback was the reaction of participants to the navigational alternatives. For example, the existence of alternative ways to access the homepage was received positively (n = 12). These alternative ways were even referred as the best thing in the web site (n = 3). However, there was one exception to this that the fifth participant (5-M-10) said he would have lessen the number of alternatives if he was given the chance although he was successful at finding alternative ways to access the homepage. On the other hand, some alternatives could not be seen by all participants, for instance, the existence of two different ways of selecting the right answers and navigating through the questions on the "Review Tests" page was not clearly understood (n = 4). Nevertheless, all participants, including the ones who could not understand, stated that it was a good thing to have these alternatives -which allow users to select the answers in the right column and/or in the left column. For example, twelfth participant (7-F-13) said *"I think it is better to have this in both sides, I mean, you can read the question on the left pane, and answer it and then pass to the next question on the right"*. Similarly, eleventh participant (7-F-12) said *"It is much better to be able to click on the answers in both sides."* Indeed, Nielsen [14] claims, based on his research, that *"children like to try many options, minesweeping the screen."* This is also not surprising since today's children are defined as digital natives by Prensky [15] and he claims that digital natives prefer random access, which makes multiple options necessary.

Fig. 3. Homepage of Vitamin

As another issue, some participants misinterpreted the *Vitamin Scores* icon -seen in Fig. 3- which shows the points gained by examining the content and completing the exercises (n = 2). For example, eleventh participant (7-F-12) thought that the icon showed how many followers you have, making an analogy to social media elements. Although this was a problem for some participants, it should be noted that despite the icon does not reveal what it represents clearly, it at least gathers attraction from children and thus they would click the icon to see what it is. It seems that it is important to get users attracted through analogies while implementing visualization methods used in icon design. This is also coherent with the study of Nielsen [14] that emphasizes on children's exploratory behavior; children like to explore in web pages.

4.4   User Satisfaction

We analyzed participants' overall satisfaction with the Vitamin platform regarding their attitudes toward using the platform, perceived difficulty, learnability, and perceived usefulness. It should be noted here that we deliberately did not use *net promoter score* since we have observed in the pilot tests that the participants did not respond well to this frame. Instead, we have used a three level scale by asking the participants whether they liked it, did not like it or were indifferent (partly liked it). The overall satisfaction level with the platform was found significantly positive.

In terms of attitudes, all the participants stated that they liked the design of the platform and would like to use it again. Among the best thing on the platform which the participants stated are listed as the following: opportunity to access interactive videos, to take exams, to be offered alternative ways to do things, to use the search bar, to access some topics also in English versions. Also, several participants made some suggestions in order for improving the platform. The first participant (4-M-10), for example, said "I would like to see a thumbs up icon when I achieve something." This can be seen as a proof to the importance of achievement badges in educational platforms. The same participant also said "When something happens that I don't like, I would like to explode it with a Minecraft Creeper." Another participant (tenth, 7-M-13) stated that it was irritating to see that all sections on the homepage were about school and lectures but there should have been also some fun content. These can be interpreted as a supporting evidence to the benefits of fun and gamification elements in online educational platforms. As another recommendation, some participants said that they would like to turn off the ads because they felt disturbed by the ads. This should also be taken into consideration since the ads seem to fail their main goal but do the opposite by irritating the user. Nielsen [14] says children have difficulty in distinguishing advertising and promotions from real content; thus advertising and promotions should be used carefully.

In terms of perceived difficulty, it was stated that it was easy to use the platform (n = 11). Exceptionally, one participant (fifth, 5-M-10) said that he found the web site partly easy to use because there were too many choices. It should be added that, this participant completed all the tasks successfully. Another issue that could be associated with perceived difficulty is learnability. In terms of learnability, only one participant (second, 4-M-10) said that it was not easy to learn how to use the platform, however, he also completed all the tasks successfully. It was also stated that learning how to use the platform was partly easy (n = 4) but learning how to use the platform was found mostly to be easy (n = 7). Regarding that the participants were successful in task completion, even they found the platform partly easy to use or to learn how to use it, this may mean that they had no difficulty to use the platform but were not satisfied at all with their experience on using it.

In terms of perceived usefulness, all the participants stated that they thought the platform was very useful, especially for their school stuff. Another issue that could be associated with perceived usefulness is recommendation of the platform. All the participants stated that they would recommend the platform to their friends. In other words, they would like their friends to try the platform since the platform is very useful.

5 Conclusion

The importance of examination of educational platforms for children is undeniable. In this study, we have examined the Vitamin platform and it can be said that the level of efficiency, effectiveness and satisfaction are found to be high. All participants have completed their tasks successfully and the level of overall satisfaction was stated as sufficient. Almost all participants stated that they liked the platform, found it useful, would like to use it again, and would recommend it to their friends.

However, it should also be noted that there are still some aspects for improvement which we have discussed in the previous section. After all, among the parameters of analysis framework, it is evidently seen that information architecture issues are at the very center of the research findings. Considering all the usability issues identified within the analysis framework, the following implications for the improvement of usability in Vitamin platform can be suggested:

- Deep level of navigation structure should be avoided since it is very confusing for children.
- Redundant sub-tabs should be eliminated, for example, if they have the same name as the tab above.
- The same named navigational elements should be used for navigating to the same pages in labeling menu items, buttons, etc. Similarly, navigational elements for navigating to different pages should be named differently.
- The labeling language should be updated in a way that children can understand easily.
- Abstract concepts should be used carefully in labeling. For example, some explanation phrases can be added to in order to associate to the names of menu items, buttons, etc.
- The video navigation bar should be placed on the bottom, taking its standard placement into consideration.
- Colors should be used in a way that provides contrast between the figure and the ground, in order to enhancing visibility.
- Color preferences can be changed in a way that would make selected sections more visible, in order to make bread crumbs on the site.
- Elements, such as navigational alternatives, which provide opportunity for children to behave exploratory should always be offered.
- Achievement badges should be used more widely.
- Gamification elements should be added more intensively.
- Advertising and promotions should be used carefully in a way that do not irritate children.

Iterative testing by children is required for the development and improvement of computer products for children [8]. Thus, we also recommend periodic usability tests for Vitamin to be conducted. Indeed, this study is the first step of a long-term research, we are planning to continue to investigate the Vitamin educational platform for different scenarios with various task for the future research agenda.

Acknowledgements. We would like to thank the Vitamin educational platform (*vitaminegitim. com*) for giving authorization us to access the web site content and supporting us to report the results in an academic environment. We would like to thank TEGV (*tegv.org*) and Hello World (*helloworld.com.tr*) for giving us a chance to work with their students. We also thank Kerem Rizvanoglu (PhD) for the fruitful discussions during the writing of this paper.

References

1. Appana, S.: A review of benefits and limitations of online learning in the context of the student, the instructor and the tenured faculty. Int. J. E-Learn. **7**(1), 5–22 (2008)
2. Barendregt, W., Bekker, M.: Guidelines for user testing with children. Technical report, Eindhoven, The Netherlands (2003)
3. Bruckman, A., Bandlow, A.: Human-computer interaction for kids. In: Sears, E., Jacko, J.A. (eds.) Human-Computer Interaction Handbook: Fundamentals, Evolving Technologies, and Emerging Applications. L. Erlbaum Associates Inc., Hillsdale (2002). ISBN: 978-0805838381, 428-440
4. Çetin, E., Özdemir, S.: A study on an educational website's usability. Procedia-Soc. Behav. Sci. **83**, 683–688 (2013)
5. Ellis, R.K.: Field guide to learning management systems. ASTD Learning Circuits. https://www.td.org/~/media/Files/Publications/LMS_fieldguide_20091
6. Fatih Projesi. http://www.fatihprojesi.com/ [Retrieved on 13 Jan 2015]
7. Gelman, D.L.: Design For Kids. Rosenfeld Media, Brooklyn (2014)
8. Hanna, L., Risden, K., Alexander, K.: Guidelines for usability testing with children. Interactions **4**(5), 9–14 (1997)
9. ISO 9241-11, Ergonomic requirements for office work with visual display terminals (VDTS) - part 11: guidance on usability (1998). https://www.iso.org/obp/ui/#iso:std:iso:9241:-11:ed-1:v1:en
10. Lazaris, L.: Designing websites for kids: trends and best practices (2009).http://www.smashingmagazine.com/2009/11/27/designing-websites-for-kids-trends-and-best-practices/
11. Markopoulos, P., Bekker, M.: On the assessment of usability testing methods for children. Interact. Comput. **15**(2), 227–243 (2003)
12. McAulay, A., Stewart, B., Siemens, G.: The MOOC model for digital practice, University of Prince Edward Island (2010). http://www.elearnspace.org/Articles/MOOC_Final.pdf
13. Mohammad, A., Repass, C., Mazarakis, P.: IMA 2 usability testing report (2014).www.khanacademy.org
14. Nielsen, J.: Children's websites: usability issues in designing for kids (2010). http://www.nngroup.com/articles/childrens-websites-usability-issues/
15. Prensky, M.: Digital natives, digital immigrants part 1. Horiz. **9**(5), 1–6 (2001)
16. Richards, G., McGreal, R., Hatala, M., Friesen, N.: The evolution of learning object repository technologies: portals for online objects for learning. J. Distance Educ. **17**(3), 67–79 (2002)
17. Yılmaz, G., Tüfekci, A.: Web temelli bir eğitim yazılımının kullanilabilirliği "ttnet vitamin ilköğretim 6.sinif matematik örneği". Ahi Evran Üniversitesi Kırşehir Eğitim Fakültesi Dergisi (KEFAD). **14**(1), 215–226 (2013)

Evaluating an Education Department Portal:
A Case Study

Xiaojun Yuan[1(✉)], Huahai Yang[2], Kathleen Moorhead[3],
and Kathleen DeMers[3]

[1] College of Computing and Information, University at Albany,
State University of New York, Albany, NY 12222, USA
xyuan@albany.edu
[2] Juji, Inc., Saratoga, USA
hyang@juji-inc.com
[3] New York State Education Department, 89 Washington Avenue,
Albany, NY 12234, USA
Kathleen.Moorhead@nysed.gov

Abstract. We performed a series of usability studies to evaluate an education department portal for New York State Education Department (NYSED) (www.nysed.gov) in order to measure the quality of a user's experience when interacting with specific sections of this Web site. This study is composed of two phases: 1. heuristic evaluation and cognitive walkthrough were carried out to evaluate 25 web pages of the site; and 2. a user testing was performed to evaluate three components of the site that have been redesigned based on the findings and recommendations from the Phase 1. The results will assist NYSED in identifying opportunities for improving customer service and enhancing the website.

1 Introduction

The Internet has become an integral part of people's lives. People rely on web-based information systems like websites to access the information that they need on the Internet. These websites generally contain an extensive amount of information on a significant number of web pages. It is very important that usability issues have already been addressed when designing such portals. International Standard Organization (ISO) 9241 defines usability as "the extent to which a product can be used by specified users to achieve specified goals with effectiveness, efficiency, and satisfaction in a specified context of use" [4]. Nielsen & Mack [10] define usability problems as "any aspect of the design where a change would lead to improved system measures". Website usability can be measured through various human-computer interaction (HCI) techniques. This paper addresses usability issues with a large government education website employing heuristic evaluation, cognitive walkthrough, and user testing.

The New York State Education Department's (NYSED) website (www.nysed.gov) provides an electronic means for a wide variety of people to access information from and conduct business with the State Education Department (SED). The Department's

© Springer International Publishing Switzerland 2015
A. Marcus (Ed.): DUXU 2015, Part III, LNCS 9188, pp. 240–247, 2015.
DOI: 10.1007/978-3-319-20889-3_23

Web presence consists of approximately 600,000 pages, including the main site and about 60 sub-sites. The scope of this site includes the Department's main entry portal (at www.nysed.gov) as well as sites maintained by various program offices.

In this study, we aim to evaluate the NYSED website by conducting a series of usability studies to measure the quality of a user's experience when interacting with specific sections of this large website. We want to find out whether or not users can accomplish their respective tasks, and measure the overall effectiveness of the resources which are offered via the internet. The results of the usability analysis will assist NYSED in identifying opportunities for improving customer service and enhancing the website.

The following sections include a discussion on previous work, details about how we conducted heuristics evaluation, cognitive walkthrough and user testing of the NYSED site, our findings, and improvement recommendations for the site.

2 Previous Work

2.1 Usability Testing Methods

Heuristic evaluation has been widely used to identify usability problems in user interface design of websites [10, 11]. A small number of evaluators will be used to examine the interface and evaluate its compliance with the widely used usability principles. Cognitive Walkthrough is a popularly used method for evaluating the design of a user interface, which addresses how well the interface supports "exploratory learning" [12].

In 2010, [14] addressed the eight golden rules of interface design, including consistency, catering to universal usability, offering informative feedback, designing dialogs to yield closure, preventing errors, permitting easy reversal of actions, supporting internal locus of control, and reducing short-term memory load. Blackmon, Polson, Kitajima, & Lewis [2] proposed the Cognitive Walkthrough for the Web (CWW) that can be used in the website design and usability evaluation.

In addition to the expert evaluation methods such as heuristic evaluation and cognitive walkthrough, researchers also rely on user testing to evaluate website usability. User testing relies on user comments and user experience of using the website, and it is usually carried out in a lab environment [16].

Iterative design of user interfaces involves redesigning the interfaces based on findings of user testing. Nielsen [9] discovered that, among four case studies, the median improvement in overall usability was 165 % from the first to the last iteration, and the median improvement per iteration was 38 %. Nielsen [9] suggested iterating through at least three versions of the interface.

2.2 Previous Related Usability Studies

Jones [5] presented a case study implementing discount usability techniques (including prototypes, heuristic evaluation, etc.) in a federal government agency on their system WISQARS (Web-based Injury Statistics Query and Reporting System). The results of the study were positive and have raised usability issues on several other Injury Center web efforts. In 2009, Zhou [17] analyzed the Canadian government website using theories of usability engineering and information architecture. The study tried to integrate a large amount of information by using a clear structure and a friendly interface within a small screen to allow users to see the information and locate it faster. Following W3C recommendations and standards, Murenin and Tabrizi [8] identified useful guidelines for interactive websites where user registrations and searching within static fields of a database are involved. The website they redesigned became optimized for viewing from different browsers and profiles, including text browsers, printing profiles of graphical browsers, and mobile devices [8].

Sutcliffe [15] employed heuristics to evaluate three airline websites and found that although attractiveness and aesthetic design are key factors in usability evaluation, further research would need to be carried out to assess how these properties affect different user groups.

In a usability test of a distance continuing education website for human service professionals, Levine & Chaparro [6] evaluated the website's ease of use, efficiency, and user satisfaction with the targeted users. The evaluation identified usability issues that were critical to know before releasing the site to the public. It addressed the need to focus on the potential consumers of the site (human service professionals) rather than just on the site's functionality [6].

McMillen and Pehrsson [7] employed a cost-effective strategy to improve the usability of the Bibliotherapy Education Project's (BEP) counselor education website. They identified three themes for improvement: graphics and visual presentation, organization of textual content, and workflow.

Akilli's study [1] focused on user satisfaction for an educational website by using only one usability technique, the Questionnaire for User Satisfaction based on OAI (Object-Action Interface) model. The study found the website user friendly but did not have flexibility and stimulating attributes.

3   Phase 1: Heuristic Evaluation and Cognitive Walkthrough

3.1   Heuristic Evaluation

Two evaluators conducted heuristic evaluation independently on 25 web pages using the adapted website checklist designed by Gaffney [3]. The heuristics considered were navigation, functionality, control, language, authority, feedback, consistency, and visual clarity. These heuristics were evaluated based on a 6-point scale: 1-Never, 2-Seldom, 3-Sometimes, 4-Frequently, 5-Always, Not Applicable (N/A).

We computed the average score for each of the eight usability categories based on the 5-point rating scale. An average score close to five indicates good usability in that area. A low score close to zero signifies bad usability. Figure 1 shows the combined average ratings of the evaluators for each of the eight aspects of usability.

Evaluators felt generally positive about the usability of the website. Results indicated that the navigation, consistency, and visual clarity aspects of the website usability need to be given more attention.

Similar ratings were given for the majority of categories by the two evaluators. Evaluator 2 is slightly more generous than Evaluator 1. Relatively large discrepancies exist with language and consistency. The disagreements were caused by a few problems identified by Evaluator 1 that Evaluator 2 was not able to detect.

3.2 Cognitive Walkthrough

An evaluator conducted cognitive walkthroughs on all of the 8 scenarios provided by NYSED. While accomplishing the tasks described in the scenario narratives, the evaluator duly recorded each of the mental and operational steps with a Cognitive Walkthrough Evaluation Sheet [13]. Overall, the site has done a good job of laying out the information, as evidenced by the high success rate of the walkthrough evaluations. Results indicated that the structure and searching functionality of the site need to be improved.

Since heuristic evaluation and cognitive walkthrough are methods that rely on opinions and evaluations from a small number of evaluators, the findings could be limited in the generalizability and exhaustiveness. In the next section, we will describe a formal user-centered experiment which involves real users to find out the usability problems and task effectiveness of the website. The results will contribute to a more robust website for targeted NYSED users.

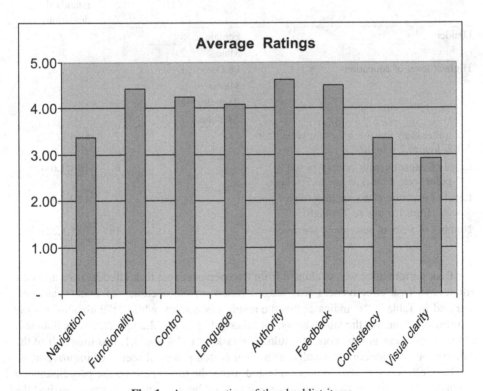

Fig. 1. Average rating of the checklist items

4 Phase 2: User Testing

User Testing was carried out based on the newly improved site based on the recommendations from the Phase 1. Seven participants evaluated three components of the site: General Education Development (GED), Office of Teaching and General, which were redesigned based on the recommended changes after the heuristics evaluation and cognitive walkthrough. These participants were recruited by NYSED. Table 1 shows the demographic information of the seven participants. NYSED also provided a total of eight tasks: three tasks for the GED site (Task 1.1, 1.2, and 1.3), four tasks for the Office of Teaching site (Task 2.1, 2.2, 2.3 and 2.4), and one task for the General site (Task 3.1). Each participant was asked to complete the eight tasks using NYSED sites. Before the study, each participant was asked to sign a consent form. Then each participant filled out a background questionnaire. Next, each participant searched the site for information to complete the eight tasks. Each participant session was recorded using TechSmith UserVue, an online service that enables the experimenter remotely observe and record participants' screens as they navigate applications and sites. We then reviewed the recordings, compiled the results and provide a report to NYSED.

Table 1. Demographic characteristics of the participants

Characteristics	Value	Count	Min	Max	Mean (standard deviation)
Gender	Female	5			
	Male	2			
Highest level of education	Ph.D.	1			
	Master	3			
	Bachelor	2			
	Associate	1			
Computer daily use (on a 7-point scale, from 1 = low to 7 = high)			1	7	6.14 (2.27)
Level of expertise with computers (on a 7-point scale, from 1 = low to 7 = high)			1	6	4.14(1.68)
Level of expertise with searching (on a 7-point scale, from 1 = low to 7 = high)			1	7	4.29(1.89)
Number of years of searching experience			1	18	7.86(5.52)

Task performance was evaluated from two perspectives: task effectiveness and task efficiency. Task effectiveness was judged based on the accuracy of results, as summarized in Table 2. "√" indicates that the result was correct, while "x" indicates that the result was wrong. As the table shows, for tasks 1.1, 1.2, 1.3, 2.2 and 2.3, more than half of the participants got the correct results. For tasks 2.1, 2.4 and 3.1, less than half of the participants got the correct results, which suggested potential areas for improvement.

Task efficiency (Table 3) was evaluated using the time spent by the participants on the tasks. "x" indicates the result was not collected because the participant finished the

Table 2. Task effectiveness – answer correctness by user by task ("√" indicates the result is correct, while "X" indicates the result is wrong).

USER	Task1.1	Task1.2	Task1.3	Task 2.1	Task 2.2	Task 2.3	Task 2.4	Task 3.1
1	√	√	√	X	√	√	√	√
2	√	√	X	X	X	X	X	X
3	X	√	√	X	√	√	X	√
4	√	√	√	X	√	X	√	X
5	√	√	√	√	√	√	X	√
6	√	√	√	X	X	√	√	X
7	X	X	X	X	X	√	X	X
Total number of correctness	5	6	5	1	4	5	3	3

Table 3. Task efficiency - time (in seconds) by user by task

USER	Task1.1	Task1.2	Task1.3	Task2.1	Task2.2	Task2.3	Task2.4	Task3.1
1	51	167	95	83	96	103	177	176
2	50	27	265	189	36	18	25	288
3	58	62	43	204	209	39	180	121
4	45	37	22	213	x	91	158	31
5	116	101	13	310	x	142	327	93
6	187	50	54	74	100	115	162	184
7	80	68	64	67	69	135	78	353
Average Time (in secs)	84	73	79	163	102	92	158	178

task 2.2 when doing task 2.1. It is not surprising to see that the tasks that were identified to have bad effectiveness (tasks 2.1, 2.4, and 3.1) had the longest completion time. This suggests that these tasks were particularly difficult for the participants. A lot of participants could not find the correct answers even though they spent much more time on these tasks.

Overall, the participants performed well for the tasks related to the GED site, but performed poorly for the tasks related to the Office of Teaching site and the General site.

5 Recommendations and Conclusions

At the end of the second phase, we recommended the following changes, including: (1) improving on how to categorize the top menus and submenus; (2) highlighting the important links; (3) restructuring website to show the requirements for different user profiles; (4) avoiding ambiguity of contents so users know how to interpret them;

(5) avoiding long pages by organizing contents in a clear structure so users will not get lost in navigation; (6) providing better clarification of link names to avoid confusion.

Our study has proved successful in identifying usability problems of the NYSED site. We conclude that it is necessary to have a series of studies, and involve stakeholders in the whole usability testing process. We were constrained by a limited number of experts and subjects, and a limited number of tasks. The only realistic way to address this issue is to investigate further if and how the user groups (e.g. teachers, parents, and students) behave differently when using the site. Despite the limitations, we believe our study made a significant effort in highlighting the critical importance of involving stakeholders in the design and content development [6], and involving a sequence of testing phases in the usability testing process of websites.

References

1. Akilli, G.K.: User satisfaction evaluation of an educational website. Turk. Online J. Educ. Technol. **4**(1), 85–92 (2002)
2. Blackmon, M.H., Polson, P.G., Kitajima, M., Lewis, C.: Cognitive walkthrough for the web. In: Proceedings of CHI, vol. 4, pp. 463–470 (2002)
3. Gaffney, G.: Web site evaluation checklist v1.1. Information and Design pty ltd (1998). www.infodesign.com.au Accessed 20 March 2007 http://www.infodesign.com.au/ftp/WebCheck.pdf
4. ISO 9241-11. Ergonomic requirements for office work with visual display terminals (VDTs): guidance on usability, International Standards Organisations (1998)
5. Jones, C.P.: Lessons learned from discount usability engineering for the federal government. In: Society for Technical Communication's 50th Annual Conference Proceedings, pp. 333–338 (2003)
6. Levine, J., Chaparro, B.S.: Usability study of a distance continuing education website for human service professionals. J. Technol. Hum. Serv. **25**(4), 23–39 (2007)
7. McMillen, P.S., Pehrsson, D.E.: Improving a counselor education web site through usability testing: the bibliotherapy education project. Counselor Educ. Supervision **29**, 122–136 (2009)
8. Murenin, C.A., Tabrizi, M.H.N.: Development of usable and accessible web-portals using W3C standards. In: Proceedings of the International Conference on Information Technology: Coding and Computing, vol. 2, pp. 829–831 (2005)
9. Nielsen, J.: Iterative interface design. IEEE. Computer **26**, 32–41 (1993)
10. Nielsen, J., Mack, R.L. (eds.): Usability inspection methods. John Wiley and Sons, New York (1994)
11. Nielsen, J.: Designing web usability. New Riders Publishing, Indiana (2000)
12. Rieman, J., Franzke, M., Redmiles, D.: Usability evaluation with the cognitive walkthrough (1995). Accessed 15 December 2010. http://www.sigchi.org/chi95/proceedings/tutors/jr_bdy.htm
13. Rowley, D.E., Rhoades, D.G.: The cognitive jogthrough: a fast-paced user interface evaluation procedure. In: Proceedings of the Conference on Human Factors in Computing Systems, pp. 389–395 (1992)
14. Schneiderman, B., Plaisant, C.: Designing the user interface: strategies for effective human-computer interaction. Addison Wesley, Boston (2010)

15. Sutcliffe, A.: Assessing the reliability of heuristic evaluation for website attractiveness and usability. In: Proceedings of the 35th Hawaii International Conference on System Sciences, vol. 5, pp. 183–198 (2002)
16. Tan, W., Liu, D., Bishu, R.: Web evaluation: heuristic evaluation vs. user testing. Int. J. Ind. Ergon. **39**, 621–627 (2009)
17. Zhou, X.-Y. : Usage-centered design for government websites. In: Proceedings of the Second International Conference on Information and Computing Science, pp. 305–308 (2009)

Designing the Playing Experience

Ads-on Games and Fake Brands: Interactions, Commercials and Playful Branding

Herlander Elias[1,2]($\boxtimes$), Ernesto Filgueiras[1,2], and Breno Carvalho[3]

[1] Online Communication Laboratory – LabCom, University of Beira Interior,
Covilhã, Portugal
HerlanderElias248@gmail.com
[2] G3Dlab - Digital Game Design and Development Laboratory,
Covilhã, Portugal
[3] UNICAP - Catholic University of Pernambuco, Boa Vista, Brazil

Abstract. Today's communication-based world relies on advertising as a positive medium, and branding is no exception. Also, the gaming industry relies on videogames as a heavy player in our time, since "narrative", "graphics" and "gameplay" are constantly worked out in the name of the best digital experiences, where the user is the center. We have noticed that a fusion is taking place between commercials, real and /or fake brands, in order to turn digital worlds more convincing for the user-player. Relying on analytics, media theory and user experience, we have conducted a study to better understand, in analytical and experimental form, what is happening between the user, the brands, the games and the outputs of such experiences in terms of interaction and playfulness. Gamification seems to be the new rule.

Keywords: Brands · Videogames · User experience · Interaction · Advertisement · Connection · Player · Gamification

1 Introduction

This paper presents the results of the analitycal phase that is part of a complex study composed by two phases (analytical and experimental). The main goal was to evaluate the influence and retention of the brands (real and fake ones), on the videogames that were not developed with the advertisement explicit objective (ex. FIFA, PES, Forza, etc.).

Main findings indicate that there is a strong connection among traditional elements from advertisement or branding for the 'videogames' narrative composition, and that recently we could verify a strong influence of the videogames on branding.

We'll start our analysis with videogames, branding, commercials and fake brands by considering some ideas, models and paradigms. Ads on games are more and more frequent, so much, that sometimes fake brands need to show up just to make the interaction between user-player as real as it gets. As far as games, branding and iconography are concerned, what we are dealing here is "in-game" branding (Cocoran, 2007, 288). It means that games work out as carriers for either fictitious or real brand messaging.

One author, such as Rushkoff, knows that "computer games may, in fact, be popular culture's first satisfactory answer to the collapse of narrative" (2013, Chapter 1,

© Springer International Publishing Switzerland 2015
A. Marcus (Ed.): DUXU 2015, Part III, LNCS 9188, pp. 251–262, 2015.
DOI: 10.1007/978-3-319-20889-3_24

117–564, para.106). Our suggestion is that ads on games provide continuity to the game narrative, sometimes in a transmedia way, and that brands, even if fictitious, increment a sense of "realness" in the game, as the footage gets closer and closer to live-action film footage.

In the realm of websites and online gaming there is a concept being used for sometime to describe the merge between gaming and advertising: "AdverGaming", despite being more children-directed, it is still prevalent (Elias, 2007, Cocoran, 2007, 282). Another issue is that "while video games do occur over linear time, they are not arched like stories between a past and the future" (Rushkoff, 2013, Chapter 1, 117-118–564, para.106).

On a very interesting study, Molloy notices the "rise of branded gaming and entertainment", and so he says that "given the popularity of games, it was logical that companies would look for opportunities to leverage the games market to advertise their brand names" (2014, LOC 1309 de 4186). Somehow, brands show on games as icons, guiding icons, beacons, they say "this could be real" or "we're communicating with you". For marketing and branding experts such as Frampton, like it or not, we're stepping in a new connected, web-like world; where everything is linked up, yet sometimes it seems complex and confusing, and rich, intimate and alive. He highlights that brands and organizations need to learn how to plug into this vast intelligence" (in Best Global Brands 2012, 2013, 3).

We are told by Heilbrunn that brands themselves may be seen not merely as signs, but as a "semiotic engine" whose very function is to constantly produce meanings and values (apud Schroeder and Salzer-Mörling 2006, 92). Indeed, semiotics has a true power, signs (*Watchdogs, Killzone: Shadow Fall*), words (*Alien: Isolation, Syndicate*) and colors (*Mirror's Edge, Fallout, WipeOut Series*) are just the basis, from our point of view. French thinker Roland Barthes knew the power of language and so he mentioned the "image-reservoirs of language" (1975, 33). Since videogames, the modern ones, are relying on the triplet mechanics-narrative-transmedia strategies, the user-experience (UX), departs on a new ground now. Because of the cutting-edge "image-reservoirs", what we are dealing with here is but language — it is communication in its regular mass media/new media form.

By putting together brands and virtual worlds, fake brands, connections and messages, icons and advertising, we found something closer to the UX domain. Marc Gobé believes that advertising should be thought of as experiences (2007, 133). And the reason why it happens this way is because a brand is way more than mere iconography (2007, 99).

On the language level, what we see is that the "'message' is not of a purely verbal nature, but constitutes a word and image text" (Forceville, 2002, 81). Basically, the "image-reservoirs", the "semiotic engine" and iconographies of brands becoming experiences turn out to be guiding vectors, and they have to be "positive" (Nöth [1987:279] apud Forceville, 2002, 68).

Having in consideration that this "intention" and "empathic" profiles of ads are a mark of advertising working out its way, it may not be disturbing to find out that in videogames, brands have to appear, in order to cause empathy and to surround the active user-player, make him feel he is being talked to. Forceville says that the aim of an advertiser is, as we have seen, to persuade a prospective client to buy (literally or figuratively) his/her product, service or idea (2002, 68). But what we have identified in the videogames, movies and TV shows, our objects of examination for this paper, is that brand iconography, whether real or virtual, is establishing a referent system of its own. Following this, the big picture is that the degree of connectivity between user-players [potential consumers of real brands or videogame worlds with their own fake brands] is not only higher but techno-dependent, as well. Due to the more common transmedia strategies [Jenkins, 2006] and the collapse of narrative, videogames allow us to stay in touch with worlds where signs, text, images, characters and stories unravel a UX with new worlds. (Elias, 2013) Then, there is also the "multi-medial character" (Forceville, 2002, 70) in all of this, since we are being told a story in many forms, both in pictorial and linguistic components. And besides, sounds, colors, layouts, billboards, soundtracks, special effects, character design and virtual logos just happen to stand out this multi-medial or transmedial nature of our context.

There are three major distinctions in brand logos. First we have typographic logos, secondly we have graphic logos, and ultimately, we have imagotypes, the latter merging both typographic and graphic logotypes. The branding iconography we have found, the most futuristic even, is minimalistic (*WipeOut*), but the conventional forms apply. Even in TV shows (*Lost* [J.J. Abrams, Jeffrey Lieber, Damon Lindelof, 2004-10]), films (*Robocop*) and games (*Watchdogs*) from some decades ago still rely on pictorial and textual elements to seem more real world-like. The reason why this branding iconography keeps appearing is that it proves that, regardless of the type of virtual world we're dealing with, and the epoch, brands are anchors.

Another relevant issue is that Forceville, for example, affirms that there is a dual nature in word and image, how they relate to each other (2002, 71). Others, such as Simon White, mention more "new trendy" phenomena such as "next-generation contextual advertising" (apud De Waele, 2013, LOC 266 de 2059). However, the fact is that, more or less customized ads, are tailoring their messages, more or less visual, in a more or less transmedial way, to reach consumers. This is why Molloy says "the line between content and advertising is sometimes blurred in games" (2014, LOC 2124 de 4186). Sometimes it is so blurred that we do not know if we are playing ads-on games or games on-ads.

Let's retrieve what Vasilache says about semiotics: she says that as the study of signs and symbols as communication elements, it is essentially something that explains how people extract meaning from words, sounds and images. She also defends that semiotics' principles, once applied to visual identity of brands, provide easy recognition, and, last but no less important, multiple layers of information (2012, 2).

Should we accept the barthesian model, then we have to see a distinction here: there is a more direct approach (literally) or more non-direct one (figuratively). The whole battle implies the "implicit" and the "explicit", "denotation" vs. "connotation". In Barthe's language advertising is what is left once one erases the connotation signs ([1986/1964:29] in Forceville, 2002, 72). This means what was more straight, minimal, simple, consumer-directed. In the images we have observed the signs being more easily identifiable are simple, and we keep recalling them after playing the games, much as it happened with TV shows (*Lost*) and movies (*T2*) applying the same logic.

Right now, the problem is but one of associations, links, displays, messages carried, UX changed by ads that are not just shown but experience-confirming elements. Lury, in her turn, believes that "brands as interfaces are a place (…) of interactivity, not of interaction" (2004, 6). What this means is that brands need to interface and interact, and that the reason why brands as a technology (Manovich), as a 'medium', or as new media (Manovich), need a place, is the very reason why they end up in cyberspace. In 2001, Lunenfeld was mentioning "brands are unfinished". What better domain to establish themselves if not the digital, beta world of videogames? The other issue here, is that this "change" is modifying people, whom then become a triptic of consumer, user and player.

2 Case Studies

This paper presents a study whose purpose is to fully understand the relationship between gaming, commercials and interaction design, if there is an application of true or fake brands. In fact, the synergy between gaming and branding is what the study aims to explain best. The results presented here reflect the heuristic analysis made by experts in videogames, digital media and interaction design.

The methodology for this work envisioned not games that work explicitly as advertising or branding carriers, such as *Gran Turismo* or *Forza*, but games that provide digital experiences where the ads, or brand iconography, foment a real-world experience. In this sense, the games we have chosen are very diverse in platform, epoch and genre, though the common point stands as games in which ads resemble or act like real ads do. Also, the timeframe is very large, but the games we have examined are chosen in most cases amongst the games with better graphic hardware capabilities. The result is a more notorious graphic presentation of advertisement, which made easier our identification, pattern recognition and interlinking with media, design and user-experience theory.

For this paper we have examined Google"s Doodles, 11 movies, 2 TV shows and 18 videogames in which ads are displayed, either about fiction brands or real world brands. We have to assume, like Jhally, that advertising operates in order to create false needs (for manufacturers and not to consumers) (1995, 15). Much as this author states, advertising is mostly about the relationship "between" people and products (Ibidem, 16), since the goods are working out as "markers" of significant social categories (Ibidem, 21). However we have to say too that this ads-on games are more than advergaming or branding entertainment, due to the process of making narrative more believable, thus the ads consolidate the fiction world, the UX becomes reliable.

Data was collected from 24 young adults aged between 18 and 25 years old (Mean = 20.96 ±1.899) of the Portuguese air force military and Portuguese university. Twelve male soldiers, of different categories (1st Corporal, 2nd Corporal or Soldier) and twelve female university students, studying in the healthcare domain, residing in dormitories of the air base and the university were selected. Each participant will be approximately six (6) months with two months of personal contact between the principal investigator and volunteers, and the remaining time implying an impersonal touch through e-mails and mobile phone.

The bedrooms were in dormitories standard of an institution, which is the case of college students and military with 2 beds in each bedroom with the same equipment room conditions (i.e. bed, mattress, air conditioning system, light level and noise).

2.1   The Ads-on Games Analysis

When it comes to films and TV shows, many examples may be provided. For instance, in *2001: A Space Odissey* (Stanley Kubrick, 1968) HAL 9000, the computer did not exist at the time in real world, whereas PAN AM (the airliner company) was real. In Ridley Scott's *Alien* (1979) Yutani, or the Weyland-Yutani Corporation, with its motto "Building Better Worlds", was fictive. Some years later, in *AVP - Alien vs. Predator* (Paul W.S. Anderson, 2004), the same fiction brands are displayed all over the sets. Other examples, like *The Amazing Spider-Man* (Marc Webb, 2012) reveal the evil Oscorp brand behind all conspiracy. In Christopher Nolan's *Batman* trilogy, the fictitious Wayne Enterprises, as in comics, makes a tie between Bruce Wayne's secret hero world and the real world New York city upon which Gotham city grounds are based. In *Blade Runner* (Ridley Scott, 1982) the gigantic *Tyrell Corporation* is the manufacturer of android brand Nexus Cocoran, (Cocoran 2007).

Of course, many examples could be provided but certain films display brands in their aesthetic and narrative as well, from the start. *Charlie And The Chocolate Factory* (Tim Burton, 2005) sells the Wonka Chocolate bars. In the latest Andrew Niccol's film, *The Host* (2013) there is a brand playing with its own name: Store Brand. Some live-action films, though full of special effects, present fake brands; *Ironman* (Jon Favreau, 2008) shows Stark Industries (as in comics), but the sequel *Ironman 2* (Ibidem, 2010) reveals a new villain: Hammer - Advanced Weapons Systems. Even if we go back to cartoons like the *Looney Toons* (Warner Bros Aimation, 1930-69), we are still witnessing fake brands like ACME every time the roadrunner and the coyote pick a fight.

The ground-breaking transmedia and post-narrative TV show *Lost* manages to introduce a new brand across all the plans of the so-called Dharma Initiative, which opens the box for Dharma Computers, Dharma Jumpsuits; not to mention the parallels of Oceanic Airways, Oceanic Airlines, and so on. In the recent Wes Ball film, *Maze Runner*, there is an army brand behind the playing of the maze (2014), called W C K D ["WICKED"]. Also, in the first of two films of *Prometheus* (I) Ridley Scott (2012) introduces again the romantic high-tech distopia of the "Alien" world being played out by characters working for Yutani, Weyland-Yutani Corporation. And again the motto repeats itself. In addition, RT01 Transport, Project Prometheus, USCSS Prometheus, among other references are shown on films and games that establish transmedia narrative link-ups.

Everybody watched *Pulp Fiction* (Quentin Tarantino, 1994) selling the Big Kahuna Burgers, but nothing compares to *Resident Evil* (AAVV, 2002-2016) films and games (Capcom, 1996-2016) and exploiting the evilness of the Umbrella Corporation. In the same trend, Paul Verhoeven's *Robocop* (1987) shows something big as well: OCP - OmniConsumer Products, which is revamped in José Padilha's latest version as Omnicorp in *Robocop* (2014). Between the 1980s and the late 1990s the trend of fake brands augments its path. In *The Terminator* (James Cameron, 1984) and *Terminator*

2: Judgment Day (Idem, 1991) Cyberdyne Systems is still the evil system, and evil brand. In both *Tron* (Steven Lisberger, 1982) and *Tron Legacy* (Joseph Kozinski, 2011) ENCOM is an overwhelming operating system designer powerhouse. Perhaps a virtual form of Google Doodled world?

When it comes to videogames some slogans are repeated. It happens in *Aliens: Colonial Marines* (2013). And in a weird way, we still see the displayed images of well-being (Jhally, 1995, 39). The revolution takes place in next-generation gaming, like in *Alien: Isolation* (2014). Many fictitious brands like Weyland-Yutani, Seegson, Daveport - RYE, Cuppa Joe's, Apollo; or Kerchner Buck, Koorlander, Sevastopol Spaceflight Terminal, and Xing Xang are presented. Others, such as Samani, Vista, The Planet Hopper, Souta Lager, Arious Computers, and Big Dog!; not to mention Watatsumi Efficient Machine Solutions, Towerlink, Tranquility and Seegson Credit Services. The bottom line here is that these brands are mostly about a supposed lifestyle, and they are mostly about technology, digital gear, services, food or cosmetics.

Says Frampton that "as living business assets", brands are something to be understood as being fluid, dynamic and somehow organic (2012, 2). This is what we see, brands across media recurring to the same semiotic language, making difficult to the viewer, user or player to fully understand which of them are real and which are not. Google's Doodles also play with this context. In *Battlefield 3* (2011), brands such as NYeye, LEAP, and WERKSHAFT are revealed like real brands. The majority is image-based. According to Jhally, modern advertising is characterized by the prevailing domain of image media (1995, 39).

In *Bioshock Infinite* (2013) Rolston Reciprocating, Rapture city, Ryan Industries, and the Plasmids as well, are part of brands existing all-around one single character. In *Borderlands* (2009) there is not much but Vladof propaganda. Same thing happens in *Fallout* (2013), since there is not much besides Nuka-Cola. Open-world games, like *Grand Theft Auto IV* (2008) uses fake brands to make the shopping world and the virtual cities more plausible, displaying brands like Sprunk, tw@ Internet Cafe and Pibwasser.

Some of the most notorious villain brands, are *Half-Life 2*'s (2004) Black Mesa Research Facility, as in the antipode we have *Infamous: Second Son*'s (2013) Roth Records. For thinkers like Zygmunt Bauman, a "Cyworld" (2011, 2) is a frightening cybernetic world extending itself. This is also exactly what one has in *Watchdogs* and in *Killzone: Shadow Fall*. The latter videogame by Guerilla Games (2013) reveals abstract totalitarian propaganda, and non exisitng brands like Three3, Ralph Von Vekta, Vekta City, and VSA. Brands outside the military theme like LEAF IT Coffee House, N-WORK ONE, Cocoon and Robionica are almost an excuse to make it look real and not a warfare simulator in the future.

Lets not forget that Rushkoff highlighted how twentieth century's had "dangerously compelling ideological narratives" (2013, Preface, 13–564, para.10). The trend of somehow dystopian brands reappears in *Oddworld: Abe's Oddysee* (Oddworld Inhabitants, 1997) with the Rupture Farms, and especially in the *Portal* games (2007-2011) with the AI of Aperture Science Laboratories menacing the player.

Minor examples are featured in *Red Faction* (2001) with the ULTOR political brand, or *Superfrog* (1993) for becoming almost an advergame selling the real Lucozade drink (Elias, 2007). It gets weird, how between fake and real world brands end up on games to consolidate the UX. For Appadurai, the "global" 'mediascapes' and the global 'ideoscapes' ([1990] apud Schroeder and Salzer-Mörling 2006, 86) are mostly relevant. In fact, videogames are becoming, more than films and TV shows, a real showcase for ideoscapes (landscapes of ideas) and mediascapes (landscapes of real brands), in our point of view.

One of the brightest examples of ads-on games is the First Person Shooter (Elias, 2009) *Syndicate*, a revamped version of and old school game (2012) where brands such as Aspari, Cayman Global, and mostly EuroCorp occupy a special spot. They are not just advertising nor branding. They are the gamespace itself. Once, Jean-Paul Sartre said that the future arrives at man through objects, in the same way it previously did before ([1976] in Jhally, 1995, 66). Some games are more than this. They are also future-focused (Rushkoff, 2013, Chapter 1, 26–564, para.9). One key example is Ubisoft's *Watchdogs* (2013) showing MAPE, Blume brands in a world concerned with privacy and surveillance culture.

Relying on Freedman's arguments, to wherever we drive our attention to, there is the story, the experience. Images become a meaningful text in their own right (apud Kackman et al., 2011, 207). This takes place in the *WipeOut* future-driven racing game for PlayStation Systems in the late 1990s and 2000s. From *WipeOut* (PSX-PS3) to *Wip3out* (1996), and also in *WipEout HD* (2008), and in *WipEout: Pure* (2005), highly modern brands [supposedly conceived in fictitious form by the The Designers Republic studio] like ADVANCE, BOOOND, ag-5 International, Goteki 45, Feisar, Icoros, [QIREX-RD], Assegai Developments, Auricom, MGD, PIRANHA, AG-5Y5 and QIRDX mesmerize the user-player audience. It is sure, for new media researcher Lev Manovich, that brands may be regarded as the effect of hyperlinking, which in fact is the principle driving interactive media (apud [2001, 61] Lury, 2004, 10). Thus, needless is to say, that much has to be thought of concerning user-experience.

During the heuristic analysis, we need to identify the participation of branding elements in the narrative content of the analysed videogames. This analysis allowed the experts to identify two main components for branding characterization:

a. Neutral Branding: Related with the neutral, positive or passive participation of the branding on the narrative, in which one can verify the exposition of brands and companies' products (fake or real products), only to draw up an aesthetical and realistic scenario (i.e. product posters in a movie theater).
b. Evil Branding: Negative participation of the branding for the narrative content of the analysed videogames. In these cases, the companies that are presented on the videogames are responsible for the negative consequences presented on the narrative and usually are associated to the greed for profits, absence of scruples in scientific research, political propaganda through products and consumer goods and indifference to the consequences of the actions marketing and aggressive advertising.

This classification allowed experts to a better evaluation of the need to develop us fictitious brands related to the videogame. The Table 1 presents the results of the heuristic analysis of reference videogames from different game platforms:

What we conclude from this analysis is that the majority of videogames being resourceful to fictitous, fake brands, are the games in which graphic engines and game

Table 1. Heuristic analysis results for brands on games in most common devices

Games	Issue-products	Issue-services	Issue-propaganda	Neutral Branding	Evil Branding	Semiotics	Real Branding	Fictitious Brands
Aliens: Colonial Marines	X	x	√	x	√	√	x	√
Alien: Isolation	X	√	√	x	√	√	x	√
Battlefield 3	√	√	x	x	√	√	x	√
Bioshock Infinite	√	x	√	x	√	*	x	√
Borderlands	X	x	√	x	√	√	x	√
Fallout	√	x	x	x	√	√	x	√
Grand Theft Auto IV	√	√	x	x	√	√	x	√
Half-Life 2	X	√	x	x	√	√	x	√
Infamous: Second Son	√	√	√	*	*	√	x	√
Killzone: Shadow Fall	√	√	√	x	x	√	x	√
Oddworld: Abe's Oddysee	X	x	√	x	√	*	x	√
Portal	X	x	√	x	√	√	x	√
Portal 2	X	x	√	x	√	√	x	√
Red Faction	X	x	√	x	√	√	x	√
Resident Evil	X	x	√	x	√	√	x	√
Superfrog	√	√	√	√	*	√	√	x
Syndicate	√	√	x	√	x	√	x	√
Watchdogs	X	√	√	√	x	√	x	√
WipeOut	X	√	√	√	x	√	x	√
Wip3out	X	√	√	√	x	√	x	√
WipEout HD	X	√	√	√	x	√	x	√
WipEout: Pure	X	√	√	√	x	√	x	√

√ = Verified | X = Not verified | * = Not applied

narrative, and mechanics as well, are more recent. A feature of open world games and action-paced games is the resort to brand iconography or propaganda iconography to make the virtual world seem more credible and also aesthetic. Games in which the hardware allows massive environments, first or third person points of view, big narratives, immense mini-game puzzling and creative environments are also using very much fake brands, propaganda and colorful, high-tech design in their unravelings.

2.2 Gamification, Google Doodles and UX

According to Elali et al. (2012), the company's mutations display a strategy needed for to establish their relevance in a highly competitive world, and turned itself into a fast-paced information rhythm. Research on branding present the term "customer engagement" (Bosovsky, 2013, 59), being one of the directives the positioning of a brand in a corporation. Such engagement, mostly applied in the gamification process of a brand, it is most needed, in order to turn the client into a loyalty-based consumer, attached to the brand actions.

As the Web and IT advance, and mobile media, the usage of brand versatility as a means for expression and communication towards the public, in a more dynamic and participative mode in the computer grid, it becomes frequent as a brand philosophy in the present day's organization agenda (Kreutz, 2011, 2).

Until now, only one company dared to provide more than one configuration possibility to the mutations of the very logotype itself, without compromising its legibility and visibility. Google's choice in applying a versatile strategy for the brand reveals that, much as its users, their brand is a living entity, something playful, creative, aspired by the world and geeks (Elali et al., 2012, 200).

In 2010, Google, the search engine online, released one of its Doodle variations to pay a tribute to one of the most memorable games for 8bit generation players: *Pac-Man*. In this approach to the user, the brand transforms itself in a playable mutating logotype, its identity elements are mixed with the game scenario (Carvalho et al., 2014). Thus, Google unraveled more than a brand mutation mixing brands logos, ads and games.

With the mutating and playable brand approach a new experience was provided to Google users, not just occupying space on Google's homepage, but also triggering a strong appeal in emotional and communicational terms (Carvalho et al., 2014, 75). As we see, brands, games, user experience and the border between the non-real ad, or the real brand ad, and the IT is getting blurred.

Relying on the Analysis Model of Dynamic Identity (AMDI) (please see Table 2) developed by Carvalho (2014), the authors define a playable dynamic brand as a versatile identity, in which traces of a matrix signature may be observed; along with graphic data from the brand. In this sense, the brand gamification process is by no means limited to resorting to engagement elements, such as scoring, diversion, to stimulate a new emotional relationship between user and brand; whether it is through bonus campaigns, or actions mediated by apps; or even the use of advergames in a wider-angle strategy for branding (Elias, 2007), which means a fusion across artifacts in digital media designing a new bond between brand signature, audience and corporate interests. Even if logotypes, ads, games, are fake, they are already rooting on a new ground where brands become games, and the secret for that is user experiences itself with a coherent and contemporary form, going beyond the insertion of audiovisual and interactive resources, coordinated by clear-focused goal narrative. Rules also propose the decision calling to the user in a certain time-space, and contemplate the player with quantitative results.

In this sense, the brand gamification process is by no means limited to resorting to engagement elements, such as scoring, diversion, to stimulate a new emotional relationship between user and brand; whether it is through bonus campaigns, or actions mediated by apps; or even the use of advergames in a wider-angle strategy for branding, which means a fusion across artifacts in digital media designing a new bond between brand signature, audience and corporate interests. Even if logotypes, ads, games, are fake, they are already rooting on a new ground where brands become games, and the secret for that is user experience.

Table 2. Final Model of analysis for dynamic, static, playful and toy-like brands

Mutation type	Authors	Characteristics
Static Brand	Paul Rand (1991), Per Mollerup (2000), Cauduro (2001), Elizete Kreutz (2005), Strunck (2007), Campos (2007), Rezende (2010), Ulrike Felsing (2010) Irene Nes (2012), Alina Wheeler (2012)	• Keeps signs of the original identity; • It is consistent, contemporary and easy to remember; • Allows flexibility of identity elements (logo, type, color) and also allows to be recognizable; • Addition / subtraction of graphics or image, new features; • Enables visibility and readability of the logo in the used media.
Dynamic Brand	Per Mollerup (2000), Strunck (2007), Andrea Pol (2012), Alina Wheeler (2012), Elizete Kreutz (2005), Ulrike Felsing (2010), Irene Nes (2012)	• The visuals elements are animated to electronic or digital media; • Use sound or sound effects; • Presents a lively narrative
Like a toy Brand	Elizete Kreutz (2005), Ulrike Felsing (2010), Irene Nes (2012) Vygotsky (1984), Santos (1999), Huizinga (1993),	• Allows to explore objects, discover new concepts; • The user interacts with graphics; • It has play activity, safe, out of ordinary life
Playful Brand	Huizinga (1993), Abt (1970), Avedon & Sutton-Smith (1971), Crawford (1982), Suits (1990), Costikyan (1994), Parlett (1999), Caillois (2001), Salen & Zimmerman (2012)	• There are rules that limits the users; • It has objectives and needs users' decision taking; • It has quantifiable results, reward the user with visual elements without material gain; • There is more than one level of interaction and challenge in a determined time / space

3 Conclusions

Results attained in the phase of the study allowed authors to conclude that, on one hand, the analysis made by the experts showed that there is a deep need to involve branding components to compose the narratological map of videogames that do not have characteristics of associate advertising to finance themselves (like in sports games and racing). It can be linked to the game designers needs in reproduce with high fidelity the reality of the consumer society to increase the immersion of the players and the players' empathy with the narrative of the game. On the other hand, the creation of false trademarks and fictitious companies is a common feature in all cases where there are the combination of negative factors to companies or products that are necessary for the context of the game.

Regarding real branding, there is a increased need for gamification of brands and actively associate them to the game, in other words, the brand of many companies ceased to be a backdrop to enhance the reality of the game and now becomes the game itself, through the playable branding. This new application can demonstrate that these two components (videogames and brands) are closely linked and require more attention from developers as the impact of both is usually ignored.

As a continuation of this study, it is being developed in Digital Game Design and Development Lab (G3Dlab at the University of Beira Interior - Portugal) a new research that aims at studying the association and the insights between real and fictitious brands made by the players during their interaction with videogames.

References

Ayas, N., et al.: A prospective study of sleep duration and coronary heart disease in women. Arch. Intern. Med. **163**, 205–209 (2003)

Barthes, R.: The pleasure of the text, pp. 33–35. Hill & Wang, New York (1975)

Bauman, Z.: Consuming Life. Polity Press, Malden (2011)

Bosovsky, G.: El pulso de la marca. In: Costa, J. (ed.) Los 5 pilares del branding, anatomía de la marca. Colección Joan Costa, p. 59. Barcelona CPC, Barcelona (2013)

Carvalho, B.: Doodle game: análise da marca mutante jogável da Google (Master dissertation in Federal University of Pernambuco, Brazil) (2014). www.ufpe.br/sib/ (Accessed 2 March 2015)

Cocoran, I.: The art of Digital Branding. Allworth Press, New York (2007). Apple iBookStore (ebook) (Accessed October 2014)

Cooke, P.: UNIQUE - Telling Your Story In The Age Of Brands And Social Media. Regal, Ventura (2012)

Crawford, C.: The art of computer game design [1982] (2015). www.van-couver.wsu.edu/fac/peabody/game-book/Cov-erpage.html (Accessed 15 January 2015)

De Waele, R., Campbell, L.: SHIFT 2020 - How technology will impact our future. Kindle version (2014). Amazon.com

Elias, H.: Post-Web: The Continuous Geography Of Digital Media. Formal Press, Odivelas (2013)

Elias, H.: First Person Shooter – The Subjective Cyberspace. Labcom Books, UBI, Covilhã (2009)

Elias, H.: "The advergames report". In: Néon digital – um discurso sobre os ciberespaços [Digital neon: a discourse on cyberspaces]. Labcom Books, UBI, Covilhã, Portugal (2007)

Elali, L., et al.: Logomorphism and liquid logos: an analysis of google doodles. In: Gonçalves, G. (ed.) The Dialogue Imperative: Trends And Challenges In Strategic And Organisational Communication, pp. 183–206. Labcom Books, Covilhã, UBI (2012)

Forceville, C.: Pictorial metaphor in advertising [1996]. Routledge, London (2002)

Frampton, J.: Branding in the post-digital world. creating and managing brand value. Interbrand (2012) www.interbrand.com (Accessed July 2013)

Gobé, M.: Brandjam - Humanizing Brands Through Emotional Design. Allworth Press, New York (2007)

Jhally, S.: Os códigos da publicidade - o feiticismo e a economia política do significado na sociiedade de consumo [The codes of advertising - fetishism and the political economy of meaning in the consumer society, 1987]. Edições Asa, Porto, Portugal (1995)

Kackman, M., et al.: Flow TV: Television In The Age Of Media Convergence. Routledge, New York (2011)

Kreutz, E.: "O discurso multimodal das marcas mutantes". In: XIV Congresso brasileiro de ciências da comunicação, p. 2. Intercom – Sociedade Brasileira de Estudos Interdisciplinares da Comunicação, Recife, Brazil (2011)

Lunenfeld, P.: The Digital Dialetic - New Essays on Media [1999]. MIT Press, Massachussets, Massachussets of Technology (2001)

Lury, C.: Brands - The Logos Of The Global Economy. Routledge, International Library of Sociology, London (2004)

Molloy, S.: Appvertising. How apps are changing the world. US: Saatchi & Saatchi, Crispin Porter, Bogusky, The Walt Disney Company (2014)

Rushkoff, D.: Present Shock - When Everything Happen Now Current - Penguin Books, US (2013). iBook (ePub) version @ Apple iBooks Store

Schroeder, J.E., Salzer-Mörling, M.: Brand culture. Routledge, New York (2006)

Vasilache, J.: Semiotics rising. In: Interbrand (2012). Interbrand.com (Accessed August 2013)

Heartbeat Jenga: A Biofeedback Board Game to Improve Coordination and Emotional Control

Yu-Chun Huang[1(✉)] and Chung-Hay Luk[2]

[1] Graduate Institute of Design Science, Tatung University,
No 40, Sec 3 Zhongshan N. Rd., Taipei, Taiwan
ych@ttu.edu.tw
[2] Augmedix, 1161 Mission Street Suite 210,
San Francisco, CA 94103, USA
luk@chunghay.com

Abstract. In most biofeedback interfaces, the user learns his/her biometric reading, but does not need it to guide consequent motor control. Here we demonstrate a game that requires the user to actively adjust his/her play in response to his/her heartbeat. The game is based on Jenga, where players take turns removing a wooden block from a tower of blocks and putting it on the top without causing the tower to collapse. Heartbeat Jenga's added biofeedback component changes the difficulty of the game based on real time monitoring of the player's heart rate during the player's turn. If heart rate increases (indicating that the player is not calm), the platform holding the blocks shakes and the room lights dim, making the game harder to play. Through such manipulation, the player actively prompts him/herself to calm down, while improving coordination.

Keywords: Biofeedback · Board game · Heart rate monitoring · Tangible interfaces · Soft circuits

1 Introduction

Biofeedback games are games, in which players use their bio-signals to alter dynamics in the game. Often these games are designed to heighten self-awareness of players' combined mental and physical states, and hence lend themselves nicely for psychotherapy.

Current products address various aspects of mental health, from improving concentration to overcoming anxiety. Thus far, games promoting concentration use brainwaves to manipulate game dynamics. Star Wars' the Force Trainer has the player concentrate to levitating a ball and lifts the ball depending on differences in several bands of brainwaves [1]. Mattel's MindFlex is similar, using brainwaves to navigate a ball through an obstacle course [2]. In the realm of gaming, NASA and SmartBrain Technologies have created a game controller that responds to neurofeedback [3]. Players are taught to concentrate more, as the controller becomes harder to move when the player becomes less focused (measured as more slower brain waves).

© Springer International Publishing Switzerland 2015
A. Marcus (Ed.): DUXU 2015, Part III, LNCS 9188, pp. 263–270, 2015.
DOI: 10.1007/978-3-319-20889-3_25

Another application of biofeedback games is as a way to overcome anxiety. Emanuel Andel's Knife.Hand.Chop.Bot puts the player's fears to the test [4]. The player puts his/her hand on a metal surface with fingers spread. Then a robot moves a sharp knife in between the fingers with the exact stub location determined by the galvanic skin response of the player. A less intense game to tackle angst is HeartBeat, a hide-and-seek-like game for children [5]. Each child has a sensor worn around the chest. If his/her heart rate goes above a threshold, a radio signal is transmitted to opposing teammates and the hiding spot becomes revealed. Our project shares this element of fear, in that the game becomes harder to play when players are anxious. Like Knife.Hand.Chop.Bot, our project uses the player against him/herself, though in subdued manner.

Rather than emphasizing angst, some games promote the converse – calmness. Mindball pits two players in a tug-of-war-like game to see who is more relaxed [6]. Journey to Wild Divine, a biofeedback computer game, fosters calmness in its general goal to train mediation skills and self-awareness [7]. Instead of a joystick or mouse, the controller consists of three sensors on the fingers that record heart rate and galvanic skin response. To navigate through the virtual world in a first-person adventure, the player must adjust his/her bio-signals depending on the level. Active Ingredient's Ere Be Dragons is another first-person adventure game, but for the personal digital assistant (PDA) [8]. The player sets a target heart rate, and the virtual world fades in and out depending of how off he/her heart rate is from the target. Again, it emphasizes self-awareness and trains users to adjust their calmness.

Our project has overlapping goals with its intent on training players to adjust their emotional state and remain calm. But our project requires more: players must dual-task, keep calm while coordinating their movements in response to a changing environment. This additional component potentially makes Heartbeat Jenga most similar to future games for the Nintendo's Wii Vitality Sensor, a heart rate finger clip extension to the Wiimote [9]. However, to date, the first game still under development that utilizes the sensor Heartbeat

2 Implementation

2.1 Heartbeat Jenga Game

Heartbeat Jenga is a modified game of Jenga. Like Jenga, players take turns removing blocks from a tall tower and placing them at the top. The tower subsequently grows taller and less stable from gaps created by the removed blocks. The game ends when a player causes the tower to fall.

The set-up is also similar to Jenga. It consists of 54 rectangular blocks, placed in groups of three to form individual stories of the 18-story tower. The alignment of each story's blocks is perpendicular to the alignment of the adjacent stories, so from the side view, you would see the short ends of three blocks in one story and the long end of one block in the story above and the story below. In our version, the tower rests on a vibrating platform that shakes in time with heartbeats. A faster beating heart causes more shakes, whereas a slower beating heart causes less shakes. An additional modification is that the lighting in the room is controlled by the player's heart rate. A fast rate dims the lights, ultimately turning them off, while a slow rate brightens the lights.

2.2 Scenario Demonstration

The game is played in a dark room and just relied on ambient lighting. At the beginning of a player's turn in Heartbeat Jenga, the player puts on a bio-sensing necklace device (see Fig. 1-A). Securing the necklace around the neck initiates the player's turn, which is visualized by the surface surround the tower illuminating by optical fabric during the duration of the turn (see Fig. 1-B). The computer subsequently begins collecting and processing the player's heartbeat signal. Each time a heartbeat is detected, an ornament on the player's necklace lights up, and the vibrating platform under the tower of blocks shakes a random amount. The lighting also changes subtly over time to match the fluctuations of the player's heart rate. For example, when user's heartbeat rate goes higher, it means he/she is getting nervous. In the mean time, he will lose lighting and the desk will shake more (see Fig. 1-C). While these changes are occurring, the player is removing a block from the tower and placing it at the top. If he/she successfully does so, the illuminated surface around the tower turns off. The vibrating platform ceases to shake, the ambient lighting returns to its brightest setting, and it becomes the next player's turn (see Fig. 1-D).

Our necklace device is worn by the player, whose turn it is, and serves as the on-off switch for the vibrating platform and ambient light. It is also soft and flexible, from the use of conductive thread rather than wire for the circuitry (see Fig. 1-A).

When a player starts his/her turn, he/she puts the necklace on. The magnetic clasp at the back clamps down on a force-sensing resistor (FSR), initiating the player's turn. The top of the vibrating platform lights up as well whenever the necklace is worn.

Next the player sticks the two extending branches of the necklace on his/her chest. Our necklace device measures electrical activity from the heart in the form of electrocardiography (ECG or EKG), and the current prototype uses surface electrodes (OTC^{TM} Reusable TENS electrodes, Koalaty Products, Inc.). One electrode goes by the heart, the other one further away, i.e. over the other breast. (The exact location does not matter, because this electrode is the reference point and carries no pulse signal.)

Lastly, the player connects the ribbon connector from the necklace to the ribbon cable that connects to the Arduino. The ECG signal exits the necklace via this ribbon cable and enters a chip that amplifies and filters the signal (Small 2-lead ECG analog front-end breadboard, Open ECG Project). The processed signal is then fed into Arduino for further processing to isolate the actual heartbeat signal.

Each time a beat is detected, the LED ornament on the necklace lights up. This provides other players with a sense of how calm or stressed the current player is.

2.3 Devices

The devices include heartbeat signal sensor, LED ambient lighting, servo motor, optical fabric and necklace (see Fig. 2).

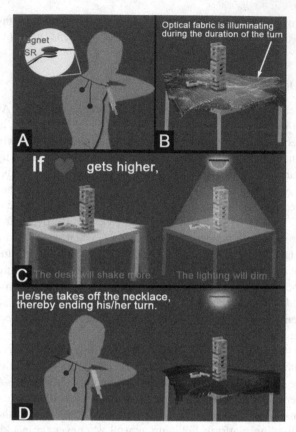

Fig. 1. Scenario demonstration: (A) At the beginning of the Jenga game, user puts on a bio-sensing necklace device; (B) The optical fabric is illuminated during the duration of the turn; (C) If heart rate goes higher, the platform shakes more, and the lighting dims; (D) When user takes off the necklace, his/her turn ends.

2.4   Heartbeat Jenga Installation

Our set-up consisted of three components: a small table with a vibrating platform in the center, circuit boards hidden beneath, and a light above the table to create the ambient lighting. We set an Arduino board and a heartbeat circuit as media to transfer signal from physical input (FSR and bio-signal) to digital output (including LED necklace, vibrating platform by using servo motor, and control of ambient lighting). After getting the bio-signal from the heartbeat circuit, the computer then sends the command to Arduino to adjust the ambient lighting and the shaking rate of the platform (see Fig. 3).

To make the platform on the table shake, we found a tray with wheels. We constrain its movement by placing a ring around it. To create the shaking movement, we attached a servo motor underneath and added extensions to the motor that push the platform upward against the tabletop to create a shake (see Fig. 4).

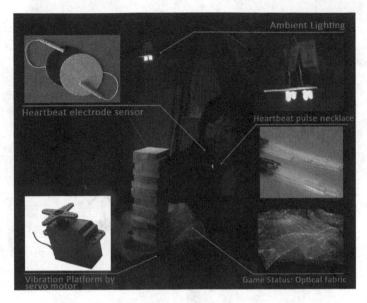

Fig. 2. Devices

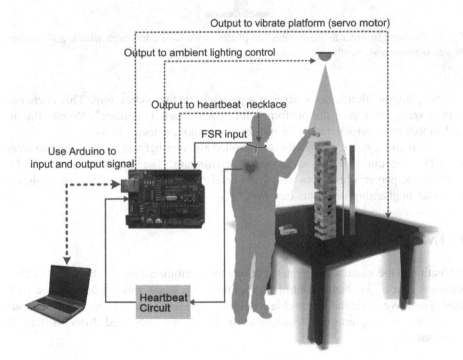

Fig. 3. System framework

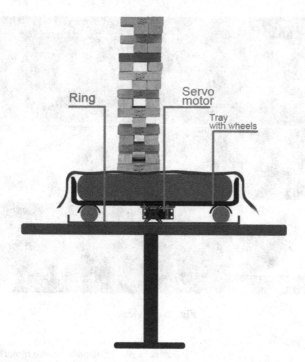

Fig. 4. Platform: in order to create vibration platform, we used a tray with wheels and attached the servo motor underneath.

The platform illuminates whenever a player is taking his/her turn. This is created from covering on top of the platform with optical fabric (Luminex®, Roman Illumination) that turns on whenever the bio-sensing necklace device is worn.

For our prototype of the heartbeat-controlled ambient lighting, we attached an array of LEDs over our table by an arched wire structure. The brightness of the LEDs followed the player's heart rate with faster heart rate dimming the lights, and a slower heart rate brightening the lights (see Fig. 5).

3   Evaluation

Evaluation of the game was conducted during the exhibition days for the Tangible User Interface course. To better control the lighting, the game was set-up inside a dark (dusty) tent. We made but one necklace device, so player experience was limited to one of us. She was questioned. Additional feedback was obtained from visitors in conversation.

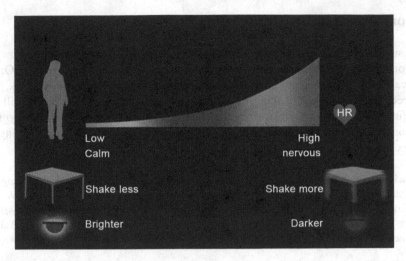

Fig. 5. The relationship between heart rate, the ambient lighting, and shake rate of the platform

4 Results

Player experience in the current set-up is not particularly comfortable. Because we needed to control for light, the set-up had to be condensed within a tent, and sitting on the floor is not as comfortable as sitting on chairs. Further, the player's movements were limited, as everything was wired. In contrast, the necklace was comfortable and felt like a scarf.

In terms of technical issues, we need more work interfacing wires to fabrics. The reoccurring problem is that conductive thread looses its tension. A possible fix is covering seams with bias tape as recommended by Ali Crockett at Aniomagic [Boyd, personal communication]. More advance signal processing will also cut down on false pulses.

The benefits of the biofeedback game began early on. Improvements in coordination were observed within twenty minutes of demonstrating the game to visitors. In contrast, no noticeable ability to control heart rate was observed during the 3-4 h of demonstration. More playtime may be needed.

From conversing with visitors, it seemed like the game was straightforward to follow. Most people noticed the changes we made linked to heartbeat. The shaking platform was the easiest to pick-up on, then the blinking LED on necklace, and lastly the changes in ambient light. Everyone understood the added difficulty of our game that punished players for stressing out. One visitor liked the potential application of Heartbeat Jenga to teach young kids to control their emotions. We also received suggestions for improving and augmenting our game. One recommendation was to have each player wear his/her own necklace and use a token to denote whose turn it is [Goodman, personal communication]. An interesting extension to the game to make it more social was to have all players' heartbeats involved in the game. A player could then purposely and suddenly increase his/her heart rate during another player's turn to make the game harder for an opponent [Ryokai, personal communication].

5   Conclusions

The concept for Heartbeat Jenga was well received. People understood the game and could pick-up on the effects caused by the player's pulse reasonably quickly. On the technical side, the connecting point between the necklace and wires was a weak point and needs further work. Changing to wearable conductive fabric electrodes will also make future evaluation possible, since the sharing of sticker electrodes lacks hygiene. Additional evaluation from other people wearing the pulse necklace and playing the game is needed.

Acknowledgements. We thank Professor Kimiko Ryokai, Elizabeth Goodman, Keng-Hao Chang, and the Tangible User Interface classmates for their feedback and suggestions. We also thank Eric Boyd for collaborating on the research leading up to the current heartbeat-sensing necklace prototype. Financial support of this research by Tatung University, Taipei, Taiwan, under the grant B103-DD1-027 is gratefully acknowledged.

References

1. The Force™ Trainer, Uncle Milton Industries, Inc. http://unclemilton.com/starwarsscience/
2. Mindflex™, Mattel, Inc. http://mindflexgames.com/
3. Video game SMART systems, SmartBrain Technologies. http://www.smartbraintech.com/store/pc/viewCategories.asp?idCategory=3
4. Andel, E.: Knife.Hand.Chop.Bot. No date. http://5voltcore.com/typolight/typolight257/index.php?id=1&articles=33
5. Magielse, R., Markopoulos P.: HeartBeat: an outdoor pervasive game for children. In: Proceedings of CHI 2009, pp. 2181–2184 (2009)
6. Mindball Game, Interactive Productline. http://www.mindball.se/product.html
7. The Journey to Wild Divine Adventure Gaming Series, Wild Divine. http://www.wilddivine.com/meditation-products.html
8. Davis, S.B., Moar, M., Cox, J., Riddoch, C., Cooke, K., Jacobs, R., Watkins, M., Hull, R., Melamed, T.: Ere be dragons: an interactive artwork. In: ACM Multimedia, pp. 1059–1060, ACM, New York, NY, USA (2005)
9. Beaumont, C.: E3 2009: Nintendo's Wii Vitality Sensor measures player's heart rate. Telegraph Jun. 2009. http://www.telegraph.co.uk/technology/e3-2009/5432684/E3-2009-Nintendos-Wii-Vitality-Sensor-measures-players-heart-rate.html Accessed 15 December 2009
10. Heartbeat, Capybara Games (Not yet released). http://www.capybaragames.com/heartbeat-2/

Evaluation of User Experience in Interaction with Computer Games

Tihana Lapaš and Tihomir Orehovački[✉]

Faculty of Organization and Informatics, University of Zagreb,
Pavlinska 2, 42000 Varaždin, Croatia
{tihana.lapas,tihomir.orehovacki}@foi.hr

Abstract. Positive user experience (UX) is considered to be one of the main predictors of users' loyalty. In the context of Massively Online Battle Arena (MOBA) games, absorption & dissociation, immersion, presence, flow, and social play constitute a set of essential user experience (UX) facets. With an objective to determine to what extent the aforementioned UX dimensions contribute to MOBA games players' continuance intentions, an empirical study was carried out. Participants in the study were randomly selected MOBA games players. Data were collected by means of an online post-use questionnaire. The psychometric features of the conceptual model that reflects an interplay of UX facets and players' loyalty were examined by means of the partial least squares (PLS) structural equation modelling (SEM) technique. Implications for both researchers and practitioners are presented and discussed.

Keywords: Massively Online Battle Arena (MOBA) · Computer games · User experience · Empirical study · Post-use questionnaire · Conceptual model · SEM-PLS

1 Introduction

In the last two decades, information and communication technology (ICT) has become the constituent part of many different aspects of human life. Regardless of whether ICT serves as an aid in business and learning or is employed in leisure time for relaxation and fun, an interaction with it results in user's subjective perception which is commonly referred to as user experience (UX).

When reasoning about the definition of UX, researchers can be grouped in two main streams. The first one defines UX as a synonym for usability and user-oriented design. As one of the main representatives of this stream, Bevan [3] argues that usability evaluation contributes to better understanding of users' needs, improves software performance, and in turn creates positive UX. In addition, Alben [2] stated that successful, interesting, and valuable UX is affected by both software development and interaction with software criteria. The second stream defines UX as a concept which is separated from usability and represents added value to software in terms of fulfilling users' needs and desires [17]. For instance, Hassenzahl and Tractinsky [16] emphasize that UX facets go beyond instrumental and are orientated on satisfying hedonic human needs related to beauty, invocation, stimulation, growth, etc. In that

© Springer International Publishing Switzerland 2015
A. Marcus (Ed.): DUXU 2015, Part III, LNCS 9188, pp. 271–282, 2015.
DOI: 10.1007/978-3-319-20889-3_26

respect, UX monitoring and testing should be included in all phases of the software lifecycle [31].

Specific piece of information and communication technology are computer games. Today, they are used in leisure time for entertainment purposes as well for learning and gaining diverse skills. Facer [10] claims that learning through computer games is easier and more fun because they provide information through graphics, animations and videos which is more interesting than pure text used in regular learning materials. Moreover, educational computer games are challenging in a way that they enable students to solve real-life issues in a safe environment [22, 29]. By anticipating possible moves that one will make, a computer game can predict events that might occur [38] and are due to this feature used for training purposes in organizational [7] and military settings [11]. Considering that Massively Online Battle Arena (MOBA) genre of computer games have implemented all of the set forth features and can be employed in numerous contexts, they have been used as a representative sample in our empirical study on assessment of specific UX facets.

The remainder of the paper is structured in following way. In the second section, a brief overview of relevant and recent studies on UX assessment together with the proposed research framework and hypotheses is offered. Employed research design is described in the third section. Results of the empirical study are presented in the fourth section. Discussion of study findings and concluding remarks are contained in the last section.

2 Background to the Research

2.1 Literature Review

Recent research related to the UX in interaction with computer games was mainly focused on exploring aspects such as flow, fun, immersion, presence, tension, attention, frustration and addiction. Some studies also examined impact of playing with others and effect of game elements such as story, gameplay and game mechanics on UX [8, 20, 33, 34]. In the light of the aforementioned, Takatalo et al. [37] developed fifteen scaled questionnaire to measure two aspects of game playing. The first one is adaptation which is manifested by physical presence, attention, and interest while the second one is flow and quality which is represented by playfulness, game challenges, impression, and enjoyment, among others. The same authors [36] developed another questionnaire, Presence-Involvement-Flow-Framework (PIFF), which was used for evaluating the impact of presence, involvement and flow on UX. Nacke et al. [26] measured seven different dimensions (sensory and imaginative immersion, tension, competence, flow, negative affect, positive affect, and challenge) of UX with their Game Experience Questionnaire (GEQ). Desurvire et al. [8] developed Heuristics Evaluation of Playability (HEP) framework meant for evaluating game story, game play, game mechanics and game usability. Very similarly, Hunicke et al. [20] conducted a research in which they explored Mechanics, Dynamics, and Aesthetics (MDA) of a computer game. Results of a study carried out by Lazzaros [23] have shown that challenges (overcoming obstacles), grabbing attention (curiosity, excitement, and adventure), altering states (emotions and sensations) and presence of other players (competition and co-operation with others) are the main aspects of a computer game that have impact on UX. Roth et al. [32] developed a questionnaire in a form of a multidimensional self-reporting scale which purpose was to examine the influence of interactive stories on UX. The aim of the research conducted by Hannu et al. [15] was to investigate the influence of various elements of user experience such as challenge, competition and fellowship, and sympathy and thrill on playfulness and pleasure, in the context of computer games. Choi and Kim [5] carried out a research in which they analyzed the effect of personal and social interaction, flow and absorption on users' loyalty. Finally, Lee [24] completed a study whose purpose was to examine the influence of player's motivation to participate, addictive behavior, flow and immersion experience, role-playing and achievements on player's loyalty.

2.2   Research Model and Hypotheses

The aim of the research presented in this paper was to identify to what extent different facets of UX affect user's continuance intention related to playing MOBA genre games. For that purpose, the research framework that illustrates an interplay among five UX facets and user's loyalty was designed. Four UX facets (absorption & dissociation (A&D), flow (FLW), immersion (IMS), and presence (PRS)) were adopted from Nacke et al. [26] and subsequently enhanced with questionnaire items that were proposed by Takatalo et al. [36, 37]. Social play (SPL) was measured with items designed by Isbister [21] whereas loyalty was evaluated with items that were adopted from Agarwal and Karahanna [1].

Immersion is a specific state of becoming engaged in the gaming experience while still retaining some awareness of surroundings, but in a way that surrounding distractions can be successfully and easily ignored [26]. Prior research [8] showed that immersion represents deeper engagement with the game and is result of positive experience that occurs during the game play. Study conducted by Hannu et al. [15] revealed that trait of successfully ignoring surroundings is constitutive part of playfulness. In that respect, we hypothesize the following:

H1.   Immersion will positively influence absorption & dissociation.

Flow is a state achieved when one's skills and capabilities are in balance with heaviness of game objectives. According to Sánchez et al. [33], flow is one of the influential factor of player's loyalty towards online games. In addition, Lee [24] found that well-build game elements such as role-playing and achievements have great influence on flow. Considering that player will be more motivated to gain specific skills if he or she establish deeper emotional connection with an avatar, we proposed following hypothesis:

H2.   Flow will positively influence presence.

Social play refers to any form of socialization through joint game play, including competition, collaboration and assistance [23]. Several studies [21, 24] discovered that avatars, which form one's virtual identity and represent him or her in interaction with others, helps one to feel more connected with and included into game. Playing with others eventually results in deeper relationship between players in form of virtual friendship. Choi and Kim [5] stated that one's desire for spending time with friends will result in continuance intention related to playing the game. In the light of the afore-mentioned, we proposed following hypotheses:

H3.   Social play will positively influence presence.

H4.   Social play will positively influence loyalty.

Presence can be described as a state of being aware of real surroundings and at the same time having experience of being inside the virtual environment. The set forth can be achieved by empathizing the plot or identifying with the avatar (its appearance, abilities and skills). By making a connection with the game, player willingly becomes present in it [36]. As a result of their research, Lombard and Ditton [25] concluded that media attributes (e.g. color and sound richness, camera angle, extent of social realism) influence to a certain degree on one's presence perception in the context of the virtual world. Based on the aforesaid, the following hypothesis is proposed:

H5.   Presence will positively influence absorption & dissociation.

Absorption & dissociation refers to a state in which one's mind detaches from reality in a way that he or she identifies himself or herself with an avatar and stops having any awareness of real surroundings while playing the game. Prior work suggests that excessive immersion into the game can lead to absorption in a way that person adopts and mimics appearance, behavior, and thinking of favorite avatar in everyday life situations [4]. In their research, Poels et al. [28] discovered that dissociation can manifest as anxiety when one is not able to play the game, excessive excitement when talking or thinking about the game, and anticipation of being able to play the game again. Taking the set forth into account, following hypothesis was defined:

H6.   Absorption & dissociation will positively influence loyalty.

3   Methodology

Research subjects were randomly selected players of MOBA games. The sample of study participants was composed of individuals who play MOBA games on regular basis as well of individuals who used to play this genre of computer games. The research included 158 MOBA players of which 91.77 % completed the questionnaire correctly. Majority (71.72 %) of study participants were male while 28.28 % of them were female. The age of players ranged from 10 to more than 50 years where majority (71.03 %) of them had between 20 and 29 years.

Data were collected by means of the post-use questionnaire that was designed with KwikSurveys online survey builder. Link to the questionnaire was published at several websites and forums dealing with popular MOBA games such as Defense of the Ancients 2 (DOTA2) and League of Legends (LOL). It was also posted to gaming community Steam and official fan pages of the aforementioned MOBA games on social networking sites Facebook and Twitter. The questionnaire was available for three weeks during August 2014.

Questionnaire was comprised of two main parts. Demographic data about MOBA players were collected in the first part of the questionnaire. The second part contained 24 statements related to six dimensions of the proposed research framework. The answers were modulated on a four-point Likert scale ranging from (1) "strongly disagree" to (4) "strongly agree".

Considering the exploratory nature of conducted empirical study, the psychometric features of the proposed research framework and associated hypotheses were examined by means of the partial least squares (PLS) structural equation modeling (SEM) technique. The reasoning behind the choice of PLS-SEM over its covariance-based counterpart (CB-SEM) relies on the fact that PLS-SEM does not require sound theoretical foundations and achieves high level of statistical power even when the sample size is relatively small and data significantly deviate from normal distribution [14]. Data analysis was conducted with SmartPLS 2.0 M3 [30] software.

4 Results

PLS-SEM algorithm performs path analysis in two stages. The first one is iterative approximation of measurement model parameters while the second one is the estimation of standardized partial regression coefficients which are part of the structural model [9]. Consequently, the assessment of psychometric characteristics of the research framework was two-step procedure.

The quality of the measurement model was evaluated by examining the reliability of manifest variables (items), reliability of latent variables (constructs), convergent validity, and discriminant validity. Reliability of manifest variables was estimated by exploring the standardized loadings of manifest variables with their respective latent variable. The purification guidelines suggested by Hulland [19] indicate that manifest variables should be removed from the model if their standardized loadings are below threshold value of 0.707. The same author argue that exception can be made in the case of exploratory studies in which composite reliability values above 0.600 are considered acceptable. Results of the confirmatory factor analysis (CFA) presented in Table 1 indicate that standardized loadings of 23 manifest variables were greater than recommended cut-off value, except of SPL1 whose standardized factor loading was 0.6920. However, since this manifest variable presents an important dimension of social play and its omission would significantly reduce the validity of the research framework, it was retained in the measurement model. Standardized loadings of manifest variables were in the range from 0.6920 to 0.8925 which indicates that latent variables explained between 47.89 % and 79.66 % of their manifest variables' variance.

Reliability of latent variables was tested using the Cronbach's alpha (α) coefficient and composite reliability (CR). Opposed to Cronbach's alpha (α) which assumes that weightings of items are equal, CR includes actual item loadings and consequently indicates better estimate of internal consistency. Hair et al. [14] recommended thresholds of 0.707 for both CR and Cronbach's α. Data provided in Table 1 imply that estimated values for all six latent variables were above the aforementioned cut-off value.

Table 1. Standardized factor loadings and cross loadings of manifest variables

Manifest variables (MVs)	Latent variables (LVs)					
	Absorption & dissociation (A&D)	Flow (FLW)	Immersion (IMS)	Loyalty (LOY)	Presence (PRS)	Social play (SPL)
A&D1	**0.8391**	0.3525	0.5963	0.3021	0.2376	0.3770
A&D2	**0.8253**	0.1861	0.5495	0.2959	0.2583	0.2293
A&D3	**0.7276**	0.3254	0.3661	0.3331	0.3076	0.2717
A&D4	**0.7516**	0.3516	0.4293	0.3102	0.3875	0.3321
FLW1	0.2846	**0.7919**	0.2989	0.1844	0.2910	0.3199
FLW2	0.3401	**0.8436**	0.2065	0.3093	0.3461	0.2950
FLW3	0.3248	**0.8480**	0.2643	0.2767	0.3439	0.3007
IMS1	0.5004	0.1987	**0.8117**	0.2390	0.2476	0.2886
IMS2	0.3787	0.1857	**0.7782**	0.2952	0.2217	0.3454
IMS3	0.5694	0.3379	**0.8566**	0.3167	0.1906	0.2799
IMS4	0.5696	0.2629	**0.8472**	0.2884	0.0926	0.3487
LOY1	0.2197	0.1835	0.2585	**0.8072**	0.1848	0.5380
LOY2	0.4541	0.3250	0.4026	**0.8915**	0.4122	0.5766
LOY3	0.3601	0.3068	0.2953	**0.8810**	0.1966	0.5197
LOY4	0.2925	0.2536	0.2148	**0.8462**	0.2956	0.5713
PRS1	0.3849	0.3025	0.2629	0.3217	**0.8925**	0.3703
PRS2	0.2621	0.3353	0.1477	0.2962	**0.8662**	0.3388
PRS3	0.3134	0.3919	0.1544	0.2210	**0.8327**	0.3091
SPL1*	0.3526	0.2524	0.3353	0.5960	0.2108	**0.6920**
SPL2	0.4091	0.2985	0.3392	0.4558	0.4553	**0.7668**
SPL3	0.1567	0.2674	0.2189	0.3786	0.2855	**0.8021**
SPL4	0.3075	0.3121	0.2118	0.4737	0.2931	**0.7894**
SPL5	0.2560	0.2574	0.3346	0.4852	0.2761	**0.7621**
SPL6	0.2081	0.2618	0.2423	0.4857	0.2364	**0.7005**

*given that standardized factor loading is in a range that is acceptable for exploratory studies, this manifest variable was retained in the measurement model

Convergent validity was examined using the average variance extracted (AVE). According to Fornell and Larcker [12], AVE values above 0.50 are considered acceptable because they indicate that shared variance between specific latent variable and its manifest variables is larger than variance of the measurement error. As can be seen in Table 2, all constructs have met this criterion.

Discriminant validity is defined as an extent of dissimilarity among latent variables in the measurement model. Two measures were used to evaluate discriminant validity [14]. The first one are cross loadings according to which manifest variables should load higher on latent variable they are assigned to than on any of other latent variables in the model. As depicted in Table 1, loadings of all manifest variables on their respective latent variables are higher than their loadings on all remaining latent variables which indicates that all manifest variables have met this criterion of discriminant validity. The second measure is the Fornell-Larcker criterion [12] according to which the square root of the AVE of each latent variable should be greater than its highest correlation with remaining latent variables in the model. Table 3 clearly illustrates that each latent variable shares greater amount of variance with their manifest variables than with other latent variables in the model which implies that all latent variables have met the second criterion of discriminant validity. All the aforementioned confirms reliability and validity of the measurement model.

Table 2. Convergent validity and internal consistency variables

Latent Variables (LVs)	Average Variance Extracted (AVE)	Composite Reliability (CR)	Cronbach's Alpha (α)
Absorption & dissociation (A&D)	0.6199	0.8667	0.7945
Flow (FLW)	0.6859	0.8675	0.7714
Immersion (IMS)	0.6790	0.8942	0.8436
Loyalty (LOY)	0.7346	0.9171	0.8791
Presence (PRS)	0.7468	0.8984	0.8302
Social play (SPL)	0.5675	0.8870	0.8469

Table 3. Discriminant validity of latent variables

	A&D	FLW	IMS	LOY	PRS	SPL
A&D	**0.6199**					
FLW	0.1471	**0.6859**				
IMS	0.3891	0.0938	**0.6790**			
LOY	0.1534	0.0988	0.1188	**0.7346**		
PRS	0.1397	0.1572	0.0488	0.1049	**0.7468**	
SPL	0.1485	0.1345	0.1436	0.4149	0.1548	**0.5675**

In the second step of evaluation, the quality of structural model was estimated by means of endogenous latent variables' determination coefficient, path coefficients' significance level, exogenous latent variables' effect size, and exogenous latent variables' predictive relevance.

The determination coefficient (R^2) refers to the proportion of endogenous latent variables' variance explained by the set of predictors. According to Orehovački [27], R^2 values of 0.15, 0.34, or 0.46 for endogenous latent variables in the structural model can be, as a rule of thumb, interpreted as weak, moderate, or substantial, respectively. As shown in Fig. 1, 22.83 % of variance in presence was explained by flow and social play, 44.77 % of variance in absorption & dissociation was explained by immersion and presence while 43.91 % of variance in loyalty was explained by social play and absorption & dissociation. Considering the set forth, predictors of absorption & dissociation and continuance intention have moderate explanatory power while predictions of presence have weak explanatory power.

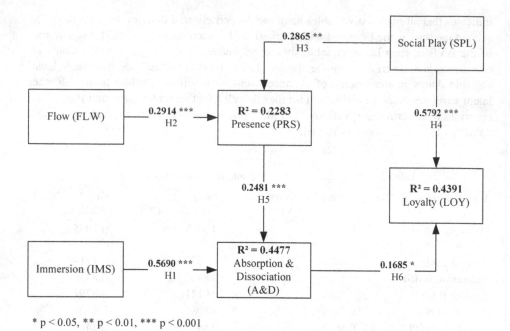

* p < 0.05, ** p < 0.01, *** p < 0.001

Fig. 1. PLS estimates for structural model

The evaluation of path coefficients' goodness was carried out with an aim to examine the hypothesized associations among latent variables. One-tailed t-statistics derived from a bootstrapping resampling procedure was used to determine significance of path coefficients. The number of bootstrap samples was 5.000 while the number of cases was equal to the sample size.

Results of hypotheses testing are shown in the first five columns of Table 4. Data analysis revealed that both flow ($\beta = 0.2914$, $p < 0.001$) and social play ($\beta = 0.2865$, $p < 0.01$) significantly contribute to the presence thus providing support for H2 and H3. It was also discovered that immersion ($\beta = 0.5690$, $p < 0.001$) and presence ($\beta = 0.2481$, $p < 0.001$) significantly affect the absorption & dissociation thereby supporting H1 and H5. Finally, it appeared that absorption & dissociation ($\beta = 0.1685$, $p < 0.05$) and social play ($\beta = 0.5792$, $p < 0.001$) have significant impact on players' loyalty thus demonstrating support for H6 and H4.

The effect size (f^2) reflects the change in the endogenous latent variable's determination coefficient. According to Cohen [6] values of 0.35, 0.15, or 0.02 imply that specific predictor has large, medium, or small influence on endogenous latent variable, respectively. As presented in the sixth column of Table 4, immersion strongly ($f^2 = 0.54$) affects absorption & dissociation while presence has small impact ($f^2 = 0.10$) on this endogenous latent variable. Both flow and social play have small influence ($f^2 = 0.09$) on presence. Finally, the effect of social play on loyalty is large in size ($f^2 = 0.49$) whereas it turned out that absorption & dissociation has small effect ($f^2 = 0.04$) on loyalty.

Table 4. Results of testing the hypotheses, effect size, and predictive validity

Hypotheses	β	t-value	p-value	Supported	f^2	q^2
H1. IMS → A&D	0.5690	9.4879	***	Yes	0.54	0.25
H2. FLW → PRS	0.2914	3.4963	***	Yes	0.09	0.07
H3. SPL → PRS	0.2865	3.2527	**	Yes	0.09	0.06
H4. SPL → LOY	0.5792	11.3698	***	Yes	0.49	0.30
H5. PRS → A&D	0.2481	3.5578	***	Yes	0.10	0.05
H6. A&D → LOY	0.1685	2.5187	*	Yes	0.04	0.02

$* \ p < 0.05, \ ** \ p < 0.01, \ *** \ p < 0.001$

The predictive validity of exogenous latent variables was tested with non-parametric Stone's [35] and Geisser's [13] cross-validated redundancy measure Q^2 that based on blindfolding reuse technique predicts indicators of endogenous latent variable. Changes in Q^2 indicate relative impact (q^2) of exogenous latent variables in predicting manifest variables assigned to endogenous latent variable. Values of 0.35, 0.15, or 0.02 signify substantial, moderate, or weak predictive relevance of a specific exogenous latent variable [18]. Taking into account data presented in the last column of Table 4, immersion has moderate relevance ($q^2 = 0.25$) while presence has weak relevance ($q^2 = 0.05$) in predicting absorption & dissociation. Moreover, flow and social play have weak relevance ($q^2 = 0.07$ and 0.06, respectively) in predicting presence. Finally, social play has moderate relevance ($q^2 = 0.30$) whereas absorption & dissociation has weak relevance ($q^2 = 0.02$) in predicting loyalty.

5 Discussion and Concluding Remarks

The objective of this paper was to identify to what extent different facets of UX (immersion, flow, presence, absorption & dissociation, and social play) have influence on users' loyalty in terms of a continuance intention to play Massively Online Battle Arena (MOBA) games. For that purpose, a research framework which illustrates interference among aforementioned latent variables was proposed. Its psychometric characteristics were examined by means of the partial least squares (PLS) structural equation modeling (SEM) technique. Considering that measurement and structural model have met all criteria prescribed by Hair et al. [14], validity and reliability of the proposed research framework were confirmed.

Given that reported findings add to the extant body of knowledge, they offer several implications for researchers and practitioners. Researchers can use introduced framework as a foundation for future studies in the field. On the other hand, designers and developers can employ the post-use questionnaire in order to determine to what extent games they implemented have met specific criteria of user experience. In addition, the analysis of the proposed framework revealed several designing aspects which developers should take into account when developing a MOBA game. Firstly, they have to assure that the player does not feel frustration or boredom when playing a game. The set forth can be easily achieved by balancing heaviness of in-game assignments and one's capabilities which would eventually lead player to a flow state. The attention should be also paid to the development of avatars and the plot so the player could bound with game on emotional level thus reaching a game presence. In addition, a game should be successful in attracting one's attention in a manner that nothing can distract him or her when playing a game. The state of immersion and a feeling of a game presence together indicate that one is completely involved in a virtual world and detached from reality when playing a game. Finally, if a MOBA game supports connecting and playing with others and is capable to bring a player into a state of absorption & dissociation, he or she will be eager to play a game again and recommend it to others.

Considering that topic of this paper were MOBA games and that presented results are part of an ongoing research, in our future work we will enhance the proposed research framework with additional UX dimensions and then explore its validity and reliability on the representative sample of diverse game genres.

References

1. Agarwal, R., Karahanna, E.: Time flies when you're having fun: cognitive absorption and beliefs about information technology usage. MIS Q. **24**(4), 665–694 (2000)
2. Alben, L.: Defining the criteria for effective interaction design. Interactions **3**(3), 11–15 (1996)
3. Bevan, N.: Classifying and selecting UX and usability measures. In: Law, E., Bevan, N., Christou, G., Springett, M., Lárusdóttir, M. (eds.) Valid Useful User Experience Measurement (VUUM) Proceedings of the International Workshop on Meaningful Measures, pp. 13–18. Institute of Research in Informatics of Toulouse (IRIT), Toulouse (2008)
4. Brockmyer, J.H., Fox, C.M., Curtiss, K.A., McBroom, E., Burkhart, K.M., Pidruzny, J.N.: The development of the game engagement questionnaire: a measure of engagement in video game-playing. J. Exp. Soc. Psychol. **45**(4), 624–634 (2009)
5. Choi, D., Kim, J.: Why people continue to play online games: in search of critical design factors to increase customer loyalty to online contents. Cyber Psychol. Behav. **7**(1), 11–24 (2004)
6. Cohen, J.: Statistical power analysis for the behavioral sciences. Lawrence Erlbaum Associates, Hillsdale (1988)
7. Cone, B.D., Irvine, C.E., Thompson, M.F., Nguyen, T.D.: A video game for cyber security training and awareness. Comput. Secur. **26**(1), 63–72 (2007)
8. Desurvire, H., Caplan, M., Toth, J.: Using heuristics to evaluate the playability of games. In: CHI 2004 Extended Abstracts on Human Factors in Computing Systems, pp. 1509–1512. ACM (2004)
9. Vinzi, V.E., Trinchera, L., Amato, S.: PLS path modeling: from foundations to recent developments and open issues for model assessment and improvement. In: Vinzi, V.E., Chin, W.W., Henseler, J., Wang, H. (eds.) Handbook of Partial Least Squares, pp. 47–82. Springer, Heidelberg (2010)
10. Facer, K.: Computer games and learning (2003). http://admin.futurelab.org.uk/resources/documents/discussion_papers/Computer_Games_and_Learning_discpaper.pdf

11. Fong, G.: Adapting COTS games for military simulation. In: Proceedings of the 2004 ACM SIGGRAPH International Conference on Virtual Reality Continuum and Its Applications in Industry, pp. 269–272 (2004)

12. Fornell, C.G., Larcker, D.F.: Structural equation models with unobservable variables and measurement error: algebra and statistics. J. Mark. Res. **18**(3), 328–388 (1981)

13. Geisser, S.: The predictive sample reuse method with applications. J. Am. Stat. Assoc. **70** (350), 320–328 (1975)

14. Hair, J.F., Ringle, C.M., Sarstedt, M.: PLS-SEM: indeed a silver bullet. J. Mark. Theo. Pract. **19**(2), 139–151 (2011)

15. Hannu, K., Montola, M., Arrasvuori, J.: Understanding playful user experience through digital games. In: International Conference on Designing Pleasurable Products and Interfaces, pp. 274–285 (2009)

16. Hassenzahl, M., Tractinsky, N.: User experience-a research agenda. Behav. Inf. Technol. **25** (2), 91–97 (2006)

17. Hassenzahl, M.: User Experience (UX): Towards an experiential perspective on product quality. In: IHM 2008 Proceedings of the 20th International Conference of the Association Francophned Interaction Homme-Machine, pp. 11–15. ACM, Metz (2008)

18. Henseler, J., Ringle, C.M., Sinkovics, R.R.: The use of partial least squares path modeling in international marketing. Adv. Int. Mark. **20**, 277–319 (2009)

19. Hulland, J.: Use of partial least squares (PLS) in strategic management research: a review of four recent studies. Strateg. Manag. J. **20**(2), 195–204 (1999)

20. Hunicke, R., LeBlanc, M., Zubek, R.: MDA: a formal approach to game design and game research. In: Proceedings of AAAI Workshop on Challenges in Game AI, pp. 01–04 (2004)

21. Isbister, K.: Enabling social play: a framework for design and evaluation. In: Bernhaupt, R. (ed.) Evaluating User Experience in Games, vol. 2010, pp. 11–22. Springer, Heidelberg (2010)

22. Ke, F.: A qualitative meta-analysis of computer games as learning tools. Handb. Res. Eff. Electron. Gaming Educ. **1**, 1–32 (2009)

23. Lazzaro, N.: Why we play games: Four keys to more emotion without story (2004). http://www.xeodesign.com/whyweplaygames/xeodesign_whyweplaygames.pdf

24. Lee, C.W.: Influential factors of player's loyalty toward online games for achieving commercial success. Australas. Mark. J. (AMJ) **18**(2), 81–92 (2010)

25. Lombard, M., Ditton, T.B., Crane, D., Davis, B., Gil-Egui, G., Horvath, K., Rossman, J., Park, S.: Measuring presence: a literature-based approach to the development of a standardized paper-and-pencil instrument. In: Third International Workshop on Presence, Delft (2000)

26. Nacke, L.E., Drachen, A., Kuikkaniemi, K., Niesenhaus, J., Korhonen, H.J., van den Hoogen, W.M., Poels, K., IJsselsteijn, W.A., Kort, Y.: Playability and player experience research. In: Proceedings of DiGRA (2009)

27. Orehovački, T.: Methodology of Evaluating the Quality in Use of Web 2.0 Applications, Ph. D. thesis (in Croatian: Metodologija vrjednovanja kvalitete u korištenju aplikacijama Web 2.0) (2013)

28. Poels, K., IJsselsteijn, W., De Kort, Y., Van Iersel, B.: Digital games, the aftermath: qualitative insights into postgame experiences. In: Bernhaupt, R. (ed.) Evaluating User Experience in Games, vol. 2010, pp. 149–163. Springer, Heidelberg (2010)

29. Prensky, M.: Computer games and learning: digital game-based learning. Handb. comput. game stud. **18**, 97–122 (2005)

30. Ringle, C.M., Wende, S., Will, A.: SmartPLS 2.0 M3 (2005)

31. Robert, J.M., Lesage, A.: A designing and evaluating user experience. In: Boy, G.A. (ed.) The Handbook of Human-Machine Interaction: A Human-Centered Design Approach. Ashgate Publishing, London (2012). http://atibook.ir/dl/en/Engineering/other% 20Engineering/9781409411710_the_handbook_of_human-machine_interaction.pdf
32. Roth, C., Vorderer, P., Klimmt, C., Vermeulen, I.: Measuring the user experience in narrative-rich games: towards a concept-based assessment for interactive stories. In: Entertainment Interfaces (2010)
33. González Sánchez, J.L., Padilla Zea, N., Gutiérrez, F.L.: From usability to playability: introduction to player-centred video game development process. In: Kurosu, M. (ed.) HCD 2009. LNCS, vol. 5619, pp. 65–74. Springer, Heidelberg (2009)
34. Sicart, M.: Defining game mechanics. Game Stud. 8(2), 1–14 (2008)
35. Stone, M.: Cross-validatory choice and assessment of statistical predictions. J. Roy. Stat. Soc. B 36(2), 111–133 (1974)
36. Takatalo, J., Häkkinen, J., Kaistinen, J., Nyman, G.: Presence, involvement, and flow in digital games. In: Bernhaupt, R. (ed.) Evaluating user experience in games, pp. 23–46. Springer, London (2010)
37. Takatalo, J., Häkkinen, J., Kaistinen, J., Nyman, G.: Measuring user experience in digital gaming: theoretical and methodological issues. In: Proceedings of SPIE-IS&T Electronic Imaging, vol. 6494. SPIE (2007)
38. Williamson Shaffer, D., Squire, K.R., Halverson, R., Gee, J.P.: Video games and the future of learning. Phi Delta Kappan 87(2), 104–111 (2005)

Doctor Who: Legacy, an Analysis of Usability and Playability of a Multi-platform Game

Rennan Raffaele[1(✉)], Renato Alencar[1], Iran Júnior[1], Bruno Colley[1],
Gabriel Pontes[1], Breno Carvalho[1,2], and Marcelo M. Soares[2,3]

[1] Catholic University of Pernambuco, Rua do Principe, Recife PE, Brazil
{rennan_updown, brunoviski648}@hotmail.com,
{renatopdalencar, soaresgp16, breno25}@gmail.com,
iranbarbosa@live.com
[2] Federal University of Pernambuco, Av Academio Helio Ramos,
Recife PE 50670-420, Brazil
[3] Loughborough University, Loughborough, England, UK
soaresmm@gmail.com

Abstract. Doctor Who: Legacy is a multiplatform game, available for web and smartphones, which pays tribute to the sci-fi adventure serial Dr Who from the British Broadcasting Corporation (BBC) as part of the 50th anniversary co-memorations of the program. The game is a Puzzle Quest, in which the user has to destroy blocks by turns, full of collectible characters. The central plot features the "Doctor" who has to travel through time and space to bring together all his friends and ex-assistants so as to prevent a war that threatens the universe. This study sets out to investigate the gameplay and usability of the game on mobile and web platforms, grounded on the concepts set out by Preece, Rogers and Sharp, and by observing the interactions that users engaged on.

Keywords: Multi-platform · Social games · Usability and gameplay · User's experience · Doctor who

1 Introduction

Multi-platform games are games created for more than one medium, ranging from those for consoles to games for mobile devices. An example of multiplatform game was Miner 2049ers, created in 1982 by the company, Big Five Software [1]. In it, the player needs to control Bounty Bob, a member of the Royal Canadian Mounted Police, and the mission is to search through all of Nuclear Ned's abandoned uranium mines for the treacherous Yukon Yohan. The mine is full of futuristic obstacles, and Bob has to avoid the radio-active creatures which live in the mine.Miner was released at the time of Apple II, Atari 2600, Atari 5200, Atari 8-bit, Commodore VIC-20, Commodore 64, ColecoVision, Fujitsu FM-7, NEC PC-8801, PC Booter, Sharp X1, Sony SMC-777, Thomson MO5 Thomson to7, TI-99 / 4th, Super Cassette Vision, Game Boy. Later, in 2012, it was re-launched by Magmic Inc for the iPhone, Apple's smartphone, in which it received a new visual style both in the character and the graphics besides new scenarios.

© Springer International Publishing Switzerland 2015
A. Marcus (Ed.): DUXU 2015, Part III, LNCS 9188, pp. 283–291, 2015.
DOI: 10.1007/978-3-319-20889-3_27

Casual games are simple, easy-to-learn games that are successful among people with no experience in games. Unlike console games, they do not require the player to be very skillful nor to commit and dedicate time to evolve in the game [2]. The first game to be considered casual was Pac-man, created by Tohru Iwatani for Namco in 1980, in the golden age of arcade games (Pinball) [3]. The first game to be considered casual for the computer was Microsoft Solitaire (Patience), which is still played today by over 400 million people. [4]

In addition to their success on consoles and computers, casual games have also achieved good results when released for mobile phones. The first game in this sense to achieve widespread acceptance from the public was Snake in its late 1990 s version, though originally it had been created by Gremlin Industries, an arcade game manufacturer, in 1976. Another factor that motivated the production of games for mobiles is to make it possible for people to be able to use their phones in different situations e.g. when standing in line at banks, in waiting rooms and during long-distance journeys.

With the advance of mobile technology, simple phones were transformed into mini-computers, whether when using more complex operating systems, or when improving storage capacity and processing images with 16 million colors (24-bit). Furthermore, there has been the advance of touchscreen technology, which enables games to be finger-controlled. Currently two operating systems for mobile devices stand out worldwide and there are specific stores for selling and distributing software and games for smartphones and tablets: the IOS system (Apple) which uses the ITUNES Store and Android (Google) which has Google Play.

Games such as Candy Crush Saga from the developer King, released on April 12, 2012 on the social network Facebook and on November 14 of the same year for smartphones; Clash of Clans, from Supercell, August 2012, and Subway Surfers, from Kiloo and Sybo Games, on May 24, 2012, are some of the most successful casual games today. Besides the use of simple mechanisms for gameplay, they are fun and allow users to compare points and compete with each other. Another aspect of this market are the micro-transactions within the games, in which players can buy special items with real money.

2013 saw the launch of the multiplatform game Doctor Who: Legacy, available on the web via the Facebook page and via the iTunes store and Google Play for smartphones with iOS and Android operating systems. The game is a tribute to the BBC's sci-fi adventure series as part of the TV program´s 50th anniversary. [5] Doctor Who is a Puzzle Quest, adventure and puzzle in which the user must destroy blocks by turns, full of collectible characters. The central plot features the Doctor on a journey through time and space to re-unite all his friends and ex-companions in order to prevent a war that threatens the universe.

2 The Game Doctor Who: Legacy

The storyboard, characters and all the content of the game Doctor Who: Legacy, the object of study of this research, is based on the BBC television series Doctor Who which premiered on November 23, 1963, on BBC TV. Doctor Who is the longest-running science-fiction television series in the world. It is still being broadcast today, after more than 30 seasons and has generated a film and various special broadcasts. The first six years of the series were transmitted in black and white, and it was only in 1970, by then in its seventh season that it began to use a color system (Fig. 1). One of the reasons for the great longevity of the series is the fact that the producers, on realizing that the main actor (William Hartnell) would leave the program due to illness, developed the concept that the race of the protagonist regenerates into a new body when it dies and thus has several "lives", thereby permitting a constant change of the main actors [5].

To date, 13 actors have played the Doctor (the protagonist of the series) on television. On November 23, 2013, the 50th anniversary of the series, a special episode of celebration was transmitted, and shown in the cinemas of over 200 cities around the world, thus earning the record for the most extensive simultaneous transmission in its history. Following in the wake of this huge success, the developer Tiny Rebel Games launched the game Doctor Who: Legacy [6]. The game is a puzzle in the match 3 style, in which the user has to match pieces on a board to meet objectives (Fig. 2). In the game in question, the combinations serve to attack enemies because the game has fighting, unlike most games of the same style. In addition to fighting, the player can find and create teams with different characters from the TV series and from derived media such as comic books, audiobooks, and so forth.

A.   B.

Fig. 1. A. The first doctor, interpreted by William Hartnell. B. Scene in the cold war episode of the commemorative series. (source: site bbcamerica.com).

The game has a storyboard developed especially for this, thereby allowing the characters from all eras and media of the Doctor Who franchise to interact with each other. It also has an RPG (Role Playing Game) aspect because the player can evolve, improve and change the appearance of the characters that he/she has. The game has more and more content and variety, and in one of its updates there is a separate adventure, fully produced in the pixel art style. The game is going from strength to strength and despite there being no download fee, it offers the sale of a "fan area", which allows the user access to various advantages, such as items to accelerate improving its characters, as well as to get new characters or different appearances for them. Despite this paid facet, everything can be achieved after playing the game for some time, which makes the "fan area" attractive for those who really like the game and want to contribute to its growth, and not a necessity, as is the purchase of items in many games that are free of charge.

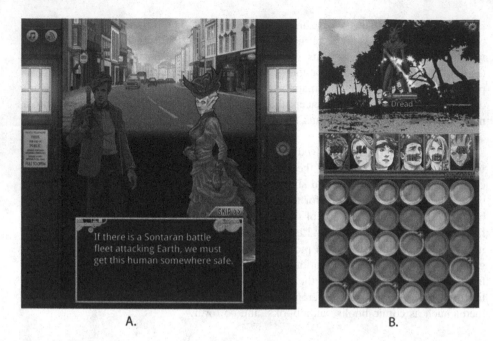

Fig. 2. A. The interface of the game on the social network facebook. B. Interface of the game on the mobile platform. (source: screens captured by the author).

3 Methodology Used in the Test of Usability and Gameplay

For the study of usability and playability of a multiplatform game, the concepts of the Jennifer Preece diagram (Fig. 3) on the user's goals of usability and experience were used as the basis. The objective is to understand specific criteria of usability (e.g. efficiency) and to explain the quality of the experience undergone. According to Preece et al. [7], making this experience enjoyable and effective in the design of interactive media has led to the ever greater involvement of psychologists, sociologists, graphic designers, photographers, artists and entertainers, etc.

The concepts of being fun, easy to understand, efficient to use, aesthetically pleasing and motivating were used. The objective was to analyze if a game is more efficient on one platform than on another and also how the user feels with regard to the interaction of the platform used.

As to the goals of usability used, they are linked in the user's perspective: they are easy to use, efficient and pleasant. As to the goals focusing on the user's experience, they refer to how the user will feel in the human-machine interaction, considering subjective aspects such as satisfaction. This interaction aims to develop designs from the application of Preece's concepts, based on observing the experiences and tests with users.

According to Walter Cybis [8], currently there is enough accumulated knowledge on how to perform usability analyses and usability tests involving the user. In this case the focus of the analysis is to verify whether or not the interface of two platforms is an

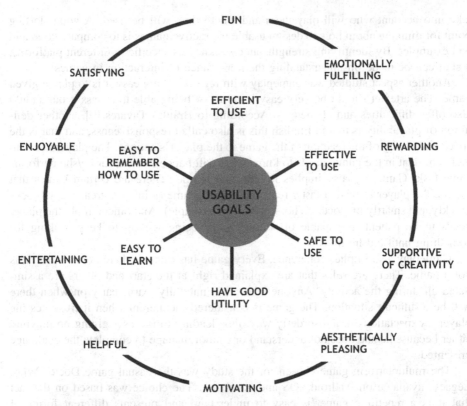

Fig. 3. Jennifer Preece's diagram on the user's goals of usability and experience. (source: site www.sharritt.com/CISHCIExam/preece.html).

obstacle between the user and his/her goals, whether it is easy to use and whether it helps the user in his/her task. This is the main perspective of the analysis of an interface for games nowadays because basically they deal with interfaces that should make it possible for the user to perform a given task or mission.

In the matter of gameplay, the author says that the focus of ergonomic interventions changes in games, because this is not only about developing interfaces that help the user to perform in a direct and objective way the tasks given to him/her. The objective in games is to provide entertainment and the right amount of challenges in an immersive environment. Very often it is challenges posed at the right pace that make it worth playing a particular game. A general principle of games is to maximize the time and effort devoted to the objectives to be achieved (gameplay goals) and to minimize the time and effort used to learn to play (usability goals). As it was a single game with two different platforms that was analyzed, it was observed that the gameplay goals are the same on both platforms and the usability goals are different.

Since the focus is to analyze a multi-platform game that is usable, which generically means games that are easy to learn, are effective in use, and provide the user with a pleasant experience. It was possible to determine whether the game to be chosen would have a good interaction design on both platforms. Usable interactive games require to take into account who will play them and where they will be used. A good starting point for thinking about how to design usable interactive games is to compare good and bad examples. By identifying strengths and weaknesses specific to different platforms, a start can be made on understanding the importance of interaction in games.

Another aspect studied was gameplay with regard to how easy it is to play a given game. The artefact should be very easy in terms of being able to access it but should also offer difficulties and challenges. According to Bráulio Tavares [9], another definition of playability is that in English this is also called responsiveness, and that is the speed and clarity of the reaction of the game to the player's actions. The player needs to feel confident in the game, needs to know what will happen whenever he/she performs some task. Gameplay also implies rhythm and tempo. There are certain games that require the player to have a faster reaction response time (joining a great many blocks quickly and smartly in Doctor Who: Legacy, for example). And others imply the player needs to be patient, is capable of waiting or of being willing to keep looking for something until he/she finds it.

Gameplay also implies coherence. Every game has rules; if there are no rules, it is not a game. There are rules that are explained right at the start and others are assimilated all during the activity. Anyone who plays naturally learns early on when there will be a difficult situation. The game is considered incoherent when it frustrates the player's expectations in a disorderly way, thus leading to the user giving up playing, either because he/she does not understand or cannot manage to complete the challenge presented.

The multiplatform game chosen for the study was the casual game Doctor Who: Legacy, available on Android, iOS and Facebook. The choice was based on the fact that it is a repetitive game, is easy to understand and presents different forms of challenge to the user, in addition to having platforms with different modes of gameplay, namely, keyboard and mouse on a desktop and touchscreen on a mobile device.

According to the data of the second edition of the Game Brazil survey in 2015 [10], smartphones are now the preferred platform of Brazilian gamers, with 82.8 % of mentions, against the 71.3 % share of PCs and notebooks. These data encouraged the investigation of how games work on two different platforms. Another piece of information obtained by Game Brazil is that although the smartphone is the most widely used platform, the Brazilian player is multi-platform, i.e. most (78.6 %) of those who took part in the survey conducted by Game Brazil 2015 [10]. play on more than one device. Given these differences in platforms, several questions beg to be asked (e.g. which one has the best response time? In what way was the game was adapted to a given platform?). Another reason that attracted our attention was the fact that the game is based on the storyboard of a television series that has existed for over 50 years.

To conduct the survey, we selected 10 people at random, 7 men and 3 women, aged between 14 and 28 years old. Half of the sample did not know the game from the BBC series. Participants had to play the tutorial and two stages of the game, on mobile platforms and, soon after, on the web. In the first of these, a smartphone, model Samsung Galaxy S3, was used; in the second, a desktop computer with keyboard and mouse. The two platforms required an internet connection. During testing, the way in which the interviewees were playing was observed by two members of the research group. This type of observation is very important because even if the user says that the game is easy or that he/she liked it, the reactions obtained while he/she is playing can demonstrate otherwise.

Before the player interacts with the applications, they were informed that it would be possible for the researchers to intervene or help participants achieve the objectives, in order to obtain greater reliability in the results. After playing on both platforms, each interviewee answered a questionnaire with 14 questions, which were designed to evaluate their experience with regard to the criteria for gameplay, usability and user experience, indicated in the Preece diagram.

4 Findings

The following data were found after observation and analyzing the users' answers to the questionnaire. Of the ten respondents, only four did not know the series and the game Doctor Who: Legacy. After becoming familiar with the game, all respondents played on the PC platform and mobile and gave their opinions on Doctor Who. Most thought it was a creative idea that there is a game for a television program. 60 % of respondents say that the game is nostalgic, because they feel themselves to be playing the story of the episodes that they had just seen on TV, in addition to praising the mechanics and strategies to be used to advance to the next phase. In the case of this game, each phase corresponds to one episode. All respondents said they did not have difficulty in interacting on the PC or mobile device, but 30 % claimed that there is a big difference in the feel of playing when using the mouse and the touch of the smartphone. They said it is quicker with the touchscreen. 80 % of the people who played found the game fun.

On the question of the motivation that the game offers the user, a balanced percentage was obtained. 50 % say the game motivated then because there is always something to do such as collecting characters and clothes to be collected, and for those who like to complete all steps, the biggest challenge is to leave all the characters at a maximum level. In addition to the collections, there is also always something new in every episode launched in the series.

One respondent pointed out that the game has an intriguing storyboard, which motivates the player to seek progress and find out how the story unfolds, something almost nonexistent among social games. 50 % said they were not all that excited with the game, since they did not know the story, or that the stages to gain some characters are very repetitive. 20 % of respondents had difficulty understanding the history of *Doctor Who: Legacy*, and claimed it was complicated to understand the history of the game, leading the game to be considered boring because it is only yet another casual game. Another interviewee said it was complicated to join all the spheres that you want. The other 80 % said the tutorial explains well what you have to do and how to play. 80 % of respondents say that even those who do not know the series should play because the game is fun, addictive and captivating even for those who do not know the series. They also claimed that the model of the game is simple and many people like it. So it would not be necessary to know the series in order to manage to play the game.

One respondent said that her sister did not like the BBC series, but still played *Doctor Who: Legacy* and that today she is another fan of the Doctor Who series.

In other words, the game and its plot induced a player to watch the same series that she did not previously like. The game also had a part in winning over more fans to the television program. 100 % of players said that the game does not have any error whatsoever, thus showing that it is fully functional and problem-free. Although half of the players interviewed did not notice any difference in the PC and mobile platforms, the other half noticed the only difference in the game: the audio controllers that on the desktop platform are at the top of the game while on the mobile, to disable or enable the audio, the user must enter the settings menu. 70 % of respondents said the interface of the game was easy to manipulate, pointing out that via the home screen menu, all areas of the game, from stages to character information and settings, can be accessed. Others said it was very demonstrative and direct, but they would like the back button to be more visible.

The other 30 % said the interface was very complex and that there are several submenus with names that only those who watch the show will understand. 90 % of respondents said that the game has good aesthetics, and claim the design of the game is very faithful to the fiction of Doctor Who and that this is very important. There were also many compliments about how beautiful and attractive the designs of the characters and scenarios are.

What caught the attention of users is the possibility of editing areas of the game, in which the theme of their spheres may be chosen. One respondent said that the game, when launched, was not as beautiful and pleasant as it is today, because there were many complaints in the forum of the game upon its release in 2013. The complaints helped developers to improve the game, thus making it more pleasing to the users in its latest version.

Once again, the respondents did not present any difficulty in interacting with the game. All they mentioned was that the tactile sensation with the touchscreen is more perceptible than that with the mouse. Although the mouse offers greater accuracy, respondents prefer the speed of the touch technology. All respondents were satisfied with the legibility presented on both platforms, but would very much like that the game could be played optionally in Portuguese since Doctor Who is only available in English.

5 Final Remarks

Since the 1980 s, casual and multi-platform games have been captivating their users through interactions, narratives and empathy with the characters created. The need to reach a large share of audiences, either by using computers connected to the internet, or mobile devices with touchscreen technology, led game developers to the challenge of creating interfaces and mechanisms to define screens and distinct commands on various platforms, but which allow users the same experience of interaction.

The development team of the game Doctor Who: Legacy managed to create a game that fits the platforms investigated without the vast majority of users realizing it. Because of the test performed, it can be seen that the issue of the multi-platform platform did not adversely affect the experience of interaction, since it satisfied a good number of players in the category of comfort both on the mobile platform and on the

PC. The storyboard was well worked out and therefore grasps the fan's attention and that of anyone who has never seen the series, as can be seen in the search results. The game in itself does not present any difficulties in its gameplay since it combines an interaction with simple movements and a light interface. The strategy of developing the art of the game similar to that of the original Doctor Who series pleased most of those investigated. The game Doctor Who: Legacy fulfills its role of entertaining fans of the Doctor Who series besides being a digital artifact that appeals to new users who are not interested in it because of the old or current series.

From the research using the Preece diagram, even though most users do not identify differences in visual and physical interaction with the game, the touchscreen technology enabled the players to play at greater speed and with greater precision. As Cybis [8] shows in the surveys on video games and experiences that arise from this interactive universe, this leads researchers in usability and playability to leave the comfort zone by showing that being concerned with only the user interface is not enough to understand a good experience of using a multi-platform game.

The knowledge available and the existing techniques and tools for assessing the aspects of usability and gameplay together need to advance and improve in order to include the users of games in touchscreen technology devices as opposed to the interaction with the classical computer.

References

1. Miner 2049ER por My Abandonware. http://www.myabandonware.com/game/miner-2049er-2jn
2. Fleury, A., Nakano, D., Cordeiro, J.H.D.: Mapeamento da Indústria Brasileira de Jogos Digitais. Pesquisa do GEDIGames, NPGT, Escola Politécnica, USP, para o BNDES, São Paulo (2014)
3. Q & A: Pac-Man criador reflete sobre 30 Anos de Dot-Eating por KSHOSFY. http://www.wired.com/2010/05/pac-man-30-years/
4. Leitor no Contro, os jogos casuais por Patrick Mattos. http://abrindoojogo.com.br/leitor-no-controle-os-jogos-casuais
5. Doctor Who por BBC America. http://www.bbcamerica.com/doctor-who
6. Doctor Who:Legacy. http://www.tinyrebelgames.com
7. Preece, J., Rogers, Y., Sharp, H.: Design de interação: além da interação homem-computador. Bookman, Porto Alegre (2005)
8. Cybis, W.: Ergonomia e usabilidade: conhecimentos, métodos e aplicações/ Walter Cybis, Adriana Holtz Betiol, Richard Faust, 2nd edn., Novatec Editora, São Paulo (2010)
9. A jogabilidade por Braulio Tavares. http://revistalingua.uol.com.br/textos/67/artigo249097-1.asp
10. Pesquisa: o smartphone é a principal plataforma de games no País por Proxxima. http://www.proxxima.com.br/home/mobile/2015/02/09/Pesquisa-o-smartphone-e-a-principal-plataforma-de-games-no-Pais.html

Newsgames: Gameplay and Usability in Simulation Games

Carla Teixeira[1,2(✉)], Breno Carvalho[1,2], Jarbas Agra[1],
Valeska Martins[1], Anthony Lins[2,3], Marcelo M. Soares[1],
and André Neves[1]

[1] Federal University of Pernambuco, Av Academio Helio Ramos, S/No.
g50.670-420, Recife PE, Brazil
{carla.teixeira3, breno25, jarbasagra, valeskamartins,
soaresmm, andremneves}@gmail.com
[2] Catholic University of Pernambuco, Rua do Príncipe, 526, Boa Vista, Recife
PE CEP, 50050-900, Brazil
thonylins@gmail.com
[3] UFRPE, Recife, Brazil

Abstract. Newsgames are a game format that use the news as a basis for constructing their narrative. Observations made between 2012 and 2014 indicated a gap in the observation of gameplay and usability of this kind of game, which has arisen as a different format of publishing information. The objective of this study was to analyze the usability and playability of newsgames produced since 2000, for which three simulation newsgames were chosen: *Iced - I can end deportation*, *Heartsaver* and *The Candidate*. The analysis was based on studies by Niesen and Preece and Rogers, who observed users interacting with newgames. From the results obtained we intend to investigate other genres of newsgames, with a view to improving the game experience.

Keywords: Newsgames · Gameplay · Usability · Simulation games

1 Introduction

Newsgames are a game format that use the news as a basis for constructing their narrative. The first experiments began around 2001 with the publication of the independent newsgame Kabul Kaboon produced by the game designer and researcher Gonzalo Frasca. The game is a criticism of the American bombing in Kabul, Afghanistan. In 2003, September 12th. was published by NewsGaming.com, a company that produces games and was managed by Gonzalo Frasca. The game simulates a bombing and during the game makes it clear that it is impossible to hit only (military targets), thus criticizing the American attacks in the war on terror by demonstrating the effects of the war on civilians. More than 500,000 people played this newsgame [1]. Seabra [2] indicates that in fact the first experiments started from 2004, with the publication of Madrid by the Spanish newspaper El País. Produced in one day, it was a reaction to the terrorist attacks in the Spanish capital on 11 March 2004. Between 2004 and 2009 special attention was drawn to the newsgames published by CNN

© Springer International Publishing Switzerland 2015
A. Marcus (Ed.): DUXU 2015, Part III, LNCS 9188, pp. 292–302, 2015.
DOI: 10.1007/978-3-319-20889-3_28

(Presidential Pong in 2007), MTV (Darfur is Dying in 2006; Debt Ski, in 2009), by The New York Times (Food Import Folly in 2007) and El País (Madrid, 2004), and by the magazine Wired (Cut-throat Capitalism, 2009). In Brazil, between 2007 and 2011, the production team of the magazine Superinteressante published several newsgames with topics ranging from science to philosophy.

For this research study, three games produced since 2000 were chosen from the list of games presented in the directory Newsgame Vault [3]. It holds information and links on newsgames and serious games published in countries all over the world. The project is maintained by Jornalistas da Web, a news from Brazil website, created in 2000 and dedicated to cover the relationship between journalism and new technologies. It has statistics on countries that record productions of this type and, which, amongst these, have the highest number of publications. The list comprises: the United States (45), Brazil (19), UK (15), Italy (7), France (4), Uruguay (4), Australia (2), Netherlands (2), Austria (1), Canada (1), Chile (1), Denmark (1), Germany (1), India (1) and Japan (1). The United States began production in 2002 and remained relatively constant until 2014. From this observation, three simulation games produced in the USA were chosen at random.

2 Newsgames: Typology and Rhetoric

Sicart [4] evaluates newsgames as serious games designed to illustrate a specific and concrete aspect of news using a procedural rhetoric with a view to prompting participation and public debate. Their characteristics should be: to encourage citizens to participate in them, to be developed in a short period of time, to be played in accordance with the conditions/mechanics of games and to be ephemeral. Seabra [2] emphasizes that newsgames are a genre of online game that are produced rapidly in response to current events that can also prompt social mobilization. Bogost [5] analyzes the different perspectives and usabilities of digital games, and classifies newsgames into seven major categories.

For this study, three of them were selected: Infographics: they arise from the evolution of journalistic infographics, in which players can simulate different scenarios and situations which are based on real events; Documentaries: The authors argue that there can be an approximation of the sensation of realism and the veracity of game documentaries in relation to documentary film. For video games, "realism" typically refers to the visual form of something. They tackle historical or current facts in a similar way to documentaries and investigative reports; Puzzles: These are crossword puzzles, in which the concept of play and the news are brought together in a digital format. Another digital format is that of questionnaires – a quiz. The model presents "a number of issues that supposedly helps to locate the participant in some social category" [5].

3 Newsgames Analyzed

Simulation games seek to offer an experience closer to the real condition of the player, reproducing in an identical way, or almost so, characteristics, reactions, variables and situations encountered in reality [6]. In a simulation, the user must take action in a short space of time, by using interfaces – ranging from buttons and commands to viewing and camera focus. Their playability is varied and can combine aspects of action games, strategy or adventure. For this research study, the games ICED - I can end deportation [7]; Heartsaver [8] and the Candidate [9] were selected. They are all played by a single player. The Newsgame Vault directory classifies them as simulation games.

Iced (Fig. 1) is of the documentary genre. Edited by Breakthrough in 2008, with a platform for Macintosch and PC, it uses flash language. The objective is to become a US citizen. As an immigrant teenager, the player must avoid the ICE agents, make choices and answer questions about immigration. He/she can be arrested and deported. ICED teaches players about current immigration laws on detention and deportation that affect all immigrants: legal permanent residents, asylum seekers, students and undocumented people by violating human rights and denying due process.

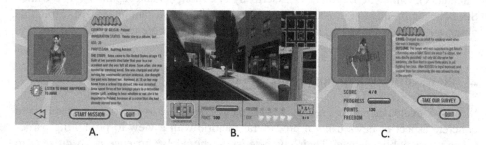

Fig. 1. A. Screen for choosing the character. B. Interface of the game. C. Result in case of defeat. (source: screens captured by the author).

Heartsaver (Fig. 2) is of the infographic format. It has flash language and is geared to the Web platform. It deals with the chances of surviving a heart attack in New York City. The mission is to save as many heart attack victims as possible by taking them to the emergency room in time. The game was made by ProPublica in April 2013 during one of GEN's Hackdays.

Finally, The Candidate (Fig. 3), 2013 is a quiz. It uses jquery language and was published by Bayporta.com. The game has six stages, divided by months: June, July, August, September, October and November. The objective of the player/candidate is to be elected to Congress. To ensure victory, the player must raise money and choose problems so as to manage to receive the approval of different groups of voters.

4   Methodology Adopted for Analyzing Newsgames

After selecting the newsgames, the research team played each of them, and took note of the extent of their usability and playability. The usability analysis was based on Nielsen's usability heuristics [10]:

Visibility of the state of the system: the system always keeps users informed about what is happening by providing appropriate feedback within a reasonable time;

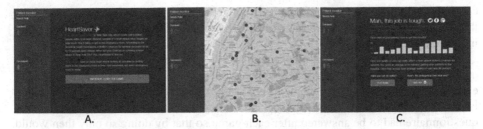

Fig. 2. A. Home screen of the Heartsaver newsgame with initial instructions. B. Format reproduces map of New York City. C. Results screen offers indicators after the end of the game. (source: capture screens by the author).

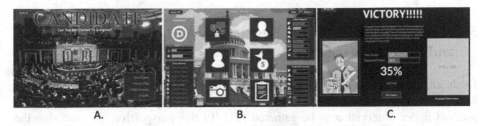

Fig. 3. Opening screen of the newsgame. B. First phase of the campaign. C. Results of the election. (source: screens captured by the author).

Mapping between the system and the real world: the system speaks the user's language using words, phrases and concepts which are familiar to him/her instead of using terms orientated towards the system; **User's freedom and control**: the system provides ways for users to get out of any unexpected places in which they find themselves easily by using clearly identified "emergency exits"; **Consistency and standards**: these avoid users having to think about whether words, situations or different actions mean the same thing; **Error prevention**: where possible, this prevents the occurrence of errors; **Recognizing rather than recalling**: making objects, actions, and options visible; **Flexibility and efficiency of use**: this provides invisible accelerators for inexperienced users, which, however, allow the more experienced to accomplish tasks more quickly; **Aesthetic and minimalist design**: this avoids using irrelevant or rarely necessary information; **Support for the user to recognize, diagnose and recover from errors**: this uses simple language to describe the nature of the problem and suggests a way to solve it; **Help and documentation**: this provides information that can be easily found and help via a series of concrete steps that can be easily followed.

Regarding playability, the parameters sought, drawing on Preece [10], to understand the user's experience, considering as concepts if newsgames were pleasant, fun, interesting and motivating. Also if they offered an immersive environment capable of prompting the desire to remain or continue the game. These matters were considered because, in some cases, games use a negative procedural rhetoric while the game is being played. Similarly, in the interaction with the proposed challenges, newsgames can make it impossible to win the game. The fact of not knowing this characteristic of the game or of not reaching the stage of perceiving this, can lead to the user becoming indifferent or frustrated.

Heuristic analysis and that of playability were the bases of the guidelines of the questionnaire on the test with users. Ten people between 19 and 50 years old, of whom eight were men and two were women were randomly selected. The test took place in a laboratory with one of the researchers present, whose only guidance was that the questionnaire had to be answered after each game so that by doing so only then would avoid interfering with the experience of the game. Participants played on PC computers connected to the internet and provided with a sound system, monitor, mouse and keyboard. Each user had to complete all phases of the game, and to keep to an interval of 10 min between each newsgame.

5 Heuristic Analysis of the Newsgames *Iced, HeartSaver* and *the Candidate*

Evaluating usability by means of heuristics enables the user's relations with the product and systems to be analyzed, as well as information on particular situations of the product under observation to be gathered [11]. In this perspective, on analyzing the usability of the three genres of simulation newsgames, the interaction conditions of the games could be verified, while taking the players' various levels of experience into account.

5.1 Iced

As to the Visibility of the State of the System, the first of Nielsen's heuristics, the researchers found that it meets the requirement because it offers sound and visual feedback and the interface shows the player's status and his/her location (on a map located at the top right of the screen). When detained, there could be feedback if the character goes to solitary, a mechanism indicating the passage of time. The legibility of the typography is flawed. With respect to the Mapping of the System, there are similarities with other games in relation to the logic, mechanics, and language directed to the public. The User's Freedom and Control was considered satisfactory (the quit button is present on most screens, but on the game screen the only way to get out of it is to use the ESC key. This is not clear to a beginner player). The loading screen cannot be cancelled. You can only get out by closing the application.

In Consistency and Standards, the game is reasonable, as it displays consistency, including the visual one (as to colors, fonts, the forms of buttons). However, on some screens the Advance button appears on the bottom left and, on others, on the top right. Prevention of errors is satisfactory. When closing the application screen, there is no confirmation prompt asking if the player really wants to end the game. In Recognizing, instead of recalling, there are, at most, in-game icons which serve for scoring, this requirement being almost nonexistent. The evaluation of the Flexibility and Efficiency of use was considered poor. The only existing shortcut is ESC to exit the main screen.

On the tutorial screens, for example, the screen can only be changed by mouse and not by the arrows. Nor do these screens (rules and credits) allow the player to go back. The player must go to the end of the sequence of screens to get out of any of them. This point is also classified as a lack of user control.

The heuristic of Aesthetic and Minimalist Design was classified as good: the choice of the colors, and the pleasant art style that does not interfere or hinder any moment of the game. Support for the user to recognize, diagnose and recover errors, if the point of view of the system is considered, does not have many options for loss of data. The Help and documentation is fairly complete. At several points, there are detailed explanations about how to play, and what to do with information before and during the game.

5.2   HeartSaver

The Heartsaver newsgame is relatively simple. Basically, the mechanics require the player to drag the victim of the heart attack to the nearest hospital. Visibility can be seen to be flawed because feedback is not displayed when the mouse passes over the patient icon (main action of the game). It only changes after the player drags the icon. The exact location of where to take the patient is also unclear. Sometimes, the patient can be saved, and, at others, is not, and the player does not know if he/she erred in time or location. As the game is simple and the level of interaction is low, there is little to be assessed as to the heuristic of mapping. The user has no Freedom nor control. Although the game, in practical terms, consists of only one screen, the application does not allow the player to pause or exit the game via some command or button.

As for Consistency and Standards, this is present mainly in the color pattern, shapes and typography. Prevention of errors is quite confusing. It is not clear why the player made an error, and, even after playing several times and changing the tactics of the game, not all patients can be saved. The Recognize factor instead of recalling is benefitted by applying colors, which is very efficient and smart for a type of game that requires speed. The heuristic of Flexibility and efficiency of use was considered not to exist. As for the Design, the visuals of the game are simple, but very pleasant and clear. There is no support whatsoever for the user to recognize, diagnose and recover mistakes. From the point of view of the application, there is no loss of data or errors because its structure is simple. But as a game, there is a lack of clarity and the application does not help to solve this problem. As to Help and documentation, an animated gif shows how to play. Given the ease of the task, it can be said that the instrument is sufficient. However, this is the only help that the player encounters throughout the newsgame.

5.3   The Candidate

Visibility is good. The initial step of the game provides players with outline information, thus enabling the user to choose the profile of his/her candidate for the game, and gives options regarding their electoral platforms. The questions are linked to the image of a possible voter, a public figure, a lobbyist or a journalist. There is, in the case of victory, comment on the steps undergone and main challenges after being elected. In defeat, the text comments on the possible errors of the campaign. There is sound and visual feedback which marks the phases. Background music does not contribute to the atmosphere.

The Mapping between the system and the real world is compatible with the user because the player uses clearly identifiable icons. But there is no difference of background images between the phases. Each question carries an explanatory text that gives guidance on the practices or situations that happen during elections in the United States. The user´s Freedom and control is nonexistent. There is no way to go to or back from another level if the player regrets having taken some action. The system presented error after one of the questions because the candidate did not have any more money for the campaign. Despite the Continue button, it stayed on the same level and the only alternative was to restart. The Help button does not work for this case. The analysis also applies to the heuristic of Error Prevention. There is also no Support for the player to recognize or recover errors.

It was observed with regard to Consistency and Standards that the same graphic pattern was adopted in all phases of the game, which makes playability monotonous. As to Recognizing instead of Recalling, the newsgame presents visible objects and actions, but during the stages, it is not possible to have access to numbers won over. Flexibility and efficiency of use are non-existent: there are no accelerators, the game has the same pace without balancing between the challenges. As to Design, important visual information is suppressed such as an avatar for the candidate that would make the game more interesting. The same Help button is available at all stages, but when it is opened the game field cannot be seen.

During the heuristic evaluation, the characteristics of playability could be observed. The player's experience was observed, and consideration given to whether the newsgames were pleasant, fun, interesting and motivating. Iced, because of its visual characteristics, the feedback provided and the fact that it is played in the first person, allows greater interaction with the game. The graphical representation of the city and the prison is close to reality and is pleasing. There are five characters, two women and three men, thereby generating greater identification. The age range is 20–23 years old. They have stories and are from different countries: Haiti, Poland, India, Mexico and Japan.

A summary of the personality of each character can be read before starting the game so as to support which one to choose, thereby awakening interest in the situation of each of them. There is also the possibility of listening to them talking about themselves, in the accent of their country of origin. While the game loads, a text explains the way of life of people in the US. The same text is heard by the player. Navigation simulates the streets of a city in 3D. There are challenges - questions about immigration and deportation in the US - and extra points.

With regard to Heartsaver, it presents identical difficulties in relation to playability in different operating systems (MacOSX and Windows). Even when the hospital icon is green (indicating that it would be apt to choose it to receive a patient), the victim did not survive. The final message congratulated me on my performance, even though it was weak. There is no way to make it clear what all the decision criteria are that should be used when choosing a hospital. The use of negative procedural rhetoric makes the experience less fun because the rules are not at all clear.

Finally, The Candidate. It is considered motivating for the public it is aimed at but depending on the player it can end up generating disinterest due to the amount of text there is to read and analyze. The mechanics of point-and-click in the options (topics and answers) makes the game easy. As there is no time counter, a player can analyze the options and look for the best decisions. There is a flaw in the final screen of the game when the outcome of the election comes up. In case of victory or defeat, the candidate's image appears, but the image in the Table which should show the figure of the opponent does not appear.

6 Testing the Newsgames with Users

The material collected during the laboratory tests enabled the analysis to be made in greater depth, thereby generating data on the users' level of involvement in the game, usability and playability.

6.1 Iced

Of the three newsgames analyzed, the one that most stimulated users was Iced, which seemed to cause the greatest immersion and generate the most fun. The game has different levels of challenges and each wrong answer increases its degree of difficulty, because ICE agents appear who hunt for the immigrant. In the case of detention, new challenges appear. However, they are not clearly visible. A small number of test participants, 30 %, realized that the green circles on the map displayed indicated small tasks, thus increasing their score and reducing their time in prison.

Iced provided the longest game. It was played for more than 30 min, suggesting that immersion in the game environment was more effective. Of the test participants, 70 % rated the game as good and 30 % as excellent. Of the 70 % of respondents who gave an opinion on the strong points of the game, the vast majority (70 %) mentioned the good playability. Among the reasons for this were the fact that it is dynamic, fun, provides visual feedback and has movement commands that those who are not familiar with controls found easy to use. Other aspects deal with the context in which the player is inserted, which deals with illegal immigration, this being very informative and offering the possibility of choosing characters.

40 % of respondents gave responses about negative aspects in Iced. Among them, 50 % deal with the quality of the graphic representation, which they consider is average. The other 50 % indicated that the game has insufficient data (25 %) and that there is a lack of information on how to avoid getting caught by agents (25 %). It is observed that the heuristic on prevention of errors was not considered in its entirety.

Another 40 % of the respondents gave suggestions for enhancing the experience of the game: improvement in interaction with the items of the scene, making the ultimate goal clearer, improving the background of the game, since the context is the US, having access to the rules and a tutorial during the game and a prison that corresponds to character's gender. About playing Iced, users defined it as easy (40 %), average (40 %) and difficult (20 %). In the case of Iced, there is no use of negative procedural rhetoric.

About feedback and information during the game, the level was considered good by 60 % of the respondents, satisfactory by 30 % and excellent by 10 %. The possibility of following the hunt in real time with the feedback provided by the system favors the immersion in the environment and makes it fun to play. Verbal reports of the registered players during the test expressed the emotion of trying to escape from those pursuing them, and the frustration at having been caught.

Error prevention was considered good (40 %) and satisfactory (20 %). However, 30 % considered this item was poor and 10 % that it was terrible. Playability got the grades of good (40 %), satisfactory (30 %) and excellent (30 %).

6.2   Heartsaver

In the test with Heartsaver, it was observed that the participants played more than one game in an attempt by to improve their score. A point in common between the verbalized comments was with regard to the speed of the game, which was progressive, and to the frustration at being unable to save all lives. In the evaluation of the proposed questionnaire, 10 % of participants considered the game was excellent; of the other 90 % 30 % defined the newsgame as being poor, 30 % as satisfactory and 30 % as good. When commenting on the strong points of Heartsaver, participants mentioned the visuals, playability, the speed at which feedback on who is being saved appears and the challenge of saving lives. Also cited as positive points were: encouraging decision-making and the educational message, besides comparison with other players' scores being given. Only one of the respondents indicated that he realized that the mechanics of the game impedes all patients being saved and that if this is the main objective, the game manages to transmit this.

On the negative points of the game, it is precisely the impossibility of saving all heart attack victims that is observed: of the 60 % of participants who gave an opinion, 80 % indicated this point, while 10 % reported a lack of obstacles as a problem and 10 % found use of the mouse troublesome. On improvements, only 50 % of participants made observations: the inclusion of an enemy to make the game more exciting (10 %) and the possibility of really saving lives (10 %).

The suggestions converge for three of Nielsen's heuristics: visibility of the status of the system: 10 % of respondents indicated that feedback should be improved when the characters are saved or die, and disappear more quickly from the game; help and documentation: a tutorial and rules of the game with the possibility of their also being accessed during the game, besides clearer information about the differences between the hospitals; aesthetic and minimalist design: because it has the form of a map, the game features a simple and informative layout. However, the suggestion of one of the participants deals precisely with offering a flashier and more attractive layout for the player, thereby increasing interactivity. 40 % found the game easy, even when they did not manage to win.

The perception on the level of feedback and information provided by the game indicated the need to improve the newsgame: 20 % considered it good, while 40 % said it was satisfactory and the other 40 % that it was poor. On prevention of errors, 50 % of the players indicated that this was poor, 20 % that it was very poor and 20 % that it was satisfactory. Since there are no clear indicators on, for example, the quality of the hospitals to which the characters are being taken, there is no way to be sure if the patient will be saved or not. Playability was considered satisfactory by 40 % of the interviewees.

6.3 The Candidate

Despite being a game of strategy for simulating the decisions to be taken during an election campaign, it appears that test participants in this newsgame found it neither fun nor interesting. Of these, 40 % consider it good; 20 % satisfactory; 20 % poor; 10 % excellent and 10 % very poor.

The strong points commented on by 70 % of participants (30 % did not give an opinion) concern having the power to take decisions freely when choosing alternatives; learning by playing, the instructive way that the political landscape is reported; the well-explained tutorial, the possibility of switching the music on and off and gender equality, since it is possible to choose candidates of both genders; understanding of the issues involved in the elections, attributions of the government and ethics; proximity to the reality of an election campaign, when presenting choices and decisions that a candidate would have to take.

On the negative points, 60 % of respondents reported: the visuals; the similarity with language tests done online; it is not fun, it does not stimulate engagement and there is no feedback; it offers few alternatives as responses; the impossibility of leaving the game and returning to the menu while playing; the objective of getting votes but not managing to please all voters. Only 30 % of the universe of test participants gave suggestions for improving the game, which included improving the visuals of the game, more options of response and being able to choose an avatar who will be the face of the politician. These three suggestions can be related to the heuristics on the system's compatibility with the real world.

As to ease in playing, 60 % also considered the game was average. The level of information and feedback was considered satisfactory by 50 % of the interviewees, while 20 % defined them as excellent and the remaining 30 % as good, poor and very poor. The prevention of errors is indicated as good by 30 % of the respondents and 20 % consider it satisfactory. Another 30 % consider it poor and 20 % very poor. Once again, 40 % of respondents considered the playability satisfactory.

7 Conclusion

The newsgames analyzed meet the prospects of being serious games that offer some type of learning and are related to items of news and world reality. Elections, deportation and the warning about the need for immediate care in case of heart attack, with the situations that arise in each of these cases, are simulated and approximate to what happens in the real world. However, attention given to the content of the games seems to be counterpointed to the need to improve their usability and gameplay. Of the three games analyzed, only one, Iced, satisfies most of the heuristics chosen for the study and was also capable of causing test participants to feel pushed towards greater interaction, involvement and excitement.

In the evaluation of the researchers, the fact that Iced offers different levels of challenges, increases the difficulty throughout the game and offers appropriate feedback while the game is running, and is played in first person, made the experience more fun. The results found for, specifically, this game indicate that users were able to understand the situation of illegal immigrants in an experiment the meaning of which was built based on the immersion in the character and on the environment of the game.

From the results obtained we intend to investigate other newsgame genres in order to build a theoretical framework leading to enhancements in this type of game by observing the criteria of gameplay and usability in the development phases of the product.

References

1. de Andrade, L.A.: Games em pauta: a relação entre jogos eletrônicos, weblogs e jornalismo online. CONECO RIO – 3º Congresso de Estudantes de Pós-Graduação em Comunicação, Rio de Janeiro, UERJ (2008). https://www.academia.edu/7310832/Games_em_Pauta_A_relacao_entre_jogos_eletronicos_blogs_e_jornalismo_online. Accessed 3 May 2013
2. Seabra, G.: Newsgames: demarcando um novo modelo de jornalismo on-line. http://www.slideshare.net/blognewsgames/newsgames-demarcando-um-novo-modelo-de-jornalismo-onlinepdf. Accessed 10 July 2013
3. Newsgamevault. http://www.newsgamevault.com/. Accessed 5 November 2014
4. Sicart, M.: Newsgames: theory and design. In: Stevens, S.M., Saldamarco, S.J. (eds.) ICEC 2008. LNCS, vol. 5309, pp. 27–33. Springer, Heidelberg (2008)
5. Bogost, I., Ferrari, S., Schweizer, B.: Newsgames: Journalism at Play. MIT Press, Cambridge (2010)
6. Sato, A.K.O., Cardoso, M.V.: Além do gênero: uma possibilidade para a classificação de jogos. http://www.sbgames.org/papers/sbgames08/ad/papers/p08.pdf. Accessed 8 December 2014
7. Iced. http://www.icedgame.com/. Accessed 8 January 2015
8. Heartsaver. http://sisiwei.github.io/gen-hackday-propublica/. Accessed 8 January 2015
9. The Candidate. http://bayreporta.com/files/candidate/index.html. Accessed 8 January 2015
10. Preece, J., Rogers, Y., Sharp, H.: Design de interação: além da interação homem-computador. Bookman, Porto Alegre (2005)
11. Roepke, G.A.L. et al.: A importância da ambientação na avaliação da usabilidade de produtos. In: Conferência Internacional de Integração do Design, Engenharia e Gestão para a inovação, Anais. UDESC, Florianópolis (2012)

Improving Song Guessing Games Through Music Track Composition

João Marcelo Teixeira[1,2]([✉]), Dicksson Almeida[1],
Edvar Neto[1], and Veronica Teichrieb[1]

[1] VOXAR Labs, Center of Informatics,
Federal University of Pernambuco, Recife, Brazil
{jmxnt, droa, excvn, vt}@cin.ufpe.br
[2] DEINFO, Federal Rural University of Pernambuco, Recife, Brazil

Abstract. In this work we propose a different scheme for music guessing games, based on a constructive approach. By analyzing current available mobile games, we show the barriers that must be surpassed to make such games viable and how novel this work is. We have implemented a game prototype called "What's the Song" and performed user tests with both usual and constructive approaches. A Likert questionnaire was answered by all users and it points out that the constructive approach improves game engagement and overall user experience.

Keywords: Game experience · Music guessing games · Casual games

1 Introduction

What is the difference between music and sound? Music is the art of sound. Sound is invisible waves moving through the air around us. When something vibrates, it disturbs the air molecules around it. Music is sound that is organized by people on purpose, to dance to, to tell a story, to make other people feel a certain way, or just to sound pretty or be entertaining [1, 2].

From the player's perspective, the most important theories are [3]:

- Sounds aid the learning curve for gamers - interactivity is crucial in a game, feedback sounds (positive and negative ones) are important to mark how players progress during the game
- Sounds affect the degree of game immersion - auditory and positioning sounds give certain clues and shape the perception a player has in any given situation. Games sounds enhance the extension of the physical body
- Sounds create a community outside the game itself - music can be customizable and players can share their own music remixes with an online community

These theories threat sound as a game accessory, giving support to the game's main features, but what happens when the music itself is the key of the game? Music games most commonly challenge the player to follow sequences of movement or develop specific rhythms. Some games require the player to input rhythms by stepping with their feet on a dance pad (e.g. Dance Dance Revolution), or using a device similar to a

A. Marcus (Ed.): DUXU 2015, Part III, LNCS 9188, pp. 303–314, 2015.
DOI: 10.1007/978-3-319-20889-3_29

Fig. 1. Screenshots from the game prototype: initial screen, main screen, positive and negative result screens

specific musical instrument, like a replica drum set (e.g. Guitar Hero, Rock Band, DJ Hero). These games have changed the way players interact with their consoles by making the gaming experience more active and sociable, and paving the way for exergaming [4–6] (e.g. Lips, Just Dance, Dance Central).

When music meets casual games in mobile platforms and web, the music guessing games (MGGs) genre arise. This can be considered a mix of two distinct game genres: music games and trivia games. Trivia games are constantly growing in popularity, especially in mobile phones where people may only have a few minutes to play the game. In trivia games, the object is to answer questions with the goal of obtaining points. In music guessing games, the main question to be answered is "What is the song being played?".

According to [7], Consumer Musical Intelligence (CMI) is a multi-faceted construct whose core components comprise the capacity to feel the emotion expression in music, to respond to musical stimuli, and to understand the music in a discerning manner. They also propose three factors underlying CMI:

- *Affective Musical Intelligence* is the extent of spontaneity and intensity with which people identify with emotional content in music
- *Behavioral musical intelligence* is the extent of semiconscious motor reactivity to musical stimuli
- *Cognitive musical intelligence* constitutes the efficiency of the processes in the perception, encoding, and recall of musical information

This work focuses on the cognitive musical intelligence factor. We try to answer the following question: "How to make MGGs more interesting, challenging and pleasurable to players?". Our main hypothesis is that it is possible to improve MGGs by simply altering the way music is presented to the player. Instead of playing a music section as it is, we think that a constructive approach sequentially presenting a combination of instruments being played can hold the player's attention and improve the overall game experience.

The remainder of this paper is organized as follows. Section 2 presents an analysis regarding 67 MGGs on mobile platforms, none of which use the proposed approach. Section 3 provides details on how the proposed approach was implemented, how problems were overcome and the game prototype flow. Section 4 depicts the users' experiments and the results obtained. At last, Sect. 5 concludes the paper and provides directions to future works.

2 Music Guessing Games

Currently, the most used mobile platforms are Android and iOS. Given that the majority of games have versions for both of them, and in order to facilitate the MGG analysis, we compared only iOS available games. The "AppCrawlr" App Discovery Engine (http://appcrawlr.com/) was used with the following parameters: "guess the song" as search query, "free application" as general filter, "iOS" as platform filter and "relevance" as sorting option. A total of 465 results were found, of which the first 67 were analyzed. Five different points were compared:

- *Response type*: Alternative (user has to select as correct answer one of n alternatives), Letter (user has to construct the correct song/artist name from a mixed set of letters), Typing (user has to type the answer from standard input)
- *Clues*: Yes (the game has clues to help users guess correctly), No (there are no clues available)
- *Full song playback*: Yes (player can listen to the entire song), No (only part of the song is played)
- *Content*: Single instrument (usually guitar or piano versions), Original song (part of the original song is played), No song (no song is played, user has to guess based on visual clues), Voice (player has to sing), Backwards (song in opposite direction)
- *Score calculation*: None (there is no score computed), Correct/Wrong (score is calculated based on the number of correct guesses), Correct/Wrong & Time (score also considers how much time was spent to correctly guess)

Regarding response type, the three categories analyzed (by crescent order of difficulty) were Alternative, Letter and Typing. Alternative and Letter were the most frequent ones, with 45 and 42 %, respectively, as shown in Fig. 2. Typing represents the most difficult interaction, since the user has fewer clues to guess the answer.

Most of the analyzed games provide clues to help users guessing the correct answers. As shown in Fig. 2, 78 % of the games have some type of clues to aid players, which vary from removing wrong alternatives/letters or even skipping the current song.

We also verified how many of the analyzed games played the entire music to the user or just a part of it. All the 67 games only make use of music segments. This is probably justified by the fact that small music parts tend to diminish the amount of data to be transfered over the network.

How music content is presented to players is the focus of this work. From the analysis, we could conclude that none of the 67 MGGs use the proposed constructive approach, which is to sequentially increment the number of instruments played using isolated tracks. Approximately 75 % of the games use part of the original song to be guessed. This, besides making the game easier, does not provide the player with information on how the music is composed. According to Fig. 3, 15 % do not reproduce any kind of music at all, while 3 % use voice and 6 % use a single instrument. One of the games analyzed reproduces the original music, but in backward direction.

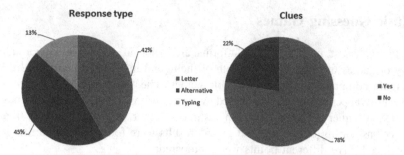

Fig. 2. Response type comparison (Alternative, Letter, Typing) (left) and comparison regarding clues provided by the games (right).

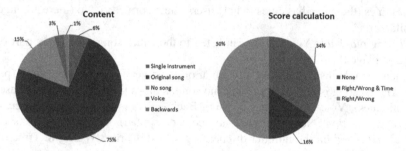

Fig. 3. Comparison on how music content is presented to players (left) and comparison on how score is calculated (right).

Regarding score calculation, three possible categories are shown in Fig. 3. There is no score calculation in 34 % of the games analyzed, which means that score is reverted to the number of songs guessed right. Also, 50 % do not take time to answer in consideration. The smallest portion (16 %) considers both time and right guesses on score computation.

3   The Proposed Approach

In order to verify this work's hypothesis, we decided to implement a MGG prototype for mobile platforms, called "What's the Song".

The base to our hypothesis is that there is available a music database composed by different song samples, each one having its tracks independently separated. Initially, the idea was to allow players to choose which tracks would play at a certain time.

The main problem with this approach is that each track would have to synchronously play in a separate processor thread. Since most songs have more than six different tracks, this would elevate the prototype processing requirements.

The *Karaoke Version* site is specialized in producing and selling music tracks for karaoke games. Once a song is bought, its owner can customize it and download each track separately or perform any track combination and then download the resulting mp3 file. Fortunately, the site provides random samples of 30 to 45 s for each music stored in its database.

In order to overcome the high processing demand stated before, we fixed a specific order in which the music would be presented to the user. This means, for example, that the first track to be heard would be the drums-based ones, followed by bass, keyboard, brass, guitar and vocal ones. To make sure that each song would have at maximum six tracks, we had to create six instrument classes for grouping the tracks, as shown in Table 1.

After creating the track groups, we implemented a web crawler using the Java language. This tool was responsible for downloading the isolated tracks from the *Karaoke Version* website, and combining them according to their group. For eachsong, a folder was generated containing song information along with up to six combined tracks. The tracks were cumulative, which means that track #6 is composed by all previous tracks (1 to 5) and the instruments from the Vocal instrument group. This allowed us to play a single mp3 every time the player listens to the music, which significantly decreased the prototype requirements and eliminated the need for syncing the song playback. The tool used for combining the mp3 tracks was the SoX (Sound eXchange) [8].

The music selection process was performed as follows. We asked 14 people (all computer science students, aged from 20 to 30) to select music known to them from the *Karaoke Version* website. After that, we created a shared table using Google Docs containing all the 274 previously selected songs. There was given edit access to all the 14 people and they were asked to mark with an "x" all the songs they knew. Based on this voting process, we ordered the songs by number of votes and selected the 100 mostly known.

The prototype was implemented in a client-server fashion. Server side was developed using PHP, while client side was developed using Objective-C, since the iOS platform was chosen as target.

The server implementation provides the mobile client with the possible answers and links to each of the tracks to be played in a turn, in an XML-like structure. Since it does not take into account which songs were already used, repetitions can occur. The link information provided is relative to the song folder. It must be concatenated to the server's initial address before accessed on the client side.

The client side was implemented as a Single View Application on XCode. The game is mainly composed by tree stages/screens, as shown in Fig. 1. Figure 4 illustrates the complete game flow.

The second screen is where most game interaction occurs. In the top of the screen it is possible to use the back button to return to the initial screen (when this happens, all score is reset and any music playing is stopped) and to view the current score on the

Table 1. Categories used to classify and combine instruments

Group	Game name
Drums	Acoustic drum kit, Bells, Body percussion, Bongos, Clap, Claves, Woodblock, Click, Congas, Cowbell, Drum kit, Drums and percussion, Eggs, Electronic drum kit, Hand clap, Intro count, Orchestral percussion, Percussion, Pitched percussion, Snap (fingers), Steeldrums, Tambourine, Triangle, Tubular Bell, Toms, Wind chimes
Bass	Bass, Bass synth, Double bass, Electric bass, Synth Brass
Guitar	Acoustic Guitar, Arr. electric guitar, Banjo, Cello, Distorted electric guitar, Electric guitar, Guitar Synth, Lead acoustic guitar, Lead electric guitar, Mandolin, Resonator guitar (Dobro), Rhythm acoustic guitar, Rhythm acoustic guitar (Arpeggio), Rhythm electric guitar, Rhythm electric guitar (Arpeggio), Strings, Violin, Viola, Appalachian dulcimer
Keyboard	Arpegiator, Electric piano, Glockenspiel, Keyboard, Marimba, Organ, Piano, Synth Lead, Synth Keys, Synth Pad, Synth Strings, Xylophone, Celesta
Brass	Brass instruments, Brass section, Flute, French Horn, Harmonica, Orchestra, Saxophone, Vibes
Vocal	Backing vocals, Lead vocal, Sound effect, Sound effects, Synth Voice, Synthesizer, Vocoder

right. The discs are shown below the score area. A total of six different discs, each one mapping to an instrument group, indicate which instruments are playing on that specific moment. In order to advance to the next track, the user must swipe from right to left. It is important to notice that the discs are stacked, to give the impression that the pile of instruments being played only grows, according to what was explained earlier. This way, a single mp3 needs to be played every time. The bottom of the screen contains the alternatives to be chosen. Since the server already scrambles the alternative positions, the client just needs to display them. The user selects the answer which seems to the correct one by directly clicking on it. When an alternative is pressed, the last track is automatically played, revealing all the instruments.

The first screen indicates the starting point of the application. At this point, only the game logo is presented and no network access is made. When the user presses the play button, information regarding a turn is requested to server and data is downloaded. As soon as the mp3 s related to the songs finish downloading, the first track starts playing. Since all tests were performed using local network, a loading screen was not necessary. In a more real scenario, we think it is important to have such a loading screen, due to the fact that approximately 3.5 MB are downloaded before starting each turn.

The third screen shows whenever the user clicks on an answer. It can show a positive or negative message, according to the answer given. When the user presses the "next" button, a new turn is started, fetching new information from the server.

The user score is cumulative, meaning that each turn score is added to the final score. The turn score is based on the number of tracks needed to correctly guess the song and on how much time was used. Considering time for score calculation makes the game more dynamic, since users feel compelled to guess faster. Only positive

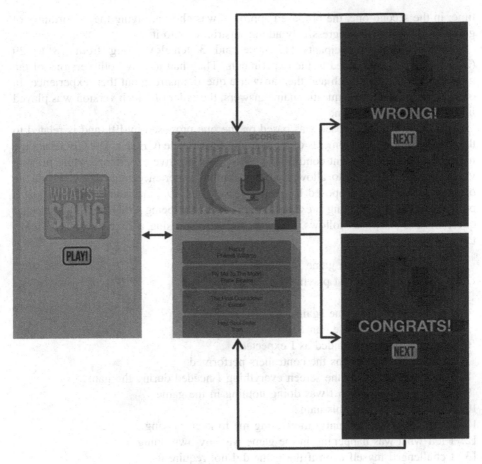

Fig. 4. "What's the Song" game flow

scores are calculated, from 0 to 100. Wrong guesses mean that the turn's score was zero that time. The core calculation uses the following formula:

$$Score = \left(1 - \frac{(CurrentTrack * TrackDuration) + TrackTime}{TrackDuration * NumberOfTracks}\right) * 100$$

4 Experiments

The primary purpose of this work was to understand if a constructive approach could contribute to a more engaging and overall better MGG. For this we conducted an experiment aiming to stimulate people to interact with the implemented MGG prototype. Two versions of the game were used: in the first one, the usual guessing game approach was chosen, in which the music was played with all instruments available at a time; in the second one, the proposed approach was chosen, giving the opportunity of guessing the song by progressively adding instruments to it.

A total of 20 participants (17 male and 3 female), aging from 18 to 29 (20.55 ± 2.79), contributed to the experiments. They had to play both versions of the game for about 5 min each and then answer a questionnaire about their experience. In order to not influence on questionnaire answers, the order of which version was played first was randomly chosen.

The questionnaire chosen was based on the one proposed by [9], and is related to the theory of the Core Elements of the Gaming Experience (CEGE). The CEGE are the necessary but not sufficient conditions to provide a positive experience while playing video-games. It is used to allow studying gaming experience objectively. From the original 38 questions proposed by them, we selected 19, since our game was just a prototype and just the song presentation approach was being evaluated. The selected questions are shown as follows. Answers were given using a Likert scale [10] containing 7 levels.

1. I enjoyed playing the game
2. I was frustrated whilst playing the game
3. I liked the game
4. I would play this game again
5. I was in control of the game
6. The controllers responded as I expected
7. I remember the actions the controllers performed
8. I was able to see on the screen everything I needed during the game
9. There was time when I was doing nothing in the game
10. I got bored playing this game
11. The game kept constantly motivating me to keep playing
12. I felt what was happening in the game was my own doing
13. I challenged myself even if the game did not require it
14. I played with my own rules
15. The game was unfair
16. I understood the rules of the game
17. The game was challenging
18. The game was difficult
19. I knew all the actions that could be performed in the game

The experimental results showed significant difference between usual and constructive approaches. Figs. 5 and 6 show the constructive approach was better scored on 13 of the 19 statements. These statements were mainly related to enjoyment, ownership and gameplay. The interaction offered by this approach may have caused this effect, expanding the sense of ownership and engagement.

The statements in which the usual approach received higher scores were mainly related to frustration and control. This could be explained by the fact that the usual version is simpler to be manipulated than the constructive one.

As it can be observed in the Table 2, the more significant differences among the answers occurred in the following questions: "17. The game was challenging" and "18. The game was difficult". Thus, we can say that players thought progressively adding instruments was 53.7 % more challenging and 75.9 % more difficult than the usual approach. According to question "13. I challenged myself even if the game did not require it", the constructive approach also promoted more sense of challenging the player (21 % more).

Table 2. Mean and Standard Deviation values for user answers in both scenarios

Question #	$\bar{x} \pm SD$	
	Usual	Constructive
1	5.25 ± 1.58	6.3 ± 0.92
2	2.45 ± 2.03	2.8 ± 2.11
3	5.45 ± 1.70	6.25 ± 0.96
4	5.2 ± 2.14	6.45 ± 0.99
5	5.65 ± 1.18	5.3 ± 1.34
6	4.9 ± 1.68	5.2 ± 1.64
7	6.6 ± 0.82	6.55 ± 0.82
8	6.15 ± 1.38	5.95 ± 1.50
9	2.85 ± 2.00	2.7 ± 2.07
10	2.5 ± 1.84	1.8 ± 1.32
11	5.25 ± 1.83	5.8 ± 1.10
12	5.7 ± 1.65	6.2 ± 1.32
13	4.75 ± 1.83	5.75 ± 1.37
14	3.9 ± 2.29	4.15 ± 2.10
15	1.4 ± 0.82	1.75 ± 0.82
16	6.45 ± 1.05	6.4 ± 1.18
17	4 ± 1.94	6.15 ± 1.30
18	2.7 ± 1.83	4.75 ± 1.48
19	6.3 ± 1.26	4.95 ± 2.00

Other results show that the constructive approach was 20 % more enjoyable (question 1) and 14.6 % more liked (question 3). Players also thought that the usual way was 38.8 % more boring (question 10), even if it had a low score. On the other hand, the users thought controlling the usual approach was 27.2 % more comprehensive than the other one (question 19), what was expected since there were fewer controls. These results meant that the difference in way of interaction did have a final impact on the level of gaming experience.

The participants were also encouraged to leave suggestions and comments after answering the questionnaire. Some participants suggested to make the usual approach more difficult and challenging, adding more songs to both approaches and dividing them by categories. The main criticisms were about the feedback given, often repeated songs (this happens because the server does not keep a record of songs already played) and the delay when the button next is touched (this delay was due to the fact there was no loading screen and as said before, was the time needed to download all mp3 tracks used on the game).

Usual approach

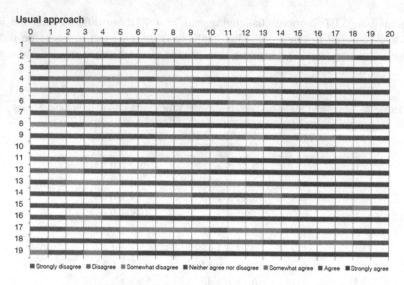

Fig. 5. Usual approach response compilation

Constructive approach

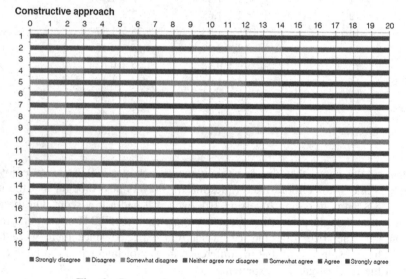

Fig. 6. Constructive approach response compilation

Many players were very enthusiastic about the constructive approach and reported that it was more interesting than the traditional version. Compliments about the user interface were also made.

5   Conclusion

This work proposed a new approach for music presentation on MGGs. The original hypothesis that players would be more engaged and have an overall better experience was validated by 20 participants during the test sessions.

The experiment showed that adding instruments progressively improved some scores of the gaming experience, such as enjoyment, ownership and gameplay. The main reason to this was that the new approach expanded the sense of difficulty, and consequently the sense of challenge of the game. Besides its simplicity, players liked the implemented prototype and most of them suggested that an enhanced version of it should be made available for public download. As future work directions, and according to the participants suggestions, we should perform the following modifications on the game:

- Group musics by genre
- Add multiplayer functionality to the game
- Allow users to post their achievements in social networks
- Implement a global rank in order to increase engagement and competitiveness among users.

Acknowledgements. The authors would like to thank all the players that helped us during experiments.

References

1. Collins, K.: Game Sound: An Introduction to the History, Theory, and Practice of Video Game Music and Sound Design. MIT Press, Cambridge (2008)
2. Schmidt-Jones, C.: Talking about sound and music February 2013. http://cnx.org/contents/a8994fb8-f743-4acf-a175-af2a4682ce63@1
3. Collins, K.: Playing with Sound: A Theory of Interacting with Sound and Music in Video Games. MIT Press, Cambridge (2013)
4. Staiano, A.E., Calvert, S.L.: Exergames for physical education courses: Physical, social, and cognitive benefits. Child. Dev. Perspect. 5(2), 93–98 (2011)
5. Peng, W., Lin, J.-H., Crouse, J.: Is playing exergames really exercising? a meta-analysis of energy expenditure in active video games. Cyberpsy., Behav, Soc. Networking 14(11), 681–688 (2011)
6. Sinclair, J., Hingston, P., Masek, M.: Considerations for the design of exergames. In: Proceedings of the 5th International Conference on Computer Graphics and Interactive Techniques in Australia and Southeast Asia, GRAPHITE 2007, pp. 289–295. ACM, New York, NY, USA (2007)
7. Krishnan, V., Machleit, K.A., Kellaris, J.J., Sullivan, U.Y., Aurand, T.W.: Musical intelligence: Explication, measurement, and implications for consumer behavior. J. Consum. Mark. 31(4), 4 (2014)
8. Bagwell, C.: Sox - sound exchance, the swiss army knife of sound processing programs February 2013. http://sox.sourceforge.net/

9. Gmez, E.H.C., Cairns, P.A., Cox, A.L.: Assessing the core elements of the gaming experience. In: Bernhaupt, R. (ed.) Evaluating User Experience in Games. HumanComputer Interaction Series., pp. 47–71. Springer, London (2010)
10. Albaum, G.: The likert scale revisited. J.-Mark. Res. Soc. **39**, 331–348 (1997)

Evaluating and Customizing User Interaction in an Adaptive Game Controller

Leonardo Torok[✉], Mateus Pelegrino, Jefferson Lessa,
Daniela Gorski Trevisan, Cristina N. Vasconcelos, Esteban Clua,
and Anselmo Montenegro

Computing Institute, Federal Fluminense University,
Rua Passos Da Pátria 156 – E – 3rd Floor, São Domingos, Niterói, Brazil
{ltorok,daniela,crisnv,esteban,anselmo}@ic.uff.br,
{mateuspelegrino,jefferson2459}@gmail.com

Abstract. When playing a game, the user expects an easy and intuitive interaction. While current game console controllers are physical pre-defined hardware components with a default number, size and position of buttons. Unfortunately, different games require different buttons and demand different interaction methods. Despite that, the play style of each player differs according to personal characteristics (like hand size) or past gaming experiences. To achieve an optimal controller configuration for each player, this work proposes a virtual controller based on a common touchscreen device, such as smartphone or tablet, that will be used as a joystick to control a game on a computer or console, collecting user input data and applying machine learning techniques to adapt the position and size of its virtual buttons, minimizing errors and providing an enjoyable experience. With the prototype controller, tests were performed with a set of users and the collected data showed considerable improvements in the precision and game performance of the players.

Keywords: Adaptive interfaces · Adaptive game control · Machine learning · User behavior · Mobile · Touchscreen

1 Introduction

Gameplay experience is one of the most important aspects for achieving the fun factor [1]. This process includes several characteristics that will determine the final impression and engagement of the user. Among many aspects, the challenges must be correctly balanced or the user can get frustrated by excessive roughness or become bored by the absence of challenge [2]. The gameplay experience is implemented by the game rules, which is executed by the player through its interface. In this sense, the interface must be engaged with the user experience, stimulating the user to interact.

While several games became infamous because of unresponsive controls or clunky and unintuitive interface solutions, others are remembered for the opposite: fast, responsive, intuitive, efficient and innovative control schemes, creating an enjoyable experience that made those games memorable. With the rise of smartphones, quickly followed by tablets, a gaming revolution was bound to happen. The computing power

© Springer International Publishing Switzerland 2015
A. Marcus (Ed.): DUXU 2015, Part III, LNCS 9188, pp. 315–326, 2015.
DOI: 10.1007/978-3-319-20889-3_30

on these mobile devices quickly improved, allowing the launch of several mobile games with complex visuals and refined interactions. A major difference was that these devices rely primarily on touch input, done on a large screen that normally covers the entire front of the device. These new technologies, both on mobile devices and in traditional gaming machines, were the starting point for a new wave of games using more intuitive control schemes, bringing millions of players that aren't interested in learning complex control schemes to electronic games. Although traditional controllers may be complex, they are reliable and precise. The new methods suffered with lack of precision in command input, slower reaction time and limitations when trying to map complex actions. The problem was clear in several mobile games, which started using virtual buttons displayed on its touchscreen to simulate a traditional controller and other input options. Among different problems of this solution, the lack of tactile feedback of a real controller is an important issue [2].

In this work we propose a new interface for electronic games, that has the large input options of a regular gamepad but with the flexibility of a virtual controller. This new input method aims to be an alternative to the traditional video game joystick with a touchscreen device with a virtual controller on its screen, creating a less cluttered and more intuitive interface to play a video game. In order to solve the lack of precision and consequently more mistakes, our solution introduces a novel control adaptation to the user's behavior. Based on an observation of basic interaction events of a specific user, such as button presses, speech input, or internal state changes, user preferences are derived. Different algorithms extract information from these basic events, such as preferences of the user or a prediction of the most likely following user action. The proposed adaptive interface employed machine learning algorithms to analyze user inputs and detect errors. After detecting how the user is missing the virtual buttons, the controller will try to smoothly fix the position and size of the buttons in order to eliminate or reduce touch errors.

2 Related Work

Mobile phones have specific hardware (camera, accelerometer, GPS, Bluetooth, Wifi) with lots of them being different from the ones found in traditional game platforms, like video games and PCs. For this reason, these devices bring new forms of user interaction however with the drawback of lacking tactile feedback [3]. On the other hand an adaptive user interface is an interactive software system that improves its ability to interact with a user based on partial experience with that user [4]. Adaptation of interactive systems describes changes of the interface that are performed to improve the usability or the user satisfaction.

Rogers et al. [5] developed models that treat uncertain input touch and use this to deal with the handover of control between both user and system. They demonstrate a finger map browser, which scrolls the map to a point of interest when the user input is uncertain. Keeping the same goal, but in a different way, Weir et al. [6] used Machine Learning approach for learning user-specific touch input models to increase touch accuracy on mobile devices. They proposed mapping data or touch location to the intended touch point, based on historical touch behavior of a specific user.

Bi et al. [7] conceptualized finger touch input as an uncertain process, and used statistical target selection criterion. They improve the touch accuracy using a Bayesian Touch Criterion and decrease considerably the error rate. However, even improving the accuracy in a higher level, the user keeps missing the buttons and the interface needs to calculate the intended target.

While personalized inputs have been commonly used, such as key-target resizing on soft keyboards [8], this type of adaptability has some disadvantages, as the needs of using only on meaning of process language, and it just adapt according to the model of language and of user typing behavior.

The use of touchscreen devices as gaming controls is relatively new, resulting in very few related works, with the most relevant ones covered in this section. When looking specifically at mobile phones with adaptive interfaces being used as gaming controls it is clear that this is an area that still remains unexplored.

3 Proposed Adaptive Interface

The proposed game control interface is composed of both a physical hardware (touchscreen device, in this case an Android smartphone) and software components that will observe the user behavior and adapt the interface components. As smartphones and tablets are common devices, they will be used as a physical component, allowing the player to use devices he already has to play games.

The touchscreen device, our first component, will represent the joystick. A mobile application was created, presenting an interface similar to a real controller and sending all button presses to the computer that runs the game. A second software, running on the PC, will receive the information about key presses and generate the corresponding keyboard events on the computer.

3.1 Control Adaptations to the User's Behavior

With our proposal, game developers may also project a specific interface for their game. However, due to time limitation, it is possible that the developer can't develop many usability tests in order to validate and adjust his interface. In our work we developed an automatic and interactive adaptation mechanism, based in machine learning concepts, in order to improve the usability or the user satisfaction and facilitate the developer process. Adaptations may be triggered by different adaptation causes, such as the context of the interaction, the experience of the user, or user behavior [9]. In this work, we focus on the adaptation of interactive game control to user behavior. From a philosophical point of view, [10] defines behavior as an internally produced movement and contrasts behavior with other movements that are produced externally. For instance, raising an arm is behavior, whereas having an arm raised by someone else is not. In this point of view, reflexive and other involuntary movements are considered as behavior. Thus, behavior does not necessarily have to be voluntary and intentional. Reflexives movements can become very common in some kinds of games where the user should perform movements of the virtual character many times quickly.

To achieve the desired adaptation to each user's play style we decided to perform two different changes in the controller's layout: size and position of buttons. These adaptations are performed at the same time for each button. The size adaptations aims to facilitate the usage of the most important buttons for the game being played, increasing the size of the most used buttons in the controller and decreasing the size of the buttons that are less used. The controller retains the data for each button press and uses this data history to determine the optimal size for each button, following maximum and minimum limits on size (predetermined as two times the original size of the button and half of its original size). The controller is also capable of reacting to changing requirements. If a button that had minimal use start being used constantly, the controller will learn with the user interaction and start increasing the size of this button. This change will be done once per iteration, but limiting for this work, by a maximum of 3 pixels each time, in order to have a more organic adaption. The controller will perform one modification per second, so it does not change too fast.

The second type of adaptation is the button's position. The basic concept here is try to detect the position for a specific button that will guarantee that the majority of users touches actually hit the button (remembering that the user will not have the physical feedback of a real controller and will not be able to keep looking at the controller to check if his fingers are hitting the correct spot of the buttons during gameplay). To perform this adaptation, we will use all the data about users' touches on the screen (both correct touches and wrong ones) and try to detect the points that represent more accurately the center of the position where the user is trying to press. After determining the positions, each one will be correlated with the closest button. It is necessary to note that some buttons may not have a new center assigned, indicating that, for now, they will not need any adaptation (this may occur when a button did not had touches or when the amount of touches in its area is insignificant compared to the full dataset of inputs). With the correlation done, the application on the smart device will start to move the button for the new correct position. This movement is done moving the button at maximum 5 pixels (considering the distance in the x and y axis) per iteration, with an interval of one second. Figure 1 shows the adaptations correcting a button's position.

To keep the interface consistent, several rules and boundaries were specified. For the changes in size, it was determined that each button could reach a maximum size of two times its original size, with a minimum limit of half its size. This rule will avoid buttons with an exaggerated size or simply too small to use. Despite that, it is necessary to deal with the presence of other buttons in the surrounding areas. If a button moves or grows in conflict with a neighbor button, the user would not be able to use the interface. To avoid that, before each button size increase, the controller will verify if its new position and size is in conflict with any of the other buttons (considering that a conflict is defined as any intersection in the area of any pair of buttons). If a change results in conflict, it will not be done. This means that if the center for the input data assigned to a button is very close to another button, in a manner that moving the button until its center is located at that point would result in an intersection, the controller will move the button as close as possible to the correct position without intersecting both buttons. If the neighbor button that created the conflict moves out of the way (something that can happen because of the adaptations performed on the neighbor), then the algorithm will continue the adaptation since the conflict is not happening anymore. With this rules, the controller will always maintain a consistent interface.

Fig. 1. The red dots represent the player's touches in the screen while the blue dots corresponds to the centroid for the cluster assigned to the button "1", the correct position. In the left side, the controller is on its default configuration. The controller will gradually move the button "1" until it reaches the position demonstrated in the right side of the figure.

3.2 Machine Learning

With the two adaptations approaches defined, it is necessary to define the method to gather user input data and translate it to meaningful results to improve the controller responding to the player's needs. The data used to evaluate the controllers correctness is a set with the entire touches log in the screen performed by the user. Each touch can be classified as correct or incorrect. A correct touch is defined as an interaction that hits any button in the screen and performs an action, while an incorrect one is defined as an action that does not hit any button, representing a situation where the user tried to perform an action and failed. To collect the necessary information about input, the mobile application uses an extra control over the interface, an invisible layer that will intercept the touches, collect data and redirect the touch for the buttons above. This layer covers the entire screen area and is mapped in Cartesian coordinates, with the y-axis representing the screen height and the x-axis representing the screen width, considering the device in landscape mode. The origin of the coordinate system is located at the upper left corner, following the convention used by the Android OS when mapping screen input. Each touch in the screen is saved in the internal SQLite database of the Android device (both the correct and the incorrect inputs) and the machine learning algorithm will use the most recent data from the database. In our tests, the algorithm always used the last 30 points. This approach allows the controller to change its behavior in response to a change in the player's needs. Both operations occur simultaneously, with the controller constantly inserting new input data in the database and the algorithm collecting the data and processing it at each iteration.

With the data being collected, the next step was defining when and how to perform adaptations. The size adaptation is the simplest case, detailed in the last section. The size will increase for the most used buttons and decrease in the least used ones. In this first case, a simple algorithm that tracked and counted the amount of times each button was used was enough, allowing the controller to easily determine which buttons would need to increase and which would need to decrease its size. The algorithm uses the list of buttons ordered by the amount of presses. This list is divided in 3 parts, with equal size. The first one contains the most used buttons while the last one contains the least used. The middle set will not suffer any size change. The buttons in the first set will start to increase at each iteration, while the buttons in the last group will start decreasing, respecting the boundaries detailed in the last section. At each iteration, the list will be updated with the user inputs and the order may change. As an example, during one iteration, the button A can be the most used, starting to increase on size. After a set of iterations, it can fall to the middle group, halting it's increase. If, after a defined delta time, the A button becomes less necessary and ends in the last group, it will start to decrease.

While the size adaptation only demanded a simple algorithm, the position correction needs a more sophisticated approach. The main objective is to find the points in the screen that represent the center of the most used areas. The objective of using the input data as points in the screen space and group the data according to its positions, finding the center for each group can be correctly modeled by the K-means unsupervised learning algorithm, which is a vector quantization method used in data mining that receives an entry set and separates these entries in K classes of co-related entries. The algorithm is NP-hard, but with several heuristics that allow a quicker solution that converges surprisingly fast to a local optimum. Given a set $X = \{x_1, \ldots, x_m\}$ the goal of K-means is to partition it into k clusters such that each point in a cluster is more similar to points from its own cluster than others from different clusters [11].

In our case, the entry set is composed by the most recent user inputs, represented as Cartesian coordinates. The objective was to separate it in K classes, with K being the number of virtual buttons in the screen. The algorithm will return several subsets of the full input dataset containing related points grouping the closest points in the same class. For each class, the K-means clustering will also detect the class centroid, which is the nearest point to all other touches that corresponds to that cluster, since it corresponds to the optimal position for a button. The users' touches will be located in the area of a button or at least close to it, since the player's objective is to hit the correct position of the button to perform actions in the game. After several interactions it is possible to observe a pattern of inputs close to each button, allowing the K-means clustering to separate inputs in classes that represent each buttons area and some of the space around it. After finding the centroids, each one will be paired with the closest button. In the case where there are two centroids where the closest button is the same, the correct pair will be created based on the minimal distance, with the other centroid remaining without an assigned button, which is a more common situation in the initial usage, based on a low amount of touch data. The paired centroid related to the button will be considered as the optimal position for that element, since it represents the middle point of all inputs directed to that button. With this data, the controller will start to move the button gradually towards the centroid of its class, until the center of the button is located precisely in the centroid for that class.

4 Usability Tests

In order to investigate our adaptation approach and the user gameplay experience, we conducted a user interaction evaluation for the adaptations presented before. These users' tests examine the effectiveness and satisfaction of the adaptations and provide empirical evidence for the application of the adaptations in the domain of game control.

4.1 Participants and Apparatus

The evaluation used two different interactive systems (one adaptive and other not adaptive) and two games genre: a platform game (Super Mario Bros) and an arcade game (Streets of Rage).

Platform games involve traveling from one direction to another, avoiding obstacles, enemies and jumping platforms (very occasionally other means are substituted for jumping, like swinging or bouncing, but these are considered variations on the same mechanic). They are most often associated with iconic video game mascots like Donkey Kong, Sonic the Hedgehog, Mario, Megaman, Samus, Crash Bandicoot and Rayman, though platform games may have any theme. Arcade games can involve several variations, being common in the 1990 s. Usually, the player must travel from one screen to another, defeating all enemies presented. Streets of Rage and Final Fight are two examples of this genre.

Fig. 2. The user interaction setup used during the evaluation sessions

A total of 16 users tested two different version of the control with two different games, totalizing four evaluation sessions for each user. Our group of volunteer participants consisted of 13 male users and 3 female users with ages ranging from 18 to 50. The user group was selected among expert computer and smartphone players. The experiment was conducted on a Motorola Moto X phone running Android OS 4.4. The capacitive touchscreen was 4.7 inches in diagonal with an aspect ratio of 9:16 and a resolution of 720 × 1280 pixels. When a finger touched the screen, the approximate centroid of contact area between the finger and the screen was reported as the touch point. Figure 2 is showing the user's interaction set up.

4.2 Procedure and Study Design

Each evaluation session was limited to 5 min of playing and approximately one minute and half of training before starting the test. The training session consisted of a free user interaction while the evaluator read a script describing the function of each button as well as the game goals. The evaluations comprise both a subjective survey by means of a questionnaire and an objective investigation by means of log data collected during the users' interactions. The subjective measures include perceived performance and usability issues. The four evaluation sessions per user took approximately 30 min.

All events caused by the user-control device interaction were written to a log file to enable an assessment of the user's behavior. The log file registered the following data: screen coordinates where the users touched for each button, error rate, score and quantity of lives spent in the game. The success rate is committed when the user performed a touch inside the area of the button. All subjects used both an adaptive and a non-adaptive version of each game genre to facilitate a comparison of the two conditions. The order in which the subjects tested the individual systems was altered to eliminate an effect of the order, for instance through a training effect. Likewise, the adaptive and the not-adaptive version were used first alternately. The same procedure was adopted for alternating the game genres order. Basically with this study design we intend to verify two main design issues: firstly how the adaptation is improving the user interaction, and secondly if the achieved adaptation pattern suffers influence from the game genre. In the next section we discuss our results.

5   Results

In this section we described our obtained results divided into two kinds of achievements: the objective results including the data log analysis and the subjective results involving the post questionnaire users' answers.

5.1   Objective Results

In order to verify how the adaptation to the user behavior is improving the user-control interaction we observed two variables: the success rate and the average of score per life. Observing Fig. 4 we can conclude the adaptive control reached better success rates than the not-adaptive version in both genres of games. For the platform game (Super Mario Bros) the adaptive control augments the precision in 6.67 %. For the arcade game (Streets of Rage) the adaptive control augments the precision in 13.7 %. In Fig. 5 we can observe the adaptive control reached better score per life than the not-adaptive version in both genres of games.

Observing the graphs of Figs. 4 and 5, we evaluated the difference between both prototypes. Since our samples could not be assumed to be normally distributed we use the Wilcoxon Signed-Rank non-parametric statistical two-tailed hypothesis test with a threshold of 0,05 for significance. Table 1 presents the results for each variable in game and the results are statistically significant.

Figure 3 (a) and (b) shows different layouts corresponding to the intersection of all users achievements at the end of the interaction for each game genre. It is possible to observe that depending on the genre of the game, the final layout may have some similarities. For instance, the platform games, which the main objective of the game is to reach the rightmost part and avoid to be hit by enemy either passing or jumping, may present the Right and the Jump buttons bigger than others. However, for arcade games, where the player must walk through scenario and hit enemies, the configuration of the controller changes slightly, where the punch button probably corresponds to the largest one, the directional buttons may vary and the Right button tends to be the largest button of the directional.

Table 1. Results of wilcoxon test

Game	Variable	P-value
Super Mario Bros.	Success Rate	0.003357
Super Mario Bros.	Score/Life	0.0155
Streets of Rage	Success Rate	3.052e-05
Streets of Rage	Score/Life	0.01443

Fig. 3. Intersection of all users achievements at the end of the interaction for (a) Streets of Rage and (b) Super Mario Bros.

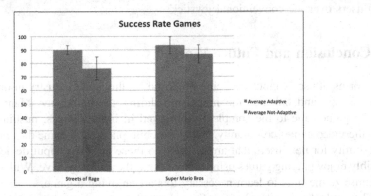

Fig. 4. Touch buttons precision measured as Success Rate

5.2 Subjective Results

After the tests, users answered a questionnaire about the usability of the adaptive control, with questions about which controller the user believes he played better, which prototype he would prefer to use to play again, the general ease of use for both controllers and if he is interested in using an adaptive controller. All users receives two identical questionnaires, one for each game played.

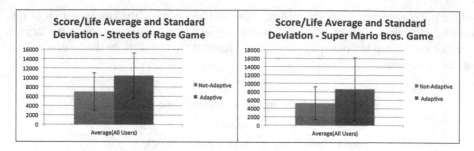

Fig. 5. Performance measured as Score/Life, where the y-axis displays the average score reached in the game for each life (a)Streets of Rage (b) Super Mario Bros.

The statistics were favorable to use this type of adaptive control. We observed that 88 % of the users prefer to play Streets of Rage using a control with adaptation and 94 % of these users prefer to use this adaptive control to play Super Mario Bros. Regarding the ease of use, the median score was 4 (where 1 corresponds to very hard and 5 to very easy, with the upper quartile equals to 5 chosen by four users and one unique minimum value equals to 2. The other question asks if the user would use the adaptive control in other possibility. The scale is again from 1 to 5, which 1 represents I would not like to use and 5 represents I would love to use again. The median of this question was 4, with the upper quartile equals to 5 and the minimum value equals to 3. From the subjective evaluations, we can conclude that the adaptive prototype was well accepted for most users. According to this subjective evaluation, the users appeared motivated to accept and change to this new way to play, even with the large experience from users over the conventional joystick.

6   Conclusion and Future Work

New forms of user's input are being proposed by the game industry in order to attract more players and enhance the immersion during the gameplay. Many users avoid playing games due to the complexity observed in input devices, pushing them away from the video games community. Using a mobile phone as a game data input gives the opportunity for new users that are resistant to these complex input devices to try and possibly enjoy playing games using a device that they already have. With that, we hope to minimize the time to learn necessary to start enjoying a game.

The evaluations not only investigated whether the proposed adaptation improves the user-control interaction, but also give insight into the general conditions under which the adaptations perform well. We can conclude that the adaptive controller brings benefits to great part of the users and from this brief evaluation we can start pointing an ideal interface. The advantages showed by the test results indicate that the participants achieved a configuration for the controller that allowed a very low standard deviation, principally playing the game Streets of Rage. Another observation comparing the user's final interface was the disposal of the buttons. Some users changed the original positions of the buttons 1 and 2 (originally placed with the button 2 slightly above the button 1) until both buttons were aligned in a position more similar the one found on controllers for video game consoles.

Another interesting finding was related to the user attention focus while playing. It was observable through video capture that in the non-adaptive version the users frequently alternate their attention focus between the control and the computer screen while in the adaptive version this frequency decreased considerably. However in the next work we hope to proof this finding by capturing more valuable and objective data of the user's attention focus for instance by using an eye tracking system.

The machine learning algorithm is another aspect where improvements can be made. The K-means implementation in use considers that the number of classes is equal to the number of buttons in the controller. However, when a game doesn't use all buttons this kind of assumption will lead to a higher than needed number of classes and centroids, affecting the adaptation process. In this direction a more flexible implementation of the algorithm that considers only the buttons in use will be investigated.

Regarding the user's experience evaluation other parameters involved in the adaptation process (such as speed adaptation, maximum change in a button position and so on) could be further investigated to fine tune the controller adaptive behavior which could lead to an optimal configuration to the controller.

Acknowledgments. We thank all participants who have contributed in our experimental studies and all colleagues at Universidade Federal Fluminense for their valuable comments to improve this work.

References

1. Koster, R.: Theory of fun for game design. O'Reilly Media Inc., Sebastopol (2013)
2. Schell, J.: The Art of Game Design: A book of lenses. CRC Press, Boca Raton (2008)
3. Joselli, M., Junior, J.R.S., Zamith, M., Clua, E., Soluri, E.: A content adaptation architecture for games. In: SBGames. SBC (2012)
4. Langley, P.: Machine learning for adaptive user interfaces. In: Brewka, G., Habel, C., Nebel, B. (eds.) KI 1997. LNCS, vol. 1303. Springer, Heidelberg (1997)
5. Rogers, S., Williamson, J., Stewart, C., Murray-Smith, R.: Fingercloud: uncertainty and autonomy handover in capacitive sensing. In: ACM CHI 2010, pp. 577–580 (2010)
6. Weir, D., Rogers, S., Murray-Smith, R., Löchtefeld, M.: A user-specific machine learning approach for improving touch accuracy on mobile devices. In: ACM UIST 2012, pp. 465–476 (2012)
7. Bi, X., Zhai, S.: Bayesian Touch – a statistical criterion of target selection with finger touch. In: ACM UIST 2013, pp. 51–60 (2013)
8. Baldwin, T., Chai, J.: Towards online adaptation and personalization of key-target resizing for mobile devices. In: IUI 2012, pp. 11–20 (2012)
9. Bezold, M., Minker, W.: Adaptive multimodal interactive systems. Springer, Boston (2011)
10. Dretske: Explaining Behavior. Reasons in a World of Causes. MIT Press, Cambridge, MA, USA (1988)
11. Smola, A., Vishwanathan, S.: Introduction to Machine Learning. Cambridge University, Cambridge (2008)

12. Malfatti, S.M., dos Santos, F.F., dos Santos, S.R.: Using mobile phones to control desktop multiplayer games. In: Proceedings of the 2010 VIII Brazilian Symposium on Games and Digital Entertainment, ser. SBGAMES 2010, pp. 74–82. IEEE Computer Society, Washington, DC, USA (2010)

13. Stenger, B., Woodley, T., Cipolla, R.: A vision-based remote control. In: Cipolla, R., Battitato, S., Farinella, G.M. (eds.) ICISTM 2012. SCI, vol. 285, pp. 233–262. Springer, Heidelberg (2010)

14. Vajk, T., Coulton, P., Bamford, W., Edwards, R.: Using a mobile phone as a wii-like controller for playing games on a large public display. Int. J. Comput. Games Technol. **2008**, 4:1–4:6 (2008). http://dx.doi.org/10.1155/2008/539078

15. Wei, C., Marsden, G., Gain, J.: Novel interface for first person shooting games on pdas. In: OZCHI 2008: Proceedings of the 20th Australasian Conference on Computer-Human Interaction, OZCHI, pp. 113–121. ACM, New York, NY, USA (2008)

16. Zyda, M., Thkral, D., Jakatdar, S., Engelsma, J., Ferrans, J., Hans, M., Shi, L., Kitson, F., Vasudevan, V.: Educating the next generation of mobile game developers. IEEE Comput. Graph. Appl. **27**(2), 96, 92–95 (2007)

New Research Methods for Media and Cognition Experiment Course

Yi Yang$^{(\boxtimes)}$, Shengjin Wang, and Liangrui Peng

Department of Electronic Engineering, Tsinghua University, Beijing, China
{yangyy,wgsgj}@tsinghua.edu.cn,
plr@ocrserv.ee.tsinghua.edu.cn

Abstract. With the development of human-brain cognition and signal processing techniques, there is more attention on media and cognitive disciplines, especially focus on human-computer interaction and human's brain function analysis. Electronic media is a new expression of human civilization, culture and arts. Media and cognition experiment course is to complete the goal of training talents through a large number of state-of-the-art methods. This paper describes the understanding of the new practical engineering projects on media and cognition course. Students were asked to complete several sets of practical engineering courses. Some optional contents are also included. After this training, we were able to select and train more high-level talents further. In fact, this kind of practical engineering course can improve the students' ability to grasp related knowledge points. Eventually they will have the ability to plan projects and solve practical problems.

Keywords: Media and cognition · Analysis of human brain · Human-computer interaction · High-level talents · Investigation of project programming

1 Introduction

Electronic information science and technology serve the people as the electronic media. The electronic media is a new human civilization carrier which will give birth to new culture and arts. Media is defined as the information carrier and can be classified as three parts [1–3]:

- Substances in materials or substances entity;
- Fluctuations signals of matter and energy;
- Symbol carrier, exist and have an effect by the means of two types of carrier mentioned above;

  Media information technology research topic included three parts:

- Text: Text retrieval, text classification, text summarization, machine translation;
- Image and video: Video encoding, video summary, target detection, tracking, identification, 3DTV;
- Voice: Speech coding, speech synthesis, speech recognition;

© Springer International Publishing Switzerland 2015
A. Marcus (Ed.): DUXU 2015, Part III, LNCS 9188, pp. 327–334, 2015.
DOI: 10.1007/978-3-319-20889-3_31

Bill Gates first proposed the concept of "natural user interface" in 2008, and he predicted that human-computer interaction will have a big change in the next few years which means keyboard and mouse will be gradually replaced by more natural module such as touch, vision and voice. At the same time, "Organic User Interface" began quietly rising which includes biometric sensor, skin display, and even directly connection between brain and computer. These technologies will undoubtedly give a significant impact on human's life. With the application of computer technology and sensors, the real world has gradually emerged its "Digital Edition" side, and natural human-computer interaction is bridge between real and virtual world.

Media and cognition course is the latest created course of the Department of Electronic Engineering of Tsinghua University. This course is to complete the goal of training talents through a large number of state-of-the-art methods. The implementation of all the projects will allow students to deeply understand the basic signal processing methods on media and cognition course. Students were asked to complete several sets of fundamental engineering projects to establish their modelling method and the algorithm programming skills through these practices. Some elective contents are also included to inspire their related fields of research and analysis capabilities. After this training, we were able to select and train more high-level talents further. In fact, this kind of practical engineering course can improve the students' ability to grasp related knowledge points. Eventually they will have the ability to plan projects and solve practical problems.

2   The Curriculum Contents of Media and Cognition

When confronted with another person, the brain immediately focus on him and identified his identity based on the experience. This process is not through hundreds of layers of decision tree to realize. The human brain is to know. A little baby is difficult to distinguish two different people, but adults can do it through years of study and training. In fact, the human brain may also be able to accurately guess their age, gender, mood, or personality. The purpose of the course is to create a human-like cognitive technology equipment and methods. The purpose of the course is to create a human-like cognitive technology equipment and methods. This technology will observe the world around it and operate and interact with a human user. It can conduct its independent study, and even affect humans to produce some new culture and art. It revolutionized human's knowledge and means by learning from and interaction with the outside world and other human beings.

To cultivate the high-level talents on this field, we design four kinds of fundamental projects as: three somatosensory entertainment or games based on human-machine interaction; Android-based human face recognition system.

2.1   Somatosensory Entertainment and Games

We designed a variety of entertainment and games somatosensory topics for students to choose and develop. The development platform is Kinect device and its SDK toolkit.

Fig. 1. Kinect device

Kinect is a motion sensing input device by Microsoft for the Xbox 360 video game console and Windows PCs which is shown in Fig. 1. Based around a webcam-style add-on peripheral for the Xbox 360 console, it enables users to control and interact with the Xbox 360 without the need to touch a game controller, through a natural user interface using gestures and spoken commands. Our projects are developed with Kinect Software Development Kit released by Microsoft for Windows 7. This SDK will allow developers to write Kinect apps in C++/CLI, C#, or Visual Basic .NET [4–6]. And the parameter index of Kinect device is:

- The output video frame rate of 30 Hz
- 8-bit VGA resolution (640 × 480 pixels)
- The best recognition region 1.2-3.5 m, 0.7-6 m extended area
- Visual area: horizontal 57 ° vertical 43 °
- Up to track 20 individuals body node

By using multi-channel media interface technology, virtual reality technologies become the future development trend of human-computer interaction. To achieve the objectives of natural human-machine interaction and multi-dimensional information space interaction which is known as "human-machine's harmony", we need to use a variety of media to identify human's body posture, gestures and voice, etc. and to determine person's intention. Somatosensory entertainment and games are good topics to bring a new awareness of students' experience which included:

1. Gymnastic Posture Correction and Scoring System:

Students need to design multiple gymnastics pose [7] by Kinect's interactive features for users to guide user's gymnastic posture by voice commands which is shown in Fig. 2. The system will compare he degree of difference between the standard and the user's skeleton node data and give the corresponding scores. According to the degree of difference, the voice interaction wrong posture correction and scoring errors is announced. This system can correct user's yoga action and correct user's body shape to keep health.

The core of Kinect skeleton track processing is CMOS sensor to perceive the environment no matter how ambient lighting conditions. Firstly, the sensor generates the depth image stream at a rate of 30 frames per second and the real-time 3D reproduction of the surrounding environment. Next, Kinect will evaluate the depth image on pixel-level to identify the different parts of human's body. Next, Kinect will evaluate the depth image on pixel-level to identify the different parts of human's body. The final step is to use these results to generate a skeleton system by tracking human's joints.

Fig. 2. Gymnastic posture correction and scoring system

2. Motorcycle Driving Games System:

With Kinect device SDK toolkit, students design a human-computer interaction motorcycle driving game [8], which is shown in Fig. 3. Students need to design a menu operation and interface operation mode for the game. The importance is the "two can always switch the operating mode":

– In the beginning, program is shown as the menu operation interface in the default mode. The user can change the gesture to select the menu's item included entry, exit and other operations;

Fig. 3. Motorcycle driving games

– After entering the game, user can do the gesture "hands together" to achieve the operating mode switch to enter the somatosensory game mode. Then the user can use his body position to play the game.

According to the body and gestures by the user to simulate the driving motor of the acceleration, deceleration and stopping. They also design the driving the process overturned and overtaking other skills.

3. Music Knocking Drum Games:

The main problem of the music rhythm interaction through PC's keyboard is that person have to imitate the "Drumming" action by pressing a key, the realistic action is too low to form a good user's experience. Realization of gestures by Kinect equipment can enable users to directly operate by imitating drumming gestures which will greatly enhance the game's experience degree. Another benefit is the exercise effect. This game is designed on the existed music knocking drum games platform, which is shown in Fig. 4. Simulating knocking drum by musical rhythm matching according to the rhythm of the music where the user data is from the human-computer interaction device. The final ranking and achievements is announced by the synthesis voice.

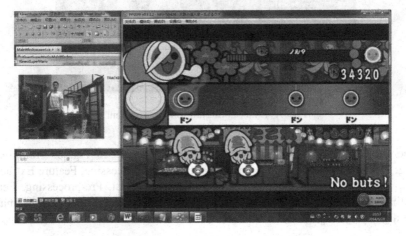

Fig. 4. Music knocking drum games

2.2   Android-Based Human Face Recognition System

Smart phones and other mobile devices are operating in increasingly rich settings that include both nearby sensors and machines [9]. The android-based human face recognition system is developed on the Linux environment [10, 11]. The Android-based human face recognition system is optional item. But what's interesting is that many students chose this topic. The Linux configuration environment is shown in Fig. 5:

Fig. 5. Linux configuration environment

After finishing the configuration of Android SDK, The Linux environment is shown in Fig. 6:

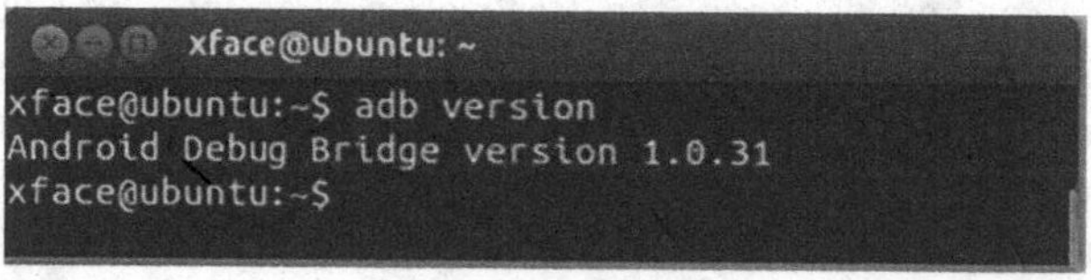

Fig. 6. Linux configuration environment

Fig. 7. Linux configuration environment

The Project included the following modules as shown in Fig. 8: Training and Testing. Training module included Face data input, Pre-processing, Feature Extracting, Feature Database; testing module included Face data input, Pre-processing, Feature Extracting, Feature matching. The project is based on principal component analysis (PCA) algorithm. (Figure 7).

– Training module: The training set is 40 individuals and each person 10 kinds of gestures selected from AT & T Laboratories Cambridge ORL face database [12]. Each two-dimensional face gray-scale image is converted into a row vector and calculate the feature vector set by saving all the row vector into one matrix. Then compute the eigenvector and eigenvalues of covariance matrix to produce the Eigen-face. Finally, the selected principal components of Eigen-face are obtained to identify the training and testing face images.
– Testing module: In the testing phase, the testing face image is projected to the Eigen-face subspace and use nearest neighbor classifier with Euclidean distance as a decision. The minimum distance between training image and test image is the criterion of matching.

The final results running in the Android platform is shown in Fig. 9. The registered users' face will be identified and achieved 80 % recognition rate above.

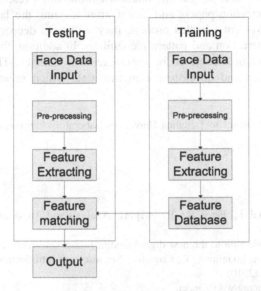

Fig. 8. Flowchart of face recognition based on Android platform

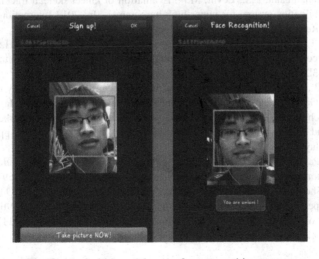

Fig. 9. Android-based human face recognition system

3 Summary

These lively and attractive media and cognition projects will encourage students to broaden their thinking and explore the unknown information researching fields. Students wrote their scientific papers and patent after learning the latest scientific and technological achievements. In this process, they will have deeper understanding of human-computer interaction and pattern recognition. In addition, the course will provide independent practical subjects for some excellent students. These students will have more discussion and development in this field which greatly stimulate their interest.

Acknowledgements. Thanks to Tsinghua University Laboratory Innovation Funding.

References

1. Nick, P., Yonghuai, L., Peter, B.: 3D Imaging. Analysis and Applications. Springer, New York (2012)
2. Wenjun, Z.: Introduction to the new digital media. Fudan University Press, Boston (2009)
3. Zheng, S., Fang, F., Jiongjiong, Y.: Cognitive Neuroscience Introduction. Peking University Press, New York (2010)
4. http://en.wikipedia.org/wiki/Kinect
5. Fabian, J., Young, T., Jones, J.C.P., Clayton, G.M.: Integrating the microsoft kinect with simulink: real-time object tracking example. IEEE/ASME Trans. Mechatron. **19**(1), 249–257 (2014)
6. Tao, G., Archambault, P.S., Levin, M.F.: Evaluation of kinect skeletal tracking in a virtual reality rehabilitation system for upper limb hemiparesis. In: 2013 International Conference on Virtual Rehabilitation (ICVR), pp. 164–165. 26–29 Aug (2013)
7. Nakamura, T., Nishimura, N., Asahi, T., Oyama, G., Sato, M., Kajimoto, H.: Kinect-based automatic scoring system for spasmodic torticollis. In: 2014 IEEE Symposium on 3D User Interfaces (3DUI), pp. 155–156, 29–30 March (2014)
8. Chaperot, B., Fyfe, C.: Improving artificial intelligence. In: 2006 IEEE Symposium on A Motocross Game, Computational Intelligence and Games, pp. 181–186. May 2006
9. Jang, M., Schwan, K., et al.: Personal clouds: sharing and integrating networked resources to enhance end user experiences. In: 2014 Proceedings IEEE INFOCOM, pp. 2220–2228. April 27–May 2, 2014
10. Kemp, R., Palmer, N., Kielmann, T., Bal, H.: Cuckoo: a computation offloading framework for smartphones. In: International Conference on Mobile Computing, pp. 59–79 (2010)
11. Ra, M.R., Sheth, A., Mummert, L., Pillai, P., Wetherall, D., Govindan, R.: Odessa: enabling interactive perception applications on mobile devices. In: Proceedings the 9th International Conference on Mobile Systems, Applications, and Service, pp. 43–56 (2011)
12. http://www.cl.cam.ac.uk/research/dtg/attarchive/facedatabase.html

Designing the Urban Experience

Learning from Hourly Household Energy Consumption: Extracting, Visualizing and Interpreting Household Smart Meter Data

Sam Borgeson[(✉)], June A. Flora, Jungsuk Kwac, Chin-Woo Tan,
and Ram Rajagopal

Sustainable Systems Lab, Department of Civil and Environmental Engineering,
Stanford University, Stanford, USA
{sborgeson, jflora, kwjusul, tancw, ramr}@stanford.edu

Abstract. In this paper, we present the Energy *Visualization and Insight System for Demand Operations and Management* platform (VISDOM), a collection of smart meter data analysis algorithms and visualization tools designed to address the challenge of interpreting patterns in energy data in support of research, utility energy efficiency and demand response programs. We provide an overview of how the system works and examples of usage, followed by a discussion of the potential benefits of using VISDOM to identify and target participants whose electricity consumption is best aligned with the goals of efficiency and demand response programs.

Keywords: Information design · Data visualization · Energy · Sustainability · Energy efficiency · Customer segmentation · Machine learning

1 Introduction

By mid- 2014, electricity smart meters had been installed for over 50 million, or 43 %, of US households and were generating in excess of 1 billion data points a day[1] [1]. Smart meter data flows into utilities at a rate approximately three orders of magnitude faster than traditional monthly meter readings, creating significant opportunities for novel forms of analysis and interpretation of energy consumption at a massive scale. In this paper, we present the Energy *Visualization and Insight System for Demand Operations and Management* platform (VISDOM). VISDOM is a collection of smart meter data analysis algorithms and visualization tools designed to address the challenge of interpreting patterns in energy data in support of utility energy efficiency and demand response programs.[2]

---

[1] Smart meters record electricity usage at 15 min or hourly intervals, with typical residential configurations defaulting to hourly.

[2] Energy efficiency programs are a wide array of publically funded programs, typically administered by utilities, designed to reduce customer energy consumption. These programs vary from conveying information, to rebates for energy efficient purchases, to online or in person household energy audits. Demand response programs are similar to efficiency programs but are designed to get customers to reduce their load temporarily during periods of grid stress.

© Springer International Publishing Switzerland 2015
A. Marcus (Ed.): DUXU 2015, Part III, LNCS 9188, pp. 337–345, 2015.
DOI: 10.1007/978-3-319-20889-3_32

This paper describes each of VISDOM's components, summarizing the algorithms used to characterize customer consumption and the interactive interface for open-ended exploration of the characteristics of large sets of customers. We provide examples of typical usage and discuss the potential benefits of segmenting and targeting customers for participation in energy programs based on the consumption characteristics available through VISDOM.

2   What Is VISDOM?

VISDOM's three main components are customer consumption feature extraction, feature exploration(i.e. interactive plots and mapping), and household segmentation and targeting (i.e. using features to filter and categorize customers). We define features as discrete pieces of categorical or numerical data known or estimated for every customer. They are designed to capture essential characteristics of customers and their energy consumption and can support self-directed learning about consumption patterns and their drivers, academic research into consumption and its correlates, or to identify households that make the best targets for specific energy interventions.

2.1   Feature Extraction

Feature extraction algorithms, implemented in R, [2], iterate through customers, record known features and derive (through statistical summaries) or estimate (through statistical and machine learning techniques) values for others. Known customer features typically include location, rate plan, and billing information. To date we have implemented several dozen derived features, including demand percentiles and variability for different time periods, daily load characteristics, and correlations between demand and external phenomena [3]. Estimated features include parameters from statistical models and machine learning algorithms performing tasks like end use disaggregation, characterizing occupancy patterns and schedules [4], recovering heating and cooling system attributes [3], and clustering and interpreting load shape characteristics[3] [5].

Figure 1 provides an illustration of the feature extraction process. Smart meter data and other information known about each customer, location, and building are the raw inputs into feature extraction algorithms. These algorithms output a list of features for each customer, potentially achieving full coverage of a utility service territory. Features can be categorized into the following loose categories.

- **Basic statistics and heuristics**, including mean, median, peak, minimum, variance, etc., computed for different time intervals.

---

[3] A load shape is the pattern of demand, or energy use profile, of a customer over a 24 h period. Load shapes are determined by operational schedules and occupancy, and thus have many applications related to understanding drivers of demand and predicting future outcomes.

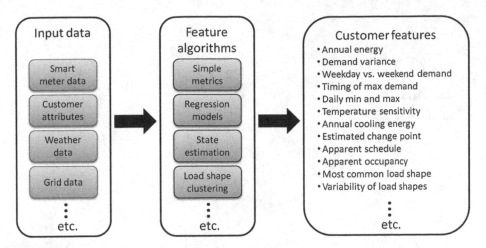

Fig. 1. Diagram of feature extraction, where pre-defined feature algorithms are run against time series meter data, augmented with supporting data, to produce an array of feature values for every customer.

- **Model outputs** of regression, state estimation, end use disaggregation, and other machine learning algorithms, including energy committed to heating and cooling, thermal balance points, occupancy patterns, hourly, day of week, and seasonal variations in consumption.
- **Load shape characteristics**, including clusters of typical consumption patterns, and metrics of load shape variability over time and across customers.

2.2 Interactive Feature Exploration

The VISDOM feature exploration interface allows users to interact with and interpret feature data for large numbers of customers. It is a web-based interactive system, implemented in Python, using Pandas [6] to manage and filter feature data and D3 [7] to create interactive visualizations.

As seen in Fig. 2, the VISDOM interface places customer filtering controls in the left column, visualizations, including maps with zip codes colored by feature values, histograms, scatter plots, cumulative sums, sorted values, and load shapes summaries, in the central column, and visualization controls in the right column. The visual data filters are used to identify specific customers based on their feature values, such as, climate, weather response, baseload, variability, and typical load shapes. Numerical features are filtered using interactive histograms and categorical data is filtered using multi-select boxes. Features drawn from filtered customers are rendered in real time to the interactive data visualizations. They can also be viewed as tabular data or exported as CSV files for further analysis or integration with external systems.

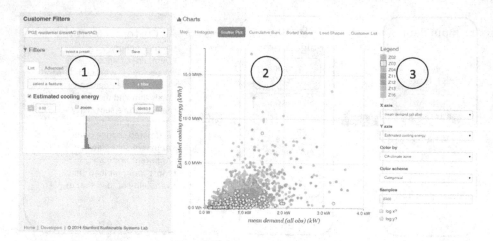

Fig. 2. Illustration of the interactive feature exploration interface. (1) Is the visual filtering interface for selecting a subset of customers with specific feature values, where (a) labels a grey histogram range filter. (2) Is the display area for the selected visualization, a scatter plot in this case, with (c) labeling the other visualizations. (3) Is the legend and the controls specific to the selected visualization, with (b) labeling an interactive feature of the legend.

Figure 2 contains a visualization comparing annual electricity consumption (x-axis) to estimated annual cooling energy (y-axis), colored by California climate zone, using the interactive legend to highlight customers from the central coast (climate zone Z03).

Typical usage moves from left to right in the interface: First, the user defines feature values that identify the group of customers he or she would like to study. Second, the user selects one of the available visualizations of customer features he or she would like to interact with. Finally, the user applies display controls specific to the selected visualization. However, it is expected that users will re-adjust filter controls, cross reference different visualizations, and update visualization control parameters as needed to spot patterns and better understand the underlying customers. Filter settings and entire views, including filter settings, visualization, and visualization settings, can be named and saved for future use or sharing with others.

3   Example Usage

Due to its diverse feature set and flexible interface, the VISDOM tool can be used to study consumption in a variety of contexts. For example: Utilities can use it to tie their infrastructure improvement plans to robust modes of customer demand; Energy Efficiency programs can be focused on the customers best suited to program offers; and city planners can better understand the needs of their citizens. This section provides several examples of VISDOM applied to a data set of 200,000 residential customers in Northern and Central California to illustrate the breadth of potential applications and uses.

3.1   Climate as a Proxy for Cooling

Current best practice for planning air conditioning efficiency programs is to focus on the hottest climates. This sensible approach can potentially overlook significant cooling loads in cooler climates and waste program recruitment resources on very low cooling loads that happen to be in hot climates.

Figure 3a provides a VISDOM map of average cooling intensity by zip code in the service territory of Pacific Gas and Electric, a California-based utility, with the hottest climate zone, CZ13, highlighted with a red outline. Here we can see that CZ13 does indeed contain significant cooling loads, but a histogram of annual cooling energy by customer in that zone, Fig. 3b, reveals a very wide diversity in cooling energy from one customer to the next. With the ability to estimate cooling energy on a per-customer basis, programs could focus on high usage customers, rather than general geography. This would lead to more effective cooling energy reduction and management programs.

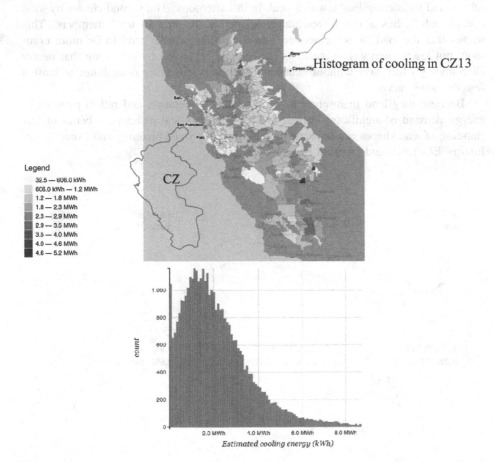

Fig. 3. (a) Map of estimated annual cooling energy for residences in Northern and Central California. (b) Histogram of individual customer annual cooling in the highlighted climate zone, CZ13.

3.2   Load Shape Characterization

Load shapes, or 24 h electricity use profiles, capture within-day variations in household energy consumption that reveal patterns in scheduling and occupancy. VISDOM clusters load shapes by similarity and provides tools for understanding the diversity of load shapes exhibited by individual customers or groups of customers.

The average load shape for each cluster can be thought of as the representative load shape for the whole group. The load shape visualization interface displays the representative load shapes for the clusters that best represent the subset of customers defined by the filter interface.

Figure 4 provides a visualization of the top 6 (by total energy) representative load shapes for residential customers in California's hot CZ13. It can be observed that most of these shapes display significant afternoon or evening peaks, with one exhibiting a secondary morning/mid-day peak. Afternoon/evening peaks are typically driven by the coincidence of occupancy as residents return home from work and school and by cooling loads, which peak in the afternoon. The second cluster by total energy, which has a flat representative shape, is the first in total members. This means that the load shapes classified into the second cluster tend to be more common, but lower energy than the first. This is best explained by observing that nearly all homes go full days without occupants, so every customer contributes at least a few flat load curves.

Because they lend themselves to behavioral interpretation and reflect patterns in energy demand of significant interest to grid operators and planners, a better understanding of load shapes can translate directly into improved planning and execution of Energy Efficiency and Demand Response programs.

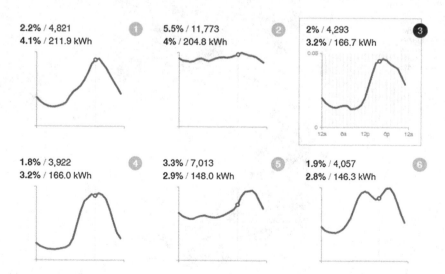

Fig. 4. VISDOM visualization displaying The top 6 load shapes, or daily energy usage profiles, for customers in California's hot climate zone CZ13.

3.3 Segmentation and Targeting

The customer segmentation and targeting features of VISDOM make use of predictive models of customer responses to energy efficiency and demand response programs [8] to identify and rank the best customers (targeting) or groups of customers (segmentation) to approach with a specific offer or incentive. Customer responses can be estimated using expert knowledge and opinion, derived from engineering principles, or based on the outputs of models trained on the observed outcomes of past programs. For example, households estimated to use large amounts of air conditioning based on their meter data would likely have the greatest cooling energy (kWh) and demand (kW) savings from participation in programs that improve the efficiency of or control over air conditioning equipment.

Alternately, the features found in VISDOM can be used as inputs into predictive response models. Features related to temperature sensitivity, cooling energy use, typical patterns of daily energy use, and physical location can be combined with ground-truth program participation and outcome data to generate a propensity score that identifies customers best able to reduce demand during periods when the grid is operating near its physical limits, i.e. when those reductions are most needed and valuable.

Figure 5 illustrates VISDOM's cumulative sum visualization. The cumulative annual cooling energy in climate zone CZ13 is calculated from values sorted from highest to lowest (upper red curve) and then again based on random sampling of the population (lower black curve). At the 25th percentile of customers (dashed vertical

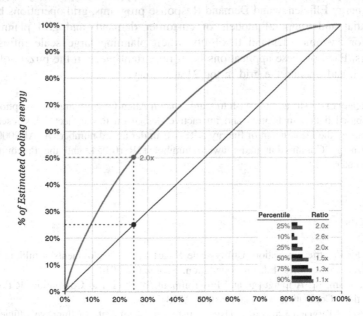

Fig. 5. Cumulative sum of estimated annual cooling for CZ13 sorted from highest to lowest values (upper, red) compared to the cumulative sum of annual cooling selected at random from the population.

line), the sorted cumulative cooling energy is two times the unsorted, indicating a significant potential return on program targeting: 50 % of cooling energy is used by 25 % of the customers, so we could expect that targeted program marketing could provide twice the savings per customer as untargeted.

4 Conclusions

The benefits latent in the extraordinary volume of smart meter data now flowing have only just begun to be realized. We have provided details of design and implementation of VISDOM, a system for extracting meaningful and actionable features from very large samples of smart meter data, including complete samples of customers in a given utility service territory or geographic region. VISDOM allows users to filter, sort and group subsets of customers using feature criteria and to display attributes of filtered customers using generic (i.e. histogram and scatter plot) or task specialized (i.e. cumulative sum and load shape) interactive visualizations.

We have provided examples of how these capabilities can be used to identify and better understand significant variability in cooling loads within hot climates, how customer load shapes (24 h energy use profiles) can be classified into clusters that share similar scheduling and occupancy characteristics, and how the features of individual customers can be used to model their expected response to energy programs so the most responsive customers can be targeted by program recruitment efforts to double program savings.

Collectively, the capabilities of VISDOM can support more precisely targeted and effective Energy Efficiency and Demand Response programs, grid operations based on robust spatial and temporal models of customer demand, and grid planning that accounts for customer demand flexibility when planning large scale infrastructure investments. Each of these applications is an important piece in the puzzle of how to plan, design, and operate the grid in the 21st century.

Acknowledgements. The authors wish to thank Shawn Allen for applying his exceptional skills in browser-based data visualization and interactive design on this project. This research was funded in part by the Department of Energy ARPA-E under award number DE-AR0000018, the California Energy Commission under award number PIR-10-054, and the Precourt Energy Efficiency Center.

References

1. Institute for Electric Innovation, Utility-scale Smart Meter Deployments: Building Block of the Evolving Power Grid, Edison Foundation, September 2014
2. Core, R., Team, R.: A Language and Environment for Statistical Computing. R Foundation for Statistical, Computing, Vienna, Austria (2013)
3. Borgeson, S.: Targeted Efficiency: Using Customer Meter Data to Improve Efficiency Program Outcomes. Dissertation, Berkeley (2013)

4. Albert, A., Rajagopal, R.: Smart meter driven segmentation: what your consumption says about you. IEEE Trans. Power Syst. **28**(4), 4019–4030 (2013)
5. Kwac, J., Flora, J., Rajagopal, R.: Household energy consumption segmentation using hourly data. Smart Grid IEEE Trans. **5**(1), 420–430 (2014)
6. McKinney, W.: Data structures for statistical computing in python. In: Proceedings of the 9th Python in Science Conference, pp. 51–56 (2010)
7. Bostock, M., Ogievetsky, V., Heer, J.: D3: data-driven documents. IEEE Trans. Vis. Comp. Graph. Proc. InfoVis, 2011
8. Kwac, J., Rajagopal, R.: Demand response targeting using big data analytics, pp. 683–690 (2013)

Defining HCI/UX Principles for Urban Environment

Pavel Farkas[✉]

Faculty of Humanities, Charles University in Prague, Prague, Czech Republic
pf@pfarkas.com

Abstract. Interaction design works successfully with several design principles that are widely implemented and used in the community of designers and theoreticians. In this article, the author argues that urban designers and architects who are designing built environment may very well face similar questions and problems as the interaction designers in Human-Computer Interaction (HCI) design. The text sets the design thinking and semiotics of interaction in a large scale and tries to outline the connections between the UX design and urban design for cities we live in. Moreover it targets means of interaction and attempts to encourage designers of to engage in turning our modern cities into more livable, user-friendly and inclusive environments.

Keywords: Architecture · Communication · City · Design thinking · Information · Interaction · Semiotics · Smart city · UX · Wayfinding

1 Introduction

We might tend to use our surroundings without thinking: our primary function in the city is less likely just traveling for pleasure and seeing the built environment: more often we travel to work, school or cultural events. We rush to get to the subway lines before our train departs, we run to the tramway before the door closes or peddle through the intersection before we hit red. Now, let's try to slow down and think about our environment the way we think when designing an interface. Let's see the design behind it, which may let us understand the built environment better, or appreciate the solutions that would otherwise go unnoticed. We may discover solutions that surprise us or enrich us in designing the user interfaces, because even city is supposedly designed with one aim in mind: to provide the inhabitant with an excellent user experience.

In this article, we will point out several conceptual similarities in information and interaction design between the built environment and user interfaces to illustrate the framework of thinking and to show how the philosophical connection between the two entities is being perceived. Further, we will consider a specific area of interaction in the built environment and draft possibilities for evolution within so called smart cities.

The nature of the problem discussed further lays in design thinking, which may be seen as a common ground for both, design of interaction in cities and design of interface interaction. Given that we can use the same terminology to describe problems in the built environment and in the design of interaction, the main research question is

© Springer International Publishing Switzerland 2015
A. Marcus (Ed.): DUXU 2015, Part III, LNCS 9188, pp. 346–356, 2015.
DOI: 10.1007/978-3-319-20889-3_33

whether or not we also can find similar solutions for problematic situations. Aside of precise demarcation of the term of interaction, there is a natural challenge to this problem, constituted by the particular differences of the character of interaction in either environments. But just as it is possible to try to build an ideal city on suggestions introduced by Alexander et al. [1], we may attempt to build a vocabulary used in the sole act of interaction among people and technologies within a built environment.

2   Basic Concepts and Principles

City is a system that works. In ideal conditions, that is. City consists of elements that provide information for a researcher, as well as for the user. Naturally, we can view the terms of information and system from very different perspectives: a Czech professor of information science Jiří Cejpek points out [4] that a person can be understood as a communicatively-information system themselves (...) whose brain processes information as some kind of metabolism. Let's presume that while a researcher may perceive an information gathered within a given city as an element of our knowledge letting us orient in the world, it is quite possible, that we expect our user to knowingly utilize only information that is intended to be read, perceived, processed and followed, as is, e.g. wayfinding information or directive signs. In this article, we will be aiming our attention to information in the physical environment that is not necessarily meant to be perceived by the receiver — instead, to information that is used inadvertently, similarly to the "flow" as described by Cooper et al. [6]. We will try to point out the similarities to the interaction design in HCI to introduce the framework of thinking and further we develop the possible benefit of interaction tenets for modern cities.

3   Basic HCI Design Terms Applied to the Built Environment

Among other authors in the area of design, Donald Norman [13] operates with well established terms for the interaction design praxis. Below, several most common principles will be revised and placed in a viewing angle of different kinds of human interaction within the built environment.

A. Visibility
It is possible to argue that if a visual lead is not present in interaction design, a signified function in fact does not exist for the user. Of course, visibility is desirable in the physical environment as well. Figure 1 shows a street situation in Berlin. The metal construction above the subway (U-Bahn) station on Fig. 1 is well visible from all directions leading to this prominent intersection in Nollendorfplatz and creates a notable node, which is a term used in urban planning by Lynch [12] in 1960. His description of the built environment is still respected today by architects and urban designers and defines basic elements of a city that provide us with clear information clues. In contrast, we may mention Microsoft and their release of the Windows 8 system, with a very few visual leads, leaving the user wondering how to navigate in the system.

Fig. 1. Street situation (left) of Nollendorf station, Berlin, Germany. (Source: Google Maps). Nollendorf U-Bahn station is a significant example of a visibility concept in the urban environment (right).

B. Natural Mapping

Mapping is a technical term meaning the relationship between two things, e.g., between the controls and their movements and the result in the world [4]. It is desirable to design the situation in a way that corresponds with the reality. Compare the situation on Fig. 2 and then imagine what a confusion would this kind of incoherency in design rules bring into the real world, for example, in a subway situation orientation system. The use of natural mapping brings significant benefits for the user in product design, information design, or geography design.

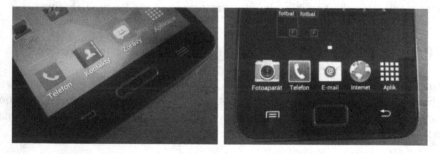

Fig. 2. LG cell phone (left) and Samsung cell phone (right). Note the opposite mapping principle represented by the position of the "back" button.

C. Affordance and constrains

We may think of a physical environment (Fig. 3) when designing an interface (Fig. 3); the philosophy behind it is actually very similar. It only lets us do this much – and not more, often for our own sake. Interaction designers want to prevent users from making mistakes, while designers of environment do the same. Physical barriers are necessary in situations where there is a risk of fall. In other situations, like in a subway, they need to design the borders using a combination of visual and tactile tools.

Fig. 3. Sarasota, Fla., 2015. Compare the constrain (left) forbidding parking in a physical environment to a similar design principle in an interface of a Czech e-mail portal (right). There is a hidden constrain in this web mail client preventing users to click into the corner of the message window. (Source Fig. 3: seznam.cz).

D. Icons and symbols

Symbols or pictograms describe the reality in a simplistic way to prevent us from too much of cognitive load processing. Great graphic precision is not necessary; instead we need the user to choose appropriate direction or action quickly and without taking time to make the decision. Remember the "flow" mentioned earlier [6]. It is necessary that they are executed in a simple yet understandable way and without too much invention. Novelty can prevent the user from understanding the meaning of a given message: trying an innovating approach in every step may create backlash.

Fig. 4. Rome, Italy, 2013. A situational tactile map in center of the city as a conceptual model of the surroundings.

E. Conceptual models

Even complicated devices can be understood better if we give the user a clear clue of how the device works. It is best if we can simply introduce a model which is then followed in the user's mind. The advantage is that we prevent making errors during actions. Let's now think of such models in our cities. They do exist: remember the tourist maps, topographical models or tactile situation maps cast in bronze (Fig. 4).

F. Feedback and confirmation of an action

In most situations, multiple actions of the same kind immediately following each other are not the way we expect the user to behave. Thus, introducing feedback following an action keeps our users certain about their actions. If they believe in the system, they will wait – as long as they have a confirmation of their action (Fig. 5). There are light and sound signals in the real world, some of them we ignore as they are meant to be used by a special group of people (those who are blind, for example), some of them we do not want to understand because we are too busy reading the newspaper or talking on a cell phone. But they do "talk" to us and we interact with them every day.

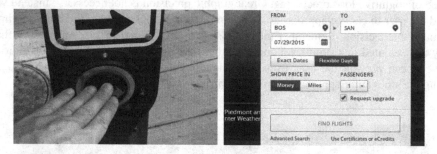

Fig. 5. Feedback of an action as provided by a traffic light in Washington, DC (2010) – red light indicated that the required action was taken. Similarly, on Fig. 5, Delta Airlines website search (2015) indicates with a "blank" color that we just have pressed the "Find Flights" button. (Source Fig. 5: delta.com).

4 Smart Cities and Technodeterminism

Previous examples showed a few of many every day situations that we encounter in both, real world and the design of interfaces. It would be certainly interesting to conduct a research on how interaction designers perceive the cities they live in and how they approve or disapprove the interaction solutions in their physical spaces. Would they change or improve something? In fact, we should ask whether they do.

Progress of the mankind inevitably introduces new elements of everyday life into our environments. Let's perceive them as a whole new layer of information — or as new means of communication, advantages, sources of disturbance, and so on. At the same time, digital technologies and new media flood the markets, supposedly to achieve a marketing success and also to help people live their lives more efficiently and comfortably. In order to be as inclusive as possible, in further text we will be not knowingly disqualifying those inhabitants-users of our cities who are not using personal digital devices, smartphones etc. In harmony with ideals of Jan Gehl [8], the professor of Urban Design program of the Royal Danish Academy of Arts, lets keep a presupposition that cities are here to encourage the idea of all people use (or even enjoy!) the environment, and communicate with each other within it.

With this in mind, one must ask what is the ideal model of our cities in the 21st century? If design can provide he perfect solution for any interaction of a user with their environment, are so called smart cities the ideal solution for the physical world we live in? How can interaction designers contribute for the life quality and what are the challenges that we face today, in the digital age? Is there still room for inexpensive and simple solutions in those smart cities, or are we too fascinated with technology driving us into the abyss of technodeterminism with a questionable functionality? (See Fig. 6) On the other hand, why is it that functional technologies whose positive effect was proven by years of usage, are sometimes disregarded? Driving experience in Vitoria, Spain is highly frustrating and finally leads drivers to totally ignore red traffic signals on the main road. Red lights there come off if no car is present on auxiliary roads, which makes the driving through this town a long and tiring ordeal.

Fig. 6. In 2014, Provincetown, Mass. introduced a solution that is aimed to improve the traffic flow in this popular resort town. Unfortunately, the operator of the largest municipal parking lot has to take a 10-minute walk in order to manually switch the signal indicating the actual situation in the parking lot. That is by switching the electric cord to another outlet.

Many elements of such smart cities are discrete and users hardly notice them at all: sensors in the road to help time the green light at the intersection, sensors in the escalators conserving energy by slowing the speed down when nobody uses the device or even those simple motion sensors that open the door of the hotel for us. But one must ask crucial questions: Who is the designer? What does the term of smart city actually mean for different communities? Do the smart city elements fulfill the basic idea of design: to make the world more usable? There is hope that designer's intentions are not driven by monetary gains, producing redundant technologies. Yet, what if it is possible to argue that the adjective of "smart" may largely be a marketing construct that improves the perceived status of a city — various charts of smart cities exist out there [5], and hopefully they might lead our understanding of which characteristics the communities cherish as key for the "smartness" of a city. From the design perspective, a quest for grasping this understanding may be the most crucial value for future generations.

Designing wayfinding information in complex environments, to mention one example, may be extremely tricky given the structural qualities of the interiors. Dealing with the U-turn is one of the most difficult situations [14] and at Prague airport, there were three different attempts introduced in four years, until one effective solution was found. This reminds us clearly of words of Arthur and Passini [2]: "In planning the layout, [architects and urban planners] are creating the setting and the wayfinding problems future users will have to solve. In articulating the setting, they are providing the users with much of the necessary information to solve the wayfinding problems at hand." Here we have a viable note of design thinking. Arthur and Passini clearly argue that all problems cannot be only approached with placing a wayfinding sign. But we all know the world is not ideal, and having this in mind, we realize that new displaying techniques like the example at Paris CDG airport in Fig. 7 may help to find the way while respecting natural mapping and lowering the cognitive load of a passenger, who is always on the run in such places...

Fig. 7. Paris, France, 2013. A smart solution of a complicated wayfinding situation at Paris CDG Airport uses a projection on the floor immediately after stepping out of the escalators, combined with an animated arrow suggesting the direction of walk.

We should be interested to see where smart interaction design stands among these values and see through the ideology behind user interfaces, just as Lefebvre [11] discusses the ideology behind space relations in cities. Is the ideology we target in this design thinking actually corresponding with the usability principles – and how can we read the city as a system? De Waal [15] is asking even more crucial question: How does our interaction with new media actually change our relationship with cities? Answering this question may get even more complex when we consider the cultural background of our user/inhabitant/visitor: habits and cultural background in general may have effect greater than expected, as Brejcha [3] found out in his study on cross-cultural UX design. There is no reason to avoid this factor in the physical environments as well (see Fig. 8).

Fig. 8. London, UK, 2014. In London Subway, it is customary to walk on the left side, just as it is to drive a car on the surface. On the contrary – in Stockholm, Sweden, many subway elevators heading to the surface are positioned left, while the surface traffic keeps right. It may be the reminder of the fact that the surface traffic there was not changed to the right until 1967 [7], while the subway first opened already in 1950 [9].

5   Consequences of Design Thinking

We may ask what may possible be the advantages of thinking of these and other design principles in both, physical environments and interfaces. Innovation is always driven by such questions. The meaning of the world is largely based on representation and metaphors and new inspiration from situations in either place can always arise. New displaying technologies as well as completely new philosophical approach may find a good use of revised use, as well as reinforcing of solutions already existing. Because – regardless the environment of interaction design – the main objective should always be introducing solutions that minimize the frustration of a user.

The connection between the physical world and interaction design practiced by interaction designers is inevitable. Inhabitants are users at the same time, and it is probably the right time for interaction designers to be employed by cities when hiring architects designing public spaces and buildings to avoid the above frustration in Vitoria just as one in Grand Rapids (Fig. 9).

In this situation, there is virtually no technology involved, and error could be so easily resolved. Systematic solutions involve tenets for to be followed by execution.

Fig. 9. Grand Rapids, MI, 2014. The communication situation that a driver experiences while approaching the bus terminal is rather puzzling and literally trapping.

Such manuals exist for the world of architecture or urban planning, but the author of this paper believes that cities would benefit from such tenets elaborated for the interaction as a separate discipline of public life. For interaction designers, this is a chance for a valuable input resulting in viable and enjoyable lives in our communities.

6   Future Work

In the future work, we tend to focus on a more precisely characterized urban interaction that would frame the area of the interest involving subtle use of technologies. From the interviews with city officials, it is obvious that the trend of city development focused on smart technologies and interaction is very desirable in Prague, the city that the author of this paper calls home. Introduction of added city elements that would match the definition of interaction discussed above has been slow. The Institute of planning and development in Prague published a new Manual for design of public spaces [10] in 2014. It is a detailed file of tenets, but the interaction there is considered mainly as a physical or a social act, i.e., an interaction with city furnishing or among people. There is still some room left for the ambient or cognitive sense of interaction in the current version of this manual. Designing of complex information systems that would deal with design principles, design of information and semiotics of interaction are missing and thus seemingly not defined at all. We am aiming to research, provide and test such tenets with hope that they will be beneficial to inhabitants of a city as well as providing a positive "user experience" to the visitors.

Interaction tenets to be included in further work shall involve:

1. Investigating and defining values of "smartness" for smart cities, while disregarding the trendy-ness of such term, keeping in mind:
2. Principles for implementing discrete technology, and
3. Principles for implementing visible, audible and tactile technology in areas as, but not limited to: mobility and wayfinding, public services, enterprising, emergency services, education, and interaction devices in general.

7 Discussion

In this short text, we tried to illustrate that the principles of interaction design may be considered in the framework of modern cities. Metaphorically, we could speak of a "language" of the city which is used to communicate with its inhabitants. We believe that interaction design has the potential to be viewed as such a mean of communication. Covering the points drafted above may help us set a standard for evaluating the philosophical, anthropological, and sociological basics for cities of the 21th century. It is intriguing to view cities as interfaces or interaction systems which are seen through a prism of qualitative and quantitative research and thus available for user experience testing and evaluation.

References

1. Alexander, C., Sara, I., Murray, S.: A Pattern Language: Towns, Buildings, Construction. Oxford University Press, New York (1977). xliv, 1171 s. ISBN 01-950-1919-9
2. Arthur, P., Romedi, P.: Wayfinding: People, Signs, and Architecture. McGraw-Hill Inc, New York (1992). 238 s. ISBN 0-07-551016-2
3. Brejcha, J.: Cross-Cultural Human-Computer Interaction and User Experience Design: A Semiotic Perspective, p. 187. CRC Press, Boca Raton (2014). ISBN 978-149-8702-577
4. Cejpek, J.: Informace, komunikace a myšlení: úvod do informační vědy. 2. přeprac. vyd. Praha: Karolinum, 233 s. ISBN 80-246-1037-x (2005)

5. Cohen, B.: The 10 Smartest Cities In Europe. Co.Exist: World Changing Ideas And Innovation. 2014 [cit. 2014-10-23]. http://www.fastcoexist.com/3024721/the-10-smartest-cities-in-europe
6. Cooper, A., Robert, R., Dave, C.: About face 3: the essentials of interaction design. [3rd ed.], Completely rev. Wiley Pub., Indianapolis, IN, xxxv, p. 610 ISBN 04-700-8411-1 (c2007)
7. Flock, E., Dagen, H.: The day Sweden switched sides of the road. The Washington Post. Washington, 2012 [cit. 2015-01-08]. http://www.washingtonpost.com/blogs/blogpost/post/dagen-h-the-day-sweden-switched-sides-of-the-road-photo/2012/02/17/gIQAOwFVKR_blog.html
8. Gehl, J.: Life between buildings: using public space, p. 207. Island Press, Washington, DC (2011). ISBN 15-972-6827-5
9. History of Stockholm Subway. Stockholm Subway (c2015). [cit. 2015-01-10]. http://www.stockholmsubway.com/history.html
10. IPR PRAHA. Manuál tvorby veřejných prostranství hlavního města Prahy (2014). [cit. 2014-12-15].   http://manual.iprpraha.cz/uploads/assets/manual_tvorby_verejnych_prostranstvi/pdf/IPR-SDM-KVP_Manual-tvorby-verejnych-prostranstvi.pdf
11. Lefebvre, H., Eleonore, K., Elizabeth, L.: Writings on Cities, p. 250. Blackwell Publishers, Cambridge (1996). vi. ISBN 06-311-9188-7
12. Lynch, K.: The Image of the City. Cambridge: The Technology Press & Harvard University Press (1960)
13. Norman, D.A.: The Design of Everyday Things. 1st Basic paperback, p. 257. Basic Books, New York (2002). xxi. ISBN 04-650-6710-7
14. Okkels, N.: Information design in public transport: Using colors, fonts and advertisement. [personal interview]. December 9th, 2011. Bredgade 45C, Copenhagen, Denmark
15. de Waal, M.: The City as Interface: How Digital Media are Changing the City, p. 208. Publishers, Rotterdam (2014). ISBN 9789462080508

Participatory Explorations on a Location Based Urban Information System

Özge Genç, Damla Çay, and Asım Evren Yantaç[✉]

Arçelik Research Center for Creative Industries, Koç University,
Istanbul, Turkey
{ogencl3,dcayl3,eyantac}@ku.edu.tr

Abstract. In this paper, we share our user research experiences from an ongoing participatory location based urban information system design study. While the geographical information system (GIS) field advanced by means of sensors, data collection and data processing, there is still a limited number of visualization studies. Here, we envision novel solutions that represent spatio-temporal data for effective use in daily life. With this intention in mind, as early stage studies in our research process, we conducted a series of participatory design (PD) workshops together with an ethnographic artifact, a custom sketchbook to identify user scenarios and explore possible visualization techniques. The main objective of the study is to explore new ways of visualizing and interacting with the complex location based data that will provide intuitive yet easier and more effective daily life information for the public.

Keywords: Participatory design · Design research · Journal · Urban information visualization · Spatio-temporal data · Ethnographic research

1 Introduction

Nowadays, location-based information systems' role is progressively gaining importance in our everyday life. With the help of social media applications and mobile technologies (Craig et al., 2002), location based content is being generated easily by the public and substantially used for several purposes such as understanding decision making process about key social, political economic and environmental facts (Porter, 2011). Especially gathering location-based information from local communities is relatively more valuable in order to create sustainable solutions for human needs and improve the quality of life (Elwood, 2008). It is obvious that different approaches such as participatory design (PD), user centered design, ethnographic research methods and participatory geographical information systems (PGIS) have common characteristics in terms of their main aim. Although these practices have been used by different disciplines, it is seen that they share the common ground of understanding the needs of human and coming up with relevant design solutions.

In our ongoing design study, our aim is to make a contribution to the participatory geographical information systems (PGIS) studies by means of novel ideas for information representation and interaction. We have been gathering both content related needs and visualization inspirations from users by conducting PD workshops and

© Springer International Publishing Switzerland 2015
A. Marcus (Ed.): DUXU 2015, Part III, LNCS 9188, pp. 357–367, 2015.
DOI: 10.1007/978-3-319-20889-3_34

individual user input by journal studies in combination. In PGIS studies; more of the participatory approaches can be seen at the information gathering stages, while public involvement has been weak during information visualization stages.

This paper shares our insights from an ongoing research study for exploring new ways of visualization and interaction of spatio-temporal data in daily urban life. Meanwhile we are also looking for sustainable and effective ethnographic data collection methods for spotting intuitive use patterns. With this perspective, our objective is to investigate possible visualization techniques by adopting PD and ethnographic research methods in our study. We envision that these insights may lead us to more sophisticated and effective participatory interactive solutions for interaction with the urban data.

2 Background and Motivation

Throughout the last 50 years, location based data has been elaborately investigated by scholars under the field of Geographical Information System (GIS). Recently, this field has discovered the importance of spatial information analysis (Maguire et al., 1991). Subsequent to spatial information analysis, making explanations and predictions related to spatial information have become much simpler (Clarke, 1997). On the other hand, public knowledge has become an important issue to identify the needs of locals (Elwood, 2008). With the help of volunteered geographic information (VGI) (Goodchild, 2007; Sui, 2008), GIS has been shifted to a more democratic approach. This is because VGI methods provide an environment where the public can be much more engaged with the production of collaborative geographical knowledge. Interactive online instruments such as Google Maps and Open Street Map create open access for the public to build and share their own maps.

While location-based applications are becoming widespread, users' needs grow and become diverse. A variety of personas use these systems and a huge number of information layers appear on maps. This situation reveals the need for studies on geographic information visualization techniques. Moreover, new contexts of usage such as mobile phones, big screens or dual screens create challenges in both visualization techniques and interaction models. One of the most commonly seen participatory geographic information visualization technique is attaching pins on the maps (Ushahidi Crisis Maps; Global Transition to a New Economy). Color-coding, using attributions of visuals elements, such as circles, squares, lines, using textures, and 3D modeling are other ways of representing geographic information on map (Roth et al., 2010; Fifa Development Globe).

An important issue in location-based information visualization studies is the lack of public participation in the evaluation process of visualization techniques. One of the instruments of public participation in design is cultural probe method. Cultural probes are a range of physical objects which participants interact with. These objects help us to understand user needs and behaviors. Probes can be notebooks, postcards or maps (Gaver et al., 1999). A cultural probe even can be a wearable prototype where direct user feedback is collected, like a wearable recorder to collect city sounds (Gaye et al., 2004). Some geographical visualization techniques were evaluated by conducting user studies (Dockerty et al., 2006; Lange, 2001; Appleton and Lovett, 2003). In addition, some researchers have done collaborative geographical visualization sessions to design much more usable systems (Brewer et al., 2000). Since the geographic visualization topics are varied and complex and technology use changes quickly, we believe that sustainable methods for learning about user mental models and user needs, as well as the need for public engagement to the visualization process is crucial. GIS tools, such as Arc View, have dominantly been used in the field of participatory GIS. These tools would be effective in order to visualize geospatial information but there would also be several usability problems due to the similarities of these kinds of software.

3   Method

With the perspective above, our main approach in this study is to explore how people intuitively perceive their presence and movement on the map, how they visualize it and how participatory methods can be used for learning from the users about these two questions. For this purpose, we collaborated with people from different design domains with a series of participatory design and journal studies in 2014. Here, in this paper, we discuss five consecutive stages (Fig. 1); workshop 1 (user needs + visualization), workshop 2 (conceptualization + visualization), workshop 3 + journal study (visualization), interview (user needs) and a table top game (mental model + information architecture).

3.1   First Stage: Workshop 1 for User Needs and Visualization

All the process started by planning a series of design workshops which were announced to designers as exploratory studies on spatio-temporal data visualization about the city and how people interact and perceive this information within their daily life.

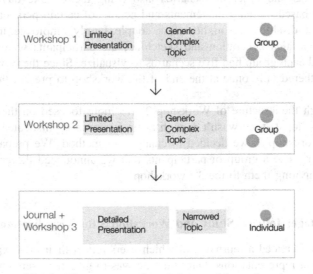

Fig. 1. The structure of workshops and journal study

Workshop 1 was announced online through an art and design institution, SALT Istanbul. Five participants who from different design backgrounds like interaction design, architecture, urban planning attended the workshop. After a presentation about data visualization, we briefed the participants about the "Design Network of Istanbul" case study. After a card sorting session to discuss about the content and information architecture of given topics, we separated them into two groups to work on issues related to data visualization (time, navigation, route, action). Working individually for a while, and then brainstorming as a group, teams gathered and presented their ideas to each other, discussed and voted for one of the ideas. Our aim in voting was to see if the competition engages participants more or not, and it ended up being time consuming and left less time for visualizing ideas. At the end, two teams presented their final ideas.

Even though there were some interesting ideas pointed out like the effects of day and night change in the city on human movement and how to visualize them; the results were not satisfying in terms of detail. Our insight from this study is that; the workshop content was too loaded for a one day practice and the participants didn't engage enough in the topic presented.

3.2   Second Stage: Workshop 2 for Conceptualization and Visualization

With a similar agenda and based on our previous experience, we held a second workshop at Koc University. The workshop was announced online to networks of design domain. Five participants; four students and one graduate attended. The workshop which started with our presentation where we briefly explained what data visualization is and showed relevant examples of it as well as the output of the first workshop. After the presentation, we asked the participants to visualize spatio-temporal information for scenarios that were presented to them. Discussions included personas and different scenarios also using factors like day/night. These scenarios were based on daily movements and actions of certain personas in the city; such as a tourist, disabled person, homeless, couple, family, employee, tradesman and local tourist. For idea generation and sketching, the participants were divided into two groups and each group had five scenarios to visualize. Since there was no voting, two groups gathered only once at the end of the workshop to present their ideas and discuss.

Even though the structure of Workshop 2 was more focused on the visualization part than Workshop 1, time wasn't enough again for more sophisticated visualization ideas. After Workshop 2, we decided to change our method. We prepared a journal (Fig. 2) and sent it to a group of participants that we announced the previous workshops, before inviting them to the 3rd workshop.

3.3   Third Stage: Journal Study and Workshop 3 for Visualization

At this stage, we created a journal with which users reflect their city experience with visual and verbal representations. Our aim here was to give the users enough time to

Fig. 2. Journals design for the participatory studies

intuitively reflect how they perceive and represent their presence and movement in the city based on their own daily experiences. There were three important questions that we were interested in this study; (1) what are the things that people choose to record?; (2) how do they visualize them?; (3) How do they perceive their presence in the city?

Journal Structure. The Journal, an A5 sized notebook, which the user can carry around while travelling, is designed with enough pages for seven days (Fig. 2). For each day, there are several parts allocated for different needs. First, there is a grayscale map of Istanbul and a blank page for free drawing. Then, there is a striped page for the user to write their experience. Finally, there is a page with questions, aiming to guide the user to think about some of the issues in the city; such as "Were there any hitches around the city?" or "What type of information did you need to achieve?"

We announced the journal study to a group of the previous workshop participants and other people with design background. During this period, we announced a third workshop. One of the main objectives is to learn about the journal users' experience with this new medium and discuss them.

Workshop 3. 9 participants, mostly from interactive media design field, attended the third workshop. The workshop lasted for 6 h and consisted of three parts; (1) presentation about visualization methods and discussion about the journal, (2) journal users' experience sharing, (3) users' selection of topics and their individual working process on visualization. The workshop started with a detailed and structured presentation about data visualization, followed by briefing on the journal. In the second part, the participants who had the journal shared their experiences. Some of the journal users addressed that they started to pay more attention to their surrounding while completing the journal. In this part, the participants, who didn't have the journal, had problems with engaging. Later on, we shared our user scenarios from the previous workshops. This was followed by a discussion and idea generation session about user needs. Afterwards, each participant selected a topic to visualize individually. Some of these topics were; historical transformation of the city, sounds of the city, events in one hour, empty areas of the city. For each topic that the participants chose, they determined 3 to 5 types of information to visualize. We imposed this limitation to participants to make them focus on visualization rather than information structure. This individual sketching session lasted for one hour. After an hour, participants presented their work and discussed their ideas all together.

3.4 Interview for User Needs

While we were conducting visualization exploration studies with designers, we also had a parallel process of long discussion sessions with the participants. However, non-designers' perspective had to be included in the study as well. Therefore we executed in-depth interviews with relatively a more heterogeneous group. The outline of the interviews was based on citizen engagement in city governance, decision-making and planning. The aim of the study was to investigate citizen activities related to social life in the city. In order to have a heterogeneous group, we contacted with political activists, journalists, city planners, students, academicians, shopkeepers, cyclists, health activists, and filmmakers and so on. Thereby we had 17 interviews. During the selection of participants, we applied snowball-sampling method. With the help of these interviews we had considerably detailed information about social movements and activities in Istanbul. We understood how and in which way people use media for taking part in the urban life, what kind of information and actions should be included. We used these insights in the next stage as user needs and mental model.

3.5 Tabletop Game for Mental Model and Information Architecture

As mentioned earlier, the intention is not only the visualization, yet how people interact with this information. Thus, apart from all the above mentioned visualization and user need explorations, we also questioned how people interact, discuss and ideate on maps. With this in mind, we conducted a custom tabletop game for citizen engagement discussions (Fig. 3). Aim of the game was to observe the user experience while citizens of a city partake in the discussion on urban issues, using computer and online-like actions such as discover, share, archive and so on. The context of the discussion was one of our on-going studies on building a citizen engagement support system application.

Fig. 3. A scene from the table top game

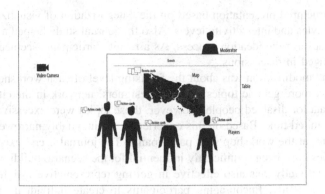

Fig. 4. Tabletop Game Setup

Briefly, the game was based on events and incidents happening in a city. Thus it was highly related to storytelling. We conducted three game sessions with minimum 4 players and a moderator in each (Fig. 4). Sessions were played around a table. In the center of the table we placed an empty Istanbul map in order to motivate the players to make discussions on map. We collected a series of real events that were related to both public and private city life, such as; a large fire of a historical building, social movements, new regulations on public transport. On each game, we opened 10 event cards one by one and gave five discussion minutes to the players. Each player had a set of action cards and they were asked to make actions with those cards based on their preference to react to the event. The action cards were built based on a previous in-depth interview study that we had conducted with 17 participants. The cards were; see, share, discover, disseminate, archive, create, interpret, argument, story, map, idea, report, group, petition, crowd funding and two jokers. Within 5 min for each event, players discussed and conducted their actions about the event.

The game acted as a useful tool to understand interaction models and build information architecture for location-based systems. With the help of the tabletop game we found an interaction pattern and applied it to our citizen engagement support system design. The result of the game sessions is an issue that requires further discussion; for this reason, we will share our findings in another paper that will be on location based citizen engagement tools.

4   Insights and Discussion

In this section, we share our insights from above-mentioned participatory exploration studies; (a) the use of workshops; (b) user needs; (c) visualization inspirations.

Regarding the evolution of workshop structures, observation of the participants' attitudes and reflections were effective in obtaining beneficial results. The first modification was about providing preliminary information for location-based visualization methods. We prepared a presentation about different methods at the beginning of each workshop as a briefing. Compared to the first two, in Workshop 3, we presented a much more structured presentation based on the categorization of visualization topics, visualization styles and interactivity levels. Also the journal study helped a lot for users to be more ready for the ideation process. As a result, participants seemed to be more willingly engaged in discussions.

The second modification was about the focusing level of each workshop. First two workshops had more generic topics such as; designers' network in the city or visualizing urban data for disabled people. However, these topics were excessively complex to study at a limited time. Based on this experience, we inevitably narrowed down and identified topics at the workshop with participants. The journal users' experiences and their true stories have been significantly influential for the scenario building process. In addition, journal study was also effective in getting representative insights about the execution of the study. Encouraging participants to create individual visual stories about daily urban life has also been effective in order to reflect more creative visualization concepts about their individual and fictional urban experiences (Fig. 5).

Apart from reflections on the PD workshop methodology, we also gained some insights about alternative user needs for urban data systems. Participants had discussing on concepts such as; spatio-temporal data about day and night change, facades of buildings as information providers, detailed information about pedestrians or urban cycle riders, transportation systems, public sphere information, environmental factors (such as noise, acoustics, waste, animal life), social issues (such as language and immigration), social and cultural events effecting the urban life, historical change of the city landscape and plan.

Although with these early studies we predominantly collected insights regarding user needs, we were also able to gather some ideas related with visualization (Fig. 6). The prominent visualization inspirations have some common features such as; color-coding, metaphoric visualization, texture usage and attributes of lines or dots. To identify different types of information (such as density, activity, pace), locations and

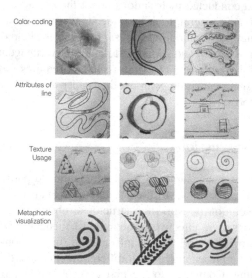

Fig. 5. Visualization sketches from PD workshops

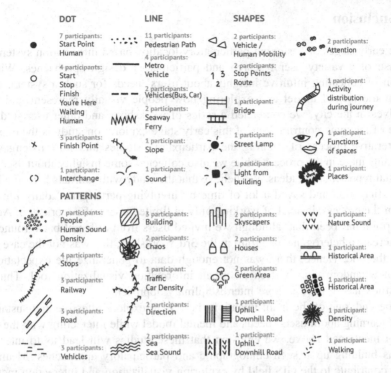

Fig. 6. Chart of visual representations from journals and workshops

actions, participants used color attributes such as; hue, saturation or alpha. Discrete geometric shapes, predominantly circles have been used to visualize human movements while in contrast; repeated amorphous shapes have been used to visualize vehicle movements. Obstacles have been visualized by patterns such as; broken lines, curved lines, zigzags and jagged lines based on their impact. Metaphoric visualization techniques have been used for noise and movement visualization. Density, place attributes and states have been visualized by using textures.

After we created an outline of the visual representation patterns, we categorized most of the visual elements from journals and workshops; into dots, lines, shapes and patterns (Fig. 6). As Bertin suggests (1983) these are basic and commonly used elements in the area of location based visualizations and maps. We looked into the visual characteristics of each element and what they were meant to stand for by the participant. After we sorted and analyzed the visual information from the journals and workshops, we built a chart. This chart contained the most commonly used elements by the participants. It also contained uncommon and remarkable representation ideas. The numbers at the top of each element indicates how many participants used that visual element. Location based visualization in relation to city context is one of our main research topic as a design research group. City by its nature is a multi-layered and complex phenomenon. In these studies, our aim is to reach self-represented visual and interaction styles that particularly coexist with the city phenomenon.

5   Conclusion

In these early stages of designing participatory location based information systems, we made use of a variety user research and participatory design approaches. With the intention of collecting intuitive insights about users' needs for such a system, understanding the mental model and exploring how people visually represent and locate themselves in the city, we conducted a series of workshops and other user studies.

One of the main contributions of this early stage exploration study is the evolution of an iterative process of running the participatory studies and how to engage the participants more in the process while we also collected some insights about user needs and visual representation ideas. We believe that the study with journals helped a lot for more participation and saved a lot of time by involving participants' daily life experience in the process, instead of working only in limited hours of a workshop. Another critical point has been that, although we invited users from different backgrounds and tried to create a heterogeneous group in the 3rd Workshop, this was not the case in the 1st and the 2nd. Hence, there was not enough data to generalize the expectations or needs of a random citizen from an urban information visualization tool. Thus, the whole study has to have a more interdisciplinary approach.

In the end, one of the main intentions here is to explore effective and sustainable ways of learning about users' needs and mental model while interacting with the urban data. As mentioned above, we envision that these studies will lead us to interactive solutions building upon such ethnographic and participatory approaches. Meanwhile we also contribute to the GIS field by exploring visualization and interaction methods. We are now planning to detail the studies with more use of journals that incorporates with interactive tools and making use of other artifacts for pre-workshop activities recruiting more diverse user backgrounds. At the same time, we are also developing prototypes to evaluate the previously collected ideas.

Acknowledgements. We would like to thank all the designers and design students who were involved in the PD workshops; Hande Özusta for the presentation structure and archiving; SALT-Galata for providing space for the workshops, Yağmur Gökçe and Başak Sucuka for proof reading; Hüseyin Kuşçu for interactive prototype development. Some of this study is connected to a Koç University, Seed Grant Funded project.

References

Appleton, K.J., Lovett, A.A.: GIS-based visualisation of rural land- scapes: defining 'sufficient' realism for environmental decision making. Landsc. Urban Plan **65**, 117–131 (2003)

Bertin, J.: Semiology of Graphics: Diagrams, Networks, Maps. ESRI Press, Milwaukee (1983)

Brewer, I., MacEachren, A.M., Abdo, H., Gundrum, J., Otto, G.: Collaborative geographic visualization: Enabling shared understanding of environmental processes. In: IEEE Symposium on Information Visualization, InfoVis 2000, pp. 137–141. IEEE (2000)

Clarke, K.: Getting Started With Geographic Information Systems. Prentice Hall, Upper Saddle River (1997)

Craig, W., Harris, T., Weiner, D. (eds.): Community participation in geographic information systems. Taylor & Francis, London (2002)

Dockerty, T., Lovett, A., Appleton, K., Bone, A., Sünnenberg, G.: Developing scenarios and visualisations to illustrate potential policy and climatic influences on future agricultural landscapes. Agric. Ecosyst. Environ. **114**(1), 103–120 (2006)

Elwood, S.: Volunteered geographic information: future research directions motivated by critical, participatory, and feminist GIS. GeoJournal **72**(3–4), 173–183 (2008)

Fifa Development Globe. Retrieved March 15, 2014. http://devglobe.fifa.com/

Gaver, B., Dunne, T., Pacenti, E.: Design: cultural probes. Interactions **6**(1), 21–29 (1999)

Gaye, L., Holmquist, L.E.: In duet with everyday urban settings: a user study of sonic city. In: New interfaces for musical expression, pp. 161–164 (2004)

Global Transition To A New Economy. Retrieved March 15, 2014. http://www.gtne.org/

Goodchild, M.: Citizens as sensors: The world of volunteered geography. GeoJournal **69**, 211–221 (2007)

Lange, E.: The limits of realism: perceptions of virtual landscapes. Landsc. Urban Plan **54**, 163–182 (2001)

Maguire, D.J., Goodchiled, M., Rhinds, D.: An overview and definition of GIS. Geogr. Inf. Syst. Principals Appl. **1**, 9–20 (1991)

Porter, J.R.: Context, location, and space: the continued development of our 'geo-sociological' imaginations. Am. Sociologist **42**(4), 288–302 (2011)

Roth, R.E., Woodruff, A.W., Johnson, Z.F.: Value-by-alpha Maps: an alternative technique to the cartogram. Cartographic J. **47**(2), 130 (2010)

Sui, D.: The wikification of GIS and its consequences: or Angelina Jolie's new tattoo and the future of GIS. Comput. Environ. Urban Syst. **32**, 1–5 (2008)

Ushahidi Crisis Maps. Retrieved March 15, 2014. http://blog.ushahidi.com/2011/04/20/crisis-mapping-japan/

Diffusion of Feedback: Perceptions and Adoption of Devices in the Residential Market

Beth Karlin[1(✉)], Angela Sanguinetti[2], Nora Davis[1],
Kristen Bendanna[1], Kristen Holdsworth[3], Jessie Baker[4],
David Kirkby[5], and Daniel Stokols[1]

[1] School of Social Ecology, University of California, Irvine 300 Social Ecology I,
Irvine, CA 92697-7075, USA
bkarlin@uci.edu
[2] Plug-in Hybrid and Electric Vehicle Research Center, University of California,
Davis West Village, 1590 Tilia Street, Davis, CA 95616, USA
[3] UCLA Institute of the Environment and Sustainability, La Kretz Crossing
Suite 300, Los Angeles, CA 90039, USA
[4] Office of Sustainability, New York University, 285 Mercer Street, 6th Floor,
New York, NY 10003, USA
[5] Department of Physics and Astronomy, University of California, Irvine 4129
Frederick Reines Hall, Irvine, CA 92697-4575, USA

Abstract. Providing households with energy feedback is widely promoted as a conservation strategy and its effectiveness has been established in field studies. However, such studies actively recruit participants and little is known about naturalistic consumers. Despite hundreds of products emerging, few have taken hold in the market. Diffusion of innovation is a theory of technology adoption that details both the general process by which innovation spreads as well as the individual process of technology adoption. The current study analyses survey data from 836 individuals through a diffusion framework to assess the current and potential market of energy feedback. Questions related to knowledge and perceptions of feedback reveal important insights about customer acceptance and statistical comparison of adopters and non-adopters identify key characteristics related to adoption. Implications for the design and marketing of feedback technologies are discussed.

Keywords: Sustainability · Feedback · Energy · Usability user experience

1 Introduction

Residential energy feedback has been highlighted as a promising strategy to promote energy conservation. Over 100 empirical studies testing feedback have been conducted over the past 40 years, with reviews finding average energy savings of 8-12 % [4–6, 17]. Effectiveness has been found to vary based on both on the way feedback is provided as well as to whom it is provided [11], yet there has been little investigation

© Springer International Publishing Switzerland 2015
A. Marcus (Ed.): DUXU 2015, Part III, LNCS 9188, pp. 368–379, 2015.
DOI: 10.1007/978-3-319-20889-3_35

into the ideal consumer of residential energy feedback or differences in the adoption, experience, and outcomes of different types of feedback.

Stern [27] observes that the impact of any climate-related action can be expressed by the equation $1 = tpn$, where I is total impact (carbon reduction); t is technical potential (reduction per single action); p is the plasticity of the action (proportion of individuals that can be induced to act); and n is the total number of individuals in the population. Research has been building a case for the technical potential of feedback, but largely neglecting the issue of its behavioral plasticity.

This paper examines the plasticity of residential energy feedback using a diffusion of innovation framework. We will introduce the framework, along with relevant literature on each step of the innovation-decision process and present findings from an online survey of active feedback adopters. Finally, implications of this research for the design and marketing of residential energy feedback will be discussed.

2 Literature Review: The Innovation-Decision Process

Diffusion of innovation is a theory of technology adoption that details the general process by which an innovation spreads and the personal process by which an individual learns about, assesses, and adopts or rejects an innovation, called the innovation-diffusion process [24]. An innovation is an idea, practice, or object perceived as new by an individual or community. It matters little if the innovation is "objectively"; the perceived newness determines its innovativeness. Groups of items or products can also be considered an innovation. A *technology cluster* consists of one or more distinguishable elements of technology that are perceived as being closely interrelated (e.g., residential energy feedback).

The innovation-decision process describes how an individual (or other decision-making unit) passes from first knowledge of an innovation (knowledge stage) to forming an attitude toward the innovation (persuasion stage), to a decision to adopt or reject (adoption stage), to use of the innovation (implementation stage), and finally to continue or discontinue use (confirmation stage). Individual characteristics and communications channels influence each of these five stages. Individual characteristics include personal and household demographics and general attitudes and values. Communication channels are interpersonal or mass media sources by which consumers learn about, receive evaluative messages about, or acquire the technology. Diffusion of Innovation has been discussed with regard to energy conservation [26], yet has not been systematically evaluated. This section will review literature related to the stages of the innovation-decision process for energy feedback.

2.1 Knowledge

Lack of consumer awareness and knowledge is cited as a barrier to feedback adoption [29]. However, there is little empirical research on knowledge and awareness of feedback among consumers, let alone systematically investigates this barrier. A recent market-scoping study found that just 10 % of individuals are very familiar with smart home products and 62 % are not familiar at all [19].

2.2 Persuasion

Since most energy efficiency studies actively recruit participants to receive feedback, little is know about active adopters (i.e., individuals who have actively and independently adopted feedback) and their attitudes toward feedback products. Liikenan [14] identified three types of motivation for adopting a load monitor: (1) determining the "truth" about home energy use; (2) identifying energy-intensive appliances; and (3) acquiring information on a single new or suspicious appliance. Other studies that inquired about motivations for using feedback among recruited participants found environmental concern ranked second to financial savings [9, 20].

2.3 Decision

The speed with which an innovation is adopted is called the rate of adoption. Rogers [24] specifies five categories of adopters: (1) innovators, (2) early adopters, (3) early majority, (4) late majority, and (5) laggards. Few studies have characterized these categories in terms of individual characteristics. Research suggests that the feedback adopters are largely male and belong to a two-adult household; education and age varied widely [9, 14]. Positive attitudes toward energy conservation [13] and past conservation behavior [2] have been found to predict feedback use among recruited study participants, but another study found no significant differences between study participants and a control group in terms of energy conservation awareness, commitment, or behavior [28]. No study to-date has systematically investigated trends in where feedback products are acquired (communication channels) or which products are adopted and many of these studies involve products that are not even commercially available.

2.4 Implementation

Problems with usability have been reported, mostly pertaining to the display of information. Mail/email feedback was reported to be unclear and not useful [23], in-home display users reported difficulty reading and interpreting numerical information and graphs provided [1, 9], and users of load monitors reported accessibility issues with certain appliances (e.g., refrigerator) whose size would block information displayed by the device [14]. Additional comments mentioned difficulties with installation, general loss of interest, and a lack of desire to change behavior [22].

2.5 Confirmation

User satisfaction has been high across feedback types. Participants report that feedback improves both their knowledge about and behavior towards energy conservation. Knowledge gains include a general increase in awareness of energy use patterns [1, 8]; learning that their energy use was either more [16] or less [9] than expected; and specific knowledge about how to reduce energy use [11, 18].

2.6   Limitations of Feedback Adoption Research

Almost all studies to-date have recruited participants to use feedback. Since widespread use requires market adoption, analysis of active adopters is vital to understanding the diffusion of this technology cluster. While over 200 feedback products are commercially available [10], less than a dozen have been tested in published studies and few have compared different product types, leaving gaps in our understanding of actual use in the market. Critical data, such as how and where users have learned about and acquired feedback, cannot be collected in experiments.

The literature review sheds light on several aspects of energy feedback diffusion, but not comprehensively or systematically linked to the innovation-decision process in a way that can broadly advance our understanding of how feedback technology is adopted in the wider marketplace. The current study, which reports results of a survey of naturalistic adopters and non-adopters of feedback, investigates multiple aspects of the adoption process in a diffusion of innovation framework.

3   Method

Data were gathered through an online survey of 838 individuals in 2010. The survey took approximately 15 min to complete and respondents were entered into a raffle for a $50 gift certificate to Amazon.com. A purposive sample of potential feedback users was recruited online via email, Facebook, and listservs. About half (53 %) found out about the survey through a personal email and the rest were recruited via listserv, website, or newsletter. Respondents were identified as *adopters* if:

1. The individual responded that s/he every used feedback
2. At least one open-ended question concerning feedback was answered.
3. The reported product was used in the home.[1]

Among the 836 survey respondents, 86 respondents met our inclusion criteria. The remainder of the sample constitutes the comparison group, *non-adopters.*

3.1   Measures

Data were collected as part of a residential energy survey, which was designed to address energy conservation behavior and its predictors and use of residential energy feedback devices. The current paper presents results from analyses of the last part of the survey (i.e., use of residential energy feedback devices) as well as demographic and psychological data. The variables examined in this study are described below:

- **Feedback Awareness and Perceptions.** Participants were presented with a definition of feedback and asked if they were aware of feedback in general and/or any specific products and their general impressions of feedback. Fixed option items inquired after reasons for not adopting feedback (e.g., *too expensive; did not know*

---

[1] If the product was unrecognizable or unspecified, subsequent responses related to energy use.

they existed) and communication channels that might influence their likelihood of feedback (e.g., *available at my local drugstore or supermarket*; *provided by my utility company*).

- **Feedback Adopters.** Participants were asked whether they had used a feedback device. If they said yes, they were asked a series of open-ended questions about the product and their experiences with it. These questions were designed to inquire about the product(s) used and address three general topics of interest: adoption (how, where, and why they obtained feedback), usability (likes and dislikes about the use of feedback), and outcomes (changes in knowledge and/or behavior due to use of feedback). If the respondent had used more than one feedback product, s/he was asked to answer these questions separately for each product.

- **Individual Characteristics.** Demographic, housing, and psychological variables were included in the survey to characterize the general sample and to compare adopters with non-adopters. Demographic items included gender, age, race, marital status, political affiliation, education, and income. Housing characteristics included housing type (detached house vs. apartment/other) and homeownership (own vs. rent). Psychological variables included: (1) a three-item environmental concern scale; a single item to assess bill consciousness; a two-item social norm scale; and three sets of two-item scales to assess motivational factors (environmental, financial, and social motivation) related to energy conservation.

4 Results

Data were analyzed using a mixed-methods approach. Individual characteristics of adopters ($n = 86$) and non-adopters ($n = 749$) were compared quantitatively via independent t-tests. Descriptive statistics and qualitative analysis (open coding followed by axial coding and derivation of common themes) were used to analyze responses related to innovation-decision stages and communication channels.

4.1 Knowledge Stage

Looking at responses about respondents' awareness of energy feedback products, they were about equally split between being completely unaware that feedback existed (37 %), being generally aware of the existence of feedback, but not aware of a specific feedback (35 %), and being aware of at least one specific product (27 %). Of those who were aware of one or more specific feedback products, 38 % had actively adopted or uses one, constituting approximately 10 % of the overall sample. We remind the reader that this sample is likely over-representative of feedback awareness and adopters due to our sampling strategy (see above).

When asked where they "found out" about each product, 24 feedback adopters indicated social means, including friends and family (17) and environmental groups (4); 21 indicated utilities; and 15 indicated a work/professional context. Additional sources of exposure included online, retail stores, magazine and newspaper articles, and displays at energy fairs/events. Environmental, or "green" sources were reported across exposure categories; these included environmental groups (5), renewable energy events (e.g., conference, fair) (3), energy audit (3), and "green" stores (2).

4.2 Persuasion Stage

When asked about general impressions of energy feedback, 42 % reported positive impressions (e.g., *wonderful idea*). 48 % responses were coded as ambivalent (e.g., *assume they make sense since utilities are promoting them*), and 10 % reported negative impressions (e.g., *doesn't seem necessary*). Many participants responded with conditional statements, stating that feedback may not be valuable *unless it is* cheap, easy to use, effective, available everywhere, etc. Non-adopters were prompted about reasons for not adopting and factors that might influence adoption. The top three reasons for not adopting were related to knowledge; additional responses included those related to time or not seeing personal benefits (Table 1). When asked about factors likely to influence adoption, the most frequent response was "available at my local drugstore or supermarket", followed by "provided by my utility company" and "somebody to help me install/use the device".

Feedback adopters were questioned further regarding their reasons for adopting. The most common reasons pertained to desire for knowledge about energy use. Analyses revealed a distinction between *tracking* and *learning*. Those motivated by *tracking* reported an interest in ongoing information about home energy use (*track energy use and compare over time more easily*). Those motivated by learning reported an interest in acquiring discrete, static facts about energy use (*trouble shoot inefficient devices; see what energy use was on a plug load*). Other reported motivations included curiosity (15), work-related reasons (9), saving energy (5), saving money (4), and because the product was free or on sale (6). None of the responses noted environmental motivations.

Table 1. Reasons for not adopting residential energy feedback

Reason	Percentage
Did not know that they existed	44 %
Did not know where to buy them	27 %
Did not know how to install/set up	18 %
Already conserving energy	16 %
Never got around to it	15 %
Too expensive	11 %
No time to install/set up	9 %
No benefit in using	5 %
Conserving energy is not a priority	2 %

4.3   Decision Stage

Type of Feedback Used. The 86 respondents reported using a total of 99 feedback products (12 reported using more than one product). They are categorized by the feedback types introduced in Karlin, Ford, & Squiers [10], as follows.

The most frequently reported type of feedback (55) were *load monitors*. Specific products reported include *Kill-A-Watt (42), Watts Up (4),* and *Square D PowerLogic (1)*. Five did not specify a product and three indicated *self-monitoring* their meter. Fifteen people reported using *in-home displays*. Specific devices reported include *The Energy Detective (TED, 9), PowerCost Monitor (2), Home Energy Cost Monitor (1), Wattson (1), ampere meter (1)* and a computer display of his wind turbine. Twelve people reported receiving feedback via an *information platform*. Specific reported products include *utility website (6), utility bill (3), Google PowerMeter (1)* and estimated feedback [4, 17] via a *online carbon footprint calculator* and a *Wattbott*. Two people reported using *energy-management networks*. Specific devices reported include *Plugwise (1)* and *Green Switch (1)*.

An additional category for *HVAC* was included in this analysis. Although they do not meet the definition of *energy* feedback, respondents reported them as feedback and referred to information provided on other home parameters (e.g., temperature) in their responses. Since we are interested in subjective user experience, they were included in the sample. Specific products reported include *automated thermostats (5), thermal sensors (4), Hobo Data Loggers (3),* and *home thermometers (1)*. Specific type of feedback used was unidentifiable for two respondents. One reported being unsure of the device was and the other indicated using a prototype.

Individual Characteristics. Independent sample t-tests revealed several differences between feedback adopters and non-adopters. Table 2 presents descriptive statistics for demographic variables. Feedback adopters were significantly more likely than non-users to be male (t = 4.14, p < .001), married (t = 2.52, p = .013), and homeowners (t = 5.73, p < .001). Feedback adopters were also significantly older ($t = 3.34, p = .001$), more liberal (t = 2.36, p = .019), higher-income (t = 2.64, p < .01), and more educated (t = 1.96, p = .05) than non-users. The only demographic variable that was not associated with feedback adoption was race (t = 1.38, p = .170).

Feedback adopters were significantly higher than non-adopters on environmental concern ($t = 3.74, p < .001$) and bill consciousness ($t = 2.09, p = .020$). Adopters were *less* motivated by financial considerations ($t = 3.40 p = .001$) and more motivated by environmental considerations ($t = 3.36 p = .001$). No significant differences were found for social norms ($t = 1.36 p = 176$) or social motivation ($t = 1.05 p = .295$).

Communications Channels. The most prevalent source of feedback acquisition was the Internet (29 %), followed by friend or family (14 %) and utility (14 %), then store (13 %), other (12 %), and manufacturer (11 %); 7 % did not recall. A recurring theme of borrowing devices emerged across acquisition categories. Two thirds of products obtained via social means (10) were borrowed. Respondents also reported borrowing devices from utility companies (2), the library (1), and the workplace (1). The most commonly borrowed products were less expensive real-time plus devices (e.g. Kill A Watt, which currently costs about $20) (Table 3).

Table 2. Demographic/housing characteristics of adopters and non-adopters

	Adopters	Non-adopters
Gender[***]	46 % female	70 % female
	54 % male	30 % male
Age[**]	45.5 years	39.9 years
Race	80 % Caucasian	82 % Caucasian
	1 % Hispanic	7 % Hispanic
	8 % Asian	6 % Asian
	1 % African-American	2 % African-American
	10 % Other/Decline	3 % Other/Decline
Marital status[*]	65 % married	51 % married
	35 % not married	49 % not married
Political affiliation[a*]	3.96	3.67
Education	18.0 years	17.4 years
Income[*]	$106,000	$88,000
Homeownership[**]	83 % own	57 % own
	17 % rent	43 % rent

[*] $p < .05$. [**] $p < .01$. [***] $p < .001$.

[a] Scale ranged from 1 = Extremely Conservative to 5 = Extremely Liberal.

Table 3. Psychological characteristics of adopters and non-adopters

	Adopters		Non-adopters	
Psychological Variables	M	SD	M	SD
Environmental				
Environmental concern[a*]	4.40	0.51	4.18	0.67
Environmental motivation[b]	3.18	1.03	2.80	0.98
Financial				
Bill consciousness[c*]	0.70	0.46	0.59	0.49
Financial motivation[b]	2.67	1.01	3.07	1.03
Social				
Social norms[a]	3.04	0.80	2.92	0.77
Social motivation	1.95	1.05	1.83	1.01

[*] $p < .05$. [**] $p < .01$. [***] $p < .001$.

[a] Scale ranged from 1 = Strongly Disagree to 5 = Strongly Agree.

[b] Scale ranged from 0 = Not at All to 4 = A Great Deal.

[c] Binary variable normalized to a maximum of 1.

4.4 Implementation Stage

Respondents reported overall positive experiences across feedback. 65 mentioned that they were happy or satisfied with the product; when asked what they *disliked* about the product, 15 said "nothing" and others emphasized ease of use (34) and the quality of information presented about energy use (29): *"Educational to my husband and other people that are not as interested in conserving energy"* (TED), *"ease of use and quick comparison information"* (load monitor). A few noted having fun using feedback: *"it was fun to see graphical info"* (Data Logger), *"very cool to see the number change when using appliances"* (TED). Additional features praised across products included multi-functionality, comparative feedback, and interactivity.

Negative responses mentioned both hardware (e.g., installation, accessibility) and software (information displayed) issues. Five responses mentioned difficulties with installation: *"totally difficult/hazardous"*, *"much more difficult to install than I thought"* (*TED*). Eight responses discussed the physical design of the product, primarily with regard to plugging in load monitors: *"have to get behind large appliances to plug it in"* (*Kill A Watt*). Adopters of both whole-home and appliance-specific feedback reported feeling as though they received an "incomplete picture" of energy use. Whole-home feedback adopters reported a desire for isolating end uses (e.g., *would be more effective if it could tell you specifically which appliance was using the most*). Adopters of appliance-specific feedback expressed a desire for whole-home information (e.g., *hard to implement for long term or whole house*).

4.5 Confirmation Stage

When asked about continued use, over half (54) responded that they still use feedback. Reasons provided included continued usefulness (5), saving energy (4), saving money (3), and because it is hard to remove (1): *"I like to check myself and make sure I'm on track"*, *"still useful, especially for measuring long-term usage on an appliance"*, *"it's become a habit."* Nine responded that they still use feedback, but to a lesser degree: *"only once in a while if I'm chasing down a draft"* (Kill A Watt).

These statements suggest a potential diminished utility of feedback as they are used over time, which was reinforced by the nearly half (46) who reported that they no longer use feedback. When asked why, 25 indicated that they are no longer in possession of the product because they borrowed it, it was removed by the company, or they moved away. Four mentioned that they no longer used feedback because they had all the information they needed: *"it's served its purpose."*

5 Discussion

This study extends previous energy feedback research by analyzing the characteristics and user experience of active adopters (and non-adopters). Both quantitative and qualitative analyses reveal patterns that can be integrated into future design, marketing, and research of residential energy feedback, as follows.

Market Segmentation. The present study revealed demographic characteristics related to the adoption of feedback products including gender, age, marital status, income and homeownership, supporting previous findings that men tend to engage more with feedback technologies [9] as well as research on demographic variables related to general energy conservation behavior [7, 18, 25]. These findings suggest market segmentation strategies should be useful in promoting residential energy conservation. Further research into the perceived barriers and benefits of energy feedback for different demographics would further inform marketing strategies.

Results also indicate difference based on motivation and attitudes. Findings support previous research that feedback adopters have high pro-environmental attitudes [13]. Adopters reported lower financial motivation than non-adopters, countering past research that found that significant financial motivation among feedback users [9, 14, 19]. However, they did not compare adopters to non-adopters. The implications of these findings are unclear; they may suggest that messages concerning financial benefits of feedback are less effective among early adopters or, conversely, greater use of financial messaging may expand the market. Further research is needed to elucidate the motivations of early adopters and non-adopters.

Feedback Acquisition. Respondents were more likely to learn about feedback though social networks and utilities than mass-media sources. It is not clear if social networks afford more effective dissemination strategies or if media sources contain little coverage of feedback (or a combination thereof). Social contacts and utilities were also significant sources of acquisition of feedback, along with both online and brick and mortal retail. Findings support social-network and utility-based marketing programs as influential dissemination venues, but also suggest the importance of developing additional diffusion strategies.

The prevalence of borrowing suggests another promising avenue for dissemination of feedback devices. Current borrowing programs are primarily through utility companies and local libraries. The findings that many feedback users report diminishing returns over time and that over half no longer use their feedback products further supports continued investigation into temporary lending programs.

Importance of Product Testing. Users reported positive experiences overall, but several usability issues were noted, including difficulty with installation, low voltage detection, and difficulty reading and interpreting displays. If a product does not undergo thorough reliability testing, early adopters will have inferior experiences and dissemination will be inhibited. This is an important concern as energy-feedback technologies are not yet widely known by the public and, therefore, product usability issues could severely diminish the likelihood of adoption by a wider population if feedback technologies acquire negative connotations early on.

Rebound Effects. Some users reported adjusting consumption upwards upon discovering they used less energy than anticipated, reflecting past research that suggests a rebound effect for gains in energy efficiency of products [3]. This is an important reminder of the need for feedback designers to acknowledge unintended consequences and also extends the potential rebound effect to not just efficiency gains, but also information sources. Further research into message-framing and motivational aspects of feedback is needed to understand ways to counter rebound effects.

6 Conclusions

This study has both practical and theoretical applications, as understanding the market for energy feedback can increase energy conservation and also contribute to our understanding of the diffusion of new technologies across sectors. By focusing on active adopters of energy feedback and collecting both quantitative and qualitative data about the user and their experiences, this study was able to address previously neglected questions about how to best to design and market feedback technologies to the public. In doing so, we found that males, homeowners, and individuals with high environmental concern were among those most likely to purchase and use feedback, which is consistent with research on other energy-conservation behaviors. Users indicated generally positive impressions of feedback devices, and their experiences revealed great promise for novel approaches to the design and marketing of feedback, including the provision of both aggregate and disaggregate energy-use information and dissemination through utility and social-network channels. Design and usability issues identified in this study indicate that this technology, despite great potential, still has some hurdles to overcome before being marketed to the general American public. Further research testing use across devices, distinguishing among non-adopters (e.g., unaware of feedback, aware but not knowledgeable, knowledgeable but have not adopted) to ascertain a more differentiated understanding of the innovation-decision process, and isolating key features of feedback will greatly enhance our understanding of its use and potential for energy conservation.

References

1. Allen, D., Janda, K.: The Effects of Household Characteristics and Energy Use Consciousness on the Effectiveness of Real-Time Energy Use Feedback. ACEEE Summer Study on Energy Efficiency in Buildings, 1–12 (2006)
2. Battalio, R.C., Kagel, J.H., Winkler, R.C., Winett, R.A.: Residential electricity demand: an experimental study. Rev. Lit. Arts Am. **61**(2), 180–189 (1979)
3. Berkhout, P.H.G., Muskens, J.C., Velthuijsen, J.W.: Defining the rebound effect. Energy Policy **28**, 425–432 (2000)
4. Darby, S.: The Effectiveness of Feedback on Energy Consumption. Oxford, UK, 2006
5. Ehrhardt-Martinez, K., Donnelly, K.A., Laitner, J.A.: Advanced Metering Initiatives and Residential Feedback Programs: A Meta-Review for Household Electricity-Saving Opportunities. Washington, D.C (2010)
6. Fischer, C.: Feedback on household electricity consumption: a tool for saving energy? Energ. Effi. **1**, 79–104 (2008)
7. Gatersleben, B., Steg, L., Vlek, C.: Measurement and determinants of environmentally significant behavior. Environ. Behav. **34**, 335–362 (2010)
8. Haakana, M., Talsi, M.: The Effect of Feedback and Focused Advice on Household Energy Consumption. Research Program on Consumer Habits and Energy Conservation Summary Report, 37–60 (1996)
9. Hargreaves, T., Nye, M., Burgess, J.: Making energy visible. Energy Policy **38**(10), 6111–6119 (2010)

10. Karlin, B., Ford, R., Squiers, C.: Energy feedback technology: a review and taxonomy. Energ. Effi. **7**(3), 377–399 (2013)
11. Karlin, B., Ford, R., Zinger, J.: The Effects of Feedback on Energy Conservation: A Preliminary Theory and Meta-Analysis (2015)
12. Kasulis, J.J., Huettner, D.A., Dikeman, N.J.: The feasibility of changing electricity patterns. J. Consum. Res. **8**(3), 279–290 (2009)
13. Kurz, T., Donaghue, N., Walker, I.: Utilizing a social-ecological framework to promote water and energy conservation: a field experiment. J. Appl. Soc. Psychol. **35**(6), 1281–1300 (2005)
14. Liikkanen, L.A.: Extreme-user approach and the design of energy feedback systems. In: International Conference on Energy Efficiency in Domestic Appliances and Lighting, pp. 1–12 (2009)
15. Lowe's 2014 smart home survey report (2014)
16. Mountain, D.C.: Real-Time Feedback and Residential Electricity Consumption (2007)
17. Neenan, B., Robinson, J., Boisvert, R.N.: Residential electricity use feedback: a research synthesis and economic framework. EPRI, Palo Alto (2009)
18. Painter, J., Semenik, R., Belk, R.: Is there a generalized energy conservation ethic? J. Econ. Psychol. **3**, 317–331 (1983)
19. Parker, D., Hoak, D., Meier, A.: How Much Energy Are We Using ? Solar Energy (2006)
20. Parker, D.S., Hoak, D., Cummings, J.: Pilot Evaluation of Energy Savings from Residential Energy Demand Feedback Devices. Florida Solar Energy Center, Mountain (2008)
21. Parks Associates. Smart home ecosystem: IoT and consumers (2014)
22. Pierce, J., Fan, C., Lomas, D., Marcu, G., Paulos, E.: Some consideration on the (in) effectiveness of residential energy feedback systems. Hu. Comput. Interact. **45**(4), 244–247 (2010)
23. Robinson, J.: The Effect of Electricity-Use Feedback on Residential Consumption (2007)
24. Rogers, E.M.: Diffusion of Innovations. Free Press, New York, NY (2003)
25. Sardianou, E.: Estimating energy conservation patterns of Greek households. Energy Policy **35**(7), 3778–3791 (2007)
26. Shama, A.: Energy conservation in US buildings: Solving the high potential/ low adoption paradox from a behavioural perspective. Energy Policy **11**(2), 148–167 (1983)
27. Stern, P.C.: Contributions of psychology to limiting climate change. Am. Psychol. **66**(4), 303–314 (2011)
28. Vollink, T.: Go for less: The effect of feedback and goal setting on household energy and water consumption (2004)
29. Williams, E.D., Matthews, H.S.: Scoping the potential of monitoring and control technologies to reduce energy use in homes. IEEE Int. Symp. Electron. Environ., 239–244 (2007)
30. Winett, R.A., Neale, M.S., Grier, H.C.: Effects of self-monitoring and feedback on residential electricity consumption. Psychology **2**(2), 173–184 (1979)

Design and Implementation of a Mobile Cloud Environmental Application for Riyadh City

Heba Kurdi[1(✉)], Amani Al-Fayez[2], Anfal Al-Tuwaim[2],
Hanan Al-Mohammadi[2], Mona Al-Mutairi[2], and Sarah Al-Kharji[2]

[1] Computer Sciences Department, King Saud University, Riyadh, Saudi Arabia
hkurdi@ksu.edu.sa
[2] Computer Sciences Department, Al Imam Muhammad Ibn Saud Islamic
University, Riyadh, Saudi Arabia
amani-cs@hotmail.com, a.altuwaim@seu.edu.sa,
{hanan.almohammadi,mona.n.almutairi,
sarah.alkhaji}@gmail.com

Abstract. Environmental problems are a global issue that everyone should contribute to minimize. As it is difficult for people in charge alone to locate all the cases of the environmental hazards and to address them on time, this paper proposes a cloud based mobile application with a user friendly interface that allows citizens to help their government make their city a better place by reporting environmental violence. The aim is to help the responsible agencies have easy and quick access to notifications provided by the community about environmental issues, so they can be addressed promptly. We choose to customize the mobile application to Riyadh City, the capital of Saudi Arabia. However, the software is generic and can be customized to any other city.

Keywords: Mobile application · Environmental software · Cloud computing · Android

1 Introduction

Environmental issues are increasingly gaining concern; any changes in the environment are likely to affect all living things, directly or indirectly [1, 2]. The growth of the population in the last years has put high demands on many of the environmental natural resources [3], which has led to many forms of pollution and environmental violations by people, intentionally or otherwise. Therefore, environmental protection becomes necessary [4] and specialized voluntary groups, environmental organizations and environmental software are emerging to address this need.

Environmental software applications are developed especially for environmental protection [5]. They offer resources and services that reduce environmental damage, increase protection acts, and raise awareness [6].

Nowadays, many people tend to use smartphone instead of PCs, which raises the importance of mobile applications. The number of active mobile phones will reach 7.3 billion by 2014. In other words, right now there are more active cell phones than there are people on the planet [7]. Therefore, the need for mobile environmental software is an important step forward to help minimize environmental damage.

© Springer International Publishing Switzerland 2015
A. Marcus (Ed.): DUXU 2015, Part III, LNCS 9188, pp. 380–389, 2015.
DOI: 10.1007/978-3-319-20889-3_36

This paper aims at increasing peoples' awareness and concern about the environment through developing an environmental mobile application that allows citizens to help their government make their cities better places. It helps the responsible agencies to have easy and quick access to notifications, provided by the community about environmental issues, so they can address and prioritize them appropriately.

Although the application can be adopted by any city, Riyadh, the capital of Saudi Arabia, was chosen to start with. Riyadh suffers from many environmental problems such as vandalism, cars left in street for a long time, dead animals on the sides of streets and a lot more. The suggested mobile application, [love]Riyadh, has the potential to increase Riyadh population's awareness about the danger of neglecting the environment and make the city of Riyadh clean, healthy and safe for the coming generations. The software has been developed and tested successfully and the preliminary evaluation results of the usability test of the software are encouraging.

2 Related Work

By searching the mobile applications market for related systems running on iOS, Android devices or both, three environmental software were found: Love Clean London (LCL) [8], myEnv [9] and Baladiya [10]. In Table 1, the main features of each application are listed and compared with [love]Riyadh.

Table 1. Comparison between environmental mobile applications

Software Feature	LCL	myENV	Baladiya	[love]Riyadh
Price	Free	Free	Free	Free
Supports built-in camera	✓	✓	✓	✓
Supports picture gallery	✓	✓	✓	✓
Supports GPS	✓	✓	✗	✓
Allows feedback/Report	✓	✓	✓	✓
Live map for all reports locations	✗	✗	✗	✓
Supports saving drafts	✓	✗	✗	✗
Displays feedbacks/reports	✗	✗	✗	✓
Displays news and events	✗	✓	✓	✗
Push-notification alerts	✗	✓	✗	✗
Help page	✓	✗	✗	✗

2.1 Love Clean London

Love Clean London (LCL) [8] is a mobile reporting tool. It is a cloud-based mobile application to report "grim crime" such as litter, potholes, graffiti, broken paving slabs, abandoned vehicles, footway and footpath defects, blocked street drains/gullies etc. The goal is to help people to report environmental crimes and keep the London boroughs clean and healthy. Figure 1 shows screen shots from Love Clean London application.

Fig. 1. Love clean London application

2.2 MyENV

My Environment (myENV) [9] application is an iPhone and Android application developed by National Environment Agency (NEA) in Singapore. This application provides useful information on the environment to the people of Singapore. This information is already available on NEAs corporate website, but the agency wanted to make it easier for users to reach important information so they can make right environmental everyday choices. Figure 2 screenshots from myENV application.

Fig. 2. myENV application

2.3 Baladiya

Baladiya [9] is a mobile application developed by Ministry Of Municipality and Urban Planning, Doha, Qatar. The application runs on iPhone or android devices, and provides several services to give Qatar citizens better and easier ways to communicate with the ministry. Figure 3 screenshots from Baladiya application.

Fig. 3. Baladiya application

3 System Design

LoveRiyadh application was developed to allow volunteers to help prevent some environmental violence, such as cars left in the street for a long time, dead animals on the sides of streets and overloaded litter bins. It also allows volunteers to report issues related to streets or districts that need to be cleaned or maintained in terms of lighting or pavements and other aspects of environmental pollution, such as car exhaust, factory smoke and water swamps.

The application acts as messaging service between volunteers and Riyadh Council. It allows volunteers to send a picture and a message (report) describing the case of the environmental hazard, showing the location of the case as a map attached to the message to the council. On receiving a message, the council responds appropriate and updates the report status so each volunteer can track the progress of his/her report(s), as shown in Fig. 4.

loveRiyadh software system is composed of a mobile application linked to a mobile database and a web-based database. The latter is connected through a web service to a server from one end and an administrator interface from the other end to help the staff in their administrative work, as shown in Fig. 5.

4 Implementation

The mobile application is implemented for Android devices using Eclipse IDE, Android Emulator and Android platform. The web database is implemented using MS SQL server 2008 and Visual studio 2010 is placed on a web server that requires authorized access and contains report information (date, current status, category name, sender information) and users' accounts. The mobile database is implemented using SQLite to store all drafts and sent reports. The web service is developed using visual studio 2010 to connect the mobile application to the web server.

The user interface is encoded in the Arabic language at this stage, although it is intended to support English in a future version. The first screen is the Logo Screen, shown in Fig. 6, which leads directly to the Sign in screen, shown in Fig. 7. From this screen, the user can sign in, go to the Sign up screen or exit the application.

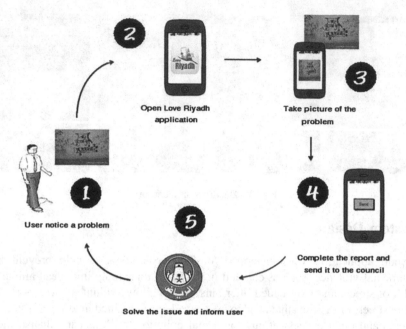

Fig. 4. Workflow of Love Riyadh application

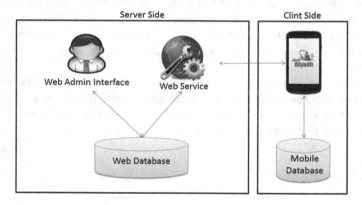

Fig. 5. ^{Love}Riyadh system architecture

In the Sign in screen, there are two fields: one for the username, which is the user ID and the other for the password. On clicking the sign in button, the application sends the data to the web database to verify user data and a message would be displayed accordingly. The Sign up screen includes four fields, as shown in Fig. 8: a username field, which is unique, so it can be used as a user ID, a password field for secure log in and e-mail and phone number fields to contact the user. After signing in successfully, the Home screen is displayed, as shown in Fig. 9. It contains six buttons: send report,

Fig. 6. Logo screen

Fig. 7. Sign in screen

saved reports, sent reports, all reports, profile and logout with each button leading to a different screen.

The Send Report screen contains a field for typing a description of the problem, a list of hazard categories to select from, a camera icon to take a picture or upload a from gallery and a location flag to indicate that the current location of the user will be automatically sent with the report, as shown in Fig. 10. There are also two buttons, one for sending the report and the other for saving the report. The Saved Reports screen presents a list of saved reports (drafts) which have not been sent yet, as shown in Fig. 11, while the Sent Reports screen displays a list of already completed and sent reports, as shown in Fig. 12.

The All Reports screen, shown in Fig. 13, has two options: one is the live map option that displays all reports that have been sent by users for this specific location on

Fig. 8. Sign up screen

Fig. 9. Home screen

the map, the other is the list of reports option, which displays a list of all reports that have been sent by all users.

5 Evaluation and Testing

For testing [Love]Riyadh application, we developed a multi-level plan that starts by testing each unit separately. Then when the whole system is completed, we test the correct integration between units. Finally, we test the functionality of the entire system. After that, we carry out the usability testing by a questionnaire to insure that the application meets the end user's expectations.

Fig. 10. Send report screens

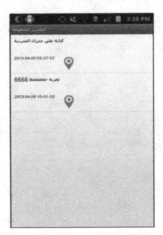

Fig. 11. Saved report screen

The work in unit testing considers each interface page in ^{Love}Riyadh application as a unit. So testing main functions for each unit was done separately, which is important in the incremental approach that followed in the software development. This test also verified that the mobile and web database are functioning as desired.

In Integration testing, we verified that all pages have correctly working links. Also, that the application is connected to the external and internal databases and able to communicate with them. After that, the entire system was tested and results were verified.

For usability testing, we developed a brief Arabic/English questionnaire to get the impression of real end users about the application. After receiving the feedback, we analyzed the results and modified the application accordingly.

Fig. 12. Sent report screen

Fig. 13. All reports screen

6 Conclusion

Due to rapid technological development and population growth, Riyadh is a city that experiences many environmental problems. The objective of this paper was to develop a mobile application that helps in preventing environmental hazards. It provides citizens with an easy and efficient way to do their part in cleaning up their city and making it a more comfortable and safe place. In addition, it lets responsible people know about the problems and start solving them immediately.

The current version of the ᴸᵒᵛᵉRiyadh mobile application supports many reporting functionalities. However, it is to be further improved in the near future to support SMS notifications, other mobile platforms and an English interface. It is also planned to generalize the application for other cities in Saudi Arabia, as well as other countries.

Acknowledgments. This work was funded by the Long-Term Comprehensive National Plan for Science, Technology and Innovation of the Kingdom of Saudi Arabia, grant number 11-INF1895-08.

References

1. Kaushik, A., Kaushik, C.P.: Environment and Ecology, in Basics of Environment and Ecology, pp. 1–13. New Age International, New Delhi (2010)
2. Pierre, Z., Fadeeva, F., Ogbuigwe, A.et al.: Visions For Change United Nations Environment Programme. Paris, France (2011)
3. Banik, S.D., Basu, S.K., Kri, A.: Environment Concerns and Perspectives. A.P.H. Publishing Corporation, New Delhi (2007)
4. Das, D., Sengupta, P.: Social cost of environmental pollution & application of counter measures through clean development mechanism with the effect of additionality & baseline — in the context of developing countries. In: Proceeding of the International Conference on Education and Management Technology (ICEMT), pp. 461–464, 2–4 Nov 2010
5. Fujita, H., Iijima, W., Koide, N.et al.: Mobile application development for environmental informatics and feedback on cooking oil use and disposal in Indonesia. In: Proceedings of the 2nd International Conference on Technology, Informatics, Management, Engineering, and Environment (TIME-E), pp. 29–33, 19–21 Aug 2014
6. Nie, Y., Zhang, J., Lei, Z., Xia, M.: Economic evaluation model and application of indoor environmental pollution. In: Proceedings of the International Conference on Computer Distributed Control and Intelligent Environmental Monitoring (CDCIEM), pp. 1478–1481, 19–20 Feb 2011
7. Digital trends. http://www.digitaltrends.com/mobile/mobile-phone-world-population-2014/
8. Love Clean London. http://www.windowsphone.com/en-us/store/app/love-clean-london/ 81a64cda-9742-e011-854c-00237de2db9e
9. The National Environment Agency (NEA). http://www.nea.gov.sg
10. Ministry of Municipality & Urban Planning. http://www.baladiya.gov.qa/cui/index.dox

How Do I Get to Room 3106?

Student Wayfinding Designs for Old Main at Wayne State University

Judith A. Moldenhauer[✉]

Wayne State University, Detroit, MI, USA
judith.moldenhauer@wayne.edu

Abstract. Built in 1895, Old Main is the oldest building on the Wayne State University campus. The building is a warren of rooms and hallways that is occupied by a wide variety of academic disciplines. However, there has never been any signage system for Old Main. Through using the experience of volunteers who specifically navigated to rooms and locations in Old Main, design students developed signage prototypes that connected the "story" of the building's information (e.g., rooms and locations, landmarks, stairs and elevators, hallways) with the "story" of the volunteers (e.g., the time it took to get to room, their use of landmarks, obstacles they encountered). This paper describes the students' design process and design work to demonstrate the importance of user-testing and the use of storytelling in design education.

Keywords: Wayfinding · Storytelling · Information design · User-testing · User-based design · Design education

1 Introduction

1.1 Where Am I to Go? How Do I Get There?

To ask for a map is to say, "Tell me a story."– Peter Turchi, *Maps of the Imagination: The Writer as Cartographer*, p. 11.

Who will help me find my way?– Paul Arthur and Romedi Passini, *Wayfinding: People, Signs, and Architecture*, p. V.

Information Design and Wayfinding. In her essay, "Chaos, Order, and Sense-Making," Brenda Dervin writes that "information is a tool designed by human beings to make sense of a reality assumed to be both chaotic and orderly." [2, p. 39] Thus– by developing strategies for people to find, understand, and use the information that they need– information designers help us make sense of the world around us. A key method in shaping effective information design is storytelling. Through finding ways to interweave the "story" of the information with the "story" of the people using the information (their experiences, background, knowledge, emotions, etc.), information designers create a new "story" that makes the information meaningful and accessible for those who need to use it. [5] This approach is especially useful for

A. Marcus (Ed.): DUXU 2015, Part III, LNCS 9188, pp. 390–399, 2015.
DOI: 10.1007/978-3-319-20889-3_37

wayfinding design. Wayfinding is about understanding, organizing, and visualizing information so that a person can spatially orient him- or herself within a location and then be able to move with confidence between places in that location. [3, p. 37] This understanding of wayfinding and the role of storytelling in information design was at the heart of the project for Wayne State University graphic design students in Fall 2013: design signage for the Old Main building on the WSU campus, a large five-story building that is a spatial maze but with no consistent signage system.

2 The Project

2.1 Old Main: The Building's Story

Designed by the architects Malcomson and Higginbotham in the American Romanesque Revival style and built in 1895 and renovated in 1997, Old Main is the oldest building on the Wayne State University campus. With its exterior of yellow brick and carved limestone, the building sits at the corner of Cass and Warren Avenues in mid-town Detroit and is home to a wide variety of art, humanities, and science disciplines. Its clock tower is an iconic symbol of the WSU campus Fig. 1.

Fig. 1. Old main from the corner of Cass and Warren avenues. The arched Cass avenue entrance is at the base of the clock tower. (Photograph courtesy of the author.)

Old Main's physical structure consists of a ground and four floors connected through several stairwells and two elevators. There are a number of entrances to Old Main, but the main entrance is a wide, rounded entrance archway on Cass Avenue that surrounds two sets of double doors. These doors open to a tiled foyer with stairs on each side leading down through arches to the ground floor and with a stairway leading up to a pair of solid metal doors that open onto the first floor. A stairway is to the left of the doors. The floors share a common central corridor with north and south wings at the eastern and western ends of the corridor; the two elevators flank the eastern end of the corridor. The north wing forms a square on the lower level and on the first two floors, but is truncated to two sides on the third floor. The south wing has two sides or arms on the ground through the third floor level. On the fourth floor, the central corridor morphs into a rectangular hallway with no wings, only a block of rooms at its east end.

General lecture classrooms populate the building's ground and first floor. The ground floor is also home to the university Planetarium and the Department of Geology; the west side hallway leads south to the graduate studios of the Department of Art and Art History and to the Elaine L. Jacob Gallery and the Schaver Recital Hall. The first floor central corridor houses the Anthropology Department and Museum while the west side of the north and south wings are occupied by Department of Music offices. Several programs in the Department of Art and Art History are located on the second, third, and fourth floors; the Department of Music has additional rooms on the second and fourth floors. The second floor corridor functions as a student lounge; classrooms and computer labs for Fashion Design and Interior Design of the Department of Art and Art History comprise the east side of the wings; music studios occupy the south wing; and faculty offices and the offices of the Dean of the College of Liberal Arts and Sciences occupy the rest of the north wing. On the third floor, classrooms and computer labs for Graphic Design, Interdisciplinary Electronic Arts, and Drawing and Painting form the eastern portions of the north and south wings. The Department of Theatre and Dance offices occupy the central corridor and the western side of these wings. On the fourth floor, the central corridor becomes a rectangle that anchor a series of music practice rooms as well as classrooms, computer labs, and darkrooms for the Photography program. The block of rooms at the eastern end of the fourth floor belongs to the Department of Communication: the Media Arts classroom, editing studios, and equipment check out for the Department of Communication.

For all the variety of its structure and occupants, there has never been any signage system for Old Main. Currently only room numbers on small placards, a small evacuation map on each floor near the elevators, and a smattering of divergent signs by the academic programs that "own" specific areas of the building serve as signage in the building. Often makeshift signage appears in the form of sheets of paper taped on the elevators, stairways, and various entryways that say things like, "dance auditions on the 3rd floor."

2.2   Old Main and User-Based Research: The First-Time Visitor's Story

On the first day of every academic term, dozens of Wayne State University students can be seen wandering the halls of Old Main, class schedule in hand, looking for their assigned classrooms. Sometimes, in desperation, they will ask another person for help. People making deliveries in Old Main or arriving at Old Main to attend or participate in an activity also do this "wayfinding dance" of scanning the environment for clues, frequently stopping to figure out which way to go, and often asking others they encounter for directions and/or re-tracing their steps. All of them experience frustration and spend more time than expected in reaching their destinations.

In Fall 2013, students in the WSU information design course directly confronted the signage deficit in Old Main through the development of prototype designs based on the experience of those trying to navigate its hallways. The design students observed volunteers – students from the College of Engineering who had never before been in Old Main – find specific room numbers (e.g., room 3106) and named locations (e.g., the Planetarium) in the building. They noted how the volunteers navigated to those places (e.g., the landmarks they used, if they re-traced their steps or backtracked, if they asked help from others in the building) and how long it took to reach each place; listened to the volunteers' comments as they searched for those places (e.g., their process for figuring out the next step); and learned details about the volunteers' experiences through a survey after arriving at their destinations (e.g., what was confusing and what was easy to follow). The students thus learned about each volunteer's wayfinding "decision plan," that is, the hierarchical problem-solving steps (from general to specific) used to arrive at his/her destination, and used that information in the development of their signage systems. [1, pp. 29-31].

Since the key to this wayfinding project was to conduct user-based research for the development of the designs and then test the designs, the project protocol, the survey instrument, the research information sheet, and volunteer recruitment materials were approved by the WSU Institutional Review Board (IRB). The students passed the Collaborative Institutional Training Initiative (CITI) basic course Responsible Conduct of Research training and read the research information sheet to each volunteer prior to his/her participation in the project. Five Engineering student volunteers participated in the project: three in the research phase of the project and two tested the prototype designs.

Each volunteer was requested to find a specific room in Old Main; everyone started inside the main Cass Avenue entrance. When presented with a room number, the first decision of the volunteers was to find the correct floor. This was the initial and most general decision of the volunteer's decision plan and the beginning of his/her story. In Old Main, room numbers have four digits, the first digit representing the floor or level; "0" stands for the ground or basement floor, "1" for the first floor, etc. One volunteer who received a ground floor room assignment initially went to the first floor because the Cass entrance, which presents the visitor with a choice of stairs going both up and down, provides no indication that the downward stairs lead to the ground floor and that the upward stairs lead to the first floor. The person assigned to find the office of the Dean for the College of Liberal Arts and Sciences (which is on the second floor) took the stairs up from the Cass Avenue entrance and continued up the staircase by the metal doors to the third floor. Not knowing the floor of the office, this individual randomly chose the third floor and nothing in the Cass Avenue entrance indicated that the elevator access lay just past the double doors. After searching unsuccessfully for the office on the third floor, the participant found the elevator and took it to the first floor. After searching in vain for a while, the participant finally asked someone for help and was directed to the second floor. The third volunteer correctly intuited from the assigned room number that it was on the fourth floor and that going through the metal doors meant finding an elevator. This participant reasoned that since most people streaming into the entrance went up the stairs and through those doors – many of whom would probably be going to the different floors – that there must be an elevator somewhere inside the building.

After arriving on the correct floor, the each volunteer stopped at the eastern end of the central corridor to figure out where to go next. It was here that he/she began to search for the number of the room and beginning the next tier of decisions in his/her decision plan. Most volunteers walked down at least one hallway only to re-trace their steps to another hallway. They could only tell the direction of the room numbering sequence for a hallway by moving close to the small signs located by the door of each room. All the volunteers took wrong turns and had to re-trace their steps. The volunteer searching for the ground floor room did not initially realize the need to go through an "exit" door to find the room. When the volunteer searching the office of the Dean for the College of Liberal Arts and Sciences got off the elevator at the second floor, that person looked down the central corridor, went down the south wing hallway until almost reaching its end, and then retracing those steps, walked down the north wing to find the office at the end of that hallway. The volunteer with the fourth floor room assignment got off the elevator and stopped, standing for almost a minute in front of a set of double doors not knowing whether to go through the doors or proceed down a short hallway to the left. Finally opting to go through the doors, this individual found the room only after walking most of the rectangular hallway there.

According to the volunteers, the most difficult aspects of their way finding task were figuring out what floor a room was on and, once on the correct floor, then figuring out which hallway the room was on. This included uncertainty about access through the double doors located at the east end of the central corridor on floors two and three. The volunteers also mentioned the need to get close to the room signs in order to see the number. When asked on the survey to state the easiest part of their way finding experience, they answered, "nothing," "not much of anything," and "wasn't very easy to find." And when asked what they would add or delete to the current Old Main signage, they responded that "large signs telling [the] range of rooms," "add more signs, have a floor map," and "add a board at the entrance of the building saying where department offices are located."

2.3   Student Wayfinding Designs

With the information gathered from the volunteers, the thirteen design students working in four teams wove the "story" of the building's information (e.g., rooms and locations, "landmarks", stairs and elevators, hallways) with the "story" of the volunteers (e.g., time it takes to get to a room, their use of "landmarks", obstacles in finding a location) into signage system prototypes that addressed experiences of the volunteers. Finished work consisted of full-scale mock-ups of at least three signage elements, a 24 × 36 inch poster describing the signage system, and a 5-7 min video documenting their design process.

Team 1. Lisa Ansteth, Caitlyn Gazarek, Kenny Szymanski, and Christopher Weber; *Team 2*. Catherine Belletini, Daniel Herrle, and Brittany Vadalabene; *Team 3*. Robyn

Eakin, Courtney Howell, and Jane Warunek; *Team 4.* Amanda Fairchild, Ashley Ratusznik, and Megan Yount.

To address the first concern and decision-making level of the volunteers – what floor is my room on? – the students designed placards that listed each floor with its corresponding room numbers, named facilities, and discipline areas. A common feature of all the students' signage systems was to place these placards in the Cass Avenue entryway, the first navigational decision point inside Old Main. One team's sign wrapped the wall space between the up and down stairs and had arrows by the floor numbers that pointed to their corresponding stairs. The teams put the placards on every floor at every major access point – stairway and elevators doors – but emphasized the respective floor number and its room numbers and facilities. Two teams also posted a version of their placard in the elevators above the floor stops buttons. A variation on the floor listing occurred for the stairwell signage. At the entry to each floor landing in a stairwell, one team placed a vertical list of all floor numbers with the current floor number reversed out of a background of the floor's designated color code. Another team simply put the color-coded number by the door, and another team posted a sign with the floor number and what was located on that floor Fig. 2.

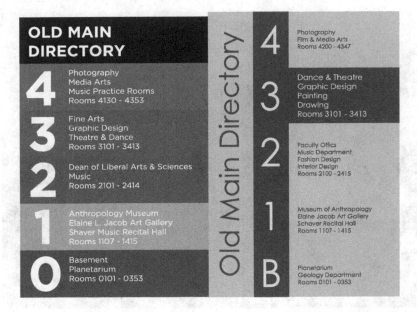

Fig. 2. Directories. cass avenue entrance: Team 2 (left) and 3rd floor: Team 3(right)

Another common design feature to the placards was color-coding. Each floor has its own color. Only one team did not use color-coding but instead used light and dark contrasts to identify floors. On those placards, light type on a dark ground indicated the current floor while dark type on light ground signaled information for the other floors. The color-coding continued throughout the building: the signage on each floor used that floor's assigned color.

There were also common issues inherent in way finding that were addressed by each team but visualized in different ways such as the use of typography and terminology. All the teams used sans-serif typefaces – Gotham, Avant Garde, Univers condensed, and Futura – to provide a high level of readability especially at a distance. Students created full-scale mock-ups that helped them choose the type weights, sizes, and spatial relationships that best signaled hierarchies of information. As to terminology, a variety of terms were used to connote the ground floor: ground, basement, or level 0; there was no research data about terminology preference.

Once on the correct floor, student designs addressed the second concern and next series of decisions for the volunteers – figuring out which hallway the room was on. The teams approached this in a variety of ways. One design team suspended a 15 × 72 inch sign from the ceiling on each floor where the eastern end of central corridor and of the north and south wings, the stair landing, and elevator access all converge. The overhead sign had a large floor number and listed room numbers and names with corresponding arrows. The information on each side of the sign was oriented to the direction in which you are facing; thus you would not see information about rooms or areas that you have already passed Figs. 3, 4, 5 and 6.

Fig. 3. Hallway banner and directory, 3rd floor (Team 1)

Other teams provided directional guides at eye level: horizontal arrows containing room numbers at the ends of hallways, 3-D illusionistic arrows with room numbers on double doors, and "you are here" or "heads-up" [4, p. 155] maps near the elevators. Two teams provided maps for each floor: one team focused on hallways and the room numbers and one focused on all the facilities of the floor, but both called out named offices and locations. One team tackled the design of the room number plates, using the

Fig. 4. Arrow on double doors, 3rd floor (Team 3)

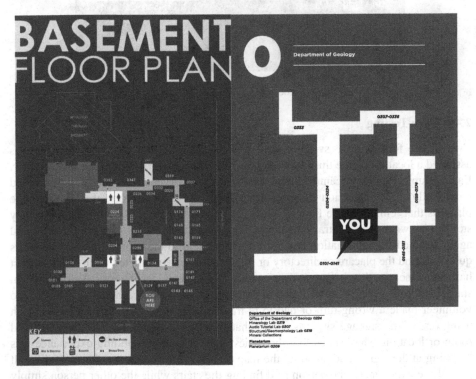

Fig. 5. Map/floor plan, ground/basement floor: Team 4 (left) and Team 2 (right)

experiences of the volunteers, the presence of makeshift signs, and the design of the current room number plates: black squares with raised white numbers in the upper left corner. Some plates include the purpose of the room, such as computer laboratory; other plates have a cutout lower portion for customizing information and often used for faculty offices and multi-purpose classrooms. The team noticed that the volunteers had to get very close to a room plate to read the number. Students also noticed announcements about activities pertaining to a classroom – a canceled class, a visiting lecture– consisted of sheets of paper taped to or near the classroom door. The students thus envisioned a room plate with larger type sizes, color-coding, and as a digital device that could display and update a variety of information.

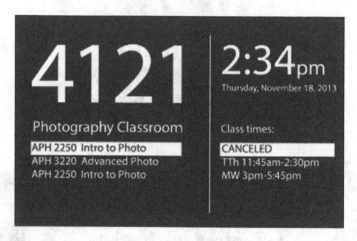

Fig. 6. Room plate, 4th floor (Team 2)

2.4   User-Testing

Two of the four signage systems were tested (Teams 1 and 2); one volunteer was assigned a location on the third floor and the other assigned a room on the second floor. Each volunteer quickly scanned the placard at the Cass Avenue entrance and proceeded confidently in the direction of the correct floor. At the elevators, they noticed the placards that reinforced the floor at which they need to arrive. Once on the floor, they stopped at where the central corridor, wings, and floor access points converge and again scanned for information that would direct them to the room. All the volunteers quickly found the placard or directory or overhead sign that directed them to the correct hallway. Once in that hallway, they readily found their destination. As one person stated on the survey, "[I] looked around for maps as soon as I reached a new floor." No volunteer made a wrong turn or had to re-trace his/her steps. All the volunteers, each using one of the signage systems, stated that they found it easy to find their assigned room or location. They stated that the easiest part of their wayfinding experience was "looking at the signs" and "reading the maps." When asked to name the most difficult part of the experience, one person said finding the stairs while the other person simply said, "it wasn't too hard."

3   Conclusions and Reflections

The user-testing showed that the volunteers took less time to find the rooms using the students' designs than it took them to find the rooms without the benefit of the designs. The stories of the volunteers (the wrong turns, the re-tracing of steps, the many stops to figure out where to go next) as they wrestled with the story of Old Main (the wide range of disciplines and facilities housed there, the different lay-out of its floors, its lack of signage) enabled the students to construct wayfinding systems that told a new story—one that makes it easy to find a room on any floor of the building. By utilizing the decision plans of the first set of volunteers, the student designs enabled the second set of volunteers to move more confidently through their decision plans. By observing how specific individuals navigated a building's interior, the students were able to create effective signage systems, as evidenced by an initial round of testing.

Ideally, the next step for the students would have been to re-work their designs for another round of testing; the design process for wayfinding in the "real world" would involve several iterations of design and testing that could extend over months or even years. Also a more extensive wayfinding project would include all of the many entrances to Old Main and the participation of more volunteers in the research and testing. The limitations of the project were due to various time and recruitment constraints. While acknowledging these limitations, the students reflected on the success of their work in the final critique as well as what could changed and/or added. All teams wanted to further develop their signage for people with special needs such as limited sight and impaired mobility. Three teams wanted to include the design of the room plates. The team with the wrap-around Cass Avenue directory wanted to better clarify where the up and down stairs lead. Other teams wanted to fine-tune such things as type and placard sizes, color choices, and the visual composition of directories.

Through this project students learned how to conduct user-based research, the importance of input from people in making effective design decisions and in creating effective wayfinding strategies. They also learned about the importance of ethics and protocols when using human subjects in research, the value of pre- and post-testing survey instruments, and insight into the amount of time required to create designs that truly meet the needs of people. The students now have a solid foundation in user-based design and understand how their work as designers can help people find their way.

References

1. Arthur, P., Passini, R.: Wayfinding: People, Signs, and Architecture. McGraw-Hill, New York (1992)
2. Dervin, B.: Chaos, Order, and sense-making: a proposed theory for information design. In: Jacobson, R. (ed.) Information Design. MIT Press, Cambridge (1990)
3. Gibson, D.: The Wayfinding Handbook: Information Design for Public Spaces. Princeton Architectural Press, New York (2009)
4. Katz, J.: Designing Information: Human Factors and Common Sense in Information Design. John Wiley & Sons, Hoboken (2012)
5. Moldenhauer, J.: Storytelling and the personalization of information: a way to teach user-based design. Inf. Des. + Doc.Design. 11, 230-242 (2002/2003)

A Practice on Wayfinding System Design with Service Design Thinking

Jing Pan[1(✉)] and Zhengsheng Yin[2]

[1] College of Architecture and Urban Planning, Tongji University,
Shanghai, China
candypj2901@gmail.com
[2] College of Design and Innovation, Tongji University, Shanghai, China
tjyzs@sina.com

Abstract. Environment around people has become more complex than ever before due to the development of society and economy. It is easy to feel lost when exposed to wide-open and unfamiliar environments. Thus, wayfinding system design becomes increasingly important. Various factors affect people's wayfinding experience. Factors such as color, symbol or material of wayfinding facilities have been discussed a lot while the importance of systematic planning of wayfinding system has been ignored. This study combined service design thinking with wayfinding system design. Different service design methods had been applied to the different stages of wayfinding system design process in order to help designers make a more comprehensive design strategy. The wayfinding system design of Tea Experience Museum had been taken as a practice to show how service design thinking was used in wayfinding system design process.

Keywords: Wayfinding system · Service system · Design · Experience

1 Introduction

Wayfinding system originated from signage, which may be just a mark on the stone. As the era developing, the boundary of this design field expanded to signage system and finally, wayfinding can into being. The terminology "Way-finding" was firstly defined by Kevin Lynch (1960) as a consistent use and organization of definite sensory cues from the external environment [1]. The basic aim of wayfinding system design is to answer the following questions: 1. Where am I? 2. Where to go? 3. How can I get there?

The current wayfinding system in general often has the following problems[1]:

1. Unreasonable information density. Too long distance between each clue may make people upset while too short distance between each clue may interrupt their experience.
2. Inconsistent information. Sometimes signage with conflicting information can be seen in the street due to inadequate on-site testing.

---

[1] Similar statements can be seen in various literatures.

© Springer International Publishing Switzerland 2015
A. Marcus (Ed.): DUXU 2015, Part III, LNCS 9188, pp. 400–411, 2015.
DOI: 10.1007/978-3-319-20889-3_38

3. Inanimate Form. The clues are usually showed in single form such signboard. Different forms of clues and more interactions should be involved.
4. Facilities out of order. Without systematic planning, new information carriers are added freely. A lot of different signage standing in chaos will make people confused.
5. No consideration of environment. Sometimes the style of wayfinding facilities is clashing with the scenery. Sometimes the design of wayfinding facility does not usable in the environment such as glass badge is difficult to read under sunshine and facilities hidden by trees are useless.
6. Neglecting the people with disability. For example, most of the wayfinding clues require visual ability, excluding the people with visual impairment.

Today in China the study of wayfinding system design is hot but still laggard. Most of the existing study remains on color, symbol or material of wayfinding facilities. Of cause these are all significant factors in wayfinding design, but another important factor that creates wayfinding problems has been ignored, which is the lack of systematic planning. Wayfinding system design is more than the separately design of wayfinding facilities.

Wayfinding system in the form of information carriers, its ultimate goal is to meet people's wayfinding needs and solve wayfinding problems. This requires us to be user-centered and plan systematically rather than focusing on each wayfinding facility separately.

Shostack put the terms "service" and "design" together in 1984 [2]. And service design launched as a design discipline for the first time in 1991 by Michael Erlhoff, a design Professor of Köln international school [3].

Service design is a user-centered system design. It serves the whole process, aiming to provide users with a complete, high-quality experience. Today, service design thinking is often use in product design as product service system design (PSSD), shifting the business focus from selling physical products alone to selling a system combining product in order to meet the specific client (both business and final user) demands [4].

For example, Diddi & Gori company provide a PSS called Digodream, from which people cannot only get the product (flooring) but an entire service, from supply and installation, to the removal. This perfectly meets the final goal of people who buys flooring: having textile flooring installed, at the same time the company also benefit from the recycling of the textile materials [5].

In this paper, wayfinding system design of Tea Experience Museum is used as a practice to show how service design thinking can be used in wayfinding system design process.

2   Background and Purpose

Tea Experience Museum is located in Huzhou, Zhejiang Province. It's base on the content of "The Classic of Tea" written LuYu, the famous tea sage in China. The museum consists of one main pavilion, a restaurant, a tea bar, a garden and a kids' park.

It not only shows the knowledge of tea but also provides visitors diverse tea experience by connecting different spaces. It was asking for a comprehensive wayfinding system, which can connect the existing resources as a whole system and meet the needs of different people, using a combination of tangible and intangible service.

Therefore, service design thinking was applied to the design process.

The aim of this study was to provide a new theoretical approach for wayfinding system design and to provide a more effective, comprehensive and interesting way-finding experience for the visitors.

3   Theory and Methods

3.1   Wayfinding System Design

The main process of wayfinding system design can be divided into three stages: Planning, Design and Implementation [6]. Planning stage consists of research and analysis, strategy and programming. In this stage, we set a clear design goals, establishing design strategy through not only the field research on the environment and traffic conditions, but also the analysis of user's needs. Preliminary plan the location and content of wayfinding facilities.

Service design methods will be used mainly in the Planning stage.

3.2   Service Design

Service design process starts from exploration to creation then reflection and finally implementation. However, it is not a linear but iterative process, each stage might be necessary to turn back to the former stages [7]. See Fig. 1.

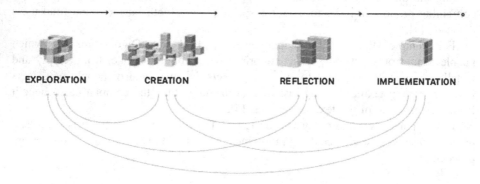

EXPLORATION   CREATION   REFLECTION   IMPLEMENTATION

Fig. 1. Service design process [7]

There are four main factors in service design:

(1) People: Human service system is the most important part. Service design starts from people and end with people. In the service system, "people" include service

end-users, service providers, partners and business users. They play different roles in the system.

(2) Environment: Environment is the service location, which includes the natural environment, social environment and cultural environment.

(3) Process: Service design process is carried out on how the service is implemented. Anything that occurred during service can be designed. Some of the processes here are material and some are immaterial.

(4) Tools: Tools are the carriers in services implementation, and they are also the potential interaction objects and service participants. Usually refers to the products, platforms and facilities provided by the service providers to end-user.

There are five principle of service design: User-centered, Co-creative, Sequencing, Evidencing and Holistic.[2]

All these factors and principles should be taken into consideration in wayfinding design process.

3.3 Apply Service Design Thinking into Wayfinding System Design

From service perspective wayfinding system can be interpreted as a service system, helping people access to the information of destination, plan their journeys with information, successfully arrived from one destination to another. Therefore, service design methods and principles can be applied into wayfinding system design process. It will help designers think and design the wayfinding system in a more user-centric and systematic way.

Firstly, literature study on both service design and wayfinding system design was done in order to form a model of wayfinding system design with service design methods (See Fig. 2). It shows which methods from service design can be used in wayfinding system design process and how they are used in each stage of the design process.

Secondly, the model of wayfinding system design with service design methods was applied into practice, taking the wayfinding system design project of Tea Experience Museum as the object:

In Research & Analysis stage of wayfinding system design process, Questionnaire, In-depth Interviews and On-site Analysis were used in order to understand the users' need and get information of the target environment and its surroundings.

In Strategy stage of wayfinding system design process, Stakeholder Map, Offering Map from service design were applied in order to define and visualize the goal of this project. Service blueprint and System Map were brought in to understand the circulation path of the users.

In Programming stage of wayfinding system design process, Persona and Storyboard were used to take different user groups into consideration and decide the location and forms of wayfinding service touch points. Prototype was used to test the whole wayfinding system.

---

[2] This is service design thinking.

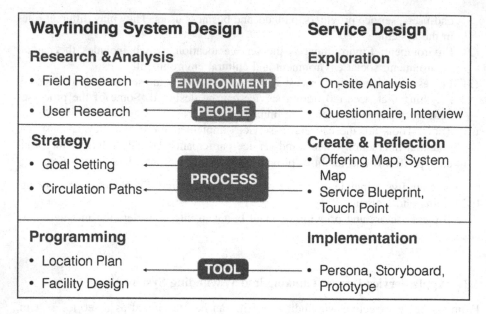

Fig. 2. Model of Wayfinding system design with service design methods

During the whole process, service design principles should be taken into consideration:

1. User-centered: During the wayfinding system design process of Tea Experience Museum, the physical needs and psychological needs of the user were the most important things need to be considered. The final goal of the wayfinding system is to serve the wayfinding needs of visitors.
2. Co-creative: Invite different user groups or even stakeholders to take part in the design process.
3. Sequencing: Services is a continuous process, so is wayfinding system. This requires directed attention be paid to user experience, avoiding problems such as unreasonable information density, inconsistent information.
4. Evidencing: Service is intangible, only through tangible goods can people "see" it. The wayfinding service was visualized by special facilities, making people aware of the existence of the service.
5. Holistic: Wayfinding service begins at the moment when visitors decide their destination. Therefore, the experience of visitors checking route information at home, determining the direction of the road, visiting the museum and going to the associated sites should be taken into account, instead of just focus on the way-finding experience inside the museum only.

4 Research on Tea Experience Museum

4.1 Field Research

Tea Experience Museum is located in Huzhou, the birthplace of Chinese tea culture. It is a topic museum based on "Experience of tea" and aimed at spreading the knowledge of tea. As a modern museum, it is no more a process of one-way teaching but a process of two-way experiment during which audience are encouraged to touch, operate, and taste. Tea Experience Museum is an important resource of tourism in Huzhou. It surpasses other resources because it could display more content of regional culture.

Tea Experience Museum is in south of the harbor, north of the administrative center, marina to the east, Zhongxing Bridge to the west. Near it, there are major cultural facilities like Huzhou Museum, Library, Science Museum, Technology Expo Centre, Grand Theatre and Music Hall. All the spaces together constitute a magnificent, fully functional cultural landscape.

Nowadays, due to development of transportation and civilization of tourism, main future visitors of Tea Experience Museum are not only local people, but also travelers from nearby cities. Huzhou has a good geographic condition, 80 km away from Hangzhou, 140 km from Shanghai, 220 km from Nanjing.

Tea Experience museum is a museum park consists of five tea theme spaces: main pavilion, tea garden, tea restaurant, tea bar and children's playground. There are also car parking lot, bike rental spot and tour bus stop in the museum park.

The building area of the main pavilion is about 3800 m^2, divided into two floors. The first floor consists of Reception, Exhibition Area, Multimedia Room, Museum Shop and Tea Room. The second floor is all Exhibition Area.

Huzhou attaches great importance to the development of tourism, with a lot of tourism resources, attracting tourists from all over the visitors. In addition to tea culture, Huzhou has a wealth of tourist attractions such as Tiefo temple, Flying tower, Long Island Park, etc.

Visitors can reach Tea Experience Museum by car or by public transportation,Since the museum haven't been open to the public yet, the author herself pretend to be a visitor, using empathy to explore the whole wayfinding process to Tea Experience Museum.

The process of people finding their way to Tea Experience Museum can be generalized in the Fig. 3. From home to Huzhou, arriving at Museum Park, entering the pavilion, going out of pavilion, visiting other scenic spots or returning home. If Tea Experience Museum is just one of many destinations in a visitor's trip plan and not the first destination, the process can go the opposite way, from other scenic spots in Huzhou to the museum and finally return home.

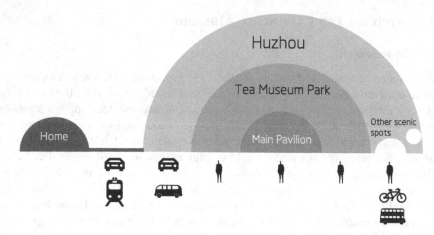

Fig. 3. The Wayfinding Process to Tea Experience Museum

4.2   User Research

Questionnaires and Interviews were used in the user research.

150 questionnaires had been distributed and 138 had been used for analysis. The questionnaire consists of four parts: basic information, understanding of tea culture, trip mode and wayfinding habits.

Five persons were selected to been interviewed in-depth based on the conclusion from questionnaire. The interview time was 1 h per person and was recorded in the form audio. The basic information of the interviewees was shown in Table 1.

Table 1. The basic information of interviewees

Name	Age	Gender	Job	Location	Other Information
TLL	24	female	student	Suzhou	
ZY	28	female	student	Shanghai	
ZHM	32	female	teacher	Shanghai	has a 5 year old son
PN	50	male	civil servant	Nanjing	has a daughter study abroad
GX	74	male	retired	Huzhou	

Insights from the user research were:

Continuous information and having wayfinding facility in the right place is the most basic needs of visitors,and they also desire for an interesting learning and interactive experience. More information about eating and accommodation is in great demand and it's better to connect other scenic spots with the museum. Different age group requires different wayfinding service. Different wayfinding stage needs different wayfinding solution

4.3   Conclusion (Opportunity)

The main stakeholders involved in the whole wayfinding process are visitors, Tea Experience Museum and government department of Huzhou. The design opportunity is in the overlapped area of the needs of theses three stakeholders (See Fig. 4).

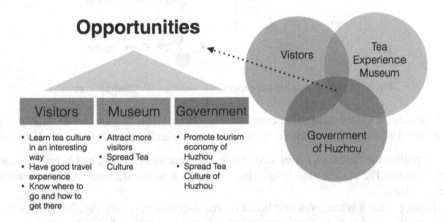

Fig. 4. Stakeholder map of tea experience museum

5   Outcomes

The visitors' main need is to learn tea culture in an interesting way and have good travel experience, to know where to go and how to get there. The main need from the museum is to attract more visitors and spread tea culture. The main need of Huzhou government department is to spread Tea Culture of Huzhou and promote tourism economy.

Therefore the design of wayfinding system should of five functions shown in the offering map (See Fig. 5).

1. Function of guidance: Information should appear in time to guide people's way.
2. Function of education: Visitors can expand their horizon of knowledge during tourist in museum.
3. Function of Advertising: Advertising board in the city could lead the way for visitors. Interesting, lovely and vivid advertisement could transfer concept of regional culture.
4. Function of Interaction: Visitors can explore by themselves via wayfinding system and gain joy of achievement.

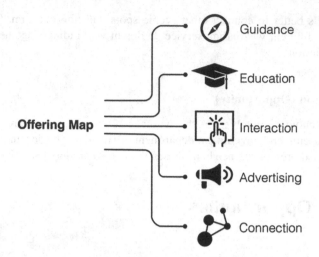

Fig. 5. Offering map of tea experience museum Wayfinding system

5. Function of Connection: The connection to other travel attracts could satisfy the demand of visitors and promotes the development of culture and economy in Huzhou.

To realize the functions mentioned above, different stakeholders had been involved in the service. The system map below (Fig. 6) shows how the stakeholders were related to each other.

Three personas were generated based on the user research (See Fig. 7). The special needs of different kinds of people revealed by drawing storyboard of different personas.

Service blueprint (Table 2) of the wayfinding system had been made to help designer understand the wayfinding process in detail and define the touch points (Fig. 8).

6   Prototype and Feedback

Some paper prototypes of the physical wayfinding facilities, such as badges and boards, had been made to test the touch points, avoiding inconsistent information. The audio guide and digital guide were explained without prototype. Two of the interviewees, ZHM and GX (see Chapter 4.2), had been invited to test the prototypes. From their feedbacks, the wayfinding information appeared in time and the diversity of wayfinding solution is welcomed. Some small adjustment about size and height of the facilities had been made to make the wayfinding experience smoother.

7   Conclusion

As a result of the rising quality of life, the wayfinding system should not only effective, but also efficient and provide smooth wayfinding experience to the users. It should meet the needs of people both physically and mentally.

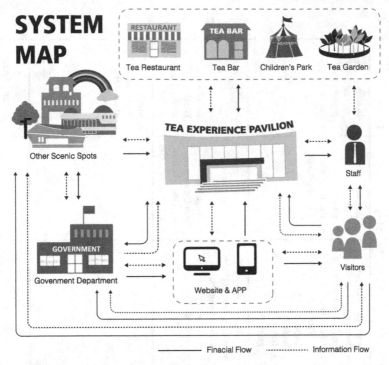

Fig. 6. System map of tea experience museum Wayfinding service

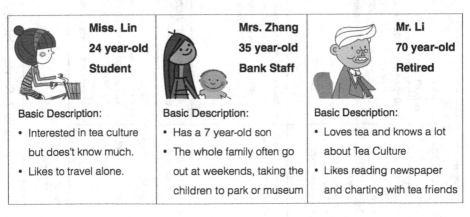

Fig. 7. Three Personas Used in Wayfinding system design process

Stakeholder	Pre-Service		During Service		After Service
	Plan	Departure	Arrival	Stay	Leave
Visitors	• Collecting information • Book tickets • Guide and activity reservation • Download App • Record route	• Departure for destination • Reference to recorded route • Use digital map or APP • Reference to wayfinding Facilities	• Enter museum park • Park cars, find main pavilion entrance • Understand the environment • Deposit coat and luggage • Get guide book/audio guide	• Visit main pavilion • Take part in activities • Visit other places in museum park	• Return • Visit other scenery spot • Give feedback
Tea Experience Museum	• Design web and APP to provide information	• Design and set the physical wayfinding system of the museum • Contact Huzhou government (departments of tourism and transportation)	• Provide relevant service (education, entertainment, catering...)	• Prepare for exhibitions and provide products • Organize activities	• Provide Feedback platform on web or APP
Huzhou government (departments of tourism and transportation)	• Add link of museum on its official website • Update city map, adding information of the museum	• Add information of the museum In tourism brochure • Put brochure and advertise in railway station • Add information of the museum to signage board in bus station • Set new bike renting point and tour bus point • Provide public wayfinding system			• Provide information of other scenic spots
Related scenic spots	• Cooperate with the museum				• Wayfinding system of other scenic spots

Table 2. Service blueprint of tea experience museum Wayfinding system

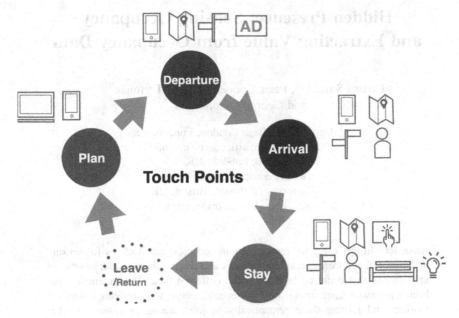

Fig. 8. Touch points in Wayfinding Process

Service design methods can be used in the planning stage of wayfinding system design process to help designers make a more comprehensive design strategy, thus design a more efficient and desirable wayfinding system to improve the visiting experience. By using service design thinking, different stakeholders are involved. This will benefit the end user (visitors), the client (museum) and also the tourism of the city.

References

1. Lynch, K.C.: The Image of the City. The M.I.T Press, Cambridge (1960)
2. Shostack, L.G.: Design Services that Deliver. Harvard Bus. Rev. **62**, 133–139 (1984)
3. Moritz, S.: Service Design: Practical Access to an Evolving Field, Lulu. com (2005)
4. Manzini, E., Vezzoli, C.: Product-Service Systems and Sustainability: Opportunities for Sustainable Solutions, pp. 4–5. UNEP, Paris (2002)
5. Manzini, E., Vezzoli, C.: A strategic design approach to develop sustainable product service systems: examples taken from the 'environmentally friendly innovation' Italian prize. J. Clean. Prod. **11**(8), 851–857 (2003)
6. David Gibdon, C.: The Wayfinding Handbook: Information Design for Public Places. Princeton Architecture Press, New York (2009)
7. Stickdorn, M., Schneider, J.: This is Service Design Thinking: Basics, Tools, Cases. BIS Publishers, Amsterdam (2010)

Hidden Presence: Sensing Occupancy and Extracting Value from Occupancy Data

Larissa Suzuki[1,2], Peter Cooper[2,3], Theo Tryfonas[3(✉)],
and George Oikonomou[3]

[1] University College London, London, UK
larissa.suzuki@arup.com
[2] Arup, London, UK
peter.cooper@arup.com
[3] University of Bristol, Bristol, UK
{t.tryfonas, g.oikonomou}@bristol.ac.uk

Abstract. In this paper we review various technical architectures for sensing occupancy in commercial real estate spaces and discuss the potential benefits of applications that could be built upon the collected data. The technical capabilities reviewed range from simple presence detection to identifying individual workers and relating those semantically to jobs, teams, processes or other elements of the business. The volume and richness of accumulated data varies accordingly allowing the development of a range of occupancy monitoring applications that could bring multiple benefits to an organization. We find that overall occupancy-based applications are underappreciated in the Smart Buildings mantra due to occupancy's inability to align to traditional building engineering silos, a lack of common view between stakeholders with respect to what is 'value' and the current client assessment tendencies which use predominantly demonstrator-based logic rather than a combination of practical demonstrators and theoretical value. We demonstrate that in commercial office buildings, occupancy-based Smart Building concepts have the potential to deliver benefits that can be orders of magnitude greater than current practice associated with silos such as energy and lighting. The directness of value in these is far more variable however, and the barriers and enablers to its realization are non-trivial. We identify and discuss these factors (including privacy, perceived additional capital expenditure, retrofitting requirements etc.) in more detail and relate them to stages of design and delivery of the built environment. We conclude that, on the presumption costs of development and implementation are relatively similar, the value streams of occupancy-based systems, while requiring more careful and bespoke design in the short term, could produce greater lifetime value in commercial office scenarios than leading smart building technologies.

Keywords: Smart built environments · Occupancy detection

© Springer International Publishing Switzerland 2015
A. Marcus (Ed.): DUXU 2015, Part III, LNCS 9188, pp. 412–424, 2015.
DOI: 10.1007/978-3-319-20889-3_39

1 A Quiet Digital Revolution Transforming the Built Environment

The optimization of urban spaces and resources has become increasingly challenging since the rapid globalization and urbanization that took place in late 20th Century, causing a tremendous transformation in cities' economy, environment and society. Since then, cities have become very powerful drivers of environmental problems [1, 2] at the local, regional and global scales.

Buildings are expensive both in financial (operational costs, real estate) and environmental (climate change, green-house emissions) terms. The built urban environment is responsible for the enormous consumption of energy and natural resources, being responsible for 68–80 % of all energy consumption and greenhouse-gas emissions in the world [3]. The US Department of Energy estimates that buildings consume 70 % of the electricity in the US [4].

Businesses seek to reduce the operational costs of buildings, transforming them into a more efficient and sustainable infrastructure. Often, buildings have multiple technology systems, possibly upward of 14 or 15 [5], and typically may have over 250 sensors going into the building management system (BMS), SCADA, and Element Management System. Nonetheless, these component systems of buildings have evolved and operated through many different paths, often separately. This scenario is clearly not optimal as one component system depends upon the other. For instance, the access control system may block the access of a particular part of the building because the fire alarm on that area was raised.

The integration of a building's component systems facilitate communication of data among systems therefore optimizing the operation and maintenance of the physical environment. In order to reduce costs, interconnect activities, and integrate systems, buildings have increased their reliance on automated machine-to-machine (M2M) interactions [5]. Such an integrated and intelligent environment has formed the basis for the concept of Smart Buildings. The term Smart Buildings covers the technologies of advanced and integrated systems for building automation, life safety and telecommunication systems.

The IoT is one of the key components in building automation systems, as buildings can be instrumented and interconnected using modern digital technologies (e.g. sensors, actuators, etc.), and often wireless communication technologies, providing information about the state and health of the physical infrastructure of buildings. This enables efficient monitoring of resources and prompt reaction to unpredicted situations. For example, pumps and motors in elevators can monitor safety limits in order to avoid damaging their infrastructure or harm their users. Energy, water, oil or gas meters can measure energy consumption in much more detail than conventional meters, offer two-way, near or real-time, information transmission between the customer and the authorized parties (e.g. utility providers, service operators, etc.).

Recent efforts have focused on making buildings more energy efficient, including research that target specific areas such as HVAC [6, 7], lighting [8] and managing IT energy consumption [9, 10] within buildings, and IoT [e.g. 7, 9, 14–18]. Most IoT solutions rely on wireless sensors network and the use of temperature sensors, air conditioning and passive infrared (PIR) technologies. In the next section we review some approaches used to detect occupancy in smart buildings. Although definitions and interpretations are of course highly varied, a building that harnesses the increased connectivity of the IoT and the increased data prevalence of big data, can be said to be a Smart Building.

2 Occupancy and Presence Detection

2.1 Occupancy Definition

In this paper we define occupancy as the combination of: (a.) the detection of presence, (b.) associated with a special context (e.g. space or activity) and (c.) associated with a time context, combined to create occupancy data. There is of course variation in the nature of occupancy depending on exactly how these three criteria are fulfilled.

Variations in the nature of (b.) and (c.) are typically one dimensional and generally result in changes in data resolution. The first point however has considerable room for multi-dimensional variation. This is far more significant, and affects what we will describe as the 'richness' of the data, demonstrated in Fig. 1.

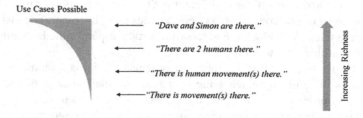

Fig. 1. Variation in richness of occupancy data.

While variation of space and time may indeed affect the performance of a use case, variation in actual presence determines, in a very binary manner, what use cases are and what use cases are not possible.

2.2 Occupancy Use-Cases

In this section we will explore a range of Smart Building use cases that harness occupancy data, spanning form those relatively understood to the most contemporary. We shall categorise these into the themes of Office Resource Management, User Experience, Analytics and Building Management.

Office Resource Management (desk allocation). Under this set we classify systems that manage non-territorial working (i.e. not firmly allocated desks per person) and distribute spare desks to arriving members of the work force. Particularly Intelligent Hot Desking Systems that undertake the above process, but with improved allocation of desks based on criteria of additional data sources, including environmental conditions, noise levels, work themes of adjacent employees, desk configuration and so on.

Analytics and Insight Development. This category includes instances of insight building through analysis and visualization of relevant data. In particular we identify:

- Desk Heat Maps– Displaying utilization of individual desks in an office;
- Origin/Destination Staff Maps– Displaying relative frequency of various internal trips of specific staff groups.
- Energy Benchmarking– developing meaningful insights on energy use.
- Real Estate Utilization Strategic Analytics– Scenario analysis for exploring reconfigurations of a staff group's location and real estate use, and expansion/consolidation of the real estate portfolio itself, both now and in varying incarnations of the future.

Building Management

- Meeting Room Management– Understanding the relationship between meeting room bookings and actual utilization, as well as suitability of meeting room configuration to use types.
- Guest Management– Improving the expectation of, greeting of and monitoring of external visitors.
- Deductive Security– Comparing automated visual recognition of individuals with the absence of the individual's ID presence data to deduce intruders.

User Experience

- Users Specific Signage – Displaying specific information or graphics on a screen depending on those in proximity.
- Geolocating Events –provide information on open, close-proximity events based on a series of predefined interests.
- Geolocating Individuals –provide locational information on individuals.
- Room User Recognition – customisation a room's setup and building services based on predefined preferences of a specific person for a specific type of room activity.

All of the above are overviewed by relative characteristics, as seen in Fig. 2.

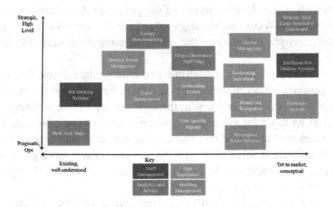

Fig. 2. A portfolio of occupancy use-cases.

3 Technologies for Occupancy Detection in Smart Buildings

Using occupancy as a driver for intelligent control of smart buildings has been increasingly investigated. Most research on occupancy detection within smart buildings focuses on the use of occupancy data to optimize energy consumption. For in-stance previous research on HVAC control systems shows that occupancy information can be used to drive a more optimized HVAC schedule [11, 12]. However, due to the difficulty in obtaining real time accurate occupancy data, many of these techniques focus on using pre-determined schedules.

The advent of low-cost wireless sensor networks has enabled wider deployment opportunities of a large number of connected sensors [13] thus allowing for improved sensing (such as occupancy detection) in buildings. Many modern buildings use passive infrared sensors (PIR) to drive lighting control and detect movement/presence of people inside rooms. PRI technologies relies on "line of sight" coverage to detect occupancy by sensing the difference in between the background space and the heat emitted by humans in motion. The current trends involve using sensor data fusion in order to gather richer details about the environment and the occupants.

For demand response HVAC control, occupancy detection needs to be accurate, reliable, and able to capture occupancy changes in real time. Estrin et al. [7] the use of microphones and PIR sensors to drive more efficient scheduling of conference rooms has been investigated. They have built a wireless sensor network to gathered data from air conditioning, temperature and microphone to estimate the utilization of conference rooms and to calculate the wastage of electricity. The test bed was developed using off-the shelf wireless sensor platform (micaZ) of crossbow. Using their solution – iSense - the WSN based conference room management solution the utility of conference room can be increased from 67 % to 90 %.

Padmanabh et al. [14] used PIR based wireless occupancy sensors to measure wasted energy in lighting even when there are no occupants [8]. They have implemented a wireless tool called LightWiSe (LIGHTting evaluation through WIreless SEnsors), which collect data from light sensors that are placed on used surfaces (desk, wall) to determine a comprehensive model of the perceived light level in the office. The authors claim that LightWiSe can highlight savings in the region of 50 % to 70 % that are achievable through optimizing the current control system or installing an alternative.

Delaney et al. [9] proposes modelling occupancy data using linear regression models. This approach involved collecting data from lighting and electrical loads, and occupancy data is estimated using a walkthrough survey of the building. This set of data were used as an input for the linear regression model which estimated occupancy for weekdays, weekends and holidays. The key limitation of this approach is to rely on energy usage to estimate if someone is present as in the case a large group of people is using a particular room, there will be no additional energy loads in the system and the model may report the room is empty.

Abushakra and Claridge [15], utilize a deployment of PIR and door sensors to obtain a binary indication of occupancy. They use a reactive strategy that adjusts the temperature based on current occupancy and estimate potential savings EnergyPlus.

Using this occupancy information as input to a simulation model of a building, they claim that the HVAC energy consumption can in fact be reduced from 10 % to 15 % using EnergyPlus. This approaches neglects the time required for a room to be brought to temperature and the impact of ventilation on energy savings.

Agarwal et al. [16] propose using a belief network for occupancy detection within buildings. By evaluating multiple sensory inputs (PIR and telephone on/off hook sensors) using a Markov Chain and an agent-based model, they determine the probability that a particular area is occupied. Markov Chain uses a transition matrix probabilities which are calculated by examining the exponential distribution of the sojourn times of the observed states. While these strategies are more suitable for predictive demand control strategies, they are are aimed for modeling occupancy for individual offices and cannot be applied to spaces with larger occupancies.

Dodier et al. [17] proposes a solution to provide input to a control strategy for energy savings in office buildings thought indoor activity recognition by using simple sensors (infrared, pressure and acoustic). Marchiori et al. [18] proposes a occupancy solution which uses a PIR sensor inside the room and one door sensor (magnetic reed switch). Nguyen and Aiello [19] use pressure pads to measure whether the user is sitting or lying on the bed as well as sitting on the desk chair, while collecting computer-related activities of the user.

Other approaches focus on using user's preference data to manage buildings consumption. For instance, Hagras et al. [20] proposes a solution to optimize the tradeoff between meeting user comfort and reduction in operation cost by reducing energy usage. Singhvi et al. [21] propose a smart building architecture that keeps track of workers' real-time location in an office and retrieve their personal preferences of lighting, cooling, and heating. Erickson et al. [23] proposes a smart building system using PIR sensing alongside algorithms supporting user profiles to determine occupancy within a smart building. The advantages of passive infrared are that they are highly resistant to false triggering, relatively inexpensive, and do not radiate any. However, they are strictly for line of sight use, and cannot see around objects, and doors, stairways and partitions have a tendency to block motion detection and reduce effectiveness.

More advanced systems for occupancy detection involves the use of cameras and computer vision algorithms. For instance, Chen et al. [22] proposed a wireless camera sensor network to determine real-time occupancy across a larger area in a building, which gathers floor-level traces of human mobility patterns in buildings. As proof of concept, they deployed a 16-node wireless camera sensor network in a multi-function building to determine the occupancy resolution. Erickson et al. [23] proposes a sonar based technique to detect the presence of computer users. This approach relies on sonar using hardware that already exists on commodity laptop computers and other electronic devices. The authors report that it is possible to detect the presence or absence of users with near perfect accuracy after only ten seconds of measurement. However, such solutions bring up concerns relating to cost, deployment and privacy issues.

CO_2-based occupancy detection has also been examined. Barbato et al. [24] pro-poses a solution to estimate actual occupancy in indoor spaces by measuring the carbon dioxide concentration of the return air and the outdoor air flow rate. Wang and chin [26] developed an algorithm based on the mass balance equation of the carbon dioxide in rooms and delivers occupants presence profiles. To evaluate the algorithm, a presence matching index (PM index) and an occupants matching index (OM index) have been introduced. Nevertheless, CO_2 buildup is slow and the sensors may take a long time to detect high levels of CO_2.

Intelligent Systems have also been used to detect occupancy in buildings. For in-stance, Hagras [20] have proposed a fuzzy expert system to learn user's preferences and to predict their needs with regards lighting intensity, temperature. The system is self-adjust its behavior when users change their habits is proposed the system. Mozer [28] applies neural networks to create a system able to optimally controlling temperature, light, ventilation and water heating within buildings based on data collected from inside the building environment.

Despite these efforts, less attention has been paid in detecting occupancy for desk usage optimization within smart buildings. Workspace management is among the most discussed subjects of facility managers, as growing cost pressures drive organizations to uncover under-utilized facilities and significantly reduce occupancy costs by downsizing and associating real estate portfolios. The current approaches used in previous work are also applicable in the workspace management scenarios, and people involved in the planning and management of buildings must innovate new ways to use the component pieces that already exists to study of how well the workstations, offices and meeting rooms are used over time within the corporate space.

4   Occupancy Value Analysis

The value types that underlie occupancy data are broadly related to the realm of smart buildings and span many stakeholder perceptions. These have been identified through relevant literature (e.g. [16, 29, 30] etc.) broken down further and can be seen in more detail Fig. 3. Identified value types have no universal equity or ranking, and different building design clients will favour them differently. For the purposes of this paper, we will exclusively examine the financial benefit of the examined use cases. To this end, we will use the commercial tenant's end profitability as the fundamental metric. Working backwards from this, we will use a traditional business metric of *profit* being decomposed as:

$$profit = (price\ of\ service/good * volume\ of\ sales) - (fixed\ costs + variable\ costs)$$

(1)

To translate the outcomes of a specific use case to a series of consequences that map as variables to formula (1), it is necessary to create a basic framework to understand the possible paths involved in the value calculations. The purpose of this framework is to create broad estimations of value, whilst taking note of confidence levels in estimation along the way. It is designed to neither be exhaustive nor rigid, but to simply categorize immediate consequences of a use case, and direct the calculation process to the final financial figure.

Due to the primarily order-of-magnitude nature of these estimates, we will rate the accuracy of estimates on a qualitative scale. This will span from 1, which is accurate to

Value Types

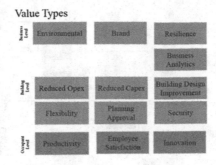

Fig. 3. Types of value cases in the smart built environment.

less than or equal to 2 orders of magnitude accuracy, to 10, with accuracy equal to, or better than, ±10 % accuracy, with a logarithmic scale spanning between each.

While we aspire to create a currency of value that is equivalent across all concepts, this ideal is of course not what is realized in practice. Not all values are equally realizable. Rather than attempt to quantify how easy-to or hard-to materialize value affects its utility, we will simply categorize any estimated value into the following categories:

Immediate Savings - These are costs for something that is on a quantity or time-basis, and as such can be easily renegotiated to suit a new, better requirement. An example of this is the reduction in electricity used to power a building; the costs can easily be realized in liquid terms at the next monthly billing date.

Intermediate Savings - These are costs for something that is on a quantity or time-basis, and as such can be renegotiated to suit a new, better requirement, albeit considerable barriers to change stand in the way. An example of this is relocating a particular business team to a different part of a company's real estate portfolio.

Capacitive Conditional - These are savings in kind that can be reused to create value elsewhere, dependent heavily on the state of other factors in the organization. An example is a time saving of middle-ranking employee hours; these could be used to work on new client work, but only if more client work exists to work on.

Capacitive Unconditional - These are savings in kind that can be reused to create value elsewhere, regardless of other conditions. An example is the saving of time of a business development employee; time savings could be reinvested in what can be assumed to be an incompletable task.

Quality Gains - This is an improvement in the quality of a product or service, without specifically creating it in a shorter period of time. An example of this is being able to charge more for a service due to an increase in its quality due to more empowered staff.

Work Volume Gains - These are value gains similar to Quality Gains, but rather than allowing you to gain more per unit for a service or product that you offer, you are able to take a larger market share. An example of this is a concept that allows you to ensure

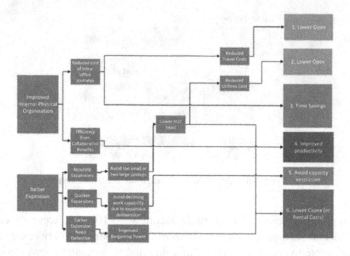

Fig. 4. Occupancy data value chain and calculation paths.

water-tight client confidentiality, thus improving client retention. The distinction here is that capacity to undertake the work is required before the value can be obtained Fig. 4.

For our scenario analysis we use the assumptions of Table 1 to explore the specific magnitude of value each instance of occupancy data use-case can realise for an organisation. These are based on figures from state of art reports such as [31, 32].

Table 1. Scenario analysis assumptions.

Staff	Value		Finances	
Employees	200		Yearly Wage Bucket	£4,921,200
Average Wage	£ 13.67		Assume Total Over-heads	2.5
Hours/Week	37.5			
Weeks/Year	48		Assume Profit Margin	0.15
			Assume Revenue	£17,962,380

Office Dimensions			Building-Specific Costs	
Desk area per capita	15m²		Gas £/m2	£ 4.57
Small Meeting Room Area	61 m²		Elec £/m2	£ 12.84
...of quantity	3		Other Space Based Over-heads £/m2	£ 5.00
Medium Meeting Room Area	84 m²			
...of quantity	2		Rent £/m2	£ 102.00
Large Meeting Room Area	137 m²		Total £/m2	£ 124.41
...of quantity	1			
Area Total	3488 m²			

We will now examine a sample use case using this logic, namely Room User Recognition. In Fig. 5 we can apply assumptions and numerical values to the chain to arrive at our estimates. The scenario assumptions are derived from real-world second

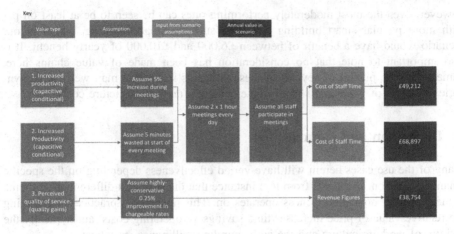

Fig. 5. Computing the benefits of a single use case through its value chain.

hand empirically reported data [31, 32] and the use case assumptions are conservative order-of-magnitude estimates. By computing all of the value chains we arrive at a value of £156,863. Reviewing the confidence level of each individual chain, and weighting this to a confidence level for the entire use case, we arrive at a value of '5' on the qualitative scale, i.e. this is believed to be accurate to 1 order of magnitude.

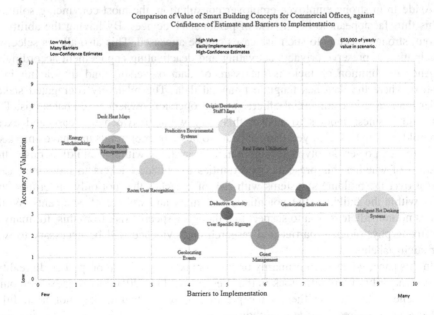

Fig. 6. A mapping of use cases across value perceptions based on value chain analysis.

Using the same method across the use case portfolio, the results of which can be viewed in Fig. 6, it can be observed that there exists no real categorization across the performance of the use cases and their results span different sizes of value. Crucially however, even the most moderately performing ones can be seen to be at least on par with more popular smart building concepts, such as Smart Lighting, which in our scenario would have a benefit of between £6,000 and £10,000 of yearly benefit. It is also important to note that no consideration has been made of value chains here, namely that the pursuit of several of these concepts in parallel may well create synergies in terms of value and shared implementation and infrastructure costs.

5 Discussion and Conclusions

Many of the use cases herein will have varied effectiveness depending on the specific tenant in question. It appears from first instance that the strongest differentiating theme is the value-per-hour the business operates on. This operates in practice by changing the relative value of price increases/time savings vs operating costs, and typically the solidity of working culture and the corresponding willingness to adjust.

As Occupancy-Based systems involve the detection of human movement, and then in turn advise the nature of further movement, additional enablers and barriers are realized over those applicable to current popular Smart Building concepts. A common consideration to all Smart Building markets, there is evidence that building occupants may oppose increased sensing in the workplace, particularly through use case categories that have highly granular datasets – occupancy, for example. This is exacerbated in commercial offices by the complex relationships of employer and employee [30].

Aside from strong employee-employer consultation, the most convincing solution to this thus far appears to be the use of personal IT devices. By having the ability to opt-out, strong objectors to such use cases can be appeased. This also allows selective participation to preserve privacy, activating and deactivating engagement accordingly.

Another common obstacle is the issue of data ownership and interfacing in a con-text where the data has tangible financial data. The relatively segregated stakeholder landscape in commercial offices (tenant, operator, owner) exacerbates this. The legal and business models to answer this vary wildly between use case and exact stakeholder setup and as of yet, there appears to be no overall trends that have emerged.

Increased power devolved to automated IT systems within a building raises the question of whether this presents opportunities to outside hackers to have increased control over the building's systems with risk of breaches that not only undermine the assets within the building, but potentially the safety and welfare of occupants. While there is no immediate reason to suspect that there is a specific risk from this, for many it is a strong physiological barrier and research and evidence will be necessary to win over such stakeholders.

In this paper we focused primarily on the context of new build properties. In reality, the vast majority of building stock in the Western world in 2050 has already been built today. The ability to use these concepts in a retrofit situation has not been fully explored and requires considerable thought.

Acknowledgements. This work has been supported by Arup Group Ltd. through the Industrial Doctoral Centre in Systems at the University of Bristol.

References

1. IBM (2011). https://www.ibm.com/developerworks/mydeveloperworks/blogs/invisiblethread/entry/it-is-time-to-make-our-cities-smarter?lang=en. Accessed 02 Dec 2013
2. United Nations, World Population Prospects: The 2010 revision. extended dataset on CD-ROM, ST/ESA/SER.A/308, Sales No. 11.XIII.7. Department of Economic and Social Affairs, Population Division, NY (2011)
3. Bose, R.K. (ed.): Energy Efficient Cities: Assessment Tools and Benchmarking Practices, World Bank, Washington, D.C. (2009)
4. DOE. Buildings Energy Data Book, Department of Energy, March 2009. http://buildingsdatabook.eren.doe.gov/
5. Sinopoli, J.: Smart buildings: a handbook for the design and operation of building technology systems, (2006)
6. Erickson, V.L., Lin, Y., Kamthe, A. Brahme. R., Surana, A., Cerpa, A., Sohn, E.M.D., Narayanan, S.: Energy efficient building environment control strategies using real-time occupancy measurements. In: Proceedings of the First ACM Workshop on Embedded Sensing Systems for Energy-Efficiency in Buildings, pp. 19–24 (2009)
7. Estrin, D., Girod, L., Pottie, G., Srivastava, M.: Instrumenting the world with wireless sensor networks. In: International Conference on Acoustics, Speech, and Signal Processing (ICASSP), pp. 2033–2036 (2001)
8. Gao, G., Whitehouse, K.: The self-programming thermostat: optimizing setback schedules based on home occupancy patterns. In: Proceedings of the First ACM Workshop on Embedded Sensing Systems for Energy-Efficiency in Buildings, pp. 67–72 (2009)
9. Delaney, D.T., O'Hare, G.M.P., Ruzzelli, A.G.: Evaluation of energy-efficiency in lighting systems using sensor networks. In: Proceedings of the First ACM Workshop on Embedded Sensing Systems for Energy-Efficiency in Buildings, pp. 61–66 (2009)
10. Agarwal, Y., Hodges, S., Chandra, R., Scott, J., Bahl, P., Gupta, R.: Somniloquy: augmenting network interfaces to reduce PC energy usage. In: Proceedings of USENIX Symposium on Networked Systems Design and Implementation (NSDI) (2009)
11. Agarwal, Y., Savage, S., Gupta, R.: Sleep server: a software-only approach for reducing the energy consumption of PCS within enterprise environments. In: Proceedings of USENIX Annual Technical Symposium (USENIX ATC) (2010)
12. Lo, L.J., Novoselac, A.: Localized air-conditioning with occupancy control in an open office. Energy Build. **42**, 1120–1128 (2010)
13. Zhu, Y., Liu, M.et al.: Optimization of Control Strategies for HVAC Terminal Boxes. In: Proceedings of 12th Symposium on Improving Building Systems in Hot and Humid Climates (2000)
14. Padmanabh, K., Malikarjuna, A., Sen, V.S., Katru, S.P., Kumar, A., Vuppala, S.P.C.S.K., Paul, S.: iSense: a wireless sensor network based conference room management system. In: Proceedings of the First ACM Workshop on Embedded Sensing Systems for Energy-Efficiency in Buildings, pp. 37–42 (2009)
15. Abushakra, B., Claridge, D.: Accounting for the occupancy variable in inverse building energy baselining models. In: ICBEO. Energy Systems Laboratory (2001)
16. Agarwal, Y., Balaji, B., Gupta, R., Lyles, J., Wei, M., Weng, T.: Occupancy-driven energy management for smart building automation. In: BuildSys (2010)
17. Dodier, R.H., Henze, G.P., Tiller, D.K., Guo, X.: Building occupancy detection through sensor belief networks. Energy & Buildings (2006)

18. Marchiori, A., Han, Q.: Distributed wireless control for building energy management. In: Proceedings of the 2nd ACM Workshop on Embedded Sensing Systems for Energy-Efficiency in Building, BuildSys 2010, pp. 37–42. ACM, NY (2010)
19. Nguyen, T. A., Aiello, M.: Beyond Indoor Presence Monitoring with Simple Sensors. In: Proceedings of the 2nd International Conference on Pervasive and Embedded Computing and Communication Systems (2012)
20. Hagras, H., Callaghan, V., Colley, M., Clarke, G., Pounds-Cornish, A., Duman, H.: Creating an ambient-intelligence environment using embedded agents, IEEE Intell. Syst. 19(6), 12–20 (2004)
21. Singhvi, V., Krause, A., Guestrin, C., Garrett Jr., J.H., Matthews, H.S.: Intelligent light control using sensor networks. In: Proceedings of the 3rd International Conference on Embedded Networked Sensor Systems, SenSys, pp. 218–229. ACM, NY (2005)
22. Chen, H., Chou, P., Duri, S., Lei, H., Reason, J.: The design and implementation of a smart building control system In: IEEE International Conference on e-Business Engineering, ICEBE. pp. 255–262 (2009)
23. Erickson, V.L., Lin, Y., Kamthe, A., Rohini, B., Surana, A., Cerpa, A.E., Sohn, M.D., Narayanan, S.: Energy Efficient building environment control strategies using realtime occupancy measurements. In: Proceedings of the First ACM Workshop on Embedded Sensing Systems for Energy-Efficiency in Buildings, BuildSys 2009, pp. 19–24. ACM, NY (2009)
24. Barbato, A., Borsani, L., Capone, A., Melzi, S.: Home energy saving through a user profiling system based on wireless sensors. In: Conference on Embedded Networked Sensor Systems, pp. 49–54 (2009)
25. Tarzia, S. P., Dick, R. P., Dinda, P.A., Memik. G.: Sonar-based measurement of user presence and attention. In: UbiComp, pp. 89–92 (2009)
26. Wang, S., Jin, X.: Co 2-based occupancy detection for on-line outdoor air flow control. Indoor Built Environ. 7(3), 165–181 (1998)
27. Calì, D., Matthes, P., Huchtemann, K., Streblow, R., Müller, D.: CO2 based occupancy detection algorithm: experimental analysis and validation for office and residential buildings. Build. Environ. 86, 39–49 (2015)
28. Mozer, M.: The Neural Network House: An Environment that Adapts to its Inhabitants. In Proceedings of the American Association for Artificial Intelligence (1998)
29. Snoonian, D.: Smart buildings. IEEE Spectr. 40(8), 18–23 (2003)
30. Hughes, W. P., Ancell, D., Gruneberg, S. Hirst, L.: Exposing the myth of the 1:5:200 ratio relating initial cost, maintenance and staffing costs of office buildings. In: ARCOM Conference, p. 12 (2004)
31. WRAP. Green Office: A guide to running a more cost-effective and environmentally sustainable office (2014)
32. Department of Business, UK Government: Analysis on UK Wages, 14 February (2015)

Designing Apps for Tourists: A Case Study

Virginia Tiradentes Souto[1]([⊠]), Caio Cristo[2], Maria Gabriela Araújo[1],
and Lucas Santos[1]

[1] Department of Design, University of Brasilia, Brasilia, Brazil
{v.tiradentes, shizen70, santoslucasls}@gmail.com
[2] Department of Computer Science, University of Brasilia, Brasilia, Brazil
caiocrivellente@gmail.com

Abstract. With the popularity of new digital media, such as smartphones and
tablets, many applications have been designed in order to help tourists at different moments of their trips. This study shows the creative process of designing
an app for tourists. The design of this mobile app is a part of a project that aims
to investigate the design of mobile apps for tourists and their implications for
interaction design and information visualization fields. It also describes the
method, the stages, and different approaches taken during the creative process.
In addition, some related studies on designing such apps are reviewed. It finally
shows some reflections on the possibilities, difficulties and challenges designers
have while trying to create an innovative app for tourists.

Keywords: Designing apps · Mobile tourist applications · Visualization
information · Creative process

1 Introduction

With the popularity of new digital media, such as smartphones and tablets, many
applications have been designed in order to help tourists at different moments of their
trips. Maps, images, graphics and augmented reality can be used to help users locate
places in a city. Tools like Google Maps offer a map service that helps tourists to plan
their trip on foot, by car, using public transport, or cycling. According to Mayer, many
Google Maps accesses (40 %) are already made from mobile devices, and Google
Maps has 150 million mobile users [1].

The tourism industry is undergoing massive changes because of the Internet,
information technology and the telecommunication industry [2]. The tendency to use
mobile devices to help users locate places has driven the design of several applications
for this purpose. Cities that receive a huge number of tourists, such as London and New
York, have several applications to help tourists. The designers of such applications are
creating new visual languages and new possibilities for interaction with users. Despite
the effort that some researchers have made to better understand the user interface with
these applications, much remains to be investigated. The way the visual elements are
presented to users differs from what they have been used to. Interaction possibilities
have been multiplied, and the control users have over the interface as well. Infographics, icons, text, 2D, 3D images, animated or not, have been created in a new

A. Marcus (Ed.): DUXU 2015, Part III, LNCS 9188, pp. 425–436, 2015.
DOI: 10.1007/978-3-319-20889-3_40

format, with new technology and with the possibility of further integration of the interface elements.

There is a growing number of tourists around the world. According to the latest UNWTO World Tourism Barometer, revenues from international tourism reached a new record in 2012 (US$ 1,075 billion), 4 % over the previous year [3]. Many authors explain the importance of mobile applications for tourists [4–8]. According to Höpken et al. [7], the importance and success of mobile applications for tourists is due to their ability to support the tourist during all stages of travel. Although mobile devices are particularly useful because of their ubiquitous nature [2] it is relevant to consider that mobile devices present usability limitations [9].

This study presents research on the design of apps for tourists. It shows the creative process of designing an app for tourists, including the method, the stages and different approaches taken during the creative process. It also describes some related studies on designing such apps. It finally shows some reflections on the possibilities, difficulties and challenges designers have noted while trying to create an innovative app for tourists.

2 Designing Apps for Tourists

Research on the design of mobile applications with a focus on tourists is not so new. It is possible to find papers dating from the mid 1990s on this topic. In the last 20 years many studies have been published in this area. As said above, tourism is one of largest business areas and technological products related to it are a big market. Malaka and Zipf [10] explains the combination of tourism and IT areas. According to them, tourism is influenced by new IT products, and IT research is applied to the tourism domain in order to research new and complex interactive information systems.

Some reviews of studies on mobile tourist applications have been done. For example, Kenteris et al. [2] reviewed the research on mobile applications used by tourists to retrieve information, navigation and guidance. Another review on the literature on mobile tourist recommendation systems was done by Gavalas et al. [11]. The aim of this paper is not to carry out another literature review on mobile tourist applications, but some research on this topic is described in order to highlight important findings as well as some characteristics of mobile tourist applications.

It seems that one of the first studies on mobile applications for tourism was conducted by the College of Computing and the Graphics, Visualization and Usability (GVU Center) at Georgia Tech, in 1996. They developed the Cyberguide project. Cyberguide is a mobile context-aware tour guide that has four main components: map, information, navigation, and communication. The tour guide plays the role of cartographer, librarian, navigator and messenger. In designing the guide, they first thought about the activities the users would do and how they could be supported by mobile technology and then they decided how the technology would have to work. They used a modular approach for system development. This modularity in the design of the project helped them in developing one component without impacting on the rest of the system.

Another example of a study of this area through the design of a mobile system is the Deep Map research framework [10]. Deep Map is a mobile system that aimed to aid tourists in navigating through the city of Heidelberg and to generate personal guided walks for tourists. Deep Map project addresses several research aspects, such as: intelligent integration of information from different data sources and services including geographical information systems, multimedia databases, and interactive Internet data sources. The researchers draw attention to usability aspects within mobile systems. They argue that usability is one of the main aspects for the success of tourism information systems, as these need to be intuitively usable. They also call attention to the system's multiple modalities for input and output. According to them, natural language is important for users that are hands-free and cannot visualize the screen. On the other hand, a graphical user interface is useful to visualize complex information, such as maps.

Like Malaka and Zipf [10], Schmidt-Belz et al. [12] also investigated maps and other services through the design of a system. The CRUMPET system was developed by the European IST project in order to create a user-friendly mobile service personalized for Tourism. The system's main functionalities are: recommendation of services (e.g. tourist attractions); interactive maps; information about tourist attractions; and proactive tips. In the interactive maps users could: overview maps of the area, find the current position of the user, pan out and zoom in on the maps, and could also have the maps highlighting sites of interest and tours. They concluded among other things that it is important both to add value by location-awareness and to provide interactive maps.

Also on researching interactive maps for tourism applications, Noguera et al. [9] designed a system that adapts the recommendations provided for users according to their current physical location and also presents a 3D map-based interface with a virtual representation of the world where the tourist is currently located. With this system they try to fulfill four tourist needs: to know where they are, which interesting items are nearby, how far they are from them, and how they reach them. The authors argue that the success of a mobile tourism system depends on both a recommender engine, and an intuitive and usable interface.

With a different approach, Kenteris et al. [2] created a categorization of mobile tourist guides aiming to extract design principles. The categorization was based on an evaluation of research and mobile applications used by tourists to retrieve information, navigation and guidance. They classified these applications into four groups: mobile guides, navigational assistants, web-to-mobile applications and mobile web-based. Based on their findings they claim that an application designer should follow at least these three principles: the information model to be used, the unique services to be provided and the input/output modalities to be incorporated in the overall project. They also claim that designers should keep in mind multilingualism. They provide a list of 'common denominator' services, such as: guided tours, communication between users and the system, e-services (e.g. currency conversion), group meeting scheduler, registering position for friends, and pre-visit and post-visit services support. Finally, they claim that more work is needed on social networking for tourist users. According to them, there is no study that connected content to social networks, such as Facebook and Twitter.

It seems that one of the most investigated kinds of mobile tourist application is the recommender system. Many studies have investigated mobile tourism recommender systems [9, 11, 13]. Recommender systems, such as Deep Map [10] and iTravel [13], are considered important as they can both offer travel recommendations to tourists and reduce the information overload. Gavalas et al. [11] made a review of the state-of-the-art in mobile tourism recommender systems (RS). They investigated the main features of mobile tourism RS studies dated from 2000 to 2012. The features analyzed were: recommendation technique, categories, items recommended, additional services offered/unique features, criteria used for recommendation, and architecture/client application implementation platform. They also proposed a classification of mobile tourism RSs with three different aspects: their chosen architecture, the degree of user involvement in the delivery of recommendations and the criteria taken into account for deriving recommendations. They conclude that mobile RSs represent a fast-evolving domain of research, and tourism in particularly is the most popular among these studies. They also highlight that the focus of these studies moved from dealing with the limitations of mobile devices, such as limited processing power and display resolution, to sensing, computational and visualization capabilities.

Still focusing on recommendation systems for tourist applications, Yang and Hwang [13] claim that most recommender systems fail to exploit information, evaluations or ratings of other tourists. According to them, most existing recommender systems use content-based approach for making a recommendation. In this approach, users state their needs based upon on selected parameters and the system then correlates their choices with catalogued destinations. The authors proposed a different approach in which mobile peer-to-peer communications (e.g. Bluetooth or Wi-Fi) are used to provide tourists with convenient means for exchanging ratings via their mobile device. They designed and tested a recommendation system for tourists using peer-to-peer communication and found that users liked the system, because having the information at the right time and in the right place helped them to make travel decisions.

The studies described above, as well as the literature reviewed on interaction design and information visualization, and an analysis of many different mobile apps with a focus on tourists were used to help us to define the application described below.

3 Designing an App for Tourists: A Case Study

In this section the project we are calling Facemap is described and discussed. The design of this mobile app is a part of a project that aims to investigate the design of a mobile app for tourists and its implications for interaction design and information visualization fields. Facemap is a mobile application that has three main functions: (1) connects people with similar interests that go to a particular event, (2) allows them to chat, and (3) helps them (by Google Map and Google Street View) to meet in a chosen place.

3.1 Defining the Concept

This project started with a discussion about mobile tourism design with researchers from different academic backgrounds. Headed by a designer researcher, also part of this project were researchers and students from different areas, such as: art media, design, computer science, software engineer, and robotics. The main question was: what are the challenges for designers to create innovative mobile applications, specially focused on tourism? In order to answer this question the state of the art of such applications and fields related to it were discussed. Then an analysis was carried out in different mobile applications, on their graphic interface, visualization, usability problems. From this perspective, we thought how we could create an app in order to investigate this area with a focus on the graphical interface of such applications. With a brainstorming section, it was considered relevant to include a social approach to this study in the investigations. It was highlighted that tourism has a social aspect and that this has not been greatly explored in this kind of app. This is in line with Brown and Chalmers [6], in a study that considered tourism a social activity, and with Kenteris et al. [2], where a literature review did not find studies that connected social networks with content for tourist users, although this was considered a relevant topic.

The ideas generated for the project were based on real situations and current problems. Some of the ideas were related to the World Cup, which was about to happen in Brazil (in June 2014), just a few months from the start of this project. The initial idea of this project was to design an app that could help the international public to find people from their own country in order to watch the games together.

Based on this initial idea, the design of the app was created. The aim was to do something new not only in the concept idea, but also in the graphical interface design. Studying the state of the art for mobile apps in general, and more in particularly for tourism, we saw that there are hugely different functions, services and approaches among them. However, what we realized is that maybe because of the restrictions of the user interface guidelines, provided by the companies of the operation systems of such apps [14, 15] they look very similar. Users can nowadays find many apps that have the same function. So, what makes one more used than another? What constitutes the success of an app? How can designers create innovative apps that help users to use them? Good usability is certainly one of the answers, and indeed usability and intuitive interfaces are considered to be two important aspects for the success of tourism information systems [9, 10].

3.2 Defining the Visualization Systems

So how should user interfaces be made intuitive? Information visualization also seems to be one of the key areas for that. Gavalas et al. [11], in a recent review of literature, mentioned in Sect. 2, found that one of the main areas of study on mobile tourism systems is their visual capability. According to them, the major design challenge for mobile recommended systems is to use adequate interface techniques to visualize recommended items [11].

One of the areas of study was the different type of visualizations for social networking. Network systems are "patterns of connections between elements in the systems" [16]. There are some research projects on this topic [17] and many samples of network visualizations [18]. It was agreed that in order to make it easier to visualize their social network for mobile use, simplicity in the visual aspect of the interface should be achieved. However, when dealing with a large size of network keeping it simple is a challenge.

At this phase of the project we decided that one of the main functionalities of the app would be to allow users to find people with a chosen profile that would be going to the same event. How to do that? And how to show the people the user is looking for?

To solve the issue of how to do that we decided to use the Facebook social network. The use of Facebook facilitates the connection among users and also allows their existing profile to be used. Therefore, the profile characteristics chosen were taken from the ones used by Facebook: where you live, where you studied, where you work, profession, age. The idea was to give users the possibility of choosing the character-istics of people they would like to meet. But how would people they were looking for appear on the display? Typically the visualization of query results is displayed as a ranked list of information items [11]. However, we did not think that a list of names would be the best way of showing this result.

We thus decided to study and analyze different types of network systems. According to Meirelles [16] there are three main methods for representing networks. They are: lists, matrices and node-link diagrams. According to her, lists are rarely used because of the large size of many networks; matrices are good for avoiding the problem of too many link crossings; whereas node-link diagrams are good for physical network systems as they "provide the spatial attribute to locate both nodes and links into the spatial structure of the diagram".

It seems that there are not many samples of diagram network visualizations for mobile applications. One of the reasons may be because they are too complex to be seen on small screens, or it may also be related to the complexity of developing such visualizations for mobile systems. Studying possible visualizations that would make it easier for the users to see the people they were looking for we found the hierarchical structure called Treemap.

Treemap is a defined as "a space-constrained visualization of hierarchical struc-tures", that "enables users to compare nodes and sub-trees" and is considered to be "very effective in showing attributes of leaf nodes using size and color coding" [19]. In this structure the shapes are organized according to their hierarchy or categorization. Treemap visualization structures have been used since the 1900s when they were created by Shneiderman [20]. One well-known sample that uses the treemap algorithm is called Newsmap, designed by Weskamp in 2004 [21]. This application takes the Google news output and shows it with a treemap, where color codes the type of news (e.g. national) and the size of the shape indicates how many stories there are on this topic [19]. Other samples and the history of treemaps can be found in Shneiderman and Plaisant [20].

The treemap algorithm was not used in the design of Facemap. However, we took the concept of this type of structure and adapted to our context. We verified two main advantages of this type of visualization for our app: (1) the fact that it is a space-efficient display of large datasets [16], which therefore makes it possible to use the whole display; and (2) the fact that it allows shapes to be organized according to their hierarchy, by using different sizes to indicate which people have a profile that is more like the profile sought. Figure 1 shows (a) the screen with the search criteria in which the participants will be ordered and (b) sample of screen with the participants ordered as defined in the previous screen.

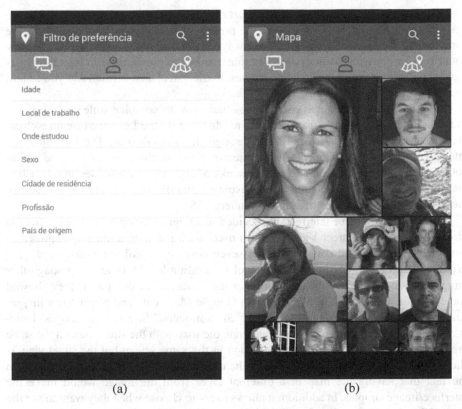

Fig. 1. (a) Screen with the search criteria in which the participants will be ordered and (b) sample of screen with the participants ordered as defined in the previous screen. Photos from the authors' personal archive.

Apart from social network visualizations and hierarchical structures another area of study was interactive maps. As said, when we are talking about apps for tourists one of the main functions is to provide a map for the users. Valuable interactive maps are considered important in a mobile system for tourism [12]. Interactive maps for mobiles have been studied by many researchers [12, 22, 23]. It is incredible how some maps like Google Maps can give us our current position, and help us to go somewhere with a precise description of the way, in different forms such as geographic maps, 3D maps, satellite maps, and street maps. The best type of map seems to be dependent on the context and on the user and her needs, among other things [24].

In the context of the app, the map would be used by two people that would be chatting and deciding where to go. A sample scenario would be of two people who do not know the city they are in, who are in different places and want to meet somewhere that would be convenient for both. For that, the map should point to the current location of each one, show the places between them, and then direct them to the place chosen. To show the current location and the places around we chose to use Google Maps. However, as the purpose of this app is not only to design a functional and appealing app, but also to investigate the state of the art of interactive maps in order to choose the best that would fit the requirements of the project, we studied and discussed how we could enhance the user's experience. What types of maps, how many types and how could they be shown? Studies points out that one of the problems with digital maps is the fact that they do not give contextual clues, as the visual area is small and you cannot see the whole map [24].

In a search for different types of maps and how to combine different maps, we found an interesting sample from the Louvre Museum. In the Louvre Museum website there is an option for users to navigate through the Virtual Tour. The tour offers an interactive visit of the galleries of the museum, allowing the users to navigate within 360 panoramic views, zooming to certain works of art. The tour provides an interactive map (located under the panoramic view displays) that displays the current position of the visitor and gives access to a chosen gallery [25].

Based on this type of interface we decided to integrate Google Maps with Google Street View. Google Street View provides users with panoramic imagery captured in hundreds of cities in 50 countries across seven continents [26]. Anguelov et al. [27] explains that Street View is a powerful tool for finding local businesses, among other things, as they can be combined with other data sources. In this paper, they showed some images with the use of 3D data, with Google Maps data and Street View images combined in the same image, resulting in "3D-annotated" Street View images. However, in our project we decided not to integrate the map with the street view in the same image. Users will see the map and the image in the same screen but the street view is shown small and will only increase when the user decides. This decision was based on the fact that having the map in a different layer from the image would make the interface/image simpler. In addition, it allows users to choose when they want to see the Street View image, and therefore provides them with contextual information whenever they want. Figure 2 shows an example of the map screen with Google Maps showing the places of the two participants and with (a) the Street View window reduced, and (b) with the Street View window expanded.

3.3   Comments About the App Development Process

It is important to highlight that although, as mentioned at the beginning of this section, researchers and students from different areas participated in some phases of the project, three designers and two programmers developed most of it. In specific issues some other professionals, designers and users were asked to contribute to the project.

Facemap is being designed with the main aim of investigating the design of a mobile app for tourists and the implications for interaction design and information visualization fields. We have not followed a particular type of methodology, because research questions that appeared during the development process would be considered, and this would have implications for the design of the app. However, the research project lasted for one year and had a deadline, and some issues could therefore not be investigated and implemented, such as map customization.

A multidisciplinary team seems to be one of the key factors for the success of such projects. Diversity in the team's academic and professional backgrounds, as well as

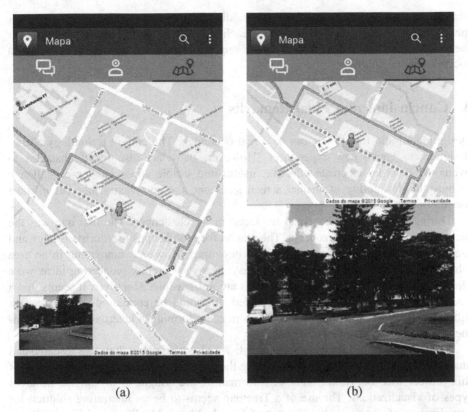

Fig. 2. An example of the map screen with Google Maps showing the places of the two participants and with (a) the Street View window reduced, and (b) with the Street View window expanded. Photo from the authors' personal archive.

mobile experience, and the presence of both men and women on the team, among others, can help to understand the problems and propose solutions in a more efficient way. Although target users were consulted about specific issues in different phases of the project, it did not happen in a systematic way. This also seems to be one of the main issues for projects with a restricted time. At the same time that it is considered relevant to have the participation of target users at different moments of the development of the app, having this participation requires time to plan, to execute and to analyze data. It seems that one way to have users' participation in the project without affecting its deadline, is to carry out informal consultations. In this approach, target users that are easy to access are from time to time asked to give an opinion, or to do a task. However, this approach should be used only to decide about smaller issues. Big issues should be analyzed with a careful and formal user test seeming to be more appropriate.

It is also important to highlight that good communication among the members of the team seems to be one of the keys to the success of a project. We noted a certain level of difficulty for the members of the team to understand the problems and the tasks of others. Although designers and programmers frequently work together on projects like this, their approaches and methods are different. Spending time to explain better the activities, thoughts and challenges of each member of the team may save time for the project and also make the team more engaged, and as a result help to design a successful final solution.

4 Conclusions and Final Remarks

Designing an app for tourists can be a real challenge. The current technology allows designers to create new experiences. However, there are also many obstacles to overcome in order to create effective, useful and usable apps, and these challenge include the desirability of smaller screen sizes and the complexity inherent in most usage contexts [28].

During the design of Facemap we faced many challenges. The first one was the definition of an innovative concept. The market for mobile apps for tourists is huge and there are many possibilities for designing new apps. However, innovating in an area where there are already so many is not easy. Many apparently pioneering ideas were already taken. In addition some good ideas are not feasible. Moreover, it seems that a good environment for innovation is needed. It should be composed of people with different points of view and previous experiences, forming a heterogeneous environment conducive to innovative ideas.

This project looked for this environment. We also carried out thorough research and analysis on the possible ways of designing the app. Considering that the key issue of this project was the visualization of information, we sought to investigate different types of visualizations. The use of a Treemap seems to be an interesting solution for visualization of query results. The use of Google Map – My Place and Google Street View displayed on the same page may help people to have a contextualized view of the place, and therefore increase their sense of assertiveness. We also worried about interaction design, trying to make the interface as intuitive as possible.

This project is in its final stage; the beta version of Facemap is almost ready, and the next step is to conduct empirical studies. The studies will be conducted in a real situation, which means we will ask people to install the app and use it during an event. Apart from checking the usability problems that the app may have, tests will be conducted in order to try to understand the perception and feelings of users in relation to the design of mobile apps in general, mobile apps for tourists in particular, and especially in relation to the visualizations.

Acknowledgements. This research was supported by the CNPq - Brazil (The Brazilian National Council for Scientific and Technological Development).

References

1. Geller, J.: Google VP Marissa Mayer dishes Google mobile stats, 150 M mobile maps users. In: BRG (2011). http://bgr.com/2011/03/13/google-vp-marissa-mayer-dishes-google-mobile-stats-150-m-mobile-users/
2. Kenteris, M., Gavalas, D., Economou, D.: Electronic mobile guides: a survey. Pers. Ubiquit. Comput. 15(1), 97–111 (2011)
3. UNWTO: International tourism receipts grew by 4 % in 2012, World Tourism Organization. UNWTO (2013). http://media.unwto.org/en/press-release/2013-05-15/international-tourism-receipts-grew-4-2012
4. Benyon, D., Quigley, A., O'keefe, B., Riva, G.: Presence and digital tourism. AI Soc. 29(4), 521–529 (2013)
5. Bødker, M., Browning, D.: Tourism sociabilities and place: challenges and opportunities for design. Int. J. Des. 7(2), 19–30 (2013)
6. Brown, B., Chalmers, M.: Tourism and mobile technology. In: Kuutti, K., Karsten, E.J., Fitzpatrick, G., Dourish, P., Schmidt, K. (eds.) Proceedings of the Eighth Conference on European Conference on Computer Supported Cooperative Work (ECSCW 2003), pp. 335–354. Kluwer Academic Publishers, Norwell (2003)
7. Höpken, W., Fuchs, M., Zanker, M., Beer, T.: Context-based adaptation of mobile applications in tourism. J. Inf. Technol. Tour. 12(2), 175–195 (2010)
8. Rodríguez, B., Molina, J., Pérez, F., Caballero, R.: Interactive design of personalised tourism routes. Tour. Manag. 33(4), 926–940 (2012)
9. Noguera, J.M., Barranco, M.J., Segura, R.J., Martinez, L.: A mobile 3D-GIS hybrid recommender system for tourism. Inf. Sci. 215, 37–52 (2012)
10. Malaka, R., Zipf, A.: DEEP MAP - challenging IT research in the framework of a tourist information system. In: Fesenmaier, D., Klein, S., Buhalis, D. (eds.) Proceedings of ENTER 2000 on Information and Communication Technologies in Tourism 2000, pp. 15–27. Springer, Vienna (2000)
11. Gavalas, D., Konstantopoulosb, C., Mastakasb, K., Pantzioub, G.: Mobile recommender systems in tourism. J. Netw. Comput. Appl. 39, 319–333 (2014)
12. Schmidt-Belz, B., Laamanen, H., Poslad, S., Zipf, A.: Location-based mobile tourist services - first user experiences. In: Proceedings of the International Conference on Information and Communication Technologies in Tourism (2003)
13. Yang, W., Hwang, S.: iTravel: a recommender system in mobile peer-to-peer environment. J. Syst. Softw. 86(1), 12–20 (2013)
14. Apple: iOS Human Interface Guidelines. https://developer.apple.com/library/ios/documentation/UserExperience/Conceptual/MobileHIG/
15. Android Design. http://developer.android.com/design/index.html
16. Meirelles, I.: Design for Information: An Introduction to the Histories, Theories, and Best Practices Behind Effective Information Visualizations. Rockport Publishers, Beverly (2013)
17. VIDI group: Visualization and Interface Design Innovation (ViDi) research group. http://vidi.cs.ucdavis.edu/about
18. Ortiz, S.: Twitter Company One week of conversations at Twitter Co. From 2/15/13 to 2/22/13. http://moebio.com/newk/twitter/
19. Human-Computer Interaction Lab: Treemap, Human-Computer Interaction Lab, University of Maryland (2003). http://www.cs.umd.edu/hcil/treemap

20. Shneiderman, B., Plaisant, C.: Treemaps for space-constrained visualization of hierarchies: Including the History of Treemap Research at the University of Maryland. Human-Computer Interaction Lab, University of Maryland (2014). http://www.cs.umd.edu/hcil/treemap-history/
21. Weskamp, M.: Newsmap. http://newsmap.jp/
22. Abowd, G.D., Atkeson, C.G., Hong, J., Long, S., Kooper, R., Pinkerton, M.: Cyberguide: a mobile context-aware tour guide. Wirel. Netw. 3(5), 421–433 (1997)
23. Poppinga, B., Magnusson, C., Pielot, M., Rassmus-Grohn, K.: TouchOver map: audio-tactile exploration of interactive maps. In: Proceedings of the 13th International Conference on Human Computer Interaction with Mobile Devices and Services (MobileHCI 2011), pp. 545–550. ACM, New York (2011)
24. Santos, F.A., Souto, V.T.: Mapas digitais e impressos: um estudo sobre a facilidade e a preferência de uso. In: Interaction South America 2012, São Paulo. Anais do Interaction South America 2012 (2012)
25. Musée du Louvre. Virtual Tour (2015). http://musee.louvre.fr/visite-louvre/aideENG.html
26. Google: Street View. https://www.google.com/maps/views/streetview?gl=us
27. Anguelov, D., Dulong, C., Filip, D., Frueh, C., Lafon, S., Lyon, R., Ogale, A.S., Vincent, L., Weaver, J.: Google street view: capturing the world at street level. IEEE Comput. 43(6), 32–38 (2010)
28. de Sá, M., Churchill, E.F.: Mobile augmented reality: a design perspective. In: Huang, W., Alem, L., Livingston, M.A. (eds.) Human Factors in Augmented Reality Environments, pp. 139–164. Springer, New York (2013)

Designing the Driving Experience

Designing for the Naturalistic Driving Experience

Wanda Eugene[1(✉)], Jerone Dunbar[1], Alison Nolan[1], Juan E. Gilbert[1],
and Renesha L. Hendrix[2]

[1] Computer and Information Science and Engineering Department, University of
Florida, P.O. Box 116120, Gainesville, FL 32611, USA
{weugene, jerone, alisonlnolan, juan}@ufl.edu
[2] Computer Science, Jackson State University, 1400 John R. Lynch St, Jackson,
MS 39217, USA
rlhendrixl@gmail.com

Abstract. We designed a naturalistic driving study to compare voice-texting alternatives. The design accounts for the nuances we have discovered through research in our simulations studies and through the literature. We then conducted a pilot study to gauge the practice implications of our design. In this paper, we present the problems we encountered, solutions we developed, and other challenges faced in moving from a simulator experience to a real-world naturalistic study. Leveraging these findings, we put forth a set of design principles that will inform future research endeavors and provide instructions for conducting naturalistic driving studies. We hope this research serves as a comprehensive design guide for an effective naturalistic distracted driving study.

Keywords: Naturalistic driving study · Road safety · Transportation · Distracted driving · Design guidelines

1 Introduction

Distracted driving contributed to an estimated 421,000 accidents in the year 2012 [8]. It is estimated that 9 % of drivers are using a cell phone or manipulating an electronic device while operating a motor vehicle. According to the National Highway Traffic Safety Administration, this is almost 660,000 drivers that are driving distracted at any particular time [15]. The "100 Car Naturalistic Study" found that secondary tasks were performed during 40 % of all trips [8]. Secondary and tertiary tasks are activities that are not immediately important to the act of driving - including eating, using a cell phone, talking with a passenger, and interacting with in-vehicle infotainment systems (IVIS). Distraction contributed to 78 % of accidents or near-accidents in the 100 car naturalistic study [8]. This study was conducted prior to the more recent increase in touchscreen interfaces, which contribute to longer periods of time that the eyes are off the road. It is difficult to find accurate data on true causes of distracted driving accidents, but one can muse that the IVIS touchscreen displays play a role.

A new study by Virginia Tech Transportation Institute (VTTI) and Insurance Institute for Highway Safety (IIHS) examined the relationship between cell phone

© Springer International Publishing Switzerland 2015
A. Marcus (Ed.): DUXU 2015, Part III, LNCS 9188, pp. 439–449, 2015.
DOI: 10.1007/978-3-319-20889-3_41

usage and accidents or near-accidents. Not surprisingly, drivers were 17 % more likely to be involved in an accident or near-accident when reaching for, interacting with, or talking on their cell phone. It is interesting to note, however, that while talking on the phone, drivers had their eyes off the road only slightly less than their baseline driving. This stresses the importance of cognitive load and begs the question of when distraction was highest - and when the accidents or near accidents occurred. The researchers also took this a step further and found that drivers were unlikely to engage in other distracting behavior when using their cell phone. When not using their cell phone, however, drivers still engaged in distracting behavior. The biggest distracting behavior besides cell phone use was talking with a passenger [9].

All of the distractions in the vehicle prompt research questions such as "What is causing distracted driving and how can we prevent it?", and "What technologies can be implemented to lower distracted driving?". To answer these questions we decided to conduct user studies. The studies must be effectively designed so that not only can researchers have appropriate metrics to measure, but also have tangible data to apply to future technologies and studies. The more common method for conducting driving studies is to use a driving simulator. The simulators are typically relatively cheap, portable, and have minimal hardware installations. Some simulators, such as the National Advanced Driving Simulator in Iowa, are much more involved and help to mimic actual driving [7]. These expensive technologies include the movement of an actual car, 360-degree views, and give a nearly-perfect experience of actual driving. The driving simulators are able to provide some insight to how drivers will respond to distractions however all driving simulators currently share the same limitation, it is not truly driving. Thus ideally, to truly observe driver road behavior a study should include an actual car, on a real road, to most closely exemplify the driving experience. This is known as a naturalistic study.

When setting out to create our naturalistic driving study, we looked at others who have tackled the problem. It was surprising to find that there had been little research regarding naturalistic driving study design principles and guidelines to set standards. Within distracted driving research, we encounter standards in everything - subjective measures (Likert) of feeling distracted, Lane Change Task (LCT) to calculate lane deviations, International Organization of Standards (ISO) standards, etc. A number of naturalistic driving studies have been conducted, but little in terms of standards are available to help streamline the validity of these studies. As such, we decided to compile a preliminary list of naturalistic driving study principles based on the literature and conduct a pilot study to put them to the test. We present the lessons learned from our study in an attempt to create a set of standards to be adopted by all others conducting a naturalistic driving study experience.

2 Literature Review

2.1 Distracted Driving

The issue of driver distraction has been a growing problem in recent years and is still a serious problem today, resulting in numerous accidents and road fatalities [2, 5]. Driver distraction is viewed as the diversion of attention from activities that are necessary to safely operate a vehicle [5]. In the VTTI study, 100 cars were unobtrusively equipped with sensors and video cameras for 12–13 months. The study showed that almost 80 % of all crashes and 65 % of near-crashes involved the driver looking away from the roadway right before the crash [8]. Therefore, it is evident that many accidents occur when there is some form of distraction away from the forward roadway. The issue of distracted driving is a daunting task that is extremely difficult to completely study and address considering the plethora of distractions in the vehicle.

2.2   Laws and Responses

Reducing the use of mobile devices while driving has been the major focus in the effort to address distracted driving. As phone prevalence and use in the car has increased, governmental agencies and regulators have attempted to enforce texting while driving and phone use bans in some states in the US [4]. This was predicted to stop or scare drivers from phone use in the car. It has become apparent, however, that prohibiting drivers from texting has led to more distractions and accidents [1, 6]. Some of these bans actually increase the number of accidents on the road since drivers who use their phone while driving make the effort to hold their phones down and out of the sight of police officers, which essentially reduces their peripheral view thus leading to more accidents. It is very important to address the drivers needs while keeping them safe and less distracted from the primary task of driving [1]. As it become apparent regardless of laws and repercussions we cannot directly stop drivers from engaging in tasks deemed as distracting, many entities have moved to how do we provide them with the technologies that will safely assist them in accomplishing their intended tasks in a seamless manner.

2.3   Solutions

These revelations have prompted several entities, including car manufacturers, mobile app developers, etc., to dive deep into alternatives, such as eyes-free, hands-free technologies. There are numerous solutions that aim to limit driver distraction with respect to phone use in the car. A few of these applications include DriveSafe.ly, Cellcontrol, DriveScribe, tXtBlocker, Voiceing among many others. Some require users to look at or touch the phone, while others have a hands-free, eyes-free driven interface. Other applications aim to block phone use while the vehicle is in motion. As a result of the handheld phone use bans in some states, this has led to many of these hands-free, eyes free applications where users can use their voice to send and receive messages and applications that block some phone activities in a moving vehicle. Research has shown that applications such as Voiceing are one of the few applications that truly support hands-free, eyes free. Some applications have hands-free features but still require the user to touch the device at specific times. Voiceing, previously called VoiceTEXT is a hands-free, eyes free application developed by researchers at Clemson University that allows users to send and receive messages using their voice [10]. The advantage that Voiceing has over many other voice applications is that transcription from human voice to text is not the main focus of the application. The Voiceing system works by sending a recording of the sender's actual voice to the recipient of the message. The transcribed text is also available for later viewing if necessary. The notion of emphasizing on the recording of verbal messages is the key difference with Voiceing. In addition, some of these other applications read emails, texts and other incoming media out loud to the driver. They also allow drivers to utter a response and transcribe the message in order the limit the need to manually input text with the phone. These applications aim to limit distraction and touching the phone while operating a motor vehicle.

Despite the technological advances, a recent study sponsored by AAA Foundation for Traffic Safety claimed that even hands-free, eyes-free solutions to texting and tertiary tasks was still mentally demanding and hindered driving performance [12]. As more and more weigh in to address the current issue of distracted driving attributed to mobile phone use along with IVIS steadily increasing in number, the need to study and develop feasible strategies to keep drivers safe is dire. Yet, there currently exist little guidance in terms of standards for designing a naturalistic driving study to assess this phenomenon.

3 Road Study Design: Simulator vs. Naturalistic Study

Numerous studies are conducted across the country to explore the impacts of secondary tasks on driving performance. The majority of these studies are done with the assistance of a simulator. Simulator studies have competitive advantages to naturalistic studies; the biggest factor is safety. Simulator environments can be controlled, the simulator software records data, and it is much easier to analyze and replicate the experiment. A more direct method to evaluating the driving experience, however, is captured by naturalistic studies in the car. A naturalistic environment entails studying a driver in as much of their natural driving state as possible. In this natural environment, there are many factors not present in a simulator study: limited repeatability, uncontrollable variables, crashes and injury to participants, data prone to noise that do not perform well in varying conditions, etc. [7]. Because of these limitations, along with the high risk-low fidelity nature of naturalistic driving studies, such studies are few. This can be problematic for researchers designing naturalistic studies for the ever changing landscape of IVIS and other secondary in-car tasks performed by drivers as there is little guidance to the process. In addition, there are also numerous challenges transferring knowledge gained from research into effective practices [3].

Simulator studies involve the use of a steering wheel, accelerator, and brake. Some systems are more advanced and have an entire cabin of a car incorporated to the design. A lower-budget system has a single front screen that shows a driving environment and reacts to driver input. Advanced systems like NADS are an entire 360° view for a much more realistic experience. The simulator studies have a secondary task, like Lane Change Task (LCT) that attempt to mimic real driving behavior. Simulator studies are very easy to control. The conditions are always the same since it is an indoor environment, the road surface is exactly the same, and even the tasks can be manipulated to the exact same moment for every participant. There are very limited confounding variables that would influence results since simulator studies allow so much researcher input. The naturalistic studies have many other variables that can cause difficulties, as we discuss below.

4 Design Principles

Due to the high-risk nature of a naturalistic study and the amount of resources, logistics and manpower required a detailed design strategy is a necessity. There are many elements that researchers must explore in planning and designing a naturalistic driving study. The principle design guidelines that we will focus on below, will place emphasis on the study design and data collections as those were the sections we found more challenging to navigate as we designed our naturalistic driving study. As the origins of most user studies are derived from a question, we will begin our exploration of design principles with the research question. The 100-Car Naturalistic Driving Study [8] is one of the most cited naturalistic road studies. As such we use [14] "Design of the in-vehicle driving behavior and crash risk study: in support of the SHRP 2 Naturalistic Driving Study" as a benchmark to guide the design principles we put forth. Below we will present some of the design principles we found in the literature along with our pilot design, which was our attempt to implement these principles in a small scale study.

4.1 Research Question

Research questions guide the process of a naturalistic study design. Strategic planned research questions will allow for data produced in the study to answer these questions within the known project constraints and limitations such as funding and time. In a naturalistic driving/road study, research questions can be organized in at least 11 different categories [14] (see Table 1).

The research questions we developed for our study fall within the Infotainment-system-based and nomadic-device-based category:

- Of the three following mobile telecommunication methods: manually texting, voice texting (Siri/Vlingo), and Voiceing, which offers a less distracting form of communicating while driving?
- Is Voiceing less distracting form of communication for a driver than voice texting?
- Is Voiceing less distracting form of communication for a driver than manual texting?

Table 1. Research Question Category

Research Question Category	
Traffic-, roadway-, and environment-based questions	Vision-, attention-, and distraction-based questions
Vehicle-based questions	Speed- and speeding-based questions
Driver- or driver-error-based questions	Crash-countermeasure-based questions
Passenger-based questions	Passing-maneuver-based questions
Multifactor/multivariate questions	Infotainment-system-based and nomadic-device-based questions
Aggressive-driving-based questions	

4.2   Design Plan

Reference [14] paper defines the design plan by two broad areas the participant sample population and the data collection site. In addition we have included the study content.

Participants Sample Population. In determining the sample population there are several factors to consider in addition to a standard study design. In recruiting participants you must weigh the pros-and cons of using a representative versus risk-prone sample. So for example participant sample population you will have to consider the correlation age to traffic infractions as it relates to research question. In addition the sample population will also affect the vehicle model selection as the effects of vehicle selection to traffic infractions as it relates to research question (sedan vs. truck): passenger cars (sedans, coupes, hatchbacks, and station wagons), pickup trucks, sport utility vehicles (SUVs; including crossover vehicles), and minivans. If your study resources allows for participant compensation the total cost of data collection versus the cost per data-year and the cost per participant versus the ability to enhance participant attraction and retention via meaningful compensation amounts has to be considered.

Data Collection Sites. In a naturalistic road driver study you want your data collection site to resemble the natural environment in which your study is situated as much as possible. There are several things that factor into the data collection site selection to determine feasibility such as geography, weather, state/county law, road types, obstructions, land usage (e.g., urban versus rural) etc. Thus the [14] paper recommends the use of a data collection site coordinator. If doing a naturalistic study within an entity with limited resources it is not always feasible to have a site contractors as used and described in the VVTI study. However having a dedicated team member to fulfill similar responsibilities, we later discovered, is essential. Selecting and securing a data collection site proved to be a challenge in our study. Because our study was a pilot we choose to do one without a coordinator. Due to our location there were limited road options that fit the outlined study requirements in terms of road distance, location, traffic activity, etc. However once we were able to identify roads that would suitable, several additional barriers were encountered as we worked to secure access to a road, included the state passing a no texting while driving law. In our study, the data collection site used, a low traffic rural road lined with trees homes and shrubs, revealed a major flaw in our study design. The rural road along with heavy tree coverage gravely impacted cell reception for several of our study participants. Thus proving to be very problematic for our study as participants struggled to receive and send text's.

Content. Many naturalistic studies look to evaluate drivers' road performance with varying environmental conditions. In our study we were interested in studying the distraction caused by varying methods of texting. Thus for this we used a texting script used by the researcher and the participant. It is important that the length, style and subject matter of the text was perceived as realistic communication amongst our targeted audience. Figure 1 below is an example of one such exchange.

Data Collection. *Driver Demographics and Vehicle Inventory.*

Driver demographic collected would vary based upon research question and target demographic, however, this will not be very different from the type of driver

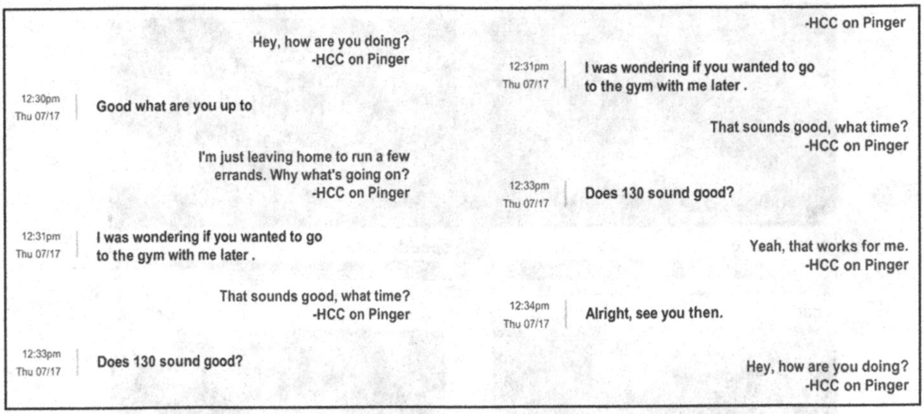

	Hey, how are you doing? -HCC on Pinger			-HCC on Pinger
12:30pm Thu 07/17	Good what are you up to	12:31pm Thu 07/17	I was wondering if you wanted to go to the gym with me later .	
	I'm just leaving home to run a few errands. Why what's going on? -HCC on Pinger			That sounds good, what time? -HCC on Pinger
12:31pm Thu 07/17	I was wondering if you wanted to go to the gym with me later .	12:33pm Thu 07/17	Does 130 sound good?	
	That sounds good, what time? -HCC on Pinger			Yeah, that works for me. -HCC on Pinger
12:33pm Thu 07/17	Does 130 sound good?	12:34pm Thu 07/17	Alright, see you then.	
				Hey, how are you doing? -HCC on Pinger

Fig. 1. Sample text dialog from a distracted driving study

demographic information a researcher might collect for a simulated study. Most naturalistic driving studies are conducted from vehicles that are similar to those statistically in use among targeted demographic in the studied user case. For example in our study, distracted driving traffic incidents that have occurred more frequently were in sedans. Ideally, for a naturalistic study it is best for participants to use their own vehicle because it reduces the amount of variability in the results that can be attributed to the lack of familiarity to the vehicle. However because our study was a pilot, with limited resources we rented a sedan. This was to reduce the chances for error and time to set up and take down the study instrumentation in participant's vehicles. In our study, the majority of drivers drove a sedan so the learning gap should not be that large as a result of direct manipulation. Direct manipulation is a well-known Human-Computer Interaction principle [11] and a good e.g. is the task of driving. The basic driving task is relatively easy to understand regardless of vehicle or country as a result of it being a direct manipulation task. For example, there are specific critical driving functions a driver can perform in every vehicle (drive forward, turn left, turn right, reverse etc.). Therefore driving is transferrable across vehicles as a result of direct manipulation. It is obvious that the notion of IVIS and additional vehicle features may lead to a completely new and much more detailed discussion, but in reference to the basic task of driving, this is very similar across most vehicles. Since distracted driving was a primary interest to the study, in addition to collection basic vehicle inventory information such as make, model, safety features, etc. we were also interested in infotainment features the participants had from previous experience.

Driver Assessment. Regardless of the research question, driver assessment is an important step in a naturalistic driving study. Understanding study participants driving functionalities under best-case scenario serves as a control and a baseline to gauge and adapt study results per participant. Because of the heighten risk factors associated with naturalistic driving studies driver assessment also allows for a means for participant selection as you can target individual differences or impairments as they relate to cognition; visual perception; various visual–cognitive, physical, and psychomotor abilities; personality

Fig. 2. Data acquisition system

factors; sleep- related factors; medicines and medical conditions; driving knowledge; and history. Depending upon the nature of the study a researcher might choose to categorize and separately administer Visual Perception Assessments, Visual-Cognitive Assessments, Cognitive and Psychomotor Assessments, physical Assessments.

Data Acquisition System. As previously stated naturalistic study design like most studies are driven by their question. As such to help illustrate a setup method we will describe our set up below. In a four door sedan, we used four GoPro cameras to provide visual feedback (Fig. 2), a dashboard camera in a separate surveillance vehicle, a steering column camera facing the speedometer, a camera on the back of the rearview mirror facing the road ahead (to measure lane deviation) and finally a dashboard camera facing the driver. An audio signal that could be heard on all cameras was used to sync the cameras' for each study run for the purpose of data analysis. In simulated road studies visual stimulus, such as road barriers or signs to adjust speed are frequently used to detect moments of distraction, and assess when the participants cognitive load is being impacted such as in the case of inattention blindness. Inattention blindness occurs when an observer fails to see an unexpected object or event in plain view because their attention is diverted to something else. Thus they can look at, but not see an object or event. We used three Adafruit NeoPixel Digital RGB LED strips lights that were programmed to flash randomly in the vehicle. In the vehicle the strips were set such that the driver could see all three strips, without having to turn their head, equally using peripheral and standard vision. One strip was placed across the front dashboard, the second to the left side of the vehicle and the third on the right side of the vehicle (Fig. 3). Study participants were instructed when they saw the LEDs on either side of the vehicle flashed green to slow down and engage the turn signal for that respective side of the vehicle. Participants were instructed when they saw the LED strip

Fig. 3. Adafruit NeoPixel digital RGB LED strips light set up (Color figure online)

in the front flashed red they were come to a complete stop. The LED strips were programmed to flash while the participant is engaged in a conversation via texting using both voice texting and manual input.

5 Discussion

There were several challenges encountered from our guided pilot study that will provide feedback in how we design future naturalistic driving road studies. One of the most problematic of the challenges we encountered was phone reception on out test road. We decided to have participants use their personal mobile phone to reduce the amount of variability/unknown in the data collected that could be attributed to the participant using a phone they were not accustomed to. This correlated with the test road selected resulting in several participants having poor to no cell reception along the test road. As a result of some quick thinking by the team we were still able to get some good data by timing the sent and received text to correspond with moments of coverage. Another challenge encountered was with the design of our stimuli, and their placement in the vehicle. For example, our stimuli were visual and we conducted studies over the course of a six-hour day we needed to better factor in the position of the sun and visibility. It would have been beneficial to the study to do a pre-pilot study just on the positioning of the LED strips in the vehicle. Lastly, due to several adjustments during the course of the study that required a bit more time than originally calculated, we ran into a challenge in charging the cameras while out in the field. After the first day of the study the team adjusted by scheduling more dead time between study participants to allow for ample time to charge the cameras. There are, however, many other ways we could have redesigned the study to avoid these problems in the first place. Guidelines for designing a naturalistic study would have surely helped our team execute the study more effectively from the start.

6   Conclusion

From our research and attempts to conduct our naturalistic pilot study there were several lessons learned. Not only lessons, but also we have identified a set of guidelines that may be very helpful to those conducting or planning to conduct a naturalistic driving experiment. Extensive pilot testing is one thing that became very evident in the process of trying to conduct a pilot study. We mentioned the issues with phone service, the sensitivity with LED lights and issues with the GoPro's keeping the charge. Even though we conducted numerous pilot tests, these are events that would not necessarily show up until later on. This one is almost self-explained, but the more testing the better, and researchers will also need to think outside of the box even more when designing a naturalistic study. For e.g. even though two phone carriers worked during pilot test, it was important to potentially examine the phone reception of all major phone carriers on the test track. From our design principles, it is clear there are numerous factors that researchers need to be aware of when conducting naturalistic experiments including, but not limited to participant sample population, driver assessment and the data acquisition system. These guidelines and tips presented in this paper are not meant to be a definitive solution for every single experiment, but a guide for researchers in this space, that may help to limit some of the potential problems that could arise when conducting a naturalistic driving experiment.

References

1. Alvarez, I., Alnizami, H., Dunbar, J., Jackson, F., Gilbert, J.E.: Help on the road: effects of vehicle manual consultation in driving performance across modalities. J. Int. J. Hum. Comput. Stud. **73**, 19–29 (2014)
2. Gordon, C.P.: Crash Studies of Driver Distraction, in Driver Distraction: Theory, Effect and Mitigation, pp. 281–304. CRC Press, Taylor & Francis Group, London (2009)
3. Hanowski, R.: The naturalistic study of distracted driving: moving from research to practice. SAE Int. J. Commer. Veh. **4**(1), 286–319 (2011). doi:10.4271/2011-01-2305
4. Harding, C.J.: The failure of state texting-while-driving laws. J. Technol. Law Policy **XIII**, 1–17 (2013)
5. Lee, J.D., Regan, M.A., Young, K.L. (eds.): Defining Driver Distraction. CRC Press, Boca Raton (2008)
6. Lima, S.H., Junwook, C.: Are cell phone laws in the U.S. effective in reducing fatal crashes involving young drivers? Transp. Policy **27**, 158–163 (2013)
7. NADS: Simulator vs. on-road evaluation. National Advanced Driving Simulator (2014). http://www.nads-sc.uiowa.edu/media/pdf/NADS-Simulator_vs_On-Road_Evaluation.pdf. Accessed 11 January 2014
8. National Highway Traffic Safety Administration: The 100-Car Naturalistic Driving Study: A Descriptive Analysis of Light Vehicle-Heavy Vehicle Interactions from the Light Vehicle Driver's Perspective, US Department of Transportation (2006)
9. Rader, R.: State texting bans don't reduce crashes, insurance data show. Insurance Institute for Highway Safety, Highway Loss Data Institute. Status Report, vol. 45, no. 10, 28 September 2010 (2010). http://www.iihs.org/iihs/sr/statusreport/article/45/10/1. Accessed 11 January 2014

10. ScienceDaily. http://www.sciencedaily.com/releases/2010/02/100216142332.htm
11. Shneiderman, B., et al.: Designing the User Interface Strategies for Effective Human-Computer Interaction. Addison-Wesley Publishing Co., Cambridge (2009)
12. Strayer, D., Cooper, J., Turrill, J., et. al.: Measuring Cognitive Distraction in the Automobile, AAA Foundation for Traffic Safety (2013). https://www.aaafoundation.org/sites/default/files/MeasuringCognitiveDistractions.pdf. Accessed 11 February 2014
13. National Safety Council. http://www.nsc.org/DistractedDrivingDocuments/Cognitive-Distraction-White-Paper.pdf
14. Anti, J., Lee, S., Hankey, J., Dingus, T.: Design of the in-vehicle driving behavior and crash risk study. In: Support of the SHRP 2 Naturalistic Driving Study. Transportation Research Board of the National Academies, Washington, D.C. (2011). http://onlinepubs.trb.org/onlinepubs/shrp2/SHRP2_S2-S05-RR-1.pdf
15. National Highway Traffic Safety Administration. http://www.nhtsa.gov/About+NHTSA/Press+Releases/NHTSA+Survey+Finds+660,000+Drivers+Using+Cell+Phones+or+Manipulating+Electronic+Devices+While+Driving+At+Any+Given+Daylight+Momentv

Exploring User Experience in the Wild: Facets of the Modern Car

Dimitrios Gkouskos[1(✉)], Ingrid Pettersson[1,2], MariAnne Karlsson[1], and Fang Chen[1]

[1] Chalmers University of Technology, Gothenburg, Sweden
{dimitrios.gkouskos,mak,fang.chen}@chalmers.se
ingrid.pettersson@volvocars.com
[2] Volvo Car Corporation, Gothenburg, Sweden
ingrid.pettersson@volvocars.com

Abstract. Experiential approaches to technology create opportunities for facilitating a wider range of in-car user experiences, however holistic knowledge regarding experiences that car users find enjoyable is lacking. We present the experience themes of *the car as a caretaker, the car as a space for relatedness, the car as a space for stimulation, and the car as a space for transition,* collected through a holistic study of 16 drivers, using contextual interviews, reflexive photography and the UX curve method. The use of the themes is exemplified through a design example. The experience themes can help designers empathize with users and create design solutions that can support positive in-car experiences, while the methodology used, serves as an example of how user's experiences with technology can be studied.

Keywords: User experience · Automotive · Qualitative · Holistic · HMI

1 Introduction

A growing amount of technology aimed at addressing users' experiential needs is continuously introduced into our lives. The modern car is one space that reflects this technological evolution. Modern vehicles can facilitate a variety of activities supported by the ever more connected and interactive human machine interface (HMI) of the cars. The vehicle industry has a comprehensive history of researching safety, ergonomics, and to an extent usability issues in vehicles. However, due to the connected and interactive environment, User Experience (UX) has become a topic of growing interest for researchers and car manufacturers [1]. In contrast to safety, vehicle makers do not yet have strong foundations for designing systems with UX in focus [2]. These parameters make the car context an interesting and unique space for studying user experiences in.

In addition to usability and task performance, UX includes non-utilitarian dimensions such as affect, value, meaning etc. [3]. Furthermore, the subjective experience of a product is a dynamic consequence of the user's internal state (e.g. expectations, needs, motivation, mood), the characteristics of the product (e.g. complexity, novelty, functionality, aesthetics) and the context (e.g. the environment) of the interaction [3]. Due to the fact that experience is subjective and highly personal there is an emergent

© Springer International Publishing Switzerland 2015
A. Marcus (Ed.): DUXU 2015, Part III, LNCS 9188, pp. 450–461, 2015.
DOI: 10.1007/978-3-319-20889-3_42

need for holistic work of in-vehicle experience from a user's perspective. In turn, this understanding will provide knowledge of how to shape technological interactions with the user's needs in mind. Two prominent issues stand out; firstly the necessity to understand the types of experience that users find truly desirable, and secondly to identify ways that this knowledge of desirable experiences can contribute to the design process of interactions in different contexts.

In this study we have chosen to focus on the role of the car's HMI in shaping the user's experience in order to explore the types of experiences these new systems can enable. The car cockpit is a place where many of us spend a substantial amount of time during daily commutes and thus the car's HMI is a significant venue for designing for positive every day experiences. The unique vehicle context of use adds additional challenges for in-vehicle HMI developers and researchers that must balance the importance of factors such as safety, usability and pleasure of an HMI. The extensive integration of the phone into the interface of modern cars gives a significant place to the integrated functionality of the phone in the research and study design.

The goal of this paper is to identify experiences that users of modern technology enjoy today by using the car context as a use case. An understanding of these experiences can assist designers by providing knowledge of the components that facilitate positive user experiences. In turn, design teams can use this knowledge to empathize with users and hereby create solutions that better support the user's experience.

2 Related Work

User experience is developing into an established discipline, with a growing number of empirical evidence to support its theoretical foundations [4]. Different frameworks have attempted to describe the elusive nature of UX in more detail (for examples see [5]), but do not address sufficiently how one should study user experience [6]. Most researchers agree that UX is subjective, dynamic and contextual [3]. One of the principal approaches to researching user experience is the holistic approach [7], which posits that the richness of human experience cannot be reduced to a set of variables but instead should be studied as a whole and in its context. Building on the holistic standpoint, McCarthy and Wright analyze experience with technology, and describe experience as a situated, temporal phenomenon that should be studied in its entirety [7].

As experience is rich, personal and subjective in nature [8], UX research requires approaches that are able to capture the fine nuances that make experience significant for each user. In order to understand user experience, researchers must capture experiences in the context they emerge, applying an objective and open perspective to the user's interaction [8]. Forlizzi and Ford turn to user narratives as a way to capture experiences from a user perspective [9]. This approach, which is inspired by ethnographic methodology, can be found in a number of studies of user experience, but does not fully address experiences that may not be voluntarily expressed and narrated by the user.

A growing number of methods have been developed for use in empirical studies of user experience. These studies vary widely in approach and application, stretching from purely quantitative studies to solely qualitative ones, depending on the focus of the study (for example summative or formative evaluations) and the researcher's underlying framework for understanding UX. Experience over time has also been a growing focus of experience studies acknowledging the highly dynamic qualities of experience [10]. Finally, there are some studies that make an effort towards capturing the user's experience in context from a holistic standpoint, many of which focus on mobile phones [11].

2.1 Automotive UX Research

UX research in the in-vehicle domain is sparse at best, especially when it comes to applied, holistic user research. One relevant example from the field of sociology is work by Lyons and Urry who presented travelling time not only as a burden, but also as valuable time for the traveler [12]. Tscheligi et al. call for a more thorough investigation of the holistic experiences in cars further grounded in the driving context [13], as very little research in the area has taken place.

Most published studies are limited to a single interactive system: for example, Knobel et al. used an interview approach focused explicitly on capturing relatedness experiences in order to design for such an experience in the car [14]. Albeit useful, this approach focuses on experiences with a single system in the car (cruise control and navigation), or with a specific experience in mind (relatedness) and do not expand into the complexity of positive experiences to be had in modern cars. A wider approach towards in-vehicle experiences can be found in Eckholdt et al. [15], although the work was not founded on empirical user studies. Finally, Gkouskos et al. used a mixed methods approach in order to explore user experience in vehicles [16] however without the rich level of detail that user narratives can produce. The lack of studies on holistic automotive user experiences highlight the need of more research in the area in order to gain a fuller understanding of these experiences.

3 Methodology

The methodology of the present study was chosen in order to provide both holistic and detailed insights of in-vehicle user experiences, as well as to investigate the phone's contribution to these experiences, since the use of the phone in the car has been steadily increasing [17].

A research approach that combined contextual interviews [18], reflexive photography [19], and a simplified version of the UX curve [20] was applied for gaining an informed understanding of user experiences in vehicles. This mixed-method approach was shaped in order to access the subjective experiences of the participants in the study through multiple entry points, and to stimulate a deeper conversation around lived experiences in cars. Furthermore, the study encompassed three study topics; the car as a whole, the car's HMI and the phone connected to the car.

3.1 Methods

Reflexive photography, or photography conducted by the interviewee, has been used in previous research [19]. In this study, photography was used as a conversation stimulus and for adding more nuances to the interview. Specifically, participants were asked to photograph what they perceived as significant for them about their car, prior to the interview. The photographs were then used to draw attention to areas that the participants found significant enough to photograph.

The core of the study was the *contextual, semi-structured interview* [18] with the participants. Being in the use context with the user was an important aspect of the interview, as topics could be followed up more thoroughly, avoiding misconceptions and spurring conversation. A deepened understanding of the interaction in the vehicle was achieved by questions triggered by the surrounding context. Examples of questions from the interviews are the participants' choice to have an add-on GPS system in their car instead of an integrated one, or asking participants to display how they typically use the in-vehicle systems during their daily commute.

The *UX curve* is a method used for reconstructing experiences over time [20]. Typically, during the construction of a UX curve, the participant draws by using pen and paper a curve to describe how the experience about a product has changed over time. The curve drawing area consists of a vertical timeline and a horizontal line that divides positive and negative experiences. In this study, the UX curve method was employed for two reasons: firstly, for gaining insights of experience as it changed over time and secondly, as a conversation mediator. In other studies, different curves are used for several, pre-selected areas of focus. In this study, only the curve for overall experience was used in order to keep an open mind of what the user experience might include or exclude in the vehicle context.

3.2 Participants

Sixteen car users with modern, high-tech vehicles participated in the study. The selection criteria were that participants should have a car with an advanced in-vehicle HMI, no older than three years and not owned by them for less than three months.

These requirements were placed to ensure participants who could relate to the new technology that shapes today's user experiences of new premium vehicles. The participants also had to have been active in the purchase (i.e. not a car they were using without having participated in the selection process of model and in-vehicle systems). Seven women and nine men participated, aged between 29 to 66 years, with a mean of 48 years. The cars that the participants owned came from a variety of manufacturers (BMW, Volvo, Audi, Mercedes, and Volkswagen). The most common family situation was that of a family with children.

3.3 Procedure

During the booking of each interview, each participant was asked to take photos of 'things that are significant regarding the car'. In the beginning of each interview, participants were given an introduction to the interview and were asked general questions regarding work, hobbies, and their attitude towards and experience with technology. As a next step the participants discussed their experiences with their smartphone or car. Each participant was randomly assigned either with the phone part first, followed by the car and then the car HMI part, or with the car first, followed by the phone and then the car HMI part. The car and phone parts of the interview were conducted in neutral spaces, e.g. the participants' home or office, while the HMI segment of the interviews was conducted inside the participant's vehicle.

The interviews included topics regarding initial expectations from the product, first impressions, opinion of the product today, typical daily use, positive and negative experiences, and things to look for when purchasing an upgrade to the current product. Questions for each of the phone, car, and HMI segments of the interview were posed in a chronological order with the support of the UX curve. The participants' photos were used to stimulate further discussion. As an added memory aid, participants were encouraged to show or mimic the activities they were talking about (i.e. dialing phone number from the steering wheel, searching for information, or using a GPS systems).

3.4   Analysis

The narratives were analyzed using conventional content analysis, a method for characterizing and comparing content in text [21]. The coding was conducted by the first and second authors together, to ensure that consensus was reached. The data that resulted from the coding was then compiled into different experience themes. The experience themes are summaries of narratives that represent the whole of the experience as told by the participants. As the UX curve and the photos highlighted experiences that were significant for the participants, data connected to the photos and UX curves were incorporated into the analysis and contributed to the categories and UX themes.

4   Findings

To contribute to the knowledge of valuable in-vehicle user experiences, we present five major experience themes extracted from the semi-structured interviews, the photographs and the UX curves of the sixteen study participants. The themes describe types of everyday experiences the participants had in their cars.

4.1   The Car as a Space for Transition

The car as a transitional space is a theme that was apparent in eight of the sixteen participants' narratives. Time spent in the car was used as an opportunity to prepare for the next stage in their lives: *"Driving to and from work is the time for me to think about what I'm supposed to do during the day, to go from home mode to work mode, and then the same going back. I try to have at least half the drive without any thoughts of work, so that when I'm home, I'm home."* (P13). Commuting time was thus an important part of the everyday life puzzle of activities, providing a window for reflection, planning and distancing.

The use of the car as a transitional space was accomplished for instance by preparing for work through taking work related calls during the drive to work, and by catching up on emails for example during red lights: *"... you spend some time working when you're driving, doing easy things, like preparing for meetings if you didn't have time to do it before you left..."* (P5). The car cockpit functioned as an extension of the workspace where the participants undertook the simple work tasks that were perceived as safe enough perform while driving. A traffic jam was at times seen as an opportunity to prepare for the day: *"The car is like your office and you can use the time (in the traffic jam to work) to learn something new, send emails etc."* (P6).

Similarly to the need for preparing for work, participants also wanted relaxation time to prepare for their home life as mentioned by one participant (P4), who played relaxing music to de-stress from a tough work day. The ability to connect a smartphone or mp3 player to the vehicle's audio system was a major enabler of this transition to and from work. When the connection to the phone or media was not working up to expectations, the poor integration was a major source of distress in the vehicle. In some cases workarounds were found for simplifying the in-car activities. For example, one participant (P6) pre-dialed a list of people he wanted to contact while driving home from work, so that he would be able to use the recent calls list and thus have a more easily managed phone list in the infotainment system during the drive home. The theme of connected phones and media was a commonly photographed topic, depicted by eight of the participants. One participant (P8) photographed for example her USB connection because it gave her access to what she needed to make her daily travel to and from work enjoyable and efficient.

The experience of the car as a transitional space remained stable over time, with the exceptions of the participants who did not have the possibility to connect the car to their phone before. They saw this connection of car and phone as a major change in their everyday routines, resulting in spending more of their time connected to for example music services; *"It is almost easier to say when I do not use Spotify. When I get in the car, when I wake up, I connect to the Apple TV, when I leave the house it automatically connects to the car and the same music which I had (in the house) is now in the car. Then I drop my kids off ... when I arrive to the office I put my headphones on and continue."* (P2). This was a typical experience of seamless transitions. The participants wanted to be able to continue the activities started before getting into the car and in the same way continue with activities after exiting the car. The HMI of the car played an integral part in enabling transitional experiences by allowing drivers to easily and safely connect to the world outside, or by providing entertainment when needed.

4.2 The Car as a Space for Relatedness

Ten of the participants mentioned the enjoyment of utilizing their time in the car by connecting to people that matter to them. For some, the car was one of the most important places for relatedness throughout the whole day, as it was a place where they were able to have some attentive time with children or partner. The HMI of the car also provided an opportunity for relatedness to others outside the car, easily accessible through smartphone integration. This direct and seamless technology shaped daily activities; *"I talk more on the phone now than before. (...) you don't hold anything and it's like talking to a friend that's next to you."* (P8). The car "bubble" is broken by the easy accessible opportunity to bring in others into the space, for example by calling a loved one; *"If I am alone I will call my mother"* (P3), thus creating a space for maintaining relationships over time.

Participants also connected to passengers in the car through shared in-car activities, often enabled by the HMI, such as listening to music, podcasts or audio books together. For example, participants mentioned handing their smartphone to their kids and letting them select the music to play: *"When the children get tired in the car you can have them borrow your phone and pick songs on Spotify. They like that because they have the feeling that they control something"* (P14). The entertainment system was then a common focus object that enabled a social, shared activity between the car's occupants. Due to the importance of these experiences the participants considered it very negative when the phone or music integration was not working. One participant related to a highly negative experience when the phone lost connection in the car during a phone call to his young daughter, leaving her in worry and distress. Once an established habit of using the system for relatedness experiences, this experience theme appeared to be stable over time. The experiences themselves could be long term, for example enjoying listening to an audiobook with a partner was a social experience that could continue over weeks. Four of the participants' photos were exclusively about the phone connection, as an indicator of how important they experienced this functionality to be.

4.3   The Car as a Space for Stimulation

The car has persistently been a symbol of freedom and independence [22], with its ability to offer thrilling driving experiences. In addition to this, modern cars offer many interactive systems that often enhance the driving experience or enable other stimulating experiences for the users. The experience theme of stimulation was evident in fourteen of the participants' narratives. A stimulating experience was facilitated through the joy of driving for some of the participants: *"If I am alone on the road I enjoy the speed (...) I like to feel the acceleration."*(P9), as well as the car's driving behavior: *"You are like an iron on the motorway. It is really difficult to drive within the speed limits because the experience is that you just want to fly"* (P7). For other participants, the discovery of new functions, and the utilization of the interactive systems available in the car was a source of stimulation. While some interactive systems aim to inform the driver and provide a sense of control, others enhance the experience of driving through, for instance, changing the look of the car's displays and systems to match the sporty feeling that drivers may wish to achieve.

For some, the experience of stimulation was mediated through the amount of technology available through the HMI systems. *"I monitor lots of things during drives [i.e. GPS and board computer information], I think it is really interesting."* (P2). Others were initially disinterested in additional HMI systems, but nonetheless enjoyed discovering new possibilities after seeing the added value in having for instance a seamless connection between a smartphone and the car's HMI systems, or the *"magical appearance"* (P4) of the electric trailer hook.

Finally, the car's smartphone app that was available to some participants was a stimulant, and a popular topic of conversation with friends and family; *"It's mostly for showing friends what cool functionality there is in the car, and what possibilities technology can give you"* (P16). Many of the stimulating experiences, such as the discovery of new in-car technology evidently developed over time. *"I find new things all the time"* (P10).

4.4   The Car as a Caretaker

Building on the availability of many active safety systems and other advances in technology, eleven participants voiced that they enjoyed the feeling that the car was taking care of their safety, and needs while also providing convenience. However, only one photograph depicted this, as the experience often was highly contextual and sometimes physical. The experience of the caretaking car was created by features such as a seat-belt tightening in sharp corners, creating a kind of "hug", conveying a strong feeling that the car is taking care of the passenger; *"It feels like the car cares for you. It is a nice feeling. I think it may be a gimmick but it is very positive."* (P6). Another feature adding to this notion of an intelligent, caretaking car was the car's phone app available to some of the participants that contributed by providing knowledge of the cars location and status. Active safety systems and convenience systems were appreciated for saving the driver and passengers from dangers; *"A car came and parked behind me, without me knowing, but then the sensors warned first, then I looked at the camera and saw the car that wasn't there when I parked. (..) I was grateful"* (P15). These experiences of security offered by the cars' systems proved valuable for the users. Finally, the discovery of caretaking functions often took place over longer time periods; *"And then I started to discover these systems, in the beginning it was just the BLIS (Blind Spot Indication System) that I saw, and that the steering wheel was vibrating, and that the car worked back and front, that there was a rear view camera. That was what I noticed in the beginning and then I started to read about the other functionalities and how that works..."* (P16).

5   Discussion

The discussion section is organized into three subsections. Firstly, a discussion regarding the approach used in the study will be presented. Secondly, the themes, their relation to other similar factors, and how they represent a UX mindset will be outlined. Finally, we will present some design implications that the themes can have on the design process of HMI car systems.

5.1   The Approach

With the approach presented in this work, we aimed to take a holistic stance on the empirical study of experience and collect subjective, personal, and situated data that can help designers better understand and empathize with users' daily lives in order to support positive experiences for users.

The combination of the semi-structured interviews, the reflexive photography and the UX curve produced a wealth of narrative, rich in experience stories from the everyday lives of participants and their cars. The interviews worked well in collecting data around themes of interest while still allowing for the flexibility to follow interesting narrative wherever it may have lead. The photography provided an entry point for the participants to reflect on what is significant to them when it comes to their cars, while the UX curves infused an over-time perspective into the participants' narratives.

The three methods represent a holistic approach to empirically studying experiences related to topics of interest. Currently existing models relating to experience such as the model proposed by Norman [23] can be useful in structuring the study of experience but do not provide clear, specific direction as to how one should empirically collect experience data. Jordan's four pleasures framework [24] provides some directions for applied research, however lacks focus on important aspects such as the over-time experience, and the importance of the context within which the studies take place. Part of the existing empirical user experience work is based on Sheldon's list of human needs [25]. These are good at highlighting areas of importance, however they lack the rich narrative that can be found in holistic studies of experience as exemplified by the experience themes. In contrast, the methodology used in this study produced specific insights for experiences found in the vehicle domain. Moreover, the study serves as an example of a holistic approach that can also be employed in studying other interactive devices in the wild, especially relevant to technology that is being used in diverse contexts and for diverse reasons, such as smart phone technology or wearable technology.

5.2   The Experience Themes

The experience themes present and summarize experiences that our participants appreciated when using their cars. It is important to recognize that these five themes do not represent all experiences that people appreciate, but rather experiences that can inspire design that promotes positive UX.

The 'Car as a Space for Transition' exemplifies how the time spent in the car is filled with activities that prepare users for what comes next in their everyday lives. The 'car as space for relatedness' showcases another way in which users turn the time spent in the car into a significant experience by taking the opportunity to connect with loved ones outside the car – through use of a phone – or to people inside the car, through shared activities.

The 'Car as a space for Stimulation' is a good example of the significance of the design of HMI systems: users were in awe of the amount of technological possibilities packed into the HMI, and enjoyed mastering the complexity and discovering new ways in which the car's systems could support their activities. This theme is more novel to automotive UX research and it highlights the importance of longitudinal UX research, as such findings are difficult to make during brief UX studies, and impossible to evaluate unless testing is done over a substantial amount of time. Finally, the 'Car as a Caretaker' is a novel theme not recognized elsewhere as of yet, and deserves more research and design ideation in the future. The theme points out the 'alterity relation'

[26] to be had with cars, i.e. seeing them as an 'other', almost a person, who is looking out for their best. Diverse themes like these are to be found in any technology that serves a number of uses and used within different contexts, and they each deserve its own attention.

5.3 Design Implications

The experience themes can have significant impact on the ways car HMI systems are designed. During different phases of the design process of HMI systems, the experience themes can represent the user's interests in using technology, and provide indication as to how new features can cater to people's needs. The themes represent some broad areas of interest, which can later in the design process be narrowed down by applying more targeted design methods.

During the user research phase of the design process, the experience themes can help designers focus on specific issues relating to the theme that they chose to design for. In the ideation phases of the design process the experience themes can be a springboard for the generation of personas and scenarios to be used in designing HMI systems, directing the designer's attention to important enablers of the desired experience.

Finally, the experience themes can be used to evaluate design concepts in terms of their potential to fulfill user needs by aiding users to accomplish their goals, in addition to evaluating functional and task fulfillment requirements. We present a design idea titled 'contextual car modes' as an example of where a combination of the themes can lead in terms of design solutions.

5.4 The Contextual Car Mode Design Concept

The Contextual Car Mode (CCM) is a system that is able to customize the experiences that the car affords for a variety of scenarios that can better fit into people's upcoming goals. With this design, the car uses data collected from onboard sensors, along with aggregated data from social networks and calendars, in order to build a database of patterns of behavior for the car's user. In turn, the car suggests different modes that may better suit the user depending on these parameters. For instance, when the car user drives to work in the morning, the car will suggest activities that will help prepare the user for the work day, be it up-beat music to help energize the user or relevant news information that may influence the user's work life. When the workday is over, the car, using GPS location and time of day, will in turn help the user connect with people important to them, thereby supporting experiences of relatedness, or help the user relax and enjoy the drive by enabling the sports mode features on a non-congested highway. We aim to further explore this design, as the CCM is one example where, through use of the UX car themes, the car can intelligently adapt to the user's daily routines and through the support of experience of relatedness, stimulation, transition enhance the commuting experience.

6   Conclusion

This paper presented research of sixteen users' in-vehicle experiences. The study revealed a number of positive experiences that people have in cars today, and presented experience themes that exemplify activities to design for – if one is to support elicitation of positive experiences for car users. Time spent in cars is used for a multitude of reasons and goals other than transportation, many of which are enabled through the vehicle HMI systems. Therefore, the commuting time can be a foundation for valuable and meaningful experiences, especially with the imminent arrival of autonomous vehicles that will allows car users more control over their time in the car. This work presents several design implications for the HMI of the car. The methodology used provides a step towards a framework for future holistic work and design explorations of interactive systems, to be used in different phases of the design process, not only for in-car systems but also for any interactive artifact.

User experience design requires the holistic understanding of the user's current experiences in order to improve the designer's chances of bettering user's lives through further enriching positive experiences or limiting negative experiences.

Acknowledgements. We would like to acknowledge the Strategic Vehicle Research and Innovation - Swedish FFI for funding this study, as well as Sus Lundgren and Maria Håkansson for their valuable feedback.

References

1. Korber, M., Eichinger, A.: User experience evaluation in an automotive context. In: 2013 IEEE on Intelligent Vehicles Symposium (IV), pp. 13–18 (2013)
2. Gkouskos, D., Chen, F.: The use of affective interaction design in car user interfaces. Work A J. Prev. Assess. Rehabil. **41**, 5057–5061 (2012)
3. Law, E.L.-C., Vermeeren, A.P.O.S., Hassenzahl, M., Blythe, M.: Towards a UX manifesto. In: Proceedings of the 21st British HCI Group Annual Conference on People and Computers, vol. 2, pp. 205–206. British Computer Society, University of Lancaster, United Kingdom (2007)
4. Obrist, M., Roto, V., Vermeeren, A., Vaananen-Vainio-Mattila, K., Law, E.L.-C., Kuutti, K.: In search of theoretical foundations for UX research and practice (2012)
5. Hassenzahl, M.: Experience design: technology for all the right reasons. Synth. Lect. Hum. Center. Inf. **3**, 1–95 (2010)
6. Kuutti, K.: Where are the Ionians of user experience research? In: Proceedings of 6th Nordic Conference on Human-Computer Interaction Extending Boundaries - Nordic 2010, p. 715 (2010)
7. McCarthy, J., Wright, P.: Technology as Experience. The MIT Press, Cambridge (2004)
8. Forlizzi, J., Battarbee, K.: Understanding experience in interactive systems. In: Proceedings of 2004 on Conference Designing Interactive Systems Processes Practices Methods, Techniques - DIS 2004, p. 261 (2004)
9. Forlizzi, J., Ford, S.: The building blocks of experience: an early framework for interaction designers. In: Proceedings of the 3rd Conference on Designing Designing Interactive Systems, pp. 419–423. ACM (2000)

10. Karapanos, E., Jain, J., Hassenzahl, M.: Theories, methods and case studies of longitudinal HCI research (2012)
11. Fallman, D., Waterworth, J.: Capturing user experiences of mobile information technology with the repertory grid technique. Architecture **6**, 250–268 (2010)
12. Lyons, G., Urry, J.: Travel time use in the information age. Transp. Res. Part A **39**, 257–276 (2005)
13. Tscheligi, M., Meschtscherjakov, A., Wilfinger, D.: Interactive computing on wheels. Computer **44**, 100–102 (2011)
14. Knobel, M., Hassenzahl, M., Lamara, M., Sattler, T., Schumann, J., Eckoldt, K., Butz, A.: Clique trip. In: Proceedings of the Designing Interactive Systems Conference on - DIS 2012, p. 29. ACM Press, New York (2012)
15. Eckoldt, K., Hassenzahl, M., Laschke, M., Knobel, M.: Alternatives: exploring the car's design space from an experience-oriented perspective. In: Proceedings of the 6th International Conference on Designing Pleasurable Products and Interfaces - DPPI 2013, p. 156. ACM Press, New York (2013)
16. Gkouskos, D., Normark, C.J., Lundgren, S.: What drivers really want: investigating dimensions in automobile user needs. Int. J. Des. **8**, 59–71 (2014)
17. NHTSA: Driver Electronic Device Use in 2011 (2011)
18. Beyer, H., Holtzblatt, K.: Contextual Design: Defining Customer-Centered Systems. Elsevier Science, Amsterdam (1997)
19. Harrington, C., Lindy, I.: The use of reflexive photography in the study of the freshman year experience. J. Coll. Stud. Retent. **1**, 13–22 (1998)
20. Kujala, S., Roto, V., Väänänen-Vainio-Mattila, K., Karapanos, E., Sinnelä, A.: UX curve: a method for evaluating long-term user experience. Interact. Comput. **23**, 473–483 (2011)
21. Hsieh, H.-F., Shannon, S.E.: Three approaches to qualitative content analysis. Qual. Health Res. **15**, 1277–1288 (2005)
22. Redshaw, S.: In the company of cars: driving as a social and cultural practice. Contemp. Sociol. A J. Rev. **40**, 642 (2011)
23. Norman, D.A.: Emotional Design: Why We Love (or Hate) Everyday Things. Basic Civitas Books, New York (2004)
24. Jordan, P.W.: Designing Pleasurable Products: An Introduction to the New Human Factors. CRC Press, Boca Raton (2002)
25. Sheldon, K.M., Elliot, A.J., Kim, Y., Kasser, T.: What is satisfying about satisfying events? Testing 10 candidate psychological needs. J. Pers. Soc. Psychol. **80**, 325–339 (2001)
26. Ihde, D.: Technology and the Lifeworld: From Garden to Earth. Indiana University Press, Indianapolis (1990)

Drivers and Automation: A Study About Cultural and Behavioral Influence in the Interaction with Driver Assistants

Rafael Cirino Gonçalves[(✉)] and Manuela Quaresma

LEUI Laboratory of Ergodesign and Usability Interfaces, PUC-Rio University,
Rio de Janeiro, Brazil
rafaelcirinogolcalves@gmail.com, mquaresma@puc-rio.br

Abstract. ADAS or advanced driving assistant systems are rapidly gaining popularity all over the world, but in order to work properly and prevent risks, ADAS must be designed considering the context that it will be working on. The problem is that most ADAS sold in Brazil were developed based in others cultures, not considering specific issues of Brazilian traffic. This study aimed to point out the most relevant problems of interaction between Brazilian drivers and their ADAS. The results of this research concluded that the problem is not related to individual aspects of Human-Machine communication, but to social and cultural factors that misrepresents the way that people should use this kind of system.

Keywords: ADAS · Automation · Safety · Ergonomics · Drivers' behavior

1 Introduction

ADAS, or advanced driving assistant systems are automated equipments designed to support drivers in many activities while driving, being by advising the driver or even taking control of the vehicle. Young [1] and Knapp et al. [2], define ADAS as automated systems that supports the driving task. It works by giving information or by performing specific manoeuvres in order to enhance safety. For Young [1] and Knapp et al. [2] all ADAS have 5 specific characteristics: (1) support the driver in the driving task; (2) offer active longitudinal or lateral support for the vehicle with or without alerts; (3) scan and analyse the environment; (4) have complex data processing; (5) offer direct interaction with the driver.

This kind of system is rapidly gaining popularity all over the world [3], even in countries like Brazil, with a little culture of automation consumption [4]. Authors like Norman [5], Reed [3], and Young [1] believe that the technology is continuously evolving towards the autonomous driving, where Vehicles won't need drivers anymore, adding convenience and enhancing safety. Even so, safety-related and primordial conception issues about the state of art of technology makes the full autonomy of vehicles unviable, raising discussions on the subject, far from reach a consensus in the scientific community.

© Springer International Publishing Switzerland 2015
A. Marcus (Ed.): DUXU 2015, Part III, LNCS 9188, pp. 462–472, 2015.
DOI: 10.1007/978-3-319-20889-3_43

Due the fundamental gap in common ground for interpretation of the real world [5], ADAS are always susceptible to errors and interaction problems (once it cannot understand social issues, being limited to the numeric data collected by its sensors). To mitigate that issue, ADAS must be designed considering behavioral and environmental aspects of the situation that it will be working on [2]. The problem is that most ADAS sold in Brazil were developed considering others cultures and not considering specific issues of Brazilian drivers and traffic conditions. It is believed that this gap between the parameters used in the design of those systems and the Brazilian context of use may cause some interaction problems that can compromise the driving task and impair the road safety.

This study is an exploratory research that aims to point out the most relevant problems of interaction between Brazilian drivers and their ADAS.

2 Problem

According to Norman [5], there are no "intelligent systems", they are just responsive. In other words, all automation behavior is based on numeric data, gathered by their sensors, but numeric abstractions cannot always translate a real danger situation. There are many abstract variables related to social interactions that may affect the situation, and it's virtually impossible to pre-define numeric parameters for every possible situation that one system may face. Considering that fact, many authors [5–7] states that automated systems are always susceptible to errors, and that must be considered in their design.

According to Norman [5], the main cause of our inability to communicate with machines is the fact that there is no common ground of communication between us and them. The author defines the term "common ground" as a range of common knowledge necessary for the proper understanding of the message between two parties. "People and machines inhabit different universes, one of logically proscribed rules that govern the interaction, and the other one with complex actions, context dependent, where the same condition may result in different actions because the circumstances were different" [5].

The Health and Safety Executive (HSE) [6] and Norman [5] claim that interpretations made by automation are based in pre-defined standards – possible scenarios, pre-programed with their specific conditions for happening. However, this working model is only 100 % accurate when one has control of all the variables interfering with the system in order to be able to predict all possible scenarios. But complex environment like traffic have an infinite number of possible scenarios, and it is unfeasible with current technology fit them into a finite number of responses of a system.

In order to mitigate the issues related to the lack of common ground of communication, ADAS must be designed considering its specific context of use [8]. According to Knapp et al. [2] and International Standardization Organization (ISO) 26262 [8], the design process of any safety-related driver assistant system must consider specific issues related both to the drivers' behavior and to the environment of the place/region it will be used. By doing that, it is possible to adapt the task requirements to the characteristics of the context of use, reducing the fallibility of the system. Dekker [9] affirms that automation systems must be designed considering that they are susceptible to errors, and must adapt themselves to the user's workflow.

The problem presented by this study is that most of the ADAS sold in Brazil are produced in Europe and USA [4], which consider their local specificities during the design process. The issue resides in the fact that the north American and the European traffic are different from the Brazilian one. DaMatta [10] affirms that the Brazilian traffic has a lot of aspects related to its infrastructure and drivers' behavior that makes it unique. Due the fact that they are not designed with Brazilian driver in mind, many ADAS does not consider the specific issues related to that specific context, which may lead to interaction problems and impair the road safety. According to Parazuraman and Rilley [7], many problems related to Human-ADAS interaction are caused by the non consideration of the user needs during the design process, making it susceptible to failures.

Another aggravating issue is the fact that this kind of system is not fully inserted in the daily lives of many Brazilians, which may cause constraints during the interaction – once issues related to the previous experience are fundamental for the decision making in the Human-ADAS interaction [3, 11, 12].

3 Methodology

The goal of this research was to verify how this differences between the parameters used on the design of ADAS and the Brazilian traffic may affect the Human-ADAS interaction and how it can impact the road safety. The main hypothesis of this research is that the non consideration of Brazilian context on the design of ADAS may impair the interaction between the driver and the system, directly affecting road safety. The secondary hypothesis is that there is a conflict between Brazilian's aggressive driving behavior and ADAS safety boundaries.

To confirm the hypothesis, the research conducted the following methods and techniques:

A focus group with Brazilian drivers aiming to understand the relationship between drivers and ADAS, looking for constraints and common interaction issues;

An online survey based on the data collected by the focus group and the literature review, to confirm some information in a quantitative approach;

The modelling of the communication process between human-ADAS [3, 13], in order to explain the main issues that trigger interaction problems pointed by users.

The focus group's general purpose was to list the different types of constraints that occurred in the relationship between the Brazilian drivers the ADAS. According Markopoulos [14], qualitative research is mainly of an exploratory nature, and then the first step in research. This technique was suitable for research due to its controversial nature: the behavior in traffic. If interviewed individually, participants could feel cornered with questions. Markopoulos [14] states that the group often serves as a protection for the participant, so that he does not feel individually cornered, since the focus is on collective expression of thoughts.

The focus group was composed by 12 open questions divided in 3 themes: (1) relationship with technology/automation, trying to draw a profile of the interviewee regarding the use of technology; (2) relationship with the traffic, trying to understand the opinion of the interviewee about the experience of drive in Brazil, looking for the up and downsides of it; (3) interaction with ADAS, looking for understand how interviewee interact with ADAS what is his opinion and constrains about the system. The application of the technique took place on August 29, 2014, with a total of nine participants, all belonging to the same age group, with more than 40 years and owners of cars with ADAS, of different models. Nobody was reluctant to answer any questions. They all have agreed to the Personal Release Agreement.

Once collected trends and hypothesis of the qualitative research findings, it was necessary to validate the data by checking whether the information obtained was not just a specific discrepancy of the respondent sample of the focus group. For the verification of the data, an online survey was the chosen technique. According Tullis and Albert [15], an online survey is a very useful tool for the rapid collection of data from a wide range of respondents, with the only disadvantage of the low depth of the answers. This type of technique was ideal to the needs of this research stage, since the in-depth analysis had already been made during the focus group, requiring only a sample that could be taken as numeric representation for the data collected in the previous technique.

The survey was composed by 31 questions, being 3 of them open-ended. The questions were divided in 4 different groups: (1) preliminary questions, aiming to filter respondents that don't fit in the frame of this research (non drivers/non ADAS users); (2) questions aiming to identify the relationship of the respondents with the traffic, and related to road safety; (3) questions about the use of ADAS, aiming to understand the relationship between the respondents and their ADAS, also looking for their most common problems during the use of the systems; (4) demographic questions, looking for a better comprehension of the sample of the respondents gathered.

To obtain a diagnosis of the main problems of interaction with ADAS in Brazil, techniques of Human-Machine-task modelling ([13]) were used to depict the process of interaction between the driver and their ADAS in order to characterize each of the elements that compose the relationship between the parties involved.

All the models were based in real stories of interaction problems reported by users during the focus group or in online interview with some specific respondent of the survey that claimed to have constant problems with his ADAS. Those storylines were modelled using a flowchart, identifying all the stages of the studied scenarios. The Driver-ADAS communication process was modelled by the communication model [13], analyzing the information and reception channels of both the driver and the system, looking for problems in the way the message was being passed. For the modelling of the mental model of the driver, it was used the OODA LOOP model [3], analyzing every step of the decision-making process to get the elements that led to the error and complete the diagnosis.

In the end 3 scenarios were modelled, each one of them characterizing what is believed to be the main problems of interaction between Brazilians and ADAS. All models were compared with the findings of the survey and focus group, and after that compared with the literature reviewed about this topic.

4 Findings

The findings of this research can be divided in two main topics: drivers' opinions and reported errors.

4.1 Drivers' Opinion

The results of the focus group and the survey verified a general consensus that the Brazilian traffic is extremely chaotic, due mainly to two factors: the low infrastructure of roads compared to the number of cars and the Brazilian drivers' behavior, being extremely individualistic and inconsequential. Considering the drivers' inappropriate behavior, this opinion could be seen in sentences that were repeated several times during focus group such as: "No one respects anyone," or "if somehow one find a way to take advantage, he will always go for it". DaMatta [10] claims that this is a critical issue typical of the Brazilian traffic. Due historical factors related to individualism and problems in the supervision of traffic laws, many drivers in Brazil have a selfish behavior, often disregarding traffic regulations. Machado [16] and DaMatta [10] believe that the main cause of this kind of behavior is the conflict between the traffic regulations on paper and their appliance on real situations. According to Machado [16], when someone is inside his car, this person tends to feel "apart" of all the issues related to traffic, making excuses to himself by committing minor infractions, and most often end up unpunished, which reinforces such behavior. The survey data shows that 72 % of the respondents think that the traffic rules are not well supervised, which shows that drivers also perceive this issue in their daily life, and understand that problem.

Another issue pointed out in the results is that roadways and traffic signs in Brazil present poor infrastructure. Figure 1 shows that 65 % the survey respondents think that the Brazilian roadways have severe problems of signalling and conservation. It is

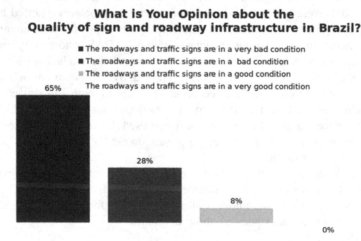

Fig. 1. Graph of the opinion about the quality of traffic infrastructure in Brazil (n = 93)

believed that it can be a factor that may lead to problems related to the ADAS workflow, impairing the correct sensor readings. It is also believed that the low infrastructure of the roadway and traffic signs may also be a problem of the social interactions in Brazilian traffic. Machado [16] claims that when there is no strong force of ruling one environment, it becomes susceptible to social interventions, diverting its use from the original project. In other words, when there is no sign to tell people what they can do, they'll do what suits to themselves, which might not be the correct action. This could lead to possible problems in the driving context, once all the rules must be applied equally to everyone, cause any action that favors only one individual over the others may compromise the whole structure of this public environment. Noriega [17] claims that environmental issues are crucial to the safety oriented driving, acting as a conditioner of drivers' behavior and problems in it may generate undesired outcomes that may impair the road safety.

It is believed that both the problems on traffic infrastructure and the drivers' inappropriate behavior may transform driving in Brazil a very stressful task. Figure 2 shows that 92 % of the respondents of the survey are unsatisfied or very unsatisfied with the stress level related to driving in urban roadways in Brazil. This stress level may affect the way people look to their ADAS, favoring sometimes features that brings comfort to the driving rather than safety-related ones. This phenomena can be perceived in phrases spoken during the focus group such as: "The traffic annoys me too much, I want something that relax me!".

Regarding drivers' opinions about their previous experience with more complex ADAS and how it may affect other interactions, when the sample of respondents of the survey is divided in 3 different groups - based on the level of complexity of their ADAS, it's possible to perceive some variations on their relationship with the systems. The fist group was composed by respondents that claimed to possess ADAS with simple data processing, generally soft automations, used to advertise the driver about some specific aspect of the driving task (e.g., Parking assistant). The second group was composed by owners of ADAS of medium complexity, capable to interfere in the driving task, but with all its readings based on specific discrete data, such as the speed of the vehicle (e.g., Cruise control systems). The third group was composed by respondents that interact with complex data processing ADAS, capable of predicting scenarios and situations to interfere directly on the driving task (e.g., Lane keeping systems).

Satisfaction with the stress level in urban roadways

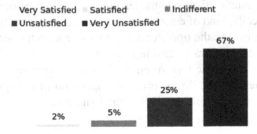

Fig. 2. Graph related to the satisfaction with the stress level in urban roadways (n = 92)

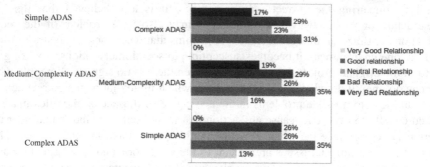

Fig. 3. Graph of the relationship of ADAS in different levels of complexity

When analyzing the answers of each group individually, it is possible to see that their affinity with ADAS is directly related to the kind of ADAS they have and their previous experience with the more complex ones. Figure 3 shows that the group with experience with more complex ADAS has good acceptance to the use of ADAS, while people with experience in the use medium-complexity ADAS have a more distributed result and the sample that owns more simple ones has almost the opposite result of the first group. According to Parazuraman [12], Degani [11], Reed [3], previous experiences in the use of ADAS are crucial for the good relationship with them. The problem resides in the fact that ADAS are still not fully adopted in the Brazilians daily lives. According to Veja [4], ADAS in Brazil are still very expensive and not affordable to most part of the population. Considering this fact, the use simple and most common ADAS may cause bad experiences to the user, compromising their trust in the systems and impairing the interaction, once trust is one of the most important factors to a smooth Human-ADAS interaction [12].

4.2 Reported Errors

The survey data found that the most common errors reported can be divided in 3 categories, as defined by of Sharit [18], Dekker [9] and Reason [19]:

1. Mode error: A specific kind of error that occurs when the driver's mental model and the actual workflow of the systems are different, making the controller misjudges the real current state of the systems, leading to unexpected outcomes.
2. Overtrust: A specific kind of error that occurs when, despite noticing an abnormality in the system functions, the operator refuses to accept such issue as an error, relying more on the system accuracy than in himself.
3. Out of the loop: A specific type of error that occurs when driver's monitoring is in low or nonexistent levels, disregarding the operation of the system thus becoming unable to react properly during an abnormal situation.

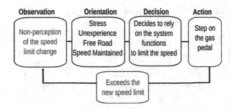

Fig. 4. Cognitive model of the first scenario (extended model available in: http://imgur.com/gOM48Pk)

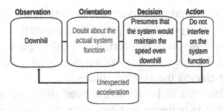

Fig. 5. Cognitive model of the second scenario (extended model available in: http://imgur.com/jn62CqZ)

For each of those kind of errors, scenarios were modelled, for better comprehension of the factors that led to the failures. The first scenario is based on a story of a user that became out of the loop by using a speed control on a freeway, and, because of that, didn't noticed the change of the speed limit when exiting it, exceeding the speed limit..

What can be perceived in this model (Fig. 4) is that the problem was caused by an observation problem, due a lack of attention. Conditioned by a successfully working system operation in the previous situation, the driver was unable to perceive the change of the speed limit. It is believed that this kind of over relaxed behavior may be caused by a previous experience of stress in traffic, making the driver look for comfort every time he is able to.

The second scenario is based on the story of a driver that misjudged the behavior of a cruise control (mode error) when he was going downhill. He thought that the speed of the vehicle would be maintained, without consider the action of the gravity, which resulted in an unexpected acceleration.

What can be perceived in Fig. 5 is a problem on the orientation process caused by a lack of experience in the use of this system. It is believed that it may be affected by the high cost of this kind of system in Brazil, making it unfamiliar for the new user. Another thing to be pointed out is that the user was in doubt about the system behavior and, even knowing that it may put himself in danger, he preferred to trust in the system rather have to act. It is believed that it may occurred because the driver was looking for comfort in the use of this system.

The third scenario was based in the history of a driver that overtrusted his lane keeping system, even in a clear problem situation. The driver clearly saw that the lanes were worn out near a curve, but even so, disregarding his own integrity, opted to not interfere, which caused the loss of control.

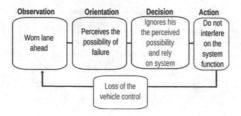

Fig. 6. Cognitive model of the third scenario (extended model available in: http://imgur.com/LfoGL2U)

According to Fig. 6, the problem occurred during the decision-making process, opting to not interfere in the system even perceiving a possible failure situation. It can be observed the driver was favoring comfort aspects, disregarding his own safety. The other problem that can be seen in this scenario is that problems in the roadway infrastructure may have caused the system failure.

Analyzing the models, it can be seen that even different, all of them had some points of similarity, and it is believed that those are the main cause of the interaction problems. The relationship between them is that all the scenarios were susceptible to one same environment, the Brazilian traffic, and all the variables inherent to it, such as the stressful conditions for the driver, the low roadway infrastructure and the high cost of ADAS, which may cause problems for the user experience. Neither of the scenarios have presented the direct communication process as a source of the interaction problems, but external factors that may have conditioned the drivers' behavior to take wrong decisions. Another issue to be pointed out is the favoring of comfort aspects rather than safety.

5   Discussion

The research concluded that there are no specific elements in the ADAS workflow not aligned to the driver's behavior, there are issues related the Brazilian traffic environment not considered in the design of this systems, which may affect the way people use this kind of system and consider their own safety. The results of this research can be split in two main points:

1. The problems of interaction are directly related to user experience with more complex ADAS. The data collected shows that people with simple and primitive ADAS complained about the alarms and the insistence of their systems, while the respondents with more sophisticated ADAS claimed to have a smooth relationship with them, even knowing that they are susceptible to the same problems. It is believed that this is a reflex of the low concern of safety issues by most of the Brazilian drivers – making the more autonomous ADAS look more attractive, and impairing the relationship with the more simple ones. So, the more complex someone's ADAS is, the better their experience with it and the fewer their concerns with problems. This is a crucial point in Brazil, since most of the ADAS sold are not

produced inside the country, which raises its costs and make them unaffordable for a big part of the population.
2. The stress related to traffic is a huge problem in Brazil [10, 16]. Most of people interviewed affirmed that driving in Brazilian traffic is a very stressful task, and at most of the times they prefer to delegate some of their activities to an ADAS than worry about all driving demands, even knowing that it could cause some eventual accidents. In other words, due to a stressful environment, once again Brazilian drivers favor comfort aspects rather than safety in the use of ADAS. Those characteristics reduce the risk perception of drivers and increase the probability of accidents.

This non consideration of the drivers' own safety may affect the way ADAS are faced and consumed in Brazil. This systems are designed to assist the driver taking control of some tasks in order to enhance safety. But, because of the stressful environment of the Brazilian traffic, combined to the high costs of the systems, ADAS are faced as luxury products, used to give drivers comfort and make the driving task more tolerable. The problem with this is that those kind of systems are not designed for that function, which may influence a non safety-oriented behavior, lowering the risk perception of the drivers.

6 Conclusion

The study was able to confirm its main hypothesis, but the secondary one was not confirmed. The main issues of the relationship between Brazilian drivers and ADAS are not related to individual aspects of Human-Machine communication, but to social and cultural factors - such as the stressful environment of Brazilian traffic, that misrepresents the way that people should use this kind of system.

It's important to remember that the results of this research are not confirmative; it has explorative data that points out for new hypothesis that must be confirmed in future researches. Even so, these results cannot be disregarded, since the analytical criteria were based on data extracted from actual users. Other researches are required to generalize the findings and treat them as a rule.

This study was part of a bigger research that aims to create guidelines for the design of ADAS better adapt to the Brazilian context in a user-centered approach. For the next steps, the research aims to confirm the findings of this study through simulator testing and understand the impact of the use of ADAS in the drivers' behavior.

References

1. Young, M.: Ergonomics issues with advanced driver assistant systems. In: Gikkas, N. (ed.) Automotive Ergonomics: Driver-Vehicle Interaction. CRC Press, Boca Raton (2012)
2. Knapp, A., Neumann, M., Brockmann, M., Walz, R., Winkle, T.: Code of Practice for the Design and Evaluation of ADAS P, Response3 (2009)

3. Reed, N.: IVIS, ADAS, OODA: joining the loop. In: Gikkas, N. (ed.) Automotive Ergonomics: Driver-Vehicle Interaction. CRC Press, Boca Raton (2012)
4. VEJA: Segurança nos Carros, o Brasil Ainda está na Beira (2014). http://veja.abril.com.br/noticia/esporte/seguranca-nos-carros-o-brasil-ainda-esta-na-rabeira. Accessed 20 March 2014
5. Norman, D.: The Design of Future Things. Basic Books, New York (2009)
6. HSE: Out of Control: Why Systems Go Wrong and How to Prevent Failure, 2nd edn. HSE Books, Noewich (2003)
7. Parazuraman, R., Rilley, V.: Human and Automation: Use, Misuse, Disuse Abuse. Hum. Factors Ergonom. Soc. **39**, 23 (1997)
8. International Standardization Organization. ISO 26262: Road Vehicles and Functional Safety (2011)
9. Dekker, S.: Ten Questions About Human Error: A New View of Human Factors and System Safety. Lawrence Erlbaum Associates, Mahwah (2004)
10. DaMatta, R.: Fé em Deus e pé na tábua, vol. 1. Rocco, Rio de Janeiro (2010)
11. Degani, A.: Taming HAL: Designing Interfaces Beyond 2001. Macmillan, Palgrave (2004)
12. Parazuraman, R., Sheridan, T.B.: A model for types and levels for human interaction with automation. IEEE Trans. Syst. **30**, 286–297 (2000)
13. Moraes, A.D., Mont'Alvão, C.: Ergonomia: Conceitos e Aplicações, vol. 4. 2AB, Rio de Janeiro (2012)
14. Markopoulos, P.: Qualitative Research Methods for Interaction Design. Crete, Heraklion, HCII International 2014 (2014)
15. Tullis, T., Albert, B.: Measuring User Experience: Collecting Analyzing and Presenting Usability Metrics, 2nd edn. Morgan Kaufman, Walthan (2008)
16. Machado, A.P.: Um Olhar da Psicologia Social Sobre o Trânsito. In: de Hoffmann, M.H. et al. (eds.) Comportamento Humano no trânsito, 2nd edn. Cosac Naif, Sao Paulo (2012)
17. Noriega, P.: Uma perspectiva ambiental de Segurança Rodoviária. Revista Portuguesa de Sinalização (2010)
18. Sharit, J.: Human error. In: Salvendi, G. (ed.) Handbook of Human Factors and System Safety. Willey, New Jersey (2006)
19. Reason, J.: Human Error. Cambridge University Press, Cambridge (1990)

Going on a Road-Trip with My Electric Car: Acceptance Criteria for Long-Distance-Use of Electric Vehicles

Julian Halbey[✉], Sylvia Kowalewski, and Martina Ziefle

Communication Science, RWTH Aachen University,
Campus-Boulevard 57, 52074 Aachen, Germany
{halbey,kowalewski,ziefle}@comm.rwth-aachen.de

Abstract. In this study we report on four focus group discussions to examine cognitions, attitudes of a broad variety of users with respect to battery electric vehicles (BEV). Specifically, we identified relevant criteria for the use of electric cars as a long distance vehicle and gathered first impressions of where users wish to locate such charging stations. Four main aspects were identified as acceptance relevant: The battery's capacity, given in the driving range in kilometers, the time it takes to regain this given range (*charging time*), the density of the charging stations grid and the attractiveness of the places where the charging stations are located, which could for example be a service area or a simple parking lot off the highway. Results of this study might provide detailed insights into conditions and technical specifications that have to be met beyond the possibility of quick charging to reach higher acceptance and a broad willingness to use BEVs for more than short-tracks in the city.

Keywords: Battery electric vehicles (BEV) · User acceptance · Quick charging · Infrastructure · Adoption of novel technologies

1 Introduction

In times of rising concerns about climate change and global warming, the automotive industry among many others is forced to find solutions for decreasing the massive exhaustion of carbon. To reach this aim, most automotive OEMs and governments all over the world consider battery electric vehicles (BEV) as the most reasonable drivetrain technology for the future. But despite high expectations as for example stated by the German government, still, the demand for electric vehicles is low. Except from the higher costs, this is assumed to be due to two main problems compared to fuel powered cars: The range is limited by the battery capacity, and recharging the battery lasts extremely long. That is why most of today's available BEVs are designed for short-track-use as a typical city car.

The possibility of quick charging might now provide a solution for the range and charging problem: With special charging stations suited with extremely high current, it is possible to regain 80 % of a battery's capacity in half an hour or less. Placed along

© Springer International Publishing Switzerland 2015
A. Marcus (Ed.): DUXU 2015, Part III, LNCS 9188, pp. 473–484, 2015.
DOI: 10.1007/978-3-319-20889-3_44

highways and in cities, such stations might enable long-distance-use of electric vehicles. However, building such an infrastructure will be expensive and given the to date low demand for BEVs for short distances it is questionable whether a quick charging infrastructure will enhance acceptance and the intention to use BEVs. For this reason the current study investigated user requirements related to a quick charging infrastructure for long-distance-use.

1.1 Actual Use of Electric Vehicles

Surveys show that the public attitude towards sustainable mobility and electric cars in particular is mostly positive [1, 2]. Still, the demand for electric cars is low, though there are several models available and expectations are high. But in Germany, only 0.03 % of the entire registered cars are battery electric ones, which is a total of about 12000 cars [3]. However, this small group of current users of BEVs can be outlined quite consistently.

The great majority of BEV users in Germany are male (89 %) and about 50 years of age. They have an income slightly above the average but there are no significant differences in the educational level compared to users of conventional cars [4]. Furthermore, most of the BEV users live in rural areas or suburbs with their families and have their own detached houses. Reasons for the purchase of such cars are usually a great interest in technology and environmental awareness, as well as rather practical issues like the low energy costs per kilometer and even the driving pleasure due to the electric drive [5].

Not only can the group of the electrically mobile people be explained in such consistency but also the use cases for BEVs. Most important, few people (users as well as non-users of BEVs) can imagine using a BEV as the only means of transportation [1, 5]. As could be expected, problems occur especially when going on holiday. This attitude matches with the fact that most of the BEV users own a second car with a conventional combustion engine [5]. Thus, having an alternative as a kind of mobility reserve seems to play an important role in the decision to buy a BEV. Besides the limited battery capacity and therefore the small driving range, the long duration to recharge the battery is mentioned as another main reason for the lack of long distance suitability.

But despite these limitations, people perceive a lot of advantages in BEVs: Most of the daily ways can be and are indeed covered by BEVs [5]. This means for example to go to work, to the supermarket or from the rural home into nearby cities, which represents a typical use case for a second car. Still it is remarkable that the average range driven with BEVs is nearly the same as the overall German average of about 43 km per day [5, 6]. This is in the range of virtually all available BEVs. According to this, it is not surprising that more than 90 % of the BEV owners park and load their cars on their own premises [5]. On the contrary, this means that existing public (slow) charging stations are hardly used to date.

1.2   How to Deal with a Limited Driving Range

There has been a lot of research concerning the question how to fit the driving range of BEVs to the people's mobility needs [7, 8]. Since batteries are expensive and heavy, the idea is to make the battery not bigger than absolutely necessary, which means to know how far people go with their cars. The main results can be explained quickly: For most of the daily mobility needs, the existing BEVs are absolutely sufficient, as explained in the section above. But longer trips remain, that cannot be done with this range.

So why do only so little people buy BEVs even as a second car, though the range is sufficient for more than 80 % of the trips done in Germany daily? Of course the higher costs will play a role, but there seems to be a psychological factor concerning the range. When it comes to electric vehicles, people subliminally fear to remain lying on the street due to an empty battery. In transportation psychology research, this fear is called *range anxiety* [9, 10]. According to the concept, not only the effectively needed driving range is crucial, but people expect an additional reserve. Transferred to current users of BEVs, this means they only use up to 80 % of the available range [11]. So not only the technical capability should be considered when designing BEVs, but also the question of how to give the consumers a feeling of security, which occurs to be a crucial aspect. How this *range anxiety* can be overcome is not safely explored yet. Besides greater battery capacities, some researchers assume especially a good public charging infrastructure to be useful as a kind of *range safety buffer* [10, 12, 13].

1.3   Research Questions and Purpose of This Study

Based on the acceptance-related research so far, the aim of this study was firstly to explore all the relevant criteria that people apply to evaluate BEVs in comparison to conventional cars. Secondly, the study was supposed to investigate the influence of a quick charging infrastructure, since this technology presents a new part in the whole concept of electric mobility and could possibly have a great impact on feelings of security and acceptance, as has been shown in the previous section. Furthermore, ideas and criteria for possible locations for quick charging stations should be collected. Finally, we wanted to deal with the question what needs to be done to make BEVs comparable to conventional ones so that they one day could replace cars with combustion engines completely.

2   Methodology

In the following section, the methodological approach of this study is detailed. Focus groups were run because this method offers the most effective approach for exploring barriers and benefits of users regarding a technology that is at an early stage of market launch [14, 15]. Three focus groups with users of BEVs were conducted and one control group with users of conventional cars. Composition of the groups and their realization are explained in the following sections.

2.1 Procedure and Participants

The selection of participants was oriented on so-called "information-rich cases" [16], which can provide diverse and multifarious information to the given topic. Therefore, the approach of this study was to gather information from current users of BEVs as they are the only ones who can evaluate the existing cars and their range and charging time and thereby anticipate future effects of quick charging.

A control group was conducted to check whether the users really differ in their opinions from the great majority of drivers of conventional cars. Overall, four different groups were formed which are described in the following.

Group 1: With only 12000 owners of electric cars in Germany, getting private BEV users to join the focus groups was not easy. But in Aachen, Germany the local transportation operator has 50 *Smart Electric Drive* at use as part of a research field trial. So via this company, four frequent users of these electric cars could be selected for the first group, accordingly a very homogeneous group of colleagues with high domain knowledge. Three of them were female, one male (mean age of 39 years).

Group 2: The second group consisted of clients of a car sharing company who often use their electric cars. These are either *Smart Electric Drive* as well, *Renault Zoe* or *Mitsubishi EV/Citroen C-Zero*. All of these cars have driving ranges of about 100 to 150 km. In this second group, all were male (mean age of 39 years).

Group 3: The third group was a mixed group out of car sharing clients, research associates from the RWTH Aachen University (mostly technical disciplines), and a (completely enthusiastic) private owner of a Tesla Model S. Except from the latter, all of them do not own BEVs, but use them frequently and therefore have experiences with the range and driving performance. This group consisted of five male participants who were, on average, 40 years of age.

Group 4: For the control group, five drivers of conventional cars were recruited (two female, three male, mean age was 31 years).

2.2 Materials

A structured interview guideline was developed with the aim of maximizing the exploration of opinions and ideas to the research questions (see Fig. 1):

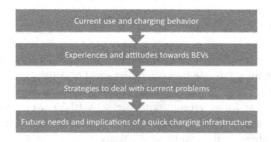

Fig. 1. Structure of the interview guideline

After a short introduction, the quick charging technology was explained briefly. Familiarizing participants with the topic, the first task of participants was to mark possible locations for quick charging stations on a city map of Aachen. Each participant was given three pins in an own color to pin on the map on a pin board.

Understanding the implicit rationale of positioning charging stations, participants were asked to explain their choices and even criticize other locations to get the discussion started. The next topic was to report about their usage behavior, especially with regard to the ways they drive with the BEVs and where they charge them so far. In this context participants were encouraged to perceived disadvantages and problems with the use of BEVs if present.

Resuming the discussion participants were asked how to deal with these existing problems and what – according to their view - needs to be done to make BEVs suitable for a wider use. Up to this point, the discussion did not explicitly refer to quick charging, but to the current state of technology and ideas for the future in general. At this point, participants were guided to include this new technique into their considerations: How could quick charging help solve the existing problems and overcome the disadvantages, related to the disadvantages they mentioned before? To put this idea even further, they were requested to report and discuss mobility needs in general and to reflect which part electric cars could take in this mobility behavior, given existing public quick charging infrastructure.

3 Results

The following section presents the results of the four focus group sessions. The findings are structured according to the expiry of topics in the interview guideline.

3.1 Current Use and Charging Behavior

Since most of the focus group participants did not own the electric cars they use, the use cases are mostly predetermined by the respective using context. For example the employees of the local transportation operator use the company's electric cars to get to work and back home or to do other business-related tours during their worktime. It is guaranteed that the employees can drive home and back to work without recharging. People who live farer away shall not use the cars. The cars are usually recharged on the company's site by 22 kW (quick-)charging stations to keep them available as much as possible. On the other hand, this means that the participants of this focus group did not have much experience with public charging stations or with longer trips.

This turned out to be quite different in the other two focus groups. Although it is intended that the car sharing cars are only recharged at the car sharing stations, some of the clients had already done longer trips where they had to recharge on the way. There were also participants who reported to have a lot of experience with electric cars and use public charging stations very frequently. Car-sharing clients declared they use the electric cars as often as possible and would drive them even more often if more of them would be available. The Tesla owner had even gone on holiday (about 800 km) with his car. But there were also other BEV enthusiasts who like to have the risk and thus make it a bit of a challenge to try out how far they can go and try to use them for as much trips as possible. So the individual use cases of participants of these two groups differed widely. Some of the car sharing clients only do short trips in the city, others use them to get to work or for business, others use them as their first vehicle for everything. Besides the car sharing sites, some of them recharge the cars at home, at public charging stations or – in case of the research associates – at the institute's own charging stations.

3.2   Experiences and Attitudes of Current Users Towards BEVs

When asked about their first experiences and their attitudes towards BEVs, the overwhelming majority commented very positively. This is mainly due to two impressions:

First of all, the *driving pleasure due to the electric drive*. This experience was mentioned most often as first impressions in all focus groups with current BEV users. For many of the participants this fact was a bit surprising since electric cars are usually associated with economical driving and saving fuel – an approach that is basically contradictory to power and driving pleasure with fuel powered cars. So many of the users appeared inspired that with BEVs, it is possible to save fuel and have fun while driving at the same time.

Secondly, a lot of the users found that BEVs are *perfectly suited for cities* – the area where most of them use them. So the BEVs used by the focus group participants meet the mobility requirements they are intended for and perform quite well.

But there are also some limitations that shape the first experiences: There are lots of details that do not work very well yet. For example, some participants reported *public charging stations that do not work, different and complicated accounting systems for charging stations* as well as an *uncertainty regarding the range* as soon as the tracks get farer than the well-known inner-city ones. Furthermore, they check the battery status a lot more often than they check the fuel gauge in conventional cars. Though also differences in the opinions showed up. While few participants – most strongly the Tesla owner – find that BEVs can satisfy all the mobility needs, others even call it an "atypical car use" only for enthusiasts. Still most participants think BEVs have their advantages in cities, but *cannot compete with conventional cars on longer trips*.

In contrast to that the control group revealed a very different impression. Most often, BEV novices expressed concerns about the driving range. The higher costs (purchase, maintenance) was another important disadvantage. Without being well informed about electric cars (self-disclosure), they had the impression that driving an electric car needs much more effort as one would always be focused on the remaining range and would have to plan where the car can be recharged. So range and costs were the dominating factors in this discussion, even if two of the participants could imagine driving a BEV in nearer future.

Especially the reported disadvantages of current BEV users and their way of dealing with them will be analyzed and explained in more detail in the following sections.

3.3   Users' Strategies to Overcome Current Problems with BEV

Some disadvantages of BEVs were already mentioned (See Sect. 3.2). The argumentation lines of the main barriers, like restricted range and the corresponding infrastructure problems, are now analyzed in more detail to find out how users deal with them at the moment and further to derive solutions for the future.

In the control group as well as in the other three focus groups, the limited driving range has been mentioned as the main disadvantage of today's BEVs. BEV novices, for example, report that they would check the battery status every few minutes even on short tracks. This fact corresponds with the explained *range anxiety* [8]. However, with increasing familiarity and daily experience with the battery range, users get accustomed to undertake short tracks without anxiety. But even those report a different feeling while driving an electric car due to a battery in comparison to a fuel tank, even on short tracks. So in general, the majority of participants reported an perceived uncertainty which appears on different levels.

First of all, there is the *general uncertainty whether the driving range is sufficient* for the track planned as soon as it is not one of the usual tracks. This effect is even strengthened since most of the participants have experienced significant variations in the driving range depending on weather, track profile and style of driving. However, they have different ways to handle this disadvantage: Especially the less experienced participants usually *keep a range reserve*, which means they only use a part of the full battery capacity. Some of the real BEV enthusiasts instead rather *take it as a challenge* to explore how far they can go or to optimize their driving style. But of course, if they have really important dates, they take a safety reserve as well. So no matter how one handles the limited range and its variations, it always leads to a *higher planning effort* compared to conventional cars. For tracks which people drive the first time or at least not usually, they *first need to plan the route* and check out how far it is. Next, they have to consider whether the driving range of their car is sufficient. If not, they either *look for recharging possibilities* on the way or use an alternative vehicle. Although planning gets easier with increasing experience the fact itself remains the same. All of the participants agreed about this *higher planning effort* and the *limited range* as a restriction to electric mobility. Having chosen the first alternative (recharging on the way), soon another uncertainty arises: Is the planned charging station free or occupied when I get there? As mentioned before, some participants even experienced though free, but broken charging stations, which increases the uncertainty even more.

However, different participants have different ways to deal with this problem. For many of the car sharing clients and the local transportation operator employees, this planning effort and uncertainty about range and charging stations is a fact that discourages them from travelling longer distances. They evaluate BEVs as beneficial for short tracks in the city, but would usually not go on longer trips with today's technical and infrastructural state of the art. Nevertheless, there was a minority – one of which was the Tesla owner – who thought differently. For those participants, the advantages weigh out the disadvantages. For the benefit of driving pleasure and the environmental effects they report to accept the cost of a higher planning effort. Thus, on the one hand, there are the rather pragmatic BEV users who do not want to accept too much extra effort or other disadvantages, on the other hand there are the electric car enthusiasts who accept some problems for the advantages they experience.

Besides range problems and connected aspects, other disadvantages – primarily mentioned in the control group - were the higher costs. Also in the control group, people wished more variety in the car models since most BEVs are small cars today. In the other groups instead, it was often mentioned that there are different accounting systems for public charging stations and that they sometimes do not work.

3.4   Future Needs and Implications of a Quick Charging Infrastructure

Based on the prior discussion, focus group participants were requested to consider potential issues to be changed to make BEVs more attractive in the future. Irrespective of this specific question, interestingly, the discussion focused on the fundamental question what an electric car can provide at all. Some participants argued that BEVs are generally only suited for short tracks and even in the future a mix of different transportation would be the only feasible solution – in line with the principle "The right car for the right purpose." Others were convinced that BEVs might completely replace fuel powered cars in the future. When asked what has to be changed in order to replace fuel powered cars in future, participants mentioned a lot of aspects that partially overlap with the stated disadvantages. Figure 2 gives an overview on the four most often mentioned aspects that have to be changed in order to enable the replacement of conventional (fuel power) cars through electric cars.

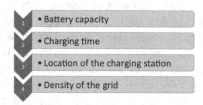

Fig. 2. The four most important aspects to enable a full usage of BEVs

First of all, all participants agreed that the **battery capacity** has to be increased, even though the vision of the future driving range varied widely across the groups. The desired range in the control group varied from 200 up to 800 km. In contrast, actual BEV users did not mention this great variety in range, they all agreed that at least medium-long tracks should be feasible. In order to use an electric car as means of transport most of the users wish at least a battery capacity that lasts for 300–500 km. As lower limit, 150 to 200 km would be barely acceptable, in order to avoid range anxiety. The desired range depended especially on the average mileage of the participants: Those who often travel longer distances considered higher ranges as necessary.

Charging time turned out to be another important factor. When the discussion came to charging, most of the participants in all groups did not find it acceptable to take any extra time to charge the car. Instead, recharging should happen while the car is parking anyway. Also, for long distance tours most participants thought of recharging the car when they have a break, anyway. Again, there were great differences between the control- and the other groups. In the control group, the requirements on BEVs were even higher than on conventional cars. They argued on base of their current travel behavior and did only want to recharge the car while they would have a break anyway. The current users of BEVs instead were mostly willing to change their habits a bit and have extra breaks to recharge. But even though, the charging time should decrease since nobody seemed willing to wait for several hours. So especially in the group with the local transportation operator employees, different ideas came up, like stations to change empty batteries for new ones or redox-flow batteries from which the electrolyte liquid can be replaced, which is basically comparable to refueling a conventional car.

When guided towards the possibility of **quick charging** it turned out that some of the current user groups were aware of the concept before, some just got to know it during the focus groups. The participants agreed that quick charging stations placed along highways have a great potential to enable long-distance use of BEVs. But even though the cars can be charged a lot more quickly than to date, quick charging a BEV still lasts longer than refueling a conventional car. Therefore, in the following discussions the question arose how quick charging along highways should be arranged, implying the question what to do while the car is plugged in. In these discussions, the **location of the charging stations** turned out to be an important factor. Some of the participants had ideas to make charging more attractive like providing free Wi-Fi. But most of them considered service areas most appropriate so that the time can be used to eat and have a good break. So again, there seems to be low acceptance to spend extra time on charging, or at least the time needs to be used effectively for other things. Furthermore, the charging time itself was discussed again, since it was recognized that there still is room for development in this aspect as well even when considering quick charging stations. Again, the users had different ideas of how quick it should be. To sum it up, most of them considered half an hour as acceptable, given that a certain range can be recovered during that time. This range was, as explained earlier, dependent from the user and his using context. Some even thought of charging more than an hour or two in a city next to the highway and have a greater break during that time.

The fourth important point in the discussion about long-distance use of BEVs was the **density of the grid**. The participants did not state this aspect as often as the others, but the fact came up very often even during the discussions about planning effort. With conventional cars, one does not have to plan where to refuel the car, as there are more than enough stations available. This would be completely different if quick charging stations had the same distances in between. Due to the lower range of BEVs one would have to plan which charging stations to use. Thus, just to enable certain routes by placing few quick charging stations along these highways would not satisfy many of the focus group participants, but instead there should be a grid so dense that one would not have to plan so much in advance. However, this was a critical point and different opinions about it arose.

Concluding, four factors turned out to be most critical for long-distance use of electric cars, given that it shall be realized by a quick charging stations grid along highways: Driving range of the car itself, charging time to regain a certain range, the locations of charging stations and distances between the stations (i.e. grid's density).

4 Discussion

The aim of this study was to explore all the relevant criteria that people apply to evaluate BEVs in comparison to conventional cars. Furthermore, the study was supposed to investigate the influence of a quick charging infrastructure on acceptance of electric vehicles. Finally, we wanted to deal with the question what needs to be done to make BEVs comparable to conventional ones so that they one day could replace cars with combustion engines completely.

In general, all users, even most of the unexperienced control group, expressed a positive attitude towards electric cars. Nevertheless, some differences appeared between users and non-users of electric cars that give fruitful implications for development and further studies. The most important benefit for users respectively people with experience in driving BEVs was the driving pleasure an electric car offers as well as economical benefits in terms of fuel saving. In contrast to that the control group that never drove an electrical vehicle focused more on arguments against buying a BEV right now e.g. limited range and higher costs. Further results showed that users are more prepared for compromises than non-users especially when it comes to charging times and battery capacity. A reasonable explanation for this difference might be the perceived benefits that one experienced when driving a BEV some times.

Another argument in favor for this assumption might be the strategy to deal with restricted range. The possible range of electric cars was considered a major drawback in this study. Although field studies have shown that the average range of an electric car would meet the mobility demands of a large amount of people [16, 17], the wish for an extended range still persists. Nevertheless, further results in this study clearly showed that although range anxiety was a major topic in the user groups it turned out clearly that people get used to deal with this problem and develop a kind of routine in planning their trips.

The major point of these results is that although battery capacity and charging time are the most critical aspects that have to be improved for more acceptance, the perceived benefits of BEVs might outweigh a higher effort in being mobile with BEVs when these technical drawbacks will be improved in future, even if BEV technology can never achieve the flexibility benchmark conventional combustion engines offer. Therefore, expanding the infrastructure by quick charging stations might be one useful solution. Improvement of battery capacity and consideration of attractiveness of locations for charging stations as well as the density of grids are the other major aspects that might lead to higher acceptance and help to overcome the phenomenon *range anxiety*.

Because of the qualitative nature of the study, quantitative follow-up studies have to be conducted. For example a choice-based conjoint study would be helpful to examine the users' preferences and trade-offs of these criteria for a long-distance-use of

BEVs, similar to the approach in [19]. Conducting a conjoint study with different levels of each criteria could help to answer questions more in detail, e.g. what is an acceptable density of the grid, when the battery capacity is sufficient for 150 km, it takes 30 min to charge and quick charging stations are located on very attractive parking lots with entertainment and food – a charging station every 120 km, 100 km or still every 50 km? Results of these trade-offs could offer technical benchmarks for developing engineers that should be achieved in order to enhance adoption of BEVs.

Another important methodological aspect of this study is the discussion process in the focus group that revealed that people are not able to adequately differentiate between infrastructure and the technology itself. When asked to evaluate their acceptance of a quick charging infrastructure, participants mostly argued on aspects that apply to the car technology itself. Thus, the process of the discussion shows that people's acceptance largely depends on the fit of the technology, independently of car type or infrastructure, focusing on their mobility needs in general. This finding though is not specifically directed to electric mobility but reflects a typical discussion behavior of focus groups that can be found also in studies in other use contexts e.g. wireless medical context [20]. Thus, when studying acceptance of a new infra-structure technology the target in use, in this case the BEV, has to be evaluated or considered as well in order to give participants an appropriate framing.

Though this study revealed insightful argumentations about users' requirements in the context of electric mobility in general and BEV in particular, naturally, this study represents only a first approach in both, scope and methodology. One limitation refers to the specificity of the user group examined here. Focus group participants (even the control group) were well educated and had comparably high domain knowledge. Findings thus might not be representative to less elaborated argumentations prevailing in a less informed public majority, which though are important for the full understanding of perceived barriers in novel car technologies. In addition, user diversity in terms of age and generation, or, gender could be a valuable addendum in this context. Finally, it is also highly probable that country-specific and cultured attitudes are underlying acceptance for BEV usage that should be addressed in further research.

Acknowledgments. This research was funded by the German Ministry of Economics and Technology (Project SLAM, reference no. 01 MX 13007F). Authors thank all focus group participants for their patience and openness to share opinions on a novel technology. Furthermore, thanks to the interdisciplinary SLAM research group for valuable input.

References

1. Ziefle, M., Beul-Leusmann, S., Kasugai, K., Schwalm, M.: Public perception and acceptance of electric vehicles: exploring users' perceived benefits and drawbacks. In: Marcus, A. (ed.) DUXU 2014, Part III. LNCS, vol. 8519, pp. 628–639. Springer, Heidelberg (2014)
2. Hoffmann, C., Hinkeldein, D., Graff, A., Kramer, S.: What do potential users think about electric mobility? In: Hülsmann, M., Fornahl, D. (eds.) Evolutionary Paths Towards the Mobility Patterns of the Future, pp. 85–99. Springer, Heidelberg (2014)

3. Kraftfahrtbundesamt. Bestand an Pkw, 1. Januar 2014 nach ausgewählten Kraftstoffarten absolut. http://www.kba.de/DE/Statistik/Fahrzeuge/Bestand/Umwelt/2014_b_umwelt_dusl_absolut.html?nn=663524
4. Pollok, P., Lüttgens, D., Piller, F.T.: Leading Edge Users and Latent Consumer Needs in Electromobility: Findings from a Nethnographic Study of User Innovation in High-Tech Online Communities. RWTH-TIM Working Paper, Germany (2014)
5. Jarass, J., Frenzel, I., Trommer, S.: Early Adopter der Elektromobilität in Deutschland. Internationales Verkehrswesen 66(2), 70–72 (2014)
6. Infas, DLR. Mobilität in Deutschland 2008 – Tabellenband. http://www.mobilitaet-in-Deutschland.de/pdf/MiD2008_Tabellenband.pdf
7. Caroll, S., Walsh, C.: The Smart Move Trial: Description and Initial Results. Cenex, Leicestershire (2011)
8. Krems, J.F., et al.: Schlussbericht zum Forschungsvorhaben Verbundprojekt: MINI E powered by Vattenfall V2.0. Technische Universität Chemnitz, Chemnitz (2011)
9. Nilsson, M.: Electric Vehicles – The Phenomenon of Range anxiety (2011). http://www.elvire.eu/IMG/pdf/The_phenomenon_of_range_anxiety_ELVIRE.pdf
10. Franke, T., Krems, J.F.: What drives range preferences in electric vehicle users? Transp. Policy 30, 56–62 (2013)
11. Franke, T., Neumann, I., Bühler, F., Cocron, P., Krems, J.F.: Experiencing Range in an electric vehicle – understanding psychological barriers. Appl. Psychol. Int. Rev. 61(3), 368–391 (2011)
12. Franke, T., Krems, J.F.: Interacting with limited mobility resources: psychological range levels in electric vehicle use. Transp. Res. Part A 48, 109–122 (2012)
13. Botsford, C., Szczepanek, A.: Fast Charging vs. Slow Charging: Pros and cons for the New Age of Electric Vehicles. International Battery, Hybrid and Fuel Cell Electric Vehicle Symposium 24. http://www.cars21.com/assets/link/EVS-24-3960315%20Botsford.pdf
14. Krueger, R.: Focus Groups: A Practical Guide for Applied Research. Sage Publications, London (1994)
15. Sutton, S.G., Arnold, V.: Focus group methods: using interactive and nominal groups to explore emerging technology-driven phenomena in accounting and information systems. Int. J. Acc. Inform. Syst. 14, 81–88 (2013)
16. Patton, M.Q.: Qualitative Research and Evaluation Methods. Sage Publications, Thousand Oaks (2002)
17. Greaves, S., Backman, H., Ellison, A.B.: An empirical assessment of the feasibility of battery electric vehicles for day-to-day driving. Transp. Res. Part Policy Pract. 66, 226–237 (2014)
18. Pearre, N.S., Kempton, W., Guensler, R.L., Elango, V.V.: Electric vehicles: how much range is required for a day's driving? Transp. Res. Part C Emerg. Technol. 19, 1171–1184 (2011)
19. Arning, K., Kowalewski, S., Ziefle, M.: Health concerns vs. mobile data needs: conjoint measurement of preferences for mobile communication network scenarios. Int. J. Hum. Ecol. Risk Assess. 20(5), 1359–1384 (2013)
20. Arning, K., Kowalewski, S., Ziefle, M.: Modelling user acceptance of wireless medical technologies. In: Godara, B., Nikita, K.S. (eds.) MobiHealth. LNICST, vol. 61, pp. 146–153. Springer, Heidelberg (2013)

A Study on a Split-View Navigation System

Jongsung Lee$^{(\boxtimes)}$, Heewon Lee, and Sung Woo Kim

Interaction Design, Grad. School of Techno Design,
Kookmin University, Seoul, Korea
{jslee0587,hiwon427}@gmail.com, caerang@kookmin.ac.kr

Abstract. CNS (Car Navigation System) provides traffic information with an intention to offer safe and comfortable driving experience. However, because too much information is presented into a single screen it often becomes information-crowded. This paper analyzed four commercial CNS products to collect information elements and conducted user studies such as focused groups, surveys and interviews to determine what information is needed for each position of the seat; the driver and the passenger seat. The result showed that there is clear difference in information priority between driver and the person on passenger seat. Based on such finding, this paper proposes using split-view based CNS. Split-view CNS contributes to enhance user satisfaction of driving experience by providing different information to needed for a driver and a passenger.

Keywords: Navigation · Split-view · Information delivery element

1 Introduction

1.1 Study Background and Purpose

With the development of digital technology, including Global Position System (GPS) and information communication, our lives have become speedy and efficient, and navigation devices have become popular. However, if too much information, other than that required, were exposed on navigation devices while driving, it would degrade drivers' "cognitive functions and deviate them from the inherent goal, thereby affecting safety driving negatively." To prevent this, selection of information in navigation devices is considered a highly important factor.

Currently, existing navigation information includes not only path guide as a primary function, but also additional information that is provided as a secondary function, which increases information complexity. In addition, because of elaborate Graphical User Interface (GUI), driver's eyes may be distracted, thereby interfering with driving and increasing the likelihood of traffic accidents. Accordingly, how to represent information on a screen is important because it is difficult for drivers to compare and judge information presented on a limited screen, and be aware simultaneously of the road conditions. In this regard, the need to study how to provide information on a screen by dividing navigation system information into two sub-screens has arisen. Thus, this study aims to prove that the importance of information delivery elements between the driver and passenger seats is different, thereby providing navigation information delivery elements customized for the driver and passenger seats.

A. Marcus (Ed.): DUXU 2015, Part III, LNCS 9188, pp. 485–495, 2015.
DOI: 10.1007/978-3-319-20889-3_45

To do this, we selected four navigation systems from local companies with high market share based on market research results, and analyzed the components of the information on the screen during driving, thereby providing a navigation system that delivers the required information delivery elements for the driver and passenger seats utilizing Split View technology.

2 Theoretical Discussion

2.1 Navigation Concept

Car Navigation System is a system that provides drivers with traffic and road information, as well as the shortest and optimum path [1]. Previous GPS-based systems that guided through a travel path only by considering current location information from satellites have evolved into advanced systems that provide safe and comfortable driving environments by collecting, analyzing, and delivering traffic information in real time based on GPS and wireless communication technologies. That is, a shortest travel path was the main goal in the past, but now this has changed to the optimum travel path. Navigation system technology is cutting-edge technology that combines various industrial technologies, such as electric, electronic, communication, and vehicular, and utilization of navigation system technology is increasingly penetrating our daily living [2].

2.2 Navigation Map Software in Korea

Development of the navigation system in Korea has been accomplished by purchasing software that is a basic electronic map installed in hardware, and then re-developing it according to the design of each company. The navigation market in Korea only had approximately ten companies in 2005, but increased to 70 companies in 2007. Among them, Thinkware and Mando Map & Soft contain map software and electronic map technologies, which are the core navigation technologies. iNavi from Thinkware and Gini from Mando Map & Soft account for 70 % of the navigation market in Korea, which makes them the leading brands in navigation systems. As the demand for navigation devices increases and the electronic map market increases, the entry of new companies has also increased, such as Atlan Map from Fine Digital and SK Energy Co. Ltd. Another trend is that more consumers are buying navigation applications (apps) through telecommunication companies, rather than buying expensive navigation devices, because smart devices have become popular (Table 1).

In this market trend, competition between companies is fierce, and the difference in technology level becomes slimmer. As a result, companies do their best effort to develop distinguished software products in order to maintain a competitive edge. Because of the fierce competition, recent electronic maps are now embedded with accurate and tremendous information database, and are capable of providing intelligent customized services that help search for destinations even without the exact name, or memorize driver habits. As such, a continuous development for user-oriented electronic map updates and services has been done [3].

Table 1. Representative map software products from Korea

Map type	Category	Map software functions	Screen example
iNavi	PND	- 40% of market share in Korea – PDA-dedicated software is mounted - Convenient search function that uses recent company name, business sector, and 114 - Travel path management function, TPEG - various auxiliary services for subways and radio - Detailed 3D screen, user customized service provided	
Gini	PND	- Manufactures own terminal - Convenient search service that uses recent company name, business sector, and 114 - Travel path management function, TPEG - Various auxiliary functions and services provided, such as game and Karaoke - Detailed 3D screen, intelligent map matching	
Atlan	PND	- New concept map developed by Fine Digital's own technology - HD grade map provided - provides user-oriented services for location search, path, and traffic services - Perfect division of screen into 2D+3D or 2D+2D	
Tmap	Mobile	- Integrated search, photo search - search by name, initial, address, or telephone number - Streaming map function - Departure time prediction function, arrival time prediction function - Report and sharing function	

2.3   Study on Split-View Definition and Analysis

Split-view technology is a type of backlit color active matrix display (TFT-LCD) where two different images are displayed simultaneously over pixels adjacent to a screen. A front side of the display is divided into two images that can be seen differently according to seat position, thereby watching two different contents simultaneously [4] (Fig. 1).

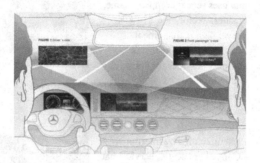

Fig. 1. Mercedes-Benz – Split view Display

2.4   Navigation Map Screen Information Components

The visual information element from the digital media information elements is divided into four elements in terms of user interaction: control, information delivery, structure, and background. Structure and background elements play a role in assisting user execution indirectly, whereas control and information delivery elements are directly related to user operational execution [5] (Table 2).

Table 2. Detailed components of map screen information

Role	Element	Detailed element
Direct role to execution	Control element	Icon, button, texts
	Information delivery element	Text, symbol, icon, pictogram, 2D, 3D, logo, background map
Indirect role to execution	Structure element	Layout
	Background element	Background color and image

3   Analysis on the Information Delivery Element in Navigations

3.1   Study Targets and Scope

In order to study a navigation map to extract information components, products from four local companies with a high market share were selected: iNavi from Map Thinkware, Gini from Mando Map & Soft, Atlan from Fine Drive, and T-map mobile navigation from SK planet. A study scope was set with information directly related to user operation executions while driving, which is provided by the selected navigation maps as a case study analysis target; furthermore, information delivery elements, with the exception of the control element, were set with a main study scope [6].

3.2   FGI

Eight Focus Group Interview (FGI) study subjects for this research are owners of vehicles equipped with the selected four navigation systems; furthermore, the subjects use their navigation systems at least weekly, and are familiar with the use of navigation systems. A second group composed of eight subjects between the ages of 20 to 39 with experience as vehicle passengers was selected to conduct the FGI.

A questionnaire process was conducted with pre-determined questions, and the survey content concerned the information delivery elements of navigation maps while driving. Individual complaints and required improvements were also recorded on the survey.

An observation experiment was conducted to determine the subjects' overall usage behavior with regards to the navigation systems, and direct observation was conducted to observe the recognition process of the information delivery elements from the navigation devices through the Think-Aloud method and their circumstances through simulated driving. As with the first group, the subjects in the passenger seats were observed   directly   using   the   Think-Aloud   method   to   determine   their navigation-watching behavior.

3.3   FGI Results

The Focus Group Interview (FGI) analysis results show that drivers and passengers can be categorized. Table 4 lists the analyzed results per position.

In the car-driving environment, drivers had a tendency to watch the navigation device when a speeding camera was present, traffic congestion occurred, driving direction needed to be changed, and entering a tollgate. In addition, passengers had a tendency to watch the navigation device when assisting support for driver was required, traffic congestion occurred, time and distance to destination were required, surrounding information was needed, and destination-related information was required. A driver observed the navigation information while driving when vehicle control was required or navigation guidance was recognized and required, whereas passengers needed auxiliary information instead of the information elements related to vehicle driving. In summary, our study results prove that the importance of the information delivery elements varies between driver and passenger.

3.4   Navigation User Survey

A survey was conducted with 260 male and female drivers (male: 179 individuals, female: 81 individuals) with a driver's license and driving experience using navigation systems, from December 10 to 16, 2014 for one week. The survey questionnaire was

Table 3. Representative navigation map information delivery elements in Korea

Information delivery element							
iNavi		Gini		Atlan		T-map	
Information	Detailed element	Information	Detailed element	Information	Detailed element	Information	Detailed element
Current location	Icon, symbol, 3D	Current location	Icon, symbol, 3D	Current location	Icon, symbol, 3D	Current location	Icon, symbol,
Start point	Icon, Text, Symbol, logo	Start point	Icon, Text, Symbol	Start point	Icon, Text, Symbol, logo	Start point	Icon, Text
End point	Icon, Text, Symbol, logo	End point	Icon, Text, Symbol	End point	Icon, Text, Symbol	End point	Icon
Traffic Signs	Icon, Text, Symbol, Pictogram	Traffic Signs	Icon, Text, Symbol, Pictogram	Traffic Signs	Icon, Text, Symbol, Pictogram	Traffic Signs	Icon, Symbol, Pictogram
No parking area	Icon, Text, Pictogram	No parking area	Icon, Text, Pictogram	No parking area	Icon, Text, Pictogram	No parking area	Icon, Text, Pictogram
High Occupancy Vehicle lanes	Icon, Text, Symbol, Pictogram	High Occupancy Vehicle lanes	Icon, Text, Symbol, Pictogram	High Occupancy Vehicle lanes	Icon, Text, Symbol, Pictogram	High Occupancy Vehicle lanes	Icon, Pictogram
Speed limit	Text	Speed limit	Text	Speed limit	Text	Speed limit	Text
Hi-pass lanes	Symbol, 3D, Logo	Hi-pass lanes	3D, Logo	Hi-pass lanes	Symbol, 3D, Logo	Hi-pass lanes	Symbol, Text
Current Speed	Text	Current Speed	Text	Current Speed	Text	Current Speed	Text
Estimated time and distance	Text	Estimated time and distance	Text	Estimated time and distance	Text	Estimated time and distance	Text
Current Time	Text	Current Time	Text	Current Time	Text	Current Time	Text
Driving Distance	Icon, Symbol	Driving Distance	Icon, Symbol	Driving Distance	Icon, Symbol	Driving Distance	Icon
Turn sign	Text, Symbol	Turn sign	Text, Symbol	Turn sign	Text, Symbol	Turn sign	Text, Symbol

The information delivery element consists of texts, symbols, icons, pictograms, and logos. Here, a difference between Personal Navigation Devices(PND) and mobile devices is that PND mostly contains elaborate icons, text, and symbols, whereas mobile devices are based on simplified graphic and icons because of their small display size.

(6) A scope of this study is mainly set to the information delivery element provided by navigation systems while driving; control, structure, and background elements were removed from the scope.

Table 4. Circumstances when driver needs to see navigation system

	Driver	Passenger
Circumstance	When speeding camera is present	When assisting support for driver is required
	When traffic congestion occurs	When traffic congestion occurs
	When driving direction needs to be changed	When time and distance to destination are required.
	When a vehicle enters a tollgate	When surrounding information is required
		When destination-related information is required

composed of questions designed to know the importance of navigation map information delivery when a driver operates a vehicle using a navigation system and watching
the map (when a speeding camera is present, traffic congestion occurs, direction change
is needed, tollgate is entered) based on the FGI analysis results (Table 3).

3.4.1 When Speeding Camera is Present

For the question regarding the importance of the navigation map information delivery
elements when a speed camera was present while driving, the subjects answered that
speed limit (41.5 %) was the most important element followed by navigation voice
information (35.4 %), distance to the speeding camera (13.8 %), and vehicle speed
(9.2 %). The results show that drivers use the camera's speed limit and voice information mainly when a speeding camera is present (Fig. 2).

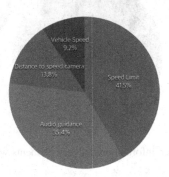

Fig. 2. Importance of navigation information delivery elements when speeding camera is
present

3.4.2 When Traffic Congestion Occurs

As shown in Fig. 3, the question regarding the importance of the navigation map
information delivery elements when traffic congestion occurs shows that current traffic
conditions (55 %) and time to the destination (28.1 %) are the two most important
elements, and accounted for 83.1 % of the responses. The next important element is

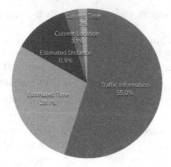

Fig. 3. Importance of navigation information delivery elements when traffic congestion occurs

distance to the destination (11.9 %), followed by current location (3.1 %) and current time (2 %), which shows that these are less important information.

3.4.3 When Driving Direction Needs to Be Changed

Regarding the question on the importance of the navigation map information delivery elements when a change in direction is required, turning direction (33.8 %), turning road lane information (33.8 %), and distance to the direction change (29.2 %) were answered with a similar degree of importance, which indicates that drivers check all three information elements (Fig. 4).

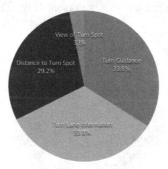

Fig. 4. Importance of navigation information delivery elements when driving direction needs to be changed.

3.4.4 When a Vehicle Enters a Tollgate

Regarding the question on the importance of the navigation map information delivery elements when a vehicle enters a tollgate, most respondents answered that high pass lane location information (52.4 %) and toll (29.2 %) are the two most important elements. That is, utilization of the navigation system is high when preparing entrance to a tollgate (Fig. 5).

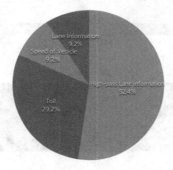

Fig. 5. Importance of navigation information delivery elements when a tollgate is entered

3.5 Interview with Passenger Seat Riders (Eight Male and Female Riders)

An interview was conducted with passenger seat riders to determine navigation utilization and the information elements that they require. The interviewees were composed of eight male and female subjects between the ages of 20 to 39 who were familiar with the use of electronics and smart devices. The interview consisted of questions designed to determine whether navigation was utilized on the way to a given destination, and which information was required after a task was given to the rider from the starting point to the destination. The interview aimed to derive the information required for passenger seat riders based on the interview results.

3.5.1 Navigation Information Elements Required for Passenger Seat Riders

The information delivery elements provided by the navigation systems were classified based on the needs produced along with the interview with passenger seat riders. Time to destination should be provided fixedly prior to and while driving for both driver and passenger, whereas weather information and destination should be provided prior to driving. While driving, rest place information should be provided fixedly for both driver and passenger, whereas traffic congestion information and toll information should be provided at the appropriate times.

4 Proposal for Navigation System Using Split-View Technology

In this paper, the navigation information delivery elements required by seat position are determined through previous studies and case studies, FGI, survey, and interview analysis, while focusing on the information delivery elements of navigation maps as described in the previous sections. Based on the results, a split-view navigation system is proposed by considering the safety of drivers and passengers, as well as the importance of information delivery elements by seat position. Here, high importance information elements are applied to the framework, and low importance information is applied or removed flexibly (Figs. 7 and 8).

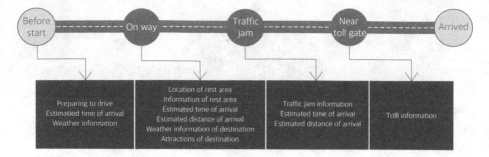

Fig. 6. Information delivery elements required when riding as a passenger

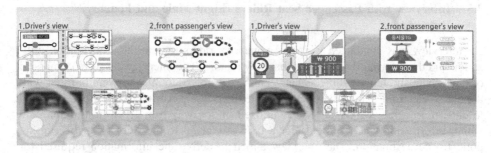

Fig. 7. During traffic congestion, split-view navigation screen.

Fig. 8. When entering tollgate, split-view navigation screen.

4.1   Examples of Split-View Navigation Utilization

4.1.1   Providing Customized Information Using Split-View Navigation During Traffic Congestion

As shown in Fig. 6, the information required for drivers and passengers is provided separately using a split view. When traffic congestion occurs, information related to the distance and time to destination is provided in the view. In the view for the passenger seat, information regarding the traffic congestion areas along with distance and time to destination, tourist attractions, and restaurants around the travel path, in addition to destination information, is provided. Distance and time to destination are provided and fixed in the screen for both driver and passenger.

4.1.2   Providing Customized Information Using Split-View Navigation When Entering a Tollgate

Highly important information, such as high pass-only lane and toll, is provided so that the driver can see the required information quickly through his/her corresponding view using a split view. For the passenger, mainly auxiliary information, such as toll gate fee and next resting place location, is provided.

5 Conclusion

The car market has changed its focus from the development of mechanical performance to the development of network and GPS technology, in addition to safety and convenience. In this trend, fast and efficient navigation devices have become increasingly popular. However, current navigation systems are unidirectional in method and form in terms of providing information, and contain unnecessary information elements that increase complexity. As a result, it is difficult for drivers to accurately compare and determine road conditions and the information presented in a limited screen space that contains information only for the driver.

To solve the aforementioned problems, this study proposed a split-view navigation system in which information is divided into separate views customized according to importance for the driver and passenger in order to allow drivers to concentrate on the driving environment and increase the satisfaction of navigation application. Through the split-view navigation system, a gap of the recognition and utilization between users and devices can be reduced, and information required for drivers and passengers can be obtained quickly and conveniently. In the future, in-depth and various driving scenarios will be set up in order to conduct more user-oriented studies, and a split-view navigation prototype will be developed to conduct experiments for comparison analysis with existing navigation systems, thereby studying driving environment concentration levels and navigation utilization satisfaction.

References

1. Park, I.G.: Study on User Interface Design Analysis of Car Navigation, p. 18 (2006)
2. Dayko, D & S, navigation system status and prospects, p. 30. JINHAN M & B, Seoul (2006)
3. Sung, J.E.: Study on Improving POI information for efficient delivery of car navigation screen information (2008)
4. Moon, Y.J.: Study on the consideration obtained for the first screen of the information presented in the Digital Maps (2006)
5. Park, M.H.: Deduction & Weight Analysis of Scenario-based Variable Information Elements for Front Window Display(Head-Up Display) in a Car
6. Münter, D., Kötteritzsch, A., Islinger, T., Köhler, T., Wolff, C., Ziegler, J.: Improving navigation support by taking care of drivers' situational needs
7. Schmidt, A., Dey, A.K., Kun, A.L., Spiessl, W.: Automotive user interfaces: human computer interaction in the car. In: CHI 2010 (2010)
8. Leshed, G., Velden, T., Rieger, O., Kot, B., Sengers, P.: In-car GPS navigation: engagement with and disengagement from the environment. In: CHI 2008 (2008)
9. Gridling, N., Meschtscherjakov, A., Tscheligi, M.: "I need help!" Exploring Collaboration in the Car
10. Lee, K.J., Joo, Y.K., Nass, C.: Partially intelligent automobiles and driving experience at the moment of system transition. In: CHI 2014 (2014)
11. Politis, I., Brewster, S.: Evaluating multimodal driver displays under varying situational urgency. In: CHI 2014 (2014)
12. -Benz – Split view Display. http://www.mercedes-benz.co.kr/

What Travelers Want: An Investigation into User Needs and User Wants on Display

Tingyi S. Lin[✉] and Chia-Nien Chang[✉]

National Taiwan University of Science & Technology (Taiwan Tech),
Taipei, Taiwan
tingyi.desk@gmail.com, chocnu@designer.org.tw

Abstract. Travel information about public transportation is essential for all commuters and travelers before and during their journey. The experience from a journey creates long-lasting impressions for each traveler. Positive impressions create good reputations for public services in and between cities. The effectiveness of public transportation often relies on brief transfers between connections. Even if they already have a clear touring map, travelers always need on-site information to confirm schedules and so on. The improvement of travel information for passengers is not only a must for enhancing transportation flow, but also a necessary condition for passengers' anxiety-free experience of transportation. Wayfinding and signage systems have been important aspects of public transportation for decades and, in recent years, have attracted more and more attention owing to rapid technology changes that allow for extraordinarily innovative creations. This information-saturated era gives us an opportunity to rethink and to re-make information so that it is more visible and more understandable.

A successful design for information delivery and communication can successfully guide users through their journey and can reduce confusion considerably. In the current study, we examine the representation of railway information relative to display-interface sections. The very first and essential step in such an examination is to consider users. Here, our aim is to define the information needs attributable to travelers during their journeys by train. In order to understand what users need and what can motivate them, we observed and interviewed users and conducted a task-based analysis—all to clarify user perceptions and reactions. The results will help future design thinking and processing in the field of information services.

Our study's results show that (1) the types of information needed for long trips differ from the types of information needed for short trips; (2) current displays suffer from several problems such as ambiguity, low legibility, and unaesthetic layouts; and (3) users like to have rapidly conveyed information at stops, on routes, and at transfers. Technical information and entertainment are of secondary importance. The two principal issues are what to show (i.e., the issue of organizing needed information) and how to show it (i.e., the issue of designing easy-to-understand information). The results and findings from this study should be references for re-design processes, and should also be key items for checking usability tests of new models for train displays. Through this passenger-focused process serving to meet travelers' demands, it is vital to take into account visual information for short- and long-distance transport networks.

© Springer International Publishing Switzerland 2015
A. Marcus (Ed.): DUXU 2015, Part III, LNCS 9188, pp. 496–504, 2015.
DOI: 10.1007/978-3-319-20889-3_46

Keywords: Railways   and   transportation   networks   ·   Wayfinding   ·
Visual-Information · User experience · Interface design

1   Introduction

The issues of wayfinding and signage system have been an important issue for at least
25 years, and ever since it has earned more and more attentions. The travel information
on public transport is essential for every commuters and travelers before and during
their journey. Especially in recent years, the rapid changes of technology have been
providing ever-changing opportunities that allow much innovative creativities to occur.
Taiwan Railways (EMU600 and EMU800) and Taipei Rapid Transit (Type C381,
Taipei Metro) started to equip with LCDs in 2006, which can represent much more
information than LED that usually shows the following stops only [1, 2]. The changes
of the ways of information representation includes new displays that larger presentation
spaces are provided, and new format that information needs to be digitalized in a way
to show. The equipment of new devices furnishes much potential ways for designing
the information to show. However, this provided opportunity also raises the question
that how to organize and to display the information for ease of accessing and understanding, rather than adding more information to fill up the spaces.

As Horn states that an effective visual information design facilitates the communication between the information itself and its receivers/users [3]. That is, skillful and
successful communication links apart information together, bridges different fields of
studies, and transfers information into knowledge. The purpose of equipment of LCDs,
for the good sake, is to satisfy users' needs, to provide correct and useful information,
to guide them through their journey, to explain what they supposed to do or not to do,
and to help them make wise decisions.

Travelers always need on-site information even they already have clear touring map
in mind. To do the double check and make any confirmation act is necessary while on
the move, no matter how much familiarity you have. Therefore, the improvement of
travel information for passengers is not only a must for enhancing the transportation
flow, but also the core for preparing an anxiety-free public service for the people.

Moreover, the experience from the journey creates long-lasting and imperceptibly
impression to every individual traveler and their friends for references. The effectiveness of public transport often relies on transferring in time between lines and modes
of transport. The positive impression invites good reputation of the public services in
and between the cities, with which takes more convenience to the visitors and commuters and more related benefits will certainly come along afterwards. In order to
satisfy this expectance, it is a preliminary but a significant step in understanding what
user needs and what design can motivate them. Since the Shalun Line, Taiwan Railways, has been claimed to be the first remodeled carriages with new LCDs for information display, four carriages a set, this five-kilometer line runs an intensive timetable
between Shalun and Tainan. This line is short but intensive used, the exterior of the
carriage is painted with four themes to demonstrate Tainan's features, including
black-faced spoonbill, lotus, Guanziling hot spring and Taijiang National Park, while
the interior installed new LCDs and flannel seats. The interface design on the newly

LCD is the key resulting in how the information is shown. As a preliminary research for a friendly information service plan, this paper aims to define the information needs for travelers during their journey on the train. Many critiques show much attention to the current interface design on the train displays. This study investigates the current interface and collects feedbacks from users, so as to understand the current condition, to define the problems that users are concurring and to know expectations that users may or may not want.

2 Information Design and User Experience

These days, people can readily search for and easily find information, but another matter entirely is whether or not the information is clear and easy to use. The field of information design therefore must graduate to a level where the focus is on not only the connections among words, icons, and images but also information systems in their entirety. In order to meet the current needs of public-transportation passengers, information-design specialists should put together a rigorous perspective on visual information and should systematize a strategy for developing a friendly wayfinding and signage system capable of enhancing the smoothness and the comfortableness of transit networks. This is not to say that basic design and fundamental forms are unimportant; the truth is that they are even more important today than in the past. The foundations of information architecture are critical: the elements of information (words, icons, and images) comprise visual sentences capable of conveying precise meanings. The spatial and temporal contexts in which visual information appears give it remarkable flexibility, so that the relationships between visual sentences continuously form new compound meanings for the large-scale conveyance of information. At the forefront of discussions concerning public transportation's effectiveness are several issues, including how to design information-dissemination systems for people on the move, how to incorporate their experiences into effective designs, and how to deliver information efficiently for average users as well as for such special-needs users as seniors, the disables, and international travelers. Designers in the field of visual information, thus, explore much more than signs and symbols themselves; designers must address Interlinked visual information that can provide sufficiently comprehensive information.

In the area of public transportation, a good design geared toward information delivery and communication can successfully guide passengers throughout their journey and can significantly reduce their confusion. This study examines display interfaces' representation of railway information, and the very first step in this study is an essential one: considering the users.

3 Method

In order to understand users' perceptions and users' wants regarding current interface representation, we have observed travelers during their train trips and we have conducted both task-based analysis and semi-structured interviews with travelers. The results of our efforts should strengthen design development for information services.

We specifically examine, in this study, twin LCDs installed above the train doors inside each of Taiwan Railways' Shalun Line carriages. Each information display measures 320 mm wide by 240 mm long (Fig. 1). Currently one LCD displays railway information, and the other one displays advertisements.

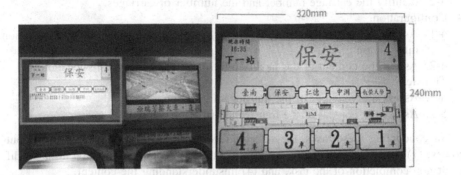

Fig. 1. The currently used interface in its real setting

3.1   Subjects

In order to undertake a first-hand analysis of targeted users' feedback, we considered data regarding twenty stakeholders who fell into one of four groups (with each group comprising five stakeholders): commuters who had been commuting more than one year, backpackers who had been traveling frequently via train and bus, travelers who made frequent transfers from and to high-speed rail (HSR), and visual-design professionals who had more than five years experience in their field.

3.2   Data Collection and Analysis

We reviewed the carriages' current interface and instructed the stakeholders to search its visual elements according to the LCDs' instructions. Thus, we conducted a task-based analysis, which involves a series of individual missions comprising a whole operational process. With this simulation of the use of the interface, stakeholders could observably explore the displays' content. Moreover, we could observe the stakeholders' behavior as they performed the tasks. Our semi-structured interview in this study helped us glean more details about users' related feelings and thoughts.

Tasks. We identified five general task-related themes (each consisting of two tasks for a total of ten tasks) that the stakeholders were to complete:

1. On the move
   1-1. Assess the visibility of the travel directions
   1-2. Assess the content concerning the travel direction and the next stop

2. Time
   2-1. Assess the visibility of the time information.
   2-2. Assess the content concerning the time information.
3. Location
   3-1. Assess the visibility of the carriage information.
   3-2. Identify the carriage number and the number of carriages.
4. Configuration
   4-1. Assess the visibility of the facility information and the configuration information.
   4-2. Assess the content of the facility information and identify its location.
5. Transfer
   5-1. Assess the visibility of the transfer information.
   5-2. Assess the content of the transfer information.

In conducting these tasks, the stakeholders could have one of four possible outcomes: (1) simple completion of the task, (2) difficult completion of the task, (3) difficult non-completion of the task, and (4) misunderstanding the content.

Observation. We conducted our observations simultaneously with the task-based testing. Our objective was to gather substantive details about stakeholders' decisions, mistakes, timing, and risk-taking. The details underlying the stakeholders' behaviors are worth analyzing because these details can clarify the stakeholders' reactions and interactions.

Semi-structured Interview. Interviews can focus on certain topics that yield authentic feedback. Such a focus can shed light on interviewees' feelings and perceptions during the interview itself [4]. Our use of the semi-structured interview in the current study helped us accurately generalize the issues to be explored. We identified five topics to discuss: (1) stakeholders' impressions and feelings from their experience of the train's LCDs; (2) stakeholders' real-world needs as drawn from the stakeholders' opinions about (a) important information and (b) secondary information; (3) stakeholders' perceptions of any glaring oversights or commissions in the LCDs; and (4) stakeholders' perceptions of future improvements in the LCD system.

4 Results

Regarding the "on the move" task-related theme, most participants found the visual travel directions; 2 participants could not. However, 8 of the 20 participants were deeply confused as to where the next stop would be. Most confusing were the directions for Bao'an Station and Rende Station. These results show that many participants —although able to find information—considered it either ambiguous or vague.

Regarding the task-related theme of "time," most of the participants found the time-related information on the interface and concluded that the time shown on the screen was the current time. However, a participant was slow to find the information, and another participant concluded that the time shown on the screen indicated the arrival time for the next stop.

As for the "location" theme, the visibility of the carriage information earned all participants' approval, though 3 participants regarded the repetition of the carriage number in the upper right-hand corner as redundant.

Only 1 participant did not find the visual information about the "configuration" task-related theme. However, 9 stakeholders noted that they needed either extra time or closer proximity to the information in order to read it. Moreover, 5 participants gave up trying to read it.

Although 8 participants could identify the interface's information pertaining to the "transfer" theme, only 1 of these 8 participants could understand the content. Finally, 6 participants could not find the information, and several participants were unable either to read or to understand the content.

4.1 Participants' Perceptions of the Current Display

The stakeholders who participated in this study expressed their satisfaction with and impression of the train's display of information. According to the interviews and keyword frequencies, stakeholders revealed that the legibility and the sound of the presented information were significant. Most participants thought that the hierarchy of font sizes in the current design worked well. The larger font size for important messages accelerated the participants' recognition and comprehension of the messages. Of all the messages, those concerning "carriage number" and "next stop" were the clearest. Participants regarded as most important the messages about "stops," "configuration of carriage," "number of carriage," "transfer information," and "current time." Moreover, most participants highly appreciated the English-language information for creating a friendly information environment and a global image.

Participants noted three major shortcomings of the currently used information display: (1) the clarity of information communication was lacking, as participants often found confusing or unexpected the information related to the "on the move" theme, the "transfer" theme, and the "configuration" theme; (2) aesthetic appearance was lacking, as participants' feedback revealed that the displays' "font use," "color composition," "style setting," and "use of icons & symbols" were inconsistent, in disarray, or in violation of graphic-design principles; and (3) needed information was lacking, as one group of participants suggested more information about "long trips," "the time of each stop," and "tour info" as well as more "English translations" whereas another group of participants regarded the quantity of current information as overloaded.

The defects of visual representation often occur with information designers' carelessness. Examples of such carelessness can be found in this case study's facility maps and construction maps. We found that the train's facility map (Fig. 2) consisted of icons and symbols added to the construction map (Fig. 3). This kind of visual representation often creates problems beyond aesthetics. Moreover, construction maps are typically designed for engineering professionals to read and, thus, are a simplified representation of structures—and are not easily comprehensible by members of the general public. Other defects in visual representation typically include unusual font type, inconsistency, and eligibility.

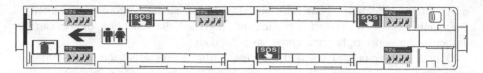

Fig. 2. Facility map for the train

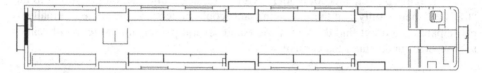

Fig. 3. Construction map for the train

4.2 Information Needs

For the current study, we identified users' information needs directly from the users (i.e., the participants) so as not only to examine the current design but also to reflect the differences between designers' tendencies and users' perceptions. We collected two sets of data regarding users' experience: for one set of data, participants would speak out loud about their impression and past experiences before seeing a sample of visual information; and for the other set of data, participants would offer suggestions about their "needs" while viewing a sample of visual information.

After conducting a cross-analysis of these two sets of data, we analyzed and organized the hierarchical information needs and the categorized information (Table 1). The four categories are (1) train on the move, (2) interior configuration of carriage, (3) carriage exterior and platform, and (4) knowledge and entertainment. The primary information and the secondary information fall into category (1) and category (2), while information for category (2) and category (3) depends on the surrounding environment. Category (4) comprises several add-ons that enrich users' experiences and enjoyment.

4.3 Visual Representation

From users' viewpoint, multi-language services[1] have been a significant part of Taiwan's culture. In fact, language-related requests and needs vary from city to city. The designs contributing to textual representation and verbal expression depend on cultural convention, as well. Because of Taiwan's multicultural vision, many train users hope

---

[1] Taiwan is home to many languages that circulate around the island and that include Mandarin, Taiwanese, Hakka, and several indigenous languages attributable to aboriginal populations. The public-transit service in major cities encourages national and international communication services—Chinese characters and English letters are used on signage systems. Broadcasts during transportation's "on the move" stage are often in Mandarin and English (buses), Mandarin and Taiwanese and Hakka and English (some metro systems), or Mandarin and Taiwanese and Hakka and Japanese and English (other metro systems).

Table 1. Hierarchical information needs and information categorization from users' viewpoint

Information Category	Primary Information	Secondary Information	Tertiary Information
A. Train on the move	Timetable for each stop, next stop, the route, transfer info, the number of carriage, reminder for door open/close	Delay information, time of service	Name of current stop
B. Interior configuration of carriage	–	Signage service for washroom	Crowd conditions; location information for water fountain, vending machine, and luggage storeroom
C. Carriage exterior and platform	Configuration map on current platform	Weather info	Attractions and nearby stores
D. Knowledge & entertainment	Breaking news	–	Discount-ticket info, railway-journey info, commercials, animated features, info on local culture

that services remain inclusive of diverse people. Even for local people, many users regard these kinds of communication services as indicative of not only high-quality transportation services but also Taiwan's various identities.

5 Conclusion

The results of our study suggest that, in order to fit users' needs, public-transportation information should be (1) multivariate, (2) instantaneous, (3) convenient, (4) flexible, (5) reflective of diverse needs, and (6) cross-regionally friendly. The results also suggest that (1) users' needs during long trips differ from users' needs during shorts trips, (2) the given train's current display suffers from such problems as poor legibility and poor aesthetic layout as well as ambiguity leading to misunderstandings, and (3) users during their journey most like to see up-to-the-minute information about stops, routes, and transfers. Scientific information and entertainment appears to be of secondary importance to users. The results and findings from this study should help designers identify "what to show" and "how to show it." Indeed, these two issues are key to testing the usability of any new train display. Through this passenger-focused process, designers can better meet travelers' demands of visual-information services for short- and long-distance transport networks.

References

1. Chen, J., Chuang, Y.: The modeling and interior design of electronic multiple units. Metro J. Biannual **35**, 49–58 (2006)
2. Railway Reconstruction Bureau. Railway Reconstruction Bureau, Ministry of Transportation and Communications (2014) Retrieved 19 November 2014. http://www.rrb.gov.tw/
3. Horn, R.E.: Information Design-Emergence of a New Profession. MIT Press, Cambridge (1999)
4. Mishler, E.G.: Research Interviewing: Context and narrative, p. 9. Harvard University Press, Cambridge, MA (1986)

Head Up Display in Automotive:
A New Reality for the Driver

Annie Pauzie[✉]

Ifsttar/Lescot, Cité des Mobilités, Allée Général Benoist "Parc du Chêne",
Case 24, 69675 Bron Cedex, France
annie.pauzie@ifsttar.fr

Abstract. In the context of automotive, Human Systems Interactions Design is
a great challenge, taking into account the road safety issues and the complexity
of the driving task under high time constraint. To support this task, existing
on-board systems display mainly visual messages, forcing the drivers to move
their eyes away from the road. This paper presents an overview of studies related
to drivers' perception and cognition when this information is displayed on the
windshield (Head-Up Display or HUD), as it can be a solution to reduce the
duration and frequency drivers look away from the traffic scene. Nevertheless,
HUD might have also shortcomings raising new critical contexts, which are
discussed. The Augmented Reality (AR) concept is also presented, as this
solution can bear HUD potential drawbacks such as the risk of occluding relevant objects of traffic as well as phenomena like perception tunneling and
cognitive capture.

Keywords: Head Up Display · Augmented Reality · Road safety · Human
factors in automotive · Advanced driver information system

1 Introduction

Driver informative and assistance systems (IVIS for In-Vehicle Information System
and ADAS for Advanced Driver Assistance Systems) for automotive have been
developed for many years now, with the aim to improve driver safety, performance,
efficiency and comfort through the support of information and communication technology. The driving activity is highly complex, partly due to time constraints for the
human to detect, perceive, process information before taking decision and react, this
activity being run in a road environment full of unpredictable events. In this framework, the display of relevant information such as "step by step guidance to the
destination", "road, traffic or weather events ahead", "road accidents or disturbances",
"distance with the previous vehicle", "danger of road holding loss", "obstacle ahead"
and so on...can be highly useful as supporting information for the driver to take
decision and to prepare the correct action. Questions for Human Factors Design rely in
the specification of the best modalities allowing conceiving efficient and effective
co-operation between the human and the machine in a context where the driving
activity is the main priority task. The efficiency or, on the contrary, the negative
consequences in terms of road safety while using these systems will depend on the

A. Marcus (Ed.): DUXU 2015, Part III, LNCS 9188, pp. 505–516, 2015.
DOI: 10.1007/978-3-319-20889-3_47

compatibility existing between their interfaces, their modes of dialogue, the road environment and the functional abilities of the drivers [1].

In terms of perception, it is well recognized that driving performance is closely linked to visual ability and visual strategy [2]. Many authors agreed upon the fact that the perceptive visual channel is the essential one for the driving task, information necessary to flawlessly accomplish the driving task being estimated to be up to 90 % perceived by the visual channel. Existing on-board systems display mainly visual messages: it can be texts, pictograms and/or cartographic displays on screens implemented on the dashboard. When the driver needs to operate these systems, they are forced to move their eyes away from the road for few seconds. The longer drivers take their eyes off the road when driving, the higher would be the possibility that a traffic accident will occur [3–5], with a duration of more than two seconds of moving eyes away from the road being the critical value linked to accident probability occurrence [6]. In broad outlines, each in-vehicle display can be considered as having an associated "visual cost", quantifiable in terms of number and duration of glances to be performed in order to get a specific information from the system [7].

As there is a gap or distance between physical spaces (e.g. the real road environment) and virtual information spaces (e.g. the in-vehicle screen), users take time and have to expend cognitive effort to adjust from one space to another. This gap is defined as the "cognitive distance" between computing and physical spaces [6]. There are two distinct components that comprise cognitive distance. The first is the cognitive effort required to move one's attention from the physical space to the information space, and to locate the appropriate information within the information space: eyes from the road toward the system. The second component is the effort required to move back from the information space to the physical space and apply the extracted information to the task at hand, such as, for example, in a typical context using GPS system, eyes from the electronic map toward the real road environment to take decision related to maneuvers and vehicle control actions. As the effort required for either of these components grows, the overall cognitive distance grows. Furthermore, if users are required to switch between these two spaces frequently, the impact of the cognitive distance can be even greater. This is particularly true for people who either have a cognitive difficulty, or are completing a task that is time-sensitive or has a high cognitive load associated with it, and certainly applies to elder drivers who may be suffering from age-related cognitive decline [6].

In this context, human factor concern is how to define criteria and efficient recommendations to support vehicle systems design displaying visual messages without distracting drivers from the driving task, taking into consideration road safety major issues [8] and knowing that the numbers of systems being implemented in automobiles are increasing every year [9, 10].

2 Head Up Display and Augmented Reality in Automotive Context

The mode of display on the windshield or Head-Up Display (HUD) can be part of the solution for displaying information from systems to the driver since it is recognized to reduce the time and frequency drivers look away from the traffic scene [11], the HUD being defined as "any transparent display that presents data without requiring users to look away from their usual viewpoints."

Furthermore, the Augmented Reality (AR) concept, where the information displayed on the windshield is matching with elements of the real road scenery and has the potential to be presented at the place where the cause for the need of information presentation is located, reduces the number of glances to get critical visual information relevant for the driver.

2.1 The Head Up Display Concept

Historically, the HUD has been used in fighters to present information without requiring pilots to look away from their usual view. In the automobile industry, General Motors employed HUD first time in 1988 for Oldsmobile Cutlass Supreme. However, even if HUD is not a new concept, various problems with the technology, the light source used, and the optics, make it not sell as well as anticipated. Today, there is a growing interest in HUD from vehicle manufacturers following considerable advances and maturity in the technology.

One of the main benefits expected to accrue from the HUD's longer focal distance is a decrease in the accommodative shift, reduced re-accommodation demands for drivers to fixate upon external targets. It is expected that the principal beneficiaries of the shorter focal transition will be the elderly, given their restricted accommodative range [6] and no longer having to look through the near correction (lower part) in their eyeglasses as required to view the instrument panel [15].

If HUD gains popularity since it reduces focal accommodation time [12], this mode of display also allows improving "eyes on the road" time by reducing the number of glances to the in-vehicle [13, 14]. Drivers' response time to an urgent event is faster with a HUD than a HDD (Head Down Display), and speed control is also more consistent [4, 16]. HUD allows more time to scan the traffic scene, quicker reaction times to external road events, earlier detection of road hinders, less mental stress for drivers and easier for first time users to use [17], lower recognition error rates and less time than using the traditional dashboard [18], and enhances understanding of the vehicle's surrounding space particularly under low visibility conditions [16]. Globally, most drivers feel safer when driving with a HUD [19].

This benefit in terms of increase situation awareness can impact the probability a driver will success in detecting a time-critical event [15].

Therefore, in the future, HUDs are expected to become an indispensable device for most drivers.

Nevertheless, some criticisms have been done concerning HUD advantages: for example, the recorded scan saving time may be valid only for low workload situation and may not generalize to higher-workload conditions [15]. Furthermore, negative impact of HUD can emerge as superimposing symbology on the forward driving scene may mask external objects via contrast interference [20], this effect depending upon the extent to which the HUD symbology fills a given viewing area, and the contrast of the HUD imagery with the visual background [15].

There is empirical evidence that the lens accommodation (i.e., optical focus of the eyes) is not at infinity when viewing the HUD, but somewhat nearer [21]. The amount of this deviation, or misaccommodation causes objects in the outside world to appear smaller and more distant [22]. This phenomenon is highly correlated with the large variations among individuals in their resting position accommodation. When the distance selected for automotive HUD imagery is designed to place it near the front edge of the car, by definition, all outside objects (e.g., other vehicles) will be at considerably greater distances than the HUD images. Sojourner & Antin [23] recognized the possibility that automotive HUDs cause the kind of size and distance misperception described by Roscoe [24]. They mentioned that the effect may be mitigated by the number of visual cues in the driving environment, "still, if, on a foggy night, the HUD imagery caused a leading automobile's taillights to be minified, resulting in their distance being overestimated, the likelihood of a rear-end collision would be increased".

In addition to HUD focal distance affecting drivers' accommodation and perception of actual objects while driving, HUD images may clutter or block drivers' view and affect visual attention [11], which can create serious safety hazards. For example, a simulator study showed that the majority of the drivers (77 %) did not want the HUD image within their focal area while driving, instead they chose to locate the HUD either to the right, below, or to the left of the immediate area looked [25]. The tradeoff between increased eyes-on-the-road time and increased visual clutter from HUD symbology, in terms of response effectiveness for safety-critical targets in the forward driving scene, remains to be determined [15].

Compared to an in-car display, a HUD has no static background. Instead, it image plane lies in the outside environment, which makes it moving when the car moves. As a matter of fact, the frame of reference of objects in the HUD is different. An object shown in a way that is appears to be standing still on the ground at a certain position moves over the HUD display. Basic psychophysical research needs to be conducted on perceptual estimations of the absolute distances of objects while participants' eyes are focused on automotive HUD imagery. The actual distances of the objects should cover a range of distances applicable to driving safety. Furthermore, the distance estimations should be obtained for the same set of participants with and without the presence of the HUD imagery, in order to anchor the effect to a naturalistic baseline and to permit an examination of potential individual differences [11].

As it was previously noted, the cognitive load due to the switching from an instrument panel or dashboard to the outside scene is much lighter with a HUD [26]. Nevertheless, HUDs overloaded with information, especially those using textual output, can create the effect known as cognitive capture [27]. Cognitive capture occurs whenever the driver is distracted due to the presence of multiple visual stimuli. These visual cues take up a significant amount of the driver's attention resources and can dilute the essential focus on the driving task. The results of cognitive capture would be to decrease the relative salience of outside objects from the real road scenery and, consequently, lower the likelihood that these objects would be noticed or detected by the driver. Overall, cognitive capture is a perturbing cognitive issue with instantaneous, adverse impact on a driver's performance and safety.

2.2   The Augmented Reality Concept

Some of the HUD shortcomings previously described can be overcome by the Augmented Reality (AR) concept. The AR extends the three-dimensional world by superimposing computer-generated virtual objects into the environment of the user [28]. This concept has been recently developed in the automotive context, allowing a matching between information displayed on the windshield with the real world, which the driver is looking on [16, 29]. The combination of objects or places and their inherent information allows for condensed information and thus for enhanced perception. The presentation of information uses new, implicit presentation schemes that require less mental load for interpretation. Especially information related to the spatial relationships in the environment of the car has the capability to be transferred to AR.

Since more than a decade, researchers have investigated and evaluated a number of AR-based visualization concepts using mobile platforms or projector-based driving simulators [30–32].

The fact that the information can be spatially related to the object of concern introduces new opportunities for fast and efficient information presentation but also generates new issues.

In comparison with HUD, AR presentations bear potential drawbacks such as the risk of occluding relevant objects of traffic as well as phenomena like perception tunneling and cognitive capture. Yet, it can be strongly argued that information presentation through this upcoming technology tends for the usage in time-critical environments.

In the following section, HUD-AR display is discussed for several types of functionalities useful in driving context.

3   HUD-AR and Driver's Assistance Functionalities

Considering the potential advantages and in order to test the perverse effects, the HUD-AR types of display have been studied for several drivers' assistance functionalities.

3.1   Drive Path Support

Lane Change. Lutz Lorenz et al. [33] tested AR display to indicate safe corridor for lane change in order for the driver to safely take over. They showed an improvement of the take over process by two positive aspects related to AR display in comparison with reference situation: (1) more drivers used the brake pedal to reduce speed, which is generally a positive indicator in terms of safety, (2) all drivers steered and braked in a very similar manner, as the trajectories showed. Nevertheless, it was not assessed how drivers would have follow an adverse recommendation, e.g. in case a car would have been located in the blind spot or approaching fast. Furthermore, this study showed that in situation of lane change, AR conditions have a tendency to make drivers to look at the side mirror later than drivers not supported by AR information, as the drivers' visual attention was firstly attracted to the AR information on the road. Indeed, it was

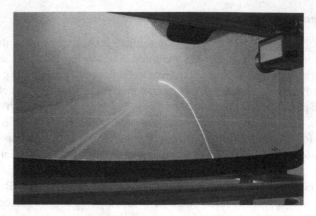

Fig. 1. HUD-AR for lane keeping support (source: http://www.wired.com/2010/03/gm-next-gen-heads-up-display)

only after interpreting this AR information that drivers started checking the side mirror to prepare for the lane change.

Lane Keeping. Lane keeping can be especially critical for inexperienced drivers and lane-keeping support can be very desirable for bad weather conditions and darkness. The AR concept allows underlining the drive path, making it then more salient for the driver.

Displaying the drive path in AR can improve lane-keeping behavior by decreasing the lane deviation [19] (Fig. 1).

3.2 Detection of Critical Road Events

Drivers have to beware of vehicles, road hazard, lanes, pedestrians and traffic signs while controlling vehicle speed and directions. All these works increase physical and mental workload, which is dangerous especially for elderly and people with slow recognition and responses. Therefore, an alarm that alerts the driver of a danger in the road can help to minimize driver workload and reduce vehicle accidents. The fact to display critical road event on the windshield can help driver's hazard event detection, in comparison with a HDD, with a 100-ms HUD advantage in participant reaction time for the detection of pop-up obstacles [34] (Fig. 2).

3.3 Night Vision

AR display can improve visualization during night, indicating location of pedestrians and obstacle, enabling effective and efficient information transfer directly understandable by the driver [32, 35].

Fig. 2. HUD-AR for obstacle detection support (source: http://www.sixtblog.fr/vehicules/affichage-tete-haute-2-0-realite-augmentee/)

Fig. 3. Example of HUD-AR for navigation signs and driving directions projected onto the windshield [36]

3.4 Navigation

The concept of projecting navigation instructions and guidance onto the windshield using HUD or AR has been investigated for some years with the objective to make decision making easier for the driver orienting himself in various traffic situations and road infrastructure complexities. Indeed, using a GPS-based navigation system displaying on-screen information creates issues of divided attention, drivers having to focus on both the information display and the road, and extra cognitive load in matching the computer-generated streets on the GPS system to the real streets in the 3-dimensional perspective that drivers have (Fig. 3).

An AR projection can be used to minimize the issue of visual distraction, divided attention and cognitive load by overlaying driving directions on the windshield and on the road, making it easier for the driver to focus attention in one single location and to translate the virtual information to effective navigation instructions.

Fig. 4. HUD-AR for contact-analog navigation arrow helping the driver to find a way in complex driving situations [37].

Fig. 5. HUD-AR for contact-analog Virtual Cable navigation assistance (source:Virtual Cable, 2014, source: http://www.mvs.net/)

Sato et al. [36] use the whole windshield surface to project navigation information such as destination and distance combined with the direction, which the driver should follow (Fig. 4).

AR-based visualization has also been employed for the purposes of supporting navigation and perception in the cases of hidden exits or roundabouts [30].

The virtual cable uses a volumetric display to create a true 3D image and superimposes it on the windscreen (Fig. 5)

Nevertheless, as the AR virtual image is, by definition, matching with the reality of the road infrastructure, the potential of anticipation for this type of display while navigating is less high than with a screen display, which can inform the driver about the next actions to proceed much more in advance than AR display, when the related infrastructure is still not in the driver's field of view. To overcome this shortcoming, SeungJun Kim, Anind K. Dey [6] imagined an AR display that allows anticipating the next actions, even if the related infrastructure was not yet in the driver's field of view. In this original concept, the AR information is superimposed on top of the real street scene, and extended with a display of the coming roads to follow appearing before the driver reaches the physical place (see Fig. 6).

Testing this display, the authors showed that, from a general point of view, elderly drivers liked the fact that the AR allowed them to look at both the navigation display and the street at the same time and mentioned that this made it easier to notice

Fig. 6. HUD-AR for navigation with anticipation of the next turns, from SeungJun Kim, Anind K. Dey [6]

pedestrians crossing the street [6]. As it was expected, AR reduces the impact of divided attention and cognitive load for elder drivers who have difficulty using navigation aids and may suffer from cognitive decline.

Nevertheless, it has to be noted that, when the visualization indicated in advance an upcoming turn, some drivers made errors and turned at an earlier intersection than the one they were supposed to. Other drivers commented that when the visualization indicated that they go straight (via a highlighted path that rises vertically up the windshield), they thought that meant they could continue to go straight, regardless of the state of the traffic lights.

4 Conclusion

Even though the HUD has been around since the 80's, it is still a rather uncommon way to display visual information in automotive context. Studies showed that the HUD display has great potential but not a high acceptance level amongst drivers [38]. One possible reason to why HUDs have not become more popular is that the design focus of the HUD has been upon implementing a technology more than accommodating the users. When considering the usefulness of a system, like the HUD, people tend to use or not use an application to the extent they believe it will help them perform their job better [39] and performance gains are often dependent upon the users' level of willingness to accept and use the system.

Design principles from classic 2D displays are no longer applicable in their full extend for this mode of display, due to the altered motion behavior of visualized objects. The information displayed on the windshield can be either continuous or discrete, displayed in 2D or 3D, spatially registered to the environment or displays unregistered symbolic content. Investigation should go on to determine which combination of design principles for HUD and AR operates best in relation to specific driving task.

Studies have to be conducted in real road environment rather than in simulator context to get better understanding of driver's level of acceptance using HUDs and to gain insight on where drivers prefer the HUD image to be located [25]. Based upon the fact that most drivers prefer user-friendly and user-centered automobile devices sensitive to their personal taste and emotions, some recent research investigates how to present HUD images that could cater to the drivers' psychological feelings and emotions [40].

Only 2 % of automobiles sold in 2012 had HUDs. However, by 2020, that rate will rise to 9 %. Japan had the highest fitment rate of car HUD systems in 2010, but Europe is expected by 2020 to take the lead. Furthermore, HUD technology combine with AR delivers a potential to overcome existing bottlenecks for increasing visual information displayed in the driving context, in comparison with in-vehicle screen display.

Based upon this perspective, the overview made in this paper underlines that HUD-AR visual display can be a great hope for supporting drivers in terms of enhanced perception and lower workload, but with a high caution while designing and implementing this information on the windshield, right in the driver's field of view. So, research in Human Factors has to be extensively conducted in order to fully understand how to optimize the great technical opportunity of the HUD-AR concept for automotive in order to keep the best and avoid the worst, taking into account the road safety issues.

References

1. Pauzié, A., Amditis, A.: Intelligent Driver Support System functions in cars and their potential consequences on safety. In: Ashgate (ed.), Safety of Intelligent Driver Support Systems: Design, Evaluation, and Social perspectives, pp 7–25 (2010)
2. Castro, C.: Visual demands and driving, in Human Factors of Visual and Cognitive Performance in Driving, CRC Press, Technology & Engineering (2008) 21 November 2008
3. Caird, J.K.: A meta-analysis of the effects of cell phones on driver performance. Accid Anal Prev. **40**(4), 1282–1293 (2008)
4. Liu, Y.C., Wen, M.H., Driving performance of commercial vehicle operators in Taiwan: Comparison of head-up display (HUD) vs. head-down display (HDD). Int. J. Hum Comput Stud. **61**, 679–697 (2004)
5. Wittmann, M., Kiss, M., Gugg, P., Steffen, A., Fink, M., Pöppel, E.: Effects of display position of a visual in-vehicle task on simulated driving. Appl. Ergon. **37**, 187–199 (2006)
6. SeungJun, K., Anind, K.D.: Simulated augmented reality windshield display as a cognitive mapping aid for elder driver navigation in: Proceeding, CHI 2009 and SIGCHI Conference on Human Factors in Computing Systems, pp. 133–142 (2009)
7. Yantis, S., Jonides, J.: Attentional capture by abrupt onsets: New perceptual objects or visual masking? J. Exp. Psychol. Hum. Percept. Perform. **27**(6), 1505–1513 (1996)
8. Wickens, C.D., Hollands, J.G.: Engineering Psychology and Human Performance, 3rd edn. Prentice Hall, Upper Saddle River, NJ (2000)
9. Bishop, R.: Intelligent Vehicle Technology and Trends. Artech House Inc., Walker, Stanton, and Young, Norwood, MA (2005)
10. Walker, G.H., Stanton, N.A., Young, M.S.: Where is computing driving cars? International Journal of Human-Computer Interaction **13**(2), 203–229 (2001)

11. Tufano, D.R.: Automotive HUDs: the overlooked safety issues. Hum. Factors **39**(2), 303–311 (1997)
12. Burnett, G.: A road-based evaluation of a head-up display for presenting navigation information. In: Proceedings of the tenth international conference on human-computer interaction pp. 180– 184. Lawrence Erlbaum Associates, New Jersey (2003)
13. Horrey, W.J., Wickens, C.D. Alexander, A.L.: The Effects of Head-Up Display Clutter and In-Vehicle Display Separation on Concurrent Driving Performance. In: Proceedings the Human Factors and Ergonomics Society Annual Meeting, p. 1880 (2003)
14. Kiefer, R.J.: Effects of a head-up versus head-down digital speedometer on visual sampling behavior and speed control performance during daytime automobile driving (SAE Tecnical. Paper 910111). Society of Automotive Engineers, Warrendale, PA (1991)
15. Gish, K.W., Staplin, L.: Human Factors Aspects of Using Head Up Displays in Automobiles:A Review of the Literature, DOT HS 808 320 (1995)
16. Charissis, V., Papanastasiou, S.: Human–machine collaboration through vehicle head up display interface. Cogn. Technol. Work **12**, 41–50 (2010)
17. Liu, Y.C.: Effect of using head-up display in automobile context on attention demand and driving performance. Displays **24**, 157–165 (2003)
18. Okabayashi, S., Sakata, M., Fukano, J., Daidoji, S., Hashimoto, C., Ishikawa, T.: Development of practical heads-up display for production vehicle application (SAE Technical Paper No. 890559.Society of Automotive Engineers, New York (1989)
19. Tonnis, M., Lange, C., Klinker, G.: Visual longitudinal and lateral driving assistance in the head-up display of cars. In: Proceedings of the Sixth IEEE and ACM International Symposium on Mixed and Augmented Reality, Nara, Japan, pp. 128–131 (2007)
20. Okabayashi, S., Sakata, M., Hatada, T.: Driver's ability to recognize objects in the forward view with superposition of head-up display images. Proceedings of the Society for Information Display **32**, 465–468 (1991)
21. lavecchia, J.H., lavecchia, H.P., Roscoe, S.N.: Eye accommodation to head-up virtual images. Hum. Factors **30**, 689–702 (1988)
22. Smith, G., Meehan, J.W., Day, R.H.: The effect of accommodation on retinal image size. Hum. Factors **34**, 289–301 (1992)
23. Sojourner, R.J., Antin, J.F.: The effects of a simulated head-up display speedometer on perceptual task performance. Hum. Factors **32**(3), 329–339 (1990)
24. Roscoe, S.: The trouble with HUDs and HMDs. Hum. Factors Soc. Bull. **30**(7), 1–3 (1987)
25. Tretten, Ph., Gärling, A., Nilsson, R. and Larsson, T.C., An On-Road Study of Head-Up Display: Preferred Location and Acceptance Levels. In: Proceedings of the Human Factors and Ergonomics Society Annual Meeting, vol. 55 p. 1914 (2011)
26. Weintraub, D.J., Ensing, M.: Human Factors Issues in Head-Up Display Design: The Book of HUD (CSERIAC state of art report) (1992)
27. Bossi, L., Ward, N., Parkes, A.: The effect of simulated vision enhancement systems on driver peripheral target detection and identification. Ergon. Design **4**, 192–195 (1994)
28. Azuma, R.: A survey of augmented Reality presence. Teleoperators Virtual Environ. **6**(4), 355–385 (1997)
29. Park, H.S., Park, M.W., Won, K.H., Kim, K.H., Jung, S.K.: In- vehicle AR-HUD system to provide driving-safety information. ETRI J. **35**(6), 1038–1047 (2013)
30. Narzt, W., Pomberger, G., Ferscha, A., Kolb, D., Muller, R., Wieghardt, J., Hortner, H., Lindinger, C.: Augmented reality navigation systems. Univ. Access Inf. Soc. **4**(3), 177–187 (2006)
31. Sawano, H., Okada, M.: A car-navigation system based on augmented reality. In: SIGGRAPH 2005 Sketches, p. 119 (2005)

32. Scott-Young, S.: Seeing the Road Ahead: GPSAugmented Reality Aids Drivers. GPS World **14**(11), 22–28 (2003)
33. Lorenz, L., Kerschbaum, Ph., Schumann, J.: Designing take over scenarios for automated driving: How does augmented reality support the driver to get back into the loop? In: Proceedings of the Human Factors and Ergonomics Society 58th Annual Meeting (2014)
34. Weihrauch, M., Melocny, G., Goesch, T.: The first head-up display introduced by General Motors (SAE Technical paper No. 890228). Society of Automotive Engineers, New York. (1989)
35. Bergmeier, U., Lange, C.: Acceptance of Augmented Reality for driver assistance information. In: Proceedings 2nd International Conference on Applied Human Factors and Ergonomics, Las Vegas (2008)
36. Sato, A., Kitahara, I., Yoshinari, K., Yuichi, O.: Visual navigation system on windshield head-up display. In: Proceedings of 13th world congress & exhibition on intelligent transport systems and services (2006)
37. Plavsic, M., Bubb, H., Duschl, M., Tonnis, M., Klinker, G.: Ergonomic Design and Evaluation of Augmented Reality Based CautionaryWarnings for Driving Assistance in Urban Environments, in Proceedings of International Ergonomics Assocation (2009)
38. Gish, K.W., Staplin, L., Stewart, J., Perel, M.: Sensory and Cognitive Factors Affecting Automotive Head-Up Display Effectiveness. Transportation Research Record 1694, Paper No. 99–0736, pp. 11-19 (1999)
39. Davis, F.D.: Perceived usefulness, perceived ease of use, and user acceptance of information technology. MIS Q. **13**, 319–339 (1989)
40. Smith, S., Shih-Hang, F.S.: The relationships between automobile head-up display presentation images and drivers' Kansei. Displays **32**, 58–68 (2011)

What Are the Expectations of Users of an Adaptive Recommendation Service Which Aims to Reduce Driver Distraction?

Nadine Walter[1]([✉]), Benjamin Kaplan[1], Carmen Wettemann[1],
Tobias Altmüller[1], and Klaus Bengler[2]

[1] Robert Bosch GmbH, Leonberg, Germany
nadine.walter@de.bosch.com
[2] Institute of Ergonomics, TU Munich, Germany

Abstract. Adaptive systems are a promising approach to reduce driver distraction caused by using functions of the infotainment system while driving. The number of operation steps can be reduced through proactive recommendations based on the user behavior in the past. We describe the methods and results conducted in the first two iterations of an user-centered design process to develop an interaction concept for an adaptive recommendation service. The result of an extensive requirements analysis is described and how different concepts perform in comparison with each other.

Keywords: Adaptation · Recommendation service · User-centered design process · Heuristic evaluation · User study

1 Introduction

Driver distraction caused by using functions of the infotainment system while driving is an increasing problem. A growing amount of infotainment functions, combined with complex menu structures leads to more driver distraction. The driver must be supported by launching the functions, but not being distracted. An approach to reach accomplishing these issues is the use of adaptive systems. An adaptive system aims to predict what function the driver wants to use and and reduce the number of operational steps involved in selecting that particular function by providing proactive recommendations. Apart from reducing driver distraction the adaptive system must also be accepted by the user. Hence, the following work will focus on how to achieve both these outcomes. This leads to the questions what requirements do users have relating to such a recommendation service in the vehicle and how different approaches perform in comparison with each other. This is answered with the help of a user-centered design process like described in the ISO 9241-210 [11].

2 Adaptive Systems and Driver Distraction

Driver distraction is caused by the conflict between the primary task of driving a vehicle and the operation of the infotainment system, which uses both cognitive

© Springer International Publishing Switzerland 2015
A. Marcus (Ed.): DUXU 2015, Part III, LNCS 9188, pp. 517–528, 2015.
DOI: 10.1007/978-3-319-20889-3_48

and visual resources for information processing [25]. Adaptive systems can reduce this load. Jameson [13] described different types of adaptive systems and several of them can be used to reduce driver distraction e.g. by filtering and summarizing information for the driver or taking over operation steps. The last type is used within this work and an interaction concept therefore is developed.

2.1   Adaptive Systems in the Vehicle

There already exist some adaptive solutions for automotive applications e.g. recommendations for driving destinations [6]. These solutions already shorten the number of operation steps within an application. A solution to reduce the number of operational steps also must account for applications that are added to the infotainment system by the user. Only a few approaches to this issue are mentioned in literature. One approach is to support the driver by using a shortcut list for recommendations and executing functions autonomously depending on the situation, developed by Garzon [4]. Results from a study show, that the shortcut list performed better in most points, for example efficiency, reliability or controllability, than the autonomous execution of applications. Another approach is the use of information agents which are designed to take over certain tasks and can be activated by the user or proactively by the system [1]. For both approaches no end-users were involved during the development process. As seen by Garzon [4] and more focused in the work of Lavie and Meyer [14] there is the possibility of different adaptation levels to support the user. Adaptation levels can be mapped to the degree of automation. Lavie and Meyer described four levels. The first level is the manual level where the user operates the infotainmenr system as usual without support. In the level "User Selection" (US) the driver can choose from a choice of recommendations like from a list of shortcuts. The level "User Approval" (UA) recommends a function to the user but needs an approval from him. The last level "Fully Adaptive" (FA) takes over operation steps automatically for the user. Several criteria e.g. the preferences of the user, characteristics of the task or the situation, influence the decision, which adaptation level is most suitable.

2.2   The Project: An Adaptive Recommendation Service for Infotainment Systems

The goal of this project is to develop an adaptive system, which recommends preconfigured functions to the driver. As described in [22] an architecture for context-sensitive warning messages is therefore extended. The interaction concept which decides "how" a recommendation is presented to the driver is one extension. This paper describes the steps taken in development of an interactive concept, utilizing a 'user-centered' design process. In our work we follow the approach of Lavie and Meyer [14] and compare different recommendation concepts with different adaptation levels referring to the requirements identified before. This approach is necessary since there can be negative aspects of highly adaptive systems e.g. loss of control or paternalism [13]. It is important to identify the requirements of the potential users and take them into account within the development process.

3   User-Centered Design Process

A user-centered design process as described in the ISO norm 9241-210 is used to develop the interaction concepts. The user should be involved in the development process very early to derive important requirements and gain more user acceptance through incorporating their feedback. With this iterative process a higher quality of the end-product can be reached through a higher usability, higher user experience or reduction of discomfort and stress [11]. Figure 1 shows the user-centered design process according to [11]. The first step is "Specify the context of use" which includes the analysis of whom the product is for and in which environment it should be used. The second step is "Analyze Requirements" wherein requirements are determined through different methods. In this work, literature research and user interviews were conducted (see Chap. 4). "Design Realization" is the third step in the development process to develop a design based on the requirements. Different prototyping methods are suitable e.g. paper prototypes, screen prototypes or functional prototypes [23] (see Chap. 5). The last step of the iteration is the "Evaluation" where it is tested if the design meets the requirements e.g. with the help of a heuristic evaluation or user interview (see Chap. 6). Afterwards a new iteration can be started at any step of the process as required.

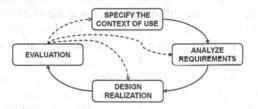

Fig. 1. User-Centered Design Process according to [11]

4   Analyze Requirements

It is very important to know the users' requirements to develop a satisfying interaction concept, especially for adaptive systems. This is due to possible negative impacts associated with adaptive systems with high adaptation levels. Therefore we need to find out what is of great importance for the users in this special case. The requirements are deduced from literature and complemented by the results of a user interview. Both are important since there is no literature especially for a user-adaptive context-sensitive recommendation service in the vehicle, which works across functions.

4.1 Literature

Since there are only few solutions in the research area of adaptive in-vehicle recommendation services like [2] or [4], we need to consider also literature from related fields like adaptive systems [3], [13], interactive systems [21] and recommendation systems [20]. Mainly this literature takes several topics into account [5]. Literature being useful for in-vehicle systems we consider guidelines like the NHTSA visual-manual guidelines [15], JAMA Guideline for In-vehicle Display Systems [12] and the European Statements of Principles on Human Machine Interface for In-Vehicle Information and Communication Systems [24]. Also ISO standards, like the ISO 9241-110 [8], the ISO 9241-11 [9], the ISO 9241-12 [10] and the ISO 15005 [7], are taken into account. The results of this literature research complemented with the results of a user study is shown in Sect. 4.3.

4.2 Interview

A second option to find out needed requirements of users for this special topic is to ask them directly. For this reason we processed a user interview with potential users to determine their requirements towards such a recommendation service in the vehicle. The interview starts with general questions and becomes more concrete in the direction of an adaptive support. An interview guideline was prepared to provide a framework but the aim was having a conversation and not asking questions like in a questionnaire. Starting, the participants need to complete a questionnaire about themselves (age, gender, attitude towards technology, etc.) and the infotainment system they use for statistical reasons. Next, the interviewer started the conversation about the functions they use most of their infotainment system, what they like or dislike, which functions the participants are missing (e.g. functions already known from the smartphone) and what the participants are doing while driving. Thirdly the participants were asked how they are supported to use these functions while driving and how they want to be supported. They were asked to imagine that the vehicle is able to adapt itself to the needs of the participants and how they can profit from this. This was conducted in the car of the participants. Six participants (2 female, 4 male) took part in this interview. Two of the participants being under the age of 30, two between 30 and 50 and two participants older than 60. The participants were regular users of modern infotainment systems with at least media player and navigation system. All of them described themselves as technically orientated and use a smartphone. The interview was recorded on audio and analyzed afterwards to document the requirements.

In a second interview with the same participants, first concepts of an adaptive recommendation service in the vehicle were introduced. This was more effective in getting requirements, since it was difficult for users in the first interview to imagine such an adaptive system on their own. The procedure of the second interview is described in Sect. 6.1, but is mentioned here since these requirements are also described in Sect. 4.3.

4.3   Summary

Requirements from the literature research and the user interviews are combined and described in Table 1. The requirements are categorized in seven categories which are named distraction, configuration, traceability, controllability, user experience, personalization &adaptivity and recommendation. The cate-

Table 1. Requirements for an adaptive recommendation system

Distraction	The operation of the adaptive system should be designed such that it has no adverse impact on the primary driving task
Visual Distraction	The adaptive system operation should be made available while driving
Legal restriction	Functions which are not allowed while driving shouldn't be suggested
Occlusion and Priority	Vehicle controls, displays and warning messages required for the primary driving task should not be obstructed by the adaptive system
Single-Handed	Single-handed operation should be possible
Sound level	No sound should be produced which masks warning from inside or outside the vehicle, or that cause distraction
Traceability	Enable the user to understand the systems status and actions
Transparency	The user should be able to understand the system behavior
Introduction	Tutorial introduction needed to explain the usage of the adaptive system
Device status	The current status and detected malfunction with an impact on safety should be presented
Intuitive and Simplicity	The driver should be able to assimilate relevant information with a few glances
Configuration	The user should have the possibility to configure the adaptive system
Reversibility	User input or configuration should be reversible
Controllability	The user should be able to control particular actions or states of the adaptive system
Freedom of choice	The user should have the possibility to choose to use a adaptation or to decline
Interruptibility	No uninterruptible sequences of visual-manual interactions should be required and an interrupted sequence should be resumable
Speed	Ability to control the speed of interaction, no time-critical response should be necessary

Table 1. *(Continued.)*

Switch off	It should be able to switch off showing non-safety related information to the driver
User Experience	The adaptive system should have a high usability and user experience
Efficiency	The user should be able to perform his tasks quickly
Effectiveness	The user should be able to finish tasks with high accuracy and completeness
Satisfaction	A usage free of impairment and support towards a positive attitude should be provided
Joy-of-Use	The use of the adaptive system should be enjoyable
Accessibility	All relevant information should easily be accessible
Feedback	For every user action, there should be some system feedback
Device Response Time	The response of the system following driver input should be timely and clearly perceptible
Recognizability	The attention of the user is directed to the needed information
Simple error handling	The user should not be able to make serious errors. The system should also offer simple error handling
Consistency	Consistent sequences of actions, identical terminology and consistent commands should be used
Compactness	Only the information which is needed to complete the intended task is shown
Personalization and Adaptivity	The adaptive system must adapt its presentation to different users (user profile), devices and situations
Changing User Behavior	The adaptive system must be able to handle change in user behavior over time
Stability	The user interface should not be modified too much
Locality	A short distance between the location of the collected information and where the adaptation is applied, is expected
Speed of Adaptation	The phase of learning should be short even when only few usage data exists
Breadth of Experience	The user should be able to operate the non-adapted system
Data Privacy	Possibility to control data collection
Recommendation	The user can be supported by giving recommendations
Proactive	The recommendation should be proactive
Scalable	A variety of functions should be supported
Unobtrusiveness	The intelligent support should not distract the user from normal usage of the application
Accuracy	Correct recommendations with a high accuracy are needed

gories represent especially the challenges of adaptive systems and the challenges which gain from the automotive field.

5   Design

Based on the state of the art, described in Sect. 2.1 and the requirements described in Sect. 4.3, several concepts for an interaction concept of an adaptive recommendation service are developed. The adaptation levels described in the work of Lavie and Meyer [14] combined with the realization of Garzon [4] are used as a basis for the concepts. The concepts are realized with different tools and revised after every iteration. Figure 2 shows the concepts which were developed after the first iteration. The adaptation level US is represented as a list of shortcuts (US1) like in the work of Garzon [4], where the user can choose out of up to four recommendations which the adaptive system considers suitable for a specific situation. The second concept (US2) belongs also to the adaptation level US, but is realized in a different way. The recommendations are displayed in form of notification, which are moved into the field of view from the side of the screen. In case the user looks at the recommendation, but is not interested at the moment and looks away again for a certain time, the notifications are minimized. The third adaptation level UA is realized as a pop-up message in which the user needs to approve or disapprove the recommendation. The last adaptation level FA is the automatic execution of a preconfigured function, which can be canceled with a cancel button which is only displayed when the displayed function is started by the adaptive system itself. For the second user interview, described in Sect. 6.1, the concepts were realized as paper prototypes. Figure 3 shows one screen of the paper prototype for the adaptation level US1. For the heuristic evaluation, described in Sect. 6.2, the concepts shown in Fig. 2 are realized as clickthrough prototypes with the tool Balsamiq[1].

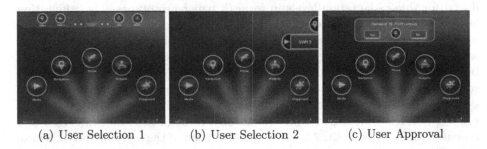

(a) User Selection 1   (b) User Selection 2   (c) User Approval

Fig. 2. Different concepts for user interfaces of an adaptive recommendation service realized as screen prototypes

---

[1] https://balsamiq.com/

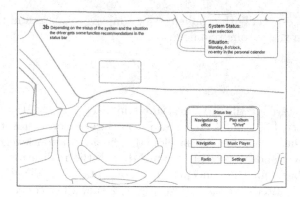

Fig. 3. Paper prototype of the concept US1 for the adaptation level User Selection

6 Evaluation

Step four of the user-centered design process is the evaluation. In this step different methods can be used depending on the stage of development. A possibility to get feedback at a very early stage is an user interview or a heuristic evaluation. For both methods no functional prototype is needed and the prototypes described in Chap. 5 are sufficient.

6.1 User Interview

To get feedback to the idea of an adaptive recommendation service in the vehicle and first ideas of an interaction concept realized as paper prototypes, a user interview was conducted.

Method. Within this interview, three different interaction concepts were introduced for three adaptation levels in form of paper prototypes. The adaptation level US was at this stage represented as a list of shortcuts (US1), UA as a pop up message and FA as the automatic execution of a preconfigured function, but without the cancel button. The concepts were always presented in this order, but additional beginning with the manual operation. First a storyline was presented to the participants to get used to the manual use of the infotainment system. The storyline (drive to the office at Monday morning and start navigating to the office while driving) was maintained through the whole interview and repeated for every concept. After each presentation of the storyline, with help of the different concepts, questions were asked. The questions addressed the general usability of those concepts, the challenges of adaptive systems and driver distraction. For example, the participants were asked if the operation is easy or not and if they perceive the concept useful while driving. At the end the participants had to compare the different concepts and choose the one they liked most. This interview was conducted in dialog form recorded on audio, instead of answering questions of a questionnaire. A total of six participants, the same as in the first user interview, described in Sect. 4.2, were interviewed, following Nielsen's proposal that five to six participants result in the best cost-benefit ratio, still addressing up to 80 percent of the usability problems to be identified [19].

Results. The results of this interview are mainly the contribution to the requirements shown in Sect. 4.3. But there are also some findings related to each concept and the comparison of the concepts. The participants described the operation of the manual infotainment system as distractive due to many operation steps, which are needed. The participants liked the concepts for the adaptation levels US and UA, but did not like the concept for the adaptation level FA. The participants rated the usage of the concept US as simple and could imagine to use it while driving. For comparison, all of them experienced the manual concept as too distractive to use while driving. The concept for UA is assessed nearly equal, but the question of what happens when a recommendation is rejected or not replied, occurred. There should be the possibility of being able to choose the recommendation later again or to configure the behavior for this case. The concept for FA has to be extended with an option to cancel an automatic execution and a one-time approval of a recommendation, hence the user can feel more in control of the adaptive recommendation service. There are different opinions about the FA concept. Some participants noted that they could think about using it when the accuracy is high enough and others would never use it. Some participants mentioned that the system behavior could not be understood e.g. why a function is recommended. The traceability needs to be increased. Based on this results the design was revised and further developed. A second realization (US2) of the adaptation level US was developed and the concepts were realized as clickthrough prototypes with Balsamiq (see Chap. 5).

6.2   Heuristic Evaluation

After the first iteration the concepts have been revised and realized as clickthrough prototypes. The next evaluation method, which we used within the user-centered design process, is the heuristic evaluation. It is a method to identify usability problems with the help of heuristics. The participants of an heuristic evaluation are experts, who have specialized knowledge and are able to put themselves in the position of the user [17].

Method. A total of six participants took part in this evaluation [19]. Experts from the fields of ergonomics, software development, design and user experience evaluated the four different concepts US1, US2, UA and FA (see Chap. 5). Nine heuristics, which are a mix of the heuristics of Nielsen [16] extended by some heuristics for driver distraction, were introduced to the participants. Afterwards the storyline (enter an address and change the radio station while driving) was presented with the help of the manual infotainment system. Next, the idea of an adaptive recommendation service is explained and the configuration of a potential service, which should be used within this study is shown in form of an explanation menu on a tablet. This enables the participants to understand the system behavior and to comprehend the current configuration. The participants are then requested to perform tasks with the clickthrough prototype for each concept on a tablet and evaluate the concept. The order in which the concepts are presented to the participants is permutated. The participants are asked to say the problems they find out loud and the interviewer write down the findings in form of a protocol. Each finding is assigned to one of the heuristics and weighted with a severity rating.

Results. The findings of the heuristic evaluation were summarized and for each problem a severity rating from 0 to 4 was given within a workshop depending on frequency, impact for the user and persistence of the problem [18]. The total number of problems is different for each concept. Concept US1 and US2 have more problems and several problems with rating 4. Figure 4 shows the distribution of the number of problems for the related severity rating and for each concept. The concepts US1 and US2 include a lot of user interaction compared to the concepts UA and FA. This is the reason why there are more problems and also problems with a higher severity. Several problems were identified for the heuristics related to control and obtrusiveness for the concept FA. The experts mentioned among other things a complete loss of control and that there is no possibility to deactivate recommendations directly. Possible countermeasures could be a menu to enable a deactivation of recommendations or a one-time approval for each recommendation for this adaptation level. Another heuristic that was called very often for the concepts US1 and US2 is the heuristic which concerns showing enough, but only necessary information. Shortcuts are small and it is a challenge to show all needed information to understand a shortcut. The experts asked for example which shortcut is most relevant in the situation. A possible solution is to arrange the shortcuts and start with the most appropriate one. As a conclusion of the heuristic evaluation, it may be stated that for the concepts US1 and US2 several points can be improved. Within the evaluation already some ideas were mentioned. For the concepts UA and FA the method was not that much effective since both concepts involve less user interaction. To improve these concepts other measures must be taken like the ones in [13], e.g. enable settings, combination of the adaptation levels in one interaction concept.

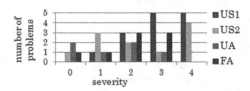

Fig. 4. Results of the heuristic evaluation according to the severity rating for each concept

7   Discussion and Future Work

Two iterations of the user-centered design process have been performed. The results of each step are important and have influenced the next step or iteration. But there are also some things which need to be criticized and discussed. The participants of both user studies could not experience the adaptive system. They had to imagine the system behavior on basis of the paper prototypes or descriptions. This is the reason why most requirements could be derived as the idea was described to the participants with the help of the paper prototypes. They liked both concepts for the intermediate adaptation levels US and UA, but we claim that they could not distinguish between these two on the given basis. The concept for FA was not assessed as good as in the first iteration, but it is a promising concept as it relieves the driver most when it has high accuracy and is accepted. To moderate the negative aspects, several measurements like described in [13] need to be taken. Only people who are described as technology-oriented were interviewed, because we expected that they are more in the position to understand such a future-oriented service. However, especially the non-technology oriented persons need support to operate the complex infotainment system. Their point of view was not considered until now. The results of the different methods are an important step in the development process of an adaptive recommendation service, but to gain reliable results for the evaluation of user acceptance and driver distraction, the adaptive system needs to be experienced by the participants. The next step in the user-centered design process is to build up a prototype to enable experiencing an adaptive recommendation service in a driving simulator environment. This will be the next step towards a prototype in real vehicle.

References

1. Ablaßmeier, M.: Multimodales, kontextadaptives Informationsmanagement im Automobil. Ph.D. thesis, Technische Universität München (2009)
2. Bader, R., Woerndl, W., Karitnig, A., Leitner, G.: Designing an explanation interface for proactive recommendations in automotive scenarios. In: Ardissono, L., Kuflik, T. (eds.) UMAP Workshops 2011. LNCS, vol. 7138, pp. 92–104. Springer, Heidelberg (2012)
3. Evers, V., Cramer, H., van Someren, M., Wielinga, B.: Interacting with adaptive systems. In: Babuška, R., Groen, F.C.A. (eds.) Interactive Collaborative Information Systems. SCI, vol. 281, pp. 299–325. Springer, Heidelberg (2010)
4. Garzon, S.R.: Kontextsensitive Personalisierung automotiver Benutzerschnittstellen : Entwicklung und Anwendung eines regelbasierten Verfahrens zur Erkennung situationsabhängiger Mensch-Maschine-Interaktionen. Ph.D. thesis, Technical University of Berlin (2013)
5. Hartmann, M.: Challenges in developing user-adaptive intelligent user interfaces. In: Proceedings of the 17th Workshop on Adaptivity and User Modeling in Interactive Systems, Darmstadt, Germany, pp. 6–11 (2009)
6. Hofmann, M., Bengler, K., Lang, M.: An assistance system for driver-and situation-adaptive destination prediction for a robust interaction with speech controlled navigation systems. VDI Ber. **1646**, 979–996 (2001)

7. ISO 15005: Road vehicles - Ergonomic aspects of transport information and control systems - Dialogue management principles and compliance procedures (2002)
8. ISO 9241–11: Ergonomic requirements for office work with visual display terminals (VDTs) - Part 11: Guidance on usability (1998)
9. ISO 9241–110: Ergonomics of human-system interaction - Part 110: Dialogue principles (2006)
10. ISO 9241–12: Ergonomic requirements for office work with visual display terminals (VDTs) - Part 12: Presentation of information (1998)
11. ISO 9241–210: Ergonomics of human-system interaction - Part 210: Human-centred design for interactive systems (2010)
12. JAMA: Guidelines for In-vehicle Display Systems - Version 3.0. Technical report, Japan Automobile Manufacturers Association (2004)
13. Jameson, A.: Adaptive interfaces and agents. In: Sears, A., Jacko, J.A. (eds.) Human-computer Interaction Handbook: Fundamentals, Evolving Technologies and Emerging Applications, pp. 433–458. Lawrence Erlbaum Associates, Hillsdale (2008)
14. Lavie, T., Meyer, J.: Benefits and costs of adaptive user interfaces. Int. J. Hum.-Comput. Stud. **68**(8), 508–524 (2010)
15. National Highway Traffic Safety Administration (NHTSA): Visual-Manual NHTSA Driver Distraction Guidelines For In-Vehicle Electronic Devices (2013)
16. Nielsen, J.: 10 Usability Heuristics for User Interface Design (1995). http://www.nngroup.com/articles/ten-usability-heuristics. Accessed 02 February 2015
17. Nielsen, J.: How to Conduct a Heuristic Evaluation (1995). http://www.nngroup.com/articles/how-to-conduct-a-heuristic-evaluation. Accessed 02 February 2015
18. Nielsen, J.: Severity Ratings for Usability Problems (1995). http://www.nngroup.com/articles/how-to-rate-the-severity-of-usability-problems. Accessed 04 February 2015
19. Nielsen, J.: How many test users in a usability study? (2012). http://www.nngroup.com/articles/howmany-test-users. Accessed 11 August 2014
20. Shani, G., Gunawardana, A.: Evaluating recommendation systems. In: Ricci, F., Rokach, L., Shapira, B., Kantor, P.B. (eds.) Recommender Systems Handbook, pp. 257–297. Springer, US (2011)
21. Shneiderman, B., Plaisant, C.: Designing the User Interface: Strategies for Effective Human-computer Interaction. Addison-Wesley, Reading (2010)
22. Siegmund, N., Altmüller, T., Bengler, K.: Personalized situation-adaptive user interaction in the car. In: Adjunct Proceedings of the 5th International Conference on Automotive User Interfaces and Interactive Vehicular Applications, pp. 105–106 (2013)
23. Szekely, P.: User interface prototyping: tools and techniques. In: Proceedings of INTERCHI 1993 (1994)
24. Union, E.: European Statement of Principles on the Design of Human-Machine Interface (ESOP 2006). Technical report (2006)
25. Wickens, C.D.: Multiple resources and performance prediction. Theor. Issues Ergon. Sci. **3**(2), 159–177 (2002)

Cross Cultural Comparison of Users' Barge-in with the In-Vehicle Speech System

Peggy Wang[1(✉)], Ute Winter[2], and Timothy Grost[3]

[1] China Science Lab, General Motors China, Shanghai, China
peggy.wang@gm.com
[2] Advanced Technical Center, General Motors Israel, Herzliya, Israel
ute.winter@gm.com
[3] Engineering, General Motors North America, Warren, USA
timothy.grost@gm.com

Abstract. The focus of this paper is user barge-in behavior during interactions with an in-vehicle speech system. This study is part of a cross-cultural research conducted in the US and China that explored the cultural differences regarding users' expectations and interactions with in-vehicle speech applications. In this paper, we describe the methodology of the field study, the interface of the prototype, the experimental set up, the analysis procedure, as well as the participants' demographics from both the US and China. We categorize the observed barge-in behavior and the typical scenarios in which it occurred, from both prompt timing and a dialog sequence perspective. After analyzing all barge-in instances, we discuss design implications for a barge-in feature and system prompts of an in-vehicle speech system that considers the different cultural norms of the two regions.

Keywords: User barge-in · In-vehicle speech system · Human-machine communication · Turn-taking · Cross cultural comparison

1 Introduction

With the increasing complexity of in-vehicle infotainment systems, interaction through speech has become an attractive alternative to visual-manual automotive interfaces. Lo and Green [1] provide an extensive overview on this situation. One of the most necessary as well as appealing concepts in speech interfaces is the use of natural language to perform tasks [2]. When users naturally utter a request to the system, they do not simply build sentences according to their own preferences but also raise their expectations for more flexibility in a dialog, such as adequate dynamic grounding, flexible turn-taking, multi-modal communication, and adaptive system capabilities, among others. Such expectations pose additional challenges on the design of the in-vehicle speech interfaces [3, 4].

Automotive companies also face the challenge of designing a speech interface for multiple markets, and in turn their various cultures and languages with the anticipated differences in user interactions. Underlying such interactions are cultural norms for communication, or "statements about conduct which are granted some degree of

© Springer International Publishing Switzerland 2015
A. Marcus (Ed.): DUXU 2015, Part III, LNCS 9188, pp. 529–540, 2015.
DOI: 10.1007/978-3-319-20889-3_49

legitimacy by participants" [5]. As such, cultural considerations are critical to the success of the discourse between the user and the speech system. In order to understand the cross cultural differences regarding user expectations and interactions with in-vehicle speech applications, we designed a multi-modal speech interface and completed an empirical study in the US and in China. Our analysis and resulting design recommendations highlight the variety of communication practices between users and the in-vehicle interface.

One of the areas that proved to be of interest for the study of cultural differences is interactional misalignments. The focus of this paper is user barge-in behavior, the different normative expectations shown by participants in the US and China, as well as the design implications for in-vehicle speech systems. Most research on barge-in as a feature in speech applications revolves around technological challenges [6–9]. However, barge-in behavior has long been linked to human turn-taking conventions [10]. Selfridge and Heeman [11] provide an interesting overview on turn-taking conventions between users and speech systems and the transformation into system models with importance for barge-in.

After introducing our field study and methodology, we discuss the barge-in behavior in both data sets from the US and China. From our analysis, we derive different cultural norms and user expectations regarding system behavior for barge-in in both countries. Finally we propose design implications for automotive speech systems.

2   Design of the Field Study

2.1   The Multi-Modal Speech Interface

For the purpose of our field study we replaced the in-car infotainment system with a multi-modal speech interface. Figure 1 below illustrates the system mounted on the air vent in the center stack.

The software provides the user with four typical in-vehicle domains of infotainment applications: phone dialing, navigation guidance, radio tuning, and music selection. The interfaces—both the spoken prompts in the speech mode and the visual-textual representations on the touchscreen—were in English for the US study and in Chinese for the China study. As there is no speech system today capable of full Natural Language Understanding at any given point of a dialog in a noisy car environment, we used a Wizard to replace the speech recognizer and semantic interpreter when the user chose the speech modality to perform the intended task. See Passonneau et al. [12] for further discussion about this approach of embedded wizardry Fig. 1.

2.2   Experimental Setup of the Field Study

The user on the driver's seat interacted via a Samsung Galaxy 10.1 in. touchscreen tablet PC mounted on the air vent in the center stack. A microphone for spoken utterances was attached on the participant's clothing and connected to a Sennheiser transmitter. The tablet PC was connected to a laptop that had the application software

Fig. 1. The multi-modal speech interface

installed. The laptop was used by the Wizard sitting on the rear seat during the interaction with the infotainment software. The Wizard heard the user's utterances via headphones which were connected to a Sennheiser receiver. A MiFi device established a wireless connection, so that the laptop and tablet PC could communicate with each other and with the Internet. The experimenter was on the passenger seat during the study. Both video and audio recordings and interaction logs from the software were used to document all interactions.

2.3   Methodology of the Field Study

In order to create situations for users to act as naturally as possible, we developed a methodology that draws on naturalistic and contextual inquiry [13–16] as well as cultural communication theory [17, 18]. We observed users in their natural car environment, driving wherever they wanted and interacting with the car and the HMI according to their own preferences. The methodology used in this study is further described in Carbaugh et al. [19, 20]. It allows for qualitative analysis of the collected data, as it is further described in Sect. 2.5.

Each participant brought their personal content to the system, such as the address book from their mobile phone, personal music collection, a list of favorite radio stations, and destinations for route guidance. After familiarizing with the multi-modal system in a closed parking area, participants were encouraged to use the multi-modal speech interface to perform tasks of their choice during an on-the-road drive of about 70 min. While driving, the only restriction was to use the speech mode except for touching the speech button or ending an application by touch. During the driving session, the experimenter on the passenger seat only responded to the driver's questions. Both in the middle and at the end of the driving session, the experimenter interviewed the driver and asked a series of open questions addressing topics of interest, such as turn-taking, grounding, interaction styles, voice preferences, among others. Observations regarding dialog sequences during the driving session as well as the participant's feedback on the speech dialog were also noted at these points.

2.4 Participants in the US and China

Twenty-six participants in the US and twenty-six participants in China were selected, keeping a balance between male and female drivers, levels of technical expertise, smartphone users and non-users, young and old, urban and rural, and overall driving experience. Early adopters of technology where also included whenever possible.

In the US study, the first 4 participants had been previously selected for a pilot study. Hence, the data from participants No. 5 through No. 26 are the basis for the data

Table 1. Descriptive statistics of participants

Variables	US (N = 26)			CN (N = 26)		
	Min	Max	Mean	Min	Max	Mean
Age (Years old)	26	64	41.6	27	62	40.6
Years of driving (Years)	1	48	24	3	35	9.7
Hours of driving per week (Hours)	1	25	9.3	1	35	12.0

analysis. In the China study, one participant showed inexperienced driving skills and the experimenter decided to terminate that driving session. Data of the remaining 25 users were used for the analysis. The following table shows the demographics of all participants Table 1.

2.5 Data Analysis

Our analysis is in its nature mostly qualitative [20] and is comprised of three levels. First, there is a descriptive analysis of the observed communication practices between the participants and the interface. Next, an interpretive analysis focuses on the meaning of said communication practices. In a last step, the comparative analysis reveals the cultural differences and similarities of the communication practices between the US and China.

We conducted a quantitative analysis as far as the data allowed only as a complementary tool to strengthen and support our qualitative findings. These results also inform where to refrain from hasty qualitative conclusions.

3 Observation of User Barge-In Behavior

The following is an example of a typical spoken interaction sequence found in the US data:

User 4:
User: ((touches microphone button and system dings)) Phone.

System: Who would you like to call?
User: R—.
System: Just a second.
System: Please confirm calling R— House.
User: Yes.
System: Calling R— House.

One rich area of analysis is the organization of turn-taking between users and the system; in particular, instances that lead to interactional misalignment. Turn-taking [21] is one fundamental process within the emerging organization of any spoken dialog. Each turn within a dialog consists of a turn-construction component, which contains dialog information, and a turn-taking component, also known as a transition relevance place (further referred to as TRP). Any TRP is a coordinating juncture in which rules for turn-taking apply. If dialog partners violate these rules, the dialog is perceived as less successful or may lead to interactional misalignments.

For turn-taking to be successful, the speech system needs to play prompts at appropriate times to create easily recognizable TRPs. In order to achieve this, the system has a predefined set of parameters. Such parameters define the system's turn-taking conventions, including for instance user response time as well as start and end of speech detection. If users do not formulate their utterances within these time frames, then the dialog suffers from interactional misalignments. One typical misalignment is user barge-in, i.e., the user self-selects as the next speaker before the end of the system prompt.

3.1 User Barge-In in the US Study

Our data from the US study contain some occurrences of user barge-in during the system ongoing prompt. As shown in Table 2, only 6.54 % of all dialogs contain user barge-in occurring in at least one utterance. These instances are distributed unevenly over participants: 3 participants barge-in in around 25 % of their dialogs, while others do not barge-in at all or do it only once. In most cases, the user intention is to promote the conversation, to move forward the interaction and complete the task at hand faster.

As Table 2 shows, user barge-in can be categorized into three different groups depending on context. The first consists of 16 instances in which users misjudge a TRP

Table 2. User barge-in behavior in the US study

	Users	Dialogs	User barge-in	Types of user barge-in		
				Repetition	Interruption and repetition	Prompt disregard
Sub-total				16 (41.0 %)	9 (23.10 %)	14 (35.9 %)
Total	21	596	39 (6.54 %)			

believing the system has selected them as the next speaker. The prompt then adds an unexpected phrase afterwards. Examples:

User 22:
System: Which number for T- : [home, work?
User: home]
User: home
User 9:
System: Sorry. I did not understand your request. [Please repeat it again
User: Fox-]
User: F- Fox news

The second category consists of 9 cases in which users believe that the system has provided sufficient information to respond and thus self-select as the next speaker. Example:

User 17:
System: Which station [or channel do you want to hear?
User: X-]
User: XM

The above two contexts are similar, and some cases maybe too close to decide whether a participant thought he was selected by the system to speak, or whether he self-selected. Clearly, participants believed to be in TRPs and had all the information about the system expectations. Together all 25 instances make 64.1 % of all observed barge-ins.

The third category consists of 14 instances that present a more distinctive characteristic. At times, users did not necessarily misjudge a pause for a TRP, but rather mostly wanted to switch tasks or contexts and did not need any system prompt. Below is one example from the 5 instances found in the data:

User 14:
System: What [kind of music do you want to hear?
User: Next track]

In 7 instances, users also provided backchannels or further comments that were not related to the information provided to the system. Example:

User 13:
System: What station?
User: 99.3
System: Tuning radio to 99.3 [FM Laser 99.3 WLZX
User: Ok]
User: There you go

There are only 2 instances that can be considered barge-in, in which the user got a relevant prompt, yet self-selected and chose to respond before getting all the prompt information. Example:

User 17:
System: ((ding))

User: Radio
System: Which [station [or channel do you want to hear?
User: e-
User: ex-
User: XM radio

Our observations indicate that there is a difference in how users react when they interrupt the system but the prompt does not stop immediately or does not stop at all. As shown in Table 2, in 64.1 % of the instances users either repeated the utterances or self-interrupted and then repeated the utterances at the end of the system prompt, which is an expected human repair mechanism to resolve interactional misalignments [22]. The examples illustrate this behavior, and furthermore show that most utterances are fairly short. On the other hand, in 35.9 % of the instances users seemed not to be irritated by the continuing prompt and did not show the self-interruption or repetition behavior described above. Rather, most of these cases involved users providing backchannels, further comments, or switching tasks, none of which depended on the ongoing system prompt.

Another important observation is the time frame in relation to a mistakenly perceived TRP, which leads to design recommendations for a barge-in feature. Frequently, misjudged TRPs occur when the system makes a pause between phrases or sentences. The average time frame between the end of the last system word and the beginning of the user response is 400–500 ms. Only one user started to talk after only 310 ms.

3.2   User Barge-in in the China Study

As Table 3 shows, there were 97 barge-in instances corresponding to 11.8 % of the interaction sequences in the China study. These instances occurred both at the opening sequence and during the course of the interaction. 9 barge-in instances occurred at the opening sequence after the user pressed the speech button and there was a pause of varying length due to a system delay. Only then the system prompted "Who would you like to call?" Users barged in shortly after the system started the prompt because they were unsure whether it was their turn Table 3. Here is one example:

User 1:
System: ((ding))
System: [Who would you like to call?
User: Make a phone call]

Table 3. User barge-in behavior in the China study

	Users	Dialogs	User barge-in	Types of user barge-in		
				Repetition	Hesitation/pause/ interruption	Prompt disregard
Subtotal				38 (39.2 %)	12 (12.4 %)	47 (48.5 %)
Total	25	822	97 (11.8 %)			

User: Mr. Chen.

The time frame between the ding sound as feedback to the user and the start of the system prompt was too long. The opening sequence was badly designed. Users in this study expressed their preference for either only an audible sound or an immediate system prompt.

Users also barged in when the system prompted a list of items, such as available songs or artists. During the system prompt, users did not wait until the end of the prompt but instead barged in right after hearing their intended item from the system. This is a natural and efficient interaction and makes the dialog advance faster. Example:

User 18:
System: What music would you like to listen to?
User: Tell me the songs by Legend of Phoenix.
System: ... Love someone who doesn't go back home]. I believe...
User: [Love someone who doesn't go back home.

Some system prompts were too long with confusing choices for the user to make:

User 13:
System: Which artist would you like to listen to?
User: Liu Dehua
System: Play Liu Dehua or select an [album.
User: The classic restored.]

Furthermore, the time provided to make a selection was too short. Consequently, if users wanted to select the second option mentioned in the prompt, they had to speak unnaturally fast before the system started playing music, which easily resulted in barge-in. There is another typical scenario in which users barged in because of their misperception of a TRP. Example:

User 13:
System: Which album would you like to listen to?
User: Black.
System: Please confirm Black [and White.
User: Con-
User: Confirm

In the following scenario, users barged in because of their delayed response to the system. The delayed response barged into the system's time-out or repetition prompt. Example:

User 13:
System: Which artist would you like to listen to?
User: ((quickly scrolls down artist list by touch))
System: [Please let me know what you would like to do.
User: Legend of Phoenix.]
User: Legend of Phoenix.

From all 97 barge-in instances, in 12 instances (12.4 %) users hesitated or paused once the system started the prompt. In 38 instances (39.2 %), users repeated their utterance after realizing they had barged in. In the remaining 47 instances (48.5 %), users simply ignored their barge-in behavior. In these instances, users did not repeat their previous utterance and proceeded as if the system had received their command. The percentage of user overt prompt disregard after barge-in is 12.6 %, which is overall higher than in the US data.

3.3   Comparison Between Data from the US and China

Socio-culturally speaking, the US data prove that barge-in behavior violates cultural norms, unless circumstances permit. This can be clearly derived from the fact that most barge-in instances occur when the user either misjudges a TRP and mistakenly self-selects as the next speaker, or once the prompt gives all the necessary information and so the user provides a relevant response. US participants appear to wait until the next TRP, when the system yields the interactional floor, or simply self-select as next speakers. Our data from China suggest that it is less normative for said users to wait until the end of the prompt. Although in both data sets participants use barge-in as a way to speed up the interaction and make it more efficient, there were many more barge-in instances in our data from China. Users often simply cut off the prompt at places which are not TRPs. This is supported by the fact that Chinese users more often talked over the system prompt in order to complete their turn, something that US users preferred not to do. US users mostly stopped their utterances and waited for the system to finish the prompt.

4   Design Implications and Conclusion

4.1   Importance of Barge-In to Users

In both cultures barge-in - if intentionally done by users - serves the purpose of advancing faster towards task completion. The US data strongly indicate that users naturally wait for a perceived TRP to abide to conversational turn-taking rules. Such user would make full use of a voice barge-in system that allows for turn-taking at any given time during the prompt only after they overcame their cultural normative behavior of waiting for a TRP. Therefore, when a user tries to barge-in, the system needs to provide feedback signaling that the user is allowed to barge-in, by immediately ending the prompt. The user may perceive this as the system's agreement to non-normative behavior. If despite user barge-in the system continues the prompt, users may understand that they need to repair a norm violation, e.g. by repeating and avoiding further barge-in behavior. The China data reveal that Chinese users do not necessarily perceive barge-in as a violation of a communication norm, at least in the contextual setting of human-machine dialog in a vehicle. They do show a significantly higher tendency to barge-in to prompts at places without transition relevance, as well as to continue to talk in parallel to the speech system while expecting the system to recognize their utterances. For Chinese users, full support of barge-in may then be of higher value than for US users.

4.2   Prompt Timing and Wording

The data provide insights for recommendations on the prompt design itself. Designing short phrases or sentences has the advantage of creating a scenario less conducive to user barge-in, since it enables users to stay within normative behavior for turn-taking, while allowing the dialog to progress at a faster pace. On the other hand, such short prompts have the disadvantage of not offering enough guidance. For example, a novice user may not sufficiently learn how to engage with the system. There are also dialog situations that demand more detailed explanation.

Prompts that exceed the length of one short sentence or phrase should avoid TRPs, and possibly also pauses that can be mistaken for TRPs. If a prompt cannot avoid this, pauses between parts of sentences and at any user perceived TRP need to be significantly shorter than 400 ms to prevent turn-taking confusions. As seen above, when users take their turn but the system does not stop fast enough, users likely enter into a repair sequence which poses difficulties on the speech recognizer. Further studies indicated that pauses shorter than 120 ms are effective. Such prompts should also avoid an intonation that suggests the end of a question or statement but rather it should signal the continuation of the prompt. The majority of users appreciates shortening prompts to phrases that provide the minimal feedback necessary for task achievement (e.g. "which radio station?", "What's the street").

The data support this recommendation through the multiple barge-in cases that resulted from users receiving the necessary information for task completion long before the prompt finished (e.g. "What station [or channel do you want to hear?"). For example, in the Chinese prompt "Call which contact number? 呼叫哪个联系人号码?" the element "number" is redundant and user barge-in would be less likely without said element. In another case, a user requested "Black", which is part of a song name, so when the system asked for confirmation, the user started to barge in right after the system said Black. The confirmation prompt could be designed as "Black [and White, right?" allowing for barge-in after the word Black to accommodate to the user. Yet another type of prompt with multiple perceived TRPs is read-aloud prompts, where the system reads out lists of artists or radio stations upon user request. It is natural and efficient for users to barge-in immediately after they hear their desired item. It would be user friendly if barge-in were allowed within a certain time frame after each item.

4.3   Proposed Solution

Even though they are culturally different to the extend described in this study, both data sets support the fact that turn-taking, and hence barge-in, is negotiable between dialog partners. Since the seminal work by Sacks et al. [21], the negotiable nature of turn-taking has been studied and is well-established. In this light, a dialog system may not always want to allow the user to take the floor and self-select as the next speaker.

This is the case for instance if the remaining prompt still contains information necessary to progress towards task completion, e.g. "I can't find a phone. Please connect your phone and try again." Additionally, some users tend to express agreement through backchannels, such as "OK". In these or similar situations, a full barge-in feature may falsely stop the prompt. We propose that the system design should allow barge-in only in certain places that are likely candidates for user barge-in, or once the system has conveyed the most important information. For example, in a prompt such as "I'm sorry, I didn't understand. What did you say?" barge-in most likely occurs from the last syllable of the first sentence through the first word of the second sentence: "I'm sorry, I didn't under[stand. What] did you say?" On the other hand, a prompt such as "Which contact [name would you like?" can allow for barge-in right after the word "contact", because users know what they need to say to complete the task. A dialog system could be designed to allow barge-in in those prominent places, while preventing it at other times of the prompt. Such approach gives the system certain control during turn-taking negotiation. It may prevent interactional misalignments or misrecognitions caused by user repair sequences at places where the prompt should not be interrupted. If designed properly, users will accept that the system sometimes continues the prompt because it needs to provide further relevant information, whereas in other instances it lets users take the turn because the situation may be more similar to negotiations from human-human dialogs.

References

1. Lo, V.E., Green, P.A.: Development and evaluation of automotive speech interfaces: useful information from the human factors and the related literature. Int. J. Veh. Technol. **2013**, 13 (2013)
2. Cohen, M.H., Giangola, J.P., Balogh, J.: Voice User Interface Design. Addison-Wesley Professional, Boston (2004)
3. Tsimhoni, O., Winter, U., Grost, T.: Cultural considerations for the design of automotive speech applications. In: 17th World Congress on Ergonomics IEA, Beijing, China (2009)
4. Nass, C.I., Brave, S.: Wired for Speech: How Voice Activates and Advances the Human-Computer Relationship. MIT Press, Cambridge (2005)
5. Carbaugh, D.: Cultural discourse analysis: communication practices and intercultural encounters. J. Intercultural Commun. Res. 36(3), 167–182 (2007)
6. Ström, N., Seneff, S.: Intelligent Barge-in in conversational systems. In: Proceedings of ICSLP, pp. 652–655 (2000)
7. Rose, R.C., Kim, H.K.: A hybrid barge-in procedure for more reliable turn-taking in human-machine dialog systems. In: 2003 IEEE Workshop on Automatic Speech Recognition and Understanding, ASRU 2003, pp. 198–203 (2003)
8. Raux, A.: Flexible Turn-Taking for Spoken Dialog Systems. Ph. D Thesis, CMU (2008)
9. Selfridge, E.O., Arizmendi, I., Heeman, P.A., Williams, J.D.: Continuously predicting and processing barge-in during a live spoken dialogue task. In: Proceedings of SIGDIAL, pp. 384–393, Metz, France (2013)
10. Heins, R., Franzke, M., Durian, M., Bayya, A.: Turn-taking as a design principle for barge-in in spoken language systems. Int. J. Speech Technol. 2(2), 155–164 (1997)

11. Selfridge, E.O., Heeman, P. A.: Importance-driven turn-bidding for spoken dialogue systems. In: Proceedings of the 48th Annual Meeting of the Association for Computational Linguistics, pp. 177–185, Uppsala, Sweden (2010)
12. Passonneau, R.J., Epstein, S.L., Ligorio, T., Gordon, J.: Embedded wizardry. In: Proceedings of the SIGDIAL 2011 Conference, pp. 248–258 (2011)
13. Holtzblatt, K.: Contextual design. In: Jacko, J., Sears, A. (eds.) The Human-Computer Interaction Handbook: Fundamentals, Evolving Technologies and Emerging Applications, pp. 941–963. Lawrence Erlbaum Associates Inc., Mahwah (2003)
14. Holtzblatt, K., Wendell, J.B., Wood, S.: Rapid Contextual Design: A How-to Guide to Key Techniques for User-Centered Design. Morgan Kaufmann, San Francisco (2004)
15. Sandelowski, M.: Focus on research methods-whatever happened to qualitative description? Res. Nurs. Health 23(4), 334–340 (2000)
16. Lincoln, Y.S., Guba, E.: Naturalistic Inquiry. Sage, London (1985)
17. Carbaugh, D.: Cultures in Conversation. Routledge, Mahwah, NJ (2005)
18. Hymes, D.: Models for the interaction of language and social life. In: Gumperz, J., Hymes, D. (eds.) Directions in Sociolinguistics: The Ethnography of Communication, pp. 35–71. Basil Blackwell, New York (1972)
19. Carbaugh, D., Molina-Markham, E., van Over, B., Winter, U.: Using communication research for cultural variability in human factor design. In: Stanton, N. (ed.) Advances in Human Aspects of Road and Rail Transportation, pp. 176–185. CRC Press, Boca Raton (2012)
20. Carbaugh, D., Winter, U., van Over, B., Molina-Markham, E., Lie, S.: Cultural analyses of in-car communication. J. Appl. Commun. Res. 41(2), 195–201 (2013)
21. Sacks, H., Schegloff, E.A., Jefferson, G.: A simplest systematics for the organization of turn-taking for conversation. Language 50, 696–735 (1974)
22. Schegloff, E.A., Jefferson, G., Sacks, H.: The preference for self-correction in the organization of repair in conversation. Language 53, 361–382 (1977)

Designing the Healthcare Patient's Experience

PostureMonitor: Real-Time IMU Wearable Technology to Foster Poise and Health

Fatemeh Abyarjoo[1], Nonnarit O-Larnnithipong[1],
Sudarat Tangnimitchok[1], Francisco Ortega[2],
and Armando Barreto[1(✉)]

[1] Electrical and Computer Engineering Department,
Florida International University, Miami, FL, USA
{fabya001,nolar002,stang018,barretoa}@fiu.edu
[2] School of Computer and Information Sciences,
Florida International University, Miami, USA
forte007@fiu.edu

Abstract. This paper presents the prototype development and verification of a simple wearable posture monitor system, based on a miniature MEMS Inertial Measurement Unit (IMU). The Inertial Measurement Unit uses accelerometers and gyroscopes to estimate the orientation of the module through sensor fusion algorithms. The system provides a warning to the user wearing it when he/she is departing by an adjustable margin from the posture indicated to the system as correct. Continuous real-time warnings of this type will help the user acquire good posture habits, which has the potential to prevent or assuage health problems caused by chronic bad posture.

Keywords: Posture monitoring · Inertial measurement system · Accelerometer · Gyrosscope · MEMS · Sensor fusion

1 Introduction

Daily activities in the modern world frequently require that individuals spend long hours in a static position. Office workers frequently sit in front of computers for long hours, many times without being able to stand or change their posture. It is well documented that maintaining an improper posture, such as 'slouching' while sitting can lead to improper alignment of the vertebrae in the spine. Improper alignment of the spine can cause damage to the discs that exist between the vertebrae and/or apply inappropriate pressure and stress to the nerves that exit the spine between the vertebrae. This, in turn, can be the cause of very significant afflictions, such as back pain, leg pain, numbness, headaches, etc. [1–6].

Therefore, it is imperative that all individuals develop the habit of maintaining a proper posture. However, many individuals tend to gradually deviate from their intended correct posture, unconsciously. It is in this context that a simple wearable device capable of providing a warning to the user when he/she is drifting away from the correct posture would be very valuable towards helping the user develop sound postural habits that would contribute to the prevention of problems stemming from chronic inappropriate posture.

© Springer International Publishing Switzerland 2015
A. Marcus (Ed.): DUXU 2015, Part III, LNCS 9188, pp. 543–552, 2015.
DOI: 10.1007/978-3-319-20889-3_50

2 Related Work

In the past, there have been several attempts to monitor the posture of the human body, pursuing a variety of goals and applications. For example, Tanaka, Yamakoshi and Rolfe [7] developed a portable instrument for long-term ambulatory monitoring of posture change, using miniature electro-magnetic inclinometers. However, the electro-mechanical inclinometers used here are delicate and therefore make this type of system more appropriate for clinical use than for ordinary consumer use.

Dunne et al. [8] developed a wearable plastic optical fiber (POF) sensor for monitoring seated spinal posture, and a garment that integrated their optical fiber sensor. While the technology used in this system is novel, it is unlikely that most individuals (e.g., ordinary office workers) would adopt the use of a special garment for the sole purpose of having their posture monitored during their daily activities. This same consideration applies to the smart garment for trunk posture monitoring developed by Wai Yin Wong and Man Sang Wong [9], which consisted of a T-shirt with three sensors attached, as well as a sizable battery pack and digital data acquisition module.

3 Inertial Measurement Units for Posture Monitoring

A key element in keeping a good posture is to preserve an adequate angle of the upper back, while standing or remaining seated. Ordinarily, most individuals will first make an effort to keep their backs 'straight', i.e., in such a way that the upper back is parallel to a vertical plane and there is no tilting of the spine to the left or to the right. The objective of a posture training system would be, therefore, to alert the user when the upper back is 'bent forward', i.e., when the subject is 'slouching', or when there is an inappropriate tilt to the left or to the right.

Fortunately, new Inertial Measurement Unit (IMU) modules have emerged in the market, which are capable of continuously monitoring, in real-time, the orientation of the module, providing digital values of the angles of rotation about three orthogonal axes. Further, these systems provide the evaluation of those, so called 'Euler Angles' of rotation, known as 'pitch', 'roll' and 'yaw', as differences with respect to initial or 'tared' values. This feature is particularly auspicious for the application at hand, because the user can reset or 'tare' the angles to zero when he/she is in the target posture, such that the reported pitch, roll and yaw will represent the corresponding angular deviations from the target orientation of the anatomical segment (e.g., the upper back), to which the IMU module is attached. Figure 1 shows the definition of the pitch, roll and yaw angles with respect to the orthogonal X, Y and Z axes, according to the convention used in our work (left-handed system).

In particular, for this work we used the 3-Space Embedded module, from YEI Corporation, which is an ultra-miniature, high-precision, high-reliability, low-cost Attitude and Heading Reference System (AHRS) / Inertial Measurement Unit (IMU) which uses triaxial gyroscope, accelerometer, and compass sensors in conjunction with advanced sensor fusion processing and on-board quaternion-based orientation filtering algorithms to determine orientation relative to an absolute reference in

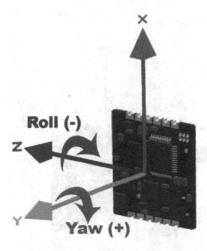

Fig. 1. Coordinate axes used, and definition of the roll and yaw angles, superimposed on the image of the 23 mm × 23 mm 3-Space YEI Embedded IMU module.

real time. This module, with dimensions of 23 mm × 23 mm x 2.2 mm (0.9 × 0.9 × 0.086 in.) is also shown in Fig. 1, with the coordinate frame (orthogonal axes) superimposed on it.

4 The PostureMonitor System

We developed the PostureMonitor system around the 3-Space Embedded module. This module has small physical dimensions and light weight (1.3 g, i.e., 0.0458 oz.), and can, therefore, be attached to the upper back of any ordinary garment worn by the user by means of Velcro glued to the bottom of the module. The specific position in which the module is attached to the upper back is not critical, since the system will be reset (or 'tared') to pitch = 0°, roll = 0° and yaw = 0° when the user adopts the target (correct) posture, initially. Figure 2 illustrates the general area and approximate orientation of attachment for the IMU module to the subject. In this figure, it can be noticed that the critical rotations which would imply an inappropriate departure from a correct posture are:

A. Bending toward the front: will result in a negative roll value (F)
B. Tilting to the right: will result in a positive yaw value (R)
C. Tilting to the left: will result in a negative yaw value (L)

According to the conventions illustrated in Fig. 2, the operation of the Posture-Monitor system only requires the 3-Space module (powered by a voltage source), an elementary user-interaction device, such as a normally-open push button which can be pressed to close its circuit, and a mechanism to provide the warning to the user, such as the speaker in an earphone (or alternatively a piezo-vibrator that could provide tactile output to the user). The 3-Space Embedded module can be supplied with 3.3 V to 6.0 V, and has minimal power consumption (45 mA @ 5 v). Therefore, it can be

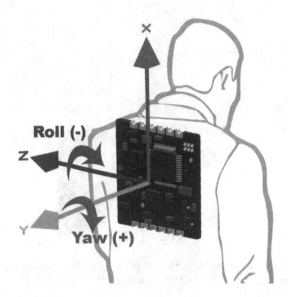

Fig. 2. Approximate position and orientation of attachment for the 3-Space module to the user (Module not to scale).

powered by a 'wrist watch battery'. In our initial prototype, we operated the 3-Space sensor in a tethered configuration in which a USB cable is attached to it, so that the power is supplied to the module from the host PC through the USB cable and commands (e.g., 'tare the sensor', 'read the current angles', etc.) and data (e.g., pitch, roll, and yaw, values estimated in the IMU module using sensor fusion of its accelerometer and gyroscope readings) are exchanged through the USB connection, under control of a C program running in the host PC. This program utilized several library functions provided by YEI Corporation to facilitate the development of applications of their IMU module.

Specifically, the PostureMonitor system operates in one of two modes:

1. INITIALIZE
2. SENSE

Figure 3 depicts the flowchart corresponding to the INITIALIZE mode. On power-up the PostureMonitor starts execution in this mode. In this mode, the system continuously waits for the activation of the push button, which will serve to indicate that the user is currently adopting the target position and the angles should be, therefore, reset ('tared') to zeros. Upon re-setting all the angles, the program branches to the SENSE mode.

In the SENSE mode the system will read the values of pitch, roll and yaw estimated by the IMU module and compare them to pre-defined (programmable) thresholds to determine if any of the 3 critical departures from correct posture exist, according to Table 1.

Then the system will determine if any of the flags (FrontFlag, RightFlag, LeftFlag) has been set and, in that case, it will assert the variable Alarm, which will cause the

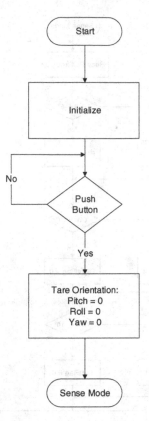

Fig. 3. Flowchart for the INITIALIZE mode

Table 1. (Programmable) Thresholds used to trigger indications of incorrect posture

Departure from correct posture	Set flag	If this condition is met
Bend toward the front (F)	FrontFlag	Roll < −5°
Tilt to the right (R)	RightFlag	Yaw > 10°
Tilt to the left (L)	LeftFlag	Yaw < −10°

warning to the user (speaker or piezo element) to be activated. The user can force the system back to the INITIALIZE mode (to be able to re-tare the angles to zero), by pressing the push button. Figure 4 shows the flowchart for the SENSE mode.

5 Verification of the PostureMonitor System

In our preliminary implementation we have tested the PostureMonitor system while still connecting the 3-Space module to a host PC through a USB cable. This provided power to the 3-Space module and allowed commands and data to be exchanged between the 3-Space module and the host PC. In this preliminary implementation the

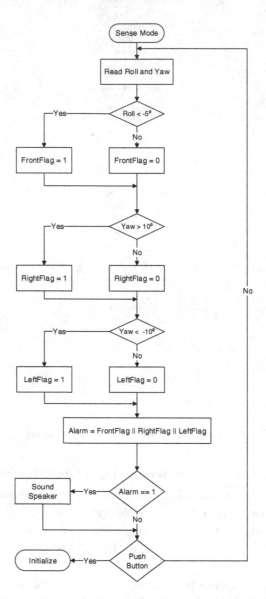

Fig. 4. Flowchart for the SENSE mode

push button was functionally substituted by a key in the keyboard of the host PC, and the actuator (speaker or piezo element) was substituted by the speaker of the host PC. Under these circumstances, we have tested the performance of the PostureMonitor system, on several volunteers, with positive results.

Figures 5 (side view, from the left of the subject) and 6 (back view) illustrate the target position (in which the sensors were 'tared') for one of the evaluations performed.

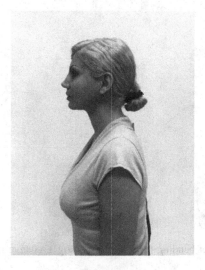

Fig. 5. Target ('tare') position - Side view

Fig. 6. Target ('tare') position - Back view

After the PostureMonitor system was initialized ('tared') in the position illustrated in Figs. 5 and 6, the system was made to change to the SENSE mode and the subject was asked to shift her position to adopt some of the typical instances of improper posture. The subject was asked to stop her movement as soon as the system activated the speaker, indicating the detection of the incorrect posture. Figure 7 shows the position in which the system reported that the subject was bending forward ('slouching'). Figure 8 displays the position in which the system activated the speaker, to report that the

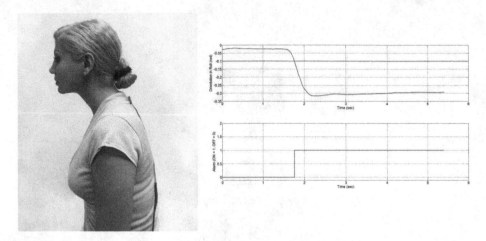

Fig. 7. Detection of subject bending forward ('slouching'), change in roll value and setting of the FrontFlag.

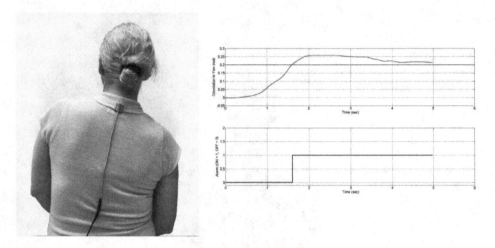

Fig. 8. Detection of subject tilting to the right, change in yaw value and setting of the RightFlag

subject was tilting to the right. Figure 9 shows the position at which the system indicated that the subject was tilting to the left.

The figures above confirm that the PostureMonitor system is sensitive enough to provide useful warnings to the user and, in that way, foster the development of good postural habits.

To visualize the operation of the SENSE mode of the system, Fig. 10 shows the changes in roll and yaw angles when the subject bent forward, then tilted to the left and then tilted to the right, causing the corresponding flags to be set. Then the subject adopted two 'combined' incorrect postures, leaning simultaneously to the front and the left and then to the front and the right.

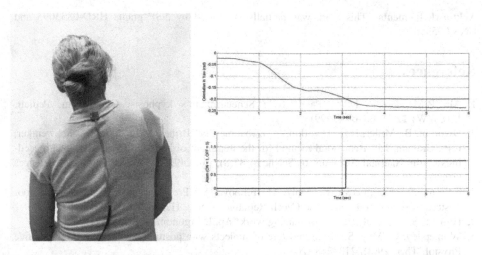

Fig. 9. Detection of subject tilting to the left, change in yaw value and setting of the LeftFlag

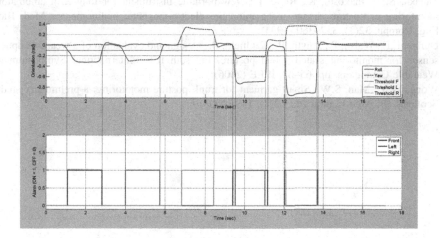

Fig. 10. Roll and yaw changes and flags set when improper postures were adopted

6   Conclusions and Future Work

This paper describes the development of a simple posture monitoring system, requiring a single MEMS IMU module (3-Space Embedded, from YEI Corp.). The verification of the system indicates that the PostureMonitor is capable of providing useful warnings to its user and therefore help him/her to develop good postural habits, which may aid in preventing or assuaging health problems derived from chronic improper posture.

Our future work will include the consolidation of the 3-Space Embedded module with a microcontroller, a miniature switch (push button), and a wrist watch battery in a fully independent wearable unit that can be connected to a headphone to provide its warnings to the user.

Acknowledgements. This work was partially supported by NSF grants HRD-0833093 and CNS-0959985.

References

1. Ali, R.M., Green, D.W., Patel, T.C.: Scheuermann's kyphosis. Curr. Opin. Pediatr. J. (LWW) **11**(1), 66–69 (1999)
2. Dworkin, B., Miller, N.E., Dworkin, S., Birbaumer, N., Brines, M.L., Jonas, S., Schwentker, E.P., Graham, J.J.: Behavioral method for the treatment of idiopathic scoliosis. In: Proceedings of the National Academy of Sciences, **82**(8), pp. 2493–2497. National Acad Sciences (1985)
3. Kratenova, J., Zejglicova, K., Maly, M., Filipova, V.: Prevalence and risk factors of poor posture in school children in the Czech Republic. J. Sch. Health **77**(3), 131–137 (2007)
4. Hignett, S.: Postural analysis of nursing work. Appl. Ergonomics **27**(3), 171–176 (1996)
5. Womersley, L., May, S.: Sitting posture of subjects with postural backache. J. Manipulative Physiol. Ther. **29**(3), 213–218 (2006)
6. Barrack, R.L., Whitecloud 3rd, T.S., Burke, S.W., Cook, S.D., Harding, A.F.: Proprioception in idiopathic scoliosis. Spine (LWW) **9**(7), 681–685 (1984)
7. Tanaka, S., Yamakoshi, K., Rolfe, P.: New portable instrument for long-term ambulatory monitoring of posture change using miniature electro-magnetic inclinometers. Med. Biol. Eng. Compu. **32**(3), 357–360 (1994)
8. Dunne, L.E., Walsh, P., Smyth, B., Caulfield, B.: Design and evaluation of a wearable optical sensor for monitoring seated spinal posture. In: 10th IEEE International Symposium on Wearable Computers, pp. 65–68. IEEE (2006)
9. Wong, W.Y., Man, S.W.: Smart garment for trunk posture monitoring: a preliminary study. Scoliosis (BioMed Central Ltd.) **3**(7), 1–9 (2008)

Robot-Era Project: Preliminary Results on the System Usability

Roberta Bevilacqua[1(✉)], Elisa Felici[1], Fiorella Marcellini[1],
Sebastian Glende[2], Susann Klemcke[2], Isabel Conrad[2],
Raffaele Esposito[3], Filippo Cavallo[3], and Paolo Dario[3]

[1] Scientific Direction, INRCA, Ancona, Italy
{r.bevilacqua,e.felici,f.marcellini}@inrca.it
[2] YOUSE GmbH, Berlin, Germany
sebastian.glende@youse.de
[3] The BioRobotics Institute, Scuola Superiore Sant'Anna, Pontedera, Italy
{r.esposito,f.cavallo,p.dario}@sssup.it

Abstract. The European project Robot-Era is an ambitious integrated project (FP7-ICT-2011.5.4), which objective is the development of advanced robotic services, integrated in intelligent environments, to provide independent living to older people.

In order to guarantee the matching of the users' need and the demands, two loops of experimentation were conceived, in realistic and real setting.

The aim of the paper is to described the methods applied and the main results coming from the first experimental loop, concerning the degree of usability of the interfaces and provide guidelines for testing socially assistive robots with older people.

Keywords: Usability assessment · Older people · HRI · HCI · Acceptability

1 Introduction

Due to the demographic increase of older people living alone and in need of care [1], a large number of research projects have been focused on the development of robotic services for ageing-well applications [2]. The support offered by the robotic applications can be related to mobility, providing household and safety maintenance and continues monitoring [3, 4].

The complexity of the robotic systems required a careful methodological consideration on how to properly approach the evaluation of the system usability and acceptability, most of all in case of system tailored for older people.

The aim of the paper is to describe the methods applied and the main results coming from the first experimental loop of the Robot-Era project (FP7-ICT-2011.5.4). As first loop of experimentation, the analysis of the usability of the interfaces has deserved a greater importance, in order to understand both the user- and the technology-oriented improvements to be made for the technical improvement. Moreover, the interest of exploring the results obtained has also to be seen in a methodological perspective,

© Springer International Publishing Switzerland 2015
A. Marcus (Ed.): DUXU 2015, Part III, LNCS 9188, pp. 553–561, 2015.
DOI: 10.1007/978-3-319-20889-3_51

in order to understand which tool can be of support to collect useful data on the usability of complex robotic systems, as the Robot-Era platform.

At this purpose, the aim of the paper is not only to report briefly the first results obtained during the system validation, but to use an extract of the results to critically analyze the methodological choices done and investigate how to implement it in the view of the second experimental loop.

1.1 The Robot-Era Platform

The Robot-Era architecture integrates a multi-robot system able to work in different environment such as outdoor, condominium and indoor [5]. It includes also a domestic Wireless Sensor Network (WSN), constituting an Ambient Intelligence (AmI) infrastructure, that supervises the home and localize the user. Other agents of the system include the elevator and the user interface sub-system. The system is composed by three different robots acting in three different environment.

The Domestic Robot (DORO) is designed to safely navigate in a domestic environment. It is equipped with a robotic arm in order to take small objects. Multicolor LEDs, mounted on the eyes, and speakers provided a feedback to the user. The robot has a removable tablet that user could use for service requests.

The Condominium Robot (CORO) navigates between floors through the elevator. It doesn't have an arm, but it is mounted a roller mechanism in order to be able to exchange goods with the Outdoor Robot.

The Outdoor Robot (ORO), designed on DustCart platform [6], is an autonomous mobile robot for objects transportation in urban environment. It is equipped with a container for the objects, a robotic head and a touch screen used primarily for human-robot interaction and sensors for obstacle detection and localization.

The users interact with the system using a web-based interface (named Graphic User Interface, GUI), from the DORO tablet or with a wearable microphone connected with a speech recognition software module.

The services offered by the Robot-Era platform are shopping delivery, reminding, communication, laundry, food delivery, object transportation and manipulation, garbage collection, surveillance, indoor escort, outdoor walking support. For the purpose of this paper, only the results of shopping delivery, reminding and communication services will be presented. The GUI of the Robot-Era system is described in details in Di Nuovo et al. [7].

2 Methodology

2.1 Recruitment and Quota Plan

The project focuses on a specific target group of elderly people, aged over 65 years old, with moderate health problems and motor and cognitive deficits, living alone or with their relatives but without a devoted caregiver.

Older people have to be able to communicate their use-preferences and opinions on the Robot-Era services, actively participating in the technical development and design of the technologies. Within the target group of elderly people, different levels of autonomy could be observed: High Level of User Autonomy (HLUA), Middle Level of User Autonomy (MLUA) and Low Level of User Autonomy (LLUA).

A method to receive fundamental statements from smaller samples in qualitative research is to set up a quota sampling [8], that means researchers are choosing the test participants based on theoretical assumptions in condition to the research question [9]. By using quotas as an orientation an arbitrary sample composition based on subjective criteria can be avoided. For the first experimental loop a number of 70 participants was prescribed. For guaranteeing the comparability between the test sides (Italy and Sweden) the sample has be divided into two equal samples (each consisting of 35 participants). The number of women and men was chosen differently because of the different life expectancy of males and females [10]. These facts lead to the assumption, that also a higher proportion of woman would potentially use the robots in the future. The operative inclusion criteria of the first experimental loop were: Older people aged $\geq$ 65 years old, positive evaluation of mental status at the Short Portable Mental Status Questionnaire [11] (cut off to be enrolled = nr. Errors $\leq$ 3), autonomy in performing daily activities with domestic tools, evaluated with the Instrumental Activities of Daily Living by Lawton [12] (cut off to be enrolled = score > 2), absence of psychiatric illness, substance abuse and communication impairments.

2.2 Tools for Measuring the Usability

Before developing the test protocol, a detailed analysis of the literature were conducted, with aim of identifying the most appropriate tools and metrics to be applied [13]. The analysis of available theories on usability evaluation has resulted in the decision of adopting a mix-methods approach, based on a quantitative and qualitative data collection.

To evaluate the overall experience and usability of the Robot-Era services, a qualitative usability test with use cases was set up. The participants tried to perform predefined test tasks, which were oriented on use cases. These use cases [14] were based on scenarios that were described in detailed step-by-step descriptions offered by the technical partners. While executing the tasks, the test persons were observed by experts who documented the difficulties. The usability test was combined with the thinking aloud technique (TAL), [15]. The use of the thinking aloud method allows the researcher to investigate in detail the overall user experience because people express their feeling, thoughts and skepticism directly when using the system. Further the Systems Usability Scale (SUS, 1996) [16] was used. This simple and not highly detailed evaluation method uses a standardized form with ten questions to assess the product's usability, on a five-point Likert scale.

In order to deeply understand the quantitative data collected, two detailed phases of video observation were conducted:

the first phase was aimed at evaluating the Human Computer Interaction (HCI) and was mainly oriented to the users' performance with the graphic user interface (GUI), running on a devoted tablet;

the second phase of observation was aimed at evaluation the overall acceptability and Human Robot Interaction (HRI).

Before starting with the analysis, a set of indicators for acceptability and HRI was selected for each service, starting from the definition of acceptability from the Unified Theory of Acceptance and Use of Technology [17] based on 13 core constructs, whose anxiety, attitude and perceived enjoyment were selected to be collected by users' free statements, as well as, the emotional reaction during the task execution, through the non verbal communication. Regarding HRI, it was decided to guide the observation through the analysis of the [18] head orientation (robot head, robot body, robot eyes, experimenter, tablet), gaze (robot, experimenter, default), body orientation (robot, experimenter, straight ahead), proxemics (approach robot, touch robot) as well as free statements of the users on the robot and its features or emotional reaction to the robot presence. The communication analysis for HRI was conducted by analyzing the presence of specific codified events.

2.3   Settings of the Pilot Sites

The tests were performed in two different pilot sites: in Peccioli (Italy) and in Örebro (Sweden). The setting with end-users in Peccioli was composed of indoor and outdoor realistic environments. The indoor environment consisted of a real apartment in a modern structure and the building consisted of two floors, the DomoCasa Lab. The outdoor environment was around the building. The Ängen Research and Innovation Apartments (Ängen-RIA) were situated in the Ängen healthcare complex in Örebro, Sweden, including senior living apartments, a retirement home for elderly in need of day-to-day care, and a local clinic.

3   Procedures

The experimental loop was conducted in Sweden and Italy, involving 67 older users. The results of the three services are available for 35 Italian users and 22 Swedish users. After the preliminary introduction, the interviewers presented the Use Cases to be executed to the participants and explained how to perform the TAL, during the use.

The Use Cases identified for the shopping delivery service were:

– send the robot go shopping
– receive the delivery from the robot;
  for the communication service:

– starting a video call;
– accept an incoming video call;
  for the reminding service:

– create a new appointment/event;
– reminding of taking the medicine.

Once completed all tasks, the SUS was administrated for each service. During the execution of the test, the two phases of observation were conducted, through videos [19].

4 Results

The subparagraphs below reported the results obtained by applying the different methods. Concerning the results of the observation, they are still under elaboration by the partners, so they are shown in the form of narratives, to offer qualitative insights to the developers. Moreover, the evaluation of the communication service was negatively influenced by the numerous technical failures of the systems during the testing phase, not allowing a proper observation of the performance of the participants. Concerning the shopping service, the results of the SUS are available only for the Italian sample. Finally, the results of the video observation on the HRI and acceptability issues are based only on the Italian sample analysis.

4.1 System Usability Scale and Thinking a Loud

In order to get an overall usability index, the SUS score is ranged from 0 to 100. From the literature [20], the following cut off were chosen, to analyze the level of the services: not usable (score < 65), usable (65 ≤ score < 85) and excellent (score ≥ 85). In addition to the overall evaluation of the services usability, the results of relevant statements were presented, whose scores are ranged from 1 to 5, as described in paragraph 3.2. As regards the overall usability of the shopping delivery service, the results of the Italian sample (n = 35) show that the proposed system is not usable for 6 elderly volunteers (M = 50.83; SD = ± 7.85), while it is usable for 8 of them (M = 77.81; SD = ± 6.74) and excellent for 21 participants (M = 90.71; SD = ± 4.04). In particular, elderly people are neither agree nor disagree about using this service frequently (M = 3.40; SD = ± 1.35). However the participants report that the GUI for the shopping service is easy to use (M = 4.03; SD = ± 1.32), and only 3 of them think that they would need the support of a technical person to use it. About communication service, 2 users of the Italian sample (n = 35) reported that the interface was not usable (M = 41.25; SD = ± 15.91), while it was considered usable for 10 users (M = 77.75; SD = ± 4.92) and excellent for 23 of them (M = 92.83; SD = ± 4.90). In addition, the results from the Swedish participants (N = 22) have shown that the communication service is considered not usable for 6 elderly volunteers (M = 50.00; SD = ± 19.17), while it is usable for 8 of them (M = 71.88; SD = ± 6.59) and excellent for 8 participants (M = 93.75 SD = ± 5.89).

Overall, it can be said that all the 57 users would be enough disposed to use the communication service without the support of a technical person, perceiving the task as very easy (IT users M = 4.49; SD = ± 0.92, SE users M = 3.73; SD = ± 1.42). Concerning the reminding service, the Italian results (N = 35) have shown that it was considered not usable for 6 users (M = 40.83; SD = ± 14.72), while it is usable for 10 users (M = 70.25; SD = ± 3.43) and excellent for 51.52 % of the sample (M = 96.62;

SD = ± 4.41). The reminding service was also tested by 18 Swedish users and it was considered mainly not usable for 55.56 % of the sample (M = 36.75; SD = ± 19.58), while it was considered usable for 6 users (M = 78.33; SD = ± 4.65) and excellent only for 2 of them (M = 87.50; SD = ± 3.54).

In the case of the Robot-Era first experimental loop, the TAL has produced not relevant information, mainly in the case of the Italian sample. Despite the positive results achieved at the SUS, that have suggested a highly degree of usability of the GUI, the qualitative analysis have highlighted some discrepancy, as detailed below.

4.2 Qualitative Usability Evaluation

During the experimentation videos were taken from three different perspectives, which show the test person, the robot and the interaction on the tablet interface. The evaluation of the usability of the Robot-Era System is mainly based on a video-interaction analysis [21] of the experimentation.

All videos taken during the experimental loop were analyzed service by service. The analysis was conducted as an explorative content analysis [22] and was validated through multiple experts in the field of usability studies. After the selection of usability problems was made, the problems were classified and weighted with regard to international usability standards and norms (e.g. EN ISO 9241-110).

To weight a usability problem the following benchmarks were used:

- Frequency of occurrence of the problem
- Influence of the problem on fulfilling the task – Was it possible for the user to complete a task or not?
- Potential of learning from the users side.

The problems then were classified from 1 (no usability problem) to 5 (major usability problem).

Usability problems related to the shopping delivery service are:
- Difficulties in understanding the concept of creating a shopping list
- Difficulties in entering the shopping list
- Difficulties in recognizing the food icons correctly
- Difficulties in finding the items under the correct category
- Purchasing more than one item
- Confusion about the ending of the task

For the communication service, no strong usability problems can be identified during the test, even if the observation was negatively influence by the system failures. Regarding the reminding service, older people failed in changing the title of the reminder, due to the fact that it was presented by a drop-down menu, where the other options are hidden. The standard title of the reminder is "Medicine". The other options "Telephone" and "Generic Alert" are only shown when the person opens it. The person did not expect that there were other options too.

4.3 Overall Acceptability and HRI Evaluation

The results reported are based on the evaluation of the Italian sample video analysis (N = 35). For the shopping service, 12 subjects were focused mainly on the robot with the head, eyes and body orientation. In one case, the user started walking around the robot for looking better at him, moving close around DORO. At the same time, 12 subjects were more oriented to the tablet, suggesting that the use of the GUI would have distracted them from the interaction with DORO. In 5 cases, it was not possible to collect the information, for the technical failure of the system. Only one user touched the fingers of the robot, as she was looking for more interaction with it, as shown also by her statements ["I'd like the robot has a human-like arm, to be adapted to my apartment"; "The robot is very nice"]. From an analysis of the communication, the majority of the users seems to like DORO and look for more speech communication with him ["Is it possible to use a courtesy communication?", "I think that it is better if the robot has the vocal command, because if I have to stay in bed, it is difficult to take the tablet", "I think I like more the robot, while tablet is still a little complicate for me. I need to exercise more"], while no one expressed openly preferences for the tablet interface. Concerning the reminding services, the principal mean of interaction was constituted by the GUI on the tablet. From the observation, it was found that just the users with a higher technological literacy were able to perform autonomously the task – 9 out of 35 –. This has influenced the acceptability of the service, that sometimes was felt as too complicated ["The menu really does not work for me!", "I don't understand this – tablet -","It's too difficult for me!", "You should do too many things for reminding something!"]. It can be understood that the majority of the sample has looked for the step by step support from the experimenter – 14 users -. The more skilled users have given input on what can be done to ameliorate the service satisfaction ["Aesthetically, it should be more similar of the shopping list, so you can choose what to remind trough icons"] and the robot communication capability for this service ["Why DORO does not say more things? For example, he can remind me also who I have to call to"]. Even if they were more concentrated on the tablet, many users have a good HRI, as shown by the adoption of a very friendly communication to DORO ["Many thanks DORO!", "I really need you, DORO!"] and free statements on its features, especially the eyes ["DORO has a really "intelligent" eyes","DORO has a funny eyes"]. In addition, an affective reaction to the robot was detected in one user ["It seems a person, it is a companion!"].

5 Conclusion

The different number of users involved in each method represents the most relevant limit to the validity of the results. Nonetheless, some considerations can be made on the methodological point of view, that can be of usefulness for improving the future assessment.

First of all, it was observed an inconsistency between the results obtained at the shopping delivery service: even if the SUS score shows a high degree of usability of the GUI, the video interaction analysis and the HRI and acceptability observation have depicted a different situation: users needed the support of the experimenter nearly step by step to complete the task. Concerning the communication service, even if the system failed many times due to technical issues, the users seems to really appreciate it, in contrast with the literature in the field of technology usability and acceptability [23]. Only the results obtained at the reminding service seems to be confirmed both at the quantitative and qualitative evaluation.

Despite the limit of the analysis already expressed at the beginning, it seems that a mix-method approach should be highly recommended, in order to deeply understand the results, avoiding the effect of social desirability on the answers given by the older users, for example [24].

From this first experience, it can be also observed that the choice of the appropriate method to adopt should be also guided by the end-users characteristics, in particular the technological affinity and the cultural predisposition to the task prescribed by the method. For example, the TAL method has produced not relevant results in the case of the Italian sample, maybe due to the unusual double-task for this population and the limited technological literacy that may have affected the overall use [23].

The HRI and acceptability observation has also highlighted the preference of the users in interacting more with the robot: the opportunity of using vocal command for completing the service is highly suggested for improving the overall system usability, switching the attention from the HCI to HRI.

From the statements of the users, in fact, it is interesting to notice the need of more social interaction, maybe mediated by the specific characteristics of the technology. Robots, in fact, may evoke in the users the feeling of empathy and reciprocity, following the theory of mind paradigm [25].

Due to this, a new metrics and benchmarks definition is conceived for the second loop, in which a higher attention is given to the Social Presence dimension [26], through combining different methods.

References

1. Van Den Broek, G., Cavallo, F., Wehrmann, C.: AALIANCE Ambient Assisted Living Roadmap. IOS Press, Amsterdam (2010)
2. Forlizzi, J.: Robotic products to assist the aging population. Interactions 12(2), 16–18 (2005)
3. Forlizzi, J., DiSalvo, C., Gemperle, F.: Assistive robotics and an ecology of elders living independently in their homes. J. HCI Spec. Issue Hum.-Robot Interac. 9(1/2), 25–59 (2004)
4. Mynatt, E.D., Essa, I., Rogers, W.: Increasing the opportunities for aging in place. In: Proceedings of the CUU 2000 Conference on Universal Usability, New York (2000)
5. Cavallo, F., Aquilano, M., Carrozza, M.C., Dario, P.: Implementation of 3D services for "Ageing well" applications: Robot-Era project. In: Proceedings of the foritaal2012 Forum, pp. 17–19. Parma, Italy, October 2012
6. Ferri, G., Mondini, A., Manzi, A., Mazzolai, B., Laschi, C., Mattoli, V., Reggente, M., Stoyanov, T., Lilienthal, A., Lettere, M.:Dustcart, a mobile robot for urban environments: experiments of pollution monitoring and mapping during autonomous navigation in urban scenarios. In: Proceedings of ICRA Workshop on Networked and Mobile Robot Olfaction in Natural, Dynamic Environments (2010)

7. Di Nuovo, A., Broz, F., Belpaeme, T., Cangelosi, A., Cavallo, F., Esposito, R., Dario, P.: A web based multi-modal interface for elderly users of the Robot-Era multi-robot services. In: 2014 IEEE International Conference on Systems, Man and Cybernetics (SMC), pp. 2186–2191 (2014)
8. Behnke, J., Baur, N., Behnke, N.: Empirische Methoden der Politikwissenschaft. Paderborn, UTB Schöningh (2006)
9. Schnell, R., Hill, P.B., Esser, E.: Methoden der empirischen Sozialforschung. Oldenbourg, München (2005)
10. Eurostat: Life expectancy at age 65 for Female 21,3 years is higher than the life expectancy of men which is 17,8 years at age 65 (2011). http://epp.eurostat.ec.europa.eu/tgm/table.do?tab=table&init=1&plugin=extraction
11. Pfeiffer, E.: A short portable mental status questionnaire for the assessment of Organic brain deficit in elderly patients. J. Am. Geriatr. Soc. 23, 433–441 (1975)
12. Lawton, M.P., Brody, E.M.: Assessment of older people: self-maintaining and instrumental activities of daily living. The Gerontologist 9(3), 179–186 (1969)
13. Bevilacqua, R., Di Rosa, M., Felici, E., Stara, V., Barbabella, F., Rossi, L.: Towards an Impact Assessment Framework for ICT-Based Systems Supporting Older People: Making Evaluation Comprehensive Through Appropriate Concepts and Metrics (2014)
14. Sarodnick, F., Brau, H.: Methoden der Usability Evaluation: Wissenschaftliche Grundlagen und praktische Anwendung, vol. 1. Huber Verlag, Bern (2006)
15. Ericsson, K., Simon, H.: Protocol Analysis: Verbal Reports as Data, 2nd edn. MIT Press, Boston (1993)
16. Brooke, J.: SUS: a "quick and dirty" usability scale. In: Jordan, P.W., Thomas, B., Weerdmeester, B.A., McClelland, A.L. (eds.) Usability Evaluation in Industry. Taylor and Francis, London (1996)
17. Venkatesh, V., Morris, M., Davis, G.B., Davis, F.D.: User acceptance of information technology: toward a unified view. MIS Q. 27(3), 425–428 (2003)
18. Mumm, J., Mutlu, B.: Human-robot proxemics: physical and psychological distancing in human-robot interaction. In: 2011 6th ACM/IEEE International Conference on Human-Robot Interaction (HRI), pp. 331–338, 8–11 March 2011
19. Nedopil, C., Schauber, C., Glende, S.: Methods of User Integration for AAL Innovations – Toolbox. AAL Association (2013)
20. McLellan, S., Muddimer, A., Peres, S.C.: The effect of experience on system usability scale ratings. Usabil. Stud. 7(2), 56–67 (2012)
21. Knoblauch, H., Schnettler, B., Raab, J., Soeffner, H.G.: Video analysis: methodology and methods Qualitative Audiovisual Data Analysis in Sociology. Lang, Frankfurt am Main (2006)
22. Mayring, P.: Qualitative content analysis. In: Forum: Qualitative social research, 1(2) (2000)
23. Sun, H., Zhang, P.: The role of moderating factors in user technology acceptance. Int. J. Hum. Comput. Stud. 64, 53–78 (2006)
24. Edwards, A.L.: The Social Desirability Variable in Personality Assessment and Research. Dryden Press, New York (1957)
25. Gordon, R.: Folk psychology as simulation. Mind Lang. 1, 158–171 (1986)
26. Biocca, F., Harms, C., Gregg, J.: The networked minds measure of social presence: pilot test of the factor structure and concurrent validity. Paper presented at the Presence, 4th Annual International Workshop, May 21–23, Philadelphia, PA (2001)

User Experience Research
on the Rehabilitation System
of Speech-Impaired Children

A Case Study on Speech Training Product

Wenyi Cai, Jun Liu, Qiang Liu, and Ting Han[✉]

School of Media and Design, Shanghai Jiao Tong University, Shanghai, China
hanting@sjtu.edu.cn

Abstract. A large number of Chinese speech-impaired children and their families face long-term tough training and lack of professional speech therapists and training products. The rehabilitation experience of preschool children in the critical period of speech learning need attention. By the analysis to the traditional treatment, it shows that young children generally have difficulty in concentration. Parents worry about time-consuming, economic pressure, fatigue from training, uncontrollable children. Speech therapists concern about the problem of searching record, limitation of treatment. Accordingly, ICT-based speech training product which suits Chinese learning has been designed to improve these stakeholders' experience. The product has interaction, gamification, professional knowledge, substitute for parents' demonstration in part, visualization of the progress and training program. By comparing using the product in the training with the traditional way, the experience has been improved in attracting the attention of children, reducing the burden of parents, lifting participation of speech therapists.

Keywords: User experience · Speech rehabilitation · Speech-impaired children and their parents · Speech therapist · ICT · Speech training product

1 Introduction

1.1 Speech Impairment

Speech has always been the most natural and most frequently used mean of human communication with the role of fulfilling the information transmission between individuals [1]. The ability of speech is not innate, but an acquired character which is formed through learning. During this process, the formation of speech skill will be influenced by the abnormal condition of central nervous system (such as brain) or peripheral system, resulting in a variety of speech impairment, such as language retardation, dysarthria and dysphonia [2].

According to the Communique on Major Statistics of the Second China National Sample Survey on Disability, in 2006, there could be 170 thousand speech-disabled

© Springer International Publishing Switzerland 2015
A. Marcus (Ed.): DUXU 2015, Part III, LNCS 9188, pp. 562–574, 2015.
DOI: 10.1007/978-3-319-20889-3_52

individuals among the schoolchildren. Moreover, the number of hearing-impaired children between 0 to 6 is about 137,000 which is growing at the pace of 23,000 per year [3]. Hearing-impairment is taken into account because it can lead to speech-impairment.

Early diagnosis of speech disorders, in either children or adults, is of prime importance for any speech therapist and the key to good chances for comprehensive rehabilitation [4]. The speech-impaired children can be rehabilitated and live a normal life by means of accurate diagnosis, prompt treatment and long-term speech training.

1.2 Speech Rehabilitation

Speech Rehabilitation includes diagnosis, assessment and training. Firstly, speech-impairment is diagnosed by the doctor. And then, the assessment of disability degree is given by the doctor and therapist, which contains the dysfunction degree of body, language and deglutition as well as the recent and long-term rehabilitation goals, to guide the formulate of physical therapy training program such as physical therapy, occupational therapy and speech therapy. After cure the physical disability, speech therapists and parents give speech rehabilitation training to the children patients. Finally, therapists will give children periodic evaluation before next course training.

The hearing and speech training institutions were regularized and the grassroots service network became better in China [5]. By the end of 2013, there were 32 provincial-level rehabilitation centers and 1,014 grassroots training institutions nationwide. 32,000 children are receiving hearing and speech training. Parent schools were further regulated. 6,448 various kinds of professionals in the field of hearing and speech training were trained. However, there is still a huge gap between supply and demand of speech therapy professionals.

1.3 User Experience

User experience is defined as a person's perceptions and responses that result from the use or anticipated use of a product, system or service [6]. During the past decade, the concept of user experience is widely used. In recent years, the concept of user experience has been transplanted to the field of medical treatment [7].

Speech rehabilitation requires not only the therapist's effects in the public health service, but also the daily training at home. The household caregiving affects the rehabilitation a lot. Meanwhile, the family also suffers from the impaired children. They do not have enough knowledge about their children's condition [8]. Simultaneously, they lack in inadequate facilities and services, which is relative to financial problems. Families felt severe sadness and loneliness [8]. What they face everyday is the stress of caregiving, confusion about the future of their children and themselves and the appeal for sharing the burden. Because of taking care of a impaired child for a long time, parents suffer from a lack of time, a lack of control and decreased psychosocial energy [9]. Their social life, working life, and family relationships are all affected [8].

1.4 ICT in HHC

Home Health Care (HHC) is a combination of contemporary high-tech and medical. The speech therapy profession has expanded rapidly, while recently making use of available Information and Communications Technologies (ICTs) [10]. Research on the ICT usage for assessment, support and rehabilitation of communication disorders have revealed positive results in disorders caused by neurological conditions, autism, hearing impairment and acquired speech and language disorders [11].

Some of the most representative studies of the last decade regarding the ICT usage in speech therapy can facilitate the life of patients with speech disorders, therapists and caregivers as well [4]. ICT is now considered a tool that assists and sometimes even achieves quicker and more efficient results where traditional therapy fails.

However, in China, the ICT has not been widely used. The assistive devices which are provided in China Disabled Person Service Net (CDPSN) only focus on assisting the speech-impairment person with communication with the outside world. This study suggested a household speech training assistive products which has not only positive effects on rehabilitation, but also a good user experience in daily rehabilitation training.

2 Experience in Traditional Rehabilitation System

This paper mainly study on the experience of the assessment and treatment process in the public healthcare service and home healthcare training. The stakeholders involved in the rehabilitation system are the speech therapists(STs),speech-impaired children who have been recovered from physiological and psychological disabilities and in the period of articulation training and their parents. The experience has been analyzed through observation, questionnaire and interview.

The ecology (actors) map [12] is a graph representing the system of the three stakeholders with their mutual relations (Fig. 1).

Fig. 1. Actor map of rehabilitation

Reference to the Picker Patient Experience Questionnaire [13] in medical field, we designed a questionnaire for parents. Figure 2 shows some of the questionnaire results.

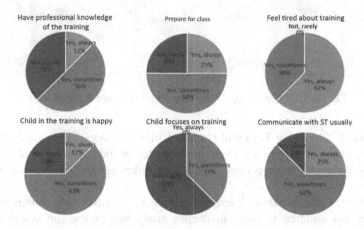

Fig. 2. Results of the questionnaire

	Before	Inquiry	Assessment	Treatment & Training	Advice
Children	1.Wait in the institution 2.Travel	Play with toy Look around Wait	2.Be praised 1.Speak out	Play with toy / Be praised Reply (repeat pronunciation) Feel boring	Wait
Parents	3.Wait in the institution 2.Travel 1.Prepare to go out	Recall and answer	2.Be praised 1.Watch	Learn the training skill Watch Can not accompany the training	listen to the ST's advice Take notes Be given new mission
ST	1.Trained other children 2.Find and review record	Ask about the progress	2.Confirm good progress 1.Talk with child	2.Ask / talk with / praise the child 1.Use toy to abstract /demonstrate 3.Demonstrate pronunciation many times	Give parents advice Take notes

Fig. 3. Experience map of the rehabilitation in public health care

Experience map describes the experience of stakeholders by representing the touch points that characterize their interaction in public and home health care (See Figs. 3 and 4).

2.1 Children

The analysis of underage children was carried out by observing the training process and description from parents and STs because of the weakness of children in expressing their subjective consciousness. One gain point and one pain point are summarized.

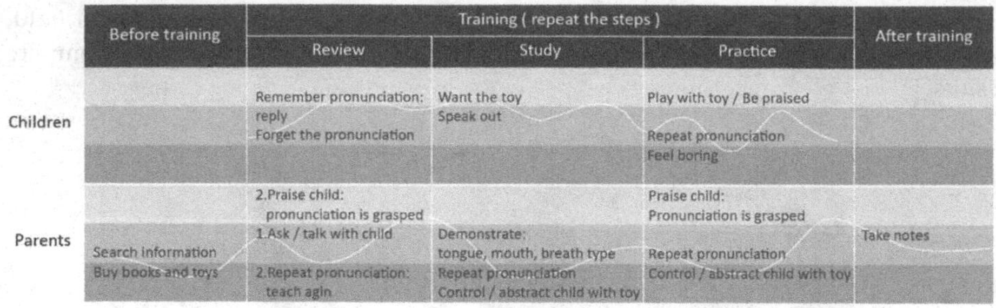

| Before training | Training (repeat the steps) | | | After training |
	Review	Study	Practice	
Children		Remember pronunciation: reply / Forget the pronunciation	Want the toy / Speak out	Play with toy / Be praised / Repeat pronunciation / Feel boring	
Parents	Search information / Buy books and toys	2.Praise child: pronunciation is grasped / 1.Ask / talk with child / 2.Repeat pronunciation: teach agin	Demonstrate: tongue, mouth, breath type / Repeat pronunciation / Control / abstract child with toy	Praise child: Pronunciation is grasped / Repeat pronunciation / Control / abstract child with toy	Take notes

Fig. 4. Experience map of the rehabilitation in home health care

- **Gain point: Attractive Toys and Games.** Children's mood is obviously improved and their attention is attracted when they have toy or food. Children intend to more actively cooperate with parents when interesting games are combined to the training.
- **Pain Point: Concentration.** Intensive training in a relative long time is necessary for impaired children in order to deepen study impression and consolidate the results. However, the attention of children is a big challenge. Distraction of children is not a rare phenomenon. A long time training is unbearable for children.

2.2   Parents

The interview and questionnaire shows the experience of parents. Pain points almost concentrate on home training. One wow point, one gain point and four pain points are summarized.

- **Wow point: Progress of Rehabilitation.** There is no doubt that it is the most delighted moment when their children make an accurate pronunciation. Similarly, it is a great stimulation to be informed of an optimistic prospect of their children's rehabilitation. Hope of rehabilitation brings confidence and courage to them to overcome difficulties.
- **Gain point: Professional Guidance.** Almost all the parents know nothing about the knowledge of speech therapy before their children are diagnosed as speech-impairment. So the process for children to receive treatment is also the process for parents to learn. Parents intend to bring their children to the hospital or professional institution because of their confidence and trust in the therapists. A majority of them search for the methods that are conductive to rehabilitation in different approaches, such as professional books, internet, service institutions or other parents' experience.
- **Pain Point: Time-Consuming.** It is the critical age for children speech and language development from 2 to 6. Since the parents need to catch that period to assist their children's rehabilitation, it costs them lots of time for searching knowledge, preparing for training, running between hospitals and home and accompanying their kids.

- **Pain Point: Economic Pressure.** Although in the stable speech training period, it is necessary for the patients to receive professional assessment from the therapists periodically. The prospect of rehabilitation process and adjusted treatment plan has positive influence on the rehabilitation efficiency. The costs for a face to face diagnosis or treatment should be quite a lot. Moreover, other expenses should be taken into account such as travelling, assistive training devices and even the hotel expenses for the family from remote areas. Comparing with the public medical institutes, the private ones charge much more. It is quite a economic pressure for the family with a speech-impaired child.

- **Pain Point: Fatigue from Training.** On account of the lack in public medical resource in China, each patient can just get the face-to-face professional training 1 or 2 times per week averagely. The rest should be given by their parents who have to demonstrate the mouth type and tongue shape, handle the toys and increase the volume unconsciously for about 3 h of daily training. It is laborious to hold such a high strength training.

- **Pain Point: Uncontrollable Children.** Another big challenge in the speech training should be controlling the mood and attention of underage children. Although toys are useful to attract the attention, it will also divert children's attention from training itself. Accordingly, the negative mood and behave will disappoint their parents as well.

2.3 Speech Therapist

The pain points of them during training are similar with those of parents. But the experience could be better for them since they are professional and experienced. Therapists concern more about inconvenience in their work and how to perform better. One gain point and two pain points are summarized.

- **Gain Point: Appreciation of Their Work.** The biggest source of their sense of accomplishment must be the progress of the speech-impaired children. From the repulsion of the child in the first time to the warmly greeting and embrace when they are familiar with each other, the establishment of an intimate relationship shows the recognition of the children, which pleasures therapists and improves training efficiency. The positive feedback from parents about the previous training can bring confidence to them as well.

- **Pain point: Searching Record.** Searching the record of cases can be an annoying problem for therapists because a therapist will admit several speech-impaired children those whose are different in terms of speech ability, rehabilitation degree, frequency of treatment and training plans. They have no systemic database or uniform record method.

- **Pain Point: Limitation of Treatment.** In order to consolidate curative effect, the therapist suggests that the patients should take training in the daily life, which can improve pronunciation accuracy and proceed to next training. However, as we told about above, the contact frequency is not high enough for the therapist to follow up on children's training. Sometimes children will meet the standard in home training but the therapist cannot know it before the next treatment. It will influence the progress. Moreover, the communication between doctors and patients is neither in time nor frequent

3 Product Design and Implementation

Based on the analysis result, this study has designed an ICT-based speech training assistive product, which contains an application software on pad to learn courses and a smart hardware doll to watch and interact, to maintain those gain points and solve those pain points of each stakeholder. This product is supposed to improve the user experience of the stakeholders in the processes of treatment or training (See Fig. 5).

Fig. 5. Actor map of rehabilitation with speech training product

3.1 Main Function

Interaction and Gamification. Interest, for long-term rehabilitation training, is very important, especially to the children. The speech training assistive item has animation, interaction and the combination of training and games. These can improve the enjoyment so that children will concentrate upon it. The virtual software can catch the phonation and the result will be expressed as a dynamic "Whac-A-Mole" game to show the score (Fig. 6). With the exception of demonstration in the training, the cartoon hardware can play audios transcribed by parents such as nursery rhyme or poem, when children interact with the roly-poly using the motion like swing, flap or rotation (Fig. 7).

Professional knowledge. Speech training knowledge is supplied by this product such as pronunciation points of consonant, training skills and announcements (Fig. 8). Moreover, a powerful database is supplied by this product to salvage parents' time which contains the data of pinyin, words, picture, tongue type and breath.

Substitute. This product can transcribe the demonstration videos of parents using the app. Then, videos will be played when the children are training (Fig. 6). Therapists can deepen children's impression on themselves by recording the videos. The video can not

Fig. 6. Learning page on App

Fig. 7. Hardware: roly-poly doll

Fig. 8. Course recording page on APP

only reduce their workload, but also display mouth types. The hardware shows the motion of tongue and its relative position to palate, which enables the patients feel directly and is convenient for parents and therapists to explain.

Visualization of the progress. The ICT-based product can record the voice of children by the speech recognition technology. The record will contain: number of pronunciation, degree of accuracy and spelling mistakes. To degree of accuracy can be count by the comparison of orthoepy and the children's pronunciation. And then the accuracy rate is counted by dividing number of all correct pronunciation by number of pronunciation so that the mastery degree of this pronunciation can be reflected. In that way, parents can see the progress directly (Fig. 9) and the therapist will get hold of the training time, mastery of pronunciation and error rate.

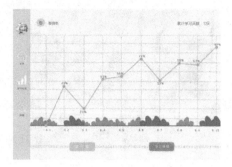

Fig. 9. Progress recorded page

Training program. The contents of home speech training in the daily life is decided by parents of patients, which is not professional and efficient adequately. Instead of that traditional way, the software of the ICT-based product intent to be set to recommend training contents that are suitable for the rehabilitation progress. Additionally, the therapists can check the situation of their patients through the remote device so that an appropriate training contents for further treatment can be sent to them. We intend to found an information sharing platform for speech-impaired rehabilitation, in which parents and therapists can communicate with each other and the training contents and plans can be uploaded and downloaded.

3.2   Use Flow

Figure 10 shows the use flow of the main function which has been realized at present:

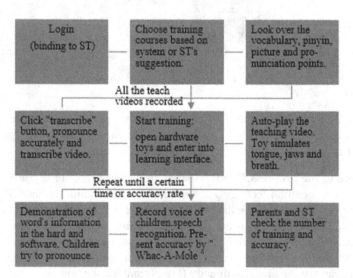

Fig. 10. Use flow of the product

4 Product Test

4.1 Usability Test

After realization of the product, this study conducted usability tests to eight speech-impaired children and their parents according to the experience problems summarizing above. Usability test had been defined as a technique to evaluate a product by the use of users [14]. The main test content is that children proceeding speech training for 5 min using the ICT-based product under parents accompaniment. Simultaneously, they do traditional speech training for 5 min as control group. During these two tests, the emotion of object children in each step is graded by researchers (from positive emotion 2 to negative one -2). The result will be convincing in combination with eye tracker test. In addition, frequency of parents demonstrating the correct pronunciation has been recorded in these two tests.

Figure 11 shows that this object's emotion improves when the pronunciation game feedbacks. Comparing with the traditional process, the emotion of tested children improve in five minutes training with ICT-based product (Fig. 12).

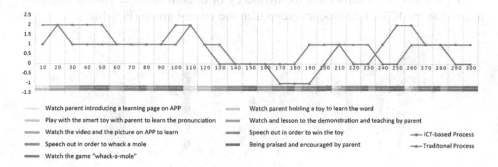

Fig. 11. Emotion map of one child in traditional and ICT-based process

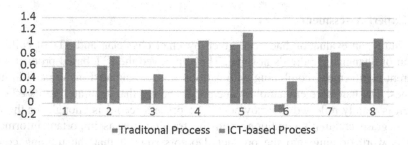

Fig. 12. Average scores of the children's emotion in 5 min

Eye tracker test had been done on the tested children letting them watching the pronunciation training interface in order to get the heat map. In the heat map, darkest areas is the representative for longest and most frequently watched places. In Fig. 13, it

Fig. 13. Heat map of the learning page

can be discovered that apart from his mother's face, the tested child prefer watching the dynamic games elements to the picture and words.

In the other hand, in the video-record step, parents can finish recording a video for one lesson smoothly in one to two minutes. Furthermore, in the training, loop playback of the pre-record videos may partly take the place of demonstrations because the children can imitate the pronunciation in the videos under guidance of their parents. The experiment result shows that the frequency of demonstration of parents had been reduced in the ICT-based product group than the control group (Fig. 14).

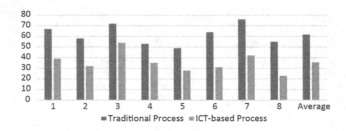

Fig. 14. Times of parents' demonstration in 5 min

4.2 Expert Assessment

In this study, an evaluation had been given by chief physician and STs of child care division of Shanghai children's hospital. They approved the ICT-based product which are parent-involvement, combining with cartoon image, animated picture and in mode of games. The hardware emulation is deemed to be not that accurate. So its effect on children is mainly reflected in enjoyment. The process record is enough for the therapists to grasp children's condition. And the training time is important information which is worth joining into the product. Doctors suggest that the training courses recommending function is quite useful for the therapist's follow-up and adjustment training plans in time. It maybe can reduce the treatment frequency in the public medical service.

4.3   Result of the Test

In allusion to usability, usability 5Es model [15] was proposed by Whitney Quesenbery: effective, efficient, engaging, error tolerant, easy to learn. Specific to this product, the ICT-based assistive product is effective because it can supply videos to children to imitate as well as pictures for understanding. The efficient is embodied in that it can reduce the time of lesson preparation, cost and demonstration times for parents. Moreover, with the help of it, ST can adjust the training plan in time so that the progress of rehabilitation will be accelerated. The engaging shows in that the design of cartoonlization and gamification improves child's interest. The product is error tolerant since the teach videos can be re-recorded if parents or therapists are not satisfied and the training lesson is free to choose. As a design for children, the use flow and interface design is easy to understand, which is proved in the evaluation experiments. In conclusion, this product fundamentally conforms to the 5Es model and with good usability.

5   Conclusion

In the system of speech-impairment rehabilitation, all of speech-impaired children, parents and therapists are noteworthy and there is an interaction among them. In this paper, the user experience of those three stakeholders in each touch point in the process of rehabilitation had been analyzed and according to this, an ICT-based assistive training product had been designed. And then this product had been implemented and verified the usability. However, there is still shortage of this research because of the difficulty of recruiting objects, privacy protection of the patients and time limitation. The product is still being modified and iterated.

Acknowledgement. This paper is sponsored by Shanghai Pujiang Program (13PJC072), Shanghai Philosopy and Social Science Program (2012BCK001), Shanghai Jiao Tong University Interdisciplinary among Hunmnity, Social Science and Natural Science Fund (13JCY02). Moreover, we thank to doctors, speech therapist, nurses from Children's Hospital of Shanghai and the students of Shanghai Jiao Tong University who contributed to this research.

References

1. Nmeth, G., Olaszy, G., Vicsi, K., et al.: Talking machines?!–. J. Infocommunications, **8** (2009)
2. Enderby, P., Philipp, R.: Speech and language handicap: towards knowing the size of the problem. Int. J. Lang. Commun. Disord. **21**(2), 151–165 (1986)
3. Application of deafness gene diagnosis to hearing loss prevention and intervention of birth defects (in Chinese). J. Chin. Sci. J. Hear. Speech Rehabil., **6**, 8–10 (2011)
4. Drigas, A., Petrova, A.: ICTs in Speech and Language Therapy. J. iJEP **4**, 49–54 (2014)
5. Statistical Communique on the Development of the Work for Persons with Disabilities in 2013(in Chinese). http://www.cdpf.org.cn
6. Standardization, I.O.F.: Ergonomics of Human-system Interaction: Part 210: Human-centred Design for Interactive Systems. ISO (2010)

7. Robert, G.: Bringing user experience to healthcare improvement: The concepts, methods and practices of experience-based design. Radcliffe Publishing, Abingdon (2007)
8. Sen, E., Yurtsever, S.: Difficulties experienced by families with disabled children. J. J. Spec. Pediatr. Nurs. **12**, 238–252 (2007)
9. Murphy, N.A., Christian, B., Caplin, D.A., et al.: The health of caregivers for children with disabilities: caregiver perspectives. J. Child: Care, Health Dev. **33**, 180–187 (2007)
10. Hoben, K., Morris, J.: PATSy: innovations in learning for speech and language therapy. J. Bulletin of the Royal College of Speech and Language Therapists (2005)
11. Danubianu, M., Tobolcea, I., Pentiuc, S.G.: Advanced Technology in Speech Disorder Therapy of Romanian Language. J. arXiv preprint arXiv:09123969 (2009)
12. Morelli, N., Tollestrup, C.: New representation techniques for designing in a systemic perspective. J. Nordes (2009)
13. Jenkinson, C., Coulter, A., Bruster, S.: The Picker Patient Experience Questionnaire: development and validation using data from in-patient surveys in five countries. J. Int. J. Qual. Health Care **14**, 353–358 (2002)
14. Nielsen, J.: Usability engineering. Elsevier, Amsterdam (1994)
15. Quesenbery, W.: Balancing the 5Es of Usability. J. Cutter IT J. **17**, 4–11 (2004)

"Keep What You've Earned": Encouraging Sailors to Drink Responsibly

Kristina Cook[1](✉), Erin Brennan[2], Colleen Gray[3], and Teha Kennard[2]

[1] Booz Allen Hamilton, Ashburn, VA, USA
cook_kristina@bah.com
[2] Booz Allen Hamilton, Washington, D.C., USA
{brennan_erin,Kennard_Teha}@bah.com
[3] Booz Allen Hamilton, Winston-Salem, NC, USA
gray_colleen@bah.com

Abstract. The U.S. Navy contracted Booz Allen Hamilton, a strategy and technology consulting firm, to develop and implement a social marketing campaign to encourage Sailors to drink responsibly. The "Keep What You've Earned" campaign, launched in April 2013, aims to encourage Sailors to drink responsibly through the use of affirmative messaging, reminding them of all they have accomplished in their Navy careers. The primary product of the social marketing campaign is a mobile application game that combines role-playing with real-life tools to help encourage Sailors to drink responsibly. Navy leadership has indicated that the Keep What You've Earned campaign, in combination with other cultural and policy-related changes, contributed to a decline in the number of reported alcohol-related incidents.

Keywords: Social marketing · Alcohol abuse prevention · Health communication model · Gamification · Behavior change · U.S. Navy

1 Introduction and Background

1.1 The Issue

According to the 2008 Department of Defense (DoD) Survey of Health Related Behaviors Among Active Duty Personnel, "binge drinking" in the Navy increased from 42 % in 2005 to 48 % in 2008 [1]. Eighteen percent of Navy respondents reported heavy drinking (more than five drinks on the same occasion at least once a week), and one in five heavy drinkers indicated that they had experienced serious consequences as a result of drinking in the past year. There are a number of serious issues and consequences associated with binge drinking, including failure to fulfill major responsibilities at work, school, or home; legal and financial problems; sexual assault and/or domestic violence; alcohol-related illness and death; and depression and suicide.

The Department of Navy Alcohol and Drug Abuse Prevention (NADAP) office launched the "Right Spirit" Campaign in 1995 to deglamorize the use of alcohol; however, NADAP recognized a need to reinvigorate the campaign after many years of

© Springer International Publishing Switzerland 2015
A. Marcus (Ed.): DUXU 2015, Part III, LNCS 9188, pp. 575–586, 2015.
DOI: 10.1007/978-3-319-20889-3_53

stagnation. An assessment of the Right Spirit Campaign was conducted in 2004 and the following observations were documented regarding alcohol abuse prevention strategies:

- Avoid moralistic and prohibitionist tones. The Right Spirit was perceived by many as having those tones.
- Target specific and definable problems, such as drinking and driving and underage drinking, for which it is possible to build a consensus.
- Target specific populations. The Right Spirit targeted the entire Navy when alcohol abuse was simply not an issue with the majority of Sailors. Identify and target those populations and situations that are really problems.
- Create an effective education and training system that is rational, has identifiable standards, is measurable and remains current. The Right Spirit only partially addressed these issues.
- Ensure that there is a data reporting system that is current, accurate, and easy to use so that trends can be identified and program and policies guided by data, not ideology [2].

These observations were used by NADAP as evidence to support the need for a revamped approach to alcohol abuse prevention efforts. NADAP contracted with Booz Allen Hamilton (hereinafter referred to as Booz Allen), a strategy and technology consulting firm (disclosure: the authors of this paper are employed by Booz Allen), for help in designing developing, and implementing its new campaign, as described in subsequent sections of this paper.

1.2   Review of Related Literature and Work

Prior to developing the campaign concept in 2012, the team conducted a landscape and literature review to better understand the challenge (alcohol misuse/abuse) and nature, extent, and efficacy of existing interventions. Key observations included:

- A number of studies reviewed documented the rise in alcohol abuse and alcohol-related incidents among young adults, especially college students. One study found that "Driving Under the Influence" infractions have increased since 1998 from 2.3 million students to 2.8 million [3]. Reported incidents of sexual assault, rape, and death involving alcohol had also increased among college students. Social norms were cited as a reason for drinking [3].
- Like the aforementioned studies, DoD and service-specific studies found evidence of binge drinking and alcohol misuse among young adult service members ages 18 −24. Specifically, the Navy conducted a study on alcohol and tobacco use to identify trends [5]. More than 50 % of binge drinking was reported by service members aged 21−25 followed by 42 % aged 26−34. In another study, conducted by the Journal of Studies on Alcohol and Drugs, service members age 21−25 were more likely to be frequent heavy drinkers than all other age groups [6].
- Many factors contribute to the probability of one's drinking habits, including demographic information such as where one grew up, the kind of family they have, experiences in childhood, etc. This study specifically concentrated on college

drinking behaviors and trends [4]. They found that there are many factors on college campuses that affect drinking, such as the local community and availability of alcohol. Other factors included biological and genetic predisposition to use, belief system and personality, and expectations about the effects of alcohol [4].

- While there are treatment programs and resources for alcohol addiction, only a small portion of programs or interventions focused specifically on alcohol abuse prevention. Even fewer such program targeted young adult service members or Sailors. Many of the existing prevention programs put the pressure on the "drinker" [7]. For example, the Department of Defense's "That Guy" campaign uses humor to show audiences that drinking affects behavior in a negative way, making the drinker look like a fool. Also, the "rethinking drinking" campaign, developed by the National Institute on Alcohol Abuse and Alcoholism (NIAAA), is a personal plan to reduce alcohol use. It begins clearly with an "are you ready" question, putting the pressure of committing to a plan on the participant [7].

- Social norm campaigns were tested on college campuses, however, it is hard to measure the effectiveness of these campaigns. Most studies reported that social norm campaigns work best when combined with other interventions [8].

- NIAAA launched a College Drinking – Changing the Culture campaign that uses a 3−1 approach. The campaign targets three different audiences (Individuals, Including At-Risk or Alcohol-Dependent Drinkers, the Student Body as a whole, and the College and the Surrounding Community) through the same campaign [4]. Research strongly supported this comprehensive approach of addressing multiple audiences with complementary campaign components [4].

- Research indicated that "anti-drinking" campaigns can often be seen as prohibitionist with moralistic tones. These types of campaigns were found to cause the very things they are trying to prevent, alcohol abuse. Some perceived these campaigns to frame all alcohol use in a negative way and those who drink it to be wrong [9].

- Smartphones were found to be underutilized as modes of alcohol abuse prevention efforts, but have shown promise in other types of health behavioral interventions, especially when best practices in designing for behavior change are adopted. Studies suggest that a number of inherent features implicit in smartphones make them good candidates for the delivery of behavioral interventions. For example, as portable devices that are highly valued by individuals, they tend to be switched on and remain with the owner throughout the day [22–24]. Therefore, they offer the opportunity to bring behavioral interventions into important real life contexts where people make decisions about their health and encounter challenges to change [23, 25, 26].

In reviewing relevant work and literature, the campaign team found that there were programs in place to treat alcohol abuse and alcoholism for Navy service members, but there had been less concentration on preventing abuse (though there are efforts underway to tackle the issue). Thus, there was a need to create a culture of responsible drinking behaviors in the Navy to curb misuse before it became a bigger problem. Furthermore, the team determined that the design of the campaign would be most effective using a socio-ecological approach, addressing the multitude of factors that influence alcohol-related beliefs and behaviors. In addition, the design needed to cater to the needs, preferences, and interests of young adult Sailors, many of whom prefer visual messages delivered through online vs. offline mediums. As such, the campaign should make use of the inherent opportunities implicit in social media, multimedia, and mobile channels. Furthermore, it should avoid messages that could be seen as prohibitionist or moralistic in tone, as well as messages that center too much on long-term health consequences (vs. more immediate job performance and career consequences).

2 Methods

In September 2011, NADAP contracted Booz Allen, to evaluate Sailors' attitudes and behaviors regarding alcohol use and to develop a health communications campaign to help decrease the number of alcohol-related incidents. The Booz Allen team was made up of health communication and digital innovation subject matter experts, who worked closely with NADAP leadership and alcohol abuse prevention personnel in the development and execution of the campaign.

Seeking to deter alcohol abuse among young, enlisted Sailors within U.S. Navy populations, the authors identified three target audiences, including Sailors (ages 18 −24), leaders, and community groups, to address both the campaign's individualistic (behavioral) and collectivist (cultural) goals, modeled similarly after the 3−1 approach found in the NIAAA campaign [4].

The primary target audience for the campaign is U.S. Navy Sailors aged 18−24 years, because formative research indicated that this population has a greater prevalence of alcohol incidents and is thus at significant risk of abusing alcohol and engaging in binge-drinking behavior [1]. A second audience for the campaign is Navy leadership, because they can have a positive influence on setting the cultural tone (norms) of responsible drinking behavior at both base and Navy-wide levels due to the hierarchical nature of the military. The third target market is community partners – including both private and public sector partners – because they (like leadership) can support the notion of responsible drinking behavior within the Navy organization culture, including disseminating messages through local bars and establishments.

This three-pronged target audience approach is based on the socio-ecological framework, which suggests that health behaviors are affected by multiple levels of influence, including the individual (e.g., Sailor), interpersonal/group (e.g., shipmates, Command), institutional (e.g., U.S. Navy), and community (e.g., fleet-concentrated regions) factors and public policy (e.g., Uniform Code of Military Justice) [10]. Research showed that community-based alcohol abuse prevention and intervention programs can have a positive impact on drinking habits [11]. Research also supported the implementation of a community partnership to reduce drinking and driving and underage drinking, given that working with the local community might encourage the Navy personnel to gain an emotional connection to their community making them feel responsible for their actions [4]. Family and friends outside of the Navy were not considered a primary audience for this campaign given that most young, enlisted service members must leave home as a function of joining the Navy and live in the barracks (military housing).

2.1   Health Communications Model

Upon establishing the target audiences, the team, using the National Cancer Institute's (NCI) Health Communications Model, conducted quantitative and qualitative research to use as the foundation for developing the "Keep What You've Earned" campaign [13]. Methods included focus groups, intercept interviews, one-on-one interviews, campaign concept testing, and a survey.

The NCI model is a science-based framework for health communications and social marketing, which is based on formative research, continuous evaluation and improvement. The stages of the communications process include:

- Stage 1: Planning and Strategy Development (e.g., communications product audit, baseline media report, literature review, intercept interviews)
- Stage 2: Developing and Pretesting Concepts, Messages, and Materials (e.g., concept/message development, focus groups)
- Stage 3: Implementing the Program
- Stage 4: Assessing Effectiveness and Making Refinements [13]

The formative research included a literature review (including works cited in Introduction and Background), materials audit, baseline media report, 396 Sailor intercept interviews, and 17 interviews with alcohol and drug abuse prevention personnel. This was followed by concept development and testing with 16 focus groups, leading to a final campaign concept, "Keep What You've Earned."

Key findings that emerged from these stages and informed the development of this campaign plan include:

- Sailors primarily drink because of stress related to the workplace, their families, and life changes (moving locations, new surroundings, new peers).
- Sailors indicated that the most significant consequence of alcohol abuse to them is Navy discipline (alcohol related incident, separation, loss of pay/rank).
- Affirmative messages/images combined with a reminder of what they could lose as a result of alcohol abuse resonated with Sailors of all ages and ranks.
- Sailors identified videos and mobile as the preferred methods of communication.
- The Navy's alcohol abuse prevention efforts need to be locally driven.
- The campaign should use the desire to avoid negative, immediate job-related consequences (vs. delayed, long-term health consequences) as the prime motivating factor to encourage to people to take positive health actions.
- Although the desired outcome (drinking responsibly) has health benefits, the connection to their job, not health, is effective in the message.

Based on the aforementioned research findings, NADAP implemented the Navy's flagship responsible drinking campaign, "Keep What You've Earned," in April 2013. The campaign uses value-affirmative messaging to remind Sailors of how hard they have worked and how much they have to lose [14]. The campaign follows a social marketing approach—a behavior change theory involving the use of commercial marketing techniques grounded by behavioral science to promote the adoption of attitudes or behaviors that will improve the health or well-being of a stakeholder group or of society as a whole [15]. Furthermore, the campaign uses the tactic of motivating people to take positive health actions using the desire to avoid a negative, near-term career consequences as the prime motivation based on the high value Sailors place on their careers in the Navy, as indicated during formative research methods [14].

A combination of traditional and non-traditional campaign elements enabled NADAP to reach key stakeholders in their communities. Through the development of 40 + tailored and targeted materials, which worked together in unison, the team increased awareness of the campaign and educated primary and secondary audiences on responsible drinking. These products provided clear and direct information to encourage Sailors to drink responsibly and were accessible across multiple platforms (online, mobile, print). Some of the most popular products of the campaign are its testimonial videos, which support research that testimonials are more effective compared to simple informational health messages [16].

2.2   Online Interventions

As indicated in the above findings, traditional print products had become a barrier to reaching younger Sailors. Instead, interviews and focus groups with Sailors revealed that they wanted to be reached on the platforms they were most engaged with—video sites, social media, and mobile applications. This is consistent with research findings observed in the initial literature review, which revealed the efficacy of online interventions on health behaviors and documented promising, albeit preliminary, results in the area of serious games for advancing health. While the average public health campaign, done well, can impact roughly 5 % of the target population's behavior, online behavior change interventions can expect to impact twice that amount based on preliminary studies [17, 18]. The results are small but statistically significant, while also offering an advantage of lower costs and larger reach [18]. However, these online interventions are most effective when they employ behavior change strategies in combination with persuasive design strategies [17].

Armed with feedback on Sailor communication preferences and literature review findings from the planning stage, the campaign utilized a combination of web 2.0 tools and tactics, "gamification" (the use of game design elements in non-game contexts, such as for responsible drinking interventions and learning), and social and traditional media outreach to engage Sailors.

The Keep What You've Earned webpage is seen as the centralized information hub on the campaign with access to all campaign materials, which results in hundreds of downloads of campaign materials each month (see full list of metrics below).

2.3   Pier Pressure Mobile Application

One of the campaign's primary platforms is "Pier Pressure," a mobile game grounded in multi-disciplinary research from the behavioral psychology, persuasive technology, mHealth, and serious game domains. Pier Pressure integrates best practices in software design and game mechanics with public health theories and cognitive behavioral research insights. It takes a "show, don't tell" approach, enabling Sailors to explore the consequences of alcohol-related decisions and behaviors on their job performance and career attainment (two factors Sailors indicated as extremely important and motivating to them) through a novel, entertaining, and safe medium.

As observed during the team's initial literature review, games have shown initial promise as a method for motivating audiences to engage in healthy behaviors [17, 18]. Although the field of serious games is still in its infancy, promising pilots have emerged in the area of games for self-care, exercise, autism, sexual and reproductive health, diabetes, asthma, confronting death, and more [20]. An empirical review conducted by Cugelman (2013) found seven common ingredients of successful gamification systems grounded in behavioral theories, including providing feedback on performance (receiving constant feedback throughout the experience), reinforcement (gaining rewards, avoiding punishments), comparing progress (monitoring progress with self and others), and fun and playfulness (playing out an alternative reality) [17]. These core persuasive ingredients of gamification were incorporated into the app through dialogue with non-player characters, leaderboards, and the alternate reality of mini-games representing the work-life and the play-life of a Sailor avatar.

This body of knowledge was called upon throughout the planning and design of Pier Pressure, a multi-part app featuring a role-playing game true to the "Navy experience." In keeping with the "fun + function" mantra, the mobile app engages Sailors in gameplay while indirectly sharing messages about responsible drinking. The game is coupled with practical resources to help Sailors practice responsible drinking behaviors in real life, including a blood alcohol content (BAC) calculator and local taxi cab search.

Through gameplay, Sailors are encouraged to think about the repercussions of alcohol abuse, and are reminded of positive steps they could take to avoid incidents, such as taking a cab and not drinking on an empty stomach. To accomplish this, the game presented a virtual environment that allowed players to explore the effects of alcohol abuse through a role-playing game and presented them with frequent, game-embedded messaging to reinforce desired concepts. Though not intended for training, the app could be accurately described as a "serious game" (i.e., a game designed for a primary purpose other than pure entertainment). While engaging and entertaining, this product's primary aim was to affect beliefs and behaviors through messaging and immersive gameplay. As a function of being a serious game, the game must be appealing and enticing enough to overcome the barriers of educational messages about responsible drinking behavior throughout gameplay [19]. In his book chapter on game-based learning, Prensky (2001) explains that the role of "fun" in the learning process in that it aids in relaxation and motivation: relaxation enables the learner to take things in easier, while motivation inspires them to put forth effort without resentment [19].

Players begin the game by selecting and customizing a Sailor avatar. The overall gameplay follows the pattern of a natural "day" where players' characters go to work and then go out to a bar with friends, making choices along the way. While "at work" players will engage in a mini-game based on the "tower defense" game genre, in which you must load crates onto Navy ships and carriers at the pier.

After work, players will make decisions about "going out" for the evening. These choices include whether and/or how much to drink and if to eat a meal before going out. The "going out" portion of the game is set in a bar scene where one plays a variation of shuffleboard (a.k.a., shufflepuck). While playing, the user is presented with "power-up" opportunities, either by choosing to drink more than previously intended or by alternating alcoholic drinks with water. But players are forewarned: choices made at the bar will affect players' level at work the next day, which in turn affects their character's evaluations. Smart drinking choices will result in achieving the next pay grade, while poor choices and performance at work result in separation from the Navy (game over).

The game also includes two of Paredes et al.'s conceptualization of games for health behavior change. There are also forced pauses after the "work game" and the "evening game" involving fictional text message conversations with the non-player characters in the game. These forced pauses and prompts allow for introspection and have been show to assist in players' reflection and increase people's awareness of their own problems [21]. The game also involves progress as a proxy for self-efficacy; the progress players see their character making as they make responsible choices and move up the ranks allows players to realize that change is possible [21].

The app features leaderboards enabling Sailors to compete with their friends and shipmates. By making responsible drinking choices, players will advance through the game and raise their score on the leaderboard, while irresponsible choices will interfere with their ability to progress through the game and advance their careers.

The mobile application game was developed using Unity3D, a third-party game development engine. Gameplay mechanics were developed by collaboratively iterating on prototypes, with the two primary mini-games being inspired by the popular mobile game "Plants vs. Zombies" and the offline game of shuffleboard, respectively. For instance, the shuffleboard game is based on a "casual game" model present in many of the most popular and addictive games. This model dictates the use of a single verb (in this case, a puck throw) and a rapid, simple feedback loop in which the player takes an action, gets immediate feedback, and adjusts his/her mental model for the next action. Similarly, the other minigame was based on design conventions for audiences seeking a more intricate experience. This design started from a proven mechanic ("tower defense"), and was iterated upon as much as possible, resulting in a game which was relatable to Navy Sailors.

2.4 Secondary Audience Outreach Activities

To engage Navy leadership, a set of leadership messaging was developed to provide key messaging and talking points to ensure that campaign messages remained new and fresh each month. Presentation briefings were also developed that provided an overview of the campaign that ADCOs, DAPAs, Navy public affairs personnel, and other military leaders can present to Sailors and their local communities to promote responsible drinking at the environmental level and enact behavior change.

In reaching the secondary audience of community partners, formal and informal partnerships were developed throughout the launch and implementation of the campaign with organizations including, but not limited to: the U.S. Navy Office of Information (CHINFO) and public affairs community, Navy and Marine Corps Public

Health Center (NMCPHC), Navy Exchange (NEX), Navy Morale, Welfare and Recreation Program (MWR), Coalition of Sailors Against Destructive Decisions (CSADD), and the Partnership at DrugFree.org. NADAP worked with official partners on promoting the website, tools and resources via their social media channels.

For example, NADAP engaged CHINFO and the Navy public affairs community to promote Keep What You've Earned messages and materials on the official U.S. Navy social media sites, including Twitter, Flickr, YouTube and Pinterest. Sample social media messages were provided to partners as an easy starting point to promote the campaign using consistent messaging, and were encouraged to tailor the posts as they saw fit. Lastly, a Virtual Partner Summit was held in early 2014 near the campaign's one-year anniversary to further collect feedback from these secondary audiences and incorporate those findings into the future development of the campaign.

3 Results

In September 2013, the U.S. Navy's 21st Century Sailor Office, which oversees NADAP, announced a 51 % decrease in alcohol incidents during the summer months (Memorial Day through Labor Day 2013) compared to the same period the previous year (2012). These figures were calculated based on the U.S. Navy's Alcohol and Drug Management Information Tracking System (ADMITS) alcohol incident numbers pulled in September 2013.

The Navy credits the Keep What You've Earned campaign, in combination with a variety of other supporting cultural and policy-related measures and changes (e.g., random breathalyzers and restricted alcohol sale hours on base), with contributing to the 51 % decline. While system limitations make it impossible to meaningfully attribute a certain percentage of the change to the campaign vs. other anti-abuse measures, leadership has cited the Keep What You've Earned campaign as playing a significant role. This impact is attributed to its social ecological framework and its deliberate use of applied social marketing and persuasive technology principles that targeted the individual and contextual factors associated with alcohol use.

The Keep What You've Earned campaign's impact has been further substantiated through a variety of other mechanisms, including feedback collected through a Navy-wide survey. The survey, conducted by NADAP and disseminated to Sailors through the Navy Personnel Research, Studies and Technology (NPRST) in April 2014, was open for six weeks and closed in May 2014. Over 1,400 Navy stakeholders participated in the survey, which was promoted through social media channels and a Navy Newsstand article. Survey participants shared information about their alcohol-related beliefs and behaviors as well as the Keep What You've Earned campaign. Findings included:

- About 1 in 3 respondents reported noticing a positive change in behavior towards drinking over the past year.
- Encouraging responsible drinking is now seen as the focus of leadership messaging (54 %) as opposed to discouraging drinking in general (16 %).

- Sailors specifically mentioned an increase in awareness of safe ride programs (45 %), which were also viewed by Sailors as the most effective measure.
- 95 % of respondents had seen or heard alcohol abuse prevention messaging in the Navy, and 76 % had heard of the Keep What You've Earned campaign.
- 31 % of respondents were motivated by the Keep What You've Earned campaign to perform a desired action (e.g., decrease consumption, talk to a Sailor).
- 80 % of respondents said the campaign is very effective or effective.

In addition to these qualitative findings, communication outcome metrics indicate that the campaign was very well received by Sailors, Navy leadership, alcohol abuse prevention personnel, partner organizations, and media from coast to coast. Communication outcomes/results from April 2013–August 2014 include:

- 47,101 + website page views and 43,212 + website unique visitors
- 9,708 + downloads of campaign materials
- 29,552 + social media interactions (likes, retweets, comments, etc.)
- 13,200 + views of campaign PSA videos on YouTube and Vimeo
- 33,790 + Flickr account views (associated with the social media posts)
- 1,450 + online pledges and 22 grassroot events
- 159 + news articles with an estimated 1 billion + impressions
- 5,000 + mobile app users/downloads and more than 25,000 + gameplay sessions
- 473,000 + estimated impressions from Navy Times mobile web ads for mobile app

These figures are better contextualized in the context of the campaign's intended primary audience of young, enlisted Sailors, which comprise about 72,000 of the estimated 266,778 enlisted Sailors in the Navy (data as of February 2015) [12]. Beyond target audience validation and behavioral change observations, the Keep What You've Earned campaign has been recognized for excellence in communication through eight industry awards, allowing the campaign to gain third-party validation, credibility, and trust.

4 Discussion

Taken together, these results (i.e., the reduction in the number of alcohol-related incidents, the positive feedback yielded through survey and focus group methods, and the campaign reach and engagement outcome measures) suggest that the Keep What You've Earned campaign has demonstrated initial success in helping to encourage responsible drinking among Sailors. Its three-pronged approach, coupled with its use of novel persuasive technology and applied social marketing techniques, is at the root of its success. Although these findings are preliminary, practitioners can consider these approaches as logical and theoretically promising, and use these methods as a basis for further experimentation and testing.

The Navy plans to build on these strengths and continue to refine and expand in the areas of socio-ecological digital-based interventions, as well as in the areas of research to further validate claims of the campaign's impact on Sailors behavior. Specifically, the team plans to continue to evolve its Pier Pressure app to include additional practical tools to support Sailors in goal setting and self-monitoring, and to refine its gameplay to increase engagement and ease of use and to promote sustained us through greater integration of social sharing and community features.

Additional evaluation methods are planned to take place over the course of the campaign to determine changes in Sailors' knowledge, attitudes, and behaviors regarding alcohol use within the Navy. These methods include follow-up focus groups and annual surveys on Sailors' knowledge, attitudes and behaviors regarding alcohol use, and further objective analysis of alcohol incidents before and after the campaign launch.

Acknowledgements. Booz Allen would like to thank the Navy Alcohol and Drug Abuse Prevention Office for their leadership and support in the development and implementation of the Keep What You've Earned campaign, and for their support in sharing these findings and best practices with communications practitioners in the research, academic, government, and professional industry.

References

1. Department of Defense (DoD). DoD Survey of Health Related Behaviors Among Active Duty Personnel (2008)
2. JHT Services. Renewing the Right Spirit, History and Assessment of the Right Spirit and a Proposal for Its Renewal, 28 April 2004
3. U.S. Department of Health and Human Services (National Institutes of Health/National Institute of Alcohol Abuse and Alcoholism). What Colleges need to know now: An update on College Drinking Research (Rep. No. 07-5010). Retrieved from National Institute on Alcohol Abuse and Alcoholism website, November, 2007. http://www.collegedrinkingprevention. gov/niaaacollegematerials/
4. National Institute of Alcohol Abuse and Alcoholism (2007). A call to action: Recommendations for addressing excessive college drinking. College drinking: Changing the culture. [Gives and overview of an alcohol abuse prevention campaign along with strategies recommended]. Accessed 19 December 2011. http://www.collegedrinkingprevention.gov/ NIAAACollegeMaterials/TaskForce/CallToAction_00.aspx
5. Newell, C., Whittam, K., Uriell, Z.: 2010 alcohol and tobacco-related behaviors quick poll. Bureau of Naval Personnel, Millington, TN: Navy Personnel Research, Studies, and Technology (2010).
6. Bray, R.M., Brown, J.M., Pemberton, M.R., Williams, J., Jones, S.B., Vandermaas-Peeler, R.: Alcohol use after forces abstinence in basic training among United States Navy and Air Force trainees. J. Stud. Alcohol Drugs **71**(1), 15–22 (2010). http://www.jsad.com/jsad/article/ Alcohol_Use_After_Forced_Ab-stinence_in_Basic_Training_Among_United_States_N/ 4409.html
7. National Institute on Alcohol Abuse and Alcoholism (n.d.). National Institute of Health: National Institute on Alcohol Abuse and Alcoholism: Frequently asked questions for the general public [Answers the most frequently asked questions from the general public about alcohol abuse and alcoholism]. Accessed on 27 December 2011. http://www.niaaa.nih.gov/ FAQs/General-English/Pages/default.aspx

8. Trent, L., Stander, V., Thomsen, C., Merrill, L.: Alcohol abuse among US Navy recruits who were maltreated in childhood. Alcohol Alcohol. **42**(4), 370–375 (2007). doi:10.1093/alcalc/agm036

9. Medical news: Anti-drinking campaigns can increase alcohol abuse [Article on medicalnewstoday.com] (2010, February 25). Accessed on 27 December 2011. http://www.news-medical.net/news/20100225/Anti-drinking-campaigns-can-increase-alcohol-abuse.aspx

10. Dejong, W., Linda, M., Langford, Sc.D.: . A typology for campus-based alcohol prevention: moving toward environmental management strategies. J. Stud. Alcohol, Suppl. 14: 140–147 (2002)

11. Toomey, T.L., Lenk, K.M.: A review of environmental-based community interventions. Alcohol Res. Health, **34**(2): 163–166. Accessed on 2011. http://pubs.niaaa.nih.gov/publications/arh342/163-166.htm

12. U.S. Navy Status of the Navy. Accessed on 2015. www.navy.mil/navydata/nav_legacy

13. U.S. Department of Health and Human Services (National Institutes of Health, National Cancer Institute) Making Health Communication Programs Work. Accessed on 2004. http://www.cancer.gov/publications/health-communication/pink-book.pdf

14. Slater, M.D., Rouner, D.: Value-affirmative and value-protective processing of alcohol education messages that include statistical evidence or anecdotes. Commun. Res. **23**(2), 210–235 (1996)

15. Andreasen, A.R.: Marketing Social Change: Changing Behaviour to Promote Health, Social Development, and the Environment. Jossey Bass, San Francisco (1995)

16. Braverman, J.: Testimonials versus informational persuasive messages: the moderating effect of delivery mode and personal involvement. Commun. Res. **35**(5), 666–694 (2008)

17. Cugelman, B.: Gamification: What It Is and Why It Matters to Digital Health Behavior Change Developers. JMIR Serious Games, **1**(1) (2013).

18. Cugelman, B., Thelwall, M., Dawes, P.: Online interventions for social marketing health behavior change campaigns: a meta-analysis of psychological architectures and adherence factors. J. Med. Internet Res. **13**(1), e17 (2011)

19. Prensky, M.: Fun, play and games: What makes games engaging, Digital Game-Based Learning. McGraw-Hill, NewYork (2001)

20. Sawyer, B.: Games for Health Blog. Retrieved from gamesforhealth.org (2014)

21. Paredes, P., Tewari, A., Canny, J.: Design principles for the conceptualization of games for health behavior change. In: CHI 2013, Paris, France (2012)

22. Miller, G.: The smartphone psychology manifesto. Perspect. Psychol. Sci. **7**(3), 221–237 (2012)

23. Boschen, M.J., Casey, L.M.: The use of mobile telephones as adjuncts to cognitive behavioral psychotherapy. Prof. Psychol.: Res. Pract. **39**(5), 546–552 (2008)

24. Patrick, K., Griswold, W.G., Raab, F., Intille, S.S.: Health and the mobile phone. Am. J. Prev. Med. **35**(2), 177–181 (2008)

25. Morris, M.E., Aguilera, A.: Mobile, social, and wearable computing and the evolution of psychological practice. Prof. Psychol. Res. Pr. **43**(6), 622–626 (2012)

26. Preziosa, A., Grassi, A., Gaggioli, A., Riva, G.: Therapeutic applications of the mobile phone. Br. J. Guidance Couns. **37**(3), 313–325 (2009)

The Use of Generative Techniques in Co-design of mHealth Technology and Healthcare Services for COPD Patients

Anita Das[1(✉)], Silje Bøthun[1], Jarl Reitan[1], and Yngve Dahl[2]

[1] SINTEF Technology and Society, Trondheim, Norway
anita.das@sintef.no
[2] SINTEF ICT, Trondheim, Norway

Abstract. People suffering from COPD commonly experience exacerbations leading to hospital admissions. mHealth technologies holds a potential for improved healthcare delivery to this group, with a possible impact on preventing COPD exacerbations. Designing appropriate technology and services for people with COPD requires an in-depth understanding of their needs, values and life situation. Co-design is an approach where users are actively involved in the design process, with democratic participation and empowerment at its center. We involved COPD patients in exploring their perspective on how mHealth technology and appurtenant healthcare services could support them. By the use of generative tools, we identified central aspects that the participants experienced to be of importance related to their health condition and disease. We here report on the main findings using this approach and on reflections on the process.

Keywords: Design thinking · mHealth · Service design · Generative techniques · COPD

1 Introduction

Co-design, also known as participatory design, is an approach where various stakeholders (e.g. end users, employees, customers and citizens) are actively involved in the design process in order to identify, create, and ensure that new solutions are according to their needs. Healthcare is a complex domain with unforeseen incidents, changing contexts, and multiple stakeholders with particular needs, interests, roles, expectations, and power. This requires a particular attention when it comes to design, development, and implementation of technology in the healthcare domain. There are a number of health information systems that have poor usability and which do not consider the contextual aspects [1, 2], due to limited understanding and knowledge about the targeted user groups needs and the products' use context. The need to get insights about user characteristics and preferences, such as insights about users experiences', emotions, dreams, desires, use contexts, and, social and cultural influences are crucial to get a holistic understanding of the targeted user group. Also, the need to explore the diverse contexts surrounding a products' use, are aspects relevant for the design development process.

© Springer International Publishing Switzerland 2015
A. Marcus (Ed.): DUXU 2015, Part III, LNCS 9188, pp. 587–595, 2015.
DOI: 10.1007/978-3-319-20889-3_54

The aim of the current study was to use generative tools in an exploring context, to identify COPD patients' needs, desires, and, aspects related to their health condition and daily life situation, as the first step of the design development process of mHealth technology and appurtenant healthcare service for this patient group. We here report on the main findings using this approach and on reflections on the process.

1.1   Chronic Obstructive Pulmonary Disease

Chronic Obstructive Pulmonary Disease (COPD) is one of the leading causes of mortality and morbidity worldwide (fourth leading cause of death), and incurs significant healthcare and societal costs [3]. People suffering from COPD commonly experience exacerbations leading to hospital admissions [4, 5]. Such admissions are associated with deteriorated health status of the individual and involve considerable costs for the healthcare services [4, 5]. One of the main objectives in COPD management is to improve or preserve the patients' health status. Increasingly, patients with COPD are being managed at home to reduce health-related costs while trying to increase patients' comfort [6, 7].

The use of online health applications has increased the last decade, and people use such applications to search for information, manage their own health and illnesses, and, communicate with peers and healthcare providers [2, 8, 9]. Increasingly, people suffering from chronic diseases, use the Internet and social media as important support tools in their daily life. In the forthcoming future, it is expected that healthcare providers and clinicians increasingly implement communication portals to facilitate and support patients in their daily life, in order to provide quality care services in cost-efficient manners.

A recent systematic review of methodologies and patients' adherence to home tele-monitoring in COPD, recommended future projects to assess patients' needs, characteristics and acceptance of the technology prior to implementation in order to adjust the intervention to the target population [10]. Also, the need for increased considerations to more easy-to-use technology for patients with COPD, and to explore the potential of the technology to change patients' self-management behaviour is required [8, 10].

Online health applications are potential solutions for improved healthcare delivery to this patient group with a possible impact on preventing COPD exacerbations. Finding appropriate solutions for how the new technology and the various elements in the healthcare service should be integrated, are key factors that need to be addressed for service delivery to this patient group.

1.2   Co-design

Co-creation refers to any act of collective creativity, i.e. creativity that is shared by two or more people, and is a broad term ranging from physical to metaphysical, and from the material to the spiritual [11]. Co-design is by Sanders and Stappers (2008) described as a specific instance of co-creation, and is the creativity of designers and lay people working together in the design development process [11]. Usually, the co-design processes are led by design professionals and are used in development processes of products, services, or organizations [11–13]. During this process, there are various techniques to how to get the participants actively involved. Sanders (2002) distinguish between three approaches of interacting with users during the design process, these being what people do, say, and make [14]. Marketing research have focused on *what people say* (focus groups, interviews, questionnaires), applied anthropology have focused on observational research in *what people do*, and participatory design have focused on *what people make* [15]. According to Stappers and Sanders (2003) generative methods can be used in the design development process together with other methods in a converging perspectives approach that draw simultaneously from these three perspectives [15].

The make tools in design research, *(what people make)*, is focused on what people create from the toolkits designers provide them with, in order to facilitate them in expressing their thoughts, feelings, dreams and desires. In exploring contexts, users are involved in so called generative sessions, which inspires and informs the design team in the early phases of the design process [16]. A generative session is a meeting in which users do generative exercises; the participants are given tools such as illustrations, post-it notes, pictures, or, sets of expressive components, in order to create artifacts that express their thoughts, feelings, and ideas. For instance, this process can involve that the participants are given a "toolkit" of words or picture images, and are requested to make collages expressing good and bad aspects of the particular situation under study. As part of the sessions, the participants present and explain their artifacts and creations, to reveal their insights, anecdotes, and stories related to the topic. The results are then used as inspiration for the design team.

2 Methods

As part of the initial stage of a technology- and service design project, we conducted five separate co-design sessions with COPD patients.

2.1 Participant Inclusion and Procedure

Participants were recruited through the hospital, where a nurse took the initial contact with the patients, and where we later took contact with the participants by phone, informing them about the study and requested participation. The study got approval from the Norwegian Social Science Data Services, and all participants provided written informed consent when participating to the study.

A sample of five subjects with COPD was included in the study, three women and two men, aged 47–76 years. All were diagnosed with COPD and had been admitted to the hospital one time or more due to COPD exacerbations.

Individual co-design sessions were conducted with five participants. Most of these meetings took place in the patients' homes, except from one that took place at our office. A week before the meeting, participants received a workbook consisting of assignments about their current situation. This was to sensitize [16] them to the topic, promote reflection about their current experiences and situation, and prepare them for the themes that would be addressed in the co-design session. The participants were instructed to fill out the assignments in the workbook and bring it to our meeting (See Fig. 1) .

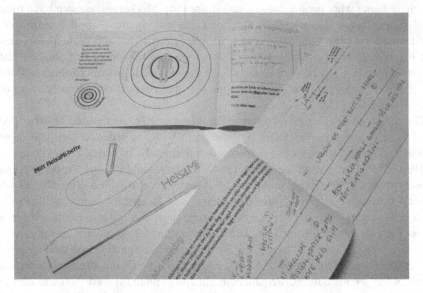

Fig. 1. Workbook that the participants completed before the individual co-design sessions

Two designers/researchers were present during each co-design session, where one had the role as facilitator and the other one as an observer. Standard procedure during each generative session was to go through the workbook before we conducted a semi-structured interview that was facilitated with the use of generative tools and activities, such as illustrations, pictures, and post-it notes. The facilitator guided the process, by asking questions and leading the conversation. The observer had the responsibility of taking notes and pictures. Each meeting typically lasted for 2–3 h each, and audio-recordings were taken during each session.

The overall theme was patients' perspectives regarding the participants' past, present and future daily life situation related to their health condition and healthcare services. More specifically we focused on their experiences, touch points and communication with the healthcare services; their needs and requirements; and technology use. Further on, the participants were to create their future scenario regarding daily life; expectations, ideas, visions, and touch points with various stakeholders and the healthcare service. Activities included: (1) construction of collages to map their feelings and experiences regarding their past and current daily life and healthcare services, e.g. used pictures and post-it notes to show previous health related and life experiences, created timeline regarding daily life, touch points, and stakeholders; (2) Making a future scenario e.g. used pictures, illustrations, and post-it notes; (3) Storytelling activities, where the participants shared their stories (See Figs. 2 and 3) .

Fig. 2. A collage created in a co-design process during a generative session to map feelings and experiences regarding past and current daily life and health condition of a participant.

Fig. 3. Participant describing a current daily-life scenario with the use of illustrations and sketches.

3   Results and Discussion

We here report on selected key findings by using generative tools and techniques in a co-design process with COPD patients. Further we reflect on the process of using such tools with this particular user group.

3.1   Key Findings

By using generative tools and techniques we identified that the participants experienced a number of challenges related to their illness, daily life activities, and communication with the healthcare services. The approach provided us with a vast and rich amount of data, and with great details about information that the participants reported that they had not articulated before. With the use of the tools provided, the participants created their past, present and future life scenario. They created collages of current services (focusing on healthcare services) with appurtenant touch points, and, of their desires related to these services, with input on technical solutions.

Selected key factors related to this was (1) the need for information about their illness, diagnose, and about how to cope with their health condition and situation, (2) the requirement to be respected and seen as a whole person (body, mind, spirit), (3) the need to get relief when it comes to organizing health related activities in communication with the healthcare services.

(1) *The patients' need of information about their illness, diagnose, and about how to cope with their health condition and situation.*

The participants expressed the need for more information about their illness, diagnose, and coping strategies related to their health condition and daily life situation. Some of the participants perceived that getting the diagnosis was a "no turn back", with limited possibilities of improved health condition in the future. However, one of the participants had experienced to turn better, and questioned if she really had COPD, as she perceived that this was impossible having the diagnosis. All the participants expressed limited information about COPD, particularly from their primary healthcare providers. The fear of stumbling over unwanted information restricted some of the participants in searching for information themselves. The need for tailor made information according to the illness development was therefore desired, and the possibility to obtain this information whenever it suited the individual was also requested.

(2) *The requirement to be respected and seen as a whole person (body, mind, spirit).*

Some of the participants reported not to be met in a dignified manner during incidents of COPD exacerbation. The desire to be seen holistic, and not merely as the person with COPD diagnosis was underlined to be important. Their personal stories revealed a need to be respected and seen holistic.

(3) *The need to get relief when it comes to organizing health related activities in communication with the healthcare services.*

The participants had various experiences regarding different stakeholders in their daily life. Some had a spouse or a family member that took good care of them, others felt alone and experienced that their illness involved a burden that they barely were capable of carrying. Some experienced that their primary care physician was an important teammate and resource, while others experienced that their physician had limited ability to see their needs. The involved participants had all experienced COPD exacerbations and emergency admittance at the hospital. The requirement of presenting their stories and experiences to each of the healthcare professional during this process was perceived to be extremely burdensome, as they commonly had breathing problems and anxiety in this situation. Also, having a chronic illness, they were regularly in contact with healthcare professionals, and experienced it as challenging to present their complete stories each and every time. As part of their illness management, the need for a reliable source or coordinator that they could rely on was therefore desired. An mHealth solution where key information about the patients previous medical history, medications etc. Was suggested to be a support tool for this means.

3.2 Reflections on Process

We experienced that the use of generative techniques provided a rich amount of data relevant for designing the future healthcare service and appurtenant technology for patients with COPD. The sensitizing task, the workbook that the participants had received before the meetings, was by most perceived as a good preparation for the meeting. However, one of the participants remarked that she had not understood much of the workbook, and explained that she had tried to complete but did not know if she had understood it correctly.

We found that the participants responded differently towards the use of generative techniques and tools during the sessions. Some were enthusiastic about being given the opportunity and tools to design their own future healthcare service and possible technology. Others were reserved and hesitated in taking part in these activities, but used the generative tools together with the facilitator after overcoming their initial scepticism. We experienced that in some instances it was important that we did not discard the generative tools that were planned, even thought the participants initially showed scepticism, as in most cases the participant just needed information and time to adopt and make use of them. However, in some cases it might be productive to use standard semi-structured interview methods as support, when or if the participant obviously is not capable or willing to use the tools provided.

We experienced that particularly the elderly participants were more skeptic and hesitating towards using the generative tools and techniques. This might have to do with their limited experience of such explorative and interactive approaches. Similar challenges with co-design activities with elderly are reported by Xie et al. [17]. According to the literature, co-designing with users is dependent on the end-users level of expertise, passion, and creativity [11]. The youngest participant that took part used the generative tools with great enthusiasm and also expressed that he enjoyed such approaches, as he had personal experience using such methods from his professional work. This underlines that experience, creativity, and motivation influences participation.

The participants that took part in this study were all diagnosed with COPD, but some were more affected by their illness than others. E.g. one of the participants had to use oxygen-supply during parts of the session due to breathing problems, and had limited ability to interact with the generative tools provided due to her physical limitations, but also that her health condition prohibited her from being able to do more at the same time than focus on the conversation. In these cases the facilitator was required to assist the participant, and write down or sketch what the participant wanted to express, as s/he was not capable of doing it herself/himself. Also, some of the other participants experienced that they were not able to stand for a long time, interacting with the tools we provided them with, and therefore needed pauses during the process. Therefore, such approaches require that the facilitators are particularly aware of the participants needs, and let the participant set his/her limitations for participation.

Consequently, the sessions took more time than anticipated. We had planned each session to last one to two hours each, but almost all the sessions lasted nearly three hours each. When planning the sessions, we had been aware that we did not want to burden the participants unnecessary, and therefore attempted to make a concise plan for the co-design sessions. However, due to various reasons, such as the fact that the participants needed time and patience to conduct the activities, we had to adjust the procedures according to the participants' health condition and creativity. Also, the participants had a lot on their mind and needed time and space to tell their stories, narrations and perceptions. This required more time than anticipated. We therefore experienced it as more important to be flexible, letting the participant set the standard for how much time and space s/he needed, rather than the need to follow a rigid time schedule.

By using generative techniques in the co-design process with participants with COPD, we could identify a number of central aspects that are crucial for the design of the future mHealth technology and appurtenant healthcare service for this group. The approach provided a rich amount of data and insights about the users' needs, requirements, dreams and desires that would be difficult to capture else way. However, we experienced that enabling generative tools and techniques are not without challenges when co-designing with elderly patients with COPD. Even though we did a number of considerations when planning the generative sessions, the need to adjust and reconsider the planned activities had to be done on site during each session.

Regardless of the challenges with using the generative techniques during co-design activities, it does not imply that the most vulnerable users should be excluded from such activities. Rather, the need to identify what tools and techniques that are the most productive and ethically dynamic for particular vulnerable user groups is still needed in order to design future mHealth technology and healthcare services.

4   Conclusion

By using generative tools and techniques we identified the experiences, needs, dreams, and desires of COPD patients regarding their health condition, daily life, and healthcare services. Selected key factors related to this is the need for information, the requirement to be respected and seen as a holistic person, and the need to get relief when it comes to organizing health related activities in communication with the healthcare services. Participating in co-design activities is resource demanding, and reflections regarding the participants' abilities to make use of the tools and techniques are important to consider when planning and conducting the activities, and the need to adjust and reconsider the planned activities has to be done on site during each session. In conclusion, the most vulnerable participants might not be eligible to enable advanced generative tools during co-design activities, and designers therefore have an important responsibility to plan and create appropriate co-design sessions with particular vulnerable user groups.

Acknowledgements. This project has been a co-operation between the R&D institute SINTEF, Trondheim municipality and St.Olavs Hospital. The project was funded by The Norwegian Research Council.

References

1. Viitanena, J., et al.: National questionnaire study on clinical ICT systems proofs: physicians suffer from poor usability. Int. J. Med. Informatics **80**(10), 708–725 (2011)
2. Jimison, H., et al.: Barriers and drivers of health information technology use for the elderly, chronically Ill, and underserved. Evidence reports/technology assessments (2008)
3. Mannino, D.M., Kiriz, V.A.: Changing the burden of COPD mortality. Int. J. Chron. Obstruct Pulmon. Dis. **1**(3), 219–233 (2006)
4. Wesseling, G., Vrijhoef, H.J.: Acute exacerbations of COPD: recommendations for integrated care. Expert Rev. Respir. Med. **2**(4), 489–494 (2008)
5. Menn, P., Weber, N., Holle, R.: Health-related quality of life in patients with severe COPD hospitalized for exacerbations - comparing EQ-5D, SF-12 and SGRQ. Health Qual Life Outcomes **8**, 39 (2010)
6. Bolton, C.E., et al.: Insufficient evidence of benefit: a systematic review of home telemonitoring for COPD. J. Eval. Clin. Pract. **17**(6), 1216–1222 (2010)
7. Titova, E., et al.: Long term effects of an integrated care intervention on hospital utilization in patients with severe COPD: a single centre controlled study. Respiratory Research, **16**(8) (2015)
8. Borycki, E.: M-Health: can chronic obstructive pulmonary disease patients use mobile phones and associated software to self-manage their disease. In: Quintana, Y., et al. (eds.) Advancing Cancer Education and Healthy Living in Our Communities. IOS Press, Amsterdam (2012)
9. Das, A., Faxvaag, A.: What Influences Patient Participation in an Online Forum for Weight Loss Surgery? A Qualitative Case Study. Interact. J. Med. Res. **3**(1) (2012)
10. Cruz, J., Brooks, D., Marqies, A.: Home telemonitoring in COPD: a systematic review of methodologies and patients' adherence. Int. J. Med. Informatics **83**, 249–263 (2014)
11. Sanders, E.B.-N., Stappers, P.J.: Co-creation and the new landscapes of design. CoDesign **4**(1), 5–18 (2008)
12. Holmlid, S.: Participative, co-operative, emancipatory: from participatory design to service design. In: First Nordic Conference on Service Design and Service Innovation. Oslo, Norway (2009)
13. Steen, M., Manschot, M., De Koning, N.: Benefits of co-design in service design projects. Int. J. Des. **5**(2), 53–60 (2011)
14. Sanders, E.B.-N.: From user-centered to participatory design approaches. In: Frascara, I.J. (ed.) Design and the Social Sciences: Making Connections. Taylor & Francis, London (2002)
15. Stappers, P.J., Sanders, E.B.-N.: Generative tools for context mapping: tuning the tools. In: Third International Conference on Design and Emotion, Taylor & Francis, Loughborough (2003)
16. Visser, F.S., et al.: Contextmapping: experiences from practice. CoDesign **1**(2), 119–149 (2005)
17. Xie, B., et al.: Connecting generations: developing co-design methods for older adults and children. Behav. Inf. Technol. **31**(4), 413–423 (2012)

Human-Computer Interaction in Bed

Gustavo Desouzart[1,2(✉)] and Ernesto Filgueiras[3]

[1] Life Quality Research Centre, Polytechnic Institute of Santarém,
Santarém, Portugal
gustavodesouzart@gmail.com
[2] Health Research Unity, Polytechnic Institute of Leiria, Campus 2 - Morro do
Lena - Alto do Vieiro Apartado 4137, 2411-901 Leiria, Portugal
gustavodesouzart@gmail.com
[3] Comunication Laboratory – LabCom, University of Beira Interior,
Covilhã, Portugal

Abstract. Sleep disorders are increasingly common view and it is a growing problem in modern societies. There are several problems that can cause this type of disturbance, being the demanding obligations of work and study, a current problem, which leads individuals to allocate more time their rest period in at home. Currently, we are seeing the replacement of handwork by mental, automated and computerized work, which translates into an increasing percentage of time spent performing repetitive static character tasks (physical effort), being able to compare yourself to your work done in industry, traditional production lines (Caetano & Vala 2002). It is no less demanding contexts of labor among which are those activities that involve the long hours spent at the computer. This paper presents a study whose objective was to research the human-computer interaction with the time spent by young adults in carrying out activities with computing devices (computer, tablet or mobile phone) in residences' bedrooms of air force military and university students in rest time periods and with ecological validation with observation method to video analysis and using a Software iSEE. A sample of 32956 observations, which corresponds to 1824 sleep-hours of 24 young adults, was classified into two (2) Interaction Categories (IC), body position while participants were awake in bed (2873 observations) and doing activities (3001 observations). The image registration was performed during the period of six months, divided into two periods with each participant, to enable the analysis of different times of the year and not just a single period can mean a higher specific activity. The results show that 38.7 % (N = 1113 observations) of the participants presented the sitting as the most common postural behavior during awake in bed when the participants doing activities. In reference of activities in bed, 49.2 % (N = 1475) used the computer, followed by Using mobile devices, with 16.7 % (N = 501) of observations. When we analyze the group of participants, the students showed 49.2 % of the period of activity in bed, using the computer, and 13.8 % used mobile equipment. In the same reference, the military also used the computer (49 %) as the main activity in bed during the night rest, but they used more mobile devices (19.4 %) than students.

Regarding the postures, students used the sitting (57.1 %) as the main active posture when in bed, however, the military was the only sitting 3rd

© Springer International Publishing Switzerland 2015
A. Marcus (Ed.): DUXU 2015, Part III, LNCS 9188, pp. 596–605, 2015.
DOI: 10.1007/978-3-319-20889-3_55

indication posture in bed, being the 1st observation of posture in bed, was the supine position with 30.7 %. This data set the type of use of computer devices in bed (studying, playing games, watching movie or playing). Findings of this study allow suggesting what graphical interface designers must seek as new strategies and solutions for posture in bed, exploring other peripheral equipment for using informatics equipment in bed position.

Keywords: Human-Computer interaction · Activities in rest period · Health care professionals' procedures · ISEE

1   Introduction

Circadian rhythms, that is one of several biological rhythms found in humans, are produced jointly by the action of various structures of the nervous system and are influenced by various environmental factors, and also by sleep quality. It would be necessary for the musculoskeletal system the period of rest (Danda et al. 2005).

For the individual get a sense of well-being or physical and mental rest, with recovery of energy, normal period of sleeping or resting is necessary, allowing the individual to perform in good physical and mental condition the next day's tasks (Rente and Pimentel 2004).

Several authors report the sleeping disorders are increasingly common view and there are several problems that can cause this type of disturbance, being the demanding obligations of work and study, a current problem, which leads individuals to allocate more time your rest period in work at home (Wright et al. 2007; Sleep Fundation 2005; Rajaratman and Arendt 2001; Guilleminaut 2005).

There are several problems that can cause this type of disorders, being the demanding obligations of work and study, a current problem, which leads individuals to allocate more time your rest period in work at home. Currently, we are seeing the replacement of handwork by mental, automated and computerized work, which translates into an increasing percentage of time spent performing repetitive static character tasks (physical effort), being able to compare yourself to your work done in industry, traditional production lines (Caetano and Vala 2002).

Some authors have shown that is necessary the analysis of postural behavior in the workplace of computer users (Brewer et al. 2006; Liao and Drury 2000), not just in terms of workplace in the company but ergonomics improvements at work in the rest period.

The behavioral and postural habits can be changed depending with the type of daily activities and they are influenced by various environmental factors, including professional or academic performance. In general, a systemic approach of activity through the analysis of all possibilities of interactions in a real context has been adopted in the ergonomic studies, and these studies has been benefited from long-term monitoring in the home environment to cope with daily variations and habituation effects (Hendrick and Kleiner 2009; Verhaert et al. 2012).

However the observation methodology based on iSEE software (Filgueiras et al. 2012) allows the classification and registration of postural behaviors for long periods of time and it can be applied in this context.

In this context, the main objectives of this study is to evaluate the human-computer interaction in postural behavior during rest period.

This knowledge will allow to: (a) understand the postural behavior in the human-computer interaction during rest period; and (b) elaborate more specific recommendations to the changes in postural behaviors and products' development.

For this paper we will present the results for interaction patterns during the use of a set of specific Interaction Category - IC, according to the methodology and tool to measure postural behavior during sleeping, proposed by Desouzart et al. (2014).

2 Methodology

This paper presents a study whose objective was to research the human-computer interaction with the time spent by young adults in carrying out activities with computing devices (computer, tablet or mobile phone) in residences' bedrooms of air force military and university students in rest time periods and with ecological validation and is based on the observation of the human interaction (with Visual Display Terminals [VDTs] and with observation method to video analysis using the Software iSEE) with postural behaviors in bed during the night period (10 h/night). We used the same group of equipment and the same model of bed, in order to analyze if there are similar patterns of interaction between users.

This study started on the 9th of April 2013 and finished on the 3rd of October 2014 and it has occurred in two distinct periods of image pickup in each group (military and students) with three days per period.

2.1 Study Site and Residence Bedrooms' Properties

Data was collected from 24 young adults aged between 18 and 25 years old (Mean = 20.96 ± 1.899) of the Portuguese air force military and Portuguese university. Twelve male soldiers, of different categories (1st Corporal, 2nd Corporal or Soldier) and twelve female university students, studying in the healthcare domain, residing in dormitories of the air base and the university were selected. Each participant will be approximately six (6) months with two months of personal contact between the principal investigator and volunteers, and the remaining time implying an impersonal touch through e-mails and mobile phone.

The bedrooms were in dormitories standard of an institution, which is the case of college students and military with 2 beds in each bedroom with the same equipment room conditions (i.e. bed, mattress, air conditioning system, light level and noise).

2.2 The Subjects and Rest Activities

A sample of 32956 observations, which corresponds to 1824 sleep-hours of 24 young adults (12 male and 12 female), aged between 18 and 25 years (mean = 20.96 + 1.899), belonged to the air base n°5 of the Portuguese air force and Portuguese university students. Twelve soldiers worked in the area of: mechanical aviation material, hospitality services and sustenance, car driver, mechanical, electrical and flight instrument work, weaponry and equipment mechanics, health service. Twelve university students, studying in the healthcare domain in the area of: physiotherapy, occupational therapy, speech therapy, nursing and dietetics.

Participants were informed about the study's objective through a group meeting and an individual approach on the day before each video recording. All video collection was authorized by the participants through a consent form and all procedures are in accordance with the Helsinki Declaration regarding the human study. The ethics committee of the University of Lisbon approved all experimental procedures.

Finally, participants were instructed to perform their tasks as usual and to not change their schedule due to the presence of the cameras.

2.3   Recording Procedure and Features

The participants' interactions with the bedroom equipment were video recorded on a normal rest period day and were assessed using: (a) one infrared digital camera (Wireless AEE Weather-proof - 2, 5 GHz – color); (b) one multiplexer video recorder (ACH MPEG-4 Realtime DVR) and (c) DVD recorder HD (LG recorder). All devices' lights were turned off or hidden and participants were informed about the placement of all cameras.

The digital video cameras turned on automatically from 11:00 p.m. to 9:00 a.m. and during the periods in which the subjects were asleep, awake, out of bed, doing activities, using a pillow, they were filmed using one plan (frontal superior) considering the best visualization of the participant and activity (Fig. 1).

In order to ensure similar interaction times in the bedroom and to not interfere in the evening activity and sleeping period, all volunteers were filmed during three days, ten hours continuously (starting at 11:00 p.m.).

Fig. 1. Images of the first plan (Frontal superior) of the bed observations

The data, collected through video using a methodology proposed by Rebelo et al. (2011), analyzed the postural behavior in real situations in bed and it was done using software developed for this purpose (Fig. 2).

The fundamental aspect of this analysis using the software ISEE was: (a) evaluate the behaviors of interaction in a real environment and for long periods of time; (b) Allow sorting at the same event an impossible number of observable in other techniques; (c) Observe activities, actions, means of interaction (equipment) and postural behavior in the same event; (d) create hierarchies allow for observable (create hierarchies allowing the observation); (e) to question the events in greater depth and detail and be able to sort all visible behaviors and test their viability during analysis by category OTHERS; among others. Following the analysis of the results of the previous phases and the observation of the collected videos, the categories were defined.

Two (2) categories of behaviors were defined, that represent the night activity in this residences' bedrooms and one another non-specific category (Fig. 2).

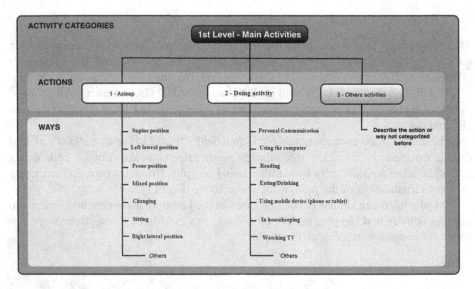

Fig. 2. Level 1 - two categories of behaviors

As mentioned, the analysis was done using software developed for this purpose. It allows classifying the IC (through video analysis) in levels (Filgueiras et al. 2012; Desouzart et al. 2014).

3   Results

A sample of 32956 observations, which corresponds to 1824 sleep-hours of 24 young adults, was classified into two (2) Interaction Categories (IC) (Graphic 1), body position while participants were awake in bed (2873 observations) and doing activities (3001 observations).

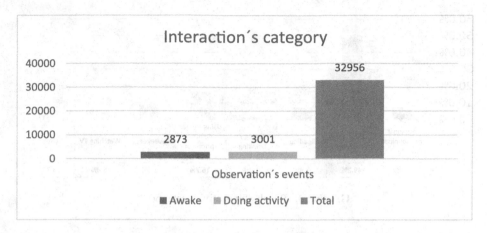

Graphic 1. Results for Interactions Categories groups

The results of category "Awake" show that 38.7 % (N = 1113 observations) of the participants presented the sitting as the most common postural behavior during awake in bed (Graphic 2).

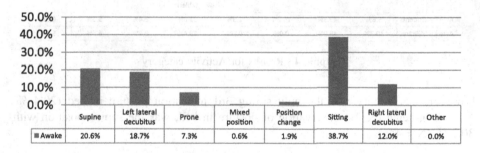

Graphic 2. Results for Awake category

When the participant stood in the "Activity" category during the video capture, the most common activity was Using a computer, with 49,2 % (N = 1475) of observation, which corresponds to approximately 30 min of computer use per participant per night, followed by Using mobile devices, with 16.7 % (N = 501) of observations (Graphic 3).

When we analyze the group of participants, the students (N = 1422) showed 49.3 % (N = 708) of the period of activity in bed, using the computer, and 13.8 % (N = 198) used mobile equipment. In the same reference, the military (N = 1564) also used the computer (49 %, N = 767) as the main activity in bed during the night rest, but used more mobile devices (19.4 %, N = 303) than students (Graphic 4).

Regarding the postures while participants were awake in bed (Graphic 5), students (N = 1422) used the sitting (57.1 %, N = 812) as the main active posture when in bed,

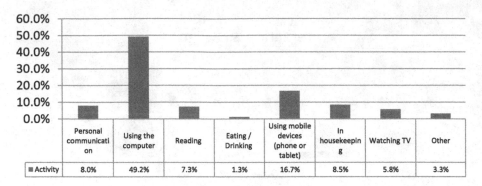

Graphic 3. Results for Activity category

	Personal communication	Using the computer	Reading	Eating / Drinking	Using mobile devices (phone or tablet)	In housekeeping	Watching TV	Other
■ Activity	8.0%	49.2%	7.3%	1.3%	16.7%	8.5%	5.8%	3.3%

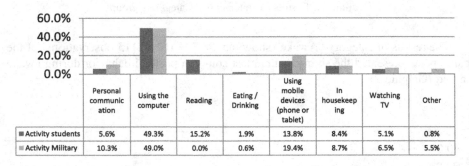

Graphic 4. Results for Activity category

	Personal communication	Using the computer	Reading	Eating / Drinking	Using mobile devices (phone or tablet)	In housekeeping	Watching TV	Other
■ Activity students	5.6%	49.3%	15.2%	1.9%	13.8%	8.4%	5.1%	0.8%
■ Activity Military	10.3%	49.0%	0.0%	0.6%	19.4%	8.7%	6.5%	5.5%

however, the military was the only sitting 3rd indication posture in bed (20.4 %, N = 301), being the 1st observation of posture in bed, was the supine position with 30.7 % (N = 446).

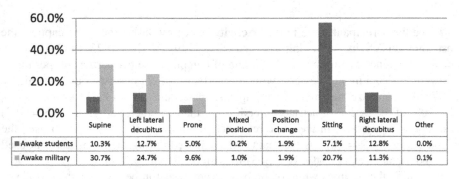

	Supine	Left lateral decubitus	Prone	Mixed position	Position change	Sitting	Right lateral decubitus	Other
■ Awake students	10.3%	12.7%	5.0%	0.2%	1.9%	57.1%	12.8%	0.0%
■ Awake military	30.7%	24.7%	9.6%	1.0%	1.9%	20.7%	11.3%	0.1%

Graphic 5. Results for Awake category

The interaction between "Posture" and "Awake" category in all participants (N = 2873) presented that the most common interactions category (IC's) were that the participants had in the sitting position using the computer with 17.23 % (N = 495), followed by sitting posture and reading with 5.99 % (N = 172) and right lateral decubitus in bed using the computer with 2.44 % (N = 70), according Graphic 6.

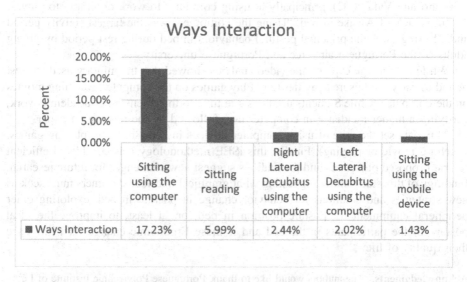

Graphic 6. Results for ways interaction

The analysis whether there is any relationship between male sample from air force military and female sample from undergraduate students.

The results showed significant difference (*p* = .000) between the postures used during the period when the participants were awake in bed and between the period when the participants were doing activity in rest period between the two groups of participants (military men and women students) within the same age group (18–25 years old), according Independent samples test (Table 1).

Table 1. Comparison of awake positions category and activity category between military and students

	Group	N	Mean	Std. deviation	Sig. (2-tailed)
Awake Posture in bed	Students	1422	4.93	2.019	.000
	Military	1451	3.26	2.278	.000
Activity	Students	1437	3.19	1.740	.000
	Military	1564	3.49	2.153	.000

4   Conclusion

The demanding obligations of work and study, is a current problem, which leads individuals to allocate more time in their rest period in work at home. Currently, we are seeing the replacement of handwork by mental, automated and computerized work, which translates into an increasing percentage of time spent performing repetitive tasks (Caetano and Vala 2002), principally in using computer to work or simply to play.

In the ICs of Awake in bed, "Using the computer" was the largest activity period and, "Sitting" was the principal postural behaviors in bed during rest period by young adults of the Portuguese air force and Portuguese university.

While held image capture, the video analysis showed that the military used the rest period to carry out leisure activities (e.g. Play games on the computer, watching movies on the computer) while Students use the same time to the extension of academic work, verifying a higher incidence in computer use, followed by the reading on paper.

This data set the type of using computer devices in bed (studying, playing games, watching movie or playing). Finally, this iSEE methodology was considered efficient for the proposed objectives and the findings suggest new challenges for future research. Findings of this study allow suggesting what graphical interface designers must seek as new strategies and solutions for behavior change in posture in bed, exploring other peripheral equipment for posture position in bed; or, at least, to improve the ideal posture of the participants in the bed and if these Ergonomic changes can influence their quality of life.

Acknowledgments. The authors would like to thank Portuguese Polytechnic Institute of Leiria and Portuguese Air Force and in particular, the Air Base n.5 as well as the General Staff of the Portuguese Air Force. The authors want to thank Magali Bordini, for her excellent contribution to the article literature review.

We would also like to thank the university student and the air force military participants for their contribution of time and effort to the research. Without them, this study would not be possible.

References

Ayas, N., White, D., Manson, J., Stampfer, M., Speizer, F., Malhotra, A., Hu, F.: A prospective study of sleep duration and coronary heart disease in women. Arch. Intern. Med. **163**, 205–209 (2003)

Bergqvist, U.: Visual display terminal work-a perspective on long-term changes and discomforts. Int. J. Ind. Ergon. **16**(3), 201–209 (1995)

Brewer, S., Van Eerd, D., Amick III, B., Irvin, E., Daum, K., Gerr, F., Rempe, D.: Workplace interventions to prevent musculoskeletal and visual symptoms and disorders among computer users: a systematic review. J. Occup. Rehabil. **16**(3), 317–350 (2006)

Caetano, A., Vala, J.: Human Resource Management. Contexts, Processes and Techniques, 2nd edn. RH Publisher, Lisbon (2002)

Danda, G., Rocha, G., Azenha, M., Sousa, C., Bastos, O.: Standard sleep-wake cycle and excessive daytime sleepiness in medical students. J. Bras Psichiatry **54**(2), 102–106 (2005)

Desouzart, G., Filgueiras, E., Melo, F., Matos, R.: Human body-sleep system interaction in residence for university students: evaluation of interaction patterns using a system to capture video and software with observation of postural behaviors during sleep. In: 5th International Conference on Applied Human Factors and Ergonomics (AHFE). CRC Press/Taylor & Francis Grou, Kraków (2014)

Desouzart, G., Filgueiras, E., Melo, F., Matos, R.: Human-bed interaction: a methodology and tool to measure postural behavior during sleep of the air force military. In: Marcus, A. (ed.) DUXU 2014, Part III. LNCS, vol. 8519, pp. 662–674. Springer, Heidelberg (2014)

Fenety, A., Walker, J.: Short-term effects of workstation exercises on musculoskeletal discomfort and postural changes in seated video display unit workers. Phys. Ther. **82**(6), 578–589 (2002)

Filgueiras, E., Rebelo, F., da Silva, F.M.: Support of the upper limbs of office workers during a daily work. Work J. Prev. Assess. Rehabil. **32**, 267–274 (2012). IOS Press

Gracovetsky, S.: The resting spine : a conceptual approach to the avoidance of spinal reinjury during rest. Phys. Ther. **67**, 549–553 (1987)

Guilleminaut, C.: Clinical Neurophysiology of Sleep Disorders. Elsevier, Amsterdam (2005)

Hendrick, H., Kleiner, B.: Macroergonomics: Theory, Methods, and Applications. Taylor & Francis Group, New York (2009)

Liao, M., Drury, C.: Posture, discomfort and performance in a VDT task. Ergonomics **43**(3), 345–359 (2000)

Rajaratman, S., Arendt, J.: Health in a 24-h society. Lancet **358**, 999–1005 (2001)

Rente, P., Pimentel, T.: A Patologia do Sono. Lidel, Lisboa (2004)

Sleep Fundation, S.: National Sleep Foundation. Sleep in America Poll. Washington, DC: WB&A Market Research, 29 March 2005

Soares, C.: Insomnia in women: an overlooked epidemic? Arch. Women's Mental Health **8**, 205–213 (2005)

Straker, L., Pollock, C., Mangharam, J.: The effect of shoulder posture on performance, discomfort and muscle fatigue whilst working on a visual display unit. Int. J. Ind. Ergon. **20**(1), 101–110 (1997)

Verhaert, V., Druyts, H., Van Deun, D., De Wilde, T., Brussel, K., Haex, B., Sloten, J.: Modeling human-bed interaction: the predictive value of anthropometric models in choosing the correct bed support. Work **41**, 2268–2273 (2012)

Wright, C., Valdimarsdottir, H., Erblich, J., Bovbjerg, D.: Poor sleep the night before an experimental stress task is associated with reduced cortisol reactivity in healthy women. Biol. Psychol. **74**, 319–327 (2007)

Rebelo, F., Filgueiras, E., Soares, M.: Behavior video: a methodology and tool to measure the human behavior: examples in product evaluation. In: Karwowski, W., Soares, M.M., Stanton, N.A. (eds.) Handbook of Human Factors and Ergonomics in Consumer Product Design:Methods and Techniques, pp. 275-292. CRC Press, Taylor and Francis Group, Flórida (2011)

Designing an Interface Agent-Based Architecture for Creating a Mobile System of Medical Care

Ariel Escobar Endara$^{(\boxtimes)}$ and Carlos José Pereira de Lucena

Pontifical Catholic University of Rio de Janeiro (PUC-RJ), Rio de Janeiro, Brazil
{aendara, lucena}@inf.puc-rio.br

Abstract. This paper presents a software-based architecture aiming to provide a mechanism for creating computer systems for telemedicine. The proposed architecture has two execution environments. First, the server environment where all the system information is centralized, processed by agents that are executed in this environment. Secondly, the mobile environment. Highlighting the interface agent, which exploits the information that is provided by the patient and the other agents in order to become a personal assistant to the patient. Together they are able to guide the patients in the care of their health and help the physician on patient's care remotely.

Keywords: Agents · Interface agents · Healthcare · Telemedicine

1 Introduction

Nowadays, in many cities around the world several problems related to the provision of health services are emerging such as:

- Increased demand of healthcare due to an increased number of elderly people
- Changed life styles leading to an increase in chronic diseases.
- The demand for increased accessibility of care outside hospitals, moving health services into the patient's own homes.
- The need for increased efficiency, individualization and equity of quality-oriented healthcare with limited financial resources.
- Difficulties of recruiting and retaining personnel in the healthcare services in general and in home and elderly care in particular. [1]

Telemedicine is thought to be a good choice to solve these problems. Telemedicine is defined as the delivery of healthcare and sharing of medical knowledge over a distance using telecommunication systems. The term telemedicine is associated with modern telecommunication systems such as: transmission of electronic medical records and images, remote monitoring of patients vital parameters, teleconferencing and interactive tele-teaching [2]. With the emergence of telemedicine, countless research and projects emerged too, which are intended to support the doctor so he can give the patient remote service. Thus to avoid the patient having to travel long distances to receive diagnoses, instead the patient could receive by a phone call, a video conference [3] or even a

© Springer International Publishing Switzerland 2015
A. Marcus (Ed.): DUXU 2015, Part III, LNCS 9188, pp. 606–615, 2015.
DOI: 10.1007/978-3-319-20889-3_56

message via internet to a Smartphone [4]. And it is precisely because of mobile devices such as Smart phones, several systems that allow the patient have direct communication with the doctor, were created, making the health care of the patient performed continuously and regardless of its location [5, 6]. However, with the establishment of these systems some problems have started to arise as well, such as the limited capacity of the patient to fully understand the systems, the impossibility of the physician to care for the patient at all times and even lack of communication that may exist between the mobile device and the information server (Fig. 1).

Due to recent technological advances, we can solve these problems by exploring software agents, more specifically interface agents.

An agent is defined as an information system that is located in some environment and is capable of an autonomous action in this environment in order to fulfill its design goals [7].

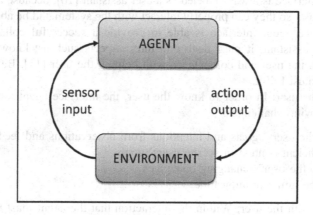

Fig. 1. An agent in its environment

Agents are information systems that have the special feature which is to be autonomous, a feature that allows them to perform tasks on their own and without requiring the direct intervention of humans [8]. As Jennings and Wooldridge affirm in their work called "Software Agents" presented in 1996, software agents have three other characteristics which are:

Social Ability: Agents should be able to interact, when they deem appropriate, with other software agents and humans in order to complete their own problem solving and to help others with their activities where appropriate.

Responsiveness: Agents should perceive their environment (which may be the physical world, a user, a collection of agents, the INTERNET, etc.) and respond in a timely fashion to changes which occur in it.

Proactiveness: Agents should not simply act in response to their environment, they should be able to exhibit opportunistic, goal-directed behavior and take the initiative where appropriate [8].

By knowing these properties and trying to take advantage of them, we propose the use of software agents applied to telemedicine problems. However, as it was appointed before, a special reference to interface agents was made, so the following section will be about such agents.

2   Interface Agents

Traditional interfaces are oriented to conversational interfaces, where the user and the agent are acting in turns [9]. Meaning the user performs an action and only after completing this action receives a response from the agent. Interface agents lead to a different design style, based on the agent being able to perform some action even when the user is in the middle of another. Meaning the user does not have to be aware of the activities the agent is performing at any given moment [9].

An agent interface is always labeled as a user assistant [10], because it has the task of guiding the user so they can properly interact with the system and be able to meet his goals. Before the agent interface is able to provide a successful collaboration and become a user assistant, it must deal with three aspects such as; knowing the user, interacting with the user and competence with helping the user [11]. Below are tasks that the agent must fulfill.

Knowing the user: In order to know the user, the interface agent must be able to fulfill the following challenges:

- Extracting the users' goals and intentions from observations and feedback
- Getting sufficient context in set the users' goals
- Adapting to the user's changing objectives
- Reducing the initial training time

Interacting with the user: Within the interaction that the agent must have with the user, it is necessary to take into account the following points:

- Deciding how much control to delegate to the agent
- Building trust in the agent
- Choosing a metaphor for agent interaction
- Making simple systems that novices can use It

Competence in helping the user: For the agent to be able to provide competent support, it must accomplish the following:

- Knowing when (and if) to interrupt the user
- Performing tasks autonomously in the way preferred by the user
- Finding strategies for partial automation of tasks

As Nwana [10] mentioned, in addition to the autonomy that characterizes any agent, interface agents must have the ability to learn because only in this way they can fulfill the three mentioned aspects above. In Fig. 2 we present a scheme in which the user, the application, the interface agent and other agents are represented with the respective links between each of them. In this figure, we can see the four ways where

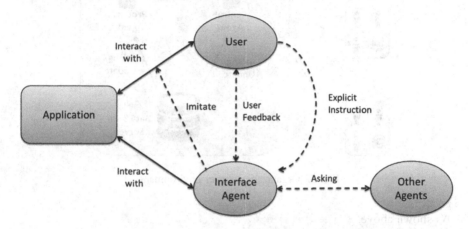

Fig. 2. How interface agents work (adapted) [12]

an interface agent learns in order to provide the user with the support it needs.

- By observing and imitating the user (learning from the user);
- Through receiving positive and negative feedback from the user (learning from the user);
- By receiving explicit instructions from the user (learning from the user);
- By asking other agents for advice (learning from peers).

3 Proposed Architecture

This proposed computational architecture is based on multi-agent systems giving more importance to interface agents who will act as patient's medical assistants. This architecture is designed in a way that can be executed on mobile devices like smart phones and tablets which communicate with a central server where it will be synchronized and processed all the information from health centers. Then it will be able to help doctors to provide patients monitoring services and preventive care in a continuous way and wherever an internet connection is available.

Within this proposal there are two environments; the server environment and mobile environment.

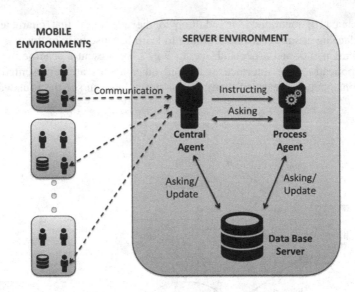

Fig. 3. Organization server environment

As shown above.

Server Environment. As illustrated in Fig. 3, the server will consist of two agents and a database which are described below.

Central Agent. This agent will be responsible for managing the connections of agents that are executed on mobile devices, being able to receive all the information concerning patients in order to store it in the master database. It will also perform the opposite function which is the continuous review of the database to do a revision to check if there is any information relevant to the patient. If the agent finds this information, it will immediately send it to the patient. It can also receive and send messages from the "Process Agent".

Process Agent. The process agent, is responsible for conducting complex information processes that are necessary to attend to a patient. It will receive orders from the Central Agent and will execute them in accordance to what is needed, but it will also fulfill a proactive and forecasting task checking the logs from the database and sending relevant information that is related to the patient to the Central Agent so it could send this information to the patient.

Data Base Server. The database of the server is the center of knowledge of the planned architecture. It will contain all the information whether, caused by agents or by the human action, meaning that this database will be fed by all of the health service records taking into account items such as the patient's clinical history, doctors records, medication records, etc. Making any information that may be useful for agents be available.

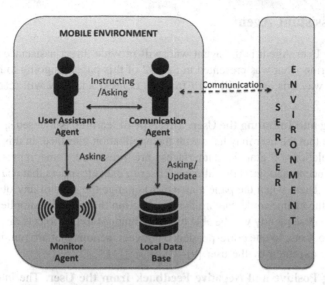

Fig. 4. Organization mobile environment

Mobile Environment. As illustrated in Fig. 4, the mobile environment will have three agents and a local data repository. Each of these components is explained below.

Monitor Agent. This will be a reactive agent, responsible to collect all the physical context of the patient and may be equipped with external devices such as sensors, GPS and Bluetooth. At the same time, it will enable the architecture to find out about events that are produced in the environment of the patient.

Communication Agent. The communication agent will be responsible to control the flow of information that may exist between the mobile environment and the server environment. This agent will define the appropriate time to send information from one environment to another depending on relevance. It and will make use of the adaptive ability of agents so that the information that was on the mobile environment will be synchronized with the server all the time. Then, if for some reason this agent fails to communicate with the server, it will wait until the moment when the connection is restored to immediately synchronize the information with the server.

User Assistant Agent. Due to the fact that this is the agent who is going to directly interact with the patient and the one that will provide all the assistance to the patient, its operation will be explained in a more detailed way in the following section.

Local Data Base. The local database of the mobile device will be the main source of knowledge for each patient. In this database, all the relevant and useful patient information will be stored. It must be said that both the relevance and usefulness of information will have to be judged depending on the application to be developed, and the interface must perform actions with the information that is not entirely relevant according to what it learned.

4   User Assistant Agent

The Assistant User Agent is the agent who will provide direct assistance to the user.

Remembering what was presented in Sect. 2 of this paper, is going to be described below by the way this agent will learn from its context and how will react about this learning.

By Observing and Imitating the User. This type of learning is focused specifically on the interaction that the user may have with the application interface. In this paradigm of direct manipulation of graphical interfaces, are presented some representations of physical or conceptual objects that allow the user to execute orders that change the state of objects [9]. Then, when the patient arrives to change the state of any object through the interface, the agent would capture the information that the user supplies to the user interface, and subsequently will be able to make changes to the objects displayed in the interface without one to one correspondence between actions that are running the agent and the orders executed by the user [9].

By Receiving Positive and Negative Feedback from the User. The interface agent must be able to learn through feedback received from the user either directly or indirectly. Indirect feedback occurs when the user leaves aside the suggestions of the agent and takes a different action instead. On the other hand, direct feedback occurs when the interface agent performs an action and the user directly indicates that it has not liked the action performed by the agent [12]. Through this type of feedback the interface agent could be able to define whether it is good or not to perform an action. In this proposed computational architecture should be noted that the interface agent will count on two types of feedback. One that will come from the patient and the other which will be received by the Communication Agent, which will come directly from the server environment, meaning that it will come from the medical staff who is responsible of the patient care.

By Receiving Explicit Instructions from the User. The user can train the agent giving it hypothetical examples of events or situations and tell the agent what to do in those cases. When this happens, the interface agent records the actions, traces the relationships between objects, and changes its sample database to incorporate the example or instruction that is given by the user [12]. Similar to the previous case, in this architecture, the interface agent may learn a lot from the instructions that are given by the patient, as per the instructions which are sent from the server by the medical team.

By Asking Other Agents for Advice. If an agent does not know what action is appropriate in a given situation, the situation can be presented to other agents and ask what measures are recommended for this situation [12]. Within the proposed architecture, if the interface agent does not know what action take, it will automatically initiate communication with the communication agent allowing it to ask the Server and find a solution for the action mentioned. Besides all of this, because it is intended to give continuous monitoring service to the patient, the agent interface will be supported on the Agent Monitor with whom will continually interact to perceive the behavior of the patient and to know as well what is the environment in which it is developing. In this way the agent will learn and perform actions that help the patient health treatment.

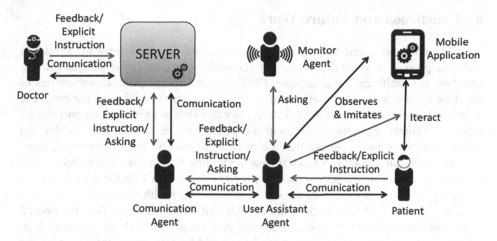

Fig. 5. Interact interface agent

5 Application Scenario

A possible case is presented where the architecture could be applied to help the patient in his health care.

As presented in the official page of World Health Organization, diabetes is a chronic disease that occurs when the pancreas does not produce enough insulin, or when the body cannot effectively use the insulin it produces. Hyper glycaemia, or raised blood sugar, is a common effect of uncontrolled diabetes and over time leads to serious damage to many of the body's systems, especially the nerves and blood vessels. [13]. It is for this reason that when it comes to a diabetic patient is vitally important to control the level of glucose in the blood. Based on this context, it can be said that the proposed architecture could help in the treatment of this disease as follows (Fig. 5).

The mobile environment can be equipped with a Bluetooth device to obtain data about the glucose in the blood [14]. In this way the Monitor Agent may continuously monitor the patient and pass the data to the interface agent who will evaluate the information according to the profile that the user has and take actions which are most appropriate. Thus, if the agent considers that the level of glucose detected in the blood can be dangerous, it will immediately ask the Communication Agent to inform the server about this issue and process the information. If the information on the server is sufficient to give an instruction to the patient, it will immediately send a response with such instructions. In the case that it is not possible to give an instruction, it is expected that the doctor be the one who sends direct instruction to the patient. On the other hand, while performing all this processing, the agent interface through alarms will alert the patient and the patient needs to take care himself to avoid problems with the glucose level.

6 Conclusion and Future Work

This paper has presented a computational architecture based on software agents, in order to propose a generalized solution for building mobile systems that provide attention and health care at a distance. Observing and studying the characteristics of interface agents, it is noted that they may act as personal assistants of patients. The example that was presented in Sect. 5 stating that this architecture could support several types of medical applications that help the patients in the care of their health. An example of this is due to the fact that it is possible to perceive the behavior the patient has, the agent can accomplish tasks such as reminding the patient the schedules when he must take medication, suggest making a direct consultation with the doctor, or even suggest performing any physical activity to improve his health.

The proposed architecture does not provide full time interaction that the medical team could perform with the system. Meaning that it is not a mobile environment from which the doctor can participate and can be assisted by software agents to attend the different problems presented with his patients. Therefore, future work would be to present an extended version of this presented architecture, where the possibility of interacting with the systems in a guided way is given to the doctor as well as the patient. On the other hand it must be taken into consideration that medical information is confidential so future enhancements should be taken into account the part of security in communications of software agents to avoid filtering problems or loss of data.

References

1. Koch, S.: Home telehealth- current state and future trends. Int. J. Med. Inf. **75**, 1–12 (2005)
2. Fischer, H.R., Reichlin, S., Gutzwiller, J.P., Dyson, A., Beglinger, C.: Telemedicine as a new possibility to improve healthcare delivery. In: Istepanian, R.S.H., Laxminarayan, S., Pattichis, C.S. (eds.) M-Health: Emerging Mobile Health Systems, pp. 203–218. Springer Science & Business Media, New York (2007)
3. Saysell, E.: Telemedicine in community-based palliative care: evaluation of a videolink teleconference Project. Int. J. Palliat. Nurs. **9**, 489–495 (2003)
4. Ferrer-Roca, O., Cárdenas, A., Diaz-Cardama, A., Pulido, P.: Mobile phone text messaging in the management of diabetes. J. Telemed. Telecare **10**(5), 282–286 (2004)
5. Gregoski, M.J.: Development and validation of a smartphone heart rate acquisition application for health promotion and wellness telehealth applications. Int. J. Telemed. Appl. **2012**, 1–7 (2012)
6. Demaerschalk, B.M.: Telemedicine or Telephone Consultation in Patients with Acute Stroke. Current neurology and neuroscience reports (2011)
7. Weiss, G.: Multiagent Systems: A Modern Approach to Distributed Artificial Intelligence. The MIT Press, Cambridge (1999)
8. Jennings, N., Wooldridge, M.: Software agents. IEE Rev. **42**, 17–20 (1996)
9. López, V.M.J.: Interfaces de Usuario Adaptativas Basadas en Modelos y Agentes de Software. Adaptive User Interfaces Based Models and Software Agents. Doctoral Tesis, Universidad de Castilla-La Mancha (2005)
10. Nwana, H.: Software agents: an overview. Knowl. Eng. Rev. **11**(3), 1–40 (1996)
11. Middleton, S.: Interface agents: A review of the field. Technical report Number (2001)

12. Maes, P.: Agents that reduce work and information overload. Commun. ACM **37**(7), 31–40 (1994)
13. World Health Organization. http://www.who.int/diabetes/en
14. Entra Health Systems. http://www.myglucohealth.net

A Study of Conversation Support System Between the Elderly Person and Young Adults by Using Facial Expression Analysis

Miyuki Iwamoto[✉], Noriaki Kuwahara, and Kazunari Morimoto

Kyoto Institute of Technology, Kyoto, Japan
cabotine.six.stars@gmail.com, nkuwahar@kit.ac.jp

Abstract. Japanese society is recently facing a problem of a super-aging population. The proportion of aged people is growing. The number of families with old couples and old singles is increasing. In some case s/he passes a day without speaking a word, and that causes a disuse of cognitive functions and a risk for dementia and/or depression. In the future, it is expected that young adults in the region will be involved with the elderly actively as a conversational partner. They focused on reminiscence technique which is effective to control dementia in order to reduce the mental burden of the partner young adult. We have already examined the difference of the mental burden and the quality of communication between the elderly and young adults when they use any photographs as content for communication support. As a result, depending on the category of the photo as a content for conversation support we are sure that there is tension in conversation. So, we went to build a conversation support system for the elderly and young adults to provide content according to the circumstances of the conversation to allow the conversation to go smoothly without feeling a sense of tension and discomfort. In previous studies, the frustration and discomfort was determined by using wearable devices (such as for heart or brain wave). However, in order to construct a system, it is necessary to use a non-contact device that can easily measure the frustration and discomfort. We measure the dissatisfaction, discomfort during a conversation using the expression analysis sensor. Therefore, in this study, it is an object of comparison and evaluation of the data obtained by measuring the dissatisfaction, discomfort in wearable devices (heart-EEG) and non-contact devices (expression analysis).

Keywords: Elderly · Reminiscence videos · Dementia · Conversation

1 Introduction

Japanese society is recently facing the problem of a super-aging population. The number of elderly people is growing [1].

The population over 65 years old, also called Baby-Boomers, is now over 30 million and it is anticipated to be 35 million in 2018 [2].

The number of families with old couples and old singles is increasing. In some cases s/he passes a day without speaking a word, and that causes a disuse of cognitive functions and a risk for dementia and/or depression.

© Springer International Publishing Switzerland 2015
A. Marcus (Ed.): DUXU 2015, Part III, LNCS 9188, pp. 616–627, 2015.
DOI: 10.1007/978-3-319-20889-3_57

We need to understand their physical and psychological characteristics in order to communicate with aged people.

Therefore we must respect their pride even though they have loss of visual, hearing and cognitive functions.

Reminiscence therapy is believed to stabilize the mental condition of elderly people suffering from dementia, and to reduce behavioral disorders. This therapy was also conducted using old tools, toys, or photos, in a group led by an experienced listening staff. The experts such as clinical psychologists, therapists or listening volunteers may deal with it in communication. In many cases, patients do not have enough conversational partners due to the decrease of staff-to-patient ratio. The number is too short for the needs.

Thus the younger generations are expected to be a talking partner to the aged people but there is a problem that they are unfamiliar with the communication with them because they grew up in a small family without grandfathers or grandmothers.

There have been some attempts to solve the problem by using a picture or a video as a trigger for a conversation [3–5].

However there is no research for the mental load of the partnering students/volunteers. That means the research has been made for the communication supporting system to improve the QOL of the aged people and the mental load of the young partners has been neglected.

Therefore we were doing the verification with regard to such an impact (feeling of burden) of young people. There is a feeling of burden or stress during the conversation.

We have been also using photos and videos as supporting tools for communication between the aged people with dementia and the students/volunteers as shown in the following figure. We noticed they made communication smoother and it is a precious chance for the aged people, even though the students/volunteers feel a mental burden (Fig. 1).

However, even in this case, there are many cases that young adults (students and volunteers) complain of a sense of burden towards the dialogue.

Fig. 1. Volunteers utilizing content for conversational support

Many caregivers and volunteers untrained in listening often feel a mental burden or they often cannot have a good conversation. There are some researches on promoting the conversation between the patients and the caregivers or volunteers, or among the patients, providing the topics sharing the photos or videos (Exam. [3–5]). They focused on reminiscence technique which is effective to control dementia in order to reduce the mental load of the partnering students/volunteers. We used the information media (media below) which provide the topics and communication supporting contents. The media in general includes photos, videos and music and their effect is unknown regarding the mental load of the caregivers or in the quality of communication between the patients and the caregivers.

We examined the difference of the mental load and the quality of communication between the patients and the caregivers/volunteers when they use photos or video in communication support contents. We have found the best medium for communication [6, 7].

2 Devised the System

2.1 Summary

We have devised a conversation support system to allow the elderly and the young people to talk without feeling each other as a burden. The overview of the system it is shown in Fig. 2.

1. The elderly and the young adults talk while looking at the common contents. (in this case, photos)
2. We set up non-invasive measuring device and recorded the facial expressions and used audio non-invasive measuring device.
3. From the data obtained from the device, it is assumed that there are situations where the elderly and the young adults feels uncomfortable.
4. We will provide a common content that the elderly and the young adults do not feel uncomfortable by an interactive control system.

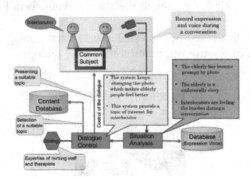

Fig. 2. Conversation support system

2.2 Method of Measuring the Burden

To measure the feeling of burden, it can be better to measure using the invasive devices such as for heart and brain waves measured accurately. Although the young adults can use the invasive devices, it is difficult to use for the elderly, and therefore, frustration and discomfort of the elderly were not able to be measured according to the heart rate and brain waves.

Therefore, by reading from the expression of elderly and young adults using the non-invasive device, it becomes possible to measure the frustration and discomfort of both the elderly and the young adults.

In this system, we decided to measure the indication that it is uncomfortable in the expression. Furthermore, the number of negative expressions was counted rather than measure the expression time. Thus, there is no dependent on the time of conversation. Therefore short conversations were considered possible to have comfortable conversation. It is possible to measure the frustration and discomfort of both the elderly and the young adults, and it is considered possible to provide a content that can allow a comfortable conversation for both.

2.3   Content

The content is generally photographic or video, but it was contemplated to use music.

From the results of experiments so far, video (movie) is less burdensome but it has been found that it is difficult to hold the conversation compared to just looking at the image. Therefore, in this system, it was decided to use the photo as a conversation content. We keep a divided photo for each content.

In this study, to database appropriate content (photos) in order to build this system, we examined the difference of the mental burden and the quality of communication between the elderly and the young adults (caregivers and volunteers) when they use photos as communication support contents.

3   Experiment

3.1   Summary

In this research young adults (caregivers, volunteers) performing a dialogue with the elderly face-to-face, in the case of using photos, for the category, we did an examination of what influences there are in the passing of time towards caregivers in the continuation of conversation, and also if there is a burden, and if there is a difference in the timing of when the burden is felt.

A camera was used to capture the expressions (nod/line-of-sight) of the elderly throughout the sessions. The expressions of the elderly were analyzed from the video recordings.

The purpose of this experiment is for young adults (caregivers and volunteers) and old couples and old singles to hardly feel a burden in any category of photos during a conversation, and also, it is to verify the quality of burden the young adults feels during the conversation or if they do not feel a burden. Thus, when constructing the system, establishing a content database is considered possible.

3.2   Evaluation Item

They answered the questions by a 5-stage subjective evaluation each time after the experiment. For the questionnaire, in addition to the questionnaire with the same content as the experiment up to now, I was asked whether they felt the burden during 10 min of conversation. The experiment's results show subjective evaluation (questionnaire, their degree of burden from the stress check sheet) and physiological evaluation (heart rate, EEG) (Fig. 4). The degree of smiling was measured for the elderly. From the interactive support experience, "Lives during the Showa Era", "electrical appliances", and "art" were added.

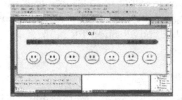

Fig. 3. Stress check sheet

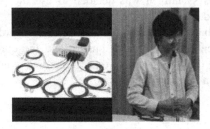

Fig. 4. Measuring device

As for subjects, one student interviewed three patients and estimated an average of the mental load excluding personal compatibilities. The partner student indicated the degree of mental load on the stress check board every minute. A check sheet that was programmed into another PC (Fig. 3) was located in a way that they elderly cannot see. The stress check sheet represented facial expressions by a 1–7-scale. Means that there was absence of any burden (stress) to continue the conversation, the right end face is meant that the person feels a lot of burden (stress). A camera was used to capture the resident's expressions and actions throughout the sessions. We compared it to her expression to see which photographs brought her pleasure or joy. Facial expressions were correlated with emotions in a previous study [7].

3.3 Subject

The partners were 5 students of 23–25 years old. Their degree of diplomacy was diagnosed in advance by the Yatabe-Guilford sociability personality diagnostic test.

The elderly were 4 senior ladies and 1 senior man of ages from 84 to 92 suffering mild dementia.

3.4 Environment of Experiment

The layouts of the experiment were shown in Figs. 5 and 6 below.

We borrowed a room in the nursing home, in which we placed chairs side by side.

We used a laptop PC in which photos categorized above were uploaded for a 10 min conversation.

We carried out checks on the degree of burden of conversation by students. A stress check seat was positioned out of sight from the elderly (Fig. 6).

Fig. 5. Experiment environment

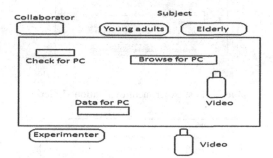

Fig. 6. The layout of the experimental environment

3.5 Expression Analysis

The expressions of the patients were analyzed from the video recordings. Analysis was carried out using the major literature "expression analysis" techniques, to understand which photos made her look happier or more joyful [8]. This document defines expressions of happiness as follows.

- Lower eyelids rise, eyes narrow
- Pupils dilate
- Wrinkles appear in the outer corners and beneath the eyes
- The mouth opens to expose the teeth as the upper lip rises and the lower lip lowers
- Grooves or wrinkles appear over the corners of the mouth from the sides of the nose

These conditions, usually in conjunction, characterized a "happy" or "joyful" expression.

In this expression analysis, we expressed the degree of smile on a frame-by-frame basis. We defined 0 % as an expressionless state that does not laugh at all, and 100 % as a state of highest laughter. We used the highest degree of smile expressed as the result for each photograph displayed.

3.6   The Contents of the Questionnaire

They answered the questions by the 5-stage subjective evaluation each time after the experiment. Questions are composed of Q1–Q10 (young adults) and Q1–Q9 (elderly) (Tables 1, 2).

Table 1. Post-experiment evaluation (Young adults)

Number	Question
1	Could you communicate naturally?
2	Was the conversation exciting?
3	Were there any interesting topics?
4	Was your partner easy to talk to?
5	Did you feel a good rapport with the elderly persons by the end of the conversation?
6	Were you interested your partner?
7	Were you interested in what your partner said?
8	Do you feel closer to your partners than you did before the conversation?
9	Did you feel any stress while communicating with your partner?
10	Would you like to talk to your partner again?

Table 2. Post-experiment evaluation (Elderly)

Number	Question
1	Could you communicate naturally?
2	Was the conversation exciting?
3	Were there any interesting topics?
4	Was your partner easy to talk to?
5	Did you feel a good rapport with the patient by the end of the conversation?
6	Were you interested your partner as an individual?
7	Do you feel closer to your partners than you did before the conversation?
8	Were you interested in what your partner said?
9	Did you feel the nostalgia of the topic in conversation?

3.7   Experimental Methods

They talk seeing a photo or a movie through the PC.

We prepared each of the 20 photos of "Food" "Events" "Playing" "Lives during the Showa Era" and "Arts" which was shown along the flow of conversation.

We prepared a 10 min movie which was displayed on the PC monitor for the 10 min conversation. The partner student indicated the degree of mental load on the stress check board every minute. The Stress check Seat was hidden from the patient's eye. Our purpose was to check the mental load of the partner in the conversation, not to check their complaints to the elderly. Thus the partner may point it without feeling any burden towards the elderly. They could judge honestly. The seat was sometimes shown in the middle of their conversation but they continued their talk while pointing was done at the moment. They answered the questions by the 5-stage subjective evaluation each time after the experiment. The partner students had their heartbeats checked to measure their mental burden. They wore the counter in advance. A camera was used to capture the expressions (nod/line-of-sight) of the elderly throughout the sessions. The expressions of the elderly were analyzed from the video recordings.

4   Results

The results of the experiment described in Sect. 3.2 are shown below. Figure 7 shows the amount of stress accumulated for each photo image category.

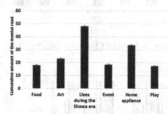

Fig. 7. Stress levels based on image type

The horizontal axis represents each photos category, respectively, and the vertical axis represents the accumulation on the numerical stress check sheet. This is a comparison of the young adults stress levels in case for each category of photos which is a comparison of the burden felt to continue the conversation as the conversation support content. Only the younger subjects' mental stress levels are shown.

The most stress was experienced when images depicting "Art" and "Lives during the Showa Era" were shown. In the "Food" "Events" "Playing" we found that there was almost the same degree of burden (stress). In addition, the result of the analysis of variance in the all categories, "Lives during the Showa Era ", "art" was out a large difference with the other items.

Figure 8 shows the results of the young adult questionnaire. The vertical axis represents the numerical value of the 5 rated questionnaire. The horizontal axis shows the questions Q1–Q10 for each category.

A more detailed examination of the results of Q9 is shown in Fig. 9. Question for "Food" for "Playing" had positive results. The opposite trend was seen in "Art" and in the "Lives during the Showa Era". There is a tendency that did not speak much in the question of whether you talk about your hobbies and interests of Q4.

Figure 9 shows the results of the question of whether one felt stress during a conversation that is asked by the questionnaire.

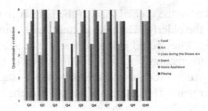

Fig. 8. Results – young adults Questionnaire (1 = No Stress. 5 = Extremely Stressful)

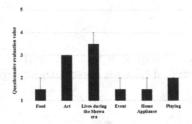

Fig. 9. Question 9 – Stress Levels (1 = No Stress. 5 = Extremely Stressful)

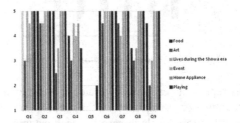

Fig. 10. Results – adults Questionnaire (1 = No Stress. 5 = Extremely Stressful)

In conversation of "Art" "Lives during the Showa Era" It has been found that they felt stress.

Figure 10 shows the results of the questionnaire for the elderly people. The vertical axis represents the numerical value of 5 rated questionnaire. The horizontal axis shows the questions Q1–Q9 for each category. A more detailed examination of the results of Q9 are shown in Fig. 11.

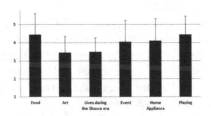

Fig. 11. Question 9 – felt nostalgia

Question for "Food" and "Playing" had positive results. The opposite trend was seen in "Art" and in "Lives during the Showa Era". There was a tendency that they did not speak much in the question of whether you talk about your partner's hobbies and interests of Q4.

Question 9 asked the question of whether they felt nostalgia. It got a good reputation of the "Food" "Event" "Home appliance" "Playing".

Were measured RR interval to measure the psychological loading of the conversation.

Figure 12 shows the RR intervals recorded during the 10-minute conversations; the RR intervals were between 746–841.

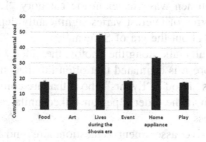

Fig. 12. RR intervals based on image categories

The RR interval in the "Lives during the Showa Era" "Art" "Home appliance" is found to be narrower.

In Fig. 13, we show the results of the expression analysis from the content of the video recorded during the experiment. As the photograph was changed roughly every 2 min, the average smile time was about 2 min per photo. Figure 13 places the contents of the video on the horizontal axis, and the degree of the patient's smile on the vertical axis.

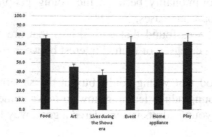

Fig. 13. The results of the expression analysis

The alphabet of the horizontal axis indicates the following.

From the results of the session shown in Fig. 13, we can see that the smile of elderly became more pronounced when we were talking about "Food" "Playing" and "Event."

The opposite trend was seen in "Art" and in "Lives during the Showa Era".

In addition, as a result of the (significance level 1 %) analysis of variance of the degree of smile in each category, we recognized a significant difference between the smiles related to each category.

5   Conclusion and Future Topics

5.1   Conclusion

We found that there is a large difference by categories of photographic images. As for what is this cause, the burden was greater in the category "Lives during the Showa Era", I found that the degree of interest varies significantly depending on whether the elderly has any fondness about the era of Showa.

Even if the young adults talk along the photos, the elderly only talk of an era that they are fond of. Therefore it is estimated that often this becomes a burden for young adults. Such as categories "Food", "Events", those that are common to any generation, it is considered that even if the elderly person talked unilaterally, the burden of the young adults might be less.

In all of the subjective assessment (Questionnaire and stress check) and the objective evaluation (EEG, Heart Rate, Expression analysis), we found that clearly there is a feeling of burden at the category "Art" and "Lives During the Showa Era" It is thought that Photos that we have used in the category of "Lives During the Showa Era" had many things that were vague, such as in a town or a house, so they couldn't determine where they could focus to talk.

On the other hand, even if items that will become part of "Lives during the Showa Era" such as "Home appliance" "Playing" as for the photos where those things were the category, we considered that the young people relatively felt less burden because the elderly felt nostalgic and the conversation went along well.

In all evaluation, it was found that when the conversation occurred with a category where there was less commonality between the young people and the elderly, the burden of the young people increases.

Regardless of age, it was found that with things that are familiar in the present environment that can be a category of mutual interest between the young adults and the elderly.

For example, the food that young adults buy at the supermarket, the elderly can make by themselves. Young adults learning how to make something from the elderly and the elderly teaching young adults is considered a good way for them to happily talk to each other.

5.2   Future Challenges

It is necessary that we make a similar experiment in other categories and will increase the categories that are appropriate for the system. We must examine in the future the mental burden of the young adults and elderly in utterance or in searching the topics. We anticipate to construct a supporting system which changes the contents of the category properly adopted to the situation to reduce the mental burden of the young adults and the elderly.

As mentioned in the overview of the system, it is necessary to have a device that the burden of both young adults and the elderly can be measured easily.

Therefore, we devised a mounting device, and we will build a system.

We suggest making a list for each category like "Food" "Events" or "Playing" in order to remove the nuisance of searching a target from an infinite data in YouTube or other pictures. Or at the point where the list of the searched result is made, an easy previewing would help to choose the one.

We are going to develop the touch panel system which would make searching a photo or a movie easy.

References

1. A Overview Ministry of Health, Labour and Welfare, a 12-year Heisei version of Annual Report on Health and Welfare, the aging of the world, the Ministry of Health, Labour and Welfare website (online)
2. Where to get. http://www1.mhlw.go.jp/wp/wp00_4/chapt-a5.html detail_recog.html (13 January 2012)
3. A Overview Ministry of Health, Labour and Welfare, a 2015 year version of Annual Report on Health and Welfare, the aging of the world, the Ministry of Health, Labour and Welfare website (online)
4. Where to get. http://www.mhlw.go.jp/topics/kaigo/kentou/15kourei/3a.html detail_recog. html (1 October 2013)
5. Astell, A.J., Ellis, M.P., Bernardi, L., Alm, N., Dye, R., Gowans, G., Campbell, J.: Using a touch screen computer to support relationships between people with dementia and caregivers. Interact. Comput. **22**, 267–275 (2010)
6. Noriaki, K., Kazuhiro, K., Shinji, A., Kenji, S., Kiyoshi, Y.: Video memories that utilize annotation of photo–application and evaluation to persons with dementia–making support. Artif. Intell. J. **20**(6), 396–405 (2005)
7. Airi, T., Noriaki, K., Kazunari, M.: Implementation of interactive reminiscence photo sharing system for elderly people by using web services. Human Interface Society (2010)
8. Miyuki, I., Noriaki, K., Kazunari, M.: Comparison between the burden of the conversation by using photographic image and that by using motion video. Human Interface Society 2012, pp. 579–584 (2012)
9. Miyuki, I., Noriaki, K., Kazunari, M.: The relationship between conversation skill and feeling of load on youth in communicate with elderly persons using video image and photographs. In: ACIT 2014 (2014)
10. Tomomi, O., Mariko, T., Mariko, A., Naoko, K., Yukikazu, S.: Expression analysis-Comparison of the characteristics of the facial expression, proposed by Ekman (2010)

The Turkish Central Doctor Rendezvous System Under Spotlight: A User Study with Turkish Senior Users

Edibe Betül Karbay$^{(\boxtimes)}$ and Kerem Rızvanoğlu

Faculty of Communication, Galatasaray University,
Ciragan Cad. No:36, 34357 Ortakoy, Istanbul, Turkey
{ebkarbay,krizvanoglu}@gsu.edu.tr

Abstract. The Central Doctor Rendezvous System (MHRS), which is one of the platforms within "Health in Transformation Project" to provide efficient health services, is promulgated by Turkish Republic Ministry of Health. The aim of this multi-method qualitative user study is to test the usability of MHRS web site with senior users. The sample includes 10 senior users. The test procedure is based on three steps: The semi-structured pre-test interview, the task observation phase and a debriefing post-test interview. The participants are asked to execute the pre-selected tasks through think-aloud protocol and the audio/mouse tracks are recorded during the navigation. The findings support the notion that the system comprises fatal problems not only for senior users who -due to relevant literature- already fight an uphill battle when interacting with any web environment, but also for a regular citizen who tries to find healthcare support.

Keywords: Usability · Healthcare · Senior users · User experience

1 Introduction

MHRS is "The Central Doctor Rendezvous System" which is promulgated by Turkish Republic Ministry of Health as one of the elements of "Health in Transformation Project" to provide efficient health services that was begun in 2009 and spread country-wide in 2011 [1]. The system offers two options to get an appointment: Via the call center service or the web site.

For the online service, users have to be enrolled to the system from the web page of MHRS. It is for free, and once someone is enrolled, s/he can register to the system whenever it is needed. MHRS system asserts that an appointment could be taken in three steps: "The first step: You can choose available doctors using search tools on the left side. The second step: You can see the doctors' working schedule when you select a doctor from the doctors' list. The third step: You can choose an available slot from the doctors' working schedule and record your rendezvous." [1].

E.B. Karbay——This study was realized under the coordination of Assoc. Prof. Kerem Rızvanoğlu with the support of Galatasaray University Scientific Research Fund (Project ID: 14.300.006).

© Springer International Publishing Switzerland 2015
A. Marcus (Ed.): DUXU 2015, Part III, LNCS 9188, pp. 628–637, 2015.
DOI: 10.1007/978-3-319-20889-3_58

This paper aims to investigate the usability of the online MHRS web site with senior users who are aged 55 and over and have specific needs to support user interaction.

2   Theoretical Background

Gualtieri [2] claimed that although there are lots of wrong or misleaded information on the websites and individuals tend to ask about health information to Dr. Google first rather than a real doctor. What she presented as a solution for medical societies or government agencies was to provide facilitated expertise guides through health web sites, and also a strong doctor-patient relationship. On the other hand, using Internet for persuasive health communication is the easiest and cheapest way to expand its effects [3]. Therefore the design of Internet-based interventions that lead to health behavior change should be explored with further studies.

Mobile health activities around the world are helping patients with chronic disease management, empowering the seniors and expectant mothers, reminding people to take their medicines on time, servicing without time and place limits, and improving health outcomes and medical system efficiency [4]. As an example, Huang et al. [5] designed and implemented a mobile health system prototype with real-time monitoring, precise positioning, rapid analysis, visualization display that can be widely used in family sickbeds, geracomiums, empty-nest elders' care, chronic disease patients and other special populations or scenes. The system had a Silverlightbased WebGIS system; a service center to monitor the location and physiological parameters of mobile monitoring terminal users, which makes alarms and reminders through spatial analysis.

Despite Turkey is notable for the majority of young people, elders are also one of the fastest growing segments in the country. According to World Aging Council gerontologist Kemal Aydın, Turkey where the population is getting older so rapidly, is taking the second place just after Indonesia: *"Now we have 6 million elders in population, furthermore we expect it to be around 12 million in 2020."* [6]. According to the research of Interactive Advertising Bureau (IAB) in 2013, the number of people above 55 years old increased by 20 % due to the previous years. Individuals, who are already experienced users of Internet, are getting older, and www seems to be a part of daily life. Thus, not only health services but also work web environment should be designed considering senior users.

There are some functional limitations associated with aging; commonly accepted ones during the normal aging process are vision decline, hearing loss, motor skill diminishment and cognition effects [7]. A senior-friendly web site is supposed to consider these limitations of the elders. On the other side, there are many seniors who were unsure about web terminology, such as page, homepage, website, or the web. This finding may be associated with the fact that seniors may use web for different reasons and that they may have started using the web without any user support [8]. Estes [8] stated that the web terms and technical jargon are especially problematic when seniors are asked to fill information up a form. The studies also showed that the users in Japan had difficulty in understanding the English web terms. In this context, it is evident that the localization process should be realized with great care and pass beyond plain translation.

Nielsen [9] collected simple measures by referring to vision, dexterity and memory criteria. He did not take into account the hearing ability because many web sites could be used fine without sound. Nielsen classified design issues and behavioral issues for senior users as follows:

Design Issues: Two most prominent design issues are readability and clickability. Considering the probability of reduced visual acuity which is one of the best known-aging problems, the websites targeting seniors should use at least 12-point font as their default set, and all of the webpages should let users increase text size as desired. Hypertext should be tracking as large and wide text, ensuing readability and making more prominent targets for clicking. Pull-down menus should walk hierarchically to prevent confusion.

Behavioral Issues: Two common behavioral issues that are observed in user studies with senior users are hesitation and discouragement: According to Nielsen [9] senior web users had discomfort and were hesitant in trying and exploring new things on the web, blamed themselves when a problem occurred rather than blaming the system, were more likely to give up on a task, and preferred to use web-wide search engines like Google to find out what they are looking for.

Nielsen [10] had recommendations for making a website easier and more engaging for seniors such as:

- Homepages that capture seniors' attention, in both the layout and content areas.
- Search design that makes finding information easy.
- Navigation considerations for the elderly who have diminished cognitive and motor skills.
- Content and web formatting techniques that help older people process information.
- Text and styles that accommodate people's diminished eyesight.
- Simplification of finding and buying items for the elderly.
- Forms that are easy to complete and not error-prone.
- Ways to reduce the number of forms to help seniors.
- Web address (URL) and browser considerations.

He also suggested offering supportive and forgiving design to encourage seniors for exploration and avoiding navigation changes to make steps catchy [9].

There is also another report, which suggests senior-friendly design of websites conducted by National Institute on Aging [11]. Hart [12] presented these guidelines as 25 usable tips for user experience practitioners [13, 14]. These parameters are as follows: Phrasing, Scrolling, Mouse clicks, Lettering, Justification, Style, Menus, Simplicity, Typeface, Color, Backgrounds, Consistent Layout, Organization of the textual content, Navigation, Help and Information, Icons and Buttons, Text Alternatives, Illustrations and Photos, Type Weight, Type Size, Site Maps, Hyperlinks, Animation/Video/Audio, Back/Forward Navigation, Physical Spacing, Search, Supportive and Forgiving Design.

3 Methodology

The purpose of this study is to explore the usability of online MHRS among senior users. A senior user is defined operationally as the person who is over 55 ages, who is a computer user, who has Internet connection at home/work and lives in Istanbul. Below is the research question of the study:

Research Question: What are the usability issues for senior users in MHRS website?

This qualitative study was based on a multi-method approach, which consisted of a pre-test questionnaire, task observation and a post-test interview. The pre-test questionnaire provided information on demographics and what s/he would expect form an online rendezvous system. The study also employed observation methods of data collection in order to gain better insight on user behaviors and attitudes. The tests were conducted with a PC laptop. Data collection instruments were semi-structured interview and tasks observation. Think-aloud protocol was used to collect behavioral data during the task execution stage. Additional behavioral data was collected by the recording of the voice, video and mouse-tracks of the participants. *Screencast-O-Matic Pro*, which is a program that records voice, video and mouse-tracks, is used as the major data collection equipment. 3 pilot tests were conducted to design the test procedure before the actual study.

The users were asked to terminate 4 different tasks during the task execution stage. First task was to "log in to the MHRS online system". The second task was to "get an appointment from the hospital located close to the home of the user". The third task was to "get an appointment from a pre-selected doctor with the following description: City: *Istanbul (Europe)* – District: *Beşiktaş* – Hospital: *Sait Çiftçi State Hospital*, Doctor: *Chest Deceases and Tuberculosis Specialist Dr. Arzu Soyhan*". The final task was to "cancel the rendezvous".

In this context, a sample of 10 senior participants (5 female, 5 male) were involved in the study. All the participants were over 55 years old (between 55 and 66) and were computer users with different educational backgrounds. One of them was graduated from the secondary school, one another was graduated from the high school and the rest had bachelor degrees. All the participants had Internet connection at home/work and lived in Istanbul.

All of the tests were conducted in the participants' own houses where they could feel comfortable. The tests were conducted by using the same laptop, mouse and online screen-recording program. The researcher adjusted the screen position according to participant's seeing abilities before starting to the user test in order to provide that all of the participants were able to see the screen easily. The participants who were not registered to the system were enrolled by the researcher's herself before the test. The researcher completed the registering process because otherwise the pilot studies showed that the task executions could take so long and result in anxiety on participants. The navigation was directly observed and recorded on a structured observation sheet by the researchers. Final structured post-test interview provided complementary findings.

The analysis framework was derived from the study of Nielsen [9, 10] and Hart [12]. The analysis framework that was derived from these two studies included the following parameters: Visibility and Affordance Issues due to Information Overload, Hard-to-Complete Error-prone Forms and Lack of User Support.

4 Results and Discussion

The findings from the background questionnaire showed that participants used www mostly for e-mail, social media and news coverage. Most of them (n = 8) have never used the MHRS before. Half of the participants had regular medical controls almost every month. The remainders seemed to have trust issues with the doctors and the hospitals. 3 participants stated that they did not prefer to go to hospitals except for emergency cases whereas 2 of them never preferred to go and see a doctor. Their relatives helped them to take their rendezvous when needed.

At the task-observation stage, the low task completion rate revealed the difficulty that the senior participants faced in using the MHRS online system. Only half of the participants were able to log in to the MHRS online system. For second task, only 4 of the participants could get an appointment from the hospital located close to the home of the user. 6 participants were able to get an appointment from a pre-selected doctor in a specific department of a hospital. However, only half of the participants could cancel the rendezvous as part of the final task.

4.1 Visibility and Affordance Issues Due to Information Overload

Visibility and affordance issues due to information overload were among the most common problems identified for older users. Too much material on the homepage made it harder for the participants to focus on relevant material.

As it can be seen on Fig. 1, in the homepage of MHRS, there is a form that has 7 different input fields to be fulfilled, each asking to choose the information from a pre-defined drop-down menu such as the city, district, hospital, district policlinic, clinic, clinic location and the doctor. Each input field has the default inline null text *"Does not matter"*. Under the form, there are 3 action buttons written in red, which are *"Clean (the input fields)"*, *"Search for rendezvous"*, *"Take a rendezvous from your family doctor"*. Next to the form, there is a welcome message and a guideline which give information about the rendezvous procedure: *"The first step: You can choose available doctors using search tools on the left side. The second step: You can see the doctors' working schedule when you select a doctor from the doctors' list. The third step: You can choose an available slot from the doctors' working schedule and record your rendezvous"*.

On the right hand, there are four buttons located separately from the form that lead to new windows when clicked: *"Past Rendezvous"*, *"Account Information"*, *"Announcements"*, *"Log out"*.

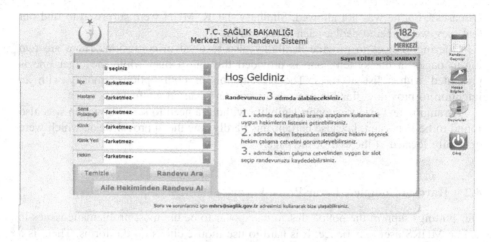

Fig. 1. Homepage of MHRS

As can be seen from the figure above, the users must fill in 7 different input fields in order to take a rendezvous. Besides the ambiguity of the labels in the forms confused the users. The input fields with the default inline null text *"Does not matter"* caused misunderstanding: *"If it does not matter, why I am supposed to fill the form?!"* (SEM), *"It does matter for me but the system does not let me choose one!"* (GUZ; MRH; MER).

There were also problems concerning the information architecture of the forms. Most of the terms were technical and users had difficulty in understanding these terms: *"What does slot mean? What is neurosurgery?"* (MUN). An onboarding process could provide users a better understanding of the system in their first visit.

In addition to that, the input flow in the form was not hierarchically designed although it had numbers that showed steps progressively. The required fields were not indicated. Thus participants thought that they needed to fill out all the input fields, which was not really necessary. In this context, the order of the input fields caused confusion: *"How can I know which policlinic my doctor works today?"* (AYN, MUN, RUH, HAY).

Canceling the rendezvous was the hardest task for participants since they looked for the "Cancel your rendezvous" button, but in fact it was hidden beneath the "Past rendezvous" button. In this sense, it is evident that the users should be provided with the action buttons carrying the relevant labels for the critical actions. Besides, the information in the system should also be supported visually. MHRS suggested visual icons, and cartoons for making the instructions simple, but this approach was not enough to support understandability.

Participants demanded smart customization features rather than an excessive load of information. They wanted the system to recognize them by their ID number and present them the information related with their demands. On the contrary, although they used their ID number in logging into the system, they were either not allowed to choose the department they preferred or they were misled to other irrelevant policlinics such as pediatrics. For example SEM wanted to take an appointment for "Allergic

Diseases", but he was not allowed. Similarly, DUR, MUN were surprised to find out that they were offered pediatrician as an option.

Offering choices to provide flexibility also resulted in confusion. There are two log-in pages in the system, one is provided through a map while the other one is presented with a list of rules. The presentation of both options –mostly with an intention to provide a flexible use- on the contrary caused confusion.

Arranging text size to support legibility without a need to scroll down/up was also found to be important, because participants hardly saw the approval links, which were generally located at the end of the page.

4.2   Hard-to-Complete Error-Prone Forms

Our findings support the notion that forms appear to be the most problematic issues in online MHRS user experience. It is hard to use mouse clicks on the forms. There is a long list embedded in the dropdown menu of each input field. Clicking any of the preferences does not work properly as well.

Senior users had difficulties in using the drop-down menus, which demanded selection from a pre-defined list. The form design was not supportive and forgiving. Once a mistake was done while filling the form, system was locked immediately. When presented with error messages, most of the participants tried a lot to recover the error. They even tried leaving the page and logging in back to clean the filled input fields. However, this unstructured trial-and-error approach mostly caused anxiety, feeling of inadequacy and guilt on senior users, which led to frustration and resulted in the abandonment of the relevant task.

There was also a systematic fail on the input field of the sign in which demanded user ID: The input field required be clicked first to fill up the ID Number. However it was not possible to click in until it was clicked to the leftmost part of the input field. In order to support the completion of the forms, keyboard focus should be on this first input field when the page is loaded.

Finally it was observed that the input fields of the form did not allow filling the form manually in case the dropdown menu didn't work properly. Participants tried to write manually to the form for several times, but the form was not designed due to this input strategy.

4.3   Lack of User Support

The findings showed that the senior participants should be supported with alternative mechanisms that could overcome the constraints caused by limited cognitive and motor abilities.

Some of the participants could not remember their password to log in. And the process to take a new password demanded excessive information based on the use of personal e-mail: *"I'm using the company's mobile phone and e-mail address. Otherwise I would not need them. And the system asks me for this information to remind me my password. What if I leave the job? What am I going to do to reach my account?"* (MUN).

Lack of onboarding in an overloaded homepage frustrated all the participants. MHRS is a technical web page due to medical terms intrinsically. However, there was neither an explanation, a glossary, a video nor a contact to lead people to the policlinic they needed to go. In this context, a live contact that offered online chat could be available for patients.

Location-based features could also simplify and shorten the rendezvous process by presenting the nearest hospitals to the user. For the second task, the user was asked to role-play as if s/he had a physical complaint of coughing and s/he was asked to take an appointment to the appropriate doctor nearby.

Since the system did not have location-based features, it was not possible to know which hospital was the closest one if the town was not well known. As the previous studies [3, 4, 13] showed that it could be possible to support ICT based systems with location-based features.

In this context the participants mostly tried to have an appointment close to their hometown or for a family doctor that they were familiar with. Especially "district" part, which was a required field, did not work properly in the system, and it was not possible to pass to the other input field without entering the district.

It was also not possible to choose a family doctor directly as it was mentioned in the guideline list of the MHRS page. It was impossible to have a rendezvous from the family doctor with the online system.

As a final note the findings showed that a proper reminder could contribute to the user experience. GUZ remarked that senior users could forget about their rendezvous. Therefore MHRS could remind them with alternative options such as telephone, e-mail etc.

5 Conclusion

The purpose of this study was to test the usability of online MHRS web site among senior users. This study revealed that MHRS has serious usability problems that disabled the senior users to use it efficiently. It was observed that the tasks, which could not be completed, were mostly related with the usability issues rather than the senior users' skills and abilities. The only difference between a senior user and a power user would be that a power user would easily understand that system did not work properly, while a senior user mostly felt anxiety, guilty and inadequacy.

Considering the usability problems observed in the study by referring to the analysis framework, the study provided the following implications for the improvement of user experience for senior users in digital health platforms:

- Beware information overload and value visibility. Make it easy to focus on relevant material in every page of the web site. Present information both textually and visually. Do not hide important functions deep within the menus without signifiers.
- Support legibility and readability. Let people adjust text size themselves.
- Value information architecture especially when presenting information with appropriate labels. Know your users. Do not adopt a technical jargon. Speak the users' language and provide consistency for language.

- Enable a hierarchical flow both for navigation and form-filling process.
- Provide easy-to-fill forms, which demand limited clicks, and support efficient data entry. Enable smart defaults and location-based features. Locate keyboard focus on this first input field when the page is loaded. Do not solely rely on drop-downs that cause both direct-manipulation and affordance issues.
- Provide flexible data entry with alternative input models.
- Be forgiving and support undoability in forms. Provide instant error feedback and tell users how to recover the problem as well.
- Present an onboarding process to emphasize the value that the system provides and teach the users to use the system quickly. Possible onboarding features could involve a demo video or a guidance system that provides sufficient information about the illnesses and leads the users to relevant departments and doctors available.
- Provide instant online help when needed. An instant messaging feature could be handy in helping the users.
- Provide reminders and alerts as cues for habitual actions.

Considering the lack of user-centered studies on senior user experience specifically in Turkey, this study contributed to the relevant literature by providing findings to improve the usability of digital health platforms for senior users. In order to a gain more insight on various aspects of senior user experience, further empirical studies with larger groups in diverse platforms should be conducted.

References

1. MHRS: Merkezi Hekim Randevu Sistemi (2014). http://www.mhrs.gov.tr/Vatandas/. Accessed January 2014
2. Gualtieri, L.N.: The doctor as the second opinion and the Internet as the first. In: Proceedings of the 27th International Conference on Human Factors in Computing Systems, Boston/USA (2009)
3. Cassell, M.M., Jacson, C., Cheuvront, B.: Health Communication on the Internet: an effective channel for health behavior change? J. Health Commun. **3**, 71–79 (1998)
4. West, D.: How mobile devices are transforming healthcare. Issues Technol. Innov. **18**, 1–14 (2012)
5. Huang, L., Xu, Y., Chen, X., Li, H., Wu, Y.: Design and implementation of location based mobile health system. In: Fourth International Conference on Computational and Information Sciences (2012)
6. ntvmsnbc: Hızla yaşlanıyoruz..., 5 October 2010. http://www.ntvmsnbc.com/id/25137919/. Accessed 23 January 2014
7. Arch, A.: Web accessibility for older users: a literature review, 14 May 2008. http://www.w3.org/TR/wai-age-literature/. Accessed 28 January 2014
8. Estes, J.: Define techy terms for older users, 24 May 2013. http://www.nngroup.com/articles/define-techy-words-old-users/. Accessed 21 January 2014
9. Nielsen, J.: Seniors as web users, 28 May 2013a. http://www.nngroup.com/articles/usability-for-senior-citizens/. Accessed 21 January 2014
10. Nielsen, J.: Senior citizens (ages 65 and older) on the web, 28 May 2013b. http://www.nngroup.com/reports/senior-citizens-on-the-web/. Accessed 22 January 2014

11. NIH: Making your website senior friendly, 17 October 2013. http://www.nia.nih.gov/health/publication/making-your-website-senior-friendly. Accessed 28 January 2014
12. Hart, T.A.: Evaluation of websites for older adults: how "senior-friendly" are they? 2003. http://psychology.wichita.edu/surl/usabilitynews/61/older_adults.htm. Accessed 29 January 2014
13. McKeown, K.R., Chang, S.-F., Cimino, J., Feiner, S.K., Friedman, C., Gravano, L., Hatzivassiloglou, V., Johnson, S., Jordan, D.A., Klavans, J.L., Kushniruk, A., Patel, V., Teufel, S.: PERSIVAL, a system for personalized search and summarization over multimedia healthcare information. In: JCDL 2001, Virginia, USA (2001)
14. West, M.: Dying to get out of dept: insolvency law and suicide in Japan. University of Michigan Law School, Michigan (2003)
15. Hart, T.A., Chaparro, B.S., Halcomb, C.G.: Evaluating websites for older adults: adherence to 'senior-friendly' guidelines and end-user performance. Behav. Inf. Technol. 27(3), 191–199 (2008)
16. Becker, S.A.: A study of web usability for older adults. ACM Trans. Comput. Hum. Interact. 11(4), 387–406 (2004)

Evaluation of Users Acceptance
of a Digital Medicine Fact Sheet:
Findings from a Focus Group

Amélia Lageiro[✉], Catarina Lisboa, and Emília Duarte

UNIDCOM, IADE – Creative University,
Av. D. Carlos I, 4, 1200-649 Lisbon, Portugal
amelia.lageiro@gmail.com,
{catarina.lisboa,emilia.duarte}@iade.pt

Abstract. Most medicine fact sheets are printed in small type and have information hierarchy and layout issues. In Europe, these sheets are individual bulletins that are put inside the packages. Users frequently report difficulties in reading the material, finding the required information and understanding the technical jargon, and/or have lost the sheet. The purpose of this study was to assess the participants' needs and major difficulties in using a medicine paper fact sheet, as well as their acceptance of a digital solution. Two focus groups sessions were conducted on a sample of 15 participants, divided into three groups (young adults, middle-aged adults, young-older adults). Differences among groups were found for difficulties with the paper version and the expectations regarding the digital version. Findings suggest that digital fact sheet may serve as a positive solution, but is mostly seen by the participants as a complement of the paper version.

Keywords: Medication · Fact sheet · Focus group · Information design · Interaction design

1 Introduction

As time goes by, health care is becoming more and more complex, and new clinical approaches are becoming available. However, little effort has been targeted at improving communication materials, such as medicine fact sheets, which may be associated to issues regarding patient medication and safety [e.g., 1–3]. This problem is particularly important for the over-the-counter (OTC) medicine, because fact sheets may be the only medium/source in which to provide users with critical information about the medication at hand.

The current strategy for OTC fact sheets, which in Europe are individual bulletins that are put inside the packages, is to include a substantial amount of information on all of the possible risks, as well as to provide guidance on proper use. In addition to this information overload, such safety communications are often designed without considering the users. As a result, the majority of these design solutions have a number of usability issues, for example: they use thin transparent paper; text in small sizes; absence of pictorials and/or illustrations; and poor organization of the information

© Springer International Publishing Switzerland 2015
A. Marcus (Ed.): DUXU 2015, Part III, LNCS 9188, pp. 638–647, 2015.
DOI: 10.1007/978-3-319-20889-3_59

(hierarchy and layout). In addition, the language used is mainly technical/complex, which does not facilitate its comprehension. Consequently, many users are not able to read and understand the information provided in the fact sheets [e.g., 7–9].

Since the population is growing old and the number of patients over 65 years of age is increasing rapidly, as well as taking medication more frequently, such usability issues need to be carefully considered. It is well recognized that older users safety may be compromised due to age-related sensory-cognitive changes [e.g., 4, 5], and therefore, may have problems in dealing with important information about the medication they take [6].

In many contexts of use, information technology has enhanced the customization and/or personalization of solutions according to the needs, limitations and expectations of individual users. In the medical domain, computer-based solutions, together with the Internet of things, can play a vital role in reducing medication-related errors, by providing information in a more effective manner [10]. Therefore, one possible solution that may override the communication problem regarding paper-based fact sheets is to turn them into digital products.

The digital fact sheet, as a product of information technology, can help to improve medication safety by preventing errors, by facilitating a more rapid response to users' doubts/needs, as well as by tracking and providing feedback. The main strategies to enhance the interaction with fact sheets could include: improving communication between clinicians and patients (e.g., creation of user profiles, personal accounts, schedules, alerts, reminders); make information more accessible (e.g., providing access to reference information) and inclusive (e.g., changing graphical properties); hierarchizing information according to relevance; assisting with the clarification of doubts (e.g., prescriptions); providing decision support; among others.

Given the large potential of a digital fact sheet, as well as the benefits and caveats involved, in this paper we present an assessment of the users' acceptance of such a solution (as a concept) for an OTC. For this purpose, focus groups were conducted with three groups of participants (young adults, middle-aged adults, young-older adults). For further reading on the application of focus group techniques for supporting design activities, readers are referred to Bruseberg and McDonagh-Philp [11], and on conducting focus groups with the elderly, are referred to Barret and Kirk [12]. This research is being conducted under the Visual and Information Design domain, according to a User Centered Design approach, and involves an iterative design process. In this early stage, participants were asked to participate in focus group sessions intended to: (a) examine their perceptions about conventional fact sheets of over-the-counter medicines, i.e., its usefulness, usability, perceived adequacy and preference; (b) examine their expectations regarding a digital fact sheet.

2 Method

2.1 Participants

Participants were recruited voluntarily by direct invitation and were chosen as representatives of the target population. When recruited, participants were informed of the study's objectives, the expected duration of the focus group session, the procedure, and all of their doubts were clarified.

A total of 15 participants (4 men and 11 women), ranging in age from 18 to 64 years old, completed the study. The mean age of the sample was 43.80 years old (SD = 15.0). Participants were recruited in three groups, based on the criteria adopted by Hancock, Rogers and Fisk [13]: young adults (18–34 years old); middle-aged adults (35–54 years old) and young-older adults (55–64 years old). There were five participants in each group (Young adults: M = 27.4 years, SD = 6.19, five females and two males; Middle-aged adults: M = 43.2 years, SD = 6.38, four females and one male; Young-older adults: M = 60.8 years, SD = 3.56, for females and one male). The disproportionate number of females is associated to the fact that such females were more available (e.g., housewives, unemployed, live longer) and open to be engaged in such studies.

2.2   Procedure

In order to minimize issues that could hinder the open discussion of the intended topics, the focus group sessions were conducted with each age group separately. All focus group sessions were held at the same facility, i.e., the meeting room of a local sports center. The facility was selected based on the following criteria: (a) location (nearby to all participants); (b) environment (quiet, warm, with daylight and well lit); and (c) equipment (have a table and at least 6 chairs, which provided easy eye contact between all participants and the moderator).

Participants were given a consent form before beginning the session. After they agreed to participate, they were given a brief presentation of the study's objectives followed by a short questionnaire to collect demographics (e.g., age, gender, education). Participants were told that there were no-wrong answers and that they were to reply freely, without constrains and in a spontaneous way. Afterwards, all participants sat around the table in order to start the session. The first author, who was the moderator, took notes regarding the critical issues and group's dynamics. All discussions were audiotaped for later analysis. When a question was asked, the participants were first asked to give their inputs one at a time, and then, only after each individual response was a group discussion encouraged. If the discussion went far off the topic at hand, the moderator reminded the participants about the topic being discussed and/or introduced a new one.

The sessions were divided into two sections that lasted approximately 30–40 min, with a 10 min break. In order to provide the participants with a context and to facilitate the discussion, two videos were displayed according to the sections' objectives; one at the beginning of each part of the session. These focus groups' objectives were to examine: for the first section – (a) perceptions of current OTC fact sheets; (b) barriers that hinder interaction with current solutions; (c) individual factors such as perceptive and/or cognitive difficulties, knowledge, attitudes and beliefs that are likely to influence behaviors towards using the fact sheets; and (d) strategies to improve the current solutions; for the second section – (e) expectations and acceptance of a digital solution.

2.3   Materials

Videos. At the beginning of each focus group section, participants were asked to watch a short video. Two videos were created for this study: video 1, related with the use of a current paper medicine fact sheet (see Fig. 1) and video 2, related with the use of a digital medicine fact sheet (see Fig. 2).The videos were filmed in a frontal point of view and showed, set by step, someone interacting with a fact sheet. In video 1 the sequence is as follows: the user grabs the medicine package, takes the fact sheet and the blister pack out of the package, unfolds the fact sheet, reads it, takes the pill, folds the fact sheet and places all materials back into the package. In video 2, the sequence is: the user grabs the medicine package, grabs the smart phone, reads the digital fact sheet, takes the blister pack out of the package, takes the pill, and places the blister pack back into the package.

Fig. 1. Screenshots from video 1, illustrating the use of a current paper medicine fact sheet

Fig. 2. Screenshots from video 2, illustrating the use of a digital (on a smart phone) medicine fact sheet.

Focus group script. The focus group followed a previously defined narrative script, which was elaborated after a literature review on the study's topics.

The first section of the session was related with the current paper fact sheets' version. In this section, participants were asked if they usually read the fact sheets; and, if so, why they do it, how often they do it, their most common difficulties while using it, and their beliefs regarding the information contained therein, as well as adverse consequences associated to their incorrect/inadequate use. After watching video 1, participants were told: "Now, please try to remember the last time you used a medicine facts sheet".

- **Reasons for using the facts sheet.** What motivated you to read it? When replying, please bear in mind: For what reason(s) did you read the facts sheet; What content do you most look for; Did you find what you needed? As exploratory and/or probative questions we had: Do you read the facts sheet before taking the medications, or only when you have doubts? Do you self-medicate yourself? If yes, how often or in what circumstances? In case of doubt, do you try to get an answer from the facts sheet or do you come into contact with healthcare workers?
- **Attitudes and beliefs.** Next, in order to assess attitudes and beliefs, participants were asked: To what extent do you believe that the facts sheet is a useful, effective and functional material for the user? As exploratory and/or probative questions we had: Do you believe that most fact sheets provide users with the answers they are looking for? Do you think that the fact sheets are needed? Do you always follow the doctor's instructions or reading the fact sheet altered your adherence to the received guidelines? Do you consider the information therein accessible, legible, and understandable to any user, regardless of his/her personal variables? What, in your opinion, could improve the fact sheets' usability?
- **Self-efficacy.** Regarding self-efficacy, participants were asked: Do you think that reading the fact sheet should become a habit and/or part of your medication process – as something that you do without conscientious consideration, similar to wearing seat belt in cars – or it is something that you need to actively think in order to be done? As exploratory and/or probative questions we had: If reading the fact sheet ensures you that you are perfectly aware of the medicines' intended use, proper way of use, and associated risks, would you be willing to read it more often?
- **Inclusiveness, availability and accessibility.** Regarding the fact sheets' inclusiveness, participants were asked: What barriers can hinder yours or others ability to effectively use the fact sheets? - (1) Medium, format and size? (2) Font/type, style, size, contrast? (3) Pictorials, graphs, illustrations? (4) Layout, structure and information hierarchy?
  When addressing the facts sheet availability and accessibility, participants were asked: Is the facts sheet normally/usually available to you when you really need it (you have it with you)? How difficult is it to obtain the fact sheet? As exploratory and/or probative questions we had: What do you think should be done in order to ensure this material's better availability and accessibility?

In the second section, participants are confronted with a prototype of a digital fact sheet and questions about its use were addressed. This set of questions was intended to gather insights on their expectations regarding such a product (e.g., functionalities, ways of interaction), advantages and disadvantages, awareness of their technology proficiency level on using such type of devices, and willingness to pay for this solution.

The participants were told: "As we had the chance" to see in the video, mobile devices (e.g., smart phones and tablets), with access to the Internet, can provide us not only with the same information contained in the current paper-based fact sheets, in a customized manner, but also with other information related with the medicine and/or the treatment, for example: our medical history/reports (risks), suggestions of other alternative medicines for the same symptomatology, costs, drug interactions, among others.

- **Relevance.** How interesting would it be for you to have such solution? Lets start with the advantages and, afterwards, with the disadvantages. As exploratory and/or probative questions we had: how useful/interesting would it be to have the chance to – (a) have a personal account with your profile; (b) have access to a database of drugs, from which you could receive warnings, alerts or other useful data regarding the medication or the treatment; (c) have a personal assistant which could help/guide you along the treatment; (d) have access to a FAQs list in which you could find the most common questions/doubts and their answers?
- **Technology proficiency.** To what extent can technology-based solutions become, to some users, an obstacle for using such type of solution? Which factors do you think may strongly affect the adoption of such a solution: (a) reliability; (b) knowledge of how to use it; (c) belief that such technology improves/enhances the process; (d) difficulty in using the application; (e) difficulty in learning how to use the application; (f) no one else (family, friend, doctor, pharmacies) is using this application?
- **Interest.** To what extent would you be interested in having this type of application? How much would you be willing to pay for it (from 0.99€ to 1.99€; 2.00€ to 3.00€).

3 Results

3.1 Reasons to Use the Facts Sheet

Most of the participants state that, although they found it difficult to use, they usually read the facts sheet. Only one participant from the middle-aged group stated not to read the fact sheet.

Regarding the reasons to read it, regardless of the group they are in, their comments were centered on three aspects: contraindications, dosage and posology. The fact sheet is also referred to as being the first option used by the participants to clarify their doubts about the medication or the medicine, followed by the Internet. The least preferred options are, and have the following order: pharmacies, other people and doctors.

3.2 Attitudes and Beliefs

All participants agreed that the majority of the current fact sheets are not effective, but they consider it very necessary. Factors such as complexity and confusion were the most referred reasons for the poor effectiveness.

Some participants stated that, due to previous negative experiences, they sometimes follow the fact sheet's instructions instead of the doctors' indications.

When asked to suggest modifications to improve the current fact sheets' design, participants suggested, firstly, a more understandable language, followed by a better hierarchy of the information, as well as a different layout and larger letters.

3.3 Self-efficacy

Participants concurred that reading the fact sheet should become a habit when taking some medication. Participants in the middle-aged groups stressed the importance of carefully reading the fact sheet, especially in what concerns children's medication, because of the risks involved.

3.4 Inclusiveness, Availability and Accessibility

The typeface size, followed by technical jargon and the information provided (which was considered scary and overwhelming) were the most referred factors for the poor interaction quality. Poor layout and graphical design were also considered as obstacles.

The middle-aged group was the only one to provide a somewhat positive evaluation of the fact sheet or, at least, to show some tolerance. In their opinions, although they sometimes spend more time and effort in order to find and/or understand the information they need, they are most of the times successful.

Regarding the accessibility, most participants stated that they usually leave the fact sheets inside the package. They rarely take it with them, and when they do take it out it is because they have doubts regarding the new medication they are taking.

3.5 Relevance

The majority of the participants in all of the groups considered the relevance of a potential digital fact sheet high. However, there were some differences among the groups. The acceptance was higher in the young-adults group, followed by the middle-aged group and, lastly, the young-older adults. On the contrary of the young adults, although considering the digital solution interesting, the middle-aged and young-older adults groups see it as a complement of the paper version.

The young-adults highlighted the quick access to the information and the mobility as the digital fact sheet's most important advantages. They also pointed out its great utility for healthcare professionals and for educational purposes. They considered the digital solution advantageous for users in general, mostly because it can be customized to users' needs and limitations, and may be accessible everywhere with a mobile device, especially with an Internet connection.

The main advantages mentioned by all of the three groups were related to the possibility of having access to information directed to their doubts, in a more intuitive and clear manner. In what regards the possibility of having a personal account, with access to a personal clinical history, it was very well accepted mostly because they considered the ability to receive alerts regarding potential interactions with substances/drugs and allergies, particularly in cases of self-medication, very positive.

They also considered the possibility of accessing information concerning alternative medicines for the same symptoms to be very useful. The personal assistant idea was a very welcomed functionality, especially if it could simplify the technical jargon. However, some participants mentioned reliability concerns regarding pre-recorded tapes or when "talking to a machine" (some form of artificial intelligence); they would rather prefer to talk (or chat) with a human expert. The young adults group also highlighted the dictionary of technical terms as an interesting functionality, since it would give them the ability to learn the terms' meanings, which could be useful when interacting with a paper-based solution.

3.6 Technology Proficiency

All of the groups agreed and expect that the older-adult population will have more difficulties in interacting with such a digital solution, because of their low technology proficiency. On contrary to the data gathered from the young-older adults group, for both of the young-adults and middle-aged adults groups, the low technology proficiency was not seen as an unsurpassable obstacle since they believe that they can learn how to use it.

Regarding their own technology proficiency level, both young-adults and middle-aged adults groups considered to have a high proficiency level, with an average of three out of five. The young-older adults considered having a low average of two out of five.

In what concerns the difficulties they usually face when dealing with applications for mobile devices, with exception of the young-older adults group which stated they do not usually interact with such applications, the two other groups shared the same difficulties: installation process, security issues, terms and conditions, as well as permissions.

3.7 Interest

Finally, in what regards the interest of using digital fact sheets, both young-adults and middle-aged groups declared they would be very interested in such an application and that they would be willing to pay (i.e., 3.00€, as previously mentioned) to have it. However, one third of the participants said they would appreciate having a trial version, even with less functionality available, in order to test their utility and usability before buying the actual application.

4 Conclusion

This paper addressed users' judgments regarding the current paper-based fact sheets and assessed their expectations and acceptance regarding a digital counterpart.

The focus groups results indicate that the participants consider the current fact sheets as non-effective due to their poor graphic design (e.g., layout, typeface size) and information issues (e.g., technical jargon, scary and overwhelming). Overall, these results are concurrent with previous findings in the literature [e.g., 2, 7–9]. However, all of the participants considered this material as very important for their safety.

Other interesting results involve the users' expectations and acceptance regarding a digital fact sheet, similar to an application connected to a database, which may be a solution to overcome the problems with the current paper-based products. With exception of the young-older adults group, the other two groups consider this a very interesting solution and provided some useful insights on what they would expect from it. The middle-aged group, however, sees it as a complement of the paper-based material.

For OTC medicines, or in cases of self-medication, important advantages were attributed to functionalities such as a personal account with connection to a personal clinical history, alerts and warnings, database of other available medicines, a personal assistant to clarify doubts, among others. Young-adults also suggested that such an application could be used by healthcare workers and/or for educational purposes. Nevertheless, they also considered such technology to have some disadvantages, mainly associated to the older adults' low technology proficiency. Some concerns regarding reliability were also discussed. But, in the end, all participants concluded that such a digital fact sheet could be relevant for increasing their safety with medication and declared to be very willing to have it and pay for it if necessary.

This study has some limitations, which can hinder the generalization of the results. One is related with the sample's representativeness. More focus groups should be run with other groups with different educational and cultural background, as well as limitations. Other methods should also be included, such as contextual interviews.

In the present study we did not evaluate the usability of a digital fact sheet prototype. According to an UCD approach, this evaluation will be required later in order to determine the solutions' quality, as part of a larger User Experience evaluation. We hope that the present study's positive results regarding the users' expectations and acceptance of a digital fact sheet for OTC medicine will help motivate/encourage additional research in this area, and thereby contribute to the promotion of users' safety.

References

1. Hellier, E., Edworthy, J., Derbyshire, N., Costello, A.: Considering the impact of medicine label design characteristics on patient safety. Ergonomics **49**, 617–630 (2006)
2. Shrank, W., Avorn, J., Rolon, C., Shekelle, P.: Effect of content and format of prescription drug labels on readability, understanding, and medication use: a systematic review. Ann. Pharmacother. **41**, 783–801 (2007)
3. Dickinson, D., Raynor, D.K., Duman, M.: Patient information leaflets for medicines: using consumer testing to determine the most effective design. Patient Educ. Couns. **43**, 147–159 (2001)
4. McLaughlin, A.C., Mayhorn, C.B.: Designing effective risk communications for older adults. Saf. Sci. **61**, 59–65 (2014)
5. Mayhorn, C.B., Podany, K.I.: Warnings and aging: describing the receiver characteristics of older adults. In: Wogalter, M.S. (ed.) Handbook of Warnings, pp. 355–362. Lawrence Erlbaum Associates Inc., Mahwah (2006)

6. Wogalter, M.S., Magurno, A.B., Dietrich, D.A., Scott, K.L.: Enhancing information acquisition for over-the-counter medications by making better use of container surface space. Exp. Aging Res. **25**, 27–48 (1999)
7. Fujita, P.T.L.: Análise da apresentação gráfica do conteúdo textual da bula de medicamento na perspectiva de leitura do paciente em contexto de uso. Setor de Ciências Humanas, Letras e Artes, Master, p. 160. Universidade Federal do Paraná, Curitiba (2009)
8. Puebla, G.d.C.: Avaliação da compreensão de bulas de medicamentis pelos usuários. Faculdade de Farmácia, Graduation, p. 33. Universidade Federal do Rio Grande do Sul, Porto Alegre (2012)
9. Spinillo, C., Padovani, S., Lanzoni, C.: Ergonomia informacional em bulas de medicamentos e na tarefa de uso: um estudo sobre fármaco em suspensão oral. Revista Ação Ergonômica **5**, 2–10 (2011)
10. Bates, D.W., Gawande, A.A.: Improving safety with information technology. New Engl. J. Med. **348**, 2526–2534 (2003)
11. Bruseberg, A., McDonagh-Philpb, D.: Focus groups to support the industrial/product designer: a review based on current literature and designers' feedback. Appl. Ergon. **33**, 27–38 (2002)
12. Barrett, J., Kirk, S.: Running focus groups with elderly and disabled elderly participants. Appl. Ergon. **31**, 621–629 (2000)
13. Hancock, H.E., Rogers, W.A., Fisk, A.D.: An evaluation of warning habits and beliefs across the adult life span. Hum. Factors **43**, 343–354 (2001)

Designing for the Healthcare Professional's Experience

An Internet of Things Application with an Accessible Interface for Remote Monitoring Patients

Chrystinne Oliveira Fernandes[(⊠)] and Carlos José Pereira de Lucena

Pontifical Catholic University of Rio de Janeiro (PUC-Rio),
Rio de Janeiro, Brazil
{cfernandes, lucena}@inf.puc-rio.br

Abstract. E-health area is a research field whose exploration can bring numerous benefits to society. In this paper, we present results from a case study performed in a healthcare environment supported by an Internet of Things (IoT) solution to automate techniques commonly used in patients' treatment and data collection processes. This solution comprises hardware prototypes including sensors, micro-controllers and software agents that work together to make hospital environments more proactive. In addition, the proposed solution provides remote storage of patient data in cloud-based platforms, allowing for any authorized person, including external professionals to work collaboratively with the local team. A web system enables real-time visualization of patient's record as graphical charts through an intuitive interface. Software agents constantly monitor collected data to detect anomalies in patients' health status and send alerts to health professionals when they occur. This work also aims to enable remote patient monitoring to increase proactivity and save resources.

Keywords: Healthcare · Medical systems · Internet of things · Multi-agent systems · E-health · Sensors · Monitoring · Accessibility

1 Introduction

In recent years, the healthcare sector has become one of the main targets for the academic community and financial market. The sector has attracted large investments, mainly because it is a field with great potential for research. The healthcare sector faces many problems such as insufficient resources, high cost of health treatments and the ineffective management of hospital resources. There are also logistical problems such as the amount of patients requiring medical care, a limited number of beds, limited hospital supplies, and few healthcare professionals. Patient monitoring is commonly performed in a reactive way, i.e., medical teams conduct treatment in reaction to the change of the patient's health condition. The reaction time is critical, since the worsening of the patient's condition can result in critical consequences.

Fortunately, these problems are associated with opportunities for improvement, many of them aided by technological resources that we have today. Within this context, our paper presents the results of a case study in a simulated environment aiming to prototype an IoT solution to tackle some of the health problems previously mentioned.

© Springer International Publishing Switzerland 2015
A. Marcus (Ed.): DUXU 2015, Part III, LNCS 9188, pp. 651–661, 2015.
DOI: 10.1007/978-3-319-20889-3_60

We named this solution Remote Patient Monitoring System (RPMS). The RPMS incorporates the use of smart devices and different software techniques in order to save resources. The general goal of this work is to contribute to a more effective management of hospital resources. The developed prototype provides an infrastructure with an accessible interface aiming to make the hospital environment more proactive, responsive and interactive. We present a technology that acts on the environment and equips it with intelligent devices.

The prototype is based on the Internet of Things (IoT). IoT is field within Computer Science that has grown substantially over recent years. It broadens the established concept of the internet, from a network that connects people to a wider network that allows for the connection between people and things, and between things, with little or no human intervention. Within the IoT context, "things" are real-world entities that are part of the IoT network. These things can vary from simple objects, such as a chair, appliances or cars, including living entities, for instance, plants, animals and persons. Our solution adopts a modeling strategy based on reactive and cognitive software agents to build the IoT application.

The remainder of this paper is organized as follows: Sect. 2 describes the theoretical groundings, discussing aspects of Ubiquitous Computing (UbiComp), IoT, Human-Computer Interaction (HCI) and Multi-Agent Systems (MAS). Section 3 describes the research method used in this study. Section 4 presents the details of the conducted case study. Section 5 concludes this paper with final remarks and future work.

2 Theoretical Groundings

This project has a multidisciplinary approach, involving a variety of research areas, such as the IoT, UbiComp and HCI. Building on these areas, we designed and constructed an e-health system to assist remote patient monitoring activity.

Before discussing the solution in detail, we present a brief overview of fundamental concepts that support the features in this work.

2.1   Ubiquitous Computing

Ubiquitous Computing (UbiComp), as defined by Mark Weiser in the early nineties [REF], relates to the concept where computing power is distributed across devices. In fact, back when Weiser coined the term Ubiquitous Computing, it represented a change of view in Computer Science. The focus changed from the machines to the human. He envisioned that computing power rather than being concentrated in supercomputers with high cost, size and power would be distributed into smaller and cheaper computing devices spread around the environment

According to Weiser, the notion of ubiquity arose from the observation of things in the real world, specifically, the office equipment used in daily activities. Weiser conceived a different approach for these computing devices based on this observation. Instead of modelling the diverse devices' functionalities within a single computer, he proposed transferring the computational power to these devices. Therefore, they would be able to process information provided to them.

According to Weiser, "ubiquitous computing it the method of enhancing computer use by making many computers available throughout the physical environment, but making them effectively invisible to the user" [2].

2.2   Internet of Things

Although the early works in Ubiquitous Computing promoted the distribution of computational power, devices were still limited because they were dependent on manual manipulation by people for making data available. These devices produced a large amount of information, but humans generally have limited time resources. This has led to a bottleneck in the process of sharing this information. This way the concept of IoT has emerged, in which things would be able to connect to the Internet and publish its information with little or no human intervention.

Considering things as a new autonomous element of network models represented a paradigm shift. It was possible to automate costly human activities, such as collecting and publishing data over the network. The IoT approach delegates these activities to things, which can interact with each other, with people and systems. Thus, interactions in the network, which before were restricted to human-to-human or human-to-computer, were extended to support other interactions like human-to-thing and thing-to-thing.

One can define IoT as a global network of smart devices that can sense and interact with their environment using the Internet for their communication and interaction with users and other systems [5]. IoT application developers may rely on a variety of communication technologies. In this work, we use RFID (Radio-Frequency IDentification), Arduino micro-controllers and sensors.

RFID is an automatic identification technology based on radio signals, used for sensing and communication [1]. A RFID system consists of two components: the transponder, which is located on the object to be identified and the interrogator or reader, which, depending on the technology used, may be a read-only or read-write device. The reader and transponder are the main components of every RFID system [8].

Arduino, is a modular open-source prototyping platform [9]. It consists of a micro-controller that can be programmed to process input and output of external electronic components connected to it. It is an embedded computing device that allows to build systems to interact with the environment through hardware and software [4].

Developers can use different types of sensors to collect useful data in IoT applications in the e-health context. These sensors can provide a variety of vital data, including heartbeat rate, blood glucose (to monitor diabetic patients), temperature, humidity, liquid level, oxygen level, carbon dioxide level, patient activities (with an accelerometer) and many others.

2.3 Multi-Agent Systems

According to Wooldridge, an agent can be defined as "a computer system that is situated in some environment, and that is capable of autonomous action in this environment in order to meet its delegated objectives" [6]. Although there is no universal definition for the term agent, there is a consensus in the literature that autonomy is a key feature to the notion of agency. In this context, the possibility of autonomous acting means that no intervention by humans or others systems is necessary for agents to decide how to perform their activities, although the set of possible actions must be set beforehand. Another relevant property of agents is learning, that is, the ability to learn from their experience.

Agents control their internal state and behavior, but they do not have full control over their environment. They have a set of actions to perform that may result in environment changes, so they may influence their environment according to the action they decide to perform. Agents autonomously decide what to do to meet their goals.

2.4 Human-Computer Interface

As defined by Preece, Rogers and Sharp, "HCI is a multidisciplinary field that is concerned with the design, evaluation, and implementation of interactive computing systems. It encompasses all aspects related to the interaction between people and computers" [7].

The quality of interactive systems involves properties such as usability, accessibility, communicability and user-experience. In this paper, we explicitly addressed the accessibility property. According to Tim Berners-Lee, the power of the Web is in its universality and the access by everyone regardless of disability is an essential aspect [10].

According to the W3C's Web Accessibility Initiative, web accessibility means that people with disabilities can perceive, understand, navigate, interact and contribute with the Web [10]. The design of the web system that is part of the RPMS solution considers some accessibility requirements. Using tools developed for visually impaired users, namely screen readers, these users are able to interact with our solution. Screen readers interpret textual content in web pages and convert them to audio format.

In terms of usability, the system supports the use of wearables, bracelets with RFID tags, as a way to interact with the system. For instance, health professionals can identify patients and their records simply by approaching a mobile device, such as tablet, smartphone, or other device with RFID reader to the patients' bracelet. The reading event triggers the display of their data through a web page, containing the medical records history and real-time status.

3 Methodology

In order to perform an in-depth analysis and clarify research challenges regarding patient monitoring through an IoT view, we have defined research questions followed by a case study to explore design and implementation issues.

3.1 Research Questions (RQ)

The following research questions were defined to tackle aspects from monitoring patients' domain that, in our point of view, are those that can bring improvements to this application domain.

RQ1. How can the use of micro-controllers, sensors and wearable devices make patient monitoring processes more proactive?

RQ2. How can the collection and distributing of real-time patient data support patient monitoring?

3.2 Hypotheses (H)

Before the empirical study, we formulated five hypothesis. At the end of this study, these hypotheses were contrasted with data obtained to be confirmed or refuted.

H1. It is feasible to use wearables devices in order to identify patients through an IoT solution

H2. One can collect patients' vital data automatically using an IoT application

H3. It is possible to detect anomalies in patients' health status in real time

H4. The patient monitoring can be done in remote mode

H5. The use of micro-controllers, sensors and wearable devices can make patient monitoring processes more proactive

4 Case Study: Remote Patient Monitoring

4.1 Problem Definition

Scientific research within the context of healthcare is a complex task. Dealing with such sensitive issues as patients' health and the risks involved in their medical treatment encompass challenges of diverse natures. Consequently, technological advances emerge more slowly than in other areas. Barriers to conducting research in this area are not limited to strictly technical matters. The direct involvement of patients in any scientific research demands the definition of an ethical protocol, which a committee may decide to approve or not. Moreover, healthcare staff and patients may be involved in design stages of a software development process, since their perspectives might contribute with practical design issues. However, these parties may be unavailable or may have little spare time for collaborating with the research.

We observe that in many cases the patient monitoring is done reactively. In this case, the medical team only takes action after detecting a decline in the patient's health. We define the term Anomaly Detection Interval (ADI) as the time interval between the moment that the patient had complications in their health status and the time of its detection by health professionals. We define as anomalies noticeable deviations in patients' health status, which requires professional intervention at the instant they occur.

The local monitoring is one of the factors that contribute to raising the ADI, since the healthcare provider needs to displace himself to the location of patients and then collect vital data for the assessment of their condition.

4.2   Proposed Solution

The RPMS is an IoT solution for patient monitoring that supports automatic collection and transferring of patient data to remote repositories. A web system provides access to this data through a user-friendly interface. This system makes use of software agents for anomaly detection, resource negotiation and dynamic reconfiguration in response to changes in the environment. Additionally, the solution helps to visualize patient data remotely stored.

4.3   Goals

We defined the following goals for guiding the development of the prototype solution, aiming to minimize the ADI:

- To reduce the displacement of health professionals in reactive monitoring;
- Automate the process of collecting vital patient data;
- To allow remote data visualization, promoting the dissemination of patient data for medical staff and external collaborators;

4.4   Results

RPMS Architecture. The RPMS is structured in three layers:

L1. Data Distribution Layer: Our solution uses a cloud-based platform to distribute data. This platform is a remote repository of patient data

L2. Data Communication Layer: Performs the communication of the IoT application (L3) with the cloud-based platform (L1) through a REST API. The application sends and retrieves data from the cloud-based platform through HTTP requests

L3. Data Management Layer: Comprises the IoT application with its six modules. It is responsible for the entire information processing in RPMS, ranging from identification, collection, storage, visualization and data monitoring to the dynamic reconfiguration of the system

Figure 1 shows an overview of the architecture of the proposed solution.

RPMS Infrastructure Elements and Technologies Used. To provide the data distribution in our solution, we use a free remote data storage service called Parse. Developers can easily configure applications' backend with this service. This cloud-based platform offers functionalities for saving data objects, file storage, push

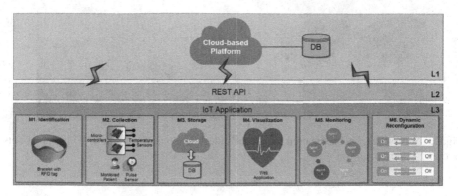

Fig. 1. The RPMS architecture with its three layers (L1-L3). The IoT Application (L3) interacts with a cloud-based platform (L1) through a REST API (L2).

notifications and user management [12]. In addition, it allows data portability, offering a way to export an application's entire data set, in the same format as the REST API. The Parse also has a feature to import data in the REST API format. The platform also has an importer, which supports JSON and CSV files. However, the platform recommends importing data in the REST API format due to its flexibility.

We use a technology called Temboo in order to enable our IoT application to interact with the cloud-based platform. The Temboo is a code virtualization platform. It is used to facilitate building applications and interacting with various APIs [13]. The Temboo has a specific library for Parse, called Parse library, with seven packages available to support code creation for consume the services offered by this cloud platform. In our solution, we are using Queries package to insert and retrieve Parse data. Thus, our IoT application uploads the patient data to the remote data repository using Parse library from the Temboo API. In addition, the application consumes this data in real time and displays them graphically on a web page.

We also use another Temboo library called Twilio to send alerts to health professionals via SMS. Twilio is a communication platform that provides web-services APIs, allowing users to build their own scalable, reliable applications for voice communication and SMS. Different solutions use Twilio, including in the healthcare context [14]. Software developers can use their web services API to make and receive calls and send and receive text messages. Twilio services are accessed via the HTTP protocol. In our application, we use Twilio service, in a simplified manner by the Twilio library from Temboo. Our application uses the SMSmessages package that allows sending and receiving SMS messages [13].

Finally, to provide the functionality corresponding to the RPMS's L3 layer, we are using some hardware and software elements. For the identification of the patient (M1 module in the IoT application), we use an RFID system. This system includes a wearable device corresponding to a bracelet with an RFID tag (Fig. 2) and an RFID reader (Fig. 4-b). The data collection module (M2), in turn, performs the patient data sensing through a hardware prototype containing an Arduino microcontroller with wireless and Ethernet network interface, a temperature sensor and a heartbeat sensor in addition to a protoboard and some male-male type jumpers (Fig. 4-a).

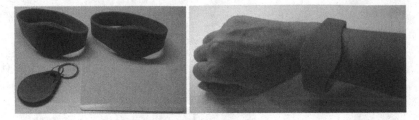

Fig. 2. Accessories that can be used for patient's identification, containing RFID tags: bracelets, card and keychain.

Fig. 3. Readings of accessories with RFID tags through our hardware prototype

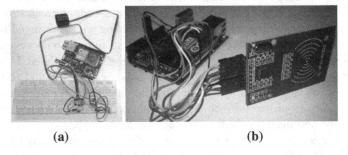

(a)   (b)

Fig. 4. (a). Prototype for monitoring patients containing temperature and pulse sensors. (b). Prototype for identification of patients through RFID automatic identification technology.

We used the Arduino Integrated Development Environment (IDE) to implement the M1 and M2 modules in the C ++ programming language. It comes with a set of libraries to build programs easily. Professionals such as designers and artists that are not professional programmers also can build systems easily using Arduino. Some sensors require the installation of external libraries, provided by their own manufacturers as the pulse sensor library used in our solution. This library can be downloaded from the manufacturer's website, along with a getting started guide [15]. We also installed the Temboo library available for download on this API's website, along with its installation manual [13].

We developed the other application modules, M3, M4, M5 and M6 in Java language. To implement software agents in the Monitoring module (M5), we used the JADE (Java Agent Development Framework) framework [11].

RPMS Model. The following table lists the elements that represent the concept of things involved in the environment in which the patient is being treated:

Thing1.   Patients;

Thing2.   Bracelets with RFID tags;

Thing3.   Health Professionals;

Thing4.   Patient's environments (Apartment, intensive care unit, Surgery room)The follow agents were modeled in the system:

Agent1.   DataVerifierAgent: Checks for anomalies in the sensored data;

Agent2.   SMSAgent: Notifies anomalies, by sending messages;

Agent3.   ResourceNegotiatorAgent: Performs negotiations with other agents to get resources;

RPMS Features. The tool is composite for six modules as follows:

M1. Patient identification: Patient identification: Performed by an RFID system, where the patient uses a bracelet with an RFID tag in order to be identified it in the system by a health professional. When health professionals read a patient's bracelet using a device such as a smartphone or a tablet, the data of this patent can be quickly visualized in their device. The RFID readings triggers the initialization of a web page with patient data (Fig 3).

M2. Collection: our application collects automatically patient data such as pulse and body temperature. This collection process is made using a hardware prototype comprising sensors and micro-controllers. The application also can collects information about patient's environment. This information can be light, humidity and noise level of environment.

M3. Storage: Once collected, the system transmits the patients' data to a cloud database service if connectivity is available. Otherwise, the application persists data locally and transmits them later on.

M4. Visualization: A web application visualizes the patient records. Any authorized person can access it from multiple devices (computer, smartphone or tablet). This application has a user-friendly interface with accessibility features for people with visual impairment. The application requests data from the cloud platform and exhibits at the web page in line charts. The plotted data is updated in real-time, in interval time settings previously. The Fig. 5 shows an example of a chart corresponding to patient temperature data.

M5. Monitoring: This module constantly monitors the collected patient data through agents that should react in case of anomalies detection. Reactive and cognitive software agents support this detection mechanism. The system has a mandatory configuration step for each patient as follows: an administrator user registers and defines the Desired Value Range (DVR) for each sensor (e.g., expected temperature and pulse values).

We call the values that are outside this range Anomalous Values (AV). The values that are close to the minimum and maximum values are associated with abnormalities. Each of these anomalies receives a representative label within the healthcare context, so

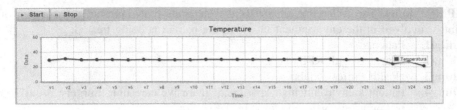

Fig. 5. Charts corresponding to the sensor readings from patients and its environment

that it makes sense to a domain expert. The goal is to enable a healthcare professional to quickly identify any problem occurring when the anomaly is detected by the system. In addition, the administrator must assign a professional to handle each anomaly, who will be alerted of its occurrence. This notification can be through e-mail or SMS. Software agents are in charge of this continuous detection of minimum and maximum anomalies, as well as sending alerts to professionals.

Cognitive agents use argumentation techniques to work collaboratively on shared resources, promoting a more effective resource management. The system outputs recommendations, such as which patient should be next in line for medical care. The agents also suggest which patient needs to receive, more urgently, medical assistance like a nursing professional to administer their medication.

M6. Dynamic reconfiguration: The collection module is context sensitive, i.e., the system can react dynamically in response to changes in the environment. The displacement from a patient to a new environment can invalidate the defined data range for the anomalies. In this case, the application will need to be reconfigured. The user can reconfigure them through the application interface or the system can reconfigure itself autonomously by intelligent agents. In the latter case, the agents will exchange information, so that new agents can learn the environment configuration, by querying other agents that already know the environment conditions.

5   Conclusions and Future Works

We can observe that the proposed solution makes the environment more proactive, since the system detects anomalies in real time and sends alerts autonomously through software agents. Responsible health professionals for handle those anomalies can take action immediately in response to these events. A possible indication of proactivity can be verified by measuring the DAI.

One can note a large human-to-thing interaction in the system, since agents (considered things in this application) are able to alert professionals about anomalies in the patients' health status. Additionally, there is a large thing-to-thing interaction, since VerifySensorDataAgent and SendSMSAgent agents, can communicate with each other effectively for achieving their goals.

One can see that this solution make the patient's identification process more efficient, since it replaces the traditional identification techniques with RFID identification technologies.

Our solution also improves the process of collecting vital patient data, since it replaces the manual data collection processes, which is more prone to errors.

The patient data distribution over the Internet allows any authorized person to consult them from anywhere at any time. This functionality also brings benefits, such as the possibility of different experts to collaborate and discuss about the patient's health status and possible treatments.

As future work, we consider using cognitive agents for performing activities such as recommendation of possible treatments and medications and predicting potential patient's health conditions that can lead to anomalies. In addition, we plan to provide remote monitoring already in ambulances during the patient's way to the hospital.

Acknowledgements. This work was supported by grants from CAPES.

References

1. Atzori, L., Iera, A., Morabito, G.: The internet of things: a survey. J. Comput. Netw. Int. J. Comput. Telecommun. Network. **54**, 2787–2805 (2010)
2. Weiser, M.: Some computer science issues in ubiquitous computing. Commun. ACM **36**(7), 75–84 (1993)
3. Kuniavsky, M.: Smart Things Ubiquitous Computing User Experience Design. Elsevier, Amsterdam (2010)
4. Norvig, P., Russell, S.: Artificial Intelligence (in Portuguese). Elsevier, Amsterdam (2013)
5. Doukas, C.: Building Internet of Things with the Arduino. CreateSpace Publisher, North Charleston (2012)
6. Wooldridge, M.: An Introdcution to MultiAgent Systems. Wiley, New York (2009)
7. Preece, J., Rogers, Y., Sharp, H.: Interaction Design, 1st edn. Wiley, New York (2002)
8. Finkenzeller, K.: RFID Handbook: Fundamentals and Applications in Contactless Smart Cards and Identification, 2nd edn. Wiley, New York (2003)
9. Arduino. http://arduino.cc/
10. W3C Web Accessibility Initiative. http://www.w3.org/WAI/intro/accessibility.php
11. JADE. http://jade.tilab.com/
12. Parse. https://parse.com/
13. Temboo. https://www.temboo.com/
14. Twilio. https://www.twilio.com/
15. PulseSensor. http://pulsesensor.com/pages/code-and-guide

Three-Dimensional Models and Simulation Tools Enabling Interaction and Immersion in Medical Education

Soeli T. Fiorini[1(✉)], Leonardo Frajhof[3], Bruno Alvares de Azevedo[1],
Jorge R. Lopes dos Santos[1,2], Heron Werner[4], Alberto Raposo[1],
and Carlos José Pereira de Lucena[1]

[1] Pontifícia Universidade Católica Do Rio de Janeiro, Rio de Janeiro, Brazil
soeli@les.inf.puc-rio.br,
{azevedo,jorge.lopes}@puc-rio.br,
{abraposo,lucena}@inf.puc-rio.br
[2] Instituto Nacional de Tecnologia - MCTI, Rio de Janeiro, Brazil
jorge.lopes@int.gov.br
[3] Universidade Federal Do Estado Do Rio de Janeiro - UNIRIO,
Rio de Janeiro, Brazil
leonardo.frajhof@gmail.com
[4] Clínica de Diagnóstico Por Imagem (CDPI), Rio de Janeiro, Brazil
heronwerner@hotmail.com

Abstract. The article proposes the creation of a library of clinical cases generated from images of minimally invasive procedures, which will enable students to experience immersive way of performing procedures enabling the implementation of a Biodesign Lab in Medicine, which will bring real cases (initially in the domain of obstetrics and cardiology) as a premise, to the virtual world, hands-on learning and experimentation of advanced technologies based on a multidisciplinary and active participation of physicians and computing engineers, experiencing and sharing experiences.

Keywords: Virtual reality · 3D modeling · Visual simulation · Minimally invasive surgery · Noninvasive diagnostic methods

1 Introduction

New forms of interaction and access to technologies previously available only to large technology centers are increasingly close to the everyday reality of the common user. Technological development has altered several practices in healthcare, covering activities such as diagnosis, treatment, management and education, and requiring the development of new skills by professionals.

Rare diseases or invasive procedures are critical in medicine because trial is limited to the number of cases, often incurs risk of life, and little training material is available. Considering the long learning curve in medical education, it is undeniable the contribution of three-dimensional models and simulation tools enabling interaction

A. Marcus (Ed.): DUXU 2015, Part III, LNCS 9188, pp. 662–671, 2015.
DOI: 10.1007/978-3-319-20889-3_61

and immersion closer to reality. Knowledge is constructed seeking information and exploring data as it existed. The minimally invasive treatment of heart disease, for example, is a lengthy process and it is very difficult to achieve the ideal positioning of medical devices such as stents. This is because the visualization process to be 2D, using fluoroscopy, while the procedure is in real 3D. Simulation of these procedures will aid the physicians when implementing this training activity.

In this context, the article proposes the creation of a library of clinical cases gene - rated from images of minimally invasive procedures, which will enable students to experience immersive way of performing procedures enabling the implementation of a Biodesign (http://www.ccbs.puc-rio.br/index.php/pesquisa/laboratorio-biodesign) Lab in Medicine, which will bring real cases (initially in the domain of obstetrics and cardiology) as a premise, to the virtual world, hands-on learning and experimentation of advanced technologies based on a multidisciplinary and active participation of doctors and computing engineers, experiencing and sharing experiences.

In cardiology, 3D physical model of the thoracic aorta and the transcatheter aortic valve implantation was chosen as a clinical case. The use of physical models in fetal research, an area in which there are few studies on digital modeling also has introduced. The result suggest a new possibility in the interaction between parents and fetus during prenatal care, physically recreating the uterus during pregnancy, showing the actual size of the fetus, as well as its anatomy. In the next sections these clinical cases are described.

2 Clinical Cases in Cardiology

The first experiments were conducted in order to understand the difficulties found during the endovascular procedure and how to produce physical 3D models could be useful in educational terms and, ultimately, for the purpose diagnostic. After performing the Computerized Tomography (CT) angiography of the aorta, and an images segmentation process, the 3D model was built by the physical rapid prototyping technique [1, 2] and a virtual simulation of the route taken by catheter into the aorta was done. This is a non- surgical alternative for aortic valve replacement in patients with aortic stenosis - taught considered unsuitable for surgery. The self-expanding transcatheter valve bioprosthetic, CoreValve has been widely used from the worldwide.

2.1 3D Physical Model - Thoracic Aorta Prototype

In order to demonstrate the possibilities provided by three-dimensional technologies, images of the thoracic region of a patient using multi-slice CT were obtained. Initially we selected the case of an aneurysm of the abdominal aorta patient, classified as complex due to anatomical reasons. The aortic aneurysm is a dilation of a segment of blood vessel. These images were handled to select only the region of interest, obtaining a three-dimensional digital model of thoraco-abdominal and thoracic aorta (Fig. 1). Thereafter, a physical model was made using additive manufacturing.

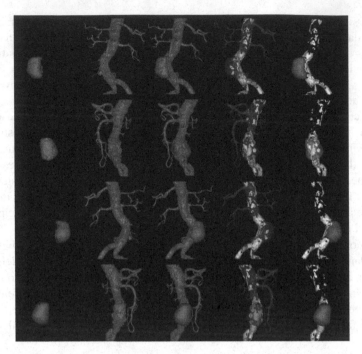

Fig. 1. A sequence of 3D software protocol was developed to target the aneurysm with high fidelity and to create a flexible aortic 3D prototype.

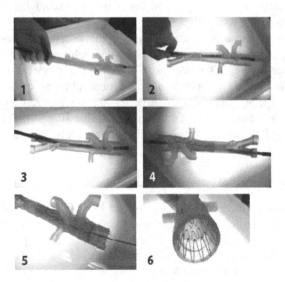

Fig. 2. Endovascular Procedure

The assay was made in order to understand the difficulties encountered during the endovascular procedure and how 3D physical model could be useful in training and, ultimately, for diagnostic purposes.

To test the viability of the aorta prototype (Fig. 2), we simulated the endovascular procedure, positioned the guide wire (Fig. 2 – number 1, 2 and 3) and insert the stent up to the desired level for their release. (Figure 2 – number 4 and 5) After the withdrawal of the guide wire, the prosthesis had been completely deployed and well positioned (Fig 2 – number 6). The procedure was a success.

2.2   A Virtual Simulation of the Route Taken by Catheter into the Aorta

In cardiology, the transcatheter aortic valve replacement – TARV, was chosen as a case study. Once a particular exam was selected, a written informed consent from the patient was obtained. The present study was registered at the National Council for Ethics in Research (CONEP), from the Brazilian Ministry of Health.

The TARV procedure has a long learning curve. Tridimensional tools, like physical models and virtual simulations may, in the near future, perform an important role in this learning process [3, 4].

An angiography-CT of the aorta was performed by Somatom Sensation 64 × 0.6 mm CT scanner (Siemens Inc., Germany). The DICOM images were transferred to the software Mimics® (Materialise, Belgium) and the aortic lumen was selected. An image segmentation process was performed as show in Fig. 3.

A physical 3D model was built by the rapid prototyping technique, using the Stratasys uPrint equipment (Stratasys, USA) with ABS plus material. This includes physical modeling of the aortic root, coronary arteries, ascending aorta, aortic arch and descending aorta.

A virtual simulation of the route taken by catheter into the aorta was implemented using the software 3ds max 2014 (Autodesk, Inc., USA). The physical and virtual model represents the patient-specific anatomy. Figure 4 shows the start of the virtual navigation process in a segment of the abdominal aorta. Figure 5 represents the lumen of aortic arch. At the top right of the image is shown the catheter in the lumen of the aorta.

After validation and reproducibility analysis, this process can be presented as a pre-step procedure to add accuracy and safety to the real transcatheter aortic valve replacement. Probably, using this procedure, it may be possible to detection of aortic diseases, like aneurysm, marked tortuosity and atheroma plaque. Thus with the VR, the doctor can navigate along the route taken by catheter into the aorta, made possible a close analysis of reality making the surgical planning or decision-making more effective.

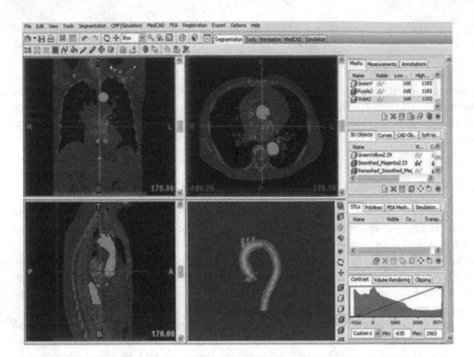

Fig. 3. Segmentation process performed in Mimics® (Materialise, Belgium)

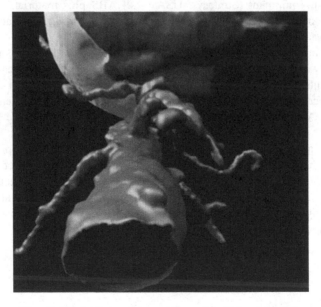

Fig. 4. Navigation process performed in abdominal aorta

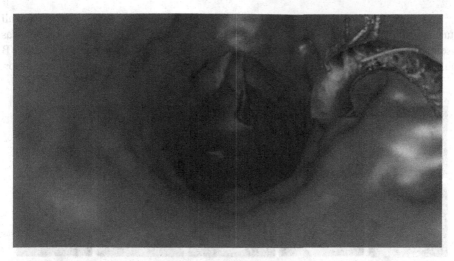

Fig. 5. Navigation process performed in the lumen of the aortic arch

3   Clinical Cases in Obstetrics

3.1   Virtual Bronchoscopy for Evaluating Cervical Tumors of the Fetus [5]

The objective was to investigate the use of magnetic resonance imaging (MRI) with virtual bronchoscopy (VB) to evaluate fetal airway patency in four fetuses with a cervical tumor (three lymphangiomas and one teratoma).

Cervical tumors (Fig. 6), although uncommon, create unique circumstances for the management of pregnant women, and are a serious medical dilemma. Although the incidence of congenital tumors is low, ultrasound (US) is effective for identifying fetal tumors [6]. Estimation of the degree of tracheal compression or distortion allows multidisciplinary planning for delivery and neonatal resuscitation [7]. Magnetic resonance imaging (MRI) with virtual bronchoscopy (VB) can provide information about the fetal airway [8].

The aim of this case was to investigate the use of MRI with VB for evaluating fetal airway patency in four fetuses with a cervical tumor.

The examinations were performed between 26 and 37 weeks gestation. All 4 fetuses were examined by ultrasound and MRI on the same day. No other fetal abnormalities were detected. MRI was performed using a 1.5-T scanner (Siemens, Erlangen, Germany). A 3D file of the airway was created by overlapping layers generated by MRI. The 3D files were converted into an OBJ extension using the 3D modeling software MAYA (Autodesk, USA). This allowed the virtual positioning of observation cameras while working with multiple windows. Using the indoor and outdoor lighting features, 3D simulation movies were generated for analysis of a virtual path.

The main outcome was the creation of 3D virtual airway paths (Fig. 7) on all fetuses and VB was successfully carried out on each case. In all 4 fetuses there was absence of invasion, compression or distortion of the trachea. Thus the MRI with VB could become a useful tool for studying fetal airway patency in cases of cervical tumor.

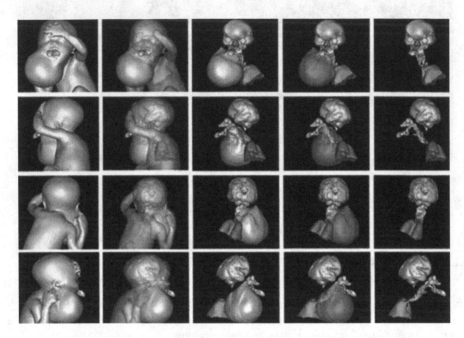

Fig. 6. Cervical teratoma, 33 weeks. 3D view of the fetus and tumor

3.2 Additive Manufacturing Models of Fetuses Built from 3D Ultrasound (3D US), Magnetic Resonance (MR) Imaging and Computed Tomography (CT) Scan Data [6]

In this study the main outcomes presented were the possibility to create 3D virtual models from 3D US, MR or CT both separately and also in various combinations. Additive manufacturing systems allow the conversion of a 3D virtual model to a physical model in a fast, easy and dimensionally accurate process [9, 10]. Additive manufacturing (AM) is the automatic, layer-by-layer construction of physical models using solid freeform fabrication.

A key concern of this study was obtaining high-quality images that could be manipulated with 3D software without loss of accuracy [11]. Fetal movements during image acquisition are one of the principal difficulties. This is less of a problem with ultrasound as the real time image can be frozen during a movement unlike MR imaging. However the lower contrast resolution with 3D US can cause difficulties at gray scale boundaries. Image quality is directly associated with the precision of the final virtual 3D mathematical data that will be used to generate the prototype. Images from medical scans are acquired by "slicing" the physical body. Superimposition of the captured slices from 3D US, MR or CT results in construction of a virtual 3D CAD (computer-aided design) model. The additive process begins when the virtual 3D CAD model is sliced in layers that are used to guide the deposition of materials, layer by layer, to generate a physical 3D model [11, 12].

The construction process transfers a 3D data file that specifies surfaces and solid internal structures to AM equipment that builds physical models through the super-imposition of thin layers of raw materials 14. This study introduced the use of additive manufacturing models into fetal research, an area where studies on digital 3D modeling have been scarce. The results suggest a new possibility for interaction between parents and their unborn child during pregnancy, by physically recreating the interior of the womb during gestation, including physical appearance, actual size and malformations in some cases.

The techniques described in this study can be applied at different stages of pregnancy and constitute an innovative contribution to research on fetal abnormalities. We believe that physical models will help in the tactile and interactive study of complex abnormalities in multiple disciplines. It may also be useful for prospective parents by recreating a 3D physical model with the characteristics of the fetus that allows a more direct emotional connection to the unborn child [13, 14].

Physical models have been used in fetal medicine for teaching purposes, but to the best of our knowledge, no examples are known that apply contemporary physical modeling technology to their production [15, 16]. Combining the different image modalities of 3D US, MR and CT may result in an increase in the interaction of both medical doctors and parents with the growing fetus, for educational and even future diagnostic purposes.

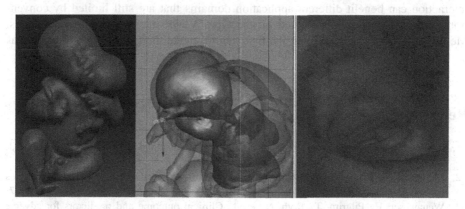

Fig. 7. Virtual bronchoscopy, 34 week fetus with cervical teratoma.

4 Conclusion

The visualization of internal anatomical structures provides substantial advances in the medical field through diagnostic imaging, reducing the subjectivity of diagnosis and taking the right treatment. These models generated in the described clinical cases help plan minimally invasive interventions and provides a great knowledge of the anatomical dimensions, facilitating the learning of health professionals. These features, when combined with additive manufacturing, creates new opportunities for scientific research and new teaching techniques in health care. The models used in cardiovascular area, for example, for in vitro test new devices and procedures generally consist on prototypes of animal origin or craft, which do not represent true human anatomy.

The increasing technological development in obtaining and viewing images trough non-invasive technologies has brought great advances in medicine, especially in viewing the fetus.

Based on our results, we believed that physical models would help in the tactile and interactive study of many medical disciplines. These techniques may be useful for prospective parents, especially visually disabled parents, as they recreate a 3D model with the physical characteristics of the fetus, as allowing a more direct emotional connection with the unborn baby.

The Virtual Reality (VR), which offers advanced interfaces capable of providing the user immersion in environments with which you can interact and explore, has permeated the area of health, bringing new possibilities for three-dimensional modeling and simulation. The feasibility of reproducing real situations without risk to patients, cost savings due to reduced use of physical objects and the ability to model, simulate and visualize impossible actions to be perceived in the real world are reasons for that VR applied to health constitutes an area of increasing interest.

If on one hand this scenario is enabling the emergence of innovative applications and new modes of interaction, on the other hand the use of 3D modeling in Medicine is still nascent. There is still relatively little knowledge about the best techniques to implement and evaluate the use of these environments, as well as how this form of interaction can benefit different application domains that are still limited by conventional interaction techniques based on the type WIMP interfaces (Windows, Icons, Menus and Pointing device), but the first step to create the clinical cases library was performed.

References

1. Pal, P.: An easy rapid prototyping technique with point cloud data. Rapid Prototyping J. **7**(2), 82–90 (2001)
2. McGurkg, M., Amis, A.A., Potamianos, P., Goodger, N.M.: Rapid prototyping techniques for anatomical modelling in medicine. Ann. R. Coll. Surg. Engl. **1997**(79), 169–174 (2007)
3. Wenaweser, P., Pilgrim, T., Roth, N., et al.: Clinical outcome and predictors for adverse events after transcatheter aortic valve implantation with the use of different devices and access routes. Am Heart Journal **161**, 1114–1124 (2011)
4. Groves, E.M., Falahatpisheh, A., Su, J.L., Kheradvar, A.: The effects of positioning of transcatheter aortic valves on fluid dynamics of the aortic root. ASAIO J. **60**, 545–552 (2014)
5. Werner, H., dos Santos, J.R., Fontes, R., Daltro, P., Gasparetto, E., Marchiori, E., Campbell, S., Belmonte, S.: Virtual bronchoscopy for evaluating cervical tumors of the fetus. Ultrasound Obstet. Gynecol. **41**(1), 90–94 (2013). Published by John Wiley & Sons, Ltd

6. Werner, H., dos Santos, J.R., Fontes, R., Daltro, P., Gasparetto, E., Marchiori, E., Campbell, S.: Additive manufacturing models of fetuses built from three-dimensional ultrasound, magnetic resonance imaging and computed tomography scan data. Ultrasound Obstet. Gynecol. **36**, 355–361 (2011)
7. Werner, H., dos Santos, J.R., Fontes, R., Daltro, P., Gasparetto, E., Marchiori, E., Campbell, S.: Virtual bronchoscopy in the fetus. Ultrasound Obstet. Gynecol. **37**, 113–115 (2011)
8. Frates, M., Kumar, A.J., Benson, C.B., Ward, V.L., Tempany, C.M.: Fetal anomalies: comparison of MR imaging and US for diagnosis. Radiology **232**, 398–404 (2004)
9. Gaunt, W.A., Gaunt, P.N.: Three Dimensional Reconstruction in Biology. Pitman Medical Press, Tunbridge Wells (1978)
10. Armillotta, A., Bonhoeffer, P., Dubini, G., Ferragina, S., Migliavacca, F., Sala, G., Schievano, S.: Use of rapid prototyping models in the planning of percutaneous pulmonary valve stent implantation. Proc. Inst. Mech. Eng. H. **221**, 407–416 (2007)
11. Robiony, M., Salvo, I., Costa, F., Zerman, N., Bazzocchi, M., Toso, F., Bandera, C., Filippi, S., Felice, M., Politi, M.: Virtual reality surgical planning for maxillofacial distraction osteogenesis: the role of reverse engineering rapid prototyping and cooperative work. J. Oral Maxillofac. Surg. **65**, 1198–1208 (2007)
12. Werner, H., dos Santos, J.R., Fontes, R., Gasparetto, E.L., Daltro, P.A., Kuroki, Y., Domingues, R.C.: The use of rapid prototyping didactic models in the study of fetal MalFormations. Ultrasound Obstet. Gynecol. **32**, 955–956 (2008)
13. Campbell, S.: 4D and prenatal bonding: still more questions than answers. Ultrasound Obstet. Gynecol. **27**, 243–244 (2006)
14. Steiner, H., Spitzer, D., Weiss-Wichert, P.H., Graf, A.H., Staudack, A.: Three-dimensional ultrasound in prenatal diagnosis of skeletal dysplasia. Prenat. Diagn. **15**, 373–377 (1995)
15. Willis, A., Speicher, J., Cooper, D.B.: Rapid prototyping 3D objects from scanned measurement data. Image Vis. Comput. **25**, 1174–1184 (2007)
16. Blaas, H.G., Taipale, P., Torp, H., Eik-Nes, S.H.: Three-dimensional ultrasound volume calculations of human embryos and young fetuses: a study of the volumetry of compound structures and its reproducibility. Ultrasound Obstet. Gynecol. **27**, 640–646 (2006)

MedData: A Mobile Application Designed for Medical Teams to Monitor Clinical Evolution of Inpatient in ICU Context

Carlos Alberto Pereira de Lucena[✉], Cláudia Renata Mont'Alvão,
and Bruno Alvares de Azevedo

Pontifical Catholic University of Rio de Janeiro (PUC-Rio),
Rio de Janeiro, Brazil
lucenapucdesign@gmail.com,
{cmontalvao,azevedo}@puc-rio.br

Abstract. Intensive Care Units inside hospitals are usually managed by different teams of physicians. Each team is in charge of a specific number of patients and are composed by physicians that cover different specialties. The information gathered by the physicians regarding each patient is crucial to their treatment and is also very valuable for the rest of their team. In the reality of the majority of the Brazilian hospitals, this type of information is recorded in paper notes and later archived in hospital records. In order to share this information with the rest of the medical team, physicians nowadays regularly create their own digital files and saves them in cloud based servers such as Drop Box or Google drive in order to give access of the data with their peers. Aiming to solve this problem, research teams from PUC-Rio university developed a mobile application named MedData. This app is currently being developed and tested, as described in this paper.

Keywords: Healthcare · Design · HCI · Mobile · E-health · Application

1 Introduction

Patients transferred to Intensive Care Unit (ICU), in the majority of hospitals, need constant care and the attendance of a qualified medical team. To make certain decisions and to plan specific treatments, this team should input, observe and interpret a huge amount of data, gathered from different sources. This information, in the reality of the Brazilian typical hospital environment, is inserted by handwriting in forms printed in paper by nurses and physicians.

After this event, the information is shared and discussed by the team in hospital meeting rooms, analyzing information printed in paper. Afterwards, in order to maintain the track record of all patients, all the information in paper is stored in hospital's archives. To gain speed in terms of sharing this type of information, medical teams usually duplicate the information that has to be formalized to hospital systems into Microsoft software spreadsheets and upload the information to Internet cloud services such as Google Drive and Drop Box. Using this method, medical teams can

© Springer International Publishing Switzerland 2015
A. Marcus (Ed.): DUXU 2015, Part III, LNCS 9188, pp. 672–681, 2015.
DOI: 10.1007/978-3-319-20889-3_62

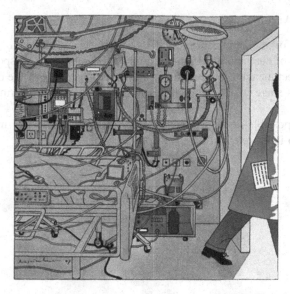

Fig. 1. Image criticizing patient data gathering in ICU's (newyorker.com/magazine/2007/12/10/the-checklist).

share and access relevant data prior to arriving the hospital. In Brazilian's main cities realities, physicians usually work in different hospitals and by sharing information online they gain autonomy and time.

Another huge challenge, in terms of data gathering in ICU's, is the use of mobile text based applications by the medical team, that need to insert a huge amount of data regarding the patient condition. In the ICU context, information has to be formalized in a very short period of time and, although mobile devices can be pretty handy in emergency environments, they lack the benefit of rapid data input through texting. This research focuses on the development of a mobile application that offers an easy way for medical teams to input and share reliable information regarding patients' conditions while interned in hospitals ICU's. The application gathers all the patients' basic information that has to be inserted in the moment that he or she enters the ICU and most importantly, a constant follow up of the clinical evolution.

2   MedData Application

In order to meet the objectives of this research, the mobile application MedData was developed during the year of 2014, in PUC-Rio (Pontifícia Universidade Católica do Rio de Janeiro), involving the departments of Informatics and Design (PUC-Rio). The first version of the application was tested inside the National Institute of Cardiology - Ministry of Health - Rio de Janeiro, Brazil. After interviews realized with physicians that used the application, the development team designed and implemented a new version of the mobile application that will be used, tested and researched during the first semester of 2015 (Fig. 1).

2.1   MedData Architecture

The architecture of the application MedData emphasizes the path from the login through the input of data about the patient, in the medical team's perspective. The first phase of the project meant to observe the usability and accuracy of the data inserted by the users. At this stage, the functionalities aimed to share the information were not looked at.

Bellow, it is possible to see the path that the user should follow inside the application in order to input relevant data (Fig. 2).

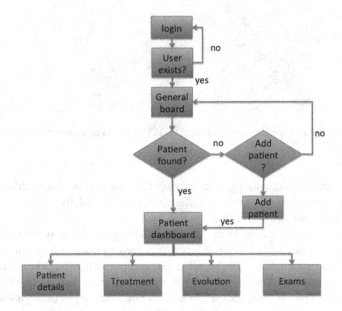

Fig. 2. MedData information architecture flowchart

2.2   MedData Initial Interface Design

Designed in the beginning of 2014, the application initial interface had to be delivered in a short period of time, in order to be tested with real users inside the hospital. To reach this goal, the first prototype was developed in iOS (Apple's mobile operating system), focused in the use via iPads. This decision was taken following the belief that the adoption of the application would be greater if the doctors could insert the information in a larger mobile display. All the data, in this version, was designed to be gathered via text.

Bellow, images that show the interfaces designed (Figs. 3, 4, 5, 6).

Fig. 3. General board - user interface

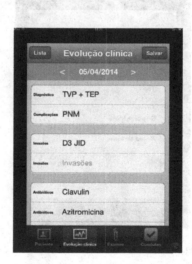

Fig. 4. Patient clinic evolution - user interface

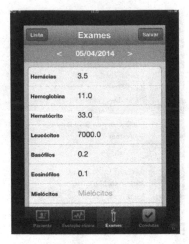

Fig. 5. Patient exams - user interface

Fig. 6. Patient treatment - user interface

3   Pilot Project

The pilot project of MedData was conducted for a period of six months during the year 2014, in the ward of a tertiary hospital in the city of Rio de Janeiro. The test was implemented and supervised by Dr. Bruno Azevedo, belonging to the clinical staff of the medical team. This ward is made up of thirty beds spread over five staff doctors and ten interns.

3.1 Pilot Project Testing

The first step in the implementation of MedData was to create a login and password for each user had access to the mobile system. After the users registration, there was a brief training of medical team and interns, when it became clear that the usability of MedData should be redesigned. Although training was brief, users were able to perform the tasks for which the system was designed.

In order to a quickly adaptation of MedData and an immediate start of use, was held the first registration of all beds by Dr. Bruno Azevedo. After the initial registration, the entire team was informed about the need for daily updates of existing fields, such as laboratory tests, discharge, transfer beds etc.

The rate of MedData utilization was constantly observed. After the first two months, there was a decrease in completing and updating the data to a percentage around 20 %. This drop occurred despite incentives and requests for the use of MedData, warning that the integration of clinical data across the medical team would result in patient safety.

Some hypotheses have been suggested to the progressive decline of MedData employment:

- Approximately 50 % of staff had Android operating system (Google Inc., CA), which precluded the adoption of MedData since its inception.
- The use of tablets was rare in the ward, about 5 % of the team, which made the data entry required only by smartphones. In this regard, when there was the need of complete fields with multiple characters, e.g., first and last name, there was a report of impracticality to perform this task on a smartphone.
- The ward, where the pilot project was carried out, already had an electronic medical record system, which is filled through desktop and is not integrated with MedData. Therefore, the completion and use of MedData represented another task to be performed during the daily medical routine.

The medical routine, either in an outpatient or hospital - emergency department, wards and intensive care units, has the characteristic of being dynamic, fast and with many crucial tasks to be performed. Any optional process or step that do not clarify its immediate utility will have difficulty in their insertion in this daily routine (Edwards et al. 2008 and Viitanen et al. 2011).

Based on the difficulties encountered on this pilot and the reporting of users, started a reengineering process of MedData. The first immediate action became the development of the application to be used also in smartphones, in multiple operational systems (i.e.: Android). In order for immediate integration into existing electronic medical record system, it was suggested to fill in some fields through photographs taken by the smartphone. Pictures will be made of papers records, which are still made with the objective of physical archiving of records. Another alternative to fill the existing fields was the data acquisition by voice. It is believed that the inclusion of data with voice, will transform this process in a spontaneous activity and facilitate its natural insertion in daily medical routine.

4   MedData Redesign

Based on the analysis of the interface testing with users during the pilot project, the MedData team decided to redesign some functionalities of the application. The new technology applied aimed to recognize and translate all the data inserted by voice and image into text, so it can be understand by the rest of the medical team. Regarding interface Design, the whole success of the use of the application depends on the easiness of use of the application. In medical contexts, anything that is faces as extra work, is not used.

The new version also bought a sense of branding to the mobile application in order to start developing the identity of the solution. Another important aspect was the planning for multiple devices, focusing in a responsive Design. The use of icons aimed in the reduction of reading, in the doctor's perspective. These issues were implemented in order to make the interface easier and faster to use.

Bellow, some examples of the new interface Design of the mobile application (Figs. 7, 8, 9, 10, 11).

Fig. 7. Login - user interface

Fig. 8. General board - user interface

Fig. 9. Patient dashboard - user interface

Fig. 10. Patient evolution - user interface

Fig. 11. Patient Evolution - user interface

5   Further Work

The full redesign of MedData will be done by April 2015. All the functionalities mapped in the application architecture will be ready to use in both Android and iOS operational systems and by multiple devices. The multidisciplinary team based on PUC-Rio University is working with a deadline to test the use of the new interface in a hospital, with a team of medical professionals, in May 2015.

Once the team of user testers is defined, the Design team will be able to apply a more structured usability test in place, using techniques such as cooperative analysis and focus groups. Dr. Bruno Azevedo has already managed to gather more information in this new test.

In parallel to the usability testing, the development team of researchers will be also focused in the social aspect of the application that will be focused in the sharing of medical data among teams of professionals.

References

Edwards, P.J., Moloney, K.P., Jacko, J.A., Sainfort, F.: Evaluating usability of a commercial electronic health record: a case study. Int. J. Hum. Comput. St. **66**, 718–728 (2008)

Viitanen, J., Hyppönen, H., Lääveri, T., Vänskä, J., Reponen, J., Winblad, I.: National questionnaire study on clinical ICT systems proofs: physicians suffer from poor usability. Int. J. Med. Inf. **80**, 708–725 (2011)

Hands On Health: How Doctors' Use Of Mobile Technology Impacts Telehealth – Infographic And Insights. Net, USA, January 2014. <http://www.handsontelehealth.com/past-issues/135-how-doctors-use-of-mobile-technology-impacts-teleheatlh-infographic-and-insights>

Ali, A.: A framework for measuring the usability issues and criteria of mobile learning applications. Net, Canada, November 2013. <http://ir.lib.uwo.ca/cgi/viewcontent.cgi?article=2585&context=etd>

Alexandru, C.A. (2010): Models to Extend the Scope of Usability Testing for Telemedicine Systems. Net, UK, November 2013. <http://www.dotrural.ac.uk/digitalfutures2012/sites/default/files/digitalfutures2012papers/Papers/Session4CUsability/Alexandru&Stevens_TelemedicineSystems.pdf>

Beijnum, B.F.J. et al (2009): Mobile Virtual Communities For Telemedicine: Research Challenges And Opportunities. Net, HOL, February 2014. <http://doc.utwente.nl/69537/1/v6i22.pdf>

Boralav, E. (2001): Design and Usability in Telemedicine. Net, Sweden, November 2013. <http://www.it.uu.se/research/publications/lic/2001-001/2001-001.pdf>

A Usability Study of a Gesture Recognition System Applied During the Surgical Procedures

Antonio Opromolla[1,2], Valentina Volpi[1,2(✉)], Andrea Ingrosso[1],
Stefano Fabri[3], Claudia Rapuano[3], Delia Passalacqua[3],
and Carlo Maria Medaglia[1]

[1] Link Campus University, Via Nomentana 335, 00162 Rome, Italy
{a.opromolla,v.volpi,a.ingrosso,
c.medaglia}@unilink.it
[2] ISIA Roma Design, Piazza della Maddalena 53, 00196 Rome, Italy
[3] Consorzio Roma Ricerche, Via Giacomo Peroni 130, 00131 Rome, Italy
{fabri,rapuano,passalacqua}@romaricerche.it

Abstract. Within an operating room, surgeons need to interact with a large amount of patient's medical information and data. In order to avoid misunderstandings among the staff and protecting the patient safety, the medical staff may use a touchless interaction system that allows the surgeons to directly interact with digital devices that visualize digital images. The RISO project aims to create a gesture recognition system for the visualization and manipulation of medical images, useful for the surgeons even during the surgical procedures. In this paper we show the main findings from a usability study carried out with the aim to evaluate, among others, the learnability of the system and the memorability of the gestures employed for the interaction.

Keywords: Touchless interaction · Gesture recognition · Usability · Surgery · Operating room

1 Introduction

Within an operating room, surgeons need to interact with a large amount of patient's medical information and data (e.g.: images, records, etc.). So, the number of computerized devices employed for accessing them is growing.

Since the electronic devices (PC primarily) are difficult to sterilize, currently a middle-person, usually a nurse, assists the surgeon by retrieving data and information through mouse and keyboard at a PC station located inside the operating room [1]. The indirect nature of this type of interaction increases the risk of causing several misunderstandings among the staff and generating an overall slowness in surgery procedures. A touchless interaction with the digital devices can represent an effective solution for surgeons, since it allows them to directly interact with digital images.

The most part of touchless systems have been implemented using voice commands and gestures. However, the speech recognition systems are limited because of their

© Springer International Publishing Switzerland 2015
A. Marcus (Ed.): DUXU 2015, Part III, LNCS 9188, pp. 682–692, 2015.
DOI: 10.1007/978-3-319-20889-3_63

difficulties to discriminate between different people talking in the same room, as well as because of their high noise sensitivity. The gesture recognition systems can be implemented through different typologies of video cameras and sensors, but they generally lack in accuracy under low light conditions. However, in comparing speech and gesture recognition systems it emerges that the latter allow a more "natural interaction"; first of all, gesture recognition systems free the surgeon from interacting with additional accessories which might cause him/her physical hindrances.

In the last years, the use of hardware and software systems in medical field has increased. These systems are used for storage, transmission, display, and printing of digital diagnostic images, such as PACS (Picture Archiving and Communication Systems). Indeed, thanks to DICOM (Digital Imaging and Communications in Medicine), a standard used in PACS, the surgeons can manipulate the diagnostic images both in 2D and in 3D [2, 3].

The RISO project (in Italian the acronym stands for "Rilevazioni Immagini in Sala Operatoria; in English, "Image Recognition in Operating Room") presented in this paper aims to create a gesture recognition system for the visualization and manipulation of medical images, useful for the surgeons even during the surgical procedures.

This paper is organized as follows. In the second section, we will discuss about the main projects that use natural interaction systems into the operating room, during a surgery. In the third section, we will describe the RISO system, focusing both on the system architecture and on the user interface and the interaction modes. In the fourth section, we will focus on the usability evaluation study conducted on the RISO system, by describing the methodology and the main findings of this analysis. Finally, in the fifth section, the conclusions.

2 Related Work

In the touchless interaction, the user inputs data without any contact between the computer components and the human body. So, gestures are suitable means to be used in touchless systems. In literature, several interaction techniques using gestures have been analysed, in order to study the different ways to recognize them, such as wearable or environmental sensors. The more common touchless interactions technique used in the operating room can be divided into two main categories: systems detecting gestures with a visual approach or with wearable sensors. The first does not require the user to wear any additional device, but it needs a direct line of sight between the user and the video capture device to let the system detect gestures. Webcam, stereo camera, ToF (Time of Flight) camera or Microsoft Kinect are some of the devices that can be used to recognize gestures. The wearable sensors instead do not require the direct line of sight. Moreover, since they allow only the person wearing the sensors to interact with the system, they avoid the possible confusion deriving from the presence of more people in the room where the system is located.

Voice commands and sensors are often used together with visual recognition systems to enable or disable particular states or mode of the system. Ebert et al. [2] developed a touchless PACS system using the Microsoft Kinect (to capture the video streaming) and a wireless microphone (to capture voice commands). The system has three main modes to control the patient's data that can be switched by using voice commands: stack navigation mode, move mode, and the window mode. All three use the movement of one or two hands.

However, in a further system implementation proposed by Ebert et al. [4], in addition to enable gestures for viewing and manipulating the medical images, the voice commands were deactivated, since the results from the previous study showed that the voice recognition were too subject to background noise and it struggled with accents (it worked poorly if the user had a non-American accent). Moreover, many users considered the required headset ungainly and distracting. The main problems encountered during the previous test were overcome by the use of finger gesture detection, by which it was possible to control the basic functionality of the medical image viewer. The finger gesture detection allows gestures such as panning, scrolling, and zooming.

Even the system designed by Ruppert et al. [5] uses the Kinect to capture the video stream, but in this case the tracked position of the user hand is used to move the mouse pointer. This allows the user to perform mouse-drag functions like 3D rotations and 2D slices change by using one or both hands. Button clicks events are also virtually generated.

Soutschek et al. [6] include the "mouse" movable cursor and click (used to measure the size of anatomical structures or specify a Volume Of Interest for further analysis) among the functional requirements considered as basic in the visualization of the medical data set (the others are rotation and translation, in order to explore and navigate 3-D data sets, and reset). These actions correspond to 5 gestures captured by a ToF camera system.

Even a simple camera positioned on the screen and a tracking module can be used to acquire and to interpret the movements, as in Gestix, a system developed by Wachs et al. [7], which recognizes both static and dynamic poses.

On the contrary, the WagO system developed by Kipshagen et al. [8] combines an image processing component, which automatically determines the user's hand and its contour position, and a gesture recognition component. Some stereo-cameras positioned below the screen and pointing to the ceiling of the operation theatre triangulate the hand positions in 3D and map them to the 2D environment of the OsiriX (an open source DICOM viewer) application. The system recognizes a set of 4 static gestures to control the file DICOM viewer OsiriX.

Hands are not the only human body parts tracked by video capture devices in order to interact with touchless medical imaging systems. Gallo et al. [9] developed an open-source system for the exploration of medical imaging data that capture both static and dynamic hand and arm gestures through a Microsoft Kinect.

Similarly, Jacob et al. [10] uses the Microsoft Kinect to capture the user's skeleton, in order to provide the positions of various landmarks placed on the human body. The system includes an intention recognition module that is able to decide whether a performed gesture is intentional or not on the basis of anthropometric and kinematic features of the human body, such as the torso and the head orientation and the hands position.

3   The RISO System

The RISO project aims to create a gesture recognition system for the visualization and manipulation of medical images.

In order to appropriately design and develop the RISO system, an accurate analysis has been conducted. It concerned both the technical solutions (mainly about the gesture recognition devices and the toolkits for the application development) and the gestures to use in a touchless interaction. The characteristics of the context of use, i.e. the operating room, was the main criterion in the selection of the technological solutions and consequently of the gestures for the interaction with the RISO system.

In details, referring to the RISO system, the interaction with the medical images occurs through the Leap Motion, a hardware sensor device that supports hand and finger motions as input. Thanks to its sensor accuracy, the Leap Motion recognizes the hands and fingers small motions, allowing a touchless interaction with the devices. This is a perfectly suitable feature for an operating room, where usually the medical team, the equipment and the machinery could hamper the surgeon movements. Furthermore the operating room is a perfect environment for the use of Leap Motion, because their surgical lights do not have IR components that interfere with the device.

Shown below the adopted solutions, concerning both the system architecture (Sect. 3.1) and the interaction modes (Sect. 3.2).

3.1   System Architecture

The hardware architecture of the RISO system is composed of a depth sensor used as input device, a computer that processes input data and manage the GUI (Graphical User Interface), and a display that shows the results. The software architecture is composed of two components: the module for gesture recognition and the module for data handling and visualization.

Input Device. The input device is the component that required more attention. In the gesture recognition field, ToF cameras (Time of Flight), also called "depth cameras", are the most used devices for image acquisition. They allow estimating the distance between the cameras and the objects in real time, by measuring the time-of-flight of a light signal between the camera and the subject for each point of the image. Using these devices allows making faster the segmentation of a hand, because they can detect skin of different colours even in conditions in which there are noisy backgrounds.

Generally, all ToF devices exploit the same technology. In details, they use in combination one or more cameras VGA and a depth sensor. The main differences that we note between the various devices are the price, the sensor accuracy, and the camera resolution.

Among all the analysed devices, Leap Motion was the most suitable for RISO. This is an innovative USB device with three IR sensors and two near IR cameras. It is designed to be placed on a flat surface under the area where hand movements are performed. It can track the movements of the fingers, palms or objects used as pointers (like pen or pencils). Movements are detected in a range between about 0.1 m and

1.0 m. Leap Motion has good performance, high precision, minimal amount of space and its price is much lower than the cost of other available devices (Fig. 1).

Fig. 1. The Leap Motion device

Libraries. Leap Motion provides a development kit that provides high-level methods for identifying hands and fingers. So, in order to develop the gesture recognition component of RISO system we used Leap Motion SDK. By using it, it is possible to perform the segmentation of the hands, feature extraction, such as fingers, palms or pointers, and finally tracking them. RISO uses Leap Motion libraries to recognize gesture and poses made by the users. These gestures and poses are mapped with the possible inputs transmitted to the module that manages clinical data.

To develop the module for clinical data handling and visualization we used the Medical Imaging Interaction Toolkit, an open-source software system for development of interactive medical image processing software.

3.2 Interaction Modes

Once defined the technological solutions to be adopted, as described in the Sect. 3.1, the 9 gestures through which the user has to interact with the RISO system were identified mainly on the basis of intuitiveness and memorability. Each gesture is named as the action that it enables: "cursor positioning" (moving along x-axis and y-axis), "moving in depth" (along z-axis), "zooming" (reshaping the image), "windowing" (changing the values on the Hounsfield scale, that is the quantitative scale describing radio-density), "image shifting" (moving the image when it is not totally visualized in the window), "resetting" (taking the cursor and the image to the starting point), "selecting" (set the focus on a specific image), "releasing" (a specific image area), "asking help". Figure 2 shows the enabled gestures.

Referring to the interaction flow, the user has to: (1) select the folder collecting the health examinations of a specific patient; (2) see the list of the examinations carried out by the patient; (3) select a specific health examination and explore it (Fig. 3).

4   The Usability Evaluation

A usability evaluation study was conducted on a prototype of the RISO system. Since a prototype version of the Leap Motion device was used during the test, in some cases the overall system lacked in stability. However, this critical condition had not invalidated the aim of the usability evaluation study.

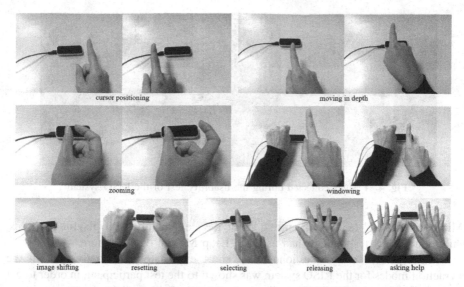

Fig. 2. The gestures enabled for interacting with the RISO system

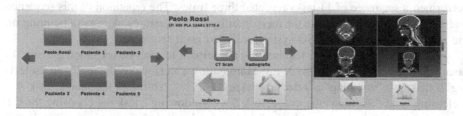

Fig. 3. The interaction flow of the RISO system. In order: (1) the user selects the folder collecting the health examinations of a specific patient; (2) he/she sees the list of the health examinations carried out by the selected patient; (3) he/she selects a specific health examination and explores it.

In details, the study aimed to evaluate the ease of learning of the system, the ease of execution of the gestures, the suitability of the employed technologies, and the memorability of the gestures.

The Fig. 4 shows some frames collected during the usability test.

4.1   Methodology

The usability tests involved (one by one) 10 users and were organized as follows.

First of all, the user filled an "entry questionnaire" (consisting of 4 closed questions and 3 open-ended questions) designed to investigate his/her confidence with the gesture recognition systems and technologies. From this questionnaire emerged that the respondents had an average knowledge of the gesture recognition systems and technologies. They mostly used the "Nintendo Wii" (a home video game console) and the

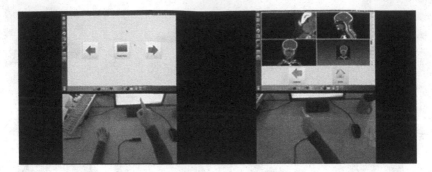

Fig. 4. Frames collected during the usability test of the RISO system

"Microsoft Kinect" (a motion sensing input device), mainly with playful purposes, while none of the respondents had used the Leap Motion device before.

Once filled the entry questionnaire, a short explanatory video focused on the interaction modes for the RISO system was shown to the test participant, in order to get him/her familiar with the RISO application and with the 9 available gestures.

Then, the user started the usability test. In particular, the participant individually performed a sequence of 11 tasks repeated three times. The repetition of this sequence had been necessary to measure the memorability of the gestures. A camera pointing on the monitor screen of the RISO system recorded each sequence.

Each task of the sequence required the participant to use one (or more) gesture. In detail: task 1 – assessing to the X-ray examination ("cursor positioning" and "selecting"); task 2 – "zooming" a selected image; task 3 – "shifting" the image; task 4 – "releasing" and "resetting" the image; task 5 – "windowing"; task 6 – choosing the CT Scan examination ("cursor positioning" and "selecting"); task 7 – "selecting" an image and "zooming" it; task 8 – "shifting" the selected image; task 9 – "windowing"; task 10 - "moving in depth" the image; task 11 – "asking help".

The usability tests were carried out in a controlled test environment (not an operating room): this condition has been a weak point of our study of usability, but it has not been an impediment to the satisfaction of its overall objective, since we mainly aimed to evaluate the learnability of the first prototype of the RISO system.

During each test session three people were taking part: a test supervisor, who taught participants the basic instructions to perform the usability test (e.g.: follow the script and run through tasks); an observer, who took notes regarding events and activities (e.g.: what the participant did, his/her facial gestures, body language, and verbatim comments, etc.); a camera operator, who recorded the test session.

Finally, the user filled an "exit questionnaire" addressed to evaluate his/her own experience in using the RISO system. The questionnaire was composed of 1 closed question, 3 open-ended questions, and a 5-point Likert scale with 21 items. Each of the 21 items was represented by a sentence describing RISO, in relation to which the respondents had to express their level of agreement or disagreement (1: strongly disagree; 5: strongly agree). Some of these sentences described RISO positively (positive position), the other sentences negatively (negative position). The evaluation of the exit questionnaire concerned: the user experience with the employed technologies and the gestures enabled for interacting with the system, the adequacy of the system features, the suitability of the RISO system within the context of use, and the user perception of the main advantages and disadvantages of the application.

4.2 Findings

Following, the main findings from the usability test analysis illustrated on the basis of the specific investigated elements.

Employed Technologies. Although the users declared they had some difficulties in understanding the operational mode of the controller (Leap Motion), they said that the activities to be performed had not been hindered by the use of this device.

Context of Application. Although the usability tests were carried out in a controlled test environment, the test participants declared that in their opinion the RISO system could be easily integrated within the real environment (the operating room). Most of the users thought that the RISO system would be able to radically innovate the context of application and to improve the work of a surgeon. However, some of the respondents pointed out the possible hindrances that could occur into the real environment conditions (e.g. low light, the distance from the Leap Motion, etc.).

Gestures. The users declared that repeating three times the same task sequence was useful in order to memorize the gestures and to perceive more natural the interaction with the system. The gestures were considered easy to perform, although some of them turned out to be not totally intuitive (especially the "windowing" gesture) or not well performing (especially the "zooming" gesture).

System Features. The users considered the system features useful for surgeon purposes. However, the test participants recommended additional features that could be implemented. Among them: sending via Internet the patient information, updating the patient information, adding comments to a selected image.

Perceived Advantages. The respondents declared that the main advantages of the RISO system were: the possibility to access the patient information without touching other instruments or compromising the hygiene of the operating room, and bypassing the misunderstandings with assistants; the higher speed in consulting patient information, with respect to the traditional tools; the large freedom of movement of the surgeon having no physical obstacles; the natural interaction, that allowed the surgeons to employ the cognitive resources only on the surgical procedures (rather than in understanding how to interact with the devices).

Perceived Disadvantages. The respondents declared that the main disadvantages of the RISO system were: the necessary training for interacting with the system; the possibility to soil the devices (primarily the Leap Motion), compromising the operation of the system; the greater lack of precision in interacting through the Leap Motion, with respect to the traditional input devices (e.g. the mouse); the time (considered too long) spent by the system in recognizing the single gestures; the general lack of "flexibility" of the system.

Improvement. As mentioned above, each of the involved users performed the tasks sequence three times, in order to measure the memorability of the gesture and, as a consequence, the improvement in interacting with the RISO system. The time spent for each task (and for each repetition) by the participants was considered as an index useful to measure these abilities. The Fig. 5 shows the average of the time (in seconds) spent by users for each task during the three repetitions.

According to these data, for 5 tasks out of 11 there was a decrease in the time spent to perform each task, from the first to the third repetition; on the contrary, 6 tasks out of 11 showed a more irregular trend.

However, if we consider the total time taken to carry out the single repetition, we note that the average of the time spent for the repetition 1 amounts to 249,3 s, 195 s for the repetition 2, and 186,8 s for the repetition 3. So, we can affirm that the average of the time spent for each repetition decreases from the first to the third one.

Moreover, we note that each task, taken one by one, shows a different average of the time spent to accomplish it (the "longer" is the task 10).

The Fig. 6 represents the average of the time (in seconds) that each user spent during the three repetitions of the 11 tasks.

According to these data, for 3 users out of 10 there was a decrease in the time used to perform each sequence of tasks, from the repetition 1 to the repetition 3; on the contrary, 6 users out of 10, show a more irregular trend. This is mainly attributed to the low stability of the system, due to the use of a prototype of the Leap Motion in this release of the RISO system.

Moreover, the participants carried out the single repetition (and the single tasks) at different times. So, we can identify three typologies of users: "Fast users" (users 2, 4,

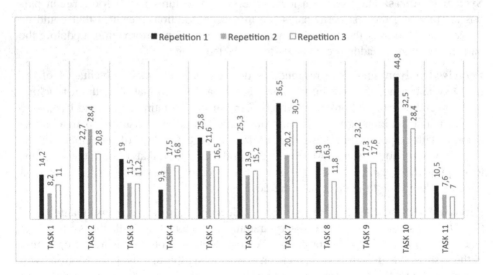

Fig. 5. The average of the time (in seconds) spent by users for each task during the three repetitions.

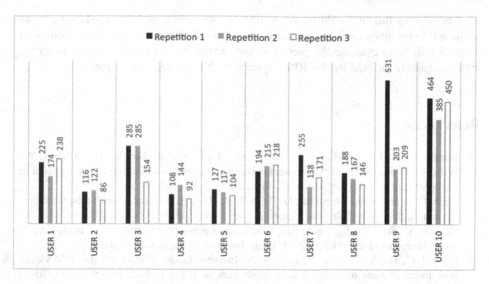

Fig. 6. The average of the time (in seconds) spent by each user during the three repetitions of the 11 tasks.

and 5), who carried out the test in a very short time; "Average users" (users 1, 3, 6, 7 and 8), who carried out the test in a longer time; "Slow users" (users 9 and 10), who carried out the test in a long time.

Success Rate. Although some tasks (i.e. the gestures employed during the interaction with the RISO system) were more problematic than others and the system was not so much stable, all the involved participants completed all the repetitions and all the assigned tasks. So, we recorded a 100 % success rate. For this reason, the effectiveness of the RISO system, represented by "the accuracy and the completeness with which specified users can achieve specified goals in particular environments" [11] can be considered as high.

5   Conclusion

In this paper, we showed the main findings of the usability study of the first prototype of the RISO system, a gesture recognition system for the visualization and manipulation of medical images during surgical procedures.

On the whole, we can affirm that the results of this study are positive, considering the learnability of the gestures enabled for the interaction and the usefulness of the system perceived by users.

The test setting had two main weak points. The first was the overall system stability, due to: the use of a Leap Motion prototype, the noise caused by IR components of the environment lighting, and the prototypal stage of the software. The second was the test environment, that was a "controlled" environment, rather than a "real" environment.

Considering this, it would be interesting to carry out a usability study on a more stable RISO prototype, within an environment very similar to an operating room. Our purpose will be to evaluate the precision, the flexibility, and the time spent in recognizing a gesture enabled by the RISO system in the real context of use.

References

1. Hartmann, B., Benson, M., Junger, A., Quinzio, L., Röhrig, R., Fengler, B., Färber, U.W., Wille, B., Hempelmann, G.: Computer keyboard and mouse as a reservoir of pathogens in an intensive care unit. J. Clin. Monit. Comput. **18**(1), 7–12 (2004)
2. Ebert, L.C., Hatch, G., Ampanozi, G., Thali, M.J., Ross, S.: You can't touch this: touch-free navigation through radiological images. J. Surg. Innov. **19**(3), 301–307 (2012)
3. Rosset, A., Spadola, L., Ratib, O.: OsiriX: an open-source software for navigating in multidimensional DICOM images. J. Digit. Imaging **17**(3), 205–216 (2004)
4. Ebert, L.C., Hatch, G., Thali, M.J., Ross, S.: Invisible touch—control of a DICOM viewer with finger gestures using the Kinect depth camera. J. Foren. Rad. Imaging. **1**(1), 10–14 (2013)
5. Ruppert, G.C., Reis, L.O., Amorim, P.H., de Moraes, T.F., da Silva, J.V.: Touchless gesture user interface for interactive image visualization in urological surgery. World J. Urol. **30**(5), 687–691 (2012)
6. Soutschek, S., Penne, J., Hornegger, J., Kornhuber, J.: 3-D gesture-based scene navigation in medical imaging applications using Time-of-Flight cameras. In: IEEE Computer Society Conference on Computer Vision and Pattern Recognition, pp. 1–6 (2008)
7. Wachs, J., Stern, H., Edan, Y., Gillam, M., Feied, C., Smith, M., Handler, J.: A real-time hand gesture interface for medical visualization applications. In: Tiwari, A., Roy, R., Knowles, J., Avineri, E., Dahal, K. (eds.) Applications of Soft Computing. AISC, vol. 36, pp. 153–162. Springer, Heidelberg (2006)
8. Kipshagen, T., Graw, M., Tronnier, V., Bonsanto, M., Hofmann, U.G.: Touch-and marker-free interaction with medical software. In: Dössel, O., Schlegel, W.C. (eds.) World Congress on Medical Physics and Biomedical Engineering, Munich, Germany, 7–12 September 2009. IFMBE Proceedings, vol. 25(6), pp. 75–78. Springer, Heidelberg (2009)
9. Gallo, L., Placitelli, A.P., Ciampi, M.: Controller-free exploration of medical image data: experiencing the Kinect. In: 24th International Symposium on Computer-Based Medical Systems, pp. 1–6 (2011)
10. Jacob, M., Cange, C., Packer, R., Wachs, J.P.: Intention, context and gesture recognition for sterile MRI navigation in the operating room. In: Alvarez, L., Mejail, M., Gomez, L., Jacobo, J. (eds.) CIARP 2012. LNCS, vol. 7441, pp. 220–227. Springer, Heidelberg (2012)
11. ISO 9241-11:1998 Ergonomic requirements for office work with visual display terminals (VDTs) - Part 11: Guidance on usability

A Novel User-Specific Wearable Controller for Surgical Robots

Carmen C.Y. Poon[1(✉)], Esther Y.Y. Leung[2], Ka Chun Lau[2], Billy
H. K. Leung[1], Yali L. Zheng[1], Philip W.Y. Chiu[1], and Yeung Yam[2]

[1] Department of Surgery, The Chinese University of Hong Kong, Shatin,
Hong Kong, The People's Republic of China
cpoon@surgery.cuhk.edu.hk
[2] Department of Mechanical and Automation Engineering, The Chinese
University of Hong Kong, Shatin, Hong Kong, The People's Republic of China

Abstract. Wearable sensors have emerged as an active field of research in
human-computer interaction. This study explores the use of wearable sensors to
detect human motion for precise control of a two-arm surgical robot designed
for gripping and dissecting tissues. The wearable sensory sheath was designed
with flexible e-textile bipolar electrodes to collect forearm electromyogram
(EMG) and inertial measurement units (IMU) to capture arm motions of the
user. Four pairs of bipolar electrodes were used to collect EMG from the
forearm muscles and two IMU for detecting rotation and translation of each arm
of the subject. Features were extracted from the EMG and linear discriminant
analysis was used as the decoding method to classify the signals of the muscles.
A calibration procedure was setup in the beginning for calibrating the IMU
sensors to familiarize the user with the working space environment and the
mapped-motions of the robot arms. A training session was then conducted for
each user to control wrist flexion, wrist extension, hand opening and hand
closure of the robot arms. Six users were asked to perform random arm and hand
movements to ensure satisfactory mapping of the movements of the surgical
robot. To evaluate the system, two tasks which were important in controlling
surgical robots were designed: (1) using the dissector to mark dots along a
straight line and (2) lifting a weight from one location to another. The results of
this study found that the performance of different users in operating the motion
controller and the wearable sensory sheath were similar in accuracy. Most users
completed the same task in a shorter time with a standard motion controller than
the wearable sensory sheath. The results show that most users adapt to a standard motion controller faster than the wearable sensors although the latter can be
calibrated individually and is a user-specific approach for the control of robot.

1 Introduction

Wearable sensors have emerged as an important tool in human computer interaction.
Physiological signals and human movements that can be captured by wearable sensors,
such as electrooculogram (EOG) [1], electromyogram (EMG) [2], electroencephalo-
gram (EEG) [3], and lip motions [4], have been proposed for controlling various types

© Springer International Publishing Switzerland 2015
A. Marcus (Ed.): DUXU 2015, Part III, LNCS 9188, pp. 693–701, 2015.
DOI: 10.1007/978-3-319-20889-3_64

of robots. Nevertheless, few studies have reported the use of wearable sensors for the control of surgical robots, which requires high precision and an ergonomic approach.

We have previously developed a surgical robot to perform advanced endoscopic procedure such as endoscopic submucosal dissection (ESD) [5]. ESD, which is a skillful endoscopic technique that allows en bloc resection of early stage gastrointestinal cancer for reducing the risk of residual cancer, involves the following working steps: marking, injection, cutting mucosa, dissection, proceeding dissection and complete resection [6]. This procedure is scar-less and effective. However, the procedure is also technically demanding and have a high risk of perforation [7]. Therefore, to assist surgeons and endoscopists to complete ESD, we have developed a robot with two arms, a gripper for lifting and a knife for dissecting tissues.

In this study, we reported the use of wearable sensors to recognize hand gestures and arm motions for intuitive control of this surgical robot. This novel way for controlling surgical robot is achieved by using flexible surface EMG bipolar electrodes and inertial measurement unit (IMU) to control discrete actions and positioning the robot respectively. For comparison, a standard motion controller is also used as the benchmark.

2   Surgical Robot and Controller Design

Figure 1 shows the surgical robot used in this study. The two robotic arms are designed with a total of nine degrees of freedom. Each arm is with a continuous structure and attached with a small surgical tool as the end effector for tissue lifting and dissection respectively.

Fig. 1. The surgical robot

Two types of controllers are used in this study: (a) a standard motion controller and (b) a wearable sheath that collects EMG and arm motions of the user. As shown in Fig. 2, the standard motion controller is designed with a 2-DOF joystick that controls the continuum section of the robotic arms, a rotational knob that controls the tilting angle of the gripper or the hinge joint of the dissector, as well as a scissor-liked knob that controls the opening and closing of the gripper. The robot arms can be translated by push buttons.

Fig. 2. Two controllers used in this study: (a) a motion controller and (b) a wearable sheath with EMG electrodes and IMU sensors.

2.1 Design of the Wearable Controller

The wearable sensory sheath in this study was designed with eight pairs of bipolar electrodes and four IMU sensors. Four bipolar electrodes to record forearm EMG and two IMU sensors to detect the motion (rotation and translation) of each arm of the subject. Figure 3 shows the overview of the control method. EMG features were extracted to control the locking function of the gripper and dissector, while the IMU sensors, which measure velocity, orientation, and gravitational forces of the operator's arm, were used to position the robotic arms.

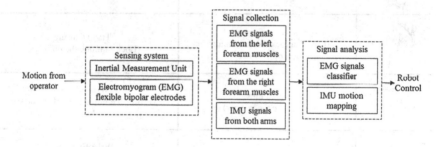

Fig. 3. Flowchart of the signal processing of the wearable controller

E-textiles materials sewn in the inner surface of the wearable sheath were used as dry electrodes for capturing EMG. Each electrode had a conducting area of 300 mm^2 and each pair of electrode has a center-to-center separation of 20 mm. As shown in Fig. 2(b), the four pairs of electrodes were arranged as follows: (1) one pair at the crest of the wrist flexor; (2) one pair at the crest of the wrist extensor; (3) one pair at the anterior distal end; and (4) one pair at the posterior distal end. Two IMU sensors were placed along the same line and parallel to each other, on the upper arm and forearm of the user respectively.

2.2 EMG Signal Recognition and Motion Mapping

Six subjects were invited to participate in this experiment. Each subject was asked to participate in a training session, during which he or she was asked to perform four motions: hand opening, hand closure, wrist flexion and wrist extension. These four postures were used to map to the discrete motion of the robot, as shown in Table 1. The subjects were asked to maintain each posture for five seconds, then relaxed for the next five seconds, and repeated the same for 5 times. The recorded EMG in the training session was used as the reference during real-time control. Mean absolute value (MAV), zero crossing (ZC), slope sign changes (SSC) and waveform length (WL) were selected as the EMG features in our study, since they have been widely verified previously in EMG prosthesis control [8, 9]. The window size for extracting features is chosen to be 150 ms. The linear discriminant analysis (LDA) [10], which finds a linear combination of features to characterize or separate two or more classes of objects or events, was used as the decoding method to classify these extracted features.

Table 1. Discrete motion control by EMG

	Left hand	Right hand
	Hand Opening (Lock / unlock the gripper)	Hand Opening (Start / stop the robot)
	Hand Closure (Lock / unlock the continuum section of the lifter)	Hand Closure (Lock / unlock the dissector)
	Wrist Flexion (Close the gripper)	Wrist Flexion (Lower the hinge joint of the dissector)
	Wrist Extension (Open the gripper)	Wrist Extension Elevate the hinge joint of the dissector

2.3 IMU Signal Recognition and Motion Mapping

The IMU sensor consisted of a three-axial accelerometer, a gyroscope and magnetometers. The IMU signals were measured continuously and processed as an independent dataset to control the rotation, translation and bending of the continuum section of the two robot arms. Two IMU sensors per arm were placed on the upper arm and forearm of each subject. By analyzing the relative motions of the upper arm and forearm, the arm movements of the user were mapped to the continuum sections of the robot arms, governed by the following equations:

$$d = K_1 \sin\alpha \qquad (1)$$

$$K = K_2 \beta \qquad (2)$$

$$\theta = K_3 \gamma \qquad (3)$$

where d is the translation distance of the robotic arm, θ is the bending angle of the continuum section of the robotic arm, K is the curvature of the continuum section of the robotic arm, K_1, K_2, K_3 are the sensitivity constant of the user's behavior obtained during the calibration section, α is the angle formed by the upper arm with the vertical plane, β is the angle formed by the forearm with the horizontal plane, and γ is the rotation angle of the forearm.

In order to familiarize the user with the working space environment and the mapped motions of the robotic arms, a calibration procedure was setup in the beginning. The user was asked to keep the initial position at the beginning of the calibration to ensure the mapping is effective. EMG signals of the user were also sent to the computer for real-time classification.

3 Subjects and Experimental Setup

Six subjects (aged 20–30 years old) participated in this experiment, where they were asked to control the surgical robot using the standard motion controller and the wearable sensory sheath in randomized order. With each controller, each subject was asked to perform two designated tasks: (1) to control the dissector to mark a dot in each and every circle shown along a straight line; and (2) to control the lifter to lift a weight from one location to another. The experimental setup is shown in Fig. 4.

After the calibration session, each subject is allocated 3 min to practice on a virtual platform as well as with the surgical robot to familiarize himself with the mapping. Between two sessions of the experiment, a rest of two minutes was given to each subject to avoid mental and muscle fatigue.

(a) Marking Dots on Papers   (b) Lifting Weights to Designated Positions

Fig. 4. Experimental setup

To compare the two control methods, i.e. using the controller and the wearable sheath with EMG and IMU sensors, the accuracy of the EMG classifier, the time to finish each task and the offset distance from each designated path were recorded. A scoring system is defined as follows: A user is considered to achieve 100 % accuracy (i.e. 100 marks) if and only if he or she can position the dissector to all designated positions. For every mark outside a designated position or any missed position, 10 marks were to be deducted.

4 Results

Figure 5 shows a typical recording of EMG of a user. For all subjects, the pattern can be clearly identified for each posture. A cross validation of the classifier in the training session achieved an overall accuracy of 99.2 ± 0.3 % for all subjects. The accuracy is considered to be sufficient to achieve a robust control during the testing session.

Table 2 reports the time of completion of each task using the motion controller and the wearable sensory sheath.

Figure 6 shows the marking results for positioning the dissector at specific locations. The average marks attained by all subjects to complete the task using the motion

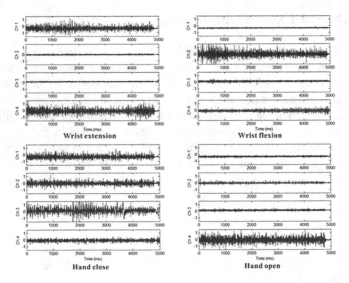

Fig. 5. Typical recording of the 4-channel EMG of a user

controller and the wearable sheath were 83 ± 15 and 83 ± 14 respectively. The average marks of lifting a weight to specified position using the traditional motion controller

Table 2. Time of completion of each task in minutes using (a) the motion controller and (b) the wearable sensory sheath.

Subject	Positioning the dissector to specified positions		Lifting weights between specified positions	
	Using the motion controller	Using the wearable sheath	Using the motion controller	Using the wearable sheath
1	2:07	2:43	2:50	7:14
2	0:58	1:33	1:30	4:17
3	1:51	2:49	0:51	4:11
4	1:46	1:44	1:21	5:14
5	1:02	2:24	1:00	3:46
6	0:58	2:52	1:02	2:17

and the wearable sheath were both 100.

5 Discussion

The average times of completing the task on positioning the dissector using the motion

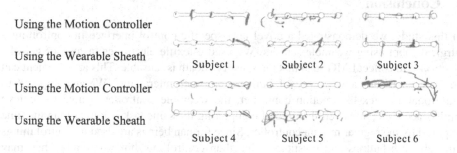

Fig. 6. Positioning accuracy of the dissector of all subjects

controller and the wearable controller were 2 min and 4 min respectively. The average times for lifting a weight from a specified position to another by either control interface were similar. On the other hand, the time required by the wearable sheath as the controller is longer than the regular motion controller. The results suggested that it is possible to use wearable sensors to control surgical robots with similar precision as regular motion controllers. Two major factors are needed for further considerations: (1) the relative motion between wrist motion and forearm rotation; and (2) the control habit of users.

5.1   Relative Motion Between Wrist Motion and Forearm Rotation

The current design uses the user's EMG signal to control the opening/closure of the gripper and the elevation/lowering of the dissector hinge joint by the wrist flexion/extension postures. Meanwhile, the left/right motions of the continuum section of the robotic arm were controlled by the rotation of the forearm. The two sets of movements induced cross-talks and can be a reason for the difficulties in the control using the wearable sheath. Therefore, the motion mapping of the datasets must be further refined, especially in understanding the correlation of the signals in different situations. In addition, increasing the number of EMG electrodes can further improve the precision.

5.2   Control Habit of Users

The traditional motion controller is designed with a one-to-one mapping, which is more definite. Although the control via the wearable sensory sheath provides a user-specific control method by analyzing the motion of the operator's arms, the subject is required to learn a designed dataset. He is required to familiarize himself in controlling his muscles with the same EMG pattern so that it can be repeatedly produced when he controls the robot. Nevertheless, the wearable controller is designed by a user-specific model and therefore, it has the potential to be adaptive to different users' behaviour if properly calibrated and setup.

6   Conclusion

In this study, we demonstrated a novel user-specific control interface in controlling a surgical robot using wearable sensors. We used e-textile electrodes instead of gel-like electrodes to collect EMG such that the sensory sheath is reusable. This arrangement can be developed into a new way of human computer interaction. When compared to traditional joystick-like motion controller, the wearable controller is able to achieve similar accuracy; however, the time of completing the same task is longer than the time required by the regular motion controller. Since human beings are used to control things through push buttons and joysticks rather than controlling things virtually, they may take a longer time to adapt to this approach. Nevertheless, the new approach allows users to move their hands freely and flexibly. The control method is also user-specific.

References

1. Barea, R., Boquete, L., Rodriguez-Ascariz, J.M., Ortega, S., Lopez, E.: Sensory system for implementing a human-computer interface based on electrooculography. Sensors 11, 310–328 (2011)
2. Gomez-Gil, J., San-Jose-Gonzalez, I., Nicolas-Alonso, L.F., Alonso-Garcia, S.: Steering a tractor by means of an EMG-based human-machine interface. Sensors 11, 7110–7126 (2011)

3. Folgheraiter, M., Jordan, M., Straube, S., Seeland, A., Kim, S.K., Kirchner, E.A.: Measuring the improvement of the interaction comfort of a wearable exoskeleton a multi-modal control mechanism based on force measurement and movement prediction. Int. J. Soc. Robot. **4**, 285–302 (2012)
4. Jose, M.A., Lopes, R.D.: Human-computer interface controlled by the lip. IEEE J. Biomed. Health Inform. **19**, 302–308 (2015)
5. Lau, K.C., Hu, Y., Leung, Y.Y., Poon, C.C.Y., Chiu, P.W.Y., Lau, J.Y.W., Yam, Y.: Design and development of a task specific robot for endoscopic submucosal dissection of early gastrointestinal cancers. In: Proceedings of International Symposium on Optomechatronic Technologies. Seattle, USA, 5–7 November 2014
6. Oka, S., Tanaka, S., Kaneko, I., Mouri, R., Hirata, M., Kawamura, T., Yoshihara, M., Chayama, K.: Advantage of endoscopic submucosal dissection compared with EMR for early gastric cancer. Gastrointest. Endosc. **64**, 877–883 (2006)
7. Teoh, A.Y.B., Chiu, P.W.Y., Wong, S.K.H., Sung, J.J.Y., Lau, J.Y.W., Ng, E.K.W.: Difficulties and outcomes in starting endoscopic submucosal dissection. Surg. Endosc. **24**, 1049–1054 (2010)
8. Hudgins, B., Parker, P., Scott, R.N.: A new strategy for multifunction myoelectric control. IEEE Trans. Biomed. Eng. **40**, 82–94 (1993)
9. Young, A.J., Smith, L.H., Rouse, E.J., Hargrove, L.J.: Classification of simultaneous movements using surface EMG pattern recognition. IEEE Trans. Biomed. Eng. **60**, 1250–1258 (2013)
10. Graupe, D., Cline, W.K.: Functional separation of EMG signals via ARMA identification methods for prosthesis control purposes. IEEE Trans. Syst. Man Cybern. SMC **5**, 252–259 (1975)

Author Index

Printed in the United States
By Bookmasters